MICROECONOMICS

Visit the *Microeconomics, fifth edition* Companion Website at **www.pearsoned.co.uk/estrin** to find valuable **student** learning material including:

- Extra practice and self-assessment problems linked to the boxes in the text
- Solutions to selected problems in the text
- An online glossary to explain key terms
- Flashcards to test your understanding of key terms
- Annotated links to relevant economics sites on the web

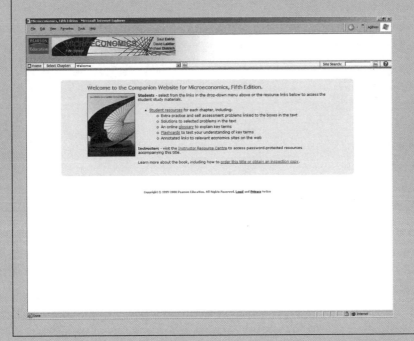

5th edition

MICROECONOMICS

Saul Estrin
London School of Economics

David Laidler
University of Western Ontario

Michael Dietrich
University of Sheffield

FT Prentice Hall
FINANCIAL TIMES

An imprint of **Pearson Education**
Harlow, England • London • New York • Boston • San Francisco • Toronto
Sydney • Tokyo • Singapore • Hong Kong • Seoul • Taipei • New Delhi
Cape Town • Madrid • Mexico City • Amsterdam • Munich • Paris • Milan

Pearson Education Limited

Edinburgh Gate
Harlow
Essex CM20 2JE
England

and Associated Companies throughout the world

Visit us on the World Wide Web at:
www.pearsoned.co.uk

First published by Philip Allan Publishing Limited 1973
Fifth edition published 2008

ISBN: 978-0-273-64627-3

British Library Cataloguing-in-Publication Data
A catalogue record for this book is available from the British Library

Library of Congress Cataloging-in-Publication Data
Estrin, Saul.
  Microeconomics / Saul Estrin, David Laidler, Michael Dietrich. – 5th ed.
    p. cm.
  Updated ed. of: Introduction to microeconomics / Saul Estrin, David Laidler. 4th ed.
  Includes bibliographical references and index.
  ISBN 978-0-273-64627-3 (pbk. : alk. paper) 1. Microeconomics. I. Laidler, David E. W.
II. Dietrich, Michael.   III. Estrin, Saul. Introduction to microeconomics.   IV. Title.
  HB172.E884 2008
  338.5—dc22

                                                                        2008002915

10 9 8 7 6 5 4 3 2 1
12 11 10 09 08

Typeset in 9/12.5 Stone Serif by 35
Printed and bound in Great Britain by Ashford Colour Press, Gosport, Hampshire

The publisher's policy is to use paper manufactured from sustainable forests.

To Jenny, Georgia, Bubble, Francis and Jo
And also to Siobhan, Liam and Asa
Not to mention Antje, Nicole and Natan

BRIEF CONTENTS

CONTENTS

* An asterisk signifies those sections that make use of calculus
and game theory, with a greater degree of difficulty signified
by two asterisks.

Supporting resources

Visit www.pearsoned.co.uk/estrin to find valuable online resources

Companion Website for students
- Extra practice and self-assessment problems linked to the boxes in the text
- Solutions to selected problems in the text
- An online glossary of key terms
- Flashcards to test your understanding of key terms
- Annotated links to relevant economics sites on the web

For instructors
- Complete, downloadable Instructor's Manual
- Detailed solutions to end-of-chapter problems in the text
- New to this edition, testbank of customisable questions for formative or summative assessment
- PowerPoints of all figures and captions in the book

Also: The Companion Website provides the following features:

- Search tool to help locate specific items of content
- E-mail results and profile tools to send results of quizzes to instructors
- Online help and support to assist with website usage and troubleshooting

For more information please contact your local Pearson Education sales representative or visit
www.pearsoned.co.uk/estrin

LIST OF BOXES

Previous editions of this book, by Saul Estrin and David Laidler under the title *Introduction to Microeconomics*, established its status as a core microeconomics text. As with these previous editions, this fifth edition is aimed at second-year undergraduates specialising in economics. The text therefore assumes that students have already taken a first level course in the subject that covers such material as the basic theory of consumer behaviour, firm behaviour in perfectly competitive markets, and the functioning of competitive factor markets. This text is designed to build on this introductory material. Among other things we therefore assume that readers know that microeconomics is concerned with the analysis of the behaviour and interactions of economic agents (primarily consumers, firms and the state), and has a central focus that involves how the decisions of agents interact to determine economic welfare. This standard approach to microeconomics is reflected in the content of this book.

The approach used in various editions of this text has evolved over time in a manner that reflects general changes in the nature of economics and teaching methods used in the subject. The first two editions used almost exclusively a verbal and geometric analysis. In the third and fourth editions calculus and game theory were introduced. This approach that combines verbal and geometric analysis along with more technical content is maintained in this new edition. Among other things this implies that students, to gain *full use* of the text, are assumed to have done an introductory course in mathematical methods for economists. But, as with previous editions, this fifth edition indicates sections that rely heavily on use of mathematics by marking this content with a *. So, for readers without a technical background this starred material can be ignored and they will still be left with a coherent discussion of microeconomic principles. But these starred sections, along with new content discussed below, are designed to allow non-mathematically inclined readers to gradually gain confidence in, and knowledge of, the formal techniques used in modern microeconomics as the book proceeds. So we urge all readers to at least work through some starred sections and in particular the early ones.

Changes to the fifth edition

New content

The fifth edition has introduced a number of important changes to the text. The material has been significantly altered to reflect contemporary teaching needs. For example, important new material has been introduced in discussions of choice in the face of risk (Chapter 7), corporate governance (Chapter 14), game theory (Chapter 17) and the economics of information (Chapter 25).

New feature

A second significant change with this edition is the introduction of new material in 'boxes'. These boxes provide worked examples or developments of key ideas and concepts. Students can use them to develop their understanding of new ideas by working through the examples and perhaps extending them themselves using slightly different numerical values. They also provide a bridge between, on the one hand, the verbal and geometric exposition, and on the other hand the formal exposition in starred sections. So the boxes are intended both to facilitate understanding for the less technical reader and to be of interest for the more mathematically able. To fulfil this role most of the worked examples use specific functional forms with numbers to illustrate key theoretical ideas. They are therefore designed to be easier to understand than abstract functional forms that are used in the starred sections.

Changes in the organisation of the material

As well as significantly altering material, the text has been through a major reorganisation to place emphasis on evolving areas of the subject whilst being mindful of retaining material introduced in previous editions. For example, we have repositioned the chapter on cost and duality (now Chapter 10) into the analysis of production and costs in Part III and the analysis of labour markets and trade unions (now Chapter 20) into Part VI on factor markets. In addition, the detailed treatment of, for example, oligopoly theory and game theory is considerably strengthened (Part V).

Of course topics that are core to standard intermediate microeconomics modules continue to be considered in this text. So the coverage involves the theory of consumer behaviour (Part I), analysis of intertemporal choice and decision making with risk (Part II), production and cost analysis (Part III), the theory of the firm (Part IV), oligopolistic and factor markets (Parts V and VI), analysis of general equilibrium (Part VII) and consideration of missing markets (Part VIII).

Using the text

Progressive levels of reading

Each chapter can be read on three levels: (1) the core material, (2) applications and developments of this material, and (3) the starred sections. Some of the core material is essentially introductory and reviews or revises what might be considered introductory level subject matter. This is particularly the case for consumer theory, production and costs, the basic theory of the firm, and the theory of factor markets. But in all cases, as well as reviewing the more basic treatment, the discussion links this to a more advanced approach. So the text can be useful for intermediate microeconomics students with differing technical needs and capabilities. The progressive organisation of the content, implied by (1), (2) and (3), is designed to be helpful both for advanced students and for those with less technical inclination.

Key words and phrases

To guide readers through the progress from basic to more advanced analysis each chapter starts with a statement of 'key words and phrases'. To some extent, these key words and phrases can be used as an *aide-mémoire* of the chapter content, but also they are useful to review understanding after reading a particular body of material.

Questions and problems

Further understanding of the material can be reinforced by use of the questions and problems that appear at the end of each chapter. Solutions to problems can be found on the book's website, **www.pearsoned.co.uk/estrin**.

Figures and illustrations

The following conventions are used throughout the book. Diagrams are referred to as either figures or illustrations. In the general text all diagrams are numbered consecutively as 'figures'. Within boxes all diagrams are numbered consecutively as 'illustrations'. All figures with captions have been reproduced in PowerPoint slides for use in lectures and can be downloaded from the password protected Instructor's Resource Centre at **www.pearsoned.co.uk/estrin**.

Equations

Equations are numbered consecutively. In the general text the numbering system involves the chapter number followed by the equation number. So the first equation in Chapter 5 would be denoted as equation (5.1). Within boxes the numbering system involves the box number followed by the equation number. So the first equation in the second box in Chapter five (i.e. Box 5.2) would be denoted as equation (5.2.1).

Choose your own route through the book

Clearly there is too much material in this book for a one semester or even a year long course in microeconomics. But the text can be used selectively by instructors or students in specialist areas. A few suggestions here are:

- A course in partial equilibrium analysis would omit Part VII.
- Key aspects of the economics of personnel are covered in Part VI.
- Industrial organisation students will find Chapters 12–17 useful.
- Those specialising in financial economics will benefit from chapters in Part II.
- Students of public sector economics and public policy will find the subject matter of Part VIII relevant.

Website

The content of this text is complemented by a website, hosted by the publisher, and is designed to be used in tandem with the text. The URL of the site is **www.pearsoned.co.uk/estrin**. The website material is intended to be used by both lecturers and students. On the lecturer part of the website the following are examples of the educational resources that can be found:

● PowerPoint slides of all the figures in the book, with captions.
● A *Lecturer's Manual* that among other things has key questions posed by each chapter, key tools and concepts for each chapter, and points of clarification for each chapter.
● A bank of multiple choice questions structured to mirror the text.

On the student part of the website the following is indicative content:

● Extra practice and self-assessment problems.
● Solutions to selected problems.
● Useful economics-related web links.
● A glossary of key terms used in the text.

ABOUT THE AUTHORS

Saul Estrin is a Professor of Management and Head of the Department of Management at The London School of Economics and Political Science. Prior to this, Saul was Deputy Dean (Faculty and Research) at London Business School for six years, and during that time served briefly as Acting Dean. He was formerly Adecco Professor of Business and Society at London Business School where he was also the Research Director of the Centre for New and Emerging Markets. He was also formerly Director of the CIS Middle Europe Centre at London Business School.

His areas of research include labour and industrial economics, transition economics and economic development. He is best known for his work on privatisation, competition and foreign direct investment. Saul has published more than one hundred scholarly articles and books. His publications include the widely cited *Privatisation in Central and Eastern Europe, Foreign Direct Investment into Transition Economies* and, recently, *Investment Strategies in Emerging Markets*. He also writes for policy journals such as *Economic Policy* and *Business Strategy Review*, of which he was for some years an editor.

Saul has considerable practitioner experience. He is currently on the Board of Barings Emerging Markets. He has been a consultant to the World Bank, European Union and OECD, DfID and NERA. He has taught on executive programmes for a number of major companies including Price Waterhouse Coopers, BT, Marks and Spencer and Deutsche Bank.

David Laidler has been Fellow in Residence at the C. D. Howe Institute in Toronto since 1991, and is also Professor Emeritus of Economics at the University of Western Ontario, where he taught from 1975 until 2004.

He was educated at the London School of Economics (B.Sc., Econ. 1959) the University of Syracuse (MA 1960) and the University of Chicago (Ph.D. 1964). Before moving to Canada in 1975 he taught at the University of California, Berkeley (Assistant Professor, 1963–66), the University of Essex (Lecturer, 1966–69) and the University of Manchester (Professor, 1969–75). He has also held visiting appointments at Stanford University, Brown University, the Stockholm School of Economics, the University of Konstanz, the Free University of Berlin and the Reserve Bank of Australia. In 1984–85 he acted as Research Co-ordinator in the area of *Economic Ideas and Social Issues* for the Macdonald Commission on Canada's economic prospects and, in 1998–99, held the position of Visiting Economist and Special Adviser at the Bank of Canada.

A specialist in monetary economics and its history, he and his co-author William Robson won the Canadian Economics Association's Douglas Purvis Memorial Prize in 1994 for their C. D. Howe Institute book *The Great Canadian Disinflation: The Economics and Politics of Monetary Policy in Canada 1988–93*. Their later book, *Two Percent Target: Canadian Monetary Policy Since 1991*, also published by the Institute, won the Donner Prize for the best book on Canadian public policy published during 2004. Professor Laidler's academic publications include numerous journal articles, some of which are reprinted in *Money and Macroeconomics: The Selected Essays of David Laidler* (Edward Elgar 1997), and *Macroeconomics in Retrospect: The Selected Essays of David Laidler* (Edward Elgar 2004).

Dr Michael Dietrich is a Senior Lecturer in the Department of Economics at Sheffield University where he teaches core Intermediate Microeconomics to over 200 students a year as well as courses in undergraduate and postgraduate Industrial Organisation. He studied at Middlesex and Sussex universities and has BA (CNAA), MA (Sussex) and DPhil (Sussex) degrees. He joined The University of Sheffield in 1992, having previously taught at the universities of East Anglia, Brighton and Northumbria.

His main interests as a microeconomist include the economics of the firm and organisation, political economy of the firm, institutional economics and firm growth and development. He is currently working on modelling firm evolution using neural networks and for some time has worked on the nature and measurement of transaction costs, evolutionary approaches to the firm, performance and organisational characteristics of UK companies and the analysis of the firm in an inter-disciplinary context.

He is co-editor of the journal *New Political Economy*. He is a Scientific Committee member for Innovations, *Cahiers d'économie de l'Innovation* and a member of the Advisory Board for *Global Business and Economics Review*. He is also the coordinator of the European Network on the Economics of the Firm.

GUIDED TOUR

Setting the Scene

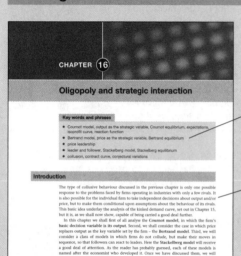

Key words and phrases emphasise the main issues covered in each chapter. Highlighted in the text when they first appear, a glossary of these key words can be found on the accompanying website.

Introductory paragraphs set the scene and outline the chapter objectives. They also demonstrate links to material you will have studied in earlier chapters and show how you can build on the content in later chapters.

Aiding your understanding

Each chapter can be **read on three levels** depending on your knowledge and understanding of the subject:

Core text introduces the topic and explains the concept in the most introductory fashion.

assumed that all small firms are equally efficient and second it is assumed in drawing its marginal cost curve as LMC that the large firm's cost advantage is such as to permit it to take the whole market for X. Nevertheless, this firm, even as the sole producer of X, has no power to raise its price above p_1. That is to say, a sole seller of a good who is in that position simply by virtue of a cost advantage is far less a 'monopolist' than one whose advantage stems from some legal barrier to competition. The latter, but not the former, can treat the market demand curve as the relevant one.

Another variation on Figure 16.6 is also worth considering. Suppose the large firm's marginal cost curve lay at LMC_1. It would produce a large part of the industry's output, but would in fact be a perfect competitor as far as its pricing behaviour was concerned.

Stackelberg equilibrium

The Cournot model discussed earlier is based on the idea that each firm takes its rival's output as given when choosing its level of production. Stackelberg analysed what would happen if one firm understood the structure of the Cournot model sufficiently well to work out how the other firm would react, and then used this information to improve upon its position in the equilibrium. Stackelberg thus analysed not 'price leadership' but 'quantity leadership', and we shall term this sophisticated firm the 'leader' and the more naive rival the 'follower'.

The **Stackelberg model** can then be developed as an extension of the Cournot framework. Firm 1, which we shall take to be the leader, seeks to maximise profits in the knowledge that firm 2, the follower, will treat firm 1's output decision as given. Hence firm 2 will always make decisions along its reaction function, while firm 1 maximises profits subject to firm 2's reaction function. The resulting **Stackelberg equilibrium** is at the tangency between firm 1's isoprofit curve and firm 2's reaction function, point 5 on Figure 16.7.

A comparison of the Cournot and Stackelberg equilibria gives us some intuition about how the leader firm uses its better knowledge to its own advantage. In the Cournot model, each party takes the behaviour of the other as given and adjusts output in response to disappointed expectations until an equilibrium of consistent expectations is reached (point C in Figure 16.7). In the Stackelberg model, firm 1 knows that firm 2 behaves in this way. It therefore chooses it output level, X_1^s, above that implied by its own Cournot reaction function in order to maximise profits subject to firm 2's reaction function. Given its expectation of X_1^s, firm 2 then responds with X_2^s, as firm 1 calculated that it would. Firm 2 in turn finds that its expectation of firm 1's behaviour is confirmed. Firm 2 is therefore misled into thinking that it is in a Cournot equilibrium, though it is producing less than X_2^s and therefore has lower profits ($\pi_2^s < \pi_2^c$). Firm 1 on the other hand is producing more than the Cournot equilibrium ($X_1^s > X_1^c$) and is therefore earning higher profits ($\pi_1^s > \pi_1^c$).

Industry profits are still not maximised at the Stackelberg equilibrium – both sides could gain from a move in a south-westerly direction along EE' in Figure 16.7. However, one suspects that the leader might be less sympathetic to the formation of a cartel in these circumstances than it would be under Cournot or Bertrand conditions, particularly if the rival's behaviour is hard to monitor.

Finally, note that, if both firms seek to be leaders, the Stackelberg model cannot yield an equilibrium. If both firms understand the other's Cournot behaviour, then they will either agree to collude or will enter a price war to determine who will act as leader and who as follower. The incentives for them to seek the former solution are obvious.

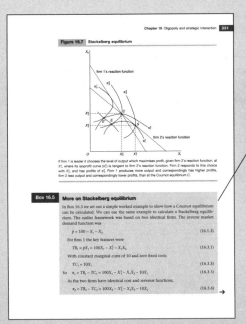

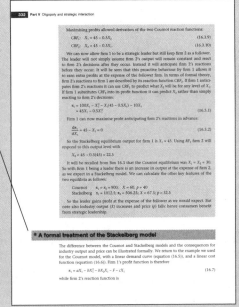

Applications and developments of the topic in **Boxes** bridge the gap between the core text and more technical mathematical analysis in * sections.

* sections take the topic further using more advanced mathematical analysis.

Each chapter closes with **Concluding comments** and **Chapter Summaries** organised by major topics.

Practising and testing your learning

Boxes provide worked examples and developments of key concepts in the text. You can use them to test your understanding of new ideas by working through the examples and extending them by using different numerical values.

End of Chapter **Problems** allow you to test your understanding. You can self-check your answers by looking at the solutions on the book's website **www.pearsoned.co.uk/estrin**.

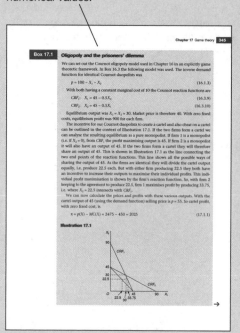

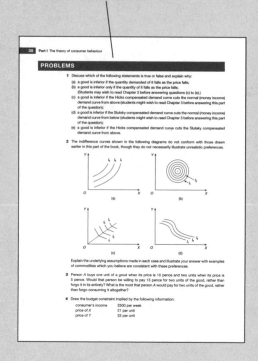

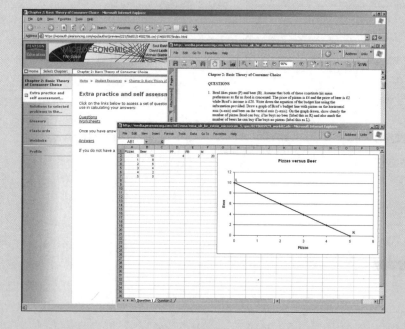

Extra practice and **self assessment problems** can be found on the book's website **www.pearsoned.co.uk/estrin** along with links to useful economics related websites.

ACKNOWLEDGEMENTS

As with all books, while the authors have been the primary source of the content and approach, they have benefited greatly from the help and advice of many people. In the preparation of previous editions the following individuals influenced the content, an influence that is still apparent in the current edition: Avner Ben-Ner, Frank Cowell, Gordon Green, Peter Holmes, David de Meza, Andrew Oswald, Michael Sumner, Jan Svejnar, Ronald Wintrobe, Amos Witzun and Ben Young. In addition the many students we have taught, while being at times inspirational and at other times exasperating, have had an important influence on this text. For the current edition the efficient management and support offered by Ellen Morgan must be acknowledged. Without her input and tactful encouragement the development of this new edition would have been a more extended and troublesome task than it turned out to be. In addition Abhijit Sharma has offered important help in the development of the website. The finalising of the manuscript has benefited from the invaluable help of Kasia Komosa and Asa Kilgarriff. Finally we must, of course, mention the support and patience of our families. Any sizeable academic project takes us away from important domestic duties and activities. But they are always present in any work we undertake: a sizeable thank you must be publicly offered.

CHAPTER ①

Introduction

Scarcity and economics

Economics is about *scarcity*. This word is used here in a special sense: it refers to a state of affairs in which, given the wants of the people who make up a society at any particular moment, the means available to satisfy them are not sufficient. If all desires cannot be satisfied totally, then choices have to be made as to which of them are going to be satisfied, and to what extent. To say that economics is about scarcity, then, is also to say that it is about choice. There is no suggestion here that the subject deals only with purely material matters, such as the production and distribution of those goods and services that happen to make up such statistical magnitudes as the gross national product. Economics is relevant here, to be sure, but its scope is much wider. Any social or private situation which involves a choice has an economic aspect.

At any time, the members of a particular society will desire a wide variety of items – food, clothing, housing, holidays, entertainment, access to countryside and seashore, to music, to art, to sporting events, to educational facilities, and so on – but the means of providing all these are limited. At a specific moment, however, the population will be of a given size, possess a particular mix of skills, and have available to it a certain array of capital equipment embodying a particular level of technology (to say nothing of having available given amounts of open space and seashore as well). In such circumstances not everyone can have all they desire of everything. For any individual to have more of one thing, they must either have less of another thing, or someone else must have less of something. Choices, individual and perhaps collective too, have to be made.

Scarcity, in short, presents a social problem of wide scope and great complexity. Given the resources available to a society, it must somehow be decided how they are to be used, which goods and services are to be produced, and in what amounts. It must also be determined how the resulting output is to be distributed among the individuals who make up that society. Moreover, though at a particular moment the society's endowment of available resources is given, it can be changed over time, both in quality and quantity by devoting part of current output to doing so. The provision of productive resources for the future is thus another of the competing ends to which current production can be devoted; and it should be noted explicitly that organising matters so that scarce resources do not sit idle, but all that are available for employment actually get used, can also present a problem.

Questions about arranging the allocation of resources among alternative uses and the distribution between economic agents of the goods and services they produce (of income, that is), providing for economic growth, coping with technical change, and maintaining full employment, are all economic in nature, because they all arise from the fact of scarcity. If all wants could be satisfied simultaneously and completely, it would not matter how resources were used, how income was distributed, how the balance was struck between the satisfaction of present and future wants, or the extent to which particular resources were utilised. But all wants cannot be satisfied, and, to repeat the message once more, economics is about the consequences of this fact, both for society and the individuals who make it up.

The ubiquity of choice

Different societies organise themselves in different ways to cope with scarcity. A purely socialist society would operate with the state in control of all scarce resources, and it would then attempt to organise its economy by formulating a coherent and consistent plan for their use and for the distribution of the resulting output. At the other extreme, a purely private enterprise system, or market economy as it is often called, would invest individuals with property rights in particular productive resources, including their own labour, and then allow them to use these resources as they saw fit. In such an economy individuals would be left free to exchange their property with one another, and/or to devote it to the production of goods and services which they could then consume, use as inputs to further production, or once more exchange with others. Within such an economy, the state's only role would be to define and establish rights to private property, protect it against theft, and lay down and operate the legal framework governing the terms on which it could be exchanged.

This book will pay a great deal of attention to the workings of market economies, so called, for the very practical reason that a great deal of the economic activity in the world around us is organised along such lines. But of course, there is no such thing as a purely market economy. Government plays a much larger role in the economic life of any actual society than simply to define and protect property rights. Nor is there such a thing as a purely socialist society. Economic activity is far too complex to have all of its details worked out and co-ordinated by a central planning bureau, let alone a single planner, and in the world around us even the most centralised of state-planned economies have always delegated many decisions to local and even individual levels.

No matter what the mix between socialism and private enterprise in any specific society's economic organisation, then, the fact of scarcity and the choices it imposes will impinge upon individual agents, be they actual people, families, capitalist firms, co-operative or state-owned enterprises, government departments, etc. All and any such agents must make choices about how to use the scarce resources under their control. An individual or a family must allocate its time between work and leisure, while bearing in mind that the income realised from work is available for the purchase of the various goods and services that it wants to consume. No firm, be it a capitalist enterprise concerned only with making profits for its owners, a socialist co-operative consciously seeking to contribute to the achievement of some collective goal for its members, or a state-owned organisation seeking to fulfil whatever goal has been laid down for it by government, has an inexhaustible supply of inputs available to it, nor will it be able to undertake the production of all conceivable types of output on any scale. A government department in charge of, shall we say, providing education, does not have unlimited resources at its disposal. Somehow those that are available to it must be divided among nursery schools, primary, secondary and tertiary education, and within each sector further decisions about how those resources are to be used must be made. In each of these at first sight disparate cases, decisions must somehow be taken about what to produce, on what scale and using what mix of inputs.

The co-ordination of individual choices

In short, the systematic understanding of the workings of any economy, no matter where it lies along the spectrum that links pure socialism to complete free enterprise, must start from an analysis of how choices are made by individual agents. But the study of individual choice, vital though it is to an understanding of how economies function, can only be a starting point. As we shall see below, it is sometimes useful and interesting to study an economy consisting of one agent – usually called a *Robinson Crusoe economy*, for obvious reasons – but there are severe limits to the application of the results of such analysis. The typical economy consists of a multiplicity of agents, and though each of them may make its own choices, these must somehow be co-ordinated. Economics is thus also concerned with how such co-ordination is (or is not) brought about, with how a solution to the problem of scarcity is (or is not) achieved at an economy-wide level, a solution not in the sense that the problem vanishes, but in the more limited sense that a particular level and pattern of use for the resources available to society emerges, along with a particular level and structure of output, not to mention a particular distribution of income as well.

In a market economy, the prices of the goods and services that are produced and traded play a crucial role in co-ordinating choices. Simple supply and demand analysis, with which most readers will already be familiar, provides an invaluable first insight into what is involved here. We shall see later in this book that, when a household makes its choices about what goods and services to consume, one outcome is an array of plans for the rate at which any specific good will be purchased that is contingent upon its income, the prices ruling in the market for other goods, and the price of the good in question. As we shall also see, holding its income and the prices of other goods constant, it is then possible to give a diagrammatic representation of how the household's plans to purchase any specific good – let us label it X – change as its own price varies. If we carry out a similar exercise for all households in the economy, and add up their planned purchases at every relevant price, we get the so-called *market* demand curve for X, which shows how much of the good buyers in the aggregate will want to purchase, contingent upon its price. We plot such a curve in Figure 1.1, where the price of X – P – is measured along the vertical axis, and the quantity that households plan to buy, per week say, is measured on the horizontal. We label this curve D, and draw it downward sloping to the right, thus capturing the idea that, as X becomes cheaper, households will plan to buy more of it. Note that in Figure 1.1 D is drawn as a straight line. This is done purely for expositional convenience. In reality the relationship between consumer demand and price is unlikely to be linear.

We shall also see later in this book that in an industry where there are many producers, each one too small to have any influence on the price at which its output sells, a condition

Figure 1.1 **Demand, supply and market equilibrium**

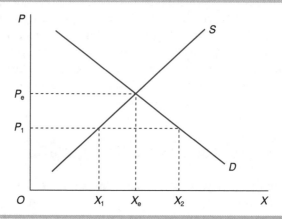

which we here assume to characterise the production and sale of X, the profit maximising decisions of each producer will lead it to formulate plans to supply a rate of flow of X to the market, again contingent upon the going price. This plan may be conceptualised as the firm's supply curve.* And we shall also see that we may add up the quantities that all firms will plan to supply at a given price to generate a market supply curve. This curve is plotted in Figure 1.1 as S, and is drawn upward sloping, to indicate that as the price of X gets higher, more of it will be produced and offered for sale. Note that, as with D, this is drawn as a straight line purely for expositional convenience.

Now a key point about Figure 1.1 for present purposes is that the choices underlying the buying plans summarised in D are made by individual households, each trying to do the best for itself and giving no thought to the consequences of its choices for others, while the production and selling plans underlying S are similarly taken by completely self-regarding firms. These individual plans are, in short, formulated with no effort on the part of those making them to ensure that they are consistent with anyone else's intentions. And yet, if the market price that faces these agents should happen to be P_e, we can see immediately that the amounts of X which households plan to buy will just add up to X_e, the very amount that firms will plan to sell. All of the plans of all of the agents involved in buying and selling this good will thus be simultaneously compatible with one another. Provided that the price of X does indeed settle at P_e, then the choices of a myriad agents, each taken in isolation and without regard to those of others, will be co-ordinated.

It is, moreover, quite plausible that the market price will settle at this *equilibrium* value, the one at which supply and demand are just in balance with one another. To get some intuition as to why this might be, suppose that at some moment the price ruling in the market for X is lower than P_e, P_1 say. In that case, the quantity of the good that households plan to buy will exceed the quantity that firms plan to supply, and this state of *excess demand* will have consequences. The amount of the good that will actually be

---

* We here set aside the complications that arise from the fact that there in fact exists an array of supply curves, depending upon the length of the time horizon relevant to the particular plans being analysed. These matters are taken up in later chapters. Nothing in the current argument hinges upon ignoring them here. Similar considerations apply to demand curves.

on the market will be X_1, that which producers plan to sell is P_1, but the amount that consumers demand at P_1 is X_2. It follows that producers will soon find that there are frustrated would-be buyers in the marketplace, willing to pay more than P_1 if they can obtain it. The pressure of their extra demand will put upward pressure on price as they compete for available supplies, and suppliers will respond to the prospect of a higher price by increasing the quantities of X they offer for sale. Such forces as these will continue to work so long as the market price remains below its equilibrium value, thus driving it upwards until P_e is reached. And, as should be obvious, had we started our story with market price above its equilibrium, these forces would have worked in reverse.

Box 1.1   ## The hog cycle or cobweb model

When analysing markets an issue that is often important is not just that market equilibrium shifts, because of changes in demand and/or supply, but the process of change from one equilibrium to another. An interesting example of when this process of change becomes important was recognised by the Hungarian economist Nicholas Kaldor, who identified in the 1930s that American pig prices behaved in a cyclical manner; hence the name hog cycle. The cobweb model is relevant when there is an obvious lag between supply responses and prices changes. A common example is agricultural markets because of a lag between planting and harvesting. A similar lag might exist in labour markets when labour supply changes respond to wage and salary changes, but the supply change might require new qualifications and skills that take time to be acquired.

Illustration 1.1

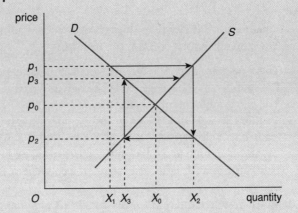

The model can be explained in terms of simple demand and supply curves, as presented in Illustration 1.1 above. We can interpret this as an agricultural market, involving for example the production of a particular vegetable. Initially the market is in equilibrium with price being p_0 and quantity demanded and supplied being X_0. Bad weather then reduces supply to X_1 (the shift in the supply curve is not shown). This reduction in supply forces up price to p_1. Farmers who grow the vegetable will observe the high price and plant vegetables to produce a high output, X_2 in the

→

diagram. When this high output eventually reaches market it forces prices down to p_2. Farmers then react to this low price by reducing planting and vegetable production to X_3. When this output eventually grows and reaches market it forces price up to p_3. It is clear from the diagram that the market cycles, but price and output changes will converge on the equilibrium.

This is called the cobweb model because the dotted lines indicating prices and quantities (allegedly) look like a cobweb. In the digram presented here the market converges to equlibrium because the supply curve is steeper than the demand curve. If the supply curve was shallow (i.e. generally very elastic) and the demand curve steep (i.e. relatively inelastic) the market cycle would move further away from equilibrium with each price and quantity adjustment i.e. the cycle would be unstable.

We can set out the market cycle in the following manner. Assume that quantity demanded in period t (X_t^D) responds to price in the same period such that the market demand curve is

$$X_t^D = 100 - 4p_t \tag{1.1.1}$$

But supply in period t (q_t^S) depends on price in the previous period, and so the supply curve is

$$X_t^S = 10 + 2p_{t-1} \tag{1.1.2}$$

Each period all supply is sold, so that $X_t^D = X_t^S$, i.e.

$$100 - 4p_t = 10 + 2p_{t-1}$$

Rearranging:

$$p_t = 45 - 0.5p_{t-1} \tag{1.1.3}$$

Equation (1.1.3) describes the period by period adjustment of price in this market. The reader can now confirm the following:

1. These demand and supply functions define demand and supply curves for which the supply curve is steeper than the demand curve.
2. The price adjustment equation $p_t = 45 - 0.5p_{t-1}$ defines price changes that get smaller through time when p_t and p_{t-1} are initially not the same. The mathematically able will recognise this price adjustment equation as a first order difference equation. In such an equation the process converges when the coefficient of p_{t-1} is between 1 and -1, and cycles when the coefficient is negative. So our model cycles and converges.
3. When the demand and supply functions are changed so that the demand curve is steeper than the supply curve the price adjustment equation has a coefficient of p_{t-1} that is smaller than -1 (remember that -2 is smaller than -1).

One criticism of this model is its assumption that producers are extremely short-sighted; they are fundamentally unable to judge market conditions or learn from their pricing mistakes that result in surplus/shortfall cycles. So the cobweb model is relevant not only when supply responds to price with a lag but also when producers are shortsighted.

Thus, market prices are a powerful means of co-ordinating the outcomes of choices that the fact of scarcity forces upon individuals who act independently of one another, because they tend to move to an equilibrium value at which these plans are mutually compatible. Here we have illustrated this point with reference to some of the properties of the market for a single good, without taking account of what is going on elsewhere in other markets, and we have therefore emphasised only some of the forces at work in the economy. We have presented what is known, for obvious reasons, as a *partial equilibrium* analysis of a particular market. By ignoring potential repercussions elsewhere in the economy of what happens in the market for X, we have been able to present a simple argument, but sceptical readers are entitled to ask whether, in setting aside so many complications, we may not have left out something of vital importance and so rendered our conclusions misleading. For example, changes in the market for oil have significant effects on many other consumer and produce markets.

The only way to be reassured about this awkward question is actually to deploy what is known as *general equilibrium* analysis. This, as its name implies, would consider simultaneously the plans made by households, not just for the consumption of one particular good, but of the whole array of goods and services that the economy is capable of producing, their plans to supply productive services to firms, and the employment and production decisions of firms, and then analyse the way in which these plans impinge upon one another. The tools needed to carry out such an exercise are developed later in this book, and there is no need to deploy them here. It will suffice to assert that the basic message yielded by our partial equilibrium analysis about the co-ordinating properties of prices does indeed carry over to this much more general framework. When all the plans of households and firms, not to mention their interactions through the market, are analysed simultaneously, it turns out that there will, under quite a broad set of circumstances, exist an array of prices that will bring about a *general equilibrium*, in which all plans of all agents are harmonised simultaneously.

A critical feature of the markets so far considered in which prices ensure that the exchange of goods and services contributes to the effective co-ordination of individual choices is that no single participant in them is large and important enough to influence the prices in question. In this very precise sense such markets are said to be *competitive*. All participants take prices from the market and try to execute their plans about quantities contingent upon them. Obviously, markets in the world around us are not always like that. Monopoly sellers and buyers (sometimes known as monopsonists) in some markets are big enough to influence prices, and will take this power into account as they make their plans, but as we shall see below, this still leads to market outcomes in which equilibrium prices harmonise plans. Whether the particular solutions for the quantities of goods and services that are bought and sold that go along with those prices have properties as desirable as those that emerge from competitive markets is another question, however, also to be taken up below.

More interesting as far as co-ordination issues per se are concerned, are markets where more than one participant is big enough to influence the prices that rule. Such agents cannot formulate plans about quantities contingent upon price as do participants in competitive markets, or plans to choose price and quantity contingent upon the plans of others who take the price that is set as given as do monopolists. Each one of them must take into account that, whatever they do, the other participants in the market are likely to react to their action, and so tailor their behaviour to what they expect those reactions to be. Here a co-ordinated outcome involves each agent's action being just what every other agent expected when their plans were formulated. This kind of inter-dependent decision making is the subject matter of game theory, and later in this book we not only provide an account of some of its basic principles, but also discuss its applications to a variety of issues – how output and price decisions might be arrived at in industries dominated by just a few firms, how wage bargaining between a strong trade union and a monopoly buyer of the type of labour it represents might proceed, and so on. But once more, when readers come to this material, they should keep it firmly in mind that the basic issue under study is the way in which choices forced on self-regarding individual agents by the fact of scarcity come to be co-ordinated with one another in a market economy.

One other important deviation from the assumptions that underlie competitive behaviour is also worth a brief mention here, and, once more, will be taken up in some detail below. This has to do with the quality of the information upon which agents base their decisions. In the market for X, briefly analysed above, it was tacitly assumed that every producer and consumer of X knew just what the properties of X were, and that the purchase or sale of one or more units of it was all that was involved in transactions between them. But not all markets are like that. Sometimes the agent on one side of a trade knows much more about the quality and reliability of the item being exchanged than the agent on the other side.

The used car market provides an obvious example of the potential importance of so called *informational asymmetries* – for example, is this car reliable, or is it a lemon? The seller probably knows better than the buyer – so does the market for insurance. Will buyers of accident insurance actually become more careless once they are covered? Here the buyer knows better than the seller – and so does the market for certain types of labour when it is difficult and expensive for the employer to monitor the quality of employees perform-ance. Is the salesperson's poor performance this week just a quirk, or is it the result of slacking? The employee knows better than the employer. Choices do get made by agents operating in such markets, and their outcomes have to be co-ordinated somehow, but informational asymmetries nevertheless pose interesting questions about how choices are made and co-ordination accomplished, that take us far beyond the simple mechanics of the competitive market.

An outline of the book

Now the above discussion does no more than give an intuitive account of the role of market prices as a central feature of the mechanisms whereby the choices made by agents operating in a free enterprise economy are co-ordinated so as to produce a coherent solution to the social problem of scarcity. It is not meant to convince anyone that such mechanisms always and everywhere work in the way outlined, not least because, as we have also suggested, they sometimes do not, particularly, though not solely, as we move away from the competitive market ideal. Rather, this brief chapter is intended only to persuade readers that the much more detailed analysis that the rest of this book presents is worth careful attention, and also to alert them to the fact that questions about choices and their co-ordination are never far below the surface of what will sometimes, but inevitably, become rather technical and lengthy discussions of particular details of the bigger picture that is microeconomic theory.

In what follows, we shall first of all deal with the behaviour of individual consumers as they face their own version of the scarcity problem – how to allocate a given income among the various goods available. We shall see how they react to changes in income and the prices of those goods, and discuss how such changes affect their economic well-being. Then we shall show how this analysis, developed to deal with current expenditure decisions, can be modified to deal with the determinants of saving behaviour, and choices involving hours of work, before going on to discuss certain aspects of choice when the outcomes of particular courses of action are uncertain. We shall complete our discussion of consumer theory by outlining an extension of it that pays particular attention to the complexity of so many modern goods and services and to the differences that exist between different brands of what are basically the same good.

Then we shall turn to questions about production, particularly in a market economy. We shall present the theory of the profit-maximising firm and the principles governing the choices it makes about levels of output and pricing under competitive and monopolistic conditions. In addition we shall pay particular attention to the interactions among the decisions that firms take in oligopolistic markets and methods of addressing the issues caused by the use of game theory. We shall also touch upon the analysis of firms that pursue goals other than profit, for example the maximisation of sales revenue, or of revenue per employee. Then we shall deal with the factors determining the prices of the inputs that firms use as an aspect of the theory of production, with a particular focus on the labour market.

Once our treatment of partial equilibrium questions is complete, we shall take up general equilibrium analysis, and discuss it extensively. Here we shall emphasise questions about how the choices of individual firms and households are co-ordinated in such a setting. We shall outline the conditions which must hold if the behaviour of firms and households are to be consistent with one another and with the overall resource constraint on the economy. Then we shall pose questions about the desirability of the resulting solution to the scarcity problem, being careful to note those conditions that might hold in an abstract model of a market economy, but are unlikely to hold in any actual economy. The problems that arise here are complex and we can only note them at this stage. First, because individuals own resources and obtain their incomes by selling the use of them, a particular income distribution is implied by any solution to the allocation problem: does this influence the judgements that we may make about the desirability of any particular allocative scheme? Second, what about the allocation of resources towards the satisfaction of those wants that are not always brought within the range of ordinary market transactions – access to the recreational facilities offered by a river, for example? How does a market economy deal, or fail to deal, with such problems?

Finally, we shall discuss some applications of economic analysis to political decision making, touching upon some highlights of what is usually referred to as *public choice* theory. As readers will see, such analysis shows that the principles of self-interested behaviour that economists have developed to analyse problems which arise from the problem of scarcity have interesting applications far beyond the traditional boundaries of economics.

PART ❶

THE THEORY OF CONSUMER BEHAVIOUR

CHAPTER 2

The basic theory of consumer choice

Key words and phrases

- objects of choice, bundles of goods, constraints on choice
- budget constraint, income, prices
- preferences, indifference curves, rationality, cardinal and ordinal utility
- consumer equilibrium, income consumption curve, normal (superior) good, inferior good, price consumption curve, substitute, complement, Giffen good
- Engel curve, income elasticity of demand
- demand curve, own price elasticity of demand, cross elasticity of demand

Introduction

The theory of consumer behaviour deals with the way in which scarcity impinges upon the individual consumer and hence deals with the way in which such an individual makes choices. This consumer may, but need not be, an individual person. Families and households also make collective consumption choices on behalf of their members. The theory as we shall present it takes the consumer unit as given. It therefore presents us with an important instance of how other social sciences, such as sociology and social psychology, which deal, in part, with the way in which people organise themselves into household and other units, could complement economics.

The theory of consumer choice has many applications. It enables us to deal with the selection of consumption patterns at a particular time and the allocation of consumption over time, and hence with saving. The individual supplying labour can be thought of as simultaneously choosing an amount of leisure time, so the same theory is relevant there as it is when we come to consider behaviour in the face of risk. Moreover, in constructing a theory to deal with problems such as these, we are forced to think carefully about, and to define precisely, such much abused terms as 'real income' and the 'cost of living', so that our theory gives us many valuable insights into matters of potentially considerable practical importance. We shall deal with all these matters, and more, in the chapters that follow.

The subject matter of this chapter

To address questions of consumer choice, we need a language of analysis, a general framework in terms of which all these apparently diverse matters can be reduced to their common elements. We shall develop such a framework in this chapter, and then we shall put it to use in deriving two relationships much used in applied economic analysis, namely, the **Engel curve** and the **demand curve**. The first of these relates the quantity of a good which a consumer purchases to the consumer's income. The second relates the quantity of a good purchased to its price, and is one of the fundamental building blocks of microeconomics.

Even so, the main emphasis in this chapter is not on these relationships in and of themselves, but rather on the theoretical structure which underlies them. The model of choice-making, from which they are derived, is of much more general interest, and provides the foundation for all of this part of the book, and for Part II as well.

In order to derive this model we need to describe first of all the logical structure of the choice problem which faces any consumer. We will find it helpful to think of that structure as being made up of three components. First, we must consider the items which the consumer finds desirable, the **objects of choice**. Secondly, since the desirability of an object does not necessarily imply that it is available to be chosen, we must consider any limitations that might be placed on the alternatives available to the consumer, the **constraints upon choice**. Finally, because choice necessarily involves a process of selection among alternatives, we must consider the way in which the consumer ranks the alternatives available, the consumer's *tastes* or **preferences**.

The objects of choice

The objects of the consumer's choice are goods and services. In the most general case we may consider patterns of consumption at each particular moment in time and over time. To keep things simple we will now confine ourselves to the choice facing an individual at a particular time, ignoring for the moment the problem of allocating consumption over time. We will also simplify the world by assuming that it contains only two goods, X and Y. This abstraction from a world with many goods to one with two is not quite so restrictive as might appear at first sight, for it is always possible to think of X as being one particular good and Y as being a composite bundle of all other goods.

Now consider Figure 2.1. On the horizontal axis we measure quantities of X per unit of time, let us say per week, and on the vertical axis quantities of Y per week. Any point in the area bounded by these two axes may be interpreted as a pattern of consumption involving a particular mixture of X and Y per week. Thus the point on the X-axis at $5X$ represents a consumption pattern of $5X$ and no Y per week, the point D represents consumption of $5X$, $10Y$ per week, and so on. In short, the objects of choice in this particular simplification of the theory of consumer choice are consumption patterns measured in terms of **bundles of goods** per week and each such bundle is represented by a particular point on a diagram such as Figure 2.1.

Figure 2.1

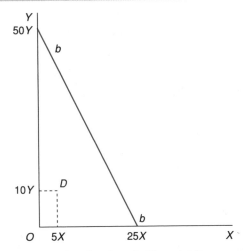

Each point of the diagram represents a bundle of goods. The point D represents a bundle made up of 5X and 10Y. The line bb is a budget constraint drawn on the assumption that a consumer has an income of £50 and faces prices for X and Y of £2 and £1 respectively. The budget constraint divides those bundles of goods that the consumer can obtain, given income and their prices, from those that cannot be obtained.

The budget constraint

Now, in principle, we may extend the axes of Figure 2.1 indefinitely and hence encompass any conceivable bundle of X and Y, but this does not mean that the consumer is in fact able to select any bundle of X and Y found desirable. Goods and services are generally not free and what a consumer can get at a particular moment is limited by available purchasing power. Suppose, for simplicity, that the only source of purchasing power is the consumer's present **income**. This may be expressed as a certain sum of money per week and it puts an upper limit on consumption. We may represent this in Figure 2.1 in the following way.

X and Y are goods that have **prices** and it is reasonable enough to suppose that these prices may be taken as constant as far as the individual consumer is concerned. Suppose that the price of X is £2 per unit and that of Y £1 per unit. Suppose also that the consumer's income is £50 per week. Then it is obvious that, if all income is devoted to the consumption of X, the consumer may have not more than 25 units of X per week; alternatively that same consumer may have 50 units of Y per week. However, there is nothing to stop X and Y being combined in the chosen consumption pattern. We can calculate how much is spent on any particular quantity (less than 25) of X, and this sum subtracted from income gives the amount left over to be spent on Y. This amount divided by the price of Y tells us the maximum amount of Y that can be bought, given the quantity of X. If we carry out this calculation for every quantity of X between 0 and 25 and link up the resulting bundles of goods, we derive the line bb in Figure 2.1 which represents the consumer's so-called **budget constraint**. This line separates all those consumption bundles that can be afforded from those that cannot be afforded. Given the prices we have assumed, it is clear that for every unit of X given up, two units of Y may be substituted. Hence the slope of this constraint is obviously the inverse of the ratio of the prices we have assumed. If X costs £2 and Y £1, then the ratio of the price of Y to the price of X is 1/2 and the rate at which Y may be substituted for X is 2/1.

Box 2.1	**Defining budget constraints**

We can specify the equation of the budget constraint as follows. We may define the consumer's money income as M, and retain as the objects of choice in our problem the goods X and Y, which sell at prices p_X and p_Y respectively. If we assume that the consumer spends all their income, it will follow by definition that income (M) equals expenditure ($p_X X + p_Y Y$). Hence

$$M = p_X X + p_Y Y \tag{2.1.1}$$

Rearranging terms to form an equation with Y expressed as a function of X, we derive

$$Y = \frac{M}{p_Y} - \frac{p_X}{p_Y} X \tag{2.1.2}$$

This equation defines a straight line – the budget constraint – with intercept M/p_Y and slope p_X/p_Y. It should be clear from an inspection of equation (2.1.2) that increases in money income shift the budget constraint outwards and parallel to itself; changes in M do not affect the slope of the constraint – p_X/p_Y. Changes in the price of X swivel the budget constraint around, pivoting it on the intercept with the Y axis (which equals M/p_Y). An increase in p_X causes it to pivot inwards. Changes in the price of Y lead the budget constraint to pivot around its intercept with the X axis (since M/p_Y alters when p_Y alters), inwards when p_Y increases and outwards when it falls. It should be stressed that in developing this formulation, we do not need to stick with the assumption that income equals expenditure, which of course implies that the consumer does not save. If consumers do not spend all their income, expenditures lie inside the budget constraint rather than on the line itself ($p_X X + p_Y Y < M$). We return to the issue of saving in Chapter 5.

The consumer's tastes

We make two assumptions about our consumer's tastes. First we assume that any two bundles of goods can be compared. The consumer can decide if bundle 1 or 2 is preferable, or whether either bundle is equally desirable. In this last eventuality the consumer is said to be *indifferent* between the two bundles. Second we assume that these comparisons are made in a *consistent* fashion. By this we mean that if, when bundles 1 and 2 are compared, 1 is preferred, and when 2 and 3 are compared, 2 is preferred, then, when 1 and 3 are compared, 1 will be preferred.

This assumption of consistent preferences is all that economists imply when they speak of the consumer being 'rational'. However, in constructing the elementary theory

Figure 2.2

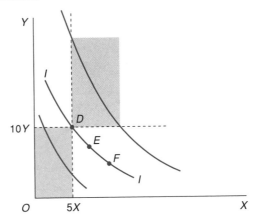

Any point in the area above and to the right of D represents a bundle of goods preferred to D. D is preferred to any point below and to its left. Thus the indifference curve II passing through D must have a negative slope. It is generally assumed that such curves are convex to the origin.

of choice, it is usual to make certain subsidiary assumptions in addition to the basic one of consistent preferences. First, having already assumed that the objects of choice are desirable, it is but a small step to the propositions that, when compared with D (the point in Figure 2.1 representing 5X and 10Y), any bundle that has either more X and no less Y or more Y and no less X will be preferred. In terms of Figure 2.2 this means that any point in the shaded area above and to the right of D will be preferred to D, and that D will be preferred to any point in the area below and to the left of it.

It follows from this that if D is one of a set of bundles of goods among which the consumer is indifferent, such bundles must lie in the areas below and to the right of D and above and to the left of D. It is usual to go further than this and argue that all such points must lie on a continuous negatively sloped line, an *indifference curve* such as the line II in Figure 2.2, a curve that is convex towards the origin. A smooth convex curve is by no means the only formulation of an indifference curve compatible with the assumption of rationality, but it is both intuitively plausible and, as we shall see below, productive of sensible predictions about behaviour. This particular shape involves what is called a *diminishing marginal rate of substitution* between the goods. This shape implies that the more X there is relative to Y in the bundle to begin with, the more X is required to compensate the consumer for the loss of a given amount of Y. Thus, in Figure 2.2 the movement from E to F involves the same loss of Y as that from D to E, but requires a larger gain in X to keep our consumer on the same indifference curve. The *marginal rate of substitution* of X for Y is the ratio of the amount of X needed to compensate for a small (in the limit infinitesimal) loss of Y to that loss of Y. It is given by the slope of the indifference curve, which is negative; and it becomes more negative (i.e. *diminishes*) as we move down the curve from left to right.

Now II is a particular indifference curve. We may think of the consumption of any bundle of goods on it as yielding a particular level of satisfaction, or *utility*, to the consumer. However, there are indifference curves passing through every point of Figure 2.2,

Figure 2.3

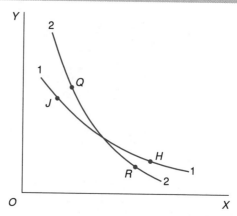

Indifference curves that cross are incompatible with the assumption that consumers order bundles of goods consistently.

each one negatively sloped and each one convex to the origin. Those which pass through points above and to the right of *D* link up bundles of goods that yield higher levels of satisfaction than those on *II*; those below and to the left yield lower levels of satisfaction. Such curves can never cross one another, for this would violate the rationality assumption. Consider Figure 2.3 in which two indifference curves have been drawn to cross and consider their interpretation. The consumer is indifferent between points *H* and *J* on curve 1 and between *R* and *Q* on curve 2. However, bundle *H* has more of both *X* and *Y* than does *R* and hence must be preferred to it; for exactly the same reason, point *Q* must be preferred to *J*. There is clearly an inconsistency here that violates the **rationality** assumption, and it obviously arises because the curves cross one another.

Box 2.2 | **More on indifference curves**

Assume that a person consumes two goods *X* and *Y*, and that the cardinal utility function is

$$U = X^{0.6}Y^{0.4} \qquad (2.2.1)$$

This is an example of a Cobb-Douglas function, characterised by constant exponents, in our case 0.6 and 0.4.

The marginal utility of *X* is

$$\frac{\partial U}{\partial X} = 0.6\left(\frac{Y}{X}\right)^{0.4} \qquad (2.2.2)$$

and the marginal utility of *Y* is

$$\frac{\partial U}{\partial Y} = 0.4\left(\frac{X}{Y}\right)^{0.6} \qquad (2.2.3)$$

It is clear that we have diminishing marginal utility because as X increases $\partial U/\partial X$ declines and as Y increases $\partial U/\partial Y$ declines. For readers that find this reasoning difficult it is straightforward to substitute particular values of X and Y and then allow the person to consume, in the one case more X and in the other case more Y, and calculate the marginal utilities that are obtained.

We can now define any of this person's indifference curves. Say, for example, we wish to derive the indifference curve for 10 units of utility. We fix $U = 10$ in (2.2.1)

$$10 = X^{0.6}Y^{0.4}$$

and rearrange this to define the 10 units of utility indifference curve:

$$Y = \frac{10^{2.5}}{X^{1.5}} \qquad (2.2.4)$$

This indifference curve has the usual property of a negative and diminishing marginal rate of substitution. To show this we can work out the slope of the indifference curve:

$$\frac{dY}{dX} = -\frac{1.5(10^{2.5})}{X^{2.5}} = -1.5\left(\frac{10}{X}\right)^{2.5} \qquad (2.2.5)$$

The indifference has a negative slope, as we would expect, and as X increases the marginal rate of substitution declines. The observant reader will have realised that we must have a diminishing marginal rate of substitution because we have diminishing marginal utility.

More generally we can define any constant level of utility $\bar{U}$. It then follows that for the utility function being used here any indifference curve is

$$Y = \frac{\bar{U}^{2.5}}{X^{1.5}} \qquad (2.2.6)$$

More on tastes – ordinal and cardinal utility

We have characterised the consumer's tastes in an *indifference map* showing how satisfaction (*utility*) varies with (*is a function of*) the consumption pattern. This *utility function* has two basic properties. Each indifference curve is convex to the origin, and as we move upwards and to the right the indifference curves represent higher and higher levels of satisfaction. Notice that, in constructing this utility function, we have said nothing about the intensity of the consumer's preferences. We have assumed that the consumer is able to rank bundles of goods with reference to their capacity to satisfy desires, but we have assumed nothing about the degree to which any bundle of goods does so.

To put it another way, in the foregoing analysis (though not in Box 2.2) we have simply noted that higher indifference curves represent higher levels of utility; we have not found it necessary to specify how much higher. We have been dealing with an **ordinal utility** function, that is, a function that tells us the *order* in which a consumer ranks bundles of goods, but tells us nothing at all about the *intensity* of likes or dislikes for particular consumption patterns. We can only use relative terms such as 'better' and 'worse', 'preferred' and 'not preferred' in this context. It is possible, however, as we did in Box 2.2, to postulate a **cardinal utility** function which, in addition to telling us about how bundles of goods are ordered, tells us about the intensity of likes and dislikes, measuring satisfaction, or utility, in precise units. To argue by analogy for a moment, in the measurement of length, an ordinal scale would tell us only that some distances were longer or shorter than (or the same length as) others. A cardinal scale would be set up in units of yards or metres and would tell us how long each distance was and hence *how much* longer (or shorter) than any other. So long as we deal with questions about choice under conditions of certainty, the ordinal utility assumption suffices as a basis for consumer theory but, as we shall see later, a cardinal utility function is extremely useful in dealing with choice in conditions of risk; indeed the existence of such a function is implicit in the possibility of such a choice. However, for the moment we are analysing consumer choice in conditions of certainty, and the idea of ordinal utility is all we require to tackle this problem.

The solution to the choice problem

We now have all the ingredients necessary for the solution of the consumer's choice problem. We have defined the objects of choice. These are bundles of goods, *consumption patterns*, made up of various quantities of X and Y. We have also derived the constraint upon choice. The consumer's money income combined with the prices of X and Y has enabled us to draw a line, a *budget constraint*, that separates those bundles of X and Y that are attainable from those that are not. Finally, the consumer's tastes have been summarised in an *indifference map*. In Figure 2.4 we bring these three ingredients together, and the solution to the consumer's choice problem immediately appears.

Figure 2.4

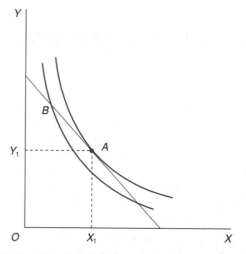

A is the bundle of goods which, of all those available, yields the consumer the highest level of satisfaction. This maximum satisfaction bundle occurs where an indifference curve is tangent to the budget constraint.

The consumer wishes to do as well as possible, to select that consumption pattern out of all those available that will yield the highest level of satisfaction – the consumer wishes to *maximise utility*. In terms of Figure 2.4 this involves selecting a consumption pattern on as high an indifference curve as possible. Clearly that pattern is given by the point A with the consumer getting X_1 of X per week and Y_1 of Y.

Consider the properties of this solution, which we call a situation of **equilibrium** for the consumer because there are no forces that would cause a move away from A. First, the point A lies *on* the budget constraint, not inside it. This happens because we have assumed that, when compared with any particular bundle of goods, a bundle with more of one good and no less of another is preferred. For any consumption pattern within the budget constraint, there is at least one on the constraint with just this property. Does this then mean that the analysis of consumer choice rules out saving? It does not, for, as we shall see in Chapter 6 it is possible to characterise saving as an act of devoting current income to future consumption. For our analysis, we made the simplifying assumption that we would not for the time being consider the choice of consumption patterns over time. Hence we have ruled out saving here for the sake of simplicity, not predicted that it cannot take place.

The second point to note about the solution depicted in Figure 2.4 is that at A an indifference curve is just tangent to the budget constraint. As readers will discover, such tangency solutions continuously occur in geometric representations of economic theory. The slope of the budget constraint tells us, as we saw above, the rate at which our consumer is permitted to substitute X for Y by the structure of prices. For every amount of Y given up some amount of X is obtained instead. The slope is equal to the ratio of the price of Y to that of X. The slope of an indifference curve at any particular point tells us the rate at which the consumer would have to substitute X for Y in order to maintain a given level of satisfaction, or to enjoy a constant level of utility. This slope is, of course, the marginal rate of substitution of X for Y. Thus we may characterise a point of tangency between an indifference curve and a budget constraint as a situation in which the marginal rate of substitution of X for Y is just equal to the ratio of the price of Y to the price of X.

That A is indeed a point of maximum satisfaction, or maximum utility, can be seen in another way. Consider the point B in Figure 2.4. Suppose the consumer started at this point for some reason. Given available income and the set of prices ruling, the consumer could get more X for a particular sacrifice of Y than is necessary to stay on the indifference curve that passes through B. Thus, by substituting X for Y along the budget constraint, the consumer can move on to higher and higher indifference curves; until, that is, A is reached. With the movement from B towards A, Y becomes progressively more valuable relative to X and the rate at which the consumer is willing to give up Y in return for X falls. At A the rate at which the consumer is willing to give up Y to get X coincides with the rate at which the price structure permits this substitution to be made. Any movement to the right of A would involve having to give up more Y than is required for the maintenance of a particular level of utility, so further substitution will not be made.

To sum up then, the utility-maximising choice involves selecting the bundle of goods where the budget constraint and the indifference curve touch tangentially. At this point both have the same slope and we can say that the rate at which the consumer is willing to substitute X for Y to maintain constant utility is equal to the ratio of the price of Y to that of X.

Box 2.3   **More on consumer equilibrium**

We can use the Cobb-Douglas utility function shown in (2.2.1) to examine consumer equilibrium. The earlier utility function was defined for two goods X and Y

$$U = X^{0.6}Y^{0.4} \tag{2.2.1}$$

Any indifference curve, defined for a constant level of utility $\bar{U}$, was

$$Y = \frac{\bar{U}^{2.5}}{X^{1.5}} \tag{2.2.6}$$

The slope, i.e. marginal rate of substitution, of any indifference curve is

$$\frac{dY}{dX} = -1.5\left(\frac{\bar{U}}{X}\right)^{2.5} \tag{2.3.1}$$

Assume that the price of X is £20, the price of Y is £5 and that total income per period is £200. We can now specify the expenditure function:

$$200 = 20X + 5Y \tag{2.3.2}$$

Rearranging the expenditure function we can define the budget constraint

$$Y = 40 - 4X \tag{2.3.3}$$

As shown in Box 2.1, in this constraint 4 is the relative price of the two goods i.e. 20/5. We know that a consumer maximises utility when the budget line is a tangent to an indifference curve, i.e. when the slope of the budget line is the same as the slope of the indifference curve:

$$-1.5\left(\frac{\bar{U}}{X}\right)^{2.5} = -4$$

Rearranging and simplifying, the utility maximising level of X is

$$X = 0.375^{0.4}\bar{U} \tag{2.3.4}$$

This, of course, defines an infinite number of solutions, each one corresponding to a different indifference curve i.e. a particular fixed level of utility ($\bar{U}$). Two steps are used to solve our consumer's equilibrium:

1. We use our optimality condition and the utility function to derive a general expression for optimal levels of both X and Y.
2. We use this general expression and the budget constraint to find the consumer equilibrium relevant for specific income and prices.

Step one

Substitute the utility maximising solution $\bar{U} = (1/0.375^{0.4})X$ into the utility function:

$$(1/0.375^{0.4})X = X^{0.6}Y^{0.4}$$

$$\left(\frac{Y}{X}\right)^{0.4} = \frac{1}{0.375^{0.4}}$$

$$Y^{0.4} = \left(\frac{X}{0.375}\right)^{0.4} \quad \text{or} \quad Y = \frac{X}{0.375}$$

Step two

Substitute $Y = X/0.375$ into the budget constraint $Y = 40 - 4X$. This allows us to define our unique consumer equilibrium: $X = 6$, $Y = 16$.

As exercises you can show that with this unique equilibrium:

1. the marginal rate of substitution is equal to the slope of the budget line, i.e. the ratio of prices;
2. the consumer spends 50 per cent more on good X than on good Y, and why this is the case.

* An algebraic solution to the choice problem

Now instead of formulating our consumer's choice problem in geometric terms, we may use algebra instead. Why, though, should we simply repeat the same result using a different technique? Do we gain anything from doing so? The answer to this perfectly reasonable enquiry is fourfold.

First, as we shall see, the use of algebra enables us to bring out one or two points of economic interpretation more sharply than does the geometric technique.

Second, as will become more apparent as this book progresses, it is easy to be misled into believing that a result that depends entirely on the particular way in which a diagram is drawn is more general in nature. It is much more difficult (but not impossible) unintentionally to bury specific implicit assumptions when algebra is used, and so its application here provides a useful check on the robustness of what has gone before.

Third, the use of geometry severely limits the number of goods with which we can deal – usually to two – but algebra enables us to extend the range of the analysis to three, four ... and indeed n goods, where n is any finite positive number. In what follows here, we shall apply algebra only to a two-good case. That will help the reader unfamiliar with elementary calculus to see clearly the relationship between what is done here and what was done in the preceding geometric analysis. However, those who feel at home with these techniques will be able to satisfy themselves easily enough that the results that follow may be easily extended to cases of many goods, and that the essential properties of the results we shall establish remain unchanged when this is done.

Finally, the techniques used here appear now for the first, but by no means the last, time in this book. Their application here is straightforward, and adds only a little to what we have derived with geometry. Later in this book, we shall meet problems whose geometric treatment would be so difficult (or even impossible) that they are much better tackled with algebra. The reader will find working through this section a useful preparation for coming to grips with these later applications.

If we continue to use the notation introduced above, so that M is the consumer's money income, X and Y are goods, and money prices p_X and p_Y, we note that any pattern of expenditure which satisfies the inequality

$$M \geq p_X X + p_Y Y \tag{2.1}$$

is feasible. Our consumer's utility function may be written as

$$U = u(X, Y) \tag{2.2}$$

Though we shall show below that the assumption is not necessary, the reader will find it helpful at this stage to think of this function as relating a cardinally measurable level of utility to the consumption of X and Y, so that its partial derivatives $\partial U/\partial X$ and $\partial U/\partial Y$, often referred to as the *marginal utilities* of X and Y respectively, have well-defined quantitative interpretations. Now note that in terms of our diagrammatic representation, each indifference curve represents combinations of X and Y for which utility levels are constant. If we take the total differential of (2.2)

$$dU = \frac{\partial U}{\partial X}dX + \frac{\partial U}{\partial Y}dY \tag{2.3}$$

then utility is constant when $dU = 0$, namely,

$$\frac{\partial U}{\partial X}dX + \frac{\partial U}{\partial Y}dY = 0 \tag{2.4}$$

The slope of the indifference curve is given by the way in which Y must change when X changes to keep utility constant, or dY/dX. Rearranging (2.4) yields

$$-\frac{dY}{dX} = \frac{\partial U/\partial X}{\partial U/\partial Y} \tag{2.5}$$

Since we denote the change in utility for an infinitesimal change in X or Y the *marginal utility* of X or Y, equation (2.5) yields the important insight that the slope of the indifference curve, or the *marginal rate of substitution of Y for X, is equal to the inverse ratio of the marginal utilities of the goods.*

The choice problem for the consumer then, is to maximise (2.2) subject to (2.1). If we limit the analysis to situations in which the consumer is *on* the budget constraint, so that (2.1) becomes

$$M - p_X X - p_Y Y = 0 \tag{2.6}$$

we may solve this problem using the method of Lagrange multipliers by forming the function

$$V = u(X, Y) + \lambda(M - p_X X - p_Y Y) \tag{2.7}$$

where λ is the Lagrange multiplier. The first-order conditions for (2.7) to be maximised are

$$\frac{\partial V}{\partial X} = \partial U/\partial X - \lambda p_X = 0 \tag{2.8}$$

$$\frac{\partial V}{\partial Y} = \partial U/\partial Y - \lambda p_Y = 0 \tag{2.9}$$

$$\frac{\partial V}{\partial \lambda} = M - p_X X - p_Y Y = 0 \tag{2.10}$$

Strictly speaking, these conditions might characterise either a maximum or a minimum of (2.2), but the assumptions we have made about tastes, namely, that more goods are preferred to fewer, and that a diminishing marginal rate of substitution rules between the two goods, guarantee that second-order conditions for a maximum are satisfied in this case. Equation (2.10) tells us that the consumer must choose a bundle of goods on the budget constraint to maximise utility, and certain other properties of this maximum may be revealed by dividing equation (2.8) by (2.9). This yields

$$\frac{\partial U/\partial X}{\partial U/\partial Y} = \frac{p_X}{p_Y} \tag{2.11}$$

Clearly the right-hand side of this expression is the ratio of the prices of the two goods. The left-hand side is the ratio of the marginal utility of X to that of Y, and as we saw is an algebraic expression for the marginal rate of substitution between the goods. Hence (2.11) is an algebraic version of the tangency solution of the consumer's choice problem depicted in Figure 2.4. It tells us that utility is maximised when the consumer equates the marginal rate of substitution between the goods to their price ratio.

Now whenever we do constrained maximisation we get a Lagrange multiplier, and that multiplier often has an economic interpretation. To consider the interpretation of λ in this case enables us to sharpen up considerably our understanding of why it sufficed to postulate ordinal utility when carrying out our geometric analysis. Equations (2.8) and (2.9) taken together yield

$$\lambda = \frac{\partial U/\partial X}{p_X} = \frac{\partial U/\partial Y}{p_Y} \tag{2.12}$$

Thus the Lagrange multiplier here tells us how utility changes as money expenditure on either X or Y is increased. It measures, therefore, the *marginal utility of money income*. The fact that λ vanishes from equation (2.11) tells us, however, that the quantitative value of the marginal utility of income is irrelevant to the solution to the consumer's choice problem. Here, then, we have an algebraic confirmation of the assertion we made earlier that we do not need to be able to measure utility cardinally in order to analyse the type of choice under consideration in this chapter. The quantitative value of utility is irrelevant to the outcome of such a choice.

The income consumption curve

Finding an equilibrium consumption bundle is the starting point of the theory of consumer choice; it is not its end point. We wish to use this analysis to derive predictions about behaviour. We wish to be able to say how the composition of the bundle of goods an individual chooses will change when the observable variables that underlie the budget constraint change in value. There are three such variables: the consumer's income, the price of X and the price of Y.

A different level of income, with the prices of X and Y remaining the same, does not imply a different slope for the budget constraint. This slope tells us the rate at which X may be substituted for Y and, as we have seen, depends only upon the ratio of the two prices. However, a different level of income does involve a different location for the budget constraint. The higher the income, the further up and to the right does the budget constraint lie, for the more bundles of goods the consumer can afford.

There is very little that can be said in general about the consequences for consumption of different levels of income. At higher levels of income the chosen consumption pattern may include more of both X and Y, more X and less Y, or more Y and less X. Any one of these solutions is compatible with an indifference map of the general form we have been

Figure 2.5

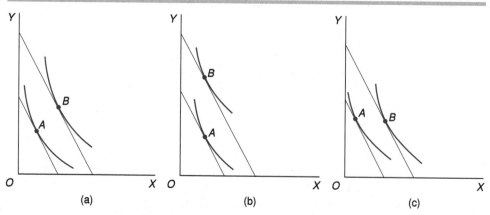

(a)	(b)	(c)

As the consumer's income increases, consumption shifts from *A* to *B*. In panel (a), this movement involves an increase in the consumption of both goods: they are both normal. In panel (b), consumption of *X* falls: it is an inferior good, but *Y* is normal. In panel (c), *X* is normal and *Y* is inferior.

assuming, as is apparent from Figure 2.5. All we can do is give labels to the possibilities. Thus, if the quantity of a good consumed falls as income increases, we call that good an **inferior good**. If it rises, we call it a **normal** (or sometimes a **superior**) good. There is no reason why a good must always be in one category or another. We can easily conceive of a good being normal at low levels of income and becoming inferior at higher levels. In Figure 2.6 we consider a variety of income levels in combination with a particular indifference map, and, linking up the points of tangency along what is called an **income consumption curve**, depict just such a case for the commodity *X*.

Figure 2.6 **An income consumption curve**

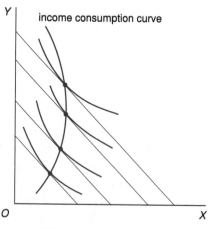

income consumption curve

As it is drawn, *Y* is everywhere normal; *X* is normal at low levels of income but becomes inferior at higher levels.

Now the analysis carried out so far has been of the behaviour of a consumer at a particular time and Figure 2.6 shows what consumption patterns would be selected at different levels of income *at that time*. This is *not* necessarily the same thing as indicating how, while relative prices remain constant, the consumption pattern will change *over time* as income changes *over time*. However, it is precisely the ability to make predictions about such changes that we seek from economic theory. If we are willing to assume that tastes remain stable over time, in other words that the indifference map does not change, and that there are no factors involved *in the movement* from one preferred consumption pattern to another that influence the consumption pattern being aimed at – and we will meet cases below where this particular assumption is inappropriate – we may treat the income consumption curve as telling us how the consumer's consumption pattern will respond to changes in income over time.

Box 2.4	**More on the income consumption curve**

In Box 2.3 consumer equilibrium was examined. For two goods X and Y we had a Cobb-Douglas utility function

$$U = X^{0.6}Y^{0.4} \tag{2.2.1}$$

With the price of X being p_X and the price of Y being p_Y we can define the expenditure function

$$M = p_XX + p_YY \tag{2.1.1}$$

As an exercise use the same technique as used in Box 2.3 to show that in this more general case consumer equilibrium will involve

$$X = \bar{U}\left(1.5\frac{p_Y}{p_X}\right)^{0.4} \quad \text{or} \quad \bar{U} = X\left(\frac{1}{1.5}\frac{p_X}{p_Y}\right)^{0.4}$$

and that in equilibrium

$$\frac{Y}{X} = \frac{1}{1.5}\frac{p_X}{p_Y} \tag{2.4.1}$$

With our Box 2.3 example $p_X = 20$ and $p_Y = 5$, and so in equilibrium

$$\frac{Y}{X} = \frac{4}{1.5} = 2.67 \tag{2.4.2}$$

We can present the equilibrium condition as in Illustration 2.1.

The ray OA is defined by $Y/X = 2.67$. With the level of utility equal to 8.88 we are in equilibrium on the $U = 8.88$ indifference curve where the budget constraint BB' is a tangent to the indifference curve. So the consumer is in equilibrium with $X = 6$ and $Y = 16$; this was the equilibrium in Box 2.3. With the level of utility equal to 4.44 we are in equilibrium on the $U = 4.44$ indifference curve where the budget constraint CC' is a tangent to the indifference curve. So the consumer is in equilibrium at $X = 3$ and $Y = 8$. It is clear that budget line CC' is parallel to BB'. So the only difference between them is that BB' involves a higher level of income of £200 rather than £100 for CC'. It follows that the ray OA is the income consumption curve.

Illustration 2.1

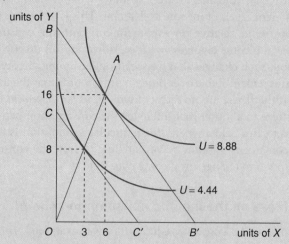

Note that the income consumption curve derived here is linear. This is an implication of the Cobb-Douglas utility function. For any set of prices, and with the utility function used here, the income consumption curve is defined using (2.4.1) i.e.

$$Y = \frac{1}{1.5}\frac{p_X}{p_Y}X \tag{2.4.3}$$

This always plots a straight line, the slope of which is determined by relative prices and how much the consumer likes X compared with Y. More complex utility functions, that are not Cobb-Douglas, can yield non-linear income consumption curves.

Price consumption curves

In addition to the income consumption curve, we may derive **price consumption curves**, one for variations in the price of X and the other for variations in the price of Y. Since the analysis is the same for each, we need only explicitly consider varying the price of X while holding the price of Y and money income constant. Clearly, when the price of X varies the point at which the budget constraint cuts the Y-axis is unchanged, since this represents the amount of Y that can be bought when all income is devoted to its purchase. What does change is the intercept on the X-axis and the slope of the constraint. As the price of X increases, less X can be bought for the same money and so the point at which the budget constraint cuts the X-axis moves nearer the origin and the slope becomes steeper. In other words, the slope of the budget constraint is given by the ratio of prices of X to that of Y. Raising the price of X increases this ratio and hence the slope of the constraint.

For every price of X there is a preferred consumption bundle and the points representing these may be linked up in a price consumption curve. Figure 2.7 shows three possible situations, all compatible with our assumptions. There is again little to be said about the shape of the curve, but note that the possibility depicted in panel (c), where over a certain range the quantity of X consumed actually falls as the price of X falls, is more an analytic

Figure 2.7

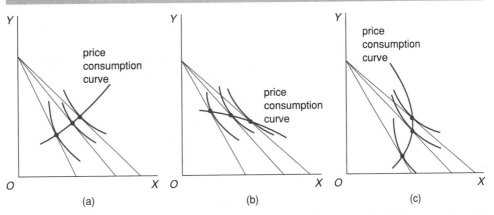

(a)   (b)   (c)

As the price of X falls the consumer moves along a price consumption curve. X and Y are complements in panel (a) and substitutes in panel (b), while X is a 'Giffen' good in panel (c).

curiosity than a practically relevant case. It is known as the **Giffen** case after the economist who first noticed the possibility of such behaviour. In panel (b) we have the quantity of Y consumed falling as the price of X declines, while in panel (a) we have a case in which the quantities of both X and Y consumed rise as the price of X declines. In the first of these cases X and Y are termed **substitutes** and in the second **complements**, for obvious reasons.[1]

Box 2.5   **More on price consumption curves**

We can continue the same example, using our Cobb-Douglas utility function, and derive a price consumption curve. We know from Box 2.4 that when our consumer is in equilibrium, consumption of X and Y will be

$$\frac{Y}{X} = \frac{1}{1.5}\frac{p_X}{p_Y} \tag{2.4.1}$$

In earlier examples we assumed $p_Y = 5$. Substituting in this price of Y, consumption of X and Y is

$$\frac{Y}{X} = \frac{1}{7.5}p_X \tag{2.4.2}$$

This expression defines a price consumption curve for X. It shows the consumption of Y and X for any price of X:

with $p_X = 20$, in equilibrium $Y/X = 2.67$,
with $p_X = 15$, in equilibrium $Y/X = 2$,
with $p_X = 10$, in equilibrium $Y/X = 1.33$.

Using our earlier income level of £200, and the first case with $p_X = 20$, $Y = 16$ and $X = 6$, so $Y/X = 16/6 = 2.67$ (see Box 2.4). We can present the price consumption curve on a diagram equivalent to Box 2.4 as in Illustration 2.2.

Illustration 2.2

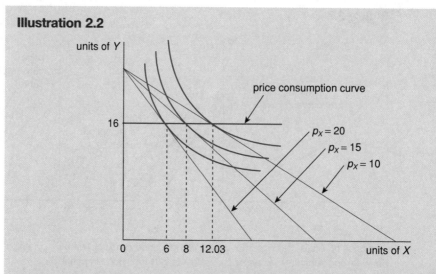

The price of X falls from 20 to 15 to 10, shown by the pivoting budget constraint. The reader can use the techniques shown in previous boxes to derive the equilibrium values of X and Y shown here. The equilibrium consumption of X increases from 6 to 8 to 12.03, and the consumption of Y remains unchanged at 16. So 16/6 = 2.67, 16/8 = 2, and 16/12.03 = 1.33. These are the equilibria calculated above. The implication, therefore, is that the price consumption curve for X is a horizontal line (as shown in the diagram). This is a characteristic of the Cobb-Douglas utility function we are using here. It implies that the two goods X and Y are neither substitutes nor complements. More complex utility functions can produce the price consumption curves shown in Box 2.4.

The Engel curve

Now from the foregoing analysis we may derive the **Engel curve** and the **demand curve** for X. The Engel curve shows the relationship between a consumer's income and the quantity of a good bought. Figure 2.8 gives an example of the derivation of such a curve, and should be self-explanatory. The slope of the Engel curve at any point is known as the *marginal propensity to consume X* and measures, for a small change (in the limiting case an infinitesimal change) in income, the ratio of the resulting change in the consumption of the good to that change in income. We may also define the *average propensity to consume* the good as the ratio of the quantity of it bought at any particular level of income to that level of income, or equivalently, given the good's price, as the proportion of income devoted to buying it. The ratio of the marginal propensity to consume the good to the average propensity to consume it is defined as the **income elasticity of demand** for the good, and measures the *proportional* change in the consumption of the good as a ratio to the *proportional* change in income that causes the variation.

Some extremely simple algebra makes this obvious enough. Let us continue to use the symbol M for income and the symbol δ to mean a 'small change in'.[2] It should be clear that the marginal propensity to consume can be written algebraically as $\delta X/\delta M$. Equally clearly, the average propensity to consume X is X/M. The ratio of the marginal propensity

Figure 2.8

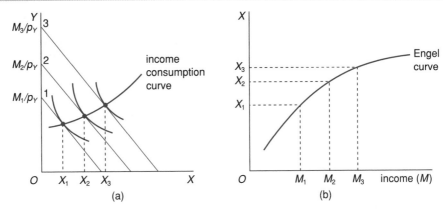

Increases in income (from M_1 to M_2 to M_3) shift out the budget constraint in panel (a) (from 1 to 2 to 3). From the income consumption curve we read off the associated levels of consumption of X (X_1, X_2 and X_3). We plot these against income in panel (b) to generate the Engel curve.

to consume X to the average propensity may then be rearranged as follows to give the ratio of a proportional change in the quantity of X demanded to a proportional change in income, the income elasticity of demand for X:

$$e_M = \frac{\delta X/\delta M}{X/M} = \frac{\delta X}{X} \bigg/ \frac{\delta M}{M} \qquad (2.13)$$

Obviously an inferior good, for which the marginal propensity to consume is negative, also has a negative income elasticity of demand, while one for which the marginal propensity to consume is positive, but lower than the average propensity to consume, has an income elasticity of demand between 0 and 1. The proportion of income spent on such a good falls as income increases. Exactly the opposite holds true for a good whose income elasticity of demand is greater than unity.

Box 2.6   Deriving the Engel curve

We can use the Cobb-Douglas utility function from previous boxes to derive an Engel curve. Earlier we assumed that a person consumes two goods (X and Y) and has a utility function:

$$U = X^{0.6}Y^{0.4} \qquad (2.2.1)$$

In Box 2.4 we found that when this person maximises utility the two goods are consumed in a ratio determined by preferences (i.e. the 0.6 and 0.4 exponents) and prices:

$$\frac{Y}{X} = \frac{1}{1.5}\frac{p_X}{p_Y} \qquad (2.4.1)$$

This condition implies that utility maximising expenditure on good Y is

$$p_Y Y = \frac{1}{1.5}p_X X \qquad (2.6.1)$$

We can now derive the Engel curve for good X by using the budget constraint that defines feasible consumption levels for X and Y:

$$M = p_X X + p_Y Y \qquad (2.1.1)$$

We can remove the expenditure on good Y by using the utility maximising condition

$$M = p_X X + \frac{1}{1.5} p_X X \qquad (2.6.2)$$

This implies the following function, which defines the Engel curve for X:

$$X = \frac{0.6}{p_X} M \qquad (2.6.3)$$

Note that the Engel curve defined by this function is a straight line because of the underlying Cobb-Douglas utility function. The slope of the curve is determined by how much the consumer likes good X, 0.6 in this case, and the price of X. The associated income elasticity of demand is

$$e_M = \frac{\partial X}{\partial M} = \frac{0.6}{p_X} \frac{M}{X} \qquad (2.6.4)$$

Using the fact that $X = (0.6/p_X)M$, $e_M = X/X = 1$. With a Cobb-Douglas utility function the income elasticity is always 1: i.e. we have normal goods with a constant income elasticity.

The demand curve

The demand curve, which relates the quantity of X demanded to the price of X, is just as easily derived; this is done in Figure 2.9 for the usual case of a non-Giffen good so that the curve is negatively sloped. Here too there is an elasticity concept to be explained. The inverse slope of the curve, $\partial X/\partial p_X$ divided by the ratio of quantity demanded to price, X/p_X, gives us the **own price elasticity of demand** for the good e_p. This measures the ratio of a *proportional* change in the quantity demanded of the good to the *proportional* change in price that brought it about. In symbols we have

$$e_p = \frac{\partial X/\partial p_X}{X/p_X} = \frac{\partial X}{X} \bigg/ \frac{\partial p_X}{p_X} \qquad (2.14)$$

Box 2.7 **More on the demand curve**

We can derive the demand curve for the Cobb-Douglas utility function used in this chapter. In Box 2.6 we derived the function for the Cobb-Douglas Engel curve

$$X = \frac{0.6M}{p_X} \qquad (2.6.3)$$

So with a fixed level of income (say $M = 200$) this defines a demand function for X

$$X = \frac{120}{p_X} \qquad (2.7.1)$$

Figure 2.9

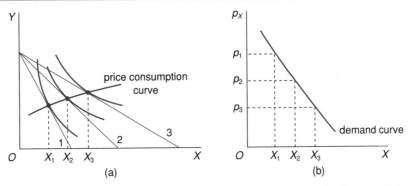

As the price of X falls (from p_1 to p_2 to p_3), the budget constraint in panel (a) shifts (from 1 to 2 to 3). From the price consumption curve we read off the associated quantities of X demanded (X_1, X_2 and X_3) and plot these against the price of X in panel (b), thus generating a demand curve. Here we hold money income and the price of Y constant.

The corresponding demand curve for X is shown below in Illustration 2.3. Note that an increase in income will shift this curve to the right because good X is normal (see Box 2.5).

We can define the associated own price elasticity of demand:

$$e_P = \frac{\partial X}{\partial p_X} \frac{p_X}{X} = -\frac{120}{p_X^2} \frac{p_X}{X} = -\frac{X}{X} = -1 \qquad (2.7.2)$$

i.e. a Cobb-Douglas utility function implies a unit elasticity demand curve.

Illustration 2.3

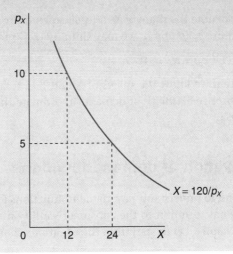

The own price elasticity of demand is negative, because the demand curve is downward sloping, i.e. $\partial X/\partial p_X$ is negative. However, we often neglect the sign of this parameter in discussing it and talk in terms of its absolute value. There is a relationship between the magnitude of the price elasticity and the volume of expenditure on a good. If the absolute value of the own price elasticity of demand for a good is equal to one, then expenditure on the good does not change as its price changes. The effect on expenditure of a lower price is just offset by the higher quantity bought. If the absolute value is greater than one, then the increase in quantity bought more than offsets the influence of the fall in price and expenditure increases, while the opposite holds true when elasticity is less than one.

Finally, it should be noted that there is a third elasticity concept in demand theory: the **cross elasticity of demand**. This measures the responsiveness of the quantity of X demanded to changes in the price of Y (or vice versa). Thus, the cross elasticity of demand for X with respect to p_Y, the price of Y, is given by

$$e_c = \frac{\partial X/\partial p_X}{X/p_Y} = \frac{\partial X}{X} \bigg/ \frac{\partial p_X}{p_Y} \tag{2.15}$$

The sign of this elasticity will be positive if the goods are substitutes and negative if they are complements, as the reader may readily verify by considering the direction of consumption changes in response to price changes in the two different cases.

The own and cross price elasticity of demand can be related to one another through the budget constraint via another simple piece of algrebra. If we take the differential of the budget constraint (2.1)

$$dM = X dp_X + p_X dX + Y dp_Y + p_Y dY \tag{2.16}$$

and assume that neither money income nor the price of Y change ($dM = dp_Y = 0$), we get

$$X dp_X + p_X dX + p_Y dY = 0 \tag{2.17}$$

Multiplying through by $p_X/M dp_X$ and noting that $1 = X/X = Y/Y$ yields

$$\frac{p_X X}{M} + \left(\frac{dX}{X} \frac{p_X}{dp_X}\right)\left(\frac{p_X X}{M}\right) + \left(\frac{dY}{Y} \frac{p_X}{dp_X}\right) \frac{p_Y Y}{M} = 0$$

If we denote the share of X in total expenditure $p_X X/M$ by α_1 and the share of Y in total expenditure $p_Y Y/M$ by α_2 we may simplify (2.17) to read

$$\alpha_1(1 + e_p) + \alpha_2 e_c = 0 \tag{2.18}$$

Hence if we know the shares of X and Y in total expenditure, we can use the value of the own price elasticity of demand to estimate the cross price elasticity of demand and vice versa.

* A formal derivation of demand functions

It is useful to understand how demand functions for goods may be derived formally from the algebraic solution to the consumer's utility maximisation problem developed earlier in this chapter. Let us start from the equations characterising that solution in terms of the equality of the marginal rate of substitution of Y for X being equal to the ratio of their prices. We may combine equations (2.5) and (2.11) to get what is often called the equilibrium condition,

$$-\frac{dY}{dX} = \frac{\partial U/\partial X}{\partial U/\partial Y} = \frac{p_X}{p_Y} \tag{2.19}$$

We know that the budget constraint must bind in equilibrium. Hence, repeating equation (2.1.1), we may write

$$M = p_X X + p_Y Y \tag{2.1.1}$$

Consumers may be presumed to know their own utility functions and incomes, while prices are given to them by the market. Hence equations (2.19) and (2.1) provide us with two equations in two unknowns, namely X and Y. They may be solved for these two variables as functions of prices and income, namely, as demand functions for the two goods in question. One way to do this is to multiply the top and bottom of equation (2.19) by the right-hand side of equation (2.2) which, the reader will recall, was a rearrangement of the budget constraint. This yields a complicated expression in X, M, p_X and p_Y,

$$\frac{\partial U(M/p_Y - Xp_X/p_Y)/\partial X}{\partial U(M/p_Y - Xp_X/p_Y)/\partial Y} = \frac{p_X}{p_Y} \tag{2.20}$$

This expression can in principle be rearranged with X as its left-hand side variable, thus yielding a demand function for X whose general form is

$$X = X^d(p_X, p_Y, M) \tag{2.21}$$

If we substitute equation (2.21) into the budget constraint and rearrange the resulting expression we get a demand function for Y of the general form

$$Y = Y^d(p_X, p_Y, M) \tag{2.22}$$

Note that it is sometimes convenient to write demand functions in what is known as the *inverse* form, with price as the dependent variable. The general form of these *inverse demand functions* is

$$p_X = X^p(X, p_Y, M) \tag{2.23}$$

and

$$p_Y = Y^p(Y, p_Y, M) \tag{2.24}$$

The foregoing analysis can be illustrated in a more specific fashion if we begin with a particular formulation of the utility function. As we have seen, a convenient and easily manipulated special case of the utility function is known as the *Cobb-Douglas* form. It may be written as

$$U = X^\alpha Y^\beta \tag{2.25}$$

with marginal utilities

$$\frac{\partial U}{\partial X} = \alpha X^{\alpha-1} Y^\beta \tag{2.26}$$

and

$$\frac{\partial U}{\partial Y} = \beta X^\alpha Y^{\beta-1}$$ (2.27)

The marginal rate of substitution between the two goods in this case is given by

$$-\frac{\partial Y}{\partial X} = \frac{\alpha Y}{\beta X}$$ (2.28)

To derive explicit demand functions for X and Y, we need the budget constraint (2.1), and the equilibrium condition, whose general form (2.19) simplifies in this special case to

$$\frac{\alpha Y}{\beta X} = \frac{p_X}{p_Y}$$ (2.29)

Multiplying the top and bottom of the left-hand side of this expression by the right-hand side of (2.2) yields

$$\alpha p_Y(M/p_Y - Xp_X/p_Y) = \beta p_X X$$

or

$$\alpha M - \alpha p_X X = \beta p_X X$$

so that we get, as the demand function for X,

$$X = \frac{M}{p_X}\left(\frac{\alpha}{\alpha+\beta}\right)$$ (2.30)

We may derive an explicit demand function for Y by substituting equation (2.30) into (2.2):

$$Y = \frac{M}{p_Y} - \frac{p_X}{p_Y}\left(\frac{\alpha M}{(\alpha+\beta)p_X}\right)$$

$$Y = \frac{M}{p_Y}\left(\frac{\beta}{\alpha+\beta}\right)$$ (2.31)

Note that, with the Cobb-Douglas utility function (as already seen in Box 2.7), the demand curves for the two goods as functions of their own prices are rectangular hyperbolae, so that their own price elasticities of demand are equal to one (strictly speaking, minus one). Moreover the demand for each good is independent of the price of the other, so the cross elasticities of demand between them are zero. Also the demand for each good is strictly proportional to income, implying income elasticities of demand equal to one.

Concluding comment

This chapter has largely been devoted to setting out a framework of analysis and defining concepts. These concepts will turn up time and time again throughout this book and the reader will see that mastering them has not been an end in itself but simply a necessary precondition for applying microeconomic analysis to what it is hoped are interesting and relevant problems. We will not use every idea developed in this chapter in each of the chapters that follows, but all of them will be used again somewhere.

Before moving on to the next chapter, the reader should have mastered the following concepts: objects of choice; budget constraint; utility function; and should understand how to use them in the derivation of income and price consumption curves. The reader should also review the derivation of the Engel curve, and particularly the demand curve, because it is to the further analysis of the latter that the next chapter is devoted.

SUMMARY

The basic theory of consumer choice

1. The objects of consumer choice are goods and services, yielding utility, which may be ordered and (in principle) measured.

2. Consumer preferences are characterised by an indifference map in which each curve links bundles of goods which yield the consumer equal levels of satisfaction. The (negative) slope of the indifference curve is called the marginal rate of substitution between goods.

3. The consumer's budget constraint shows how the upper limit on consumption (usually present disposable income) may be allocated among consumption patterns or goods at given prices. Changes in income shift the budget constraint, changes in prices alter its slope. The slope of the budget constraint gives the market evaluation of the trade-off between the two goods.

4. Maximising consumer utility generates an equilibrium where the budget constraint and the highest possible indifference curve are tangential. At any point other than equilibrium, the consumer can substitute one good for another and increase utility. In equilibrium the marginal rate of substitution between goods is equal to their ratio of prices.

5. Income consumption and price consumption curves describe how the quantity demanded of a good alters with variations in income and price.

6. If quantity demanded increases with income, we have the case of a normal good and the income consumption curve is upward sloping. For inferior goods, with demand falling as income rises, the slope is negative.

7. In a two-good world, a good whose quantity purchased moves together with changes in the price of the other good is called a substitute. That whose quantity moves in opposite directions to the other good's price change is a complement.

8. The Engel curve maps quantity demanded of one good against changes in income. The ratio of the marginal propensity to consume (slope of the Engel curve) to the average propensity to consume (ratio of quantity demanded to income) is known as the income elasticity of demand.

9. The demand curve relates quantity demanded of one good to its own price. The own price elasticity of demand is given by the slope of the demand curve (treating quantity as the dependent variable) divided by the ratio of quantity demanded to price. The cross elasticity of demand measures the proportional change in the quantity demanded of one good to a proportional price change of another.

PROBLEMS

1 Discuss which of the following statements is true or false and explain why:

(a) a good is inferior if the quantity demanded of it falls as the price falls;

(b) a good is inferior only if the quantity of it falls as the price falls;
(Students may wish to read Chapter 3 before answering questions (c) to (e).)

(c) a good is inferior if the Hicks compensated demand curve cuts the normal (money income) demand curve from above (students might wish to read Chapter 3 before answering this part of the question);

(d) a good is inferior if the Slutsky compensated demand curve cuts the normal (money income) demand curve from below (students might wish to read Chapter 3 before answering this part of the question);

(e) a good is inferior if the Hicks compensated demand curve cuts the Slutsky compensated demand curve from above.

2 The indifference curves shown in the following diagrams do not conform with those drawn earlier in this part of the book, though they do not necessarily illustrate unrealistic preferences.

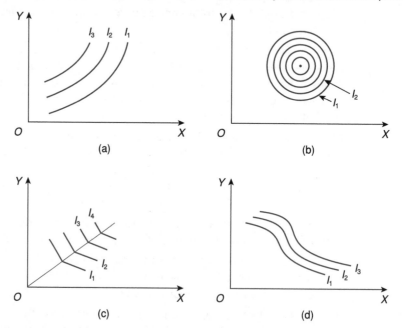

Explain the underlying assumptions made in each case and illustrate your answer with examples of commodities which you believe are consistent with these preferences.

3 Person A buys one unit of a good when its price is 10 pence and two units when its price is 5 pence. Would that person be willing to pay 13 pence for two units of the good, rather than forgo it in its entirety? What is the most that person A would pay for two units of the good, rather than forgo consuming it altogether?

4 Draw the budget constraint implied by the following information:

consumer's income	£500 per week
price of X	£1 per unit
price of Y	£2 per unit

Would the consumer be able to attain any of the following consumption patterns?

100 Y	and	200 X per week
100 Y	and	20 X per week
200 Y	and	100 X per week
200 Y	and	1600 X per month
300 Y	and	1200 X per month

How much would be left over per week from purchasing those bundles within reach? Suppose that the budget constraint instead were given by:

consumer's income	£500 per week
price of X	£1 per unit for the first 150 per week, thereafter £2 per unit
price of Y	£2 per unit

How would this affect your answers to the above questions?

5 Draw the indifference curves between X and Y where:

(a) An extra unit of X adds nothing to a consumer's satisfaction unless accompanied by an extra unit of Y.

(b) The consumer may always be compensated for the loss of one unit of X by being given two units of Y, regardless of the proportions in which they are originally consuming them.

(c) The consumer must be compensated for consuming extra units of X by being given extra units of Y, the amount of Y needed to compensate for consuming one unit of X increasing as the level of consumption of X increases.

6 Derive the relationship between the quantity of X demanded and the price of X if the consumer's indifference map *vis-à-vis* X and Y has curves concave to the origin.

Let X be games of golf per annum and Y all other goods. Draw the indifference map and budget constraint of:

(a) an amateur who pays to play golf;
(b) a professional who is paid to play golf.

May we conclude that golfers turn professional because they dislike the game?

7 Draw the budget constraints and indifference map implicit in the following observations made in two different weeks on two different consumers. Assume in each case that all income has been spent on X and Y.

Consumer A		
week 1	price of X	£2
	price of Y	£1
	income	£500 per week
	quantity of X bought	100 units per week
week 2	price of X	£2
	price of Y	£1
	income	£600 per week
	quantity of X bought	80 units per week

Consumer B		
week 1	price of X	£2
	price of Y	£1
	income	£300 per week
	quantity of X bought	110 units per week

week 2	price of X	£2
	price of Y	£1
	income	£250 per week
	quantity of X bought	110 units per week

Is X an inferior good for consumer A or B? If someone told you that consumers A and B had identical tastes *vis-à-vis* X and Y would you be able to contradict them on the basis of the above information?

8 We observe the same consumer in two successive weeks:

week 1	price of X	£10
	price of Y	£10
	quantity of X bought	10 units per week
	quantity of Y bought	10 units per week
week 2	price of X	£5
	price of Y	£15
	quantity of X bought	7 units per week
	quantity of Y bought	11 units per week

Calculate her income in the two weeks on the assumption that she spends it all on goods X and Y. Do the above observations enable you to conclude that her tastes have changed between the two weeks?

9 Is it possible when there are only two goods, X and Y,

(a) for Y to be both a substitute for X and a normal good?
(b) for Y to be both a complement to X and an inferior good?

Notes

1. As the student who reads on will discover, the possibility of complementarity can only arise in a two-good world such as we have here, because of an income effect. If we abstract from the income effect, then with normally shaped indifference curves, in a two-good world, the goods in question can only be substitutes. Possibilities for complementarity that do not hinge on an income effect do re-emerge, however, when there are more than two goods. The meaning of income and substitution effects is discussed in Chapter 3.

2. So long as we are dealing with the demand for X, holding the price of all other goods constant, the level of money income and the maximum amount of all other goods that can be bought with money income – the point at which the budget restraint cuts the Y vertical axis – move in perfect harmony with each other. The two differ only in units of measurement. Indeed, it is possible to define the units arbitrarily in terms of which quantities of all other goods are measured so that one unit of money income buys one unit of all other goods. The reader will find that a good deal of the literature on demand theory uses the symbol Y to stand interchangeably for both money income and quantities of other goods. We have used M and Y here to distinguish clearly between the two concepts. Note that in later chapters we shall use Y to stand for income.

CHAPTER 3

Money income and real income

Key words and phrases

- income effect, substitution effect
- money income, real income, compensating variation, Hicks and Slutsky real income, equivalent variation
- revealed preference, strong and weak ordering
- Slutsky equation; standard of living, cost of living, Laspèyres and Paasche price indices

Introduction

In this chapter we continue our exposition of the theory of consumer choice. We shall consider first of all those factors which can cause the demand curve for a particular good, derived in the last chapter, to shift. We shall then go on to look more closely at the relationships among the effects of price and income changes on the consumer's choice of a consumption bundle, in the process elucidating the concepts of the **income and substitution effects** of a price change. We shall then show how these concepts in turn help us to achieve a deeper understanding of such ideas as **real income**, the **standard of living**, the **cost of living** and so on, and enable us to construct and interpret various measures of these often elusive concepts.

The effect of a change in income

The demand curve derived towards the end of the previous chapter shows the relationship between the quantity of X demanded and the price of X, given the price of Y and given the consumer's money income. It follows immediately that any change in either of the latter two variables will cause the whole curve to shift. In Figure 3.1, A represents a particular equilibrium at a particular level of income and set of prices. Associated with A is a particular point on the demand curve for X.

Suppose income increases by a certain proportion. The consumer's equilibrium will shift to B. The indifference map is drawn so that X and Y are normal goods and so, at the higher income level, the consumer buys more X. Thus, with no change in the price of X the quantity demanded has increased. We can carry out this analysis for any point on the

Figure 3.1

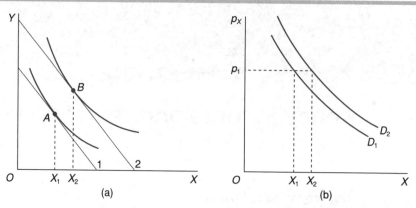

(a)   (b)

For a given price of Y and a given price of X (p_1), an increase in income shifts the budget constraint out from 1 to 2 in panel (a). The consumer's equilibrium shifts from A to B and, if X is a normal good, the quantity of it demanded at p_1 increases (from X_1 to X_2). This experiment could be repeated for any price of X and hence panel (b) shows the whole demand curve shifting to the right from D_1 to D_2.

demand curve for X, and thereby show that, for a normal good, an increase in income shifts the demand curve to the right. Readers should satisfy themselves that an increase in income shifts the demand curve for an inferior good to the left.

The effect of a change in the price of the other good

Now let us analyse the effect of a change in the price of Y. In Figure 3.2 the indifference map is drawn in such a way that X and Y are substitutes. Thus, if we again start at A, we

Figure 3.2

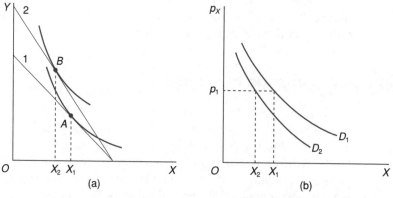

(a)   (b)

For a given level of money income and price of X (p_1), a fall in the price of Y shifts the budget constraint from 1 to 2 in panel (a). The consumer's equilibrium shifts from A to B and if X and Y are substitutes, the quantity of X demanded falls from X_1 to X_2. This experiment could be repeated for any price of X: hence, in panel (b) the whole demand curve for X shifts to the left from D_1 to D_2.

see that a fall in the price of Y shifts the consumer to a new equilibrium at which, with the same level of money income and the same price of X, less X is purchased. Once more this analysis could be carried out for each point on the demand curve for X and we can say that a fall in the price of Y, where Y is a substitute for X, causes the demand curve for X to shift to the left. Clearly, were X and Y complements, the shift would instead be to the right. Readers should derive this result for themselves.

The income effect and substitution effect

The analysis of the immediately preceding section of this chapter, and that developed towards the end of Chapter 2, has involved movements along price consumption and income consumption curves. It will be obvious to the reader that the shape of the price consumption curve for a given level of income and price of Y depends upon the precise form of the indifference map; and it will be equally obvious that the same may be said of the shape of the income consumption curve at a given set of relative prices. These apparently innocuous statements lead us directly to the next step of our analysis. They point to the *interdependence of the effects of income changes and price changes upon consumption*. Consider Figure 3.3 with the consumer initially in equilibrium at A on a budget constraint given by a line joining X_0 and Y_0. Now let the price of X fall so that the budget constraint pivots on the Y-axis and becomes Y_0X_1; the consumption pattern moves to B.

This is, of course, a movement along a price consumption curve, and it could be readily translated into a movement along a demand curve. However, B is also a point on an income consumption curve and there is another point on the same income consumption

Figure 3.3

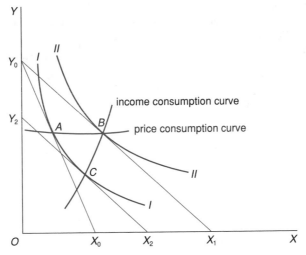

A movement along a price consumption curve from A to B may be broken down into a substitution effect around an indifference curve (from A to C) and an income effect along an income consumption curve (from C to B).

curve at C where a budget constraint, Y_2X_2, having the same slope as Y_0X_1, is tangent to the indifference curve I. This is the indifference curve on which A also lies. The movement along the price consumption curve from A to B, and hence along a demand curve for X, may therefore be looked upon as being made up of a movement around a particular indifference curve from A to C and one along an income consumption curve from C to B. The first component of this change is termed the **substitution effect** and the second the **income effect**.

It should be obvious that the substitution effect of a fall in the price of X always involves a movement round an indifference curve to a point below and to the right of A. *A negative* price change leads to a *positive* change in quantity demanded as far as the substitution effect is concerned and this effect is thus said to be *negative* in sign. This must always be the case so long as indifference curves are convex to the origin. The further to the right we move on any given curve, the more shallowly sloped it is. When the price of X falls, we find the point to which the substitution effect takes us by moving to a point at which the indifference curve on which the initial equilibrium bundle is located slopes more shallowly. This must be below and to the right of this initial bundle.

The sign of the income effect depends upon whether or not X is a normal good. If it is, then the *positive* change in income implicit in the fall in the price of X will lead to a *positive* change in the quantity of X demanded. Thus the income effect will be *positive*. This will accentuate the tendency, already implicit in the substitution effect, for the quantity of X demanded to increase as its price falls. If, on the other hand, X is an inferior good, the income effect will be *negative* and will tend to offset the substitution effect since it will work in the opposite direction. Though it is extremely unlikely, it is logically possible that a negative income effect could more than offset a negative substitution effect and lead to a fall in the quantity of X demanded as its price falls. This would give us a backward-bending price consumption curve. This case was discussed in the previous chapter as that of a Giffen good, and was depicted in Figure 2.7(c). We can now see that a Giffen good *must* be an inferior good, but there is of course no necessity that an inferior good be a Giffen good.

Now if the analysis of income and substitution effects did no more than clarify the nature of a Giffen good, it would be of little interest. However, this analysis turns out to be fundamental to such important practical matters as the distinction between money income and real income, and to the measurement of what is frequently termed the **cost of living**. The rest of this chapter is devoted to elaborating this claim.

Box 3.1	**More on income and substitution effects**

We can derive income and substitution effects for the Cobb-Douglas utility function we used in Chapter 2:

$$U = X^{0.6}Y^{0.4} \qquad (2.2.1)$$

Assume that the price of X falls from 20 to 10, but that income remains unchanged at 200 and the price of Y is unchanged at 5. With the high price of X the budget constraint is (see Box 2.3 in Chapter 2)

$$Y = 40 - 4X$$

After X falls in price the budget constraint is

$$Y = 40 - 2X$$

We know from Box 2.3 in Chapter 2 that when the price of X is 20 our consumer maximises utility when $X = 6$ and $Y = 16$. As illustrated in Box 2.4, given these levels of X and Y our consumer obtains the following utility:

$$U = 6^{0.6}16^{0.4} = 8.88$$

As an exercise show that after the price reduction to $p_X = 10$ the consumer equilibrium is

$$X = 12, \ Y = 16, \ U = 13.46$$

Note (as in Box 2.5) that when the price of X falls 6 more units of X are consumed, but the amount of Y consumed remains unchanged. This unchanged consumption of Y with the lower price of X is because of the Cobb-Douglas utility function.

We can separate the total effect of the price change, i.e. 6 extra units of X, into substitution and income effects. To derive the substitution effect we maximise consumer utility using the new price ratio, i.e. with the lower price of X, and the original level of utility:

the new price ratio = $p_X/p_Y = 10/5 = 2$
the original level of utility = 8.88

With the level of utility at 8.88

$$8.88 = X^{0.6}Y^{0.4}$$

so for this 8.88 units of utility the indifference curve is

$$Y = 8.88^{2.5}X^{-1.5} \tag{3.1.1}$$

To maximise utility with this indifference curve we need to set the MRS = p_X/p_Y.

$$\text{MRS} = \frac{\partial Y}{\partial X} = -1.5(8.88^{2.5})X^{-2.5} \tag{3.1.2}$$

Setting this MRS equal to the price ratio of 2:

$$1.5(8.88^{2.5})X^{-2.5} = 2 \qquad X^{2.5} = (1.5/2)(8.88^{2.5}) = 176.24$$

so $\quad X = 176.24^{0.4} = 7.91$

So the increase in consumption from 6 units of X to 7.91 units, i.e. 1.91 units, is the substitution effect. As the total effect of the price change involved the consumption of X increasing from 6 to 12, the income effect of the price change is $6 - 1.91 = 4.09$ units of X. So, the reduction in the price of X results in consumption increasing because of both the substitution and income effects. As we found in Chapter 2, with our Cobb-Douglas function X is a normal good.

| Box 3.2 | **Perfect substitutes and perfect complements** |

Our analysis of consumer choice in Chapter 2 was based on the assumption that the marginal rate of substitution between two goods, X and Y, was diminishing. That is to say, the amount of good X that a consumer was willing to forgo in order to receive an increment of good Y varied according to how much of X the individual had already consumed. In particular, we assumed that consumers would need more of Y to forgo a given unit of X as the amount of X that they consumed declined, which implies that the marginal rate of substitution is diminishing. However, this assumption does not always hold, and it is interesting to explore the consequences of relaxing it, especially for the analysis of income and substitution effects. We will consider two cases in this box: perfect substitutes and perfect complements. Each breaches the assumption that the marginal rate of substitution is diminishing.

Consider first the case of perfect substitutes. These are two goods that the consumer regards as identical so there is a perfect trade-off between them. There are many goods that could arguably fall into this category – makes of pen, makes of CD or DVD, even perhaps airline flights to holiday destinations on alternative cut price airlines. The situation is defined by the fact that the consumer will not mind which of the goods, X and Y, they are consuming and hence the indifference curve takes the form shown in Illustration 3.1 below, of a straight line, IC_1, IC_2, IC_3.

Illustration 3.1

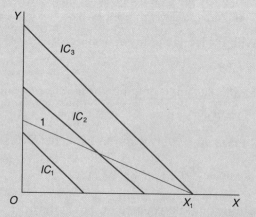

If the budget line takes the shape of 1, then the individual chooses to consume only good X, at X_1. This is referred to as a *corner solution*. It captures the intuition that, if consumers regard X and Y as perfect substitutes for each other, they will not choose to spend their budget on some combination of X and Y, but rather choose to consume only X (or, if the relative price instead favours Y, only Y).

When goods are perfect substitutes, changes in relative price will not lead to a continuous change in this consumption pattern. Instead, for relatively small changes, budget line 1 will swivel around but the consumer will continue to choose X. However, if the relative price of X relative to Y changes considerably, the consumer will stop consuming X altogether and spend all their money on Y. When the slope of the budget line is the same as that of the indifference curve, the consumer is indifferent between all possible combinations of X and Y.

The second case is that of perfect complements, when goods have to be consumed in fixed proportions. Some examples might include fountain pens and ink cartridges, torches and batteries and so forth. In this case, the consumer will not choose to purchase more of good X relative to Y when X becomes relatively cheaper, though there may still be an effect because of the increase in income. The indifference curves in this case are rectangular, as shown in Illustration 3.2.

Illustration 3.2

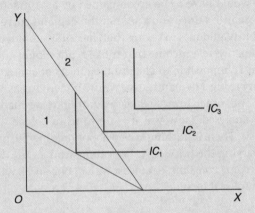

It can be seen that goods X and Y are always consumed in a fixed proportion. If the relative price of good Y falls, leading the budget line to swivel around from 1 to 2, the consumer will consume more of both X and Y but in the same proportion as previously. Hence there is an income effect but no substitution effect.

Money income and real income

Consider the following exercise. Suppose that there was a drop in the price of Y by a certain percentage, accompanied by a fall of the same percentage in the price of X. The combined effect of these two changes would be exactly the same as that of an increase of equal proportion in income with the two prices constant. This is yet another example of the interconnectedness of price and income effects in demand theory, and it should prompt us to look more closely at the nature of the demand curve with which we have so far been dealing, particularly with regard to the income concept that underlies it.

The demand curve in question is derived holding **money income** and the price of Y constant. As we move along the curve to lower and lower prices of X, we are also, in terms of an indifference curve diagram, moving to higher and higher levels of utility, to higher and higher levels of what we might call **real income**. Apparently, in order to make an individual better off, all that we need to do is lower the price of one good. Does it follow, therefore, that we could increase the living standards of the whole community by cutting the price of one good? If we simply subsidised X, could we make everyone better off? It would be appealing indeed were it possible, but there is a certain lack of plausibility about the proposal, at least in an economy operating in the region of full employment of a more or less given stock of factors of production with given technology. Yet careless use of our demand curve would suggest that the trick could be carried off.

The problem here involves the things which have been held constant in deriving the demand curve. For one individual it is possible to hold the price of Y and money income constant, lower the price of X and observe a movement along the demand curve for X. However, if the price of X was lowered to the whole community this movement along the demand curve would represent only the first stage in the story, not the end of it. The industry producing X would have to expand, and given full employment it could only do so by attracting resources from the production of Y. Thus, the expansion in the demand for X would have to be accompanied by a contraction in the supply of Y, a consequent increase in Y's price and a *shift* of the demand curve for X.

All this amounts to saying that, in a fully employed economy, for consumers viewed as a group, it is real income that is fixed, not money income, and the price of all goods save one; it is impossible to analyse the effects of changing the price of one good by a tax or subsidy using a demand curve whose underlying assumptions imply that real income can vary. The 'other things equal' assumptions we made are inconsistent with the problem being analysed. However, it is up to us to decide what things we hold constant in our analysis. There is nothing sacred about holding the price of Y and money income constant and varying the price of X. We can instead, even when dealing with an individual, hold real income constant, or at least we can once we have given precise meaning to the phrase 'constant real income'.

Constant real income and the compensating variation in money income

We have already used a real income concept in our analysis of the income and substitution effect earlier in this chapter. We there referred to the substitution effect as a movement along a given indifference curve and the income effect as a movement to a higher curve. It is reasonable to think of *constant real income* as meaning, for an individual, the ability to gain a particular constant level of satisfaction from consumption. A demand curve holding *real* income and the price of Y constant may then be derived.

Starting from A in Figure 3.4(a), let us lower the price of X, and at the same time vary money income by just enough to keep a budget constraint having the slope implied by the new price ratio in tangency with the original indifference curve (i.e. constraint 3). The required cut in money income just *compensates* the consumer for the income effect of the fall in the price of X and so the relevant cut in money income is called a **compensating variation**. The resulting demand curve is plotted in Figure 3.4(b), and clearly has *only* a substitution effect underlying it and hence *must* be negatively sloped. Equally obviously an increase in the consumption of X must be combined with a fall in the consumption of Y. When real income is held constant, X must be a substitute for all other goods taken together (although this does not rule out the possibility of X being complementary to some subset of goods in the overall bundle labelled Y). Now the movement from A to C in Figure 3.4(a) was accomplished by a compensated fall in the price of X. It could equally have been the result of an equiproportional compensated rise in the price of Y, as is shown in Figure 3.5. When real income is held constant the change in the quantity of X

Figure 3.4

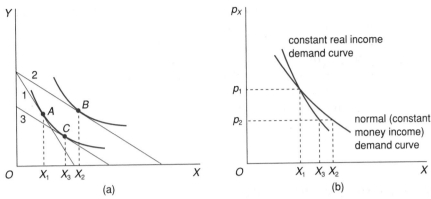

(a)

(b)

In panel (a), holding the price of Y and money income constant, a fall in the price of X from p_1 to p_2 shifts the budget constraint from 1 to 2, and the quantity of X demanded increases from X_1 to X_2. In panel (b) this shift is shown as a movement along a 'constant money income' demand curve. The substitution effect of this price change involves moving from constraint 1 to constraint 3, a change in consumption pattern from A to C and an increase in the demand for X from X_1 to X_3. This change is shown as a shift along a constant real income demand curve in panel (b). Because X is here depicted as a normal good, the income effect of the price change is positive. The constant real income demand curve relies on the substitution effect alone and hence, if X is a normal good, is steeper than the constant money income demand curve, which also contains an income effect. If X were an inferior good, the constant real income curve would be the shallower of the two.

Figure 3.5

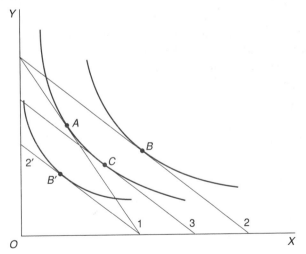

The substitution effect from A to C may be a component of the effect of one of two price changes: a fall in the price of X shifting the budget constraint to 2 and the equilibrium consumption bundle to B; or an equiproportional rise in the price of Y shifting the constraint to 2' and the equilibrium consumption bundle to B'. Recall here that the slope of the budget constraint depends only on the ratio of the prices of X and Y.

demanded as a result of a change in its price is exactly the same as it is to an equipropor-tional but opposite change in the price of Y.

This is all very well as far as it goes. We can carry out the compensating variations in income in Figures 3.4 and 3.5 and consider only substitution effects because we have already drawn an indifference map. We know how much we must shift the budget con-straint in order to restore our consumer's initial level of real income because we can see the point at which a budget constraint having the slope implied by the new prices is tangent to the old indifference curve. But if we were dealing with an actual consumer we could not do this. We could not 'see' the indifference map and therefore could not know how big a change in money income was needed to maintain the same level of utility and so compensate the consumer for the effects on real income of a particular price change.

Two measures of real income

Our lack of knowledge about the precise shape of the indifference curve would diminish the usefulness of the analysis under discussion were we not able to get around this par-ticular stumbling block by using an approximation. Instead of defining real income as the ability to purchase goods yielding a particular level of utility, let us define it instead as the ability to buy a particular bundle of goods. Thus, instead of treating any budget constraint that is tangent to the indifference curve upon which point A lies as representing a given level of real income, treat any budget constraint that passes through point A as represent-ing constant real income.

This is an approximation, to be sure, but it has the great merit of being a usable approx-imation, for, given any price for X and Y, it is clearly a routine piece of arithmetic to calculate the level of money income that will just permit the bundle of goods represented by A to be purchased. The ability to attain a constant level of utility notion of real income is sometimes referred to as **Hicks real income** and the ability to purchase a given bundle of goods concept as **Slutsky real income** after the two pioneers of modern theory who utilised these concepts in their analysis.

It should be stressed that the distinction between Hicks and Slutsky real incomes is primarily of relevance with regard to applications of the theory of consumer choice which involve discrete changes in the values of prices and quantities. If the analysis were to be undertaken algebraically, using differential calculus and limited to infinitesimal changes, the two concepts would coincide. That is to say, the extra income needed to allow a consumer, faced by an infinitesimal price increase, to maintain constant utility is the same as required to permit the consumer to continue to buy the quantities of goods initially purchased.

Earlier in this chapter, we analysed what we may now term the Hicks substitution and income effects. In Figure 3.6 we show their Slutsky equivalents. Clearly, the Slutsky substitution effect puts the consumer on a higher indifference curve than the one from which the experiment starts, and does therefore involve some increase in Hicks real income. It should be noted that this is so whether we deal with a price fall or a price increase, though only the former case is explicitly analysed in Figure 3.6. The Slutsky substitution effect is nevertheless unambiguously negative, even for an inferior good. This follows from the smooth convexity of the indifference curves. There can be no point to the left of A on budget constraint 3' that is not on a lower indifference curve than the

Figure 3.6

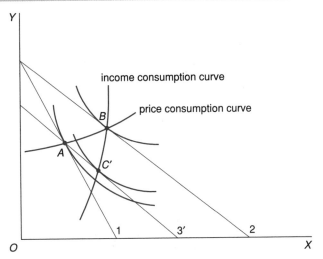

An alternative way of analysing the income and substitution effects of a price fall when 'constant real income' is defined to mean the ability to purchase a given bundle of goods rather than to achieve a given level of satisfaction. Constraint 3' passes through A. The substitution effect is from A to C' and the income effect from C' to B.

one passing through A. Similarly, there must be points to the right of A that are on higher indifference curves. Therefore, the consumer will move to the right of A, hence increasing consumption of X and decreasing consumption of Y when the price of X and hence the slope of the budget constraint fall.

The fact that a Slutsky substitution effect encompasses a small increase in Hicks real income means that we can say something about the slope of the demand curve derived holding Slutsky real income constant, as compared with that of the Hicks constant real income demand curve. Consider Figure 3.7. If we begin at a particular price p_1 and quantity X_1, then, whether we lower or raise the price of X, holding Slutsky real income constant will put the consumer on a higher indifference curve than the one from which the experiment starts. Thus, where the Slutsky constant real income demand curve that passes through p_1X_1 lies, relative to the Hicks constant real income curve that passes through the same point, will depend upon the sign of the income effect. If X is a normal good, the Slutsky curve will be tangent to the Hicks curve from above and to the right, and if X is an inferior good, from below and to the left, as the reader should easily be able to verify.

A market demand curve derived by holding individuals' real incomes constant will more easily enable us to predict the consequences for the quantity of X demanded of lowering its price by subsidy – or raising its price by tax – than will one derived from the more orthodox constant money income demand curve. The prediction will still be an approximation, however, because constant real income in the sense of a group of individuals each enjoying a given level of utility is not the same thing as constant real income in the sense of an economy producing output at a given level of productive capacity. It was the existence of an overall constraint on production that gave rise to the difficulty that led us into the foregoing analysis in the first place. However, the ability of consumers to

Figure 3.7

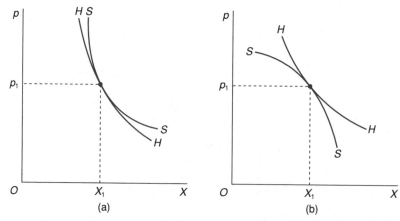

(a) If X is a normal good, then the Slutsky constant real income demand curve SS passing through p_1X_1 is tangent to the Hicks constant real income curve passing through the same point from above and to the right.

(b) If X is an inferior good, the tangency in question is from below and to the left.

consume a given bundle of goods is obviously not unrelated to an economy's ability to produce a particular composition of output: hence our assertion that a constant real income demand curve, and perhaps particularly if it is real income in the Slutsky sense that is held constant, is likely to be a useful tool in such circumstances.

Box 3.3 More on Hicks and Slutsky

The difference between Hicksian and Slutsky substitution and income effects can be calculated. If we have the Cobb-Douglas utility function we have used up to now:

$$U = X^{0.6}Y^{0.4} \tag{2.2.1}$$

we can analyse the price fall we set out in Box 3.1: p_X falls from 20 to 10; income is unchanged at £200; p_Y is unchanged at 5. In Box 3.1 we showed that the total effect of the lower p_X was 6 extra units consumes. Using a Hicksian method this was made up of: substitution effect = 1.91 units, income effect = 4.09 units. This can be compared with the Slutsky substitution and income effects.

We know that the Slutsky substitution effect is found by shifting the new budget constraint back to the original consumption point (not the original level of utility). When $p_X = 20$ we know (from Box 3.1) that the equilibrium is $X = 6$ and $Y = 16$, so with $p_X = 10$ the new budget constraint must be shifted to pass through this combination of X and Y. So using the general expression for a budget constraint:

$$M = p_XX + p_YY \tag{2.1.1}$$
$$M = 10(6) + 5(16) = 140$$

Our consumer's income must fall by £60 (i.e. 200 – 140) to pass through the original consumption point after p_x falls from 20 to 10. So, the general expression for this new budget constraint that passes through the original expenditure point is

$$140 = 10X + 5Y \qquad (3.3.1)$$

Our consumer can now maximise utility given this new budget constraint. We know from Box 2.4 (in the previous chapter) that with the utility function used here the consumer maximises utility when

$$\frac{Y}{X} = \frac{1}{1.5}\frac{p_X}{p_Y} \qquad (2.4.1)$$

Using $p_X = 10$ and $p_Y = 5$

$$Y = (2/1.5)X$$

Using the new budget constraint, our consumer's equilibrium is

$$X = 8.4, \; Y = 11.2$$

The Slutsky substitution effect therefore increases the consumption of X from 6 to 8.4 i.e. by 2.4. This is bigger than the Hicksian substitution effect of 1.91. The Slutsky income effect is the difference between the total effect on X and the substitution effect i.e. $6 - 2.4 = 3.6$. This is obviously smaller than the Hicksian income effect.

The Slutsky substitution effect has our consumer on a higher level of utility compared with the Hicksian effect (as suggested in the text). With $X = 8.4$, $Y = 11.2$:

$$U = 8.4^{0.6}11.2^{0.4} = 9.42$$

This level of utility compares to the level of utility used to calculate the Hicksian substitution effect of 8.88 (see Box 3.1).

Constant real income and the equivalent variation in money income

The analysis so far has been based on the breakdown of the response of a consumer to a price change into an income and substitution effect, the income effect in question being measured in terms of a compensating variation in money income. The response may be broken down in another way. Consider Figure 3.8. Again we start at point A, and let the price of X fall. However, instead of noting that the point B lies on an income consumption curve that must pass through the indifference curve upon which A lies, we may with equal justice note that A must lie on an income consumption curve that passes through the indifference curve upon which point B lies. The income consumption curve in question would do so at a point such as C'. We can, therefore, break down the movement from A to B as an income effect taking us from A to C' and a substitution effect taking us from C' to B.

The income effect with which we are dealing here is the result of what is known as an **equivalent variation** in income. It gets this name because the shift of the budget constraint from 1 to 3′ has an effect on real income *equivalent* to that of the price change whose effects are being analysed. It will not, in general, be quantitatively of the same order of magnitude as the income effect that we get from the compensating variation,

Figure 3.8

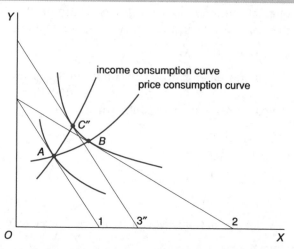

An alternative way of analysing the income and substitution effect of a fall in the price of X. The constraint moves from 1 to 2 and the equilibrium bundle from A to B. We shift the budget constraint at initial prices from 1 to 3″. This gives an 'equivalent' gain in real income, measured in terms of satisfaction, to that bestowed by the price fall. The substitution effect is then measured as C″ to B, while the income effect goes from A to C″.

and hence the size of the substitution effect will be different also. We will take up this point in more detail in the next chapter.

We may of course construct a Slutsky approximation to the Hicksian analysis contained in Figure 3.8; this is done in Figure 3.9. As with the Hicks analysis there is no need for the

Figure 3.9

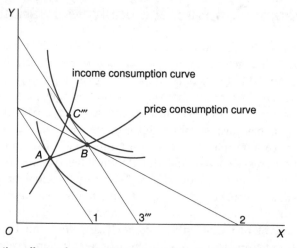

Income and substitution effects of a price fall analysed in terms of an equivalent variation when real income is defined as the ability to purchase a given bundle of goods. Constraint 3‴ goes through B. Thus C‴ to B is the substitution effect and A to C‴ the income effect of a price fall shifting constraint 1 to 2.

income and substitution effects involved here to be of the same size as those produced from an analysis using a compensating variation, but this ought not to worry the reader. When analysing the substitution effect with a compensating variation, we are dealing with the responsiveness of the demand for X to changes in its own price, with real income held constant at the level given by the ability to purchase bundle of goods A (or to maintain that level of utility yielded by A in the Hicks case). When dealing with the equivalent variation, it is the responsiveness of the demand for X to changes in its price at a different higher level of real income that is at stake. There is no reason why the responsiveness of the demand for a good to changes in its own price should be independent of the level of real income, and all that we are observing here is the lack of such independence.

Box 3.4	Hicksian compensating and equivalent variations

We know from the text that Hicksian compensating and equivalent variations measure the change in income that produces the same *utility* change as that occurring with the changed consumption of a good when its price changes. We have two measures because this change in income can be measured in terms of before change (period 1) prices or after change (period 2) prices. So:

> Hicksian compensating variation: change in income that shifts period 2 budget constraint back to period 1 level of utility.

> Hicksian equivalent variation: change in income that shifts period 1 budget constraint forward to period 2 level of utility.

The variations can be calculated if we assume a particular utility function and particular price changes:

$$U = X^{0.6}Y^{0.4} \tag{2.2.1}$$

Period 1: income = £200; p_X = £20; p_Y = £5.
Period 2: income = £200; p_X = £10; p_Y = £5.

From previous boxes we know that the equilibria in the two periods are:

Period 1: $X = 6$, $Y = 16$, $U = 8.88$.
Period 2: $X = 12$, $Y = 16$, $U = 13.46$.

To calculate the Hicksian compensating variation we use the period 2 price ratio $(10/5 = 2)$ and maximise utility on the original indifference curve $(U = 8.88)$. We know from Box 3.1 that the marginal rate of substitution of any indifference curve with this utility function is $-1.5(8.88/X)^{2.5}$. Setting this equal to the price ratio of 2:

$$1.5\left(\frac{8.88}{X}\right)^{2.5} = 2$$

So $X = 8.88 \div \left(\frac{2}{1.5}\right)^{1/2.5} = 7.91$

from which we derived our substitution effect in Box 3.1. Using this value of X and our utility function:

$$8.88 = 7.91^{0.6}Y^{0.4}$$

so $Y = 10.56$.

$\rightarrow$

This implies that $X = 7.91$, $Y = 10.56$ is the bundle of goods on the $U = 8.88$ indifference curve that is optimal given a price ratio of 2. We can now calculate the level of income that allows the consumer to purchase this bundle of goods:

$$M = 10(7.91) + 5(10.56) = £131.90$$

So, a change in income of £68.10 (i.e. 200 – 131.90) produces the same utility change as a reduction in p_X from £20 to £10 when the income change is evaluated using period 2 prices. This £68.10 is the Hicksian compensating variation.

To calculate the Hicksian equivalent variation we use the period 1 price ratio (20/5 = 4) and maximise utility on the period 2 indifference curve ($U = 13.46$). Setting the price ratio equal to the marginal rate of substitution at this level of utility:

$$1.5\left(\frac{13.46}{X}\right)^{2.5} = 4$$

So $X = 9.09$. Using this X and the utility function:

$$13.46 = 9.09^{0.6}Y^{0.4}$$

So $Y = 24.25$. Using these values of X and Y and period 1 prices:

$$M = 20(9.09) + 5(24.25) = 303.05.$$

The equivalent variation is therefore £103.05 (i.e. 303.05 – 200). With this extra income, and evaluating changes using period 1 prices, the consumer would get the same extra utility as that obtained when X falls in price from 20 to 10.

Note that the compensating and equivalent variations calculated here are different. As an exercise, explain why this difference occurs.

Income and substitution effects without indifference curves – the idea of revealed preference

Now the use of indifference curves to characterise the consumer's tastes is an innocuous enough practice as far as pure economic theory is concerned, but such relationships cannot, of course, be directly observed. Thus, it is of some interest that the basis of the foregoing analysis may be established without using them. Instead we may concentrate solely upon directly observable variables, namely, prices, income, and the quantities of goods bought by the consumer.

The basic idea needed to carry out this analysis is that of the consistency of consumer choice, discussed in the section on consumer's tastes in the previous chapter. It will be recalled that we argued there that, in the case of a consumer choosing among three bundles of goods, let us call them A, B and C, if A was preferred when A and B were compared, and B was preferred when B and C were compared, then A would be preferred when A and C were compared. This is an example of so-called **strong ordering** of bundles. **Weak ordering** permits the idea of consumer indifference to play a role, and an example of this concept at work would be a state of affairs in which the consumer definitely preferred A to B but was indifferent between B and C. In this case the idea of

Figure 3.10 **The basic analysis of revealed preference**

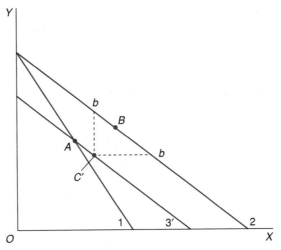

Starting at point A in constraint 1, the substitution effect of a fall in the price of X will not cause its consumption to fall, and it may increase – say to point C'. The income effect will take consumption to some point such as B on constraint 2. As drawn here, X and Y are normal goods, but note that B might lie outside bb if one of them is inferior. Note finally that Figure 3.10 is essentially the same as Figure 3.6 with the indifference curves omitted.

consistent choice would enable us to say that the consumer would unambiguously prefer A to C, and would always choose it when offered a choice between this pair of bundles.

Now consider Figure 3.10, where we draw a conventional budget constraint 1. Suppose the consumer faced by this constraint was observed to choose bundle A. Now let the price of X fall so that we get a new budget constraint 2, and then carry out a Slutsky compensating variation to obtain budget constraint 3', which passes through bundle A at the new relative price ruling between X and Y. Consider the segment of 3' above and to the left of A. Obviously our consumer could have chosen any point on this segment at the original set of relative prices underlying constraint 1. From any such point, it would have been possible to move out to constraint 1, consuming more of X for the same amount of Y, more Y for the same amount of X, or more of both; and hence, if both X and Y are desirable as we assume them to be (see Ch. 2), to reach a preferred position. However, when faced with constraint 1 our consumer chose bundle A, thus **revealing a preference** for (or at least a state of indifference between) bundle A and any other bundle available on constraint 1. Hence, the postulate of consistency enables us to deduce that the consumer prefers bundle A to any bundle on constraint 3' above and to its left.

But what about points on 3' below and to the right of A? These were not available when the consumer faced constraint 1, but by reasoning exactly similar to that used in the preceding paragraph, for any bundle below and to the right of A on 1, there is a segment of constraint 3' which permits a superior consumption pattern to be attained. We cannot say *for certain* that there exist bundles on 3' below and to the right of A which the consumer will prefer to A, but it is clearly possible. Hence, we can say, *without reference to indifference curves*, that the Slutsky substitution effect (whose limiting case for an infinitesimal price change is the Hicks substitution effect) will *never* lead to *less* of the good whose relative price has fallen being consumed, and *may* lead to *more* of it being consumed. We can, that is to say, conclude that the substitution effect is *never positive*.

What, though, about the income effect? Suppose the substitution effect took our consumer to bundle C'. Then there is clearly an array of bundles on constraint 2 (along the segment *bb*) which will be unambiguously preferred to C'. However, if X is an inferior good, there may exist even more preferred bundles above and to the left of this segment, and if Y is inferior, below and to the right. If both are normal, the ultimate equilibrium will be at some bundle such as B, inside this segment, and that is the case we have depicted in Figure 3.10.

Now this last step may seem rather vague, and clearly if we had drawn indifference curves in Figure 3.10, everything could be made more precise. Note, however, that to the extent that we cannot actually observe a consumer's indifference curves, but rather postulate them, the extra precision in question has a spurious overtone to it. As far as the general characterisation of the basic properties of the analysis of consumer choice is concerned, *revealed preference analysis*, as deployed here, establishes all the basic results: namely, that the substitution effect is never positive (and is most likely explicitly negative); that the income effect for any particular good may be either positive or negative; but that, in a multi- (including two-) good world, the income effect cannot be negative for every good.

Box 3.5   Slutsky compensating and equivalent variations

The Slutsky compensating and equivalent variations measure the change in income that allows a consumer to buy the same bundle of goods as that occurring with the changed consumption of a good when its price changes. We have two measures because this change in income can be measured in terms of before change (period 1) prices or after change (period 2) prices. So:

> Slutsky compensating variation: change in income that shifts period 2 budget constraint back to the period one bundle of goods.

> Slutsky equivalent variation: change in income that shifts period 1 budget constraint forward to period 2 level of expenditure.

We can assume the same income and prices as in Box 3.4.

> Period 1: income = £200; p_X = £20; p_Y = £5; X = 6; Y = 16.
> Period 2: income = £200; p_X = £10; p_Y = £5; X = 12; Y = 16.

To calculate the Slutsky compensating variation we use period 2 prices and the period 1 bundle of X and Y to calculate the implied level of income that would allow these purchases:

> $M = 10(6) + 5(16) = 140.$

The Slutsky compensating variation is therefore £60 (i.e. 200 − 140). Changing income by this amount would allow the consumer to buy the period 1 bundle of X and Y. This is the income equivalent of how much the consumer is better off when p_X falls and the calculation is made in period 2 prices.

The Slutsky equivalent variation uses period 1 prices and the period 2 bundle of X and Y:

$M = 20(12) + 5(16) = 320.$

The Slutsky equivalent variation is therefore £120 (i.e. 320 − 200). This is the income equivalent of how much the consumer is better off when p_X falls and the calculation is made in period 1 prices.

Note that as with the Hicksian variations the compensating and equivalent amounts of income are not the same. Also, note that the Hicksian variations are not the same as their Slutsky equivalents.

The 'standard of living' and the 'cost of living'

The compensating variation and the equivalent variation, measured according to Hicks or Slutsky, are alternative measures of the amount by which a consumer's real income changes as a result of a price change; they are alternative ways of measuring the extent to which the purchasing power of a given money income changes when a particular price changes; or to put the same point a third way, they measure the extent to which the 'cost of living' changes as a result of a change in the price of a particular good. The foregoing analysis, abstract as it is, is therefore of considerable practical relevance. It underlies most attempts to measure variations in that elusive concept, the price level, and is extremely useful in showing just why the concept is such a difficult one to capture. The price level, or cost of living, refers to the money outlay necessary for a consumer to maintain a given standard of living. A natural interpretation of the phrase 'standard of living' is surely a given level of utility, consumption along a particular indifference curve. Figure 3.11 shows yet again the consequences for consumption of changing the price of one good. The consumer has shifted from A to B. How has the cost of living changed? How has the money outlay necessary to maintain a given standard of living been affected by this price change?

There is no unique answer to this question. It all depends upon which standard of living is the given one, which indifference curve we wish to keep the individual on. Suppose it is the curve upon which A lies. Then the cost of living to our consumer has fallen by the amount by which it is possible to reduce income after the fall in the price of X and still keep the consumer on that original indifference curve. The cost of living has fallen by the amount of the Hicks compensating variation which shifts constraint 2 to 3.

Suppose instead, and there is no reason to prefer one to the other, that we decided to take the level of utility at B as the one whose cost of acquisition we were trying to measure. Then the individual's cost of living has fallen by the amount by which it would have been necessary to increase money income in order to permit a point on the same indifference curve as B to be attained at the original set of prices, to shift constraint 1 to 3″, that is to say by the Hicksian equivalent variation.

There is, as we have seen, no reason why these two measures should be the same. There is, after all, no reason why the effects of a given price change on the cost of maintaining two different standards of living should be the same. In short, the very concept of the cost

Figure 3.11

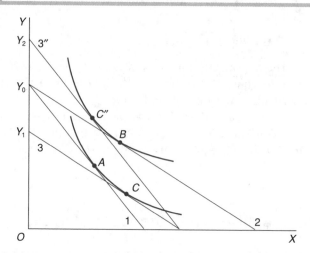

When the price of X falls and the budget constraint shifts from 1 to 2, the consumer's 'cost of living' falls. We may measure this fall in units of money by seeing how much money income must be altered to carry out the compensating variation or the equivalent variation. The first is the amount of income needed to buy $Y_0 - Y_1$ units of Y, the second the amount needed to buy $Y_2 - Y_0$ units.

of living is ambiguous. We must specify the standard of living required before we can measure changes in the cost of maintaining it. Moreover the extent of such changes for a given change in prices depends upon the shape of the indifference map and hence is specific to a particular individual. There is no such thing as a general cost of living. How a particular set of price changes affects the living standards of particular individuals with given money incomes depends very much upon their tastes, and tastes differ among individuals.

Measuring changes in the cost of living

The problem of measuring price level changes is even more difficult than the above argument would indicate, for indifference curves are not observable. There is no way of assessing quantitatively the variations in money income necessary to maintain a given level of utility, at different sets of prices. This is why the Slutsky method of analysing the income and substitution effects is important. Instead of asking questions about the cost of maintaining a given level of utility it enables us to ask questions about the cost of obtaining a particular bundle of goods. It should go without saying that our measure of how a particular price change affects the price level will depend upon the bundle of goods we choose to consider.

Suppose we chose bundle of goods A as appropriate; then, as is apparent from Figure 3.12, we would have to measure the Slutsky compensating variation if we wished to assess the effect on the cost of living of a fall in the price of X. The amount to which we could reduce money income after the fall in the price of X would be calculated by multiplying original money income by the ratio of the cost of obtaining bundle A at the new set of

Figure 3.12

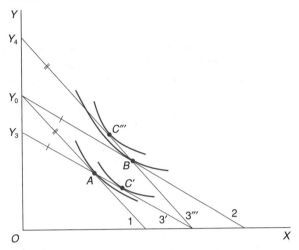

The price of X falls, shifting the constraint from 1 to 2. The change in the cost of living may be measured by the Slutsky compensating variation that shifts 2 to 3′, or the equivalent variation that shifts 1 to 3‴. The amounts of income involved would respectively purchase $Y_0 - Y_3$ and $Y_4 - Y_0$ of Y.

prices to that of obtaining it at the old set. This ratio is of course a price index, in fact the well-known **Laspèyres** or *base period* weighted index. Alternatively, we could use bundle B as the one whose cost of acquisition we were concerned with. The level of income resulting from carrying out the Slutsky equivalent variation would be given by the original level of money income multiplied by the ratio of the money income necessary to obtain bundle B at the old prices, to that necessary at the new prices. This ratio is the *inverse* of another well-known price index, the **Paasche** or *current period* weighted index. The formulae for these two index numbers are

$$\text{Laspèyres} = (p_{X_1}X_0 + p_{Y_1}Y_0)/(p_{X_0}X_0 + p_{Y_0}Y_0) \tag{3.1}$$

$$\text{Paasche} = (p_{X_1}X_1 + p_{Y_1}Y_1)/(p_{X_0}X_1 + p_{Y_0}Y_1) \tag{3.2}$$

where the subscript 0 refers to the base period, the time before the price change, and subscript 1 to the current period, the time after the price change.

These formulae will already be familiar to most readers, as will the fact that the two indices usually give different answers to questions about the cost of living. In fact, they answer questions about what has happened to the cost of acquiring particular and different bundles of goods, not a particular unambiguously defined level of utility. To all the difficulties in the cost of living concept we noted in the context of Hicks's analysis of income effects, we have added an extra problem here by substituting a given bundle of goods for a given level of utility. Whether any index of the price of a particular bundle of goods is relevant to measuring the cost of living for an individual depends very much upon the relationship between that bundle of goods and the consumption pattern of the individual. The implications of this for using allegedly general cost of living indices to measure changes in the purchasing power of the incomes of particular groups with such diverse consumption patterns as, for example, the rich, the old, students, poor families with young children, and so on, should be obvious.

Both the price indices would give qualitatively the same result in terms of Figure 3.12, both would show that the cost of living had fallen, but this need not always happen. In Figure 3.13 we start off again at A, but now permit the price of X to fall and that of Y to rise simultaneously with the net effect of a shift to B. Has the cost of living risen or fallen? The cost of obtaining bundle A is higher in the second period than in the first, so according to the Laspèyres index a positive compensating variation is required. The cost of living has increased. But initially it would have also required a higher level of income to obtain B than it does after the price changes. From the point of view of the Paasche index and the equivalent variation, the cost of living has fallen.

If we knew about the shape of the indifference map we would not face this particular ambiguity, for it would be possible to tell whether point A or B lay on the higher indifference curve. This kind of problem arises from the use of bundles of goods as approximations to given levels of utility and *may* be encountered whenever two situations are compared in which some prices are lower and others higher.

Comparisons of living costs across national boundaries, for example, often give rise to such ambiguities. Suppose that, in Figure 3.13, budget constraint 1 was interpreted as reflecting prices in Britain, and constraint 2 as reflecting American prices. Our analysis tells us that we cannot say whether the cost of living is higher in one country or the other. We can, however, conclude that the cost of a British consumption pattern is lower in

Figure 3.13

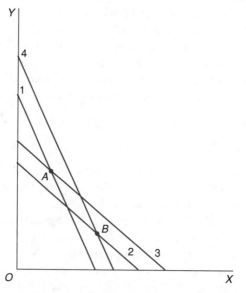

The price of X falls and that of Y rises, shifting the budget constraint from 1 to 2. The consumer is observed to shift from consumption pattern A to B. In terms of the Laspèyres index the cost of living has risen, since a compensating increase in income from constraint 2 to 3 would be needed to buy A at the new price. According to the Paasche index the cost of living has fallen, since bundle B could have been obtained at the original prices only by increasing income from constraint 1 to 4.

Britain than in America, and that the cost of an American pattern is lower in America. It is not surprising that such a state of affairs is possible, but willingness to accept this proposition involves acceptance of the fact that international comparisons of such inherently vague notions as the cost of living and the standard of living are capable of yielding ambiguous and sometimes contradictory results that must be handled with the greatest care.

Box 3.6   ## Measuring the cost of living

Let's say someone consumes two goods, X and Y. Initially (i.e. in period 0) the price of X is £10 and the price of Y is £5, and 5 units of X are consumed and 12 units of Y. By period 1 the price of X falls to £8 and the price of Y rises to £8 and the consumer responds by increasing consumption of X to 6 and reducing consumption of Y to 7.75. It is clear that money income has not changed, being fixed at £110.

With this data we can calculate the Laspèyres index of the price change that uses period 0 quantities as weights:

$$L_P = (8 \times 5 + 8 \times 12)/(10 \times 5 + 5 \times 12) = 1.2364 \tag{3.6.1}$$

and the Paasche index of the price change that uses period one quantities as weights:

$$P_P = (8 \times 6 + 8 \times 7.75)/(10 \times 6 + 5 \times 7.75) = 1.1139 \tag{3.6.2}$$

So we can say that the cost of living has gone up for this person, but we are not sure by how much.

This example can be shown in Illustration 3.3. The original bundle (5, 12) is on the period 0 budget constraint and the bundle (6, 7.75) is on the period 1 constraint. Both budget lines are defined with a level of income of £110.

Illustration 3.3

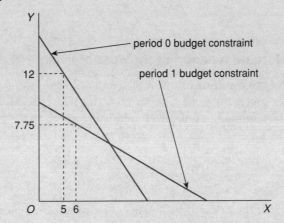

We can now see if this consumer is better off after the price change. The Slutsky compensating variation (CV_S) is measured by shifting the period 1 budget constraint parallel to the original consumption point (5, 12). This indicates that the consumer is worse off as a result of the price changes because there is a notional reduction in income from period 0 to period 1 when the two bundles are compared. If we calculate

→

this compensating variation using the method set out in Box 3.5 it is $136 - 110 = 26$. So the consumer needs to be compensated by £26 to be as well off as before the price changes, when quantities are held at period 0 levels. Using the Laspèyres price index (which also uses period 0 quantities) $110 \times 1.2364 = 136$ is the new cost of living. So the consumer needs £26 extra units of income to be as well off as before the price changes, which is the CV_S. So we can write that

$$CV_S = Y_0{}^*L_P - Y_0 \qquad (3.6.3)$$

$$\text{and} \quad L_P = \frac{Y_0 + CV_S}{Y_0} \qquad (3.6.4)$$

Y_0 = the original level of income.

We can now examine whether this person is better off using the Slutsky equivalent variation (EV_S). Referring back to the illustration we can shift the period 0 budget constraint parallel inwards to the bundle (6, 7.75), i.e. it uses period 1 quantities to see that, in this case, the consumer is worse off. We can calculate the EV_S using the method set out in Box 3.5. For this person $EV_S = 98.75 - 110 = -11.25$. So the consumer needs an equivalent reduction in income in period 0 of £11.25 to be as well of in both periods. Using the Paasche price index, which also uses period 1 quantities, $110/1.1139 = 98.75$. So the consumer needs a reduction in period 0 income of $110 - 98.75 = £11.25$ to be as well off as in period 1, which is the EV_S. So we can write

$$EV_S = \frac{Y_0}{P_P} - Y_0 \qquad (3.6.5)$$

$$\text{and} \quad P_P = \frac{Y_0}{Y_0 + EV_S} \qquad (3.6.6)$$

Box 3.7 | **More on measuring the cost of living**

We can continue the example set out in Box 3.6 and introduce a second person who consumes the same amount of X and Y in period 0 as person one, but changes the consumption bundle much more in response to the price changes so that in period 1 $X = 8.5$ and $Y = 5.25$. We can calculate the Laspèyres and Paasche price indices:

$$L_P = (8{*}5 + 8{*}12)/(10{*}5 + 5{*}12) = 1.2364 \qquad (3.7.1)$$

$$P_P = (8{*}8.5 + 8{*}5.25)/(10{*}8.5 + 5{*}5.25) = 0.9888 \qquad (3.7.2)$$

For the first person we knew that the cost of living had gone up, but not by how much. For the second person we do not even know if the cost of living has gone up or down.

The consumption bundles for both people can be shown in Illustration 3.4. The key issue here is that the original bundle (5, 12) is above the intersection of the two budget constraints, as is the first person's period 1 bundle (6, 7.75), but the second person's period 1 bundle (8.5, 5.25) is below the intersection.

Illustration 3.4

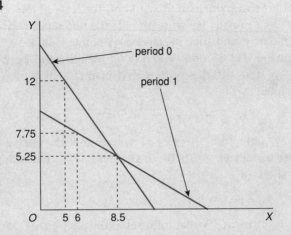

Referring back to the diagram we can see that the two consumers have the same Slutsky compensating variation (CV$_S$), found by shifting the period 1 budget constraint back to the same period 0 bundle (5, 12). Note that as the CV$_S$ is the same for both consumers the Laspèyres price index is also the same at 1.2364. But the two consumers have different Slutsky equivalent variations (EV$_S$). Shifting the period 0 budget constraint parallel to the period 1 consumption points indicates that consumer 1 is worse off after the price changes by consuming bundle (6, 7.75), whereas consumer two is better off after the price changes with bundle (8.5, 5.25). The difference in the EV$_S$ produces different results for the Paasche price index: 1.1139 for person 1 (as calculated in Box 3.6) and 0.9888 for person 2. Using the formula set out in Box 3.6 we can calculate the EV$_S$

$$EV_S = \frac{Y_0}{P_P} - Y_0 \tag{3.6.5}$$

For person 1: (110/1.1139) − 110 = −11.25.
For person 2: (110/0.9888) − 110 = 1.25.

So, although the two people face the same price changes, person 1 appears worse off by £11.25 whereas person 2 appears better off by £1.25.

✳ The Slutsky equation

The preceding analysis amounts to a series of variations on a single theme: namely, that the effect of the change in the price of a good, holding the price of other goods and money income constant, may be decomposed into a substitution effect and an income effect. This decomposition may be expressed algebraically, in the form of what is known as the **Slutsky equation**, whose label reminds us of the pioneer of consumer theory who first derived it. We have already presented a geometric treatment of this problem in terms of Figures 3.6 and 3.10 above, and the notation we use here relates to those diagrams in the following way. p_{X_1} is the price of X underlying budget constraint 1, and p_{X_2} the price of X underlying budget constraints 2 and 3'; M_1 is the level of money income underlying budget constraints 1 and 2, and M_2 the level of money income underlying budget constraint 3'; finally we write ΔX^d for the difference between the quantity of X demanded at point B and that demanded at point A, and ΔX_S^d for the difference between that demanded at C' and A, and ΔX_M for the difference between that demanded at C' and B.

We start with the consumer's demand function for X, derived formally in the previous chapter,

$$X = X^d(p_X, p_Y, M) \tag{3.3}$$

We note, from the general definition of the budget constraint that we may write the specific budget constraint 1 in Figure 3.6 – that ruling before the price change under analysis – as

$$M_1 = p_{X_1}X_1 + p_Y Y_1 \tag{3.4}$$

and constraint 3' – that ruling after the price change, and after the Slutsky compensating variation in income has been carried out – as

$$M_2 = p_{X_2}X_1 + p_Y Y_1 \tag{3.5}$$

It follows from (3.4) and (3.5) that the compensating change in money income needed to enable our consumer to buy the initial bundle of goods A at the new set of prices is

$$\Delta M = M_2 - M_1 = (p_{X_2} - p_{X_1})X_1 \tag{3.6}$$
$$\Delta M = \Delta p_X X_1$$

Using our demand function for X, the income effect associated with this compensating variation in income is

$$\Delta X_M = X^d(p_{X_2}, p_Y, M_1) - X^d(p_{X_2}, p_Y, M_2) \tag{3.7}$$

Note that this amount is negative.

Now the demand curve which holds money income constant tells us the change in the demand for X which occurs due to the change in its own price, holding money income and the price of Y constant. This amount is given by

$$\Delta X = X^d(p_{X_2}, p_Y, M_1) - X^d(p_{X_1}, p_Y, M_1) \tag{3.8}$$

Moreover, the change in the quantity of X demanded as a result of the Slutsky substitution effect, from A to C' in Figure 3.6, may be written as

$$\Delta X_s = X^d(p_{X_2}, p_Y, M_2) - X^d(p_{X_1}, p_Y, M_1) \tag{3.9}$$

Note that this amount is positive.

Equation (3.8) may now be rewritten as

$$\Delta X = \Delta X_S + \Delta X_M \tag{3.10}$$

The truth of this assertion may be checked by substituting the right-hand sides of (3.7), (3.8) and (3.9) into (3.10):

$$X^d(p_{X_2}, p_Y, M_1) - X^d(p_{X_1}, p_Y, M_1)$$
$$= X^d(p_{X_2}, p_Y, M_1) - X^d(p_{X_2}, p_Y, M_2) + X^d(p_{X_2}, p_Y, M_2) - X^d(p_{X_1}, p_Y, M_1) \tag{3.11}$$

Evidently, (3.10), which is sometimes known as Slutsky's identity, is always true.

A discrete form of the Slutsky equation may now be derived by dividing (3.10) through by Δp_X and recalling, from (3.6), that

$$\Delta p_X = \Delta M / X_1 \tag{3.12}$$

where X_1 is the initial amount of X purchased, at point A in Figure 3.6. Thus, we have

$$\frac{\Delta X}{\Delta p_X} = \frac{\Delta X_S}{\Delta p_X} - \frac{\Delta X_M}{\Delta M} X_1 \tag{3.13}$$

The second, income effect, term in this expression is written with a negative sign, because, it will be recalled, in the experiment we are here considering, the change in income ΔM needed to compensate for a fall in the price of X is negative.

Finally, it should be noted that as the change in price we are considering becomes infinitesimally small, equation (3.13) approaches

$$\frac{\partial X}{\partial p_X} = \frac{\partial X_S}{\partial p_X} - \frac{\partial X_M}{\partial M} X_1 \tag{3.14}$$

This is the usual way of writing the Slutsky equation, but its formal derivation using calculus is beyond the technical scope of this book.

Concluding comment

The underlying theme of this chapter has been the way in which the nature of a consumer's indifference map renders interdependent the effects of income, the prices of other goods, and its own price on the quantity demanded of a good. Consideration of this interdependence led us to break down movements along a price consumption curve, and therefore along a demand curve too, into income and substitution effects.

We have seen that there is more than one way to make the income – substitution effect distinction, and also how analysis of the possibilities enables us to reach a deeper and more precise understanding of such everyday concepts as 'real income', 'standard of living' and 'cost of living'.

SUMMARY

Futher analysis and applications of the theory of consumer choice

1. The effects of income and price changes upon consumption can be decomposed into substitution effects and income effects.

2. The substitution effect is always negative as long as indifference curves are smoothly convex to the origin. The income effect is positive for normal goods, and therefore augments the substitution effect when we look at the relationship between demand and price. The income effect is negative for inferior goods, and works against the substitution effect.

3. The negative income effect (increasing demand as price rises, for example) actually outweighs the negative substitution effect (decreasing demand as price rises) in the case of the Giffen good.

4. Compensating variation in money income as the price of one good falls relative to another allows us to derive the constant real income demand curve. This must be negatively sloped since it is based only upon a substitution effect.

5. Constant real income attained from a constant level of utility is sometimes referred to as Hicks real income; constant real income derived from the ability to purchase a given bundle of goods is known as Slutsky real income. The latter is an approximation to the former, and becomes identical to it for infinitesimal price changes.

6. Constant real income demand curves can also be derived using the equivalent variation in income. The shift of the budget constraint has an effect on real income equivalent to the price change in question and the income and substitution effects need not be of the same magnitude as when a compensating variation in income is employed.

7. Performing Slutsky compensating and equivalent variations in income allows us to derive alternative budget constraints. Even if we are ignorant about the indifference map we are still able to sign the income and substitution effects since there are segments of these constraints over which the consumer has revealed preferences by being observed to choose particular bundles of goods.

8. Measurement of the Slutsky compensating variation in the standard of living is possible using the Laspèyres base period weighted price index. To measure the Slutsky equivalent variation we use the Paasche current period weighted price index. Since these indices measure changes in the income needed to buy different bundles of goods, they will not usually yield the same quantitative measure of a change in the cost of living.

PROBLEMS

1 An individual is faced with a choice of buying housing in one of two markets; the private market where he may buy any amount of housing he pleases at the going price, and the public housing market where he will be offered, on a take-it-or-leave-it-basis, a particular amount of housing at a price lower than that which he would pay for it on the private market. Will he necessarily choose the public housing? If so, may we conclude that he will consume more housing than he would have purchased had he been forced to buy it on the private market? (With thanks to Dr Leslie Rosenthal.)

2 The following observations are taken on a consumer's behaviour on two successive weeks:

week 1	price of X	£10
	price of Y	£10
	quantity of X bought	10 units per week
	quantity of Y bought	10 units per week
week 2	price of X	£5
	price of Y	£20
	quantity of X bought	20 units per week
	quantity of Y bought	5 units per week

Has the consumer's money income changed between the two weeks? Calculate the Laspèyres price index for week 2 taking its value in week 1 to be 100. Calculate the Paasche price index for week 2 taking its value in week 1 to be 100. Has the 'cost of living' risen between week 1 and week 2?

(Students may wish to read Chapter 4 before answering questions 3 and 4.)

3 Suppose that it costs 12 pence a mile in *direct* operating costs to run a car.

Let X be miles per week and p be measured in pence, and an individual's demand curve for car transport be given by

$$p = 400 - 4Q$$

(a) How many miles per week will be driven?

(b) How much consumer's surplus will be gained from operating the car?

(c) Would the individual be willing to pay a fixed cost, over and above variable costs, of £60 per week to operate the car?

(d) Suppose the direct cost of operating a car rose to £2 per mile because of an increase in the price of petrol. How would your answers to questions (a), (b) and (c) change?

Use the Marshallian demand curve assumptions in answering this question.

4 Starting with an individual's Marshallian demand curve for hours of television watching and the knowledge that each hour's watching uses a given amount of electricity, show how a fall in the price of electricity will affect:

(a) the amount an individual is willing to pay to rent a television;

(b) the market demand curve for rented television.

CHAPTER 4

Utility

Key words and phrases

- consumer's surplus
- Marshallian theory
- total and marginal utility, constant marginal utility of income, marginal utility curve
- interpersonal comparisons of utility; duality

Introduction

The income effects with which we have dealt in the last chapter measure the change in satisfaction, or utility, that an individual experiences as a result of a change in the price of a particular good. We have seen that, when the price of a good falls, the individual moves onto a higher indifference curve, and that the increase in utility experienced as a result of this is equal to that gained from an 'equivalent' variation in money income. We have also seen that an alternative measure of the same gain is the amount by which money income may be diminished after the price fall in order to leave the consumer just as well off as initially, i.e. the 'compensating' variation in money income. The changes in utility which we are discussing here are often referred to as changes in **consumer's surplus**. The term is an old-fashioned one, but the concept involved is vital in understanding the response of consumers to discriminatory pricing, as it is in understanding what is involved in the application of *cost–benefit analysis* to decision making. In this chapter, we will first of all elucidate the concept in question, and then show how a particular version of consumer theory enables that concept to be analysed in a remarkably simple way. We shall also show how this particular version relates to the general model of consumer choice developed in Chapters 2 and 3 of this book.

The concept of consumer's surplus

It is a trivial implication of indifference curve analysis that if we start with the consumer out of equilibrium and permit the substitution of X for Y until a preferred bundle of goods is reached, this act of substitution makes the consumer better off. More is gained from

Figure 4.1

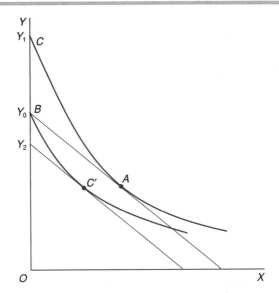

The amount of income needed to buy $Y_1 - Y_0$ of Y gives the consumer a gain in utility equivalent to the one obtained from moving from B to A, since the consumer is indifferent between A and C. The amount necessary to buy $Y_0 - Y_2$ just compensates for this ability to consume X since the consumer is indifferent between points B and C'.

increasing consumption of X than is given up in reducing consumption of Y. If we start from a situation where no X at all is consumed, as at B in Figure 4.1, where Y_0 is consumed, and move out to A, then the consumer moves from a lower indifference curve to a higher indifference curve. The increase in utility involved here is the consumer's surplus obtained from consuming X; it is the maximum gain to be made from being able to trade X for Y at the price ratio underlying the budget constraint, and it is clearly tempting to look for a means of measuring this gain in terms of money.

There are several ways of getting such a measure in terms of Figure 4.1, but we will discuss only two of them. Suppose we began with our consumer facing the price of X that is implicit in the budget constraint of Figure 4.1, and suppose that bundle of goods A was being consumed. Now suppose that we prohibited the consumption of X. We could ask the following question: by how much would we have to increase the consumer's income in order to compensate for this prohibition? Clearly, we would have to raise income by enough to enable a movement from point B to point C, an increase in consumption of Y by $Y_1 - Y_0$. If we know the price of Y, the computation of the amount of income involved here is just a matter of arithmetic. The change in income involved is just enough to *compensate* the consumer for the loss of the ability to consume X. It is one measure of the gain that accrues from being able to consume X at the going price.

On the other hand, we could think in terms of offering the consumer a choice between being forbidden to consume X or accepting a reduction in income. We could then ask how large a reduction in income would leave the consumer just as badly off as the prohibition on the consumption of X. Obviously income could be reduced until consumption was reduced to C', for here the consumer would obtain just that level of utility attainable at B. The change in income here is again easily calculated; it is the amount that would permit the purchase of $Y_0 - Y_2$ of Y. It is in fact that variation in income that has an *equivalent* effect on the consumer's utility to a prohibition on consuming X at the going price.

We have here yet another application of the ideas of compensating and equivalent variation to measuring gains and losses in real income, and there is no reason why the two measures should yield the same answers to the question, 'how much does the consumer gain from being able to consume X at the going price?' One tells us how much it would take to compensate for a prohibition on consuming X and the other tells us how big a change in income would be equivalent in its effects to such a prohibition. These sound like the same thing at first, perhaps, but they are not, as must be evident from the preceding discussion. Moreover the reader should note that, as always, which measure is called the 'compensating' and which the 'equivalent' variation depends upon the starting point for the experiment. In the above discussion we have started from point A. If we start instead from point B, as we do in the discussion embodied in the caption to Figure 4.1, the labels attached to these measures are reversed.

Box 4.1	Calculating consumer's surplus

We have seen in the text that there are two ways of calculating consumer's surplus based on compensating and equivalent variations. These two ways can be readily calculated if we have a particular utility function which allows us to calculate consumer's surplus. Therefore, assume that someone consumes two goods (X and Y) and that the utility function is

$$U = Y^{0.5}(1 + X)^{0.5} \tag{4.1.1}$$

For any given level of utility ($\bar{U}$) we can define the indifference curve for this level of utility:

$$Y = \frac{\bar{U}^2}{1 + X} \tag{4.1.2}$$

We can note that, with this indifference curve, when $X = 0$ $Y = \bar{U}^2$ and so the consumer's surplus can be calculated in the manner set out in Figure 4.1.

To calculate the consumer's surplus we need a general expression that defines utility maximisation. If the prices of X and Y are the same our consumer will maximise utility when the slope of any indifference curve is equal to 1, i.e. p_X/p_Y. The slope of any indifference curve (i.e. the marginal rate of substitution) is

$$\frac{dY}{dX} = -\frac{\bar{U}^2}{(1 + X)^2} = -\left(\frac{\bar{U}}{1 + X}\right)^2 \tag{4.1.3}$$

With $p_X = p_Y$ (as assumed), utility maximisation therefore involves

$$\left(\frac{\bar{U}}{1 + X}\right)^2 = 1$$

i.e. in equilibrium

$$X = \bar{U} - 1 \tag{4.1.4}$$

and therefore from the utility function

$$Y = \frac{\bar{U}^2}{1 + \bar{U} - 1} = \bar{U} \tag{4.1.5}$$

Using these solutions for X and Y in the budget constraint

$$M = p_X X + p_Y Y = p_X(\bar{U} - 1) + p_Y(\bar{U}) \tag{4.1.6}$$

We now have all the elements to calculate the consumer's surplus. To keep the arithmetic as easy as possible we can assume that $p_X = p_Y = 1$.

Compensating variation

In Figure 4.1 using the compensating variation to calculate the consumer's surplus involves calculating the amount of income that raises consumption from B to C. If income (M) is equal to 100, then from the condition that

$$M = p_X(\bar{U} - 1) + p_Y(\bar{U}) \tag{4.1.6}$$

and with $p_X = p_Y = 1$

$$100 = 2(\bar{U}) - 1 \tag{4.1.7}$$

So the maximum utility that can be obtained with $M = 100$ is $U = 49.5$. This equilibrium is equivalent to point A in Figure 4.1. Point B is the maximum amount of Y that can be bought with $X = 0$; with $M = 100$ and $p_Y = 1$ this is 100. We now need to find the equivalent of point C in Figure 4.1. The indifference curve with $U = 49.5$ is

$$Y = \frac{49.5^2}{1 + X} \quad \text{i.e. } Y = \frac{2450.25}{1 + X} \tag{4.1.8}$$

So with $X = 0$, point C in Figure 4.1 is $Y = 2450.25$. With $p_Y = 1$ this level of Y requires an income of 2450.25. So the consumer's surplus measured by the compensating variation, i.e. the change in income that produces the change $Y_1 - Y_0$ in Figure 4.1, is $2450.25 - 100 = 2350.25$.

Equivalent variation

Using the equivalent variation to calculate the consumer's surplus involves calculating the change in income that generates the change in Y equivalent to $Y_0 - Y_2$ in Figure 4.1. We know that Y_0 is 100. To calculate Y_2 we must find the utility maximising point C'. To do this we must find the utility generated at point B. With our utility function any indifference curve is

$$Y = \frac{\bar{U}^2}{1 + X} \tag{4.1.2}$$

With $Y = 100$ and $X = 0$, i.e. the equivalent of point B in Figure 4.1 is

$$\bar{U}^2 = 100$$

So the indifference curve at point B is $U = 10$. We already know that with our utility function, when a consumer maximises utility:

$$M = p_X(\bar{U} - 1) + p_Y(\bar{U}) \tag{4.1.6}$$

$\rightarrow$

So with $U = 10$ and $p_X = p_Y = 1$, consumer equilibrium involves $M = 19$. With this income level, our consumer maximises utility at point C' in Figure 4.1. The consumer's surplus, measured by the equivalent variation, i.e. $Y_0 - Y_2$ in Figure 4.1 starting from an income level of 100, is $100 - 19 = 81$.

An application of consumer's surplus

But why should the concept of the total gain from consuming a good be important? An example will help here. Suppose a government agency was trying to decide whether or not to provide a particular service, for example the operation of a bridge over a river. If the benefits to society of having the bridge outweighed the costs, we might all agree that it should be built. Suppose that a toll was to be charged. Would it be the case that toll revenue could be regarded as measuring the benefits consumers obtained from the bridge, so that, if such revenue did not cover the cost of operating the bridge it should not be built?

Consider Figure 4.2 and suppose that X_1 represents the bridge crossings per week made by a particular consumer at a particular toll per crossing. The actual revenue received from this consumer would be given by whatever sum of money would buy $Y_0 - Y_2$ of Y at going prices, but the *total benefit* to that same consumer of making bridge crossings could be measured by whatever sum of money would buy $Y_1 - Y_0$ of Y. That is to say, the total benefit to this consumer from operating the bridge is the *sum* of toll payments *and* consumer's surplus. In terms of Figure 4.2, $Y_1 - Y_2$ is one measure of this total benefit.

Figure 4.2

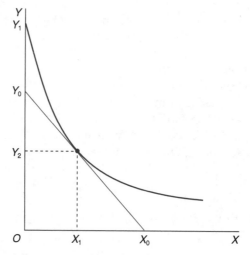

The consumer pays as much income as would purchase $Y_0 - Y_2$ units of Y in order to obtain X_1 units of X. However, consuming X_1 units of X yields the same gain in utility as would have come from consuming $Y_1 - Y_2$ units of Y. The amount of income necessary to buy this amount of Y is therefore one measure of the total benefit that the consumer gets from consuming X.

This example should suffice for the moment to establish that the concept of consumer's surplus is worth attention. The analysis embodied in Figures 4.1 and 4.2 tells us how it might be measured, but, unfortunately, only in principle. We can only find such distances as $Y_1 - Y_0$ and $Y_1 - Y_2$ if we know the shape of the indifference map. Again we are in need of some quantifiable approximation if the analysis is to be of practical value. It is to the development of one such approximation that we devote the next three sections of this chapter, an approximation that has the great advantage of utilising the shape and location of the demand curve as its analytic basis. In order fully to elucidate this approximation we must return to consider the very foundations of our analysis of consumer choice, paying particular attention to the nature of the utility function.

Marshallian consumer theory

Recall that, in Chapter 2, we discussed the concepts of *ordinal* and *cardinal* utility. It was shown there that, as far as deriving demand curves and such was concerned, it sufficed to assume ordinal utility, to postulate that the consumer could make statements about the order of preference in which different bundles of goods were ranked. It was not necessary to assume that the consumer could perceive the intensity of preferences, and measure the differences in the degree of satisfaction obtained from consuming different bundles.

The idea of cardinal utility is simply redundant in the context of the analysis carried out in Chapter 2. Nevertheless this concept was used in Alfred Marshall's version of demand theory which predates the analysis we have set out, and **Marshallian demand theory**, it turns out, enables us to develop a measure of consumer's surplus that is a usable approximation to the quantities analysed here and earlier. In order to analyse the demand for a particular good X in Marshallian terms, we make three key assumptions. First, we assume that the **total utility** gained from consuming any quantity of X is independent of the quantity of Y consumed, and vice versa. Secondly, we assume that the **marginal utility** of Y is constant, i.e. that the utility gained from consuming Y rises in strict proportion to the quantity of Y so that equal increments of Y yield equal increments of utility. Finally, we assume that the marginal utility of X diminishes as consumption of X increases, i.e. that equal increments in X yield successively smaller increments in utility.

These assumptions are difficult to take literally, to be sure, and we will see what they imply about the nature of the indifference map in a few pages; but for the moment let us pursue their other implications. In Figure 4.3 we measure on the vertical axis utility per unit of X (in terms of some arbitrary unit of measurement such as 'utils') and on the horizontal axis the quantity of X consumed per unit of time. We then plot the relationship between the marginal utility of X per unit of X and the quantity of it consumed. The area under this curve between the vertical axis and one unit of X measures the utility per unit of time gained from consuming the first unit, the area under the curve between 1 and 2 units of X measures that gained from consuming the second, and so on. Hence the total utility per unit of time gained from consuming any particular quantity of X per unit of time is found by adding up all these areas. Thus, for X_1 units, for example, this addition yields the area $OBAX_1$ as a measure of the total utility derived from consuming X_1 units of X.

Now X has a price. For each unit of X bought a certain quantity of Y must be given up because money income is given up. This means that a certain amount of utility from

Figure 4.3

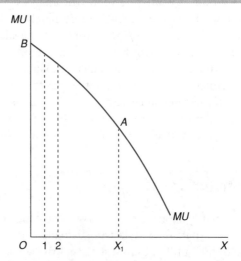

The marginal utility of X declines as the quantity of X consumed increases. The area $OBAX_1$ measures the total utility of consuming X_1 units of X.

consuming Y must be forgone for each unit of X consumed and, since the marginal utility of Y is constant, the amount of utility sacrificed is constant per unit of X obtained. The 'price' to the consumer in terms of utility forgone per unit of X consumed is **constant** and may be represented by a straight line such as SS on Figure 4.4. The area under the marginal utility curve of X is the total utility gained from consuming it and, by exactly

Figure 4.4

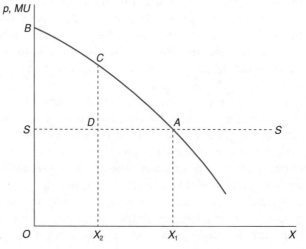

If OS measures the amount of utility that must be forgone per unit of X consumed, then utility is maximised by consuming X_1 units of X. The consumer's surplus from so doing is given by the area BAS.

similar reasoning, the area under the line *SS* is the total cost in terms of utility of acquiring it. The net gain from consuming a particular quantity of *X* is then the difference in these two areas. For example, at X_2 units of *X* this net gain is given by the area *BCDS*.

Box 4.2

Calculating the Marshallian consumer's surplus

Let us assume that a person consumes a single good (*X*) and for the purposes of this calculation has the total utility function

$$U = 100X - X^2 \qquad (4.2.1)$$

Marginal utility is then

$$MU = \frac{dU}{dX} = 100 - 2X \qquad (4.2.2)$$

Using the logic set out in Figure 4.4 we can calculate the consumer's surplus for any price of *X*. If $p_X = 5$ our person maximises utility when $MU = 5$, so

$$5 = 100 - 2X$$

which implies that $X = 47.5$.

As our *MU* curve is linear the Marshallian consumer's surplus is the area of the triangle above the price and below the curve. With $p_X = 5$ and $X = 47.5$ the area of this triangle is

$$0.5(47.5 \times 95) = 2256.25.$$

If the price of *X* falls to 4, $X = 48$ and the consumer's surplus is 2304. So the money equivalent gain in utility from the fall in price from 5 to 4 is $2304 - 2256.25 = 47.75$.

The utility-maximising consumer obviously wishes to maximise this net gain. Equally obviously in terms of Figure 4.4, this will involve consuming X_1 units of *X*, at which point the marginal gain from consuming it is just equal to its price in terms of utility forgone. The total net gain from consumption of *X* is, in this case, given by the area *BAS* and is the consumer's surplus accruing from the consumption of *X* measured in utils. It is trivially easy to translate this measure in unobservable utils into one in terms of money. With a given price for *Y*, and a given marginal utility of *Y*, we can freely translate utils into units of money. There is a strictly proportional relationship between every pound spent on *Y*, the volume of *Y* acquired, and the utility yielded by the consumption of the *Y* purchased. Thus, the 'price' in terms of utility forgone of *X* may be transformed into a price measured in pounds and pence. Similarly, the marginal utility of *X* may be measured in terms of the sum of money that would have to be devoted to the purchase of *Y* in order to yield an equivalent flow of utility.

Thus, we may substitute monetary units for utility units on the vertical axis of Figure 4.4; the price of *X* then becomes a money price, and the assumption of utility maximisation ensures that the **marginal utility curve** will relate the quantity of *X* demanded to its price. Hence the marginal utility curve becomes a demand curve. Consumer's surplus may be measured as the area under the demand curve for *X*, minus total expenditure on *X*: thus

Figure 4.5

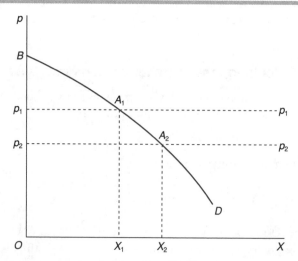

The gain in consumer's surplus as a result of the price of X falling from p_1 to p_2 is given by $p_1A_1A_2p_2$.

we have our monetary measure of consumer's surplus in terms of observable phenomena. We also have monetary measures of the change in utility that arises from changes in the price of X. Thus, if the price of X falls from p_1 to p_2 in Figure 4.5, consumption increases from X_1 to X_2 and the money value of the consumer's gain in utility is given by the area $p_1A_1A_2p_2$.

Now the measure of consumer's surplus in Figure 4.4 is apparently unambiguous, and in Figure 4.5 the measure of the change in consumer's surplus, which is just another name for the effect on real income that arises from a price change, is also unambiguous. Our careful distinction between compensating and equivalent variations seems to have vanished in the process of producing these measures of consumer's surplus in terms of areas under the demand curve for X. Let us now see how this has come about.

Marshallian analysis in terms of indifference curves

The nature of the approximations into which our search for an easily quantifiable measure of consumer's surplus has led us, and the reason why the distinction between compensating and equivalent variations has vanished, are easily seen if we translate Marshallian analysis into the language of indifference curves.

In terms of such analysis, to postulate cardinal utility means that we can label each of our indifference curves by the level of utility associated with it. The assumption that the marginal utility of Y is constant means that successive increments in Y, if the quantity of X is constant, lead to equal increments in utility, while the independence of the marginal utilities of X and Y means that these equal increments in utility are the same regardless of the quantity of X being consumed. In Figure 4.6 these assumptions are translated into an indifference map. They involve the indifference curves being equally spaced along *any*

Figure 4.6   **The indifference map implicit in Marshallian utility theory**

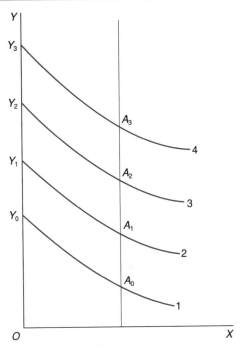

Up any line perpendicular to the X-axis (including the Y-axis itself), the indifference curves are parallel to each other. Thus, the slope of each curve is the same at Y_0, Y_1, Y_2 and Y_3, and, for example, at A_0, A_1, A_2 and A_3. At any quantity of X, successive equal increments in the amount of Y yield equal increments in utility from 1 to 2, 2 to 3, etc. The curves become more shallow as we move to the right: hence, successive equal increments in the amount of X consumed for any given quantity of Y yield successively smaller increases in utility.

line drawn perpendicular to the X-axis; this can only happen if each curve has the same slope where it cuts such a perpendicular. This obviously means that there is a zero income elasticity of demand for X. The quantity of it bought would depend only on the slope and not on the location of the budget constraint. Hence, when prices change, there is no income effect on the demand for X, only on the demand for Y.

The measure of consumer's surplus which we have dealt with in this chapter and the measures of effects on real income of price changes which we dealt with in Chapter 3 all involve measuring the vertical distance between pairs of indifference curves. Measures based on equivalent and compensating variations can differ so long as we impose no requirement that the vertical distance between given indifference curves be the same at every point. The Marshallian assumptions, however, do impose this requirement and hence, in terms of indifference curve analysis, conceptually different measures yield the same estimate of its value.

As we have seen, these same assumptions imply that various areas under the demand curve for a good may be used to measure overall levels of, and changes in, consumer's surplus. Such measurements are quite commonly used in applications of demand theory to concrete problems, but they are approximations to the much more slippery, and ambiguous, quantities analysed earlier. As the reader might expect, the closer to zero the income elasticity of demand for X, and the smaller the effect on income of whatever change is under analysis, then the better is the approximation and the more accurate will be the predictions based upon its use.

The demand curve is one of the basic relationships of economic theory, and as we have already noted, Marshall's derivation of it predates the indifference curve approach upon which this book concentrates. That is one reason why many real-world applications of the consumer's surplus concept use the demand curve, and areas under it, as their basic ingredients. It is, however, only in the limiting zero income effect special case that the area under the demand curve yields an accurate estimate of the more fundamental measures of consumer's surplus given by equivalent and compensating variations. More generally, though, there is in fact a systematic relationship among these three measures of consumer's surplus whose nature depends, as the reader might guess, upon the magnitude of the income effect.

A precise understanding of the nature of these relationships is worth having for anyone interested in real-world applications of consumer's surplus, where, as we have said, the demand curve is often used as a starting point. However, to analyse these relationships using geometry alone is very complex, but once geometry is supplemented by a little algebra matters become more straightforward. Readers who go on to the starred sections of this chapter will find this matter taken up again in more detail in the second of them.

The impossibility of comparing utility between persons

The problems in measuring consumer's surplus which we have discussed so far have all been concerned with the ambiguity of this concept when analysing the individual consumer's situation. We have, however, seen that we may produce an apparently unambiguous monetary measure of an individual's satisfaction from consuming a particular good if we make the special assumptions set out in the two previous sections of this chapter. It must be noted, however, that even making these assumptions provides no basis in economic theory for adding these measures of satisfaction over individuals to produce some global measure of the gain to the community from consuming a particular good. Even if we are willing to postulate the existence of a cardinal utility function for each member of the community, there is no basis for comparing these functions between people and hence no way of adding them up. A pound's worth of satisfaction to one person and a pound's worth of satisfaction to another may or may not be the same amount of satisfaction. There is no way of knowing. Thus, though getting a measure of consumer's surplus is one of the major problems in cost–benefit analysis, it is by no means the only one. Equally important is finding a means of comparing consumer's surplus among individuals when, as is inevitably the case, the benefits (and costs) that must be measured accrue to different individuals. This section of the book has nothing to say on this score.

Thus, to return to our bridge-building example, we now know much more than we did about the extent to which the benefits to individuals from having the services of a bridge might be measured, but we have learned nothing about how to sum these individual benefits in order to get a global measure of 'the benefit to the community' of the bridge. The problem here is one involving the distribution of economic benefits between individuals, and it is raised now only to warn the reader that it has not yet been treated in this book. We shall deal with it in a more general framework in Part VII when we take up problems involving the interaction of individuals in the economic system.

* The algebra of Marshallian analysis

We may apply the simple algebra of constrained maximisation developed in Chapter 2 to elucidating the nature of Marshallian consumer theory. The key here is to find a specific form of the utility function which has the required characteristics, that is independence of the marginal utilities of X and Y, constancy of the marginal utility of Y, and a tendency of the marginal utility of X to decline with its quantity.

Such a utility function is given by

$$U = aX^{\alpha} + bY, \ \alpha < 1 \tag{4.1}$$

As in Chapter 2, we may write the budget constraint as

$$M - p_X X - p_Y Y = 0 \tag{4.2}$$

Forming the Lagrangian expression gives us

$$V = aX^{\alpha} + bY + \lambda(M - p_X X - p_Y Y) \tag{4.3}$$

Taking the partial derivatives of (4.3) with respect to X, Y and λ, and setting these equal to zero gives us the first-order conditions characterising a maximum. These are

$$\frac{\partial V}{\partial X} = \alpha a X^{\alpha-1} - \lambda p_X = 0 \tag{4.4}$$

$$\frac{\partial V}{\partial Y} = b - \lambda p_Y = 0 \tag{4.5}$$

$$\frac{\partial V}{\partial \lambda} = M - p_X X - p_Y Y = 0 \tag{4.6}$$

Now (4.5) may be arranged to yield

$$\lambda = \frac{b}{p_Y} \tag{4.7}$$

If we hold the price of Y constant, we may define it as being equal to unity and (4.4) becomes

$$\alpha a X^{\alpha-1} - b p_X = 0 \tag{4.8}$$

We can now solve equations (4.6) and (4.8) for the unknowns Y and X as functions of M and p_X, but let us concentrate here on the demand function for X, which is the one underlying the analysis carried out in this chapter.

Equation (4.6) may be rearranged as

$$X = \frac{M - Y}{p_X} \tag{4.9}$$

and (4.8) as

$$X = Rp_X^{1/(\alpha-1)}$$

(4.10)

where

$$R = \frac{b}{\alpha a}^{1/(\alpha-1)}$$

(4.11)

Substituting (4.9) into (4.10) gives us the demand for Y as a function of M and p_X

$$Y = M - Rp_X^{\alpha/(\alpha-1)}$$

(4.12)

and substituting this back into (4.9) gives us the demand function for X

$$X = [M - M + Rp_X^{\alpha/(\alpha-1)}]/p_X = Rp_X^{1/(\alpha-1)}$$

(4.13)

Thus we have confirmed that Marshallian assumptions eliminate the income effect from the demand for X, but produce a function in which quantity demanded varies inversely with price.

** Duality – a more general treatment of equivalent variation, compensating variation and consumer's surplus

Now the Marshallian analysis is simple enough, but the assumptions about the nature of the utility function which we made to achieve that simplicity are very special indeed. At the price of extra analytic complexity, it is possible to analyse more generally the relationship between equivalent variation, compensating variation and consumer's surplus, linking them to total expenditures, and the compensated demand curve introduced in the previous chapter. It will be remembered that the (Hicksian) equivalent variation measures the impact of a change in price upon real income, measured from the new indifference curve. The (Hicksian) compensating variation measures the impact of a change on real income, measured from the old indifference curve. Changes in consumer's surplus, on the other hand, refer to triangles under the (uncompensated) demand curve.

To develop the relationship between these apparently distinct concepts formally, it is useful to specify an *expenditure function*, in which the consumer's outlay, E, varies with prices and the level of utility. We saw in Chapter 2 that consumer choice could be modelled in terms of maximising utility subject to a budget constraint. In terms of diagrams, the consumer is assumed to choose a bundle of commodities on the highest possible indifference curve, subject to the constraint that this equilibrium must lie within the feasible set of expenditures, delineated by the budget constraint. Outcomes therefore occur at the tangency between indifference curves and budget lines.

One can think of an exact **dual** to this problem, in which we predetermine the level of utility, say $\bar{u}$, and search for the minimum level of expenditure at given prices required to achieve this level of utility. Expenditures are of course indicated by the intercept of the budget constraint with the Y axis, so the problem becomes to find the bundle of X and Y on indifference curve V at which, for the given p_X and p_Y, expenditure is minimised. As before, the solution lies at the tangency of the indifference curve, $\bar{u}$, and the budget constraint. It is this minimum level of expenditure, dependent on prices and the utility level, which is expressed through the *expenditure* function. The expenditure function is written as

$$E = E(p_X, p_Y, \bar{u}) \tag{4.14}$$

which must be interpreted as the minimum of

$$E = p_X X + p_Y Y \tag{4.15}$$

subject to

$$V(X, Y) \geq \bar{u}. \tag{4.16}$$

The solution to this problem is illustrated in Figure 4.7, which, apart from the notation employed, is of course identical to our previous representations of consumer choice.

Many of the standard results of consumer theory developed in earlier chapters can also be derived in terms of this specification. We can, for example, establish that the ratio of marginal utility to price must be equalised across goods $((\partial V/\partial X)/p_X = (\partial V/\partial Y)/p_Y)$ – see equation (2.14); and that the ratio itself must equal the cost of obtaining utility at the margin. Moreover the ratio of prices (p_X/p_Y) must equal the marginal rate of substitution $((\partial V/\partial X)/(\partial V/\partial Y))$; this is, of course, the familiar tangency condition. Perhaps most importantly, we can derive compensated demand functions directly from the expenditure function, by differentiating with respect to price. Thus it can be established that

$$\frac{\partial E}{\partial p_Y} = Y^*(p_X, p_Y, \bar{u}) \tag{4.17}$$

where Y^* represents the quantity demanded, as in Figure 4.7. A simple example will help the reader grasp the intuition of the argument. Suppose we are buying 10 bars of chocolate per week and the price rises by 1 penny per bar. It is approximately true that one needs to

Figure 4.7

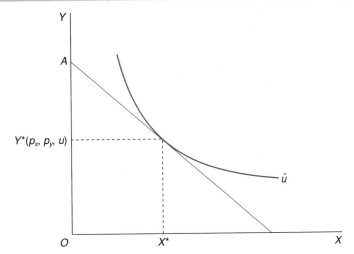

Consumer choice of X and Y around the indifference curve $\bar{u}$. Expenditure to achieve a level of utility $\bar{u}$ at prices p_X and p_Y is minimised at (Y^*, X^*). Expenditure measured in terms of Y, $E(p_X, p_Y, \bar{u})$, is given by OA.

spend 10 pence more in order to maintain the same level of utility. The compensated demand function for each good is therefore the derivative of the expenditure function with respect to its price.

The reader will have noted that this formulation of the consumer's choice problem in terms of minimum expenditures is consistent with the one adopted earlier when dealing with the compensated and equivalent variations, each of which represents changes in expenditures around a given indifference curve. Let us look at this more closely, considering once again the adjustments analysed in the previous chapter in terms of Figure 3.11. There are two possible ways of measuring the impact of a fall in the price of X, say from p_X^1 to p_X^2. The equivalent variation indicates the change in expenditure around the new indifference curve I_2 and can be written algebraically as

$$EV = E(p_X^2, p_Y, I_2) - E(p_X^1, p_Y, I_2).$$
(4.18)

In Figure 3.11, the equivalent variation equals $Y_2 - Y_0$. The compensating variation indicates the change in expenditure around the old indifference curve and can be written algebraically as

$$CV = E(p_X^2, p_Y, I_1) - E(p_X^1, p_Y, I_1)$$
(4.19)

In Figure 3.11, the compensating variation is $Y_0 - Y_1$.

Inspection of equations (4.18) and (4.19) makes clear that as the change in price from p_X^1 to p_X^2 becomes smaller, they approach *integrals* of the expenditure function with respect to price. Hence we can rewrite them as

$$EV = \int_{p_X^1}^{p_X^2} \frac{\partial E(p_X, P_Y, I_2)}{\partial p_X} dp_X$$
(4.20)

$$CV = \int_{p_X^1}^{p_X^2} \frac{\partial E(p_X, P_Y, I_1)}{\partial p_X} dp_X$$
(4.21)

and similarly for changes in the price of Y. But we know from equation (4.17) that derivatives of the expenditure function with respect to price are the compensated demand function for that good. Hence

$$EV = \int_{p_X^1}^{p_X^2} X^*(p_X, p_Y, I_2) dp_X$$
(4.22)

and

$$CV = \int_{p_X^1}^{p_X^2} X^*(p_X, p_Y, I_1) dp_X$$
(4.23)

The compensated and equivalent variations therefore represent areas under compensated demand curves, the former going through the uncompensated demand curve at the old price and the latter going through the uncompensated demand curve at the new price.

With the aid of this conceptual apparatus we can now turn to the issue of the relationship between equivalent variation, compensating variation and consumer's surplus. Consider the demand curve for the normal good X illustrated in Figure 4.8. We initially start at the price p_1, which falls to p_2. The (uncompensated) demand curve passes through X_1^* and X_2^*, the levels of demand associated with each price. The change in consumer's

Figure 4.8   The effect of a fall in the price of *X* on welfare

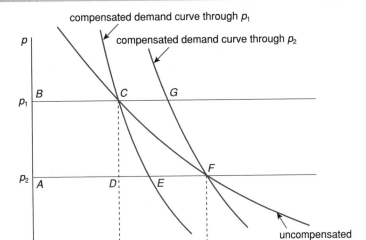

The change in consumer's surplus coming from a fall in the price of *X* from p_1 to p_2 is given by *ABCD* (the transfer from producers to consumers given by the price fall) plus *DCF*. It is less than the equivalent variation (*ABCD + DCGF*) and more than the compensating variation (*ABCD + DCE*).

surplus resulting from the price fall is given by initial expenditure (*ABCD*) plus the triangle under the uncompensated demand curve, *CDF*. The equivalent variation is the area under the compensated demand curve around the new price, p_2, between the two prices p_1 and p_2. It is given by the initial expenditure (*ABCD*) plus the rectangle *CDFG*; and is larger than the consumer's surplus. The compensating variation is the area under the compensated demand curve at the original price p_X^1 between the prices p_X^1 and p_X^2. It equals the initial expenditure (*ABCD*) plus the triangle *DCE*, and is less than both consumer's surplus and equivalent variation. (Note that *CV* and *EV* necessarily have a different sign; we here refer to their absolute values.) The change in consumer's surplus thus has an interpretation as a rough average of the equivalent and compensating variation.

This analysis has been undertaken on the assumption that the good in question is normal. As we know from Chapter 3, compensated demand curves cut normal demand curves from below when the good in question is inferior. It is left to readers to prove for themselves that the relative size of equivalent variation, consumer surplus and compensating variation is reversed when the good is inferior.

Concluding comment

This chapter has dealt with the manner in which consumer theory may be extended to deal with measuring the benefits a typical consumer obtains from consuming a particular good. The example of the toll-bridge was used to illustrate the potential importance of this problem, and the concepts of equivalent and compensating income variations were deployed to illustrate some of the difficulties inherent in it. Marshallian consumer theory, it turns out, yields benefit measures that may be derived directly from the consumer's demand curve, and hence, to the extent that demand curves are themselves measurable, are immediately applicable to real-world data. However, we have also seen that this demand theory rests on very special assumptions about the consumer's underlying utility function, assumptions which eliminate the income effect from the demand for a good and hence remove differences between the equivalent and compensating variations. Finally, readers who have worked through the final starred section of this chapter have seen in a more general way how the ideas of consumer's surplus, equivalent and compensating variations are related to one another.

Now it would be easy to conclude from all this that the measurement of economic benefits is so fraught with difficulties that it should not be undertaken. Though some might take this position we do not. Our tools are imperfect, to be sure, but they are the only ones available, and the tasks for which we need them are important. Hence we would urge, not that they never be deployed, but that when they are used it is with caution, and in full understanding of their shortcomings.

The analysis set out here, and in the preceding two chapters, constitutes in and of itself a good grounding for further work in economics, but it by no means exhausts the possibilities of consumer theory. The next section of this book, therefore, deals with further extensions of the ideas developed so far, and it is our hope that the reader will be tempted to study at least some of this material before proceeding to the theory of production.

SUMMARY

Consumer's surplus and Marshallian consumer theory

1. Compensating and equivalent variations in real income allow us to compute consumer's surplus where the shape of the indifference map is known. Where this is not possible, Marshallian demand theory provides us with a quantifiable approximation. This approach relies on cardinal utility.

2. For the two-good case, assuming total utility gained from consumption of X is independent of the quantity of Y consumed, that the marginal utility (MU) of Y is constant, and that X has diminishing marginal utility, we are able to measure consumer surplus as the area under the graph of MU_X for a given level of consumption of X less the area of the price of X in terms of (constant) utility forgone from consuming Y.

3. If MU_Y is constant there is a proportional relationship between the price in 'utils' forgone and the money price of X. The marginal utility curve of X becomes a demand curve and its price a money price. We now have a monetary measure of consumer surplus as the area under the demand curve for X minus expenditure on X.

4. Translating Marshallian analysis into an indifference map means the vertical distance between all indifference curves is equal. The compensating and equivalent variation methods of measuring these distances therefore yield identical results. Marshallian analysis represents a limiting case in which the demand for X involves a zero income effect.

5. In order to compare measures of consumer surplus with other indicators of changes in consumer welfare, we can appeal to the notion of duality. In this approach, rather than maximising utility subject to a budget constraint we study the dual expenditure

function, obtained by minimising expenditure subject to the requirement that a given level of satisfaction is to be obtained.

6. Compensated demand functions can be derived directly from this expenditure function and consumer surplus can be shown to be the rough average of the equivalent and compensated variation underlying the constant money income demand curve.

PROBLEMS

1 Suppose that good X is an inferior good. Use diagrams to illustrate the relationship between the equivalent variation, the compensating variation and the change in consumer surplus when the price of X rises from p_X^1 to p_X^2. Does the change in consumer's surplus equal the equivalent variation?

2 The price of food falls by 30 per cent and disposable income by 10 per cent. If a person spends one third of income on food, is it the case that they would be neither better off nor worse off as a result of these changes?

3 A consumer chooses weekly quantities of X and Y in order to maximise the utility function

$$U = X^{1/2}Y^{1/2}$$

Total income over the week is £100, and the prices of X and Y are £5 and £10 respectively.

(a) How much of X and Y will the consumer buy?
(b) What happens to the demand for X if the price of X rises to £10?
(c) What happens to the demand for Y if the price of X rises to £10?
(d) What is the equivalent variation and the compensating variation resulting from the increase in the price of X from £5 to £10? (Hint: calculate the utility levels at each price combination and apply the formulae in equations (4.22) and (4.23).)

PART **II**

CONSUMER THEORY: FURTHER TOPICS

CHAPTER 5

Intertemporal choice

Key words and phrases

- current and future consumption, current and future income
- capital market, the rate of interest, market opportunity curve
- present value, saving time preference, wealth, substitution and 'windfall' effects

Introduction

We now apply the theory of consumer choice to the allocation of consumption over time. We shall deal with a situation in which the individual may lend and borrow on the capital market and set out the analysis that underlies much modern work on saving decisions and the consumption function.

The basic postulate of consumer theory is that consumption alone yields satisfaction. The objects of choice in the analysis that follows are **consumption now** and **in the future**. Obviously a full characterisation of this choice problem would have us considering the time path of consumption over an individual's planning horizon, a horizon which might well be as long as a lifetime, or longer still if the individual cares about the welfare of descendents. However, we make the drastic simplification of dividing the planning period into two discrete chunks, the current period and the next period, t and $t + 1$, and consider the allocation of consumption between them.

The framework of choice without production

In this chapter we shall rule out the possibility that our individual is able to engage in production. If we make this simplifying assumption, we may characterise the individual's choice problem in Figure 5.1. There, we plot consumption in period t on the horizontal axis and consumption in period $t + 1$ on the vertical. The objects of choice in the analysis that follows are allocations of consumption between the two periods. The constraint upon choice is constructed as follows. We assume that the individual receives a particular amount of **income**, Y_t, **in time** t and expects, as if with certainty, to receive a particular

Figure 5.1

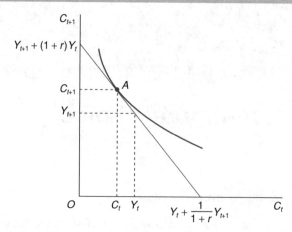

The level of saving is the result of a choice of consumption levels for now and the future. Given Y_t of income now and the certainty of receiving Y_{t+1} in the future, and faced with an interest rate of r, the individual depicted saves $Y_t - C_t$.

amount of **income**, Y_{t+1}, in **time** $t + 1$ as well. There is no reason for us to treat these two amounts of income as equal, and in Figure 5.1 we have made Y_{t+1} greater than Y_t. Now if our individual consumes all current income in each period, the consumption pattern will also be given by Y_t, Y_{t+1}, but the individual can, by borrowing or lending, reallocate consumption between periods. If we assume that the **capital market** is perfect, that the single **rate of interest** (r) at which borrowing and lending take place is completely uninfluenced by the amounts in which the individual does so, then the budget constraint, known once again as the **market opportunity curve**, is a straight line having the slope $-(1 + r)$ and passing through Y_t, Y_{t+1}.[1]

To see this, neglect questions about what might be biologically feasible and consider what would happen if the individual decided to undertake no consumption at all in the current period. All current income could then be set aside to earn interest at rate r and in the next period consumption could be equal to $Y_{t+1} + (1 + r)Y_t$. Alternatively, the individual might decide to carry out all consumption for the two periods in the current period, devoting all of next period's income to paying off the debts thereby incurred. At an interest rate of r, the maximum that could be borrowed against future income is equal to $Y_{t+1}/(1 + r)$ and maximum current consumption is $Y_t + [Y_{t+1}/(1 + r)]$. This latter sum is, for obvious reasons, known as the **present value** of the consumer's income stream. For every pound **saved** out of current income, $1 + r$ pounds of future consumption are obtained, and for every pound of future income devoted to repaying debts, $1/(1 + r)$ pounds of current consumption can be obtained: hence the market opportunity curve in Figure 5.1.

A conventional indifference map describes tastes and completes the picture set out in Figure 5.1, the slope of any indifference curve at any point defining the marginal rate of substitution between current and future goods.

Box 5.1   **More on saving and borrowing**

In previous chapters we used a Cobb-Douglas utility function to analyse consumption of two goods X and Y. We can use an equivalent utility function to analyse decisions for consumption this period (C_t) and next period (C_{t+1}):

$$U = C_t^{0.4}C_{t+1}^{0.6} \tag{5.1.1}$$

We can assume that income in the two periods is $Y_t = 100$ and $Y_{t+1} = 120$. Also we can assume that the interest rate on borrowing and lending is 5%. The market opportunity curve is therefore a straight line with slope −1.05. Using the same reasoning as set out in the text we can depict the choice problem as in Illustration 5.1.

Illustration 5.1

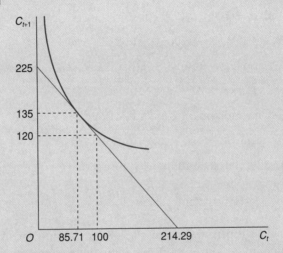

The horizontal intercept of the market opportunity curve is $214.29 = 100 + 120/1.05$. The vertical intercept is $225 = 120 + 100(1.05)$.

The decision problem is analysed in an equivalent way to that for any consumer problem. An individual maximises utility when the marginal rate of substitution of the highest indifference curve is the same as the slope of the market opportunity curve. We know that the marginal rate of substitution is the ratio of marginal utilities:

$$MRS = \frac{\partial U/\partial C_t}{\partial U/\partial C_{t+1}}$$

In turn $\dfrac{\partial U}{\partial C_t} = 0.4C_t^{-0.6}C_{t+1}^{0.6} = 0.4\left(\dfrac{C_{t+1}}{C_t}\right)^{0.6} \tag{5.1.2}$

and $\dfrac{\partial U}{\partial C_{t+1}} = 0.6C_t^{0.4}C_{t+1}^{-0.4} = 0.6\left(\dfrac{C_t}{C_{t+1}}\right)^{0.4} \tag{5.1.3}$

So $MRS = 0.4\left(\dfrac{C_{t+1}}{C_t}\right)^{0.6} \div 0.6\left(\dfrac{C_t}{C_{t+1}}\right)^{0.4} = \dfrac{0.4}{0.6}\dfrac{C_{t+1}}{C_t} \tag{5.1.4}$

Setting this *MRS* equal to the slope of the market opportunity curve:

$$\frac{0.4}{0.6}\frac{C_{t+1}}{C_t} = 1.05$$

So when our person maximises utility:

$$\frac{C_{t+1}}{C_t} = 1.575 \tag{5.1.5}$$

We now use the market opportunity curve to define the utility maximising solution. We know that consumption in period $t+1$ is income in $t+1$ plus accrued savings from period t (S_t), or minus the cost of borrowing from period t. Using our figures:

$$C_{t+1} = 120 + S_t$$

and $S_t = (100 - C_t)1.05$

So $C_{t+1} = 120 + (100 - C_t)1.05 \tag{5.1.6}$

We also know from (5.1.5) that if a person maximises utility:

$$C_{t+1} = 1.575C_t$$

Using conditions (5.1.5) and (5.1.6):

$$1.575C_t = 120 + (100 - C_t)1.05$$

This implies that utility-maximising C_t is

$$C_t = \frac{225}{1.575 + 1.05} = 85.71 \tag{5.1.7}$$

So our person consumes less than their income in period t. The resulting savings amount to $100 - 85.71 = 14.29$. With interest accrued these savings will rise to $14.29(1.05) = 15.00$. So $C_{t+1} = 120 + 15 = 135$.

Time preference and the solution to the choice problem

It is worth pausing for a moment to ask why, if the consumption goods available are identical in the two periods, the marginal rate of **substitution** between them should ever differ from -1, one unit of future goods for one unit of current goods. There are two distinct factors at work here. First, if the quantities of goods available in the two periods are not the same, there is no reason to suppose that an extra unit will be equally valued in both periods – one would expect an extra unit of goods to become relatively more highly prized the smaller was the bundle to which it was being added. This argument just restates the reasons for expecting there to be a convex indifference map in any application of the theory of consumer behaviour.

The second factor at work in this particular application is the fact that the goods in question are available at different times and for this reason alone are not the 'same' in every respect. Neglect all other differences between bundles of goods, and consider

Figure 5.2

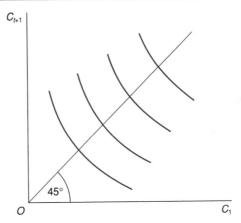

The marginal rate of substitution between present and future consumption is defined as $-(1 + \rho)$, where ρ is known as the 'rate of time preference'. The 'rate of time preference proper' is the rate of time preference where equal amounts of consumption are available in each period. If the rate of time preference proper is zero, then the indifference curves in this diagram will all cut a line drawn at 45° from the origin at right angles, since they will have a slope of –1 at that point.

situations in which equal quantities are available in each period. Consider, that is, bundles along a 45° line drawn through the origin of an intertemporal indifference map such as we have in Figure 5.2. It is not obvious that the marginal rate of substitution between present and future consumption will be –1 here; indeed many arguments, which may be summarised in the word 'impatience', have been adduced for suggesting that present goods will be valued more highly on the margin when they are available in the same quantities as future goods.

Now the marginal rate of substitution between present and future goods is frequently referred to as being equal to $-(1 + \rho)$, where ρ is defined as the *rate of* **time preference**, that is, the amount by which future goods are discounted on the margin relative to present goods for all reasons. The marginal rate of substitution between present and future goods *when equal quantities of them are available in each period* involves a particular value for ρ known as the *rate of time preference proper*, which measures the amount by which future goods are discounted on the margin *simply by virtue of their being available in the future*. A zero rate of time preference proper implies that the indifference curves all cut a 45° line drawn from the origin with a slope of –1.

In any event, the solution to our choice problem depicted in Figure 5.1 occurs at *A* with a saving out of current income equal to $Y_t - C_t$. This is a point at which, to adopt the terminology just introduced, *the rate of interest and the rate of time preference are equal to one another*. The solution has a number of characteristics worth noting.

For one thing, it tells us that current saving, and hence current consumption, depend not just upon current income but also upon future income and the rate of interest. If we use the word '**wealth**' to describe the total purchasing power currently available to an individual – the present value of the individual's income stream (in this case current income plus the value now of future income) – then the point at which the market opportunity curve of Figure 5.1 cuts the horizontal axis clearly measures wealth, and we may equivalently say that current consumption depends upon wealth and the rate of interest; these two variables are sufficient to locate the budget constraint. The implications of this for analysis which uses a simple consumption function that makes consumption depend only on current income should be obvious.

Saving and the level of the rate of interest

We may use the framework set out in Figure 5.1 to answer questions about the effect on consumption, and hence on saving, of variations in the rate of interest, being careful to distinguish between the implications of *different values of the rate of interest considered as alternatives* on the one hand and the consequences of *changes in the interest rate* on the other. Consider Figure 5.3, which is based on Figure 5.1. If the individual's income pattern in the two periods is given by Y_t, Y_{t+1} and the rate of interest is equal to r_1, then the market opportunity curve is determined and we have equilibrium at A, just as in Figure 5.1. If the rate of interest had been higher at r_2, the budget constraint would instead be given by the market opportunity line labelled 2. Clearly, our individual would, in this second case, select point B, given the nature of the indifference map. As we have drawn it, the individual would consume fewer current and more future goods at this higher rate of interest. In other words, at a higher rate of interest more is saved. Obviously, as we show in Figure 5.4, preferences could equally easily have been such as to lead to a lower savings level at a

Figure 5.3

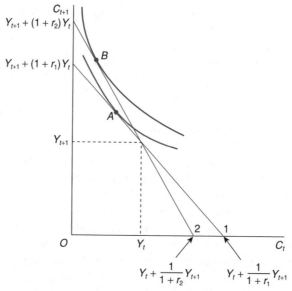

A higher rate of interest, r_2, shifts the market opportunity curve from 1 to 2, pivoting it at point Y_t, Y_{t+1} because this endowment of goods is available as a consumption bundle without borrowing or lending. At the higher rate of interest our individual will select point B rather than A.

Figure 5.4

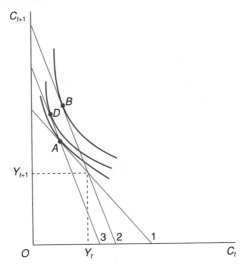

The movement from A to B at a higher interest rate may involve an increase or decrease in saving. The substitution effect, from A to D, unambiguously points to more saving but the 'windfall' effect from D to B may offset this tendency because it is reasonable to suppose that current consumption is a normal good.

higher interest rate; the influence of the rate of interest on the level of savings is therefore ambiguous.

We do not have to look too far for the source of this ambiguity. If we carry out a compensating variation in wealth to enable us to break down the difference between A and B into a **substitution effect** and an analogue to an income effect – call it a **windfall effect** – we get the constraint labelled 3 in Figure 5.4.[2] The substitution effect of a higher rate of interest from A to D clearly involves an increase in saving. It is the windfall effect from D to B that offsets this substitution effect more than completely when a higher interest rate leads to less saving. In Figure 5.3 the windfall effect was not enough to offset the substitution effect. The windfall effect works against the substitution effect because the indifference map is drawn so that both current and future consumption are normal goods.

Box 5.2 More on the windfall effect

We can continue the example set out earlier in this chapter to illustrate the windfall effect. This earlier example was based on

$$U = C_t^{0.4} C_{t+1}^{0.6} \tag{5.1.1}$$

$Y_t = 100$, $Y_{t+1} = 120$ and a rate of interest on saving and borrowing of 5%. It was shown in Box 5.1 that when our person maximises utility

$$\frac{C_{t+1}}{C_t} = 1.575 \tag{5.1.5}$$

and so $C_t = 85.71$, $C_{t+1} = 135$. It follows that saving in period one was 14.29.

→

We can now increase the interest rate to 6%. With this higher rate of interest utility maximisation occurs when

$$\frac{0.4\,C_{t+1}}{0.6\,\;C_t} = 1.06 \tag{5.2.1}$$

i.e. $\dfrac{C_{t+1}}{C_t} = 1.59$ (5.2.2)

Using the same logic as with the earlier example:

$$C_{t+1} = 120 + S_t \quad \text{and} \quad S_t = (100 - C_t)1.06$$

so $\quad C_{t+1} = 120 + (100 - C_t)1.06$ (5.2.3)

After the interest rate increase the new value of C_t can therefore be calculated:

$$1.59C_t = 120 + (100 - C_t)1.06$$

So $\quad C_t = \dfrac{226}{1.59 + 1.06} = 85.28$ (5.2.4)

i.e. C_t falls a small amount from 85.71 (with an interest rate of 5%) to 85.28 (after the interest rate increases to 6%). This implies a small increase in saving with the interest rate change.

Using the same logic as set out in Figure 5.4 we can remove the change in real income because the person is better off from the increased interest income on savings with the change from 5% to 6%. We shift the new market opportunity curve back to the original consumption point, i.e. (85.71, 135) as calculated earlier in this chapter. To calculate the substitution effect (shown by point D in Figure 5.4) we now maximise utility after this compensating variation:

$$\frac{0.4\,C_{t+1}}{0.6\,\;C_t} = 1.06 \tag{5.2.1}$$

i.e. $\dfrac{C_{t+1}}{C_t} = 1.59$ (5.2.2)

But now we have

$$C_{t+1} = 135 + (85.71 - C_t)1.06$$

$$1.59C_t = 135 + (85.71 - C_t)1.06$$

So $\quad C_t = \dfrac{225.85}{1.59 + 1.06} = 85.23$ (5.2.5)

The fall in C_t from 85.71 to 85.23 is the substitution effect of the increase in interest rates, i.e. there is more saving of 0.48. But as we are using a Cobb-Douglas function C_t is a normal good, so the extra interest income leads to an increase in C_t (and also C_{t+1}). This increase in income because of this windfall effect shifts consumption from 85.23 to 85.28 (i.e. the actual equilibrium C_t with an interest rate of 6%). This implies that the windfall effect is +0.05, i.e. increased consumption (reduced saving) because of the increase in interest income. In this case the windfall effect is smaller than the substitution effect so overall period t savings increased with an increase in interest rates. The observant readers here will have noticed that this example is based on the Slutsky (not Hicksian) substitution effect.

Saving and changes in the rate of interest

So far we have been careful to talk about the rate of interest being higher and lower, rather than rising and falling. What then does the foregoing analysis tell us about the effects of *changes* in the rate of interest on the savings rate? If savings are channelled into an institution such as a bank, in which the borrower pays a given rate of return, variations in which do not alter the capital value of savings to the lender, then the foregoing analysis is applicable without modification. However, if lending takes the form of purchasing a bond – a promise to pay *a given sum of money* in the next period – then it requires a little further thought, for here variations in interest rate do affect the current capital value of savings.

Consider Figure 5.5. Our individual starts out at Y_t, Y_{t+1} with the market rate of interest such that the budget constraint is given by 1. The preferred allocation of consumption is at A, just as in Figures 5.1, 5.2 and 5.3. However, now let the individual buy a bond in order to accomplish this reallocation, thereby moving to point A. In purchasing the bond the individual has given up $Y_t - C_t$ of current income in return for a guaranteed receipt of $C_{t+1} - Y_{t+1}$ in the next period. The issuer of the bond has promised to provide this volume of extra consumption. Thus, no matter what now happens to the rate of interest,

Figure 5.5

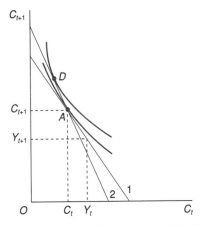

When an individual saves by buying a bond, the ability to consume at point A no matter what should subsequently happen to the rate of interest is ensured. Thus a rise in the interest rate pivots the market opportunity curve from 1 to 2 at A. The result is a pure substitution effect from A to D and an unambiguous increase in saving.

our individual saver can still stay at *A*. Now suppose, after the bond has been bought, but still during the first time period, the rate of interest rises. The individual can now move away from *A* along a more steeply sloped budget constraint than the original one. Since the constraint has pivoted at *A*, our individual is no longer in equilibrium there, and will move to *D*, buying another bond in the process on new, now more favourable, terms. Saving will unambiguously increase, for the change that we have been analysing here is clearly the outcome of a Slutsky substitution effect. Thus in this case we can conclude that there is a positive relationship between the amount of saving and the rate of interest.

Box 5.3   ### Savings, bond purchases and interest rate changes

We can bring together the elements of the examples used in this chapter to illustrate the principle that when someone saves by purchasing bonds, rather than simply using an interest bearing bank account, interest rate changes and savings are always positively related.

Previous examples in this chapter were based on $Y_t = £100$, $Y_{t+1} = £120$. With a rate of interest of 5% the utility maximising consumption levels are $C_t = £85.71$, $C_{t+1} = £135$. Rather than saving in period *t* our person can now buy a bond with a price in period *t* of £14.29 (i.e. 100 − 85.71) and a promise that in period *t+1* £15 will be received when the bond matures. This bond purchase reduces Y_t from £100 to £85.71 and increases Y_{t+1} to £135. At a rate of interest of 5% our person is in equilibrium. But with an increase in the interest rate to 6% during period *t* our consumer now has an equilibrium based on the new income levels (85.71 and 135). Using these new income levels and a rate of interest of 6%, it was calculated earlier in this chapter (in Box 5.2) that $C_t = £85.23$, i.e. period *t* equilibrium savings increase by £0.48 if a bond is purchased. This was the previously calculated Slutsky substitution effect.

Concluding comment

We have by no means exhausted the analysis of the allocation of consumption over time in this chapter. We have said nothing about the problems involved when there are durable goods; in this case the utility yielding act of *consumption* analysed in this chapter becomes separated from the act of *consumer expenditure* which is relevant for a macro theory of income determination. Nor have we said anything about how individuals might learn from each other so that their consumption patterns become interdependent, or about how they may take time to adjust their consumption patterns when the constraints facing them shift. Thus the analysis presented here, though it is fundamental to modern macro theories of consumption, does not tell the whole story about this problem area. Nevertheless we have done quite enough to show what a powerful tool our basic theory of consumer behaviour can be in this context. We have seen that a maximising individual will relate consumption plans to wealth rather than income and that they will also vary in a predictable fashion with the rate of interest. This must mean that the simple relationship between consumption and income so frequently used in elementary macro-economics is very much a first approximation to be defended only on the grounds of its simplicity.

We cannot, in a book about microeconomics, pursue these matters any further. However, there is one extension of this body of analysis worth pursuing. In the next chapter we shall discuss the consequences of opening up production as well as market opportunities to agents making intertemporal choices. Just as, in this chapter, we have laid out the microeconomic underpinnings of one macroeconomic phenomenon, namely, consumption behaviour, so, in the next, we will deal with the microeconomics of investment.

SUMMARY

The allocation of consumption over time

1. The theory of consumer choice can be applied to the allocation of consumption over time. We here consider only two periods, the present and the future, but as previously the generalisation from two to n goods or periods is straightforward. We also assume that there are no production opportunities.

2. Individuals have preferences between current and future consumption, characterised by a convex to the origin indifference curve. There is also a capital market upon which the individual can borrow or lend. From this can be derived a budget line called the market opportunity curve, with a slope given by minus (one plus the rate of interest).

3. Individuals allocate consumption between the present and the future at the point of tangency between the intertemporal indifference curve and the market opportunity curve.

4. The slope of the indifference curve gives the individual's marginal rate of substitution between current and future consumption, equal to minus (one plus the rate of time preference). In equilibrium, therefore, the rate of time preference is equated to the interest rate.

5. There is no unambiguous relationship between savings and the rate of interest. The substitution effect always implies a positive relationship here. However, this may be offset by an effect (analogous to the income effect) sometimes called the windfall effect.

6. However, when lending has already been undertaken before the interest rate changes, and takes the form of purchasing a bond, the capital value of which is affected by the interest rate, there is always a positive relationship between the level of savings and the rate of interest. This is because capital value changes brought about by the change in the rate of interest ensure that the individual's response involves only a Slutsky substitution effect.

PROBLEMS

1 Draw the two-period budget constraints implied by the following information:

(a)	income this period	$50
	income next period	$50
	rate of interest	10%
(b)	income this period	$50
	income next period	$50
	rate of interest	5%

(c)	income this period	$0
	income next period	$105
	rate of interest	10%
(d)	income this period	$0
	income next period	$105
	rate of interest	5%
(e)	income this period	$100
	income next period	$100
	rate of interest	10%
(f)	income this period	$100
	income next period	$100
	rate of interest	5%
(g)	income this period	$50
	income next period	$165
	rate of interest	10%
(h)	income this period	$50
	income next period	$165
	rate of interest	5%

2 Show that

(a) if an individual borrows by selling bonds at a particular value of the rate of interest, a fall in the rate of interest will lead to more borrowing;

(b) if current and future consumption are both normal goods, then if the individual borrows by taking out a fixed capital value loan, a fall in the rate of interest will also lead to more borrowing.

3 It is known that, were the current period's income increased by £100, an individual would increase current consumption by £80. If the rate of interest is 10 per cent, what will be the effect on the same individual's current consumption of a guaranteed increase in next period's income of £110?

Notes

1. The reader should note that, though the phrase 'market opportunity' used here is also used in discussions of the labour supply decision, the opportunities referred to differ. With labour supply decisions we are talking about labour market opportunities, and here they are capital market opportunities.

2. The phrase that comes to mind more naturally, 'wealth effect', is widely used in macroeconomics to denote a different phenomenon, namely, the effect, through its influence on the real purchasing power of consumers' assets, of a change in the price level on consumers' expenditure. That is why we avoid its use here.

CHAPTER 6

Intertemporal choice and capital markets

Key words and phrases

- investment theory, production opportunity curve, internal rate of return
- investment rules, internal rate of return rule, present value rule
- capital market imperfection

Introduction

In the previous chapter we considered the behaviour of an individual who is able to re-allocate consumption over time by borrowing or lending in a *perfect* capital market. However, instead of being limited to taking currently available resources and lending them out with a view to consuming the proceeds of the loan in the future, the individual may also have the opportunity of using those resources in a production process that yields output consumable in the future. Let us now analyse the factors that will determine whether, and to what extent, an individual will take advantage of access to such a production process. In doing so, we shall develop the basis of what, in macroeconomics, is known as 'neo-classical' **investment theory**.

In the analysis that follows, the objects of choice facing the individual remain the same as they were above, namely, consumption in the present period, C_t, and consumption in the next period C_{t+1}. The criteria in terms of which the choice is made are also the same and are summarised in exactly the same indifference map as was used there. The availability of access to a productive process (or processes) as opposed to, or in addition to, a capital market does, however, change the constraint upon choice. In this respect, the analysis we are about to carry out, which is mainly due to Jack Hirshleifer, differs from that described above.

The production opportunity curve and the internal rate of return

It is convenient to begin by considering an individual who for some reason has no access to a market in which borrowing and lending are possible and who can only transform currently available goods into goods available in the future by devoting them to production. A situation such as might face such an individual is described in Figure 6.1. First, we assume for simplicity's sake, that our individual's entire endowment of consumption goods for the two periods is available in time t. Hence, at the outset, the individual is at point Y_t on the horizontal axis in Figure 6.1. Secondly, we assume that there are available a whole array of opportunities for transforming current goods into future goods by way of production, and that as many, or as few, of these may be undertaken, and in any order. That is, we assume that production opportunities are *divisible* and *independent*. A simple example of such a state of affairs would involve an individual whose endowment of goods came in the shape of corn, which could either be consumed today, or planted in a field with a view to consuming the resulting crop. The assumption of divisible production opportunities would here mean the individual could plant just as much or as little corn as seemed appropriate, and the assumption of independence that corn could be planted in any part, or parts, of the field without the yields being in any way affected.

This assumption of independence is important because there is no reason to suppose that all opportunities facing an individual will be equally productive; in terms of our primitive example, some parts of the field might be more fertile than others. However, if production opportunities may be taken up in any order, the individual can begin with the most productive one, move on to the next most productive one, and so on. The concave-to-the-origin shape of the curve labelled pp in Figure 6.1 which we may call a **production opportunity curve**, follows from the assumption that production opportunities are undertaken in diminishing order of productivity.[1] Thus, if, starting from point Y_t an amount of resources I is devoted to production, the resulting output will be Y_{t+1}^1. If another equal amount I is added to production, the resulting output overall will be Y_{t+1}^2. However, the *increment* in output in this second case will be smaller than the initial one, the increment in output resulting from a third equal increment of amount I to the resources devoted to production would be yet smaller again, and so on.

Figure 6.1

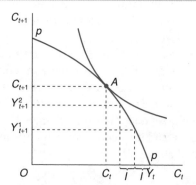

Intertemporal choice with production, pp is a production opportunity curve. Starting with an initial endowment of Y_t, successive equal investments of I in production yield diminishing increments in output. The utility-maximising investment–production–consumption plan occurs at point A, where the rate of time preference equals the internal rate of return in production.

Let us consider the slope of the production opportunity curve a little more closely. As we move up it from right to left, resources are being withdrawn from current consumption and devoted to production. These **investments** yield a payoff in terms of consumption goods in the next period in amounts that may be read off the vertical axis, and this payoff may be thought of as having two components, the first just replacing the initial outlay, and the second presenting a net return on the investment. In the previous chapter we showed that the slope of the market opportunity curve was $-(1 + r)$ where r is the market rate of interest, and defined the slope of a typical indifference curve as $-(1 + \rho)$ where ρ is the rate of time preference. By exact analogy with these arguments, we may define the slope of our production opportunity curve at any point as $-(1 + R)$ where R is the marginal rate of return on investment, or as it is usually called in the context of the analysis we are developing here, the **internal rate of return**.

The solution to the choice problem depicted in Figure 6.1 is straightforward. As in the previous chapter, the objects of choice are consumption in time t and $t + 1$, and the indifference map is identical to that used there. Because we have assumed that our individual has no access to a capital market, but does face a set of production opportunities, the production opportunity locus becomes the relevant constraint upon choice. The utility-maximising solution to our individual's choice problem clearly lies at point A, where the production opportunity curve carries the individual onto, and is just tangent to, the highest attainable indifference curve. Here the individual consumes C_t of goods in the current period, and invests $Y_t - C_t$, thus producing C_{t+1} of consumption goods for the next period. The reader might note that the fact that point A is one of tangency between an indifference curve and the production opportunity curve means that this equilibrium occurs where there is equality between the rate of time preference ρ, and the internal rate of return on investment R.

Box 6.1 ## More on present value and the internal rate of return

We can show the connection between the present value of an income stream and the internal rate of return using a simple example. Assume that someone has an investment opportunity costing £200 now and that it earns a return of £100 this year and (a known) return of £120 next year. With a single rate of interest of 5% the present value of the project is

$$PV = 100 + \frac{120}{1.05} - 200 = 14.29$$

As this project has a positive PV it is rational to pursue the opportunity. The internal rate of return is the return that generates a zero PV:

$$100 + \frac{120}{(1 + R)} - 200 = 0$$

So $1 + R = 1.2$ i.e. the internal rate of return is 20%. Any discount rate greater than 20% would make this project unviable i.e. generate a negative PV.

More generally if income this period is £100 and if a series of £10 investments can be undertaken, this period's consumption (C_t) is £100 less the total investment undertaken. In turn the investment yields a return that is used to finance next period's consumption (C_{t+1}). A possible schedule for C_t and C_{t+1} is presented in the table below.

investment	0	10	20	30	40	50	60	70	80	90	100
C_t	100	90	80	70	60	50	40	30	20	10	0
C_{t+1}	0	20	38	54	68	80	90	98	104	108	110
1+R		2	1.8	1.6	1.4	1.2	1	0.8	0.6	0.4	0.2

The reader can confirm that this schedule for C_t and C_{t+1} is consistent with a graph such as that presented in Figure 6.1. The implied internal rate of return is calculated. This person will invest until $1 + R$ is equal to the personal rate of time preference $(1 + \rho)$.

Access to a perfect capital market

Now there is really nothing very startling about the analysis just presented. What we have said is that, when excluded from borrowing and lending on the capital market, the amount that any individual will devote to productive investment will be determined by the tangency of an indifference curve to a production opportunity curve, and hence will depend upon tastes. If we do not have specific information about tastes, there does not seem to be anything very concrete that we can say about our individual's behaviour. As we shall now see, if we change the assumptions of our analysis to permit our individual to have access to a perfect capital market of the type which we analysed in the previous chapter, in addition to having access to the kind of productive opportunities we have just discussed, this conclusion changes radically. We find that we are able to make precise predictions about investment decisions without having to know anything at all about tastes beyond the usual assumption that they may be characterised by a convex to the origin indifference map.

To see why this is so, consider what would happen if we suddenly were to allow the individual whose behaviour we have been analysing to have access to a perfect capital market where one can borrow and lend at a given interest rate. Consider Figure 6.2. Suppose first of all that the individual had already moved up to point A, when access to the capital market was granted. By moving from point Y_t to point A the endowment of goods available is changed, and the first question to be settled when access to the capital market opens up these borrowing and lending opportunities is whether a further improvement upon point A is possible.

Suppose for the sake of argument that the rate of interest ruling in the capital market is higher than the internal rate of return on investment at A. Then, passing through point A is a market opportunity curve MM, a straight line with a slope of $-(1 + r)$, which is by assumption steeper than that of the production opportunity locus at A. Clearly, if our individual insists on investing $Y_t - C_t$ in production, and hence on moving to point A on the production opportunity locus, matters can now be further improved by moving from point A up to the left along the market opportunity curve as far as point A'. An amount

Figure 6.2

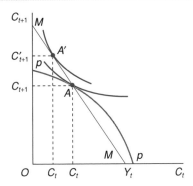

Intertemporal choice when access to a perfect capital market is made available after the individual is committed to investment–production plan A. The market rate of interest is assumed to be higher than the internal rate of return at A, so the individual rearranges consumption by further lending, moving to point A′.

$C_t - C_t'$ is now lent out on the capital market, earning in return $C_{t+1}' - C_{t+1}$. This yields a higher level of satisfaction than that achieved by investment alone.

However, this is the best that can be done *only if* the individual is already tied to the original investment–production decision at A when access is gained to the capital market. If the individual is not tied to that decision, then, by revising investment plans, an even greater gain in utility can be achieved than that depicted in Figure 6.2. The reason for this is straightforward. Wherever our individual may choose to settle on the production opportunity curve, borrowing or lending activities in the capital market may be started from that point. There is, that is to say, an attainable market opportunity curve passing through every point on the production opportunity curve. As we have drawn it, Figure 6.2 depicts a state of affairs in which the market rate of interest is higher than the internal rate of return ruling at point A, so that there is a segment of the production opportunity curve below and to the right of A that lies outside the market opportunity curve passing through that point. This means that our individual, by cutting back on the original investment plan and moving downwards to the right along the production opportunity curve, is able to move onto higher and higher market opportunity curves, and hence open up the possibility of achieving higher and higher levels of utility. Now it is obvious that the further out to the right the market opportunity curve onto which our individual moves lies, the higher is the level of utility that can be attained. Hence a utility-maximising individual is going to plan production activities in such a way as to move onto the highest possible market opportunity curve, and that in turn will be the one that is just tangent to the production opportunity curve.

The separation of investment and consumption decisions

The state of affairs just described is depicted in Figure 6.3. Here, as before, we start with an initial endowment of Y_t and face our individual with production opportunities described by the curve *pp*. In the absence of access to the capital market, our individual chose that

Figure 6.3

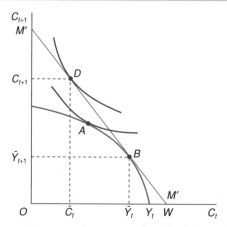

Intertemporal choice when all production opportunities are available, and access to a perfect capital market exists. The preferred investment production plan is now at point B, rather than A, and the utility-maximising consumption plan is at point D. The choice of point B is independent of the individual's tastes and may be described as the result either of equating the internal rate of return in production to the market rate of interest, or of choosing the production plan with the highest present value, denoted by W, at the market rate of interest.

combination of present and future consumption denoted by point A as the solution to both production and consumption plans; given that the individual has access to the capital market, point B is instead chosen as a solution to the production plan. $Y_t - \bar{Y}_t$ is invested in order to produce $\bar{Y}_{t+1}$, and the individual then moves along the market opportunity locus $M'M'$ to point D, which denotes the utility-maximising solution to the consumption plan. As the reader will see, this involves lending out $\bar{Y}_t - \bar{C}_t$ on the capital market in order to obtain $\bar{C}_{t+1} - \bar{Y}_{t+1}$ as a return.

Box 6.2   Separation of investment and consumption: a worked example

The intertemporal production opportunity schedule used earlier in this chapter to generate series for C_t and C_{t+1} in Box 6.1 was based on the quadratic equation

$$C_{t+1} = 110 - 0.1C_t - 0.01C_t^2 \tag{6.2.1}$$

The slope of this production opportunity schedule is therefore

$$\frac{\partial C_{t+1}}{\partial C_t} = -0.1 - 0.02C_t \tag{6.2.2}$$

If we use a utility function of the form used in the previous chapter we can apply the intertemporal choice problem set out in Figure 6.3. The utility function used earlier was

$$U = C_t^{0.4} C_{t+1}^{0.6} \tag{5.1.1}$$

It was shown in Box 5.1 that with this utility function the marginal rate of substitution along any indifference curve is

$$\text{MRS} = -\frac{0.4}{0.6}\frac{C_{t+1}}{C_t} \tag{5.1.4}$$

To identify point A in Figure 6.3, i.e. the equilibrium when only the production opportunity curve is available, we set the slope of the indifference curve equal to the slope of the production opportunity curve:

$$-0.1 - 0.02C_t = -\frac{0.4}{0.6}\frac{C_{t+1}}{C_t}$$

i.e. $\quad C_{t+1} = 0.15C_t + 0.03C_t^2 \tag{6.2.3}$

This quadratic equation defines all solutions to our utility maximising problem. We want the particular solution on our production opportunity curve (6.2.1) i.e.

$$C_{t+1} = 110 - 0.1C_t - 0.01C_t^2$$

Setting the optimal C_{t+1} equal to C_{t+1} on our production opportunity curve

$$0.15C_t + 0.03C_t^2 = 110 - 0.1C_t - 0.01C_t^2$$

so $\quad 0.04C_t^2 + 0.25C_t - 110 = 0 \tag{6.2.4}$

Equation (6.2.4) has two solutions, $C_t = 49.41$ and $C_t = -55.7$. The negative solution is meaningless in our context. So the relevant utility maximising solution, i.e. the equivalent of point A in Figure 6.3, is $C_t = 49.41$. As income is £100 (see Box 6.1) this solution implies that $100 - 49.41 = 50.59$ is invested in period t, which allows consumption in period $t+1$ of

$$C_{t+1} = 110 - 0.1(49.41) - 0.01(49.41^2) = 80.65$$

If investment and consumption decisions are separated we can solve for points B and D in Figure 6.3. Assuming a rate of interest of 10% the market opportunity locus $M'M'$ has slope -1.1. To find point B we set the slope of the market opportunity locus equal to the slope of the production opportunity curve

$$-0.1 - 0.02C_t = -1.1$$

so $C_t = 50$. This value is equivalent to $\bar{Y}_t$ in Figure 6.3. The implied $\bar{Y}_{t+1}$ is

$$\bar{Y}_{t+1} = 110 - 0.1(50) - 0.01(50^2) = 80$$

We can now define the market opportunity locus $M'M'$. We know that at the point (50, 80) and with a rate of interest of 10%

$$80 = a - (1.1)*50 \tag{6.2.5}$$

so $a = 135$ and the locus is defined by the equation $C_{t+1} = 135 - 1.1C_t$. This implies that the point W in Figure 6.3 is $C_t = 122.73$. It is now a straightforward constrained optimisation problem to calculate the equivalent of point D in Figure 6.3. Setting MRS equal to the slope of the market opportunity locus

$\rightarrow$

$$-\frac{0.4}{0.6}\frac{C_{t+1}}{C_t} = -1.1$$

So $\quad \dfrac{C_{t+1}}{C_t} = 1.65$ $\hfill$ (6.2.6)

Using the market opportunity locus $C_t = 49.1$ and $C_{t+1} = 81$. These values compare with the solution when there is no external market of $C_t = 49.41$ and $C_{t+1} = 80.65$. It follows that when there is access to a capital market and investment and consumption decisions are separated there is a positive utility gain.

Now Figure 6.3 shows that having access to a perfect capital market enables a maximising individual to separate production and consumption decisions, but it shows more than that. A moment or two spent examining the diagram in question should convince the reader that, although the solution to the consumption plan – the choice of point D – certainly depends upon our individual's tastes as depicted in the indifference map, the solution to the production plan – the choice of point B – depends solely upon the shape of the production opportunity curve and the slope of the market opportunity curve and is completely independent of tastes. That is to say, the individual's investment–production decision depends entirely upon factors that are given exogenously, these factors being the nature of the production opportunities available and the market rate of interest. Thus we can make statements about the rules that a utility-maximising individual will follow in making investment–production decisions, without referring to the precise properties of the indifference map.

Rules for selecting the optimal investment–production plan

We have seen that, in order to maximise utility from consumption, our individual must first choose an investment–production plan that makes attainable the highest market opportunity locus. One way of characterising the outcome of this production choice involves noting that the highest attainable market opportunity curve is one whose intercept with the horizontal axis of a diagram such as Figure 6.3 lies as far to the right as possible. As we showed in the last chapter, this horizontal intercept has an economic interpretation. It measures the maximum quantity of current consumption goods that our individual can command, that is, the **present value** of the income stream, or *wealth*. That is why it is labelled W. Thus the proposition that a utility-maximising individual will choose an investment–production plan so as to get onto the highest market opportunity curve available to the individual may be rephrased to say that the individual will choose that plan which *yields the highest present value*, or which *maximises wealth* at the current rate of interest. The same proposition may be rephrased to say that a production plan will be chosen at which the slopes of the production opportunity curve and the market opportunity curve are equal, at which *the internal rate of return in production is equal to the market rate of interest*. These two alternative ways of characterising the rule whereby a utility-maximising individual will formulate investment–production plans seem at first sight to be equivalent, and indeed in terms of the case considered in Figure 6.3 they are.

However, the first of them is in fact more general and yields the 'right' solution in a wider variety of cases than the second, as we shall now show.

Interdependent production opportunities

The key characteristic of the situation depicted in Figure 6.3 that makes the two decision rules seem equivalent is the assumption of *independence* among production opportunities that we made at the very outset. This assumption implies that our individual is able to take up the available production opportunities in any order, and so enables us to arrange them in order of decreasing productivity and hence to construct a production opportunity curve everywhere concave to the origin. However, there are many ways in which this assumption of independence may be violated, and Figure 6.4 depicts two of them.

In panel (a) of that figure we show what would happen if there were some indivisibility in production such that the individual was forced to choose between two sets of production

Figure 6.4

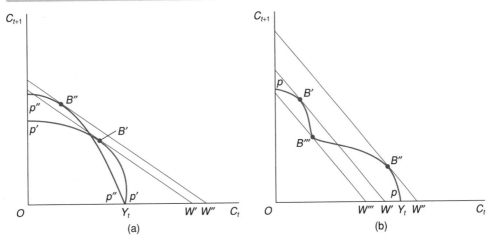

Two situations in which the rule 'equate the internal rate of return to the market rate of interest' will not necessarily find the best investment–production plan, but in which the rule 'maximise the present value of the plan at the market rate of interest' will do so:

(a) The production opportunity curves $p'p'$ and $p''p''$ are mutually exclusive. Points B' and B'' both satisfy the internal rate of return rule, but B'' has a higher present value, W'', than does B', whose present value at the market rate of interest is W'.

(b) The production opportunity curve pp has a convex section that results from a lack of independence among the production opportunities available. Here, the internal rate of return rule cannot distinguish between any of the three tangencies shown, though B''' whose present value is W''' is clearly a utility-*minimising* rather than maximising plan. Application of the present value rule enables plan B'' whose present value is W'' to be identified as superior to B' whose present value is W'. The reader with some knowledge of calculus will recognise that the 'internal rate of return' rule corresponds to the application of first-order conditions for a maximum, that the application of second-order conditions would rule out B''' in panel (b), and that the application of the 'present value' rule involves the application of conditions capable of finding a global, as opposed to merely local, maximum.

opportunities, and was unable to mix them together in any way. Such a state of affairs would arise in the context of our earlier example if for some reason our corn planting individual had to choose between two fields for the crop and, having chosen one of them to be planted, was excluded from any use of the other. If one field had some extremely fertile patches, and some not so fertile, its use might face our individual with a production opportunity curve such as $p'p'$, and if the other was of more even fertility, but with its best patches inferior to those of the first field and its worst patches better, the curve relevant to it would be the less concave one labelled $p''p''$. Our individual must now choose which production opportunity locus to be on, as well as where to locate on it. As the reader will see from inspecting Figure 6.4(a), the rule 'maximise present value' does enable the individual to select both the better production opportunity locus, and the best point on it, while the rule 'equate the internal rate of return to the market rate of interest' enables the individual to find only the best point on each production opportunity curve but not to choose between them.

Panel (b) of Figure 6.4 depicts a situation in which the individual faces only one set of production opportunities, but is not free to take them up in any order, being forced to undertake some rather low productivity opportunities (the flatter central section of the curve) before certain high productivity opportunities become available. Such a situation might arise in our example if, for reasons of fertility maintenance, a particular balance of production had to be adopted, so that, in order to go beyond a certain acreage of corn, it was first necessary to grow some less productive, but fertility restoring, crop such as grass, if additional corn plantings were to be undertaken. Such a situation as we are here describing gives rise to a production opportunity curve that is convex rather than concave to the origin over that segment where lower productivity opportunities must be taken before those with higher productivity. Again, simple inspection of the diagram will enable the reader to see that the 'maximise present value' rule will enable the individual to find the best investment–production plan, while the other rule will select three possible plans. One of these (at point B''') is the *worst* available rather than the best, and the other two are the best available on their own particular concave segment of the curve. However, the rule 'equate the internal rate of return to the rate of interest' gives no guidance as to how the choice between the latter two should be made.

Capital market imperfection

The qualifications to our analysis that we have just discussed do not affect the basic conclusion established earlier that it is possible to discuss the factors affecting the choice of the best investment–production decision independently of the consumption decision, and hence to analyse investment decisions in terms of such objective factors as the market rate of interest and the nature of available productive opportunities. However, we did note that this conclusion was conditional upon the individual being faced with a perfect capital market, and it is now time to consider this important qualification in more depth. A perfect capital market is one in which the individual can borrow and lend, up to limits imposed only by the need to remain solvent, at a given rate of interest, which is the same regardless of whether the individual is borrowing or lending and regardless of the scale at which either is being done. Only with capital market perfection can we draw the market opportunity curve as a straight line in the way that we have done throughout this and the previous chapters. If we drop this assumption, the independence of consumption and production decisions vanishes, as we shall now see.

There are many types of **capital market imperfection** that we could introduce into our model, but to make the point it will suffice to deal only with one quite simple case. Let us therefore assume that the market interest rate faced differs, depending upon whether the individual is a borrower or a lender, and that it is higher in the former case. To keep the analysis simple, let us also assume that the rate of interest at which the individual who chooses to lend can do so, that it does not vary with the amount involved, and that the borrowing rate faced is similarly constant (albeit at a higher level). Finally, and again purely for the sake of simplicity, let us assume that the production opportunities facing the individual are independent of one another so that the production opportunity curve is concave to the origin.

Figure 6.5 depicts the state of affairs implicit in these assumptions. Once more the individual starts with Y_t of resources and faces a production opportunity curve pp. However, instead of one market opportunity curve (or rather one set of market opportunity curves each passing through a different point on pp) we now have two. One set has a slope determined by the rate of interest at which the individual can borrow, and the other set has a slope fixed by the rate at which the individual can lend. BB represents the highest borrowing opportunity curve that can be reached, and it is tangent to the production opportunity curve at b, while LL is the highest lending market opportunity curve, being tangent to the production curve at l. Because the individual can only borrow at the rate of interest underlying BB, points above and to the left of b on that line are not available.

Figure 6.5

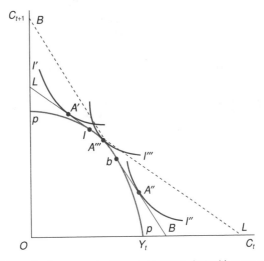

Intertemporal choice with production opportunities given by pp, but with access to an imperfect capital market where the borrowing rate of interest exceeds the lending rate. Here the optimal investment–production plan for a would-be borrower will be point b, for a lender it will be point l, or for an individual who chooses neither to borrow nor lend it will be at a point such as A'''. I', I'', I''' are *alternative* indifference curves typical of these three possible cases, and A', A'' and A''' represent the corresponding alternative consumption plans. Thus, when the capital market is imperfect, the choice of an investment–production plan comes to depend upon the individual's tastes.

By similar reasoning, the inability to borrow at the same low interest rate at which lending is possible rules out all points on *LL* below and to the right of *l*. These unattainable segments are drawn as dotted lines, and the effective constraint upon our individual's choice is made up of the discontinuous line consisting of the lower (solid) part of *BB*, the segment *bl* of the production opportunity curve, and the upper (solid) part of *LL*.

What production plan will this individual choose? If the indifference map is characterised by shallowly sloped curves such as *I'*, then being a lender on the capital market will appear desirable and the production–investment decision will be at point *l*. If the relevant indifferent curves are steep, like *I''*, and the individual wishes to be a borrower, then the investment–production plan will have point *b* being chosen. If they are of some intermediate slope like that of *I'''*, and are tangent to the production opportunity curve somewhere in the segment *bl*, then a point such as *A'''* will characterise both the production and consumption plans, and the individual will be neither a borrower nor a lender in the capital market. In any event, however, the investment–production decision that our individual makes depends upon the nature of tastes in the cases we have analysed here in a way that it does not when the capital market is perfect.

Concluding comment

As in the previous chapter, so here too we have laid out only the basics of the analysis of a fascinating application of microeconomic principles. Thus we have said nothing about what happens when the individual is able to hire other productive services – for example, labour – to co-operate in production plans, or about what happens when production is undertaken for the market rather than home consumption. Moreover we have said nothing about how this analysis relates to those special types of investment in 'human' capital known as 'training' and/or education. Nevertheless, we hope that we have carried the analysis far enough both to generate results which readers find interesting and to convince them of the close relationship between microeconomics and macroeconomics.

SUMMARY

Intertemporal choice with production opportunities and the role of the capital market

1. In this chapter, we continue the analysis of intertemporal choice. However, now the individual also faces production opportunities in which the proceeds of forgone current consumption can be invested.

2. Production opportunities are summarised by a curve which is concave to the origin because it is assumed that additional investment opportunities yield always declining increments to output. This property, in turn, follows from the assumption that available investment opportunities are independent of one another and may be taken up in any order.

3. If the individual does not have access to a capital market, utility is maximised at a point of tangency between the intertemporal indifference curve and the production opportunity curve.

4. The slope of the production opportunity curve is equal to minus (one plus the internal rate of return). In equilibrium without a capital market, the rate of time preference equals the internal rate of return.

5. An individual who can lend or borrow on a perfect capital market separates consumption and production decisions. Production and investment plans involve equalising the internal rate of return to the market rate of interest, while intertemporal consumption plans involve, as before, equalising the interest rate and the rate of time preference.

6. Utility maximising individuals will maximise the present value of their income stream, or their wealth. This is usually equivalent to equalising the internal rate of return and the market interest rate. However, the latter rate will be ambiguous if there are indivisibilities or interdependences among production opportunities. Then maximising the present value of the income stream will still yield unambiguous results.

7. These results do not necessarily go through if the capital market is not perfect, that is, if individuals cannot borrow or lend at will at the same market rate of interest. Suppose, for example, that borrowing incurs a higher interest rate than lending. The independence of consumption and production plans is lost in this event, and the individual's choice in each case will depend on tastes.

PROBLEMS

1 Two individuals have the same tastes *vis-à-vis* consumption now and in the future, and the same endowment of resources. One of them can engage in home production at a constant rate of return of 5 per cent, but is excluded from the capital market to which the other has access and where the rate of interest is 6 per cent. Can we predict which one will enjoy the higher level of consumption in the initial period?

2 We have information on the consumption choices between X and Y of an individual in two successive time periods. In each she spends all of her income. In the first time period, the price of X is £100, the price of Y is £100 and she consumes 10 units of X and Y respectively. In the second time period, the price of X is £150 and of Y is £150. She consumes 7 units of X and 11 units of Y respectively. Do we have enough information to conclude that her tastes have changed between the two periods?

3 An individual, A, survives for two time periods, 1 and 2. In the first, he works, earns W and consumes C_1. In the second, he is retired and receives a pension, out of which he consumes C_2. We assume that the pension is non-contributory, and the rate is set to ensure that post-retirement earnings equal half of wages during his working life. The individual's utility function is $U(C_1, C_2) = C_1^{1/2} C_2^{1/2}$, and the rate of interest is 10 per cent.

   (a) How much does individual A save during his working life (period 1)?
   (b) What is the impact on A's savings during period 1 of an increase in the rate of interest to 15 per cent?
   (c) What is the impact on A's savings during period 1 of an increase in the non-contributory pension rate to three-quarters of the wage in period 1?
   (d) Suppose that there were another individual, B, who attached relatively less weight to consumption during the retirement period, so $U(C_1, C_2) = C_1^{2/3} C_2^{1/3}$. If we return to an interest rate of 10 per cent and a 50 per cent non-contributory pension in period 2, does person B save more than person A?

Note

1. Note that the phrase 'production opportunity' refers to a different phenomenon from that used when discussing labour supply decisions. There the opportunity involved transforming leisure into income. Here it refers to transforming present consumption goods into future consumption goods.

Choice in the face of risk

Introduction

The subject of this chapter is not so much an application of our basic consumer theory as an extension of it. Up to now we have analysed choice-making behaviour on the assumption that the individual making the choices is certain about the outcome of any choice, or at least acts as if such certainty ruled. This is clearly a highly simplifying assumption and if we continue to make it we will be completely unable to analyse some important economic phenomena. For example, if the outcome of every choice was certain, there would be no role for insurance companies to play. After all, the basic service they provide is that of taking risks on behalf of their customers. We now go on to examine the question of choice in risky situations. Our first step will be to show that the ability to make consistent choices in conditions of risk implies the existence of a form of cardinal utility function; when this has been established, we shall use this function to analyse choice-making behaviour.

The idea of expected utility

Let us consider as simple a choice involving **risk** as it is possible to conceive of. Suppose we face an individual with the choice between receiving either the sum of £1 with certainty of a chance or winning £100 in a draw of some sort. Which alternative is chosen will depend upon the **probability** of winning the £100; a very small chance of winning will tend to make the individual select the certain alternative, while a very large chance of winning will point to the selection of the risky alternative. It is equally plausible that there is some value for the probability of winning £100 that just makes the individual indifferent between the certain and the risky alternative. It is the consequences of assuming that such a probability does exist that we now examine.

If our choice maker is able to express indifference between £1 with certainty and winning £100 with a particular probability, this is equivalent to saying that the alternatives will yield the same gain in satisfaction, the same increase in utility. The notion of £1 yielding a given increase in utility is relatively straightforward, but what do we mean by the utility associated with a risky situation?

To say that the probability of winning a particular draw is, for example, 0.2 implies that if the draw were repeated an indefinitely large number of times then two out of ten outcomes would be wins and eight out of ten would be losses. If it were a draw for £100, then £100 would be obtained two times in ten, and nothing would be gained eight times in ten. Hence the utility of a gain of £100 would accrue to the person involved in the draw two times in ten. On average, 0.2 times the utility of £100 would be obtained per repetition (on the assumption that a zero gain yields zero utility). The assumption that we make about behaviour is that our individual treats the average utility that would be obtained from many repeated tries of the risky alternative as the gain in utility to be assigned to participating in it on any one occasion. This is an *ex ante*, or before the event, idea. Once the draw is made the individual gets the utility either of £100 or of nothing, and so it is only before the draw is made that the *ex ante* average or **expected utility** concept is relevant. We did not need to distinguish between *ex ante* and *ex post* (after the event) utility levels in dealing with choice under conditions of certainty, for there the two were always the same. The consequences of making a particular choice were fully known before any choice was made. However, the distinction is obviously a vital one in dealing with situations involving risk.

Probability and cardinal utility

If our choice maker is able to say that there is a particular probability of winning £100 that is exactly equivalent to receiving £1 with certainty, that individual is also saying that the utility of one extra pound is equal to the expected utility of the risky alternative. Mathematically speaking, expected utilities are calculated by multiplying the utility of each possible outcome by the probability of its occurrence, and then adding these products together. This process yields a *probability weighted average of utilities*. In the particular case being analysed here, this **expected utility** is equal to the probability of winning £100 times the utility of a gain of £100 plus the probability of winning nothing times the utility of a zero gain. If we let $U(£1)$ be the utility of £1 extra and p_1 be the probability of winning £100 then we have:

$$U(£1) = p_1 \, U(£100) + (1 - p_1)U(0) \tag{7.1}$$

Now if it is possible to find a probability value that satisfies the above equation, it is presumably equally possible to find a value, call it p_2, that would make the utility of a chance at the draw equivalent to the utility of £2 extra with certainty, and so on all the way up to £100 (at which point the value of p would clearly have to be equal to one).

We could write down a whole array of equations as follows:

$$U(\pounds 1) = p_1 \, U(\pounds 100) + (1 - p_1) \, U(0)$$
$$U(\pounds 2) = p_2 \, U(\pounds 100) + (1 - p_2) \, U(0)$$
$$\cdots \cdots$$
$$\cdots \cdots \tag{7.2}$$
$$U(\pounds 99) = p_{99} \, U(\pounds 100) + (1 - p_{99}) \, U(0)$$
$$U(\pounds 100) = 1 \, U(\pounds 100) + (0) \, U(0)$$

If there is no gain in utility attached to getting zero extra pounds, then $U(0)$ is equal to zero and these expressions can be rearranged to read

$$U(\pounds 1) \, \frac{1}{U(\pounds 100)} = p_1$$

$$U(\pounds 2) \, \frac{1}{U(\pounds 100)} = p_2$$

$$\cdots \cdots \tag{7.3}$$

$$U(\pounds 99) \, \frac{1}{U(\pounds 100)} = p_{99}$$

$$U(\pounds 100) \, \frac{1}{U(\pounds 100)} = 1$$

When we put it this way, it is clear that the probability indices on the right may be used as **cardinal** indicators of the utility of various sums of money. To be sure, everything is here being **measured** relative to the utility of gaining £100 with certainty; the analysis implies no absolute scale for measuring utility. We could equally well conceive of experiments that would measure the utility of gaining various sums of money relative to the utility of gaining £200 or £300 or any other amount. We are in no position to say that one sum of money yields twice the utility of some other sum, for such a statement could only be made if we knew where to put zero on our utility scale; but we can say that the **difference in the utilities** yielded by two amounts of money is twice the **difference in utilities** of two other amounts.

The measurement of utility is thus rather like the measurement of temperature. A temperature which is twice the number of degrees of some other temperature on the Celsius scale will not be twice the number of degrees on the Fahrenheit scale: 'twice as hot' does not mean anything. However, the relative size of differences between particular levels of heat is the same on the two scales. The difference between 30°C (86°F) and 20°C (68°F) is twice the difference between 10°C (50°F) and 5°C (41°F) no matter which scale is used. Utility and temperature are measurable in the same sort of way and to exactly the same extent.

Diminishing marginal utility and expected utility

Now the purpose of the foregoing analysis is to show that it is legitimate for us to draw a diagram such as Figure 7.1 in which the utility accruing to an individual is related to wealth. The units of measurement on the vertical axis are arbitrary, as is the location of the origin, but to exactly the same extent as if temperature were being measured there.

| Figure 7.1 | A utility function displaying diminishing marginal utility (*U*) of wealth (*W*) |

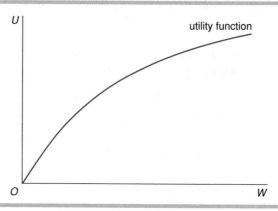

This arbitrariness is irrelevant to the analysis that follows. The relationship is drawn on the assumption that successive equal increments of wealth yield diminishing increments in utility. It displays *diminishing* **marginal utility of wealth**. The consequences of making alternative assumptions will be considered later. We may use this utility of wealth function to analyse the nature of the choice facing an individual who must decide in a risky situation whether or not to insure against the risk in question. Suppose that the individual faces a 50–50 chance of losing a certain amount of wealth ($W_1 - W_0$) within a particular time period. In terms of Figure 7.2, given an initial level of wealth, W_1, our choice maker will end the period in question either at W_1 with an associated utility level of $U(W_1)$ or at

| Figure 7.2 | |

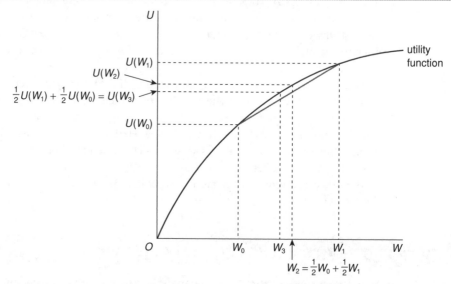

Ex ante, the individual faces a choice between a 50–50 chance of W_0 and W_1 and the certainty of W_2, which lies halfway between them. The expected wealth involved in the two alternatives is the same, but the expected utility of the certain alternative is higher by $U(W_2) - [\frac{1}{2}U(W_1) + \frac{1}{2}U(W_0)]$. A measure of the consumer's surplus gained by selecting the certain alternative by insuring is $W_2 - W_3$.

W_0 with an associated utility level of $U(W_0)$. *Ex ante* there is a 50 per cent chance of ending up in either situation. The expected value of wealth therefore is $\frac{1}{2}W_0 + \frac{1}{2}W_1 = W_2$. But it is not wealth *per se* that is relevant to our individual but the *utility* that this wealth yields. **Expected utility** in the risky situation is given by $\frac{1}{2}U(W_0) + \frac{1}{2}U(W_1)$. This measures the *ex ante* utility accruing to our individual, at the beginning of the time period under consideration.

Box 7.1 ### Utility of wealth functions

A general utility of wealth function that is useful to illustrate choice in the face of risk is $U = W^a$, where U is utility, W is wealth and a is a parameter that defines the nature of the function. Any value of parameter a less than one produces a utility function of the form presented in Figure 7.2, i.e. $a < 1$ exhibits diminishing marginal utility of wealth. We will return to the importance of this parameter later in the chapter. For arithmetic ease we will assume $a = 0.5$, so the utility function is $U = \sqrt{W}$. If our person has a 50–50 chance of having a wealth of £1600 or a wealth of £900, the important features of the utility function can be presented as follows:

Expected wealth = 0.5(1600) + 0.5(900) = 1250
Utility of £1600: $U(1600) = 1600^{0.5} = 40$
Utility of £900: $U(900) = 900^{0.5} = 30$
Expected utility of the wealth = 0.5(40) + 0.5(30) = 35

These basic features of our utility function can be presented in Illustration 7.1, which is equivalent to Figure 7.2.

Illustration 7.1

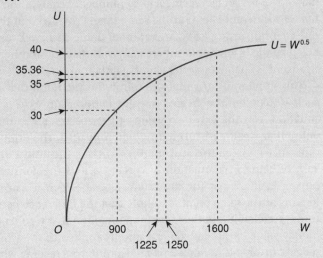

It is clear from this diagram that if our person had wealth of £1250 for certain, rather than this being an expected wealth, the utility of this amount would be higher than 35 at $1250^{0.5} = 35.36$. Also it is clear that a utility of 35 can be obtained with a certain income less than 1250 at $35^2 = 1225$. So a monetary measure of the utility loss because the wealth level is uncertain is 1250 − 1225 = 25.

Insurance and gambling

Now suppose that the individual can buy insurance against risk. Suppose that, in return for a premium paid at the beginning of the period, some agent guarantees to reimburse the individual completely for any loss incurred during the period. For payment of a fee a situation of certainty can be obtained. By reducing the level of wealth with which the period is begun by the amount of this fee our individual can be guaranteed to end the period with that same level of wealth. The utility of this alternative is clearly the utility of having W_1 minus the premium with certainty. Faced with the choice of insuring or not insuring, the individual will presumably choose the alternative that will yield the higher level of *ex ante* utility. In terms of Figure 7.2 so long as the insurance premium is less than $W_1 - W_3$ the individual would prefer to buy insurance. W_3 is the level of wealth which, if available with certainty, yields the same utility as a 50–50 chance of W_0 or W_1.

If we ignore the administrative costs of actually buying and selling insurance – we will return to these costs later – the maximum amount that this individual will pay for insurance is more than the minimum the agent providing insurance will accept by way of premium, always provided that the agent in question has a large number of customers, each facing similar, but independent risks. The minimum acceptable premium is one that will enable the insurer just to break even. If a large – strictly speaking indefinitely large – number of 50–50 risks are being covered, then half of the clients will have claims and a premium set at 50 per cent of the loss on any one claim will just cover the insurer's outgoings. That is to say, *if we ignore any costs that the insurance agent incurs in running the business*, that agent will be able to offer the client what is usually called 'a **fair bet**'. A fair bet is one on which, were it to be repeated an indefinitely large number of times, both participants would expect, in the long run, to break even. The agent selling **insurance** to many people is in fact facing a large number of trials of the same situation, not over time, but over different clients at the same time. Provided that there is no connection between one client incurring a loss and another doing so as well, and provided also that the risks taken by the insurance agent are *independent* of one another, to use a statistical term, then the agent is enabled to offer clients fair bets.

This implies in turn that the minimum premium that an insurer will charge will be such as to permit the insured to enjoy with certainty the level of wealth that, in the risky situation, was the expected value of that person's wealth. Because the individual may enjoy that wealth with certainty when insured, the utility level now is $U(W_2)$ and the difference between this and $\frac{1}{2}U(W_1) + \frac{1}{2}U(W_0)$, the utility when not insured, measures the gain of being in a situation of certainty; it is the consumer's surplus that arises from buying insurance at the minimum rate at which it can be provided. Another way of looking at the same point is to note that the difference between the minimum premium that is acceptable and the maximum premium that would be paid $(W_2 - W_3)$ measures the money value of this consumer's surplus and hence the scope available to a monopolistic seller of insurance to make a positive profit from dealing with this individual and to cover the administrative costs of the transaction.

Now the assumption of diminishing marginal utility of wealth is crucial to the foregoing analysis. As Figure 7.3 shows, a linear utility function – constant marginal utility of wealth – implies that the individual is indifferent between insuring and not insuring at the minimum premium that an insurer would offer, and would prefer not to insure at any

Figure 7.3

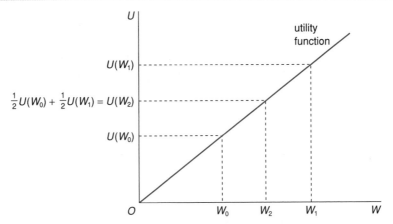

When the marginal utility of wealth is constant, not only the expected values of wealth involved in the certain and uncertain situations are the same, but also the expected utility. The alternatives here are a 50–50 chance of W_0 or W_1, or W_2 with certainty.

higher premium. It is equally clear from Figure 7.4 that increasing marginal utility of wealth will involve the individual in refusing insurance at any feasible premium. The risky alternative will be chosen rather than the safe one and hence the individual may be said to '**gamble**'.

Figure 7.4

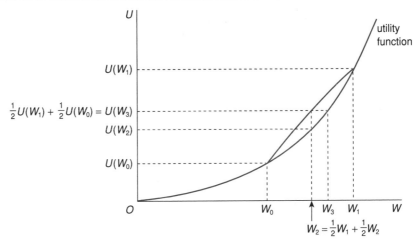

Increasing marginal utility of wealth makes the risky alternative preferable. Only the utility function distinguishes the analysis contained in this diagram from that depicted in Figures 7.2 and 7.3. Here a gain of $W_1 - W_2$ would add more to utility than an equal-sized loss ($W_2 - W_0$) would subtract from it. Thus, a 50–50 chance of such a gain or loss has a higher expected utility than the certainty of W_2. $W_3 - W_2$ measures the money value of the extent to which the uncertain alternative is preferred.

Box 7.2 **Maximum insurance outlay**

We can continue the example earlier in this chapter based on the utility function $U = W^{0.5}$ to calculate the maximum insurance premium our person is willing to pay. This person may face a wealth loss because of flood risk. If a flood occurs, wealth falls from £1600 to £900, i.e. the costs incurred with a flood are £700. We saw in the previous example that if the probability of a flood is 0.5, expected wealth is £1250 and expected utility is 35. If our person now buys insurance to cover the flood risk we can calculate the maximum policy cost that they are willing to pay and the minimum the insurance company is willing to charge.

By buying insurance, uncertainties over wealth are removed, but at a cost. Without insurance our person has an expected utility of 35. This utility can be generated by a certain wealth of $35^2 = 1225$. It follows that as long as our person's wealth, after insurance, does not fall below £1225 utility will increase by buying an insurance policy. So the maximum amount our person is willing to pay for an insurance policy to guard against flood risk is $1600 - 1225 = £375$. If the cost of insurance is any more than this, utility will be higher by bearing the flood risk without insurance and have an expected value of 35.

The minimum an insurance company needs to charge to be willing to offer a policy, i.e. the fair insurance price, is the expected value of the payout that would result if a claim is made against the policy. In our example when a flood occurs our person's wealth falls from £1600 to £900, i.e. the costs incurred with a flood are £700. As the probability of a flood is 0.5, the expected payout from a policy is $0.5(700) = £350$. This is the minimum price that an insurance company would be willing to accept. If follows that the difference between the minimum and maximum prices is $375 - 350 = £25$. As we saw earlier in the chapter, this £25 is a monetary measure of the utility loss because the wealth level is uncertain, or (what amounts to the same thing) a measure of the maximum utility (i.e. consumer surplus) gain by making an uncertain event certain by buying insurance. Some or all of this £25 might be claimed by the insurance company as monopoly profit.

Insurance and gambling: further analysis

If it is the case that increasing marginal utility of wealth implies gambling behaviour and decreasing marginal utility implies insuring, it would appear that an individual would always do one or the other. That is to say, a person who insures against large risks will also insure against small risks; a person who insures a house will insure every other risk as well, and will not fill in football coupons; a person who backs horses will carry only the minimum legal motorcar insurance. Such predictions are contrary to even casually observable facts and present something of a problem for the analysis which we have just described. One way of dealing with such awkward facts, proposed by Friedman and Savage, is to suggest that though, in general, the marginal utility of wealth diminishes overall, it may increase locally.

The shape of the utility function implicit here is displayed in Figure 7.5. An individual might experience increasing marginal utility of wealth in the region of W_2 and hence gamble small amounts – this includes not insuring against small risks – and yet find that,

Figure 7.5

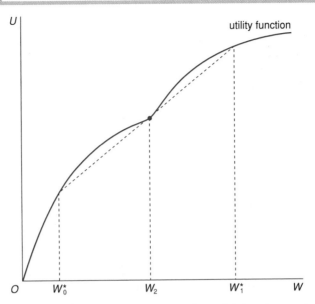

A utility function displaying successively decreasing, increasing and decreasing marginal utility of wealth. If an individual who has such a utility function is faced with the choice between W_2 with certainty and the 50–50 chance of W_0 and W_1, where the expected value of the uncertain outcome is W_0, then the risky alternative will be selected so long as W_0 and W_1 fall within the bounds given by $W_0^* W_1^*$. The individual will prefer the certain alternatives if they lie outside these bounds. This is a special case of a general tendency of individuals with such a utility function to take risks when the variations in wealth involved are relatively small and to insure when the variations are relatively large.

for risks involving the possibility of large losses, the tendency of the utility function to display diminishing marginal utility of wealth was the dominant factor in the decision. The difficulty with this solution is that there seems to be no particular tendency for people at one particular level of wealth to gamble more on small amounts than do those who are better or worse off. It would be quite a coincidence if the working of the economic system produced a distribution of wealth which gave each individual just that level of wealth at which its marginal utility was increasing. Virtually everyone, at every level of wealth, insures against some risks but not against others – hence gambling by default – nor does there appear to be any marked relationship between wealth and a propensity to engage in active gambling on the outcome of sporting events and games of chance.

Perhaps a more satisfactory approach to one aspect of this problem is to look more closely at the costs of running an insurance business. There obviously are administrative costs involved in selling insurance policies, and an insurance agent must cover these out of premium income. Thus, the agent can, in fact, never quite offer a fair bet to a customer. A premium must be charged that takes some of the consumer's surplus that would accrue to the customer were a completely fair bet offered. Now as the reader ought to be able to see easily enough, the smaller the loss which a particular consumer might face, the smaller the surplus accruing from buying insurance at a 'fair' premium. Thus, the less that consumer will be willing to pay above that fair premium to cover the insurance agent's costs of handling the transaction. But there is no reason to suppose that these costs decline in any kind of simple proportion as the value of the loss against which insurance is being sought declines. It might easily take the same amount of time and trouble to deal with the paperwork on a small policy as on a large one, and the same amount of work to assess the risk involved and calculate the fair premium. For insurance involving small amounts, these administrative costs might well exceed the consumer's surplus available to cover them.

In short, for some risks the gain from having the insurance at a 'fair' premium is outweighed by the administrative costs. Hence it is not bought, and the consumer gambles. This possibility is illustrated in Figure 7.6. The argument here is surely a plausible explanation of why individuals who insure against large risks nevertheless gamble by failing to buy cover against smaller ones. However, the argument does not explain why people *actively* undertake gambles. One avoids transaction costs by not filling in football coupons, and by not placing bets on horses. One incurs them by doing so, and they are, of course, covered by the football pool company or bookmaker shading the odds they offer in their own favour and away from a fair bet. Hence, to take account of transaction costs is to make it even more difficult to explain this type of gambling in terms of the analysis presented in this chapter. Only if one postulates that active gambling yields satisfaction to the individual who undertakes it over and above that obtained from consuming winnings (if any) can one explain its occurring. This amounts to saying that some people gamble because they like gambling and is perilously close to being no explanation at all of the phenomenon.

Figure 7.6

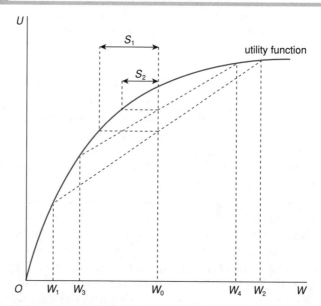

The gain from buying insurance at a fair premium against a 'large' risk: that of losing $W_2 - W_1$ with a 50 per cent probability is given by S_1. For a 'small' risk, that of losing $W_4 - W_3$ with a 50 per cent probability, the gain from insuring at a fair premium is S_2. For the smaller risk, the surplus available to pay administrative costs associated with taking out insurance is also smaller. Hence the individual is less likely to insure against small risks.

Further analysis of risk

In this chapter we have seen that a person with a utility of wealth function exhibiting diminishing marginal utility may insure against risks by buying insurance, as long as the cost of insurance is not too high. This section will take this analysis further. A preliminary point is that we must link the earlier analysis to **attitudes to risk**. Any individual can have one of three attitudes to risk: risk averse, risk neutral or risk loving.

Risk averse

Risk aversion implies that the uncertainty of a risky outcome reduces utility. It follows that any risk averse individual prefers a certain payoff to the same expected payoff with a risky outcome. We saw earlier that someone with diminishing marginal utility of wealth who faces a risky prospect has a reduction in utility because of the risk. This is why the expected utility and the expected wealth in Figure 7.2 did not coincide. It follows that someone with diminishing marginal utility of wealth is risk averse. Any risk averse person can increase utility by buying insurance and so removing the uncertainty, as long as the cost of the insurance is not too high.

Risk neutral

A person is risk neutral if they are indifferent between all alternatives offering the same expected value. This implies that the risk itself does not affect their utility directly as with a risk averse person. As long as expected values are the same a risk neutral person is indifferent towards risk. A risk neutral person, therefore, gains no advantage from buying insurance. This occurs when there is a constant marginal utility of wealth.

Risk loving

A risk loving person has a preference for an uncertain prospect with a particular expected value to a certain return with the same expected value. This implies that risk loving people get positive utility from the risk itself, i.e. they actually like taking risks. It follows that if the risk is removed by insurance there would be a reduction in utility. So, a risk loving person has an increasing marginal utility of wealth.

With these definitions we can re-examine the demand for insurance but at a more detailed level. Assume that someone has wealth of W_H (with the subscript H denoting 'high') but has to face a particular risk (for instance of flooding) that results in a reduction in wealth to W_L (with the subscript L denoting 'low'). Using the flood example, it follows that the cost of recovering from a flood is $W_H - W_L$. This suggests that the value of this person's wealth depends on the state of the world, i.e. the possibility of a costly event occurring. Using the flood risk example, the possible states of the world that affect wealth levels are the occurrence or non-occurrence of a flood. The wealth levels W_H and W_L define the endowment point E in Figure 7.7.

Earlier in this chapter we defined the fair cost of an insurance policy as a cost the same as the expected value of the payout from the policy. This fair cost implies that in the long run neither the consumer nor the firm makes money from the policy. Hence we can define fair insurance as a price set at fair cost. So, with a 50:50 chance of a flood occurring

Figure 7.7

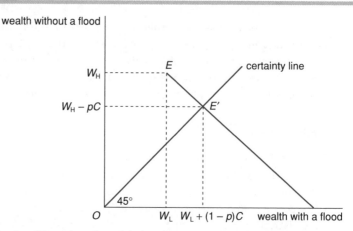

The certainty line is a 45° ray from the origin. It defines all wealth levels that are the same in both states of the world. So there is no uncertainty about the size of wealth on the certainty line. The endowment point E implies a wealth of W_H without a flood and W_L if a flood occurs. All points on the line from E and through E' have the same expected value of wealth. With fair insurance this line is the budget line for differing amounts of insurance cover.

this suggests that with a policy that covers the full $W_H - W_L$ loss the expected cost to the insurance company is $0.5(W_H - W_L)$. A fair insurance policy would therefore cost this amount. More generally we can define:

   r as the policy cost per £ of cover (i.e. the policy price)
   p as the probability of making a claim on an insurance policy.
   and C as the amount of cover bought ($W_H - W_L$ in the above example).

We can now define fair insurance as occurring when the cost of a policy (rC) is equal to the expected payout (pC):

   $rC = pC$, or $r = p$.   (7.4)

Fair insurance therefore requires that the premium rate is equal to the probability of loss.

   Using this formulation we can now examine the demand for fair insurance in more detail. We start by defining a budget constraint. Buying £C worth of insurance cover costs rC. The exact value of C is a matter we consider in a moment. Using the earlier example, this implies that, when insurance is bought, wealth without a flood is equal to £$(W_H - rC)$. This is equal to £$(W_H - pC)$ because with fair insurance $r = p$. If a flood occurs a claim is made on the policy and so £C is received, but the policy cost of £rC is still paid. So, the gain from the policy in the event of a flood is £$(C - rC) = £C(1 - r) = £C(1 - p)$ (because of fair insurance). It follows that if fair insurance is purchased the budget constraint starts from point E in Figure 7.7 and passes through a point such as E'. The slope of this budget constraint is the vertical distance divided by the horizontal distance:

   $[W_H - (W_H - pC)] \div [W_L - (W_L + (1 - p)C)]$
i.e. $-p/(1 - p)$ (7.5)

With fair insurance, and so $r = p$, the slope of the budget line is the probability of the contingency on the horizontal axis divided by the probability of the contingency on the vertical axis. Note that a characteristic of the fair insurance budget line shown in Figure 7.7 is that any point on it has the same expected value. To see this we can compare points E and E'. The expected value at point E is

$$EV(E) = (1 - p)W_H + pW_L = W_H - p(W_H - W_L) \tag{7.6}$$

The expected value at point E' is

$$EV(E') = (1 - p)(W_H - pC) + p[W_L + (1 - p)C] = W_H - p(W_H - W_L) \tag{7.7}$$

It follows that $EV(E) = EV(E')$, and both are equal to wealth without the risky event (W_H) minus the expected loss if the risky event occurs i.e. $p(W_H - W_L)$. This is true for all values of C, i.e. anywhere on the fair insurance budget line.

To examine the demand for insurance we need to specify the nature of preferences and so indifference curves that apply with insurance. To represent indifference curves a first task is to define a **certainty line**. This is shown in Figure 7.7 as a 45° ray from the origin. Why this is drawn as passing through point E' is a matter we consider in a moment. The key characteristic of a certainty line, and why it has this name, is that any point on the certainty line has the same wealth in both states of the world. It follows that wealth is certain only on the certainty line. Anywhere off the certainty line the value of wealth changes, depending on which state of the world occurs.

For a risk averse individual, indifference curves defined over two states of the world have two key characteristics:

1. The marginal rate of substitution (i.e. the slope of the indifference curve) on the certainty line is equal to $-p/(1 - p)$, where p is the probability of the state of the world defined on the horizontal axis. If we have fair insurance the slope of the budget line is $-p/(1 - p)$. So with fair insurance any indifference curve is a tangent to the budget line on the certainty line.
2. Indifference curves are convex to the origin.

We will consider these two characteristics in turn. With respect to characteristic (1) consider Figure 7.8. This presents two indifference curves, U_1 and U_2; otherwise it the same as Figure 7.7. Indifference curve U_1 is consistent with the first characteristic just outlined; in particular, it is at a tangent to the fair insurance budget line on the certainty line. Indifference curve U_2 is not consistent with the first characteristic, as the marginal rate of substitution on the certainty is (in absolute terms) greater than $p/(1 - p)$. If a risk averse individual had an indifference curve like U_2 it would imply that the same utility is obtained at point E' as at E''. Point E' is characterised by no uncertainty (it is on the certainty line) whereas E'' has some uncertainty as wealth is greater with a flood than without it. But both E' and E'' are on the same fair insurance budget line. We saw earlier that anywhere on this budget line has the same expected value. But it is not possible for a risk averse person to get the same utility from a certain event as an uncertain event with the same expected value because of the disutility of the uncertainty itself. It follows that a risk averse individual will get lower utility at E'' than at E'. For a risk averse individual this lower utility occurs at any point along a budget line that is off the certainty line. So utility at E must be lower than at E'. The only way that this can be ensured is if indifference curves are like U_1, i.e. they are a tangent to a fair insurance budget line on the certainty line.

Figure 7.8

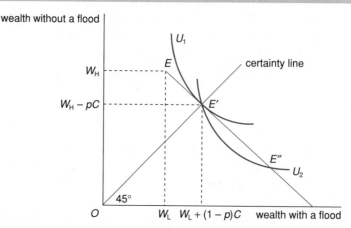

Indifferene curve U_1 defines a constant level of utility for a risk averse person. The slope of U_1 is equal to $-p/(1-p)$ on the certainty line, where p is the probability of a flood. With fair insurance utility is maximised on the certainty line, i.e. a person would buy insurance to equalise wealth in both states of the world. A risk averse person cannot have an indifference curve such as U_2, as this would imply the same utility from a certain event and an uncertain event with the same expected value, which is inconsistent with risk aversion.

We can now turn to the second characteristic of risk averse indifference curves identified above, i.e. they are convex to the origin. Consider Figure 7.9, which presents two types of indifference curve, convex and concave to origin; it is otherwise the same as Figure 7.7. With the convex indifference curves utility at E' is greater than at E, i.e. the certain wealth is preferred to the uncertain wealth. With the concave indifference curves

Figure 7.9

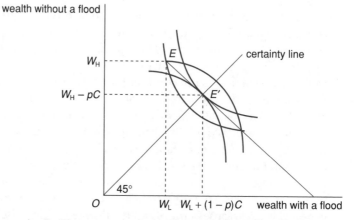

A risk loving person has indifference curves that are concave from the origin. The slope of any indifference curve is $-p/(1-p)$ on the certainty line, where p is the probability of a flood. Point E' is not utility maximising as a higher level of utility can be obtained by not buying insurance and hence being at the endowment point E.

greater utility occurs at point E rather than E', i.e. the uncertain wealth is preferred to the certain wealth. Given our earlier definitions of attitudes to risk it follows that the convex indifference curves must represent risk aversion and the concave curves a risk loving individual. As an exercise the reader can establish two things:

1. that with the risk loving indifference curves their slope on the certainty line is $-p/(1-p)$;
2. that a risk neutral person has linear indifference curves that have slope $-p/(1-p)$.

Equilibrium demand for insurance

We can now use our indifference curve framework to investigate the equilibrium **demand for fair insurance**. It is clear from Figure 7.5 that a risk averse individual maximises utility at E', i.e. equilibrium occurs on the certainty line. The amount of cover purchased, i.e. the value of C, can easily be calculated. As equilibrium occurs on the 45° ray we know that

$$W_H - pC = W_L + (1-p)C$$
i.e. $\quad C = W_H - W_L$ \hfill (7.8)

This suggests the very important result that with fair insurance a risk averse individual will buy insurance so that the policy covers the full value of the possible loss from the risk. This guarantees that wealth is the same in both states of the world, i.e. an individual will be *fully insured*.

Note that this result, that a risk averse person will be fully insured with fair insurance, is independent of exactly how risk averse a person is. If we compare two people who differ in how risk averse they are – in non-technical terms they differ in how much they dislike uncertainty – the indifference curves of the more risk averse individual will exhibit a greater degree of convexity away from the certainty line. But, for reasons set out above, the marginal rate of substitution is equal to $-p/(1-p)$ on the certainty line for both individuals. This implies that both individuals will be fully insured with fair insurance. One final point can be made about the demand for fair insurance. It is clear from Figure 7.9 that a risk loving individual will never buy insurance as maximum utility is attained at point E, i.e. the endowment point. Such a person will therefore always bear risks rather than buy insurance to eliminate risks.

As noted earlier in this chapter, insurance is unlikely to be fair in practice. This means that we must extend the analysis presented here to the possibility of **unfair insurance**. This more likely case involves the cost of an insurance policy being greater than the expected value of the payout from the policy. Or more briefly $r > p$, where r is the premium rate per £ of cover and p is the probability of the risk occurring. The effect of unfair insurance is that the slope of the budget line for insurance is no longer $-p/(1-p)$ but is now $-r/(1-r)$. As $r > p$ the budget line with unfair insurance is steeper than with fair insurance. This is shown in Figure 7.10 using the same example as that used above of flood risk. Note that in this diagram both indifference curves have a slope of $-p/(1-p)$ on the certainty line. It is clear from Figure 7.6 that with unfair insurance equilibrium is above the certainty line. This implies that an individual is better off without a flood, i.e. is not fully insured. In the diagram insurance to the value of less than pC is bought, and as $p < r$ the actual value of the policy cover is insufficient to fully cover the losses if a flood occurs. The result is that with a flood some money is accrued from the policy, as equilibrium wealth is greater than W_L, but this is insufficient to cover the full flood loss.

Figure 7.10

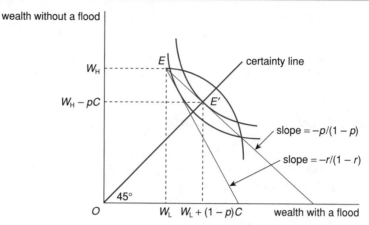

With fair insurance equilibrium is at E'. With unfair insurance the price of insurance is greater than the probability of a flood and the slope of the budget line is steeper than $-p(1 - p)$. Equilibrium with unfair insurance is to the left of the certainty line. A consumer would not be fully insured and so would have higher wealth without a flood.

We can consider one final point in this section. We found earlier that with fair insurance a risk averse individual will be fully insured and that this is independent of how risk averse any person is. With unfair insurance the situation is different. Consider Figure 7.11, which expands the relevant part of Figure 7.10 and presents indifference curves for two

Figure 7.11

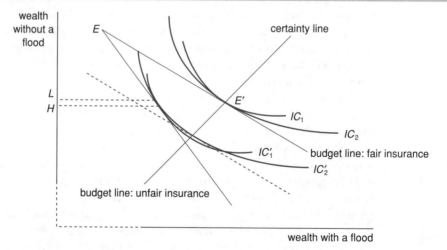

All indifference curves have the slope $-p(1 - p)$ on the certainty line. Indifference curve IC_2 has a lower degree of risk aversion than IC_1. With unfair insurance, a person who is more risk averse buys more insurance than someone who is less risk averse. This is shown by the indifference curve IC_1', which indicates a level of wealth H without a flood compared with L with IC_2'. The difference $H-L$. shows that more insurance is purchased by a more risk averse person.

individuals. Indifference curve IC_1 is based on a greater degree of risk aversion than IC_2. But note that both indifference curves have a marginal rate of substitution equal to the slope of the budget line for fair insurance on the certainty line. With unfair insurance the budget line is steeper. The indifference curves IC_1' and IC_2' define the utility maximising equilibria with unfair insurance. Note that IC_1' and IC_2' also have slope equal to $-p/(1-p)$ on the certainty line as indicated by the dashed line that is parallel to the budget line for fair insurance. The resulting equilibria are indicated as L for IC_2' and H for IC_1'. The L and H denote low and high risk aversion. Someone with high risk aversion (our H) buys more insurance when this is unfair. This greater cover results in a higher payout with a claim on the insurance.

A note on moral hazard and adverse selection

Other problems arise in the economics of insurance not because the information held by the two parties to the trade is less than certain but because it is **asymmetric**. For example, an insurance company does not have the same information as the individuals being insured. Two specific examples will serve to introduce the point. Suppose individuals have some influence over the probability that the unfavourable outcome will occur. When they are insured, they will pay inadequate attention to ensuring that the insured-against outcome does not occur. This problem is called **moral hazard**, and can severely restrict the formation of a free market in insurance. For example, we may drive relatively more carelessly if we are insured against the consequences of a crash, and may be relatively less security conscious in the home if we are insured against burglary. Insurance companies obviously respond to this problem by specifying more precisely the responsibilities of the people purchasing insurance, for example by making the first £100 of damage in the event of a car crash the responsibility of the insured, or by requiring them to fit window locks.

A second problem in insurance markets is known as **adverse selection**, which arises where the very act of selling insurance leads to demand for it by bad risks. Suppose there are two types of drivers, 'safe' and 'dangerous', with the latter having a higher probability of crashing. Clearly the insurance company would like to identify each separately and to sell insurance to the more risky group at a higher price. However, suppose there is no way for the insurance company to distinguish between the two groups of individuals, and that it offers to sell insurance at prices appropriate for low-risk individuals or for an average of dangerous and safe drivers. Either price would be cheap for high-risk individuals, who would try to buy insurance in disproportionate numbers and thereby lead the company to make a loss. The solution here of course is for the company to investigate the characteristics of 'dangerous' drivers, and to associate these with easily distinguishable features – age, gender, region of the country where they live, and so forth – which can form a basis for dispersion in insurance prices. We return to the questions of moral hazard and adverse selection in much greater detail in Chapter 26.

Concluding comment

The analysis set out in this chapter has many applications to the behaviour of capital markets and insurance markets as well as of firms and individuals. We therefore return to these issues in the later chapters of this book. It also underlies much modern work on inventory theory and on the monetary aspects of macroeconomics. As the reader will appreciate, then, this chapter has provided only the briefest introduction to a most important branch of modern micro theory.

SUMMARY

Choice in the face of risk

1. Expected utility is the *ex ante* average of the utility associated with a series of risky outcomes. Expected utility is measured by the sum of the utilities associated with all possible outcomes multiplied by their probabilities.

2. The probability weighted average of utilities can be reduced to a series of relative cardinal indicators of utility. This relative measure of cardinal utility allows us to construct a marginal utility of wealth function. Usually we assume diminishing marginal utility when we do so.

3. Where insurance is available, the decision maker who faces a risk of losing some amount of wealth will be prepared to pay an insurance premium up to a certain maximum amount in order to be certain of ending the period with the same wealth they began with (less the premium in question).

4. The maximum premium the choice maker will be willing to pay is the level of wealth which, if available with certainty, yields the same reduction in utility as would the loss insured against, times the probability of its occurring.

5. Abstracting from administrative costs, the provider of insurance will be able to offer a premium less than this maximum amount when the risks against which insurance is sold are statistically independent of one another.

6. Where the marginal utility of wealth is increasing, the decision maker is likely to gamble. We do not normally observe universal risk taking or universal insuring among individuals. The marginal utility of wealth may, therefore, diminish overall but increase locally. Alternatively, if the administrative costs of insurance exceed the gain to decision makers who might buy it, they will choose to remain uninsured, that is, to gamble.

7. Risk averse, neutral and loving individuals will have utility of wealth functions that are, respectively, concave from below, linear and convex.

8. While with fair insurance a risk averse individual is always fully insured, with unfair insurance the demand for insurance depends on the degree of risk aversion and the cost of any policy.

9. Two problems in the market for insurance are moral hazard and adverse selection. If the insured has some control over the probability of the unfavourable outcome insured against occurring, they may pay inadequate attention to averting this outcome. Similarly, where the insurer cannot distinguish between bad and good risks, the very act of offering insurance at a rate appropriate for the average level of risk attracts bad risks for whom this premium is relatively cheap.

PROBLEMS

1 Consider the following lottery tickets:

   (a) ticket 1 gives a return of £600 with a probability of 0.03 and a zero return otherwise;
   (b) ticket 2 gives a return of £100 with a probability of 0.18 and a zero return otherwise;
   (c) ticket 3 gives a return of £36 with a probability of 0.5 and a zero return otherwise.

   Individual A is willing to pay prices P_1, P_2 and P_3 for tickets 1, 2 and 3 respectively. Suppose that individual A is risk averse. What can we say about the absolute and relative values of P_1, P_2 and P_3? In what ways will the answer be different if the individual is risk neutral?

2 An individual has the utility function $U = W^{1/2}$, where W denotes wealth, and is considering a bet in which there is a 30 per cent chance of winning £49 clear, and a 70 per cent chance of winning nothing.

   (a) Will the individual take the bet if it costs £5?
   (b) Will they take it if it costs £2?
   (c) Will they take it at a cost of £5 if the utility function takes the form $U = W$?
   (d) Will they take it at a cost of £20 if the utility function takes the form $U = W$?
   (e) Will they take it at a cost of £20 if the utility function takes the form $U = W^2$?

3 Discuss why people typically choose to underinsure the contents of their houses in their domestic insurance policies.

PART III

PRODUCTION AND COSTS

Production functions

Introduction

Up to now, the analysis presented in this book has concerned itself with consumer choice, and in particular with the allocation of income among expenditures on various goods and services. It hardly needs pointing out that the goods and services which consumers purchase do not simply materialise out of the blue. In large measure they have to be produced. Moreover we have also seen that important elements in consumer decision making involve not the purchase of goods and services, but the sale of productive services, not least labour services. Of course, it is these very services that are used in the production of goods which in turn become the objects of the consumer's demand. In short, the analysis of consumer behaviour, vital though it is to an understanding of economic life, cannot tell us the whole story. The study of consumption needs to be supplemented by a study of production, and it is to the analysis of production and costs that the next section of this book is devoted.

The essential fact about production is so obvious that it hardly needs stating: it involves the use of services of various sorts to generate output. However, productive services do not usually come together spontaneously; their use is typically organised in some way. Clearly, the manner in which production is organised has important social and political, as well as economic, aspects, and much of what follows is relevant to more than one form of social and economic organisation. Production costs are, after all, as relevant to the manager of a state owned enterprise as to the manager of a privately owned firm. Nevertheless, the following chapters do take certain social and political conditions for granted inasmuch as they are overwhelmingly concerned with decisions about the production of goods and services as they arise in the context of an economy where such decisions are taken by privately owned, and (in the main) profit-oriented firms. We have already noted that production involves the organisation of flows of inputs in order to generate flows of output, and we are going to analyse the decisions that underlie such organisation as they are taken by privately owned firms. Now of course, in the real world, firms come in many shapes and sizes ranging from the family-owned corner business all the way to the giant multinational, multiproduct corporation, and there is no way in which a book as brief as this one could come to grips with all the manifold details of the organisation and operation of such a wide variety of concerns. Thus, the theory of the firm as we shall present it will be abstract and will concentrate on certain properties, one hopes the essential ones, that all such enterprises have in common.

Ownership, control and the entrepreneur

The **firm**, as we shall analyse it, is a social entity that carries out three activities. It buys productive services, organises them so as to produce output, and then sells the output. Its task is to take the decisions upon which the organisation of production depends, and economists have often found it useful to personify this decision-making role in the form of a being called the **entrepreneur**. There is no need literally to postulate that any one human being in a particular firm takes all the decisions about input purchases, the choice of technology, and the marketing of output, to make the concept of an entrepreneur a useful one. It is sufficient to realise that in any undertaking such decisions must be made in a mutually consistent way in order to see that it might be a useful abstraction to think about those decisions 'as if' they were all taken by one individual.

One thing that the reader should be careful about here is not to confuse the entrepreneur with another personification of a particular social function who sometimes turns up in discussions of the behaviour of market economies, namely, the 'capitalist'. Capitalists certainly exist as far as the following analysis is concerned, but only in the background. It is their role to own the capital equipment used by the firm in the production process, and to sell its services to the entrepreneur. Their income is derived from their ownership of capital, and is just as distinct from the entrepreneur's income as is their function in the organisation of production. The entrepreneur's '**profit**' is what is left from the proceeds of sales after the labour force has been paid for its services and capitalists have been paid for the use of their equipment.

To say that it is the task of the entrepreneur to plan and oversee the execution of the productive activities undertaken by the firm against the background of a market economy raises the following issue. It is often argued that a market economy operates so as to organise in a harmonious way the activities of numerous individual agents without any person or institution having to formulate an overall plan for the economy as a whole. The information and incentives conveyed to individual agents by prices are supposed to be sufficient to ensure that each one of them, pursuing their own self-interest, acts in a way that is compatible with the activities of everyone else without supervision of any sort. We analyse this proposition in Part VII. Such an argument, taken to an extreme, would seem to rule out the existence of firms as social institutions and to give no scope for entrepreneurial activity. It is after all of the very essence of a firm that those who provide productive services to it act under supervision, in accordance with a plan laid down by the entrepreneur, rather than as free agents making voluntary choices about their activities at each and every instant in response to price signals.

The apparent paradox involved here was first noted by Karl Marx, who used it to help justify the usefulness of what we would now call socialist planning for an industrial economy. He argued that if planning is useful at the level of the firm, it must be useful at the level of the economy as a whole as well. Much modern work in the field of industrial organisation, particularly that pioneered by Ronald Coase, rests upon an alternative response to this same paradox. The basis of that response is to note that whether any particular set of activities will be co-ordinated within a firm on a planning basis, or between individual agents by the use of market mechanisms, will depend on the relative costs of doing so in one way or the other. According to this view, market transactions *per se* are costly to undertake, so that if an entrepreneur can plan and co-ordinate aspects of individuals' behaviour more cheaply than they can be organised by market mechanisms, they can be compensated in the incomes they receive for the sacrifice of freedom they make in committing themselves in advance to obeying orders for the period of time for which they agree to work. In short, production activities come to be organised within firms when it is economical to do so.

This line of reasoning has enabled economists to begin to come to grips with a whole range of problems having to do with the factors that determine the extent of vertical and horizontal integration within industries and the way in which mergers between firms come about, not to mention many aspects of the behaviour of bureaucratic organisations in both the private and the public sectors. To deal with this wide range of subject matter would take us far beyond the scope of this book, but as readers work through the analysis of the behaviour of the firm that follows, they should constantly bear in mind that the analysis in question simply takes it for granted that firms exist. A deeper treatment of the way in which firms operate might go into the question of why they exist, and how they might evolve over time, along the lines so briefly described in the last few paragraphs. As we have already noted, such analysis does exist, and the material that follows in this book should therefore be regarded as constituting an introduction to the analysis of the behaviour of firms and industries, rather than as being anything approaching a comprehensive account of this branch of microeconomics.

Production

Just as market prices and income constrain the behaviour of households, so the technological possibilities of **production** constrain the decisions taken by the entrepreneur about the behaviour of the firm. The basic framework of the theory of the firm must concern itself to an important degree with the technical relationships involved in the transformation of such inputs as the services of labour and capital equipment into outputs of goods and services. That is why we devote this part of the book to dealing with these production relationships.

The notion of production is very general. Not only are physical goods produced, but also services, such as transportation, education, insurance and so forth. Any process which involves the transformation of one kind (or kinds) of good or service into another may be thought of as a process of production. However, as with consumption, so with production we can reduce the situation to an extremely basic and simple form and deal in detail with a fairly special case in order to get to grips with fundamental issues.

Therefore, in this chapter we will consider the production of good X, and will presume that there are but two inputs to its production. We will refer to these inputs, **factors of production** as they are usually called, as **capital** (K) and **labour** (L). It should be noted at the outset that just as the production of X is to be thought of as a *flow* of output, so the inputs into the production process should also be thought of in flow terms: K and L represent machine-hours and man-hours of productive services, not a stock of capital and a labour force.

The reader should not infer that it is possible to add together the services of all the manifold types of equipment and inventories used in a modern production process to give one unambiguous index number that measures the 'quantity of capital services' employed. Nor may one necessarily aggregate the hours worked by people of many different skills directly involved in production, to say nothing of those indirectly involved in a management or sales promotion role, into some unambiguously measurable quantity called 'the services of the labour force'. Nevertheless, the results of the two input/one output special case are both useful and often capable of being generalised, and are therefore well worth the reader's attention.

Activities and the isoquant

We start with the most primitive concept in the analysis of production, an **activity**. Carrying on an activity means combining flows of factor services per unit of time in a particular proportion and getting a rate of flow of output from doing so. Thus, in Figure 8.1 we depict an activity that involves combining machine services and labour services in the

Figure 8.1

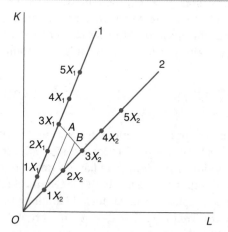

Inputs K and L are combined in given proportions along rays 1 and 2 in 'activities' that yield equal increments in the output of X for equal increments to inputs. Activity 1 and activity 2 may be combined at level of output $3X$ (or at any other level of output) to make any combination of capital and labour along the line $3X_1$, $3X_2$ available as a means of producing that level of output.

ratio 2/1 by a line labelled 1, and another that combines them in equal proportions by a line labelled 2. It is a reasonable initial simplifying assumption that if one doubles the quantities of inputs in any particular activity one will also double output, or, to put it more generally, that equiproportional increases in inputs will lead to equiproportional increases in output. This is the assumption of *constant returns to scale*. An equal distance moved along each activity line in Figure 8.1 thus represents an equal increase in both inputs and output.

Now there is no obvious reason why a firm should be confined exclusively to one production activity or another. It could presumably mix them. Thus, in Figure 8.1 it could produce an output of say $3X$ units of X by using all activity 1, all activity 2, or, by combining these activities in different proportions, it could obtain that level of output by combining capital and labour services anywhere along the line joining $3X_1$ and $3X_2$. For example, $3X$ units of X could be achieved by producing $2X$ units by activity 1 and $1X$ by activity 2, thus ending up at point A. The same output could be reached by producing $1X$ unit with activity 1 and $2X$ units with activity 2, thus ending up at point B. When readers work through Chapter 13 they will recognise the similarity between this analysis and that set out there, where we consider the possibilities of mixing different brands of a particular good in order to obtain a mixture of attributes between those available from exclusive consumption of one brand or another.

There is no reason to confine the analysis to the case of a firm having just two activities available to it. In principle, the analysis can be extended to an indefinitely large number of activities, but, for the sake of clarity alone, in Figure 8.2 we depict the case of four available activities, each using capital and labour services in different proportions. Any pair of activities may be used together, and so we have linked up each available pair of activities with straight lines as we did in Figure 8.1.

Figure 8.2

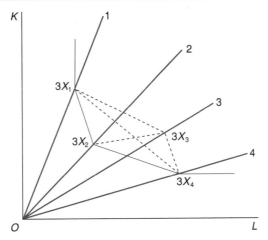

With four activities, any pair of them may be combined. Here the solid kinked line passing through $3X_1$, $3X_2$ and $3X_4$ shows the minimum combinations of capital and labour that will produce $3X$ units of output. Above activity line 1 this isoquant becomes vertical, and to the right of activity line 4 it becomes horizontal, because further additions to inputs in these directions add nothing to output.

At this point in the argument, even when apparently dealing with purely technological matters, we must introduce an assumption about the firm's motivation and behaviour if we are to proceed further. This assumption is that, whatever motivates those running the firm, they will never use more units of input than are necessary to get a given output. As we have drawn Figure 8.2, any output plan that utilises activity 3 requires more inputs for a given output than any plan that does not use it. This activity is said to be *technically inefficient* and will not be used by a firm seeking to minimise the inputs used for any output. Moreover any combination of 1 and 4 uses more inputs than combinations of 1 and 2 and 3 and 4, or 1, 2 and 4 alone. Thus, the kinked line linking the points $3X_1$, $3X_2$ and $3X_4$ gives the locus of the minimum combinations of factor inputs required for an output of $3X$ given prevailing technology. The line becomes vertical beyond $3X_1$ and horizontal beyond $3X_4$ to indicate that further increases of capital and labour beyond these points add nothing to output.

This kinked line is a simple special case of a much used analytic device in the economics of production. The output of X is the same at any point on it, and hence it is known as an 'equal product curve' or an 'iso-product curve' or, most frequently, an **isoquant**. The most important property of an isoquant is already implicit in the simple analysis carried out in Figure 8.2. It will never be concave towards the origin, and will in general be convex. In terms of Figure 8.2, the isoquant would have been concave to the origin if activity 3 had been used in its construction, for it would have contained the segment $3X_2$ $3X_3$ $3X_4$, but this segment is not part of the isoquant, because for any point on it there is a point on the line $3X_2$ $3X_4$ at which the same amount of output could be produced using fewer inputs.

In Figure 8.1, with two technically efficient activities we have a straight line isoquant; in Figure 8.2, with three such activities we have an isoquant that is kinked convexly to the origin. But we have already remarked that there is no need to confine ourselves to considering small numbers of activities. The more technically efficient activities there are, each using capital and labour services in different proportions, the more kinks there will

Figure 8.3 **A smooth production function**

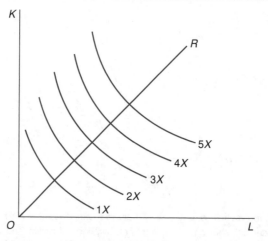

The isoquants show the maximum level of output to be had for each combination of inputs. As we move out along any ray (such as *OR*) drawn from the origin, inputs of capital and labour increase in equal proportions.

be in the isoquant, and the more will it come to resemble a smooth curve, convex to the origin. Just as along a particular consumer's indifference curve we plot all those bundles of goods the consumption of which will yield equal satisfaction, so along a smooth isoquant we plot all those combinations of factor services that will yield an equal level of output. A great deal of analysis is considerably simplified, with no important loss of accuracy, if we treat the various technically efficient factor combinations that will produce a given level of output as lying along a smooth curve such as, for example, 3X in Figure 8.3.

The production function

The previous section of this chapter was concerned with the various ways in which a particular level of output, 3X units of X, could be produced. The choice of this output level was, of course, quite arbitrary, and we could have carried out exactly the same analysis for any other level of output. Hence, there is not just one isoquant implicit in the foregoing analysis, but a whole family thereof, one for each conceivable level of output. A map of such isoquants is shown in Figure 8.3, which is a geometric representation of a **production function**. The output of X depends on – that is to say, is a *function* of – inputs of capital and labour services into the process. The isoquant map of Figure 8.3 tells us, for any combination of factor inputs, what the maximum attainable output of X will be. Equivalently, it also tells us, for any given level of output of X, what are the minimum combinations of inputs necessary to produce it. Provided that we are willing to think of inputs as being divisible into infinitely small units and of output as being similarly divisible, then we may also think of there being a smooth continuous isoquant passing through every point in Figure 8.3. However, as with the indifference map in consumer theory, it suffices for analytic purposes to draw only a selection of these. The rest of this chapter is devoted to looking at the properties of the production function in more detail.

Box 8.1   **Deriving isoquants**

We can readily derive the function for any isoquant from a Cobb-Douglas production function. Assume that the relationship between inputs (L and K) and output (X) is defined as follows:

$$X = AL^{0.75}K^{0.25} \tag{8.1.1}$$

This function is similar to that used to analyse consumer behaviour in earlier chapters. But a key difference is to include A on the right-hand side. This parameter defines 'total factor productivity' and shows the way in which output is determined, in part, by factors other than the factor inputs L and K. We can assume, without loss of generality, A = 10.

Using this function any isoquant can be derived. Rearranging the production function:

$$K^{0.25} = \frac{X}{10L^{0.75}}$$

so $$K = \frac{X^4}{10^4 L^3} \tag{8.1.2}$$

→

This expression defines the isoquant for any particular level of X. Fixing output to 10 units, the combinations of K and L required are defined by

$$K = \frac{1}{L^3}$$

Fixing output to 20 units, the combinations of K and L required are defined by

$$K = \frac{2^4}{L^3}$$

As an exercise readers can assume particular levels of L, calculate the corresponding required levels of K to produce 10 or 20 units of output, and show in a graph that the values of L and K define an isoquant that has the same general shape as shown in Figure 8.3.

Long-run and short-run analysis

Before proceeding, it will be useful to distinguish in general terms between two types of analysis: **long-run** analysis, which concerns the period when all inputs can be varied simultaneously, and **short-run** analysis, when some factors are assumed to be fixed and increments to output are assumed to derive solely from changes to variable factors. If the inputs are assumed to be capital and labour, then capital is taken to be the fixed factor in the short run, and labour the variable one. If we consider Figure 8.3 as a contour map for a three-dimensional diagram, with output rising vertically from the origin O, the long-run properties of the production function describe the shape of the whole hill. Within that context, we will be concerned with **returns to scale**, which describe the slope of the hill along a fixed capital–labour ratio (such as OR) from the origin, and the degree of *substitutability* between inputs, which has to do with the curvature around the hill at a given level of output, or the shape of the isoquant. The *short-run production function* describes the relationship between output and labour input for a given level of capital, and can be imagined as being characterised by a slice through the hill at any given level of capital $\bar{K}$. The relevant property of the short-run production function concerns how output varies with labour input alone or, more generally, **returns to a factor**.

The long-run production function: some preliminaries

Algebraically, we specify the two-input production function depicted in Figure 8.3 as

$$X = f(L, K) \tag{8.1}$$

We typically assume $f(\cdot)$ to be a *monotonic* function, one in which X rises as either L or K, or both, rise. It should always be possible to produce at least as much output as in an initial situation by using at least as much of each input as in that situation. This proposition implies that the firm can always dispose costlessly of inputs which are surplus to the minimum required to produce a given level of output, a characteristic sometimes referred to as *free disposal*.

Much of the analysis which follows will draw on the relationship between two variables which characterise the production function (8.1). First, the *average product* of a factor is output per unit of time divided by factor input per unit of time: X/L for labour and X/K for capital. These ratios are sometimes referred to, rather loosely, as labour and capital *productivity* respectively. Second, the *marginal product* of a factor is the increment to output per unit of time an increment of a factor input per unit of time, holding the other factor input constant. In the limit, when the increments become infinitesimal, they are therefore the partial derivatives of the production function (8.1). Hence $\partial X/\partial L$ is the marginal product of labour and $\partial X/\partial K$ is the marginal product of capital.

| Box 8.2 | **Calculating factor productivities** |

We can use the Cobb-Douglas function defined earlier in this chapter to calculate factor productivities. With

$$X = AL^{0.75}K^{0.25} \tag{8.1.1}$$

the average products of the factors are

$$\frac{X}{L} = \frac{AL^{0.75}K^{0.25}}{L} = \frac{AK^{0.25}}{L^{0.25}} = A\left(\frac{K}{L}\right)^{0.25} \tag{8.2.1}$$

$$\frac{X}{K} = \frac{AL^{0.75}K^{0.25}}{K} = A\left(\frac{L}{K}\right)^{0.75} \tag{8.2.2}$$

The marginal products of the factors are

$$\frac{\partial X}{\partial L} = 0.75AL^{0.75-1}K^{0.25} = 0.75A\left(\frac{K}{L}\right)^{0.25} \tag{8.2.3}$$

$$\frac{\partial X}{\partial K} = 0.25AL^{0.75}K^{0.25-1} = 0.25A\left(\frac{L}{K}\right)^{0.75} \tag{8.2.4}$$

In these expressions K/L measures the capital intensity of production, and L/K the labour intensity. If capital intensity increases we move upwards around any one isoquant indicating the increasing K/L. As this happens the average and marginal products of labour increase and average and marginal products of capital will fall. In short the productivity of any factor is determined (in part) by the levels of other inputs that are used. A second feature of these expressions is that as L increases $\partial X/\partial L$ declines and as K increases $\partial X/\partial K$ declines, i.e. we have diminishing marginal productivity.

Returns to scale

The concept of 'returns to scale' refers to what happens to output when every input is increased in equal proportion. In terms of a diagram such as Figure 8.3, equiproportional increases in both inputs involve moving out along a straight line, a ray, drawn from the origin. In general, we may speak of production functions displaying decreasing returns to scale, constant returns to scale, and increasing returns to scale. If successive equal increments of all factor inputs yield successively smaller increases in output, we have decreasing (or diminishing) returns to scale, if they yield equal increments in output we have constant returns to scale, and if they yield successively increasing increments in output we have increasing returns to scale.

The notion of returns to scale can be related to the production function (8.1) in the following way. Take equation (8.1) and note that if we start with a given level of inputs K and L, we will have some level of output X. Now, multiply K and L by some factor t, and note that output will change by some related multiplicative factor α. Thus we may write

$$\alpha X = f(tL, tK) \tag{8.2}$$

If, as we vary t, α varies in the same proportion, we have constant returns to scale; if it varies proportionately more, we have increasing returns; and if it varies proportionately less, we have decreasing returns.

Strictly speaking, statements about returns to scale characterise what happens over a particular range along a given ray through the origin, and do not necessarily describe the whole production function. If all we require of our isoquants is that they be smooth and convex to the origin, then it is easy indeed to construct a production function which yields constant returns along some rays and diminishing (or increasing) returns along others, or which yields successively increasing, constant and diminishing returns along the same ray. Nevertheless, there are special types of functional relationship for which what is true of one section of one ray through the origin is true of all sections of all rays. One class of such functions is called **homogeneous functions**.

Mathematically speaking a production function is homogeneous of degree k if

$$t^k X = t^k f(L, K) = f(tL, tK) \tag{8.3}$$

where k is a constant, $t > 0$ and, in terms of the notation used in (8.2), $t^k \equiv \alpha$.

Homogeneity implies two characteristics in the two input case. The first is that *all* the isoquants that cut *any one* ray through the origin do so with the same slope. This characteristic is known as **homotheticity**. Homothetic isoquants which are equidistant from one another along any one ray are also equidistant along any other. To move from one isoquant to another represents a definite cardinally measurable change in the level of output. The second characteristic of a homogeneous production function is that it displays the same returns to scale characteristics along any ray regardless of the input combination represented by that ray. Figure 8.4 depicts a special case of such a relationship: the constant returns to scale special case. Such a production function displays *homogeneity of degree one*. As the reader will see by comparing equations (8.2) and (8.3), $\alpha = t^k = t$ where $k = 1$, so that $d\alpha/dt = 1$.

Box 8.3	**More on returns to scale**

We can use the Cobb-Douglas function introduced in this chapter to derive an important result about returns to scale. The function used above is

$$X = AL^{0.75}K^{0.25} \tag{8.1.1}$$

If we double both inputs, i.e. using the notation just introduced set $t = 2$, we can define the corresponding change in output, i.e. α in the notation just introduced:

$$\alpha X = A(2L)^{0.75}(2K)^{0.25}$$

$$\alpha X = 2^{0.75}2^{0.25}AL^{0.75}K^{0.25} = 2AL^{0.75}K^{0.25}$$

as $\quad X = AL^{0.75}K^{0.25}$

$$\alpha X = 2X$$

i.e. $\quad \alpha = 2$

With our function, when inputs are doubled the output produced doubles, i.e. there are constant returns to scale. This result follows because the exponents sum to one with the result that $2^{0.75}2^{0.25} = 2$. If the exponents summed to more than one the production function would exhibit increasing returns to scale. With a sum less than one it would exhibit decreasing returns. This characteristic of a Cobb-Douglas production function is set out in general terms at the end of this chapter. The result derived here indicates a shortcoming of the Cobb-Douglas function: it cannot exhibit varying returns to scale.

If we return to thinking of the production function diagrammatically as a contour map of a hill, we can see that the assumption of homogeneity makes life a lot easier for us in describing the shape of the hill. It means that, as we move up the hill in any fixed direction (along OR, for example, Figure 8.3), the slope is changing at a constant rate. If we have constant returns to scale, that constant rate of change of the slope is in fact zero: that is, a slice through the hill from the origin along a K/L ray plots a straight line. Constant returns to scale are therefore a characteristic of what is often called *linear* production technology. The property of homotheticity implied by homogeneity means that the rate of change of the slope of the hill is not just constant but is the same along every possible K/L ray from the origin. The convenience of the assumption of homogeneity is

Figure 8.4 **A 'homogeneous of degree one' production function**

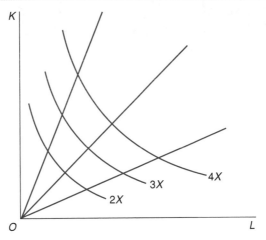

As we move out along any ray through the origin, equal increments in input yield equal increments in output. All isoquants have the same slope as they pass through any particular ray.

this. It enables us to provide a simple summary statistic, a single number measuring the degree of homogeneity of the function, that describes the way in which output changes with all inputs. This statistic is independent both of the level output of used and of the capital–labour ratio. These properties are so convenient that homogeneity is a commonly made assumption in applied work on production functions.

Homogeneity is a very strong assumption to make about the nature of technology, however. It is not hard to think of examples where returns to scale are initially increasing with output, and then become either constant or diminishing beyond a certain point. In the former case the output level where increasing returns change into constant returns is called *minimum efficient scale* of production. We will return to this notion again when we consider the shape of *cost functions*, the nature of which will be shown to be directly associated with the returns to scale characteristics of the production function. The point to note at this stage is that though homogeneity implies homotheticity as a characteristic of a production function, homotheticity does not require homogeneity. To put it precisely, homogeneity is sufficient for homotheticity, but it is not necessary. Homotheticity is in fact a weaker assumption, which can be retained even after the assumption of homogeneity has been relaxed.

Box 8.4	Constant returns with a Cobb-Douglas function

We know from Box 8.3 that when we use a Cobb-Douglas function in which the exponents sum to one it exhibits constant returns to scale, i.e. it is homogeneous of degree one. The important characteristic of such a function shown in Figure 8.4 can be readily illustrated with the following function:

$$X = AL^{0.75}K^{0.25} \tag{8.1.1}$$

As above we can assume $A = 10$. We know from Box 8.1 that with a fixed level of output $\bar{X}$ the isoquant is defined as

$$K = \frac{\bar{X}^4}{10^4 L^3} = \frac{\bar{X}^4}{10^4}L^{-3} \tag{8.1.2}$$

The slope of this isoquant is shown by its first derivative:

$$\frac{dK}{dL} = \frac{-3\bar{X}^4}{10^4}L^{-4} = \frac{-3\bar{X}^4}{10^4 L^4} \tag{8.4.1}$$

So, for example, with 10 units of output the slope of the isoquant for this output level is defined for any particular value of L by

$$\frac{dK}{dL} = \frac{-3}{L^4}$$

and, again for any value of L, for 20 units of output isoquant its slope is

$$\frac{dK}{dL} = \frac{-3(2^4)}{L^4}$$

To see the property that the slopes of the different isoquants are the same along any ray from the origin (as set out in Figure 8.4) we can recognise that any ray from the origin defines a constant capital labour ratio (K/L), i.e. constant capital intensity. We can define the capital intensity using the Cobb-Douglas production function (8.1.1). Multiplying the top and bottom of the right hand side of the production function by $L^{0.25}$:

$$X = \frac{10L^{0.75}L^{0.25}K^{0.25}}{L^{0.25}} = 10L\left(\frac{K}{L}\right)^{0.25}$$

Rearranging:

$$\frac{K}{L} = \frac{X^4}{10^4 L^4} \tag{8.4.2}$$

Combining this expression for the capital labour ratio with the slope of any isoquant (8.4.1):

$$\frac{dK}{dL} = \frac{-3\bar{X}^4}{10^4 L^4} = -3\frac{K}{L} \tag{8.4.3}$$

It follows from (8.4.3) that, with our production function, if we expand along a ray defined by a constant capital intensity, i.e. unchanged K/L, the slopes of all the isoquants are the same at $-3(K/L)$. This is the key characteristic of a function that is homogeneous of degree one, i.e. exhibits constant returns to scale. The value -3 in this final expression is determined by the relative sizes of the exponents in the production function.

Factors leading to variable returns to scale

Now the production function derived from activity analysis obviously displays constant returns to scale, and the question must arise as to how any production function could display any other characteristic. The key simplifying assumption that yields this property is that it is possible to carry on any activity, with equal efficiency, at any level of output. This need not always be so. In agriculture, for example, it is not the case that, simply by halving all inputs, including the size of the field, one also halves output, nor that output can be doubled merely by doubling all inputs. There are technical indivisibilities here that make it impossible to utilise certain types of technology at small output levels and that make it preferable to switch from one technical process to another as the scale of output changes. The type of harvesting equipment used on large North American type farms cannot be used effectively on the small farms that at one time dominated British agriculture, and are still widespread in continental Europe. Or, to give another example, in the battery production of eggs, if one wishes to double the number of hens housed, it is far from clear that it is technically most efficient to double the air space of the buildings in which they are housed. There is no reason to suppose that the amount of inputs needed to heat the henhouses in question will be doubled for, even if one did just double the air space of the building by, for example, doubling its floor area, one would not double the area of its outside surfaces, nor would one double its propensity to heat loss. Nor, of course, would one double the building materials required to erect the building by doubling its air space.

We could multiply examples like this *ad nauseam*, but enough ought now to have been said to convince the reader that a production function that everywhere displays constant returns to scale is a special case, albeit, perhaps, a useful and relevant special case. A priori, there is nothing in general that can be said about the returns to scale characteristics of production functions. One can have decreasing, constant or increasing returns to scale, or indeed a combination of all three in any production function. It depends upon the nature of the technology that is available to a particular industry.

Substitutability

Substitutability, the second key property of production functions to which we referred earlier, characterises the rate at which capital can be used to replace, or can be **substituted** for, labour (or vice versa) in the production process, while holding output constant. Two limiting cases of substitutability can easily be identified.

Suppose first that the firm has only one production activity available to it. For example, suppose we require the services of three machines and five people to produce one unit of *X* per unit of time; six machines and ten people to produce two units of *X*; and so on. If we have only six machines, the maximum attainable output level is therefore 6*X*, regardless of the number of workers available. Additional workers can produce nothing without equipment to operate. Similarly, if the labour force is 25, output has a fixed maximum of five, even if we have 30 or 40 machines. Additional capital cannot increase output without additional labour made available in *fixed proportion* to capital. In this case there is no possibility of substituting workers for capital, or vice versa, in the production process. The degree of substitutability between the factors is zero. Assuming constant returns, the isoquant map for this case is illustrated in Figure 8.5(a). The production

Figure 8.5

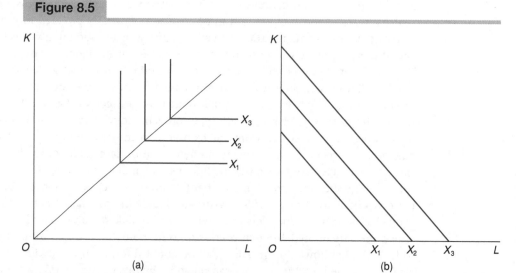

(a) Fixed proportions technology, with constant returns to scale.

(b) Inputs are perfect substitutes, with constant returns to scale.

function for fixed proportions technology, sometimes called *Leontief* technology in reference to the economist who first analysed it in detail, may be written as

$$X = f(L, K) = \min(L, K) \tag{8.4}$$

Suppose, on the other hand, that technology is such that a unit of the capital equipment used can do exactly the same job as a certain number of workers. Such a case might arise if capital equipment took the form of robots. From the point of view of output, we could therefore use either an additional robot or a certain number of additional people to produce a given increment of production. In this case, capital and labour are said to be *perfect substitutes* for each other, and the isoquants of a production technology characterised by perfect substitutability are illustrated in Figure 8.5(b). The relevant production function may be written in the following general form:

$$X = f(L, K) = aL + bK \tag{8.5}$$

In the special case where inputs can be substituted at a ratio of 1:1, $a = b = 1$, and the isoquants will cut the L and K axes with an angle of 45°.

Figures 8.5(a) and 8.5(b) illustrate the limiting cases of zero and perfect (infinite) substitutability respectively. As we have seen, if production possibilities are adequately described by an array of activities which can be operated independently, then weighed averages of pairs of activities provide feasible ways of producing output, as well as the use of a single activity. It is this possibility which underlies the common assumption that isoquants are *convex* to the origin, as they are drawn in Figure 8.3. Such a technology is characterised by less than perfect, but more than zero, substitutability between factors.

The elasticity of substitution

To investigate the concept of substitutability further, consider the slope of the isoquant. This slope is referred to as the **marginal rate of technical substitution (mrts)** between inputs. The marginal rate of technical substitution between labour and capital is denoted $mrts_{LK}$. It measures the rate at which the firm will have to substitute one input for another in order to keep output constant. A precise formula for the marginal rate of technical substitution can be derived by first of all taking the total differential of production function (8.1):

$$dX = \frac{\partial X}{\partial L}dL + \frac{\partial X}{\partial K}dK \tag{8.6}$$

Note that, along any isoquant, inputs are varied while the level of output is fixed. The slope of the isoquant is thus dL/dK when $dX = 0$. Rearranging (8.6) on the assumption that $dX = 0$ yields

$$mrts_{KL} = \frac{dL}{dK} = \frac{\partial X/\partial K}{\partial X/\partial L} \tag{8.7}$$

The marginal rate of technical substitution of labour for capital at any point therefore equals the ratio of the marginal product of capital to that of labour, and vice versa. For the case of fixed proportions, the marginal products are not defined and the discontinuous *mrts* is therefore also not defined. For the case of perfect substitutes, from (8.5), $\partial X/\partial L = a$ and $\partial X/\partial K = b$. The slope of the isoquant (dL/dK) is therefore given by the constant ratio $-b/a$.

As we noted in our discussion of the demand curve in Chapter 2, the slope of a curve is an unsatisfactory number with which to characterise the sensitivity of quantity demanded to price, because it is not independent of the units of measurement. The need for a measure whose value is independent of units of measurement arises also when we characterise the degree of substitutability between factors. In the case of the demand curve, the concept of the *elasticity* of demand provided us with a useful and unit-free measure of the sensitivity of quantity demanded to price. In the case of the isoquant, there is an analogous notion, the **elasticity of substitution**.

Assuming that isoquants are convex, the marginal rate of technical substitution of labour for capital will decline in algebraic terms, and increase in absolute value, as labour is substituted for capital along the isoquant. At the same time, of course, the capital–labour ratio will be diminishing. The *elasticity of substitution* is a pure number which is defined as the proportionate change in factor proportions (K/L) that takes place as we move around an isoquant, divided by the proportionate change in the marginal rate of technical substitution that simultaneously occurs. Hence denoting the elasticity of substitution by σ, we have

$$\sigma \equiv \frac{\partial(K/L)}{K/L} \frac{\partial(mrts_{LK})}{mrts_{LK}} \equiv \frac{\partial(K/L)}{K/L} \bigg/ \frac{\partial(\partial K/\partial L)}{\partial K/\partial L} \tag{8.8}$$

As the reader will intuitively see, the more easily capital is replaced by labour, the less will be the proportional change in the marginal rate of technical substitution of labour for capital as the capital–labour ratio falls, and the greater in absolute value will our measure of the elasticity of substitution be. In the limiting case of perfect substitutability, the *mrts* will not change at all, and the elasticity of substitution will be infinite.

Box 8.5 **The elasticity of substitution**

Any elasticity measures the response of one variable to a change in another, for example demand in response to price or income, investment in response to interest rate changes. In all cases the changes are measured in proportionate terms and so any elasticity is a unit free measure of responsiveness. The elasticity of substitution follows these basic principles and can be explained in terms of Illustration 8.1. We have an isoquant defined for the fixed output level X_1. As we move round the isoquant from point A to point B we see that the slope of the isoquant (the marginal rate of technical substitution) changes and simultaneously the capital labour ratio (K/L) declines. The elasticity of substitution measures the extent to which labour can be substituted for capital (or vice versa) by combining these two changes.

As set out in the text the elasticity of substitution is

$$\sigma = \text{(proportionate change in } K/L)/\text{(proportionate change in } mrts)$$

$$= \frac{\partial(K/L)}{K/L} \bigg/ \frac{\partial(\partial K/\partial L)}{\partial K/\partial L}$$

Illustration 8.1

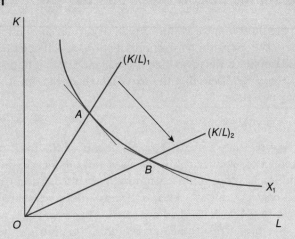

We can calculate this elasticity of substitution using the Cobb-Douglas function introduced above:

$$X = 10L^{0.75}K^{0.25} \tag{8.1.1}$$

Assume that a firm becomes less capital intensive with a reduction in K/L from 2.5 to 2. The proportionate change in K/L, i.e. the numerator in the formula for σ, is therefore

$$\frac{2.5 - 2}{2.5} = 0.2 \tag{8.5.1}$$

We know from Box 8.4 that with our Cobb-Douglas function the *mrts* is

$$\frac{\partial K}{\partial L} = -3\frac{K}{L} \tag{8.4.3}$$

With $K/L = 2.5$ the *mrts* $= -7.5$, and with $K/L = 2$ the *mrts* $= -6$. So the proportionate change in the *mrts* is

$$\frac{-7.5 - (-6)}{-7.5} = 0.2 \tag{8.5.2}$$

It follows that with our Cobb-Douglas function

$$\sigma = \frac{0.2}{0.2} = 1 \tag{8.5.3}$$

Readers can use different values for the change in K/L but will always find that with a Cobb-Douglas function $\sigma = 1$. This finding is presented in general terms at the end of this chapter. It implies that the slopes of the isoquants with a Cobb-Douglas function are always defined by the characteristic that for any move around an isoquant the percentage change in capital intensity is the same as the percentage change in *mrts*.

The short-run production function and returns to a factor

In the short run, we assume capital to be held constant while only labour and output can vary. The short-run production function, which describes the interaction of labour input and output, is thus two-dimensional and is easier to analyse. It is depicted geometrically in Figure 8.6. Denoting the fixed capital stock by $\bar{K}$, the short-run production function may be written

$$X = f(L, \bar{K}) \tag{8.9}$$

We typically assume that increments to the fixed capital stock *increase* the average product of labour, or shift the short-run production function upwards. (The reasons for and implications of this assumption are discussed in Chapter 18.) More important than this characteristic, however, is the upward convex shape we have given to the function in Figure 8.6, which we shall now discuss in some detail.

The production function, whether long-run or short-run, is basically a technical relationship; economics takes it as given and classifies the characteristics it may display. However, this does not mean that it displays no dominant characteristics of particular importance to economics. When it comes to *returns to a factor*, which characterise the short-run production function, we may say something very definite about its nature, namely, that in the region that is relevant for analysing the behaviour of competitive firms, the short-run production function displays *decreasing* or **diminishing returns to a**

Figure 8.6

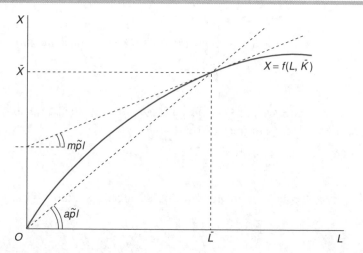

$X = f(L, \bar{K})$ is a short-run production function showing how output varies with labour input when capital is held constant at $\bar{K}$. The average product of labour at each level of employment is given by the slope of a line from the point on the production function to the origin. When $L = \bar{L}$, $X = \bar{X}$ and hence the average product of labour, $a\tilde{p}l$ is given by $\bar{X}/L$. The marginal product of labour is the slope at the tangent to the production function at each level of employment. When $\bar{L} = \bar{L}$, $\partial X/\partial L = m\tilde{p}l$. Concavity of the short-run production function implies that the average product always exceeds the marginal product of labour.

factor. The concept of returns to a factor refers to what happens to output as successively equal increments of one input are combined with a fixed quantity of other inputs; about what happens as we move along the short-run production function. It is this characteristic of diminishing returns which is embodied in the convex shape of the relationship portrayed in Figure 8.6.

This property of diminishing returns relates the way that the marginal product of a factor changes with its level of employment. More formally as in the case of labour it may be described in terms of the sign of the derivative of the marginal product of labour with respect to labour which is the second derivative of the short-run production function and second partial derivative of the long-run one, again with respect to labour. What is sometimes called 'the law of diminishing returns' therefore refers to the assumption that

$$\frac{\partial}{\partial L}\left(\frac{\partial X}{\partial L}\right) = \frac{\partial^2 X}{\partial L^2} < 0 \tag{8.10}$$

This assumption is satisfied when the short-run production function is upwards convex, as in Figure 8.6. In terms of Figure 8.7, we use an isoquant map to illustrate diminishing returns to a factor. We ask what happens to output as we move along a line drawn perpendicular to the capital axis, and hence what happens to output as we vary labour and hold capital constant. To postulate diminishing returns to labour (indeed to either factor) involves postulating successively decreasing increments in output for equal increments in the factor in question, labour in this case.

Figure 8.7

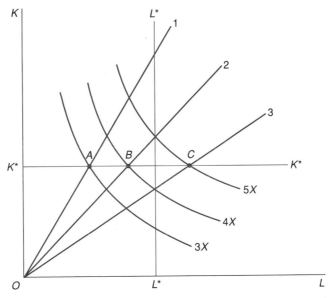

This homogeneous of degree one production function displays constant returns to scale but diminishing returns to a factor. Thus, as we move along K^*K^*, the movement from A to B to C involves successively greater increases in labour input for equal increments in output. Note that this movement takes us from ray 1 to 2 to 3, so that the isoquants become progressively less steep as we move to the right.

More on diminishing returns

To say that diminishing returns to a factor always exist in the region that is relevant for analysing the behaviour of the firm is to say two things: first, that it is usual for production functions to display in some region diminishing returns to a factor regardless of their returns to scale characteristics; second, that firms behave in such a way as to ensure that such a tendency exists in the region of the production function upon which they choose to operate. Since we have not yet said anything about what motivates this behaviour of firms, we cannot take up this second point at this stage, but it is easy to show that the tendency to diminishing returns is present in almost any production function.

In Figure 8.7 the production function which we have drawn displays constant returns to scale along any ray drawn out from the origin, and the isoquants that describe it are convex to the origin. These two properties are enough to ensure diminishing returns to both capital (as we move along $L*L*$) and to labour (as we move along $K*K*$) because along either of these lines isoquants showing successively equal increases in output are growing further and further apart. That this must be the case is easily seen. Let us consider the case of increasing labour inputs. The isoquant that cuts $K*K*$ at C is more shallowly sloped than that which cuts it at B, which in turn is more shallowly sloped than A. The further to the right we move along $K*K*$ the more rapidly is each isoquant moving away from the one to the left of it, and the wider the horizontal gap between successive curves. Only if the isoquants were straight lines touching both axes would there be no tendency for diminishing returns to a factor when returns to scale are constant.

Even the simple isoquant map based on the existence of two activities presented in Figure 8.1, and drawn here as Figure 8.8, would display diminishing returns, and in a

Figure 8.8

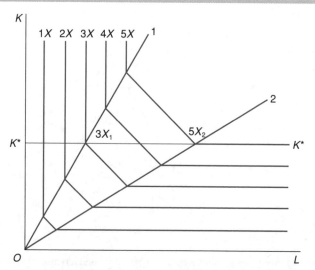

Diminishing returns to labour with but two constant returns to scale activities. Equal increments in labour yield equal increments in output along $K*K*$ until point $3X_1$. Thereafter, increments to output continue but at a smaller size until point $5X_2$. Thereafter, further increments to labour inputs add nothing to output.

dramatic way. With a given quantity of capital of $K*$ we would have constant returns to labour up to output $3X$. Here there is enough labour to make activity 1 fully viable. We would then have constant positive returns to labour (but at a lower rate) between level of output $3X$ and level of output $5X$. At the latter point, activity 2 would be the only one in use and further increments of labour could not be productively employed without adding to the capital stock. In short, returns to labour, holding capital constant, would suddenly diminish to zero at output level $5X$.

If returns to a factor always end up diminishing when returns to scale are constant, it should be obvious that they also diminish when returns to scale decrease. If, in terms of Figure 8.7, successive increments of capital or labour, holding the other factor constant, lead to successively smaller increases in output when equal movements along any ray through the origin yield equal increments in output, they must also do so when equidistant movements out from the origin yield successively smaller increments in output. Diminishing returns to scale accentuate the tendency of a production function to display diminishing returns to a factor. If a production function displays increasing returns to scale this can offset the tendency to diminishing returns to a factor, and indeed as we show below it is mathematically possible to write down equations for production functions in which returns to scale increase so rapidly that returns to a factor never begin to diminish. However, what is mathematically possible is not always empirically plausible, and such cases are logical curiosities rather than practically relevant examples.

In the real world, it is clear that the tendency to diminishing returns to a factor is ubiquitous. No matter what the technical process of production is like, and no matter what might happen to its productivity if all inputs into it are increased in proportion, if only one input is increased, sooner or later that input is going to find it harder and harder to find units of other inputs to co-operate with; it may even begin to get in the way of production simply by its physical presence. The contribution of extra units of this factor to production is then inevitably going to diminish. One cannot indefinitely cram more and more machines into a given building with a given labour force; one cannot indefinitely add workers to a production line; one cannot put more and more hens into a given henhouse; one cannot put more and more fertiliser on a given plot of land, and not expect to see the extra units of the input that is being varied make a diminishing contribution in terms of additions to output.

The general Cobb-Douglas function

In this chapter we have developed a large number of categories and definitions of relevance to producer theory, which have wide theoretical use and considerable empirical relevance. In both theoretical and empirical work, analysts frequently simplify matters by assuming that technology takes a specific form. A particularly convenient specification of the production function, which we have already used in several boxes, is the *Cobb-Douglas*, named after its originators. Our purpose in this section is to use the Cobb-Douglas function as an example to illustrate the material which went before, and to derive the key parameters of interest in production theory.[1]

The **Cobb-Douglas production function** takes the form

$$X = f(L, K) = AL^{\alpha}K^{\beta} \tag{8.11}$$

The parameter A translates units of inputs into units of output, while α and β determine the responsiveness of output to increments in factor inputs. The Cobb-Douglas function has been widely used in empirical work. By taking logs of (8.11) we obtain

$$\ln X = \ln A + \alpha \ln L + \beta \ln K \tag{8.12}$$

The Cobb-Douglas function thus specifies technology as linear in the logarithms of variables, and this property renders it particularly amenable to econometric analysis.

Let us investigate the returns to scale characteristics of this function with more generality than we did in Boxes 8.3 and 8.4. Let us suppose first that

$$\alpha + \beta = 1, \text{ so } \beta = 1 - \alpha$$

In this case (8.11) becomes

$$X = A \left(\frac{L}{K} \right)^{\alpha} K \tag{8.13}$$

If we increase L and K in equal proportions, their ratio does not change, so the term $A(L/K)^{\alpha}$ remains the same. However, K has changed by a given proportion, and equation (8.13) implies that X will change in the same proportion. For example, a doubling of both inputs will exactly double output. Hence the assumption $\alpha + \beta = 1$ implies that the Cobb-Douglas function displays constant returns to scale.

More generally, we may take the differential of (8.11):

$$dX = \alpha A L^{\alpha-1} K^{\beta} dL + \beta A L^{\alpha} K^{\beta-1} dK \tag{8.14}$$

which, substituting from (8.11) can be rewritten as

$$dX = \alpha \frac{X}{L} dL + \beta \frac{X}{K} dK \tag{8.15}$$

The notion of returns to scale refers to the way in which output changes as both inputs vary, holding factor proportions, the ratio K/L, constant. Suppose then, that

$$\frac{dL}{L} = \frac{dK}{K} \tag{8.16}$$

Hence (8.15) becomes

$$dX = X \frac{dL}{L} (\alpha + \beta) = X \frac{dK}{K} (\alpha + \beta) \tag{8.17}$$

or

$$\frac{dX}{X} = \frac{dL}{L} (\alpha + \beta) = \frac{dK}{K} (\alpha + \beta) \tag{8.18}$$

If $\alpha + \beta = 1$, as we have already seen, output increases in strict proportion to labour (or capital) input so long as the capital–labour ratio is held constant, and we have constant returns to scale. If $\alpha + \beta > 1$, output increases proportionately more than labour (or capital) input and we have increasing returns to scale. On the other hand, $\alpha + \beta < 1$ implies diminishing returns to scale.

In the Cobb-Douglas case, so long as α and β are each less than one, the marginal products of factors decline as their use increases, and bear a constant proportion to average products. From (8.15), when $dK = 0$, we have, as the marginal product of labour,

$$\frac{\partial X}{\partial L} = \alpha \frac{X}{L} \tag{8.19}$$

Similarly when $dL = 0$,

$$\frac{\partial X}{\partial K} = \beta \frac{X}{K} \tag{8.20}$$

Note that X/L and X/K are the average products of labour and capital respectively. The second derivatives are

$$\frac{\partial^2 X}{\partial L^2} = \alpha(\alpha - 1)\frac{X}{L^2} \tag{8.21}$$

and

$$\frac{\partial^2 X}{\partial K^2} = \beta(\beta - 1)\frac{X}{K^2} \tag{8.22}$$

respectively. Hence, if α and β are less than 1, these second derivatives are negative and so marginal products (the first derivatives) diminish. We therefore confirm that diminishing returns to a factor will coexist with constant returns ($\alpha + \beta = 1$) and diminishing ($\alpha + \beta < 1$) returns to scale, and may coexist with increasing ($\alpha + \beta > 1$) returns to scale. Note, however, that if α or β were to be greater than 1, labour or capital respectively would yield increasing returns as it was varied, holding the other input constant. Thus the 'law of diminishing returns' is an economic proposition about the empirical properties of real-world production processes. It is not a mathematically necessary property of any logically conceivable production function.

Now let us consider the elasticity of substitution (see 8.7). The marginal rate of technical substitution in the Cobb-Douglas case is given by

$$mrts_{LK} = \frac{dL}{dK} = -\frac{\partial X/\partial K}{\partial X/\partial L} = \frac{-\beta X}{K} \bigg/ \frac{\alpha X}{L} = \frac{-\beta}{\alpha} \frac{L}{K} \tag{8.23}$$

Convexity of the isoquant implies that the slope of the isoquant ($-dL/dK$) increases as L/K increases. This will hold provided $\alpha, \beta > 0$.

The elasticity of substitution can be derived as follows. Recall that

$$\sigma \equiv \frac{\partial(K/L)}{K/L} \bigg/ \frac{\partial(\partial K/\partial L)}{\partial K/\partial L} \tag{8.8}$$

From (8.23) we have

$$\partial K/\partial L = -\frac{\alpha K}{\beta L} \tag{8.24}$$

so

$$\frac{\partial K/\partial L}{K/L} = -\frac{\alpha}{\beta} \tag{8.25}$$

Differentiating $\partial K/\partial L$ with respect to K/L yields

$$\frac{\partial(\partial K/\partial L)}{\partial(K/L)} = -\frac{\alpha}{\beta} \tag{8.26}$$

Hence, substituting (8.25) and (8.26) into (8.8) we have

$$\sigma \equiv -\frac{-\alpha}{\beta} \bigg/ \frac{-\alpha}{\beta} = 1 \tag{8.27}$$

The Cobb-Douglas production function therefore is always characterised by an elasticity of substitution of unity. This holds regardless of its returns to scale characteristics, or, more generally, of the values attached to the parameters α and β.

We have already noted that the short-run Cobb-Douglas production function, $X = AL^\alpha \bar{K}^\beta$, with a fixed capital stock $\bar{K}$, displays a diminishing average and marginal product of labour provided $\alpha < 1$. The marginal product is, as we have seen, $\alpha X/L$ and the average product is of course X/L. We noted previously that diminishing returns to a factor implies that the marginal product is regularly less than the average product. In this case,

$$\frac{X/L}{\partial X/\partial L} = \frac{1}{\alpha} \tag{8.28}$$

so

$$\frac{X}{L} > \frac{\partial X}{\partial L} \text{ provided that } \alpha < 1 \tag{8.29}$$

Finally note that the effect of an increase in the capital stock on the marginal product of labour is given by substituting (8.11) into (8.19) and differentiating with respect to K, to obtain

$$\frac{\partial^2 X}{\partial L \partial K} = \frac{\alpha \beta X}{LK} > 0 \text{ provided that } \alpha, \beta > 0 \tag{8.30}$$

Hence in the Cobb-Douglas case, increases in capital shift the short-run production function upwards, and increase the marginal (and average) product of labour. It is also the case that

$$\frac{\partial^2 X}{\partial K \partial L} = \frac{\beta \alpha X}{KL} > 0 \text{ provided that } \alpha, \beta > 0 \tag{8.31}$$

which establishes that the cross derivatives of the Cobb-Douglas function are symmetric. An increase in labour input has the same impact on the marginal and average products of capital as does an increase in capital inputs on the marginal and average products of labour.

Concluding comment

It might be helpful to summarise the points developed in this chapter. We have argued that the production function is a technical relationship between the rate of flow of factor services put into a production process and the rate of flow of output emerging from it.

When inputs are increased in equal proportion, we describe the consequences for output in terms of the concept of returns to scale, and we have seen that a production function may be characterised by decreasing, constant, or increasing returns to scale. Indeed, it may exhibit a combination of these characteristics as output increases over different ranges.

A second important property of the long-run production function is the degree of substitutability between the inputs required to produce a given level of output. Technology can display a range of degrees of substitutability from zero to perfect substitutability. This property of substitutability is measured by the elasticity of substitution.

When we analyse the short-run production function, and only one factor is varied, holding constant the quantities of all the others, we speak of the consequences in terms of returns to that factor. Though certain production functions *may*, logically speaking, display a tendency to increasing returns to a factor, the overwhelming general tendency here is for returns to a factor to diminish, and as we shall see below, competitive firms always operate in the region of the production function where they do diminish. The importance of all this, as far as the behaviour of firms is concerned, is that the production function provides a vital link between their behaviour in goods markets with that in markets for factors of production. We shall begin to investigate this link in the remainder of this part.

SUMMARY

Properties of the production function

1. The decision-making role in the firm is often personified in the form of the entrepreneur. The entrepreneur is assumed to make the decisions upon which the organisation of production depends, such as setting the price at which the product is to be sold, or deciding on the quantities to be supplied.

2. If the market will organise in an efficient way the co-ordination of production and consumption decisions, why do firms exist? The answer to this question, given by Ronald Coase, was that activities will be co-ordinated either within the firm or by the market depending on relative costs.

3. The decisions of entrepreneurs are constrained by the technological possibilities of production. We therefore need a way to describe the technical relationships involved in the transformation of such inputs as the services of labour and capital equipment into outputs of goods and services. These technical relationships are summarised in the production function.

4. A production function can be represented geometrically by a map of isoquants. We often assume that isoquants are smooth and convex to the origin. Each isoquant describes the technically efficient combination of factors required to produce a given output; it tells us the minimum combinations of inputs necessary for the production of a given quantity of X.

5. Economists use two key properties to characterise production functions. The first refers to how output adjusts when the quantity of all inputs is increased. Production functions are said to yield constant, diminishing or increasing returns to scale. The second is the degree of interchangeability between the inputs required to produce a given level of output. This property is characterised with reference to the elasticity of substitution.

6. The distinction between the short-run and the long-run production function is important. When we analyse the short-run production function, one input, usually capital, is assumed to be constant, while labour is varied. In the long run, both capital and labour inputs are varied.

7. The increments to output that occur as we change the variable factor, holding the fixed factor constant, are referred to as returns to a factor. If productivity on the margin declines with input of the variable factor, it is said that the variable factor yields diminishing returns.

8. It is sufficiently common to assume diminishing returns to a factor that we often speak of a 'law' of diminishing returns. However, this 'law' is an empirical generalisation, not a logically necessary property of any conceivable production function.

9. With Cobb-Douglas technology, we find that diminishing returns to a factor are consistent with diminishing, constant and increasing returns to scale. However, increasing returns to a factor may arise in the presence of sufficiently rapidly increasing returns to scale.

PROBLEMS

1 A firm uses capital and labour to produce a single output, and its production function displays increasing returns to scale at all levels of output.

(a) Does this imply that the average products of labour and capital are increasing?
(b) Does this imply that the marginal products of labour and capital are increasing?
(c) Does this imply that the short-run average cost curve is downward sloping?
(d) Does this imply that the long-run average cost curve is necessarily downward sloping?

2 (a) Do diminishing marginal returns to a factor imply diminishing average returns to a factor?
(b) Do diminishing marginal returns to a factor imply diminishing returns to scale?
(c) If every factor generates diminishing marginal returns to a factor, does that imply factors are perfect substitutes for each other?
(d) If every factor generates diminishing marginal returns to a factor, does that imply that factors are perfect complements?

3 'Since an entrepreneur can always build the same factory next door, there is no reason to believe that long-run average costs will actually ever increase as output rises.' Discuss.

4 Suppose that the long-run production function which describes how labour and capital generate output is homothetic and displays constant returns to scale.

(a) Will the expansion path be upward sloping and convex for given input prices?
(b) Under what conditions will the long-run average cost curve be downward sloping?

Note

1. The reader will recall that we used the Cobb-Douglas form as a special case of the utility function in Chapter 2.

CHAPTER 9

Cost functions

Key words and phrases

- cost minimisation
- wages, machine rental price
- cost functions, expansion path, total, average, and marginal cost
- long-run and short-run cost functions, the envelope, U-shaped long-run average cost curve, fixed and variable costs

Introduction

The cost function is central to the economics of the firm. It is the relationship that enables us to translate market prices of individual factors of production into costs of production for output, and to derive from market prices of output the prices which firms are willing to pay in order to obtain factors of production. This chapter uses the production function to clarify the way in which production costs vary with the level of output.

As the reader might guess, it is always logically possible to construct peculiar special case production functions that in turn yield peculiar relationships between output levels and costs. In what follows, we normally stick to dealing with homogeneous (or at least homothetic) production functions (described in Chapter 8) in order to keep the analysis manageable. Some results are not therefore quite general. Nevertheless, they are sufficiently widely applicable to provide an adequate basis for the analysis of firm behaviour that is dealt with in later chapters.

We said earlier that a firm would seek to produce any given output utilising no more inputs than were necessary. Such behaviour is a consequence of a more basic proposition about the behaviour of firms, namely that whatever level of output they choose to produce, they will do so at the minimum possible cost. This in turn is an implication of the basic assumption of the so-called neo-classical theory of the firm, that the entrepreneur's motive is to maximise profit. We will discuss this assumption at some length below but, for the moment, the reader need only accept the weaker **cost minimisation** hypothesis as a basis for the following analysis.

Expenditure on inputs and the cost function

Let us continue to assume that the firm whose behaviour we are to study produces only good X, and uses the services of labour and capital in its production. Let us further assume that, in relation to the markets for these inputs, the firm stands in very much the same way as did the consumer of Part I in relation to the markets for X and Y. That is to say, the prices the firm must pay for labour services and for capital services do not vary with the amounts bought. Input prices are therefore exogenous to the firm.

The measurement of input prices, though straightforward, is worth explicit attention. As we have seen, inputs are measured in flow terms – in hours worked per week or per month as far as labour is concerned; as to capital, the appropriate input measure is also a flow, for example machine hours or machine weeks per week or month. Thus, the relevant price for labour is the **wage** per hour worked, denoted w, and the relevant price of capital is emphatically *not* the price of a new machine. Rather it is the hourly or weekly rental price of a machine, denoted r. Though machinery is sometimes leased, it is more typically owned by the firm that uses it, but in this case the reader might find it helpful to think of the firm renting the machine from itself. The **rental price of the machine** is given by what the firm forgoes, per hour, or per week, by owning the machine. That amount is clearly the interest that the firm could earn per hour or per week on the funds tied up in the machine (the normal net rate of return on capital in the economy times the value of the machine) plus any depreciation (or minus any appreciation) in its value. The rental price of the machine is the *opportunity* cost of owning it.

Total cost can be defined as the sum of outlays on labour, L, and capital, K:

$$C = wL + rK \tag{9.1}$$

A **cost function**, however, describes how the *minimum* total cost of production C changes with the volume of output and with input prices:

$$C = C(X, w, r) \tag{9.2}$$

Even with input prices given, the move from (9.1) to (9.2) requires us to know two things: first, the quantities of factor inputs chosen by the firm, which we assume is done on the basis of cost minimisation; second, the way those quantities of inputs, optimally chosen in the long-run case where all inputs are variable and denoted K^* and L^*, are transformed into output via the production function,

$$X = f(L, K) \tag{9.3}$$

We shall be particularly interested in whether or not properties of the production function described in the previous chapter have implications for the shape of the cost function (9.2).

Long-run cost minimisation

Formally, the long-run cost function (9.2) is the solution to the minimisation problem:

$$\min_{LK} C = wL + rK \tag{9.4}$$

subject to

$$X = f(L, K) \tag{9.3}$$

This procedure of minimising costs subject to the constraint imposed by the production function is analogous to the constrained utility maximisation of Chapter 2. We provide a formal algebraic solution to this problem in Chapter 10. In this chapter we confine our attention largely to results which we can derive on the basis of geometry. We can get most of the conclusions in which we are interested with these methods. Nonetheless, those who want to go further in their study of economics should be aware that algebra is more powerful and general in its application, and the next chapter is therefore worth their attention.

We can obtain an intuitive understanding of the solution to the cost minimisation problem by using a diagram which illustrates both the firm's tradeoffs in the choice of inputs, and the technological constraints which it faces. The latter we characterise in terms of an isoquant map, such as Figure 10.4. Tradeoffs between inputs available to the firm are formalised in terms of *isocost* curves, which describe the quantities of capital and labour services that can be bought per unit of time for a given cost outlay. Figure 9.1 illustrates an isocost curve, where we let the prices of capital and labour services per week be £100 and £50 respectively. Then, for an outlay of £1,000 per week, the firm can acquire 10 units of capital, 20 units of labour, or any combination of inputs along a line joining $10K$ and $12L$.

Algebraically, we may rearrange equation (9.1) to read

$$K = \frac{C}{r} - \frac{w}{r} L \tag{9.5}$$

For any given outlay, $\bar{C}$, this equation defines a straight line with intercept $\bar{C}/r$ and slope $-w/r$ ($dK/dL = -w/r$). In terms of our previous numerical example, we would have $C = 1,000$, $r = 100$. Hence $C/r = 10$, and the slope of the isocost line is given by $-50/100 = -0.5$. From equation (9.5) we note that the isocost curve shifts up parallel to itself as outlays rise, that changes in labour's price alter the slope of the curve, but not its intercept with

Figure 9.1

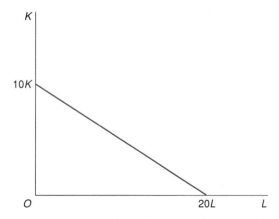

An isocost curve showing the quantities of capital and labour services that can be bought per unit of time for an outlay of £1,000 per unit of time when their prices are £100 and £50 per unit respectively.

Figure 9.2

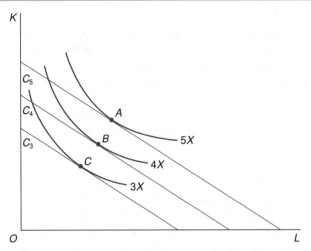

A family of isocost curves superimposed upon the production function. At point A we have the cheapest way of producing output $5X$ since any other point on that isoquant must be above isocost curve C_5. Equivalently, an output of $5X$ is the maximum output that can be had for an outlay of C_5 on factors of production. Any point other than A on isocost line C_5 is on a lower isoquant than $5X$. Similarly, C_3 and C_4 are the minimum costs of producing $3X$ and $4X$ units of output.

the capital axis, while changes in capital's rental price r change both its slope and its intercept with the capital axis.

Minimising the cost of production of X means two equivalent things. One may say that the firm, for a given outlay on factors, maximises production of X, or that, for a given level of output, it minimises the cost of obtaining the factors necessary to produce that level of output. In Figure 9.2 we show that, in geometric terms, cost minimisation takes place where an isoquant representing a particular level of output is just tangent to an isocost curve. By exact analogy with arguments developed in Chapter 2, we may say that *costs are minimised where the marginal rate of substitution between inputs in production, the slope of the isoquant, is equal to the ratio of factor prices, the slope of the isocost curve.* Any other combination of factors along the isoquant in question, other than that at which this condition holds, will result in more expense for no extra output, and any other point on the same isocost curve will mean the same expense for less output. So much should be obvious from inspection of Figure 9.2.

Box 9.1 ### Equilibrium in production with a Cobb-Douglas function

It is straightforward to illustrate the nature of equilibrium in production using a Cobb-Douglas function with a specific budget constraint. We can use the isocost curve set out in the text: $r = £100$, $w = £50$ and $C = £1,000$. In this case the equation for the isocost curve is

$$K = (1,000/100) - (50/100)L = 10 - 0.5L \tag{9.1.1}$$

The 0.5 in this function is relative input prices w/r. In addition we can use the Cobb-Douglas function examined in the previous chapter:

$$X = 10L^{0.75}K^{0.25} \tag{8.1.1}$$

We know that with this production function the marginal products are (see Box 8.2)

$$MP_L = \frac{\partial X}{\partial L} = 0.75(10)\left(\frac{K}{L}\right)^{0.25} \tag{8.2.3}$$

$$MP_K = \frac{\partial X}{\partial K} = 0.25(10)\left(\frac{L}{K}\right)^{0.75} \tag{8.2.4}$$

The slope of any isoquant (the marginal rate of technical substitution) is

$$\frac{MP_L}{MP_K} = \left[0.75(10)\left(\frac{K}{L}\right)^{0.25}\right] \div \left[0.25(10)\left(\frac{L}{K}\right)^{0.75}\right] = 3\frac{K}{L} \tag{9.1.2}$$

Note that the 3 in this expression for the *mrts* is the ratio of the exponents in the production function.

Using the logic set out in the text we know that equilibrium in production requires

$$mrts = w/r$$

Using (9.1.1) and (9.1.2):

$$3\frac{K}{L} = 0.5$$

This defines the optimal capital intensity

$$\frac{K}{L} = 0.167 \tag{9.1.3}$$

or $K = 0.167L$ and $L = 6K$

With a cost of £1,000 (as in the example used here) the isocost function is

$$K = 10 - 0.5L \tag{9.1.1}$$

So efficient production implies

$$K = 10 - 0.5(6K)$$

$$K = 2.5 \quad \text{and} \quad L = 15$$

In this least cost equilibrium total output is

$$X = 10(15^{0.75})(2.5^{0.25}) = 95.84$$

It is straightforward to show that if the firm does not produce at this efficient K/L and keeps costs the same, there is an efficiency loss in terms of lower output. For example if the firm operates with $K/L = 0.2$, then $K = 0.2L$ and $L = 5K$. With a cost of £1,000

$$K = 10 - 0.5(5K)$$

$$K = 2.86 \quad \text{and} \quad L = 14.29$$

→

Output is therefore

$$X = 10(14.29^{0.75})(2.86^{0.25}) = 95.58.$$

This is clearly less than efficient output.

These solutions are set out in Illustration 9.1. Efficient production occurs at the tangency between the isoquant and the isoquant line and so defines the optimal $K/L = 0.167$. Inefficient production, with $K/L = 2$, involves lower output, as indicated by the isoquant that cuts the isocost line.

Illustration 9.1

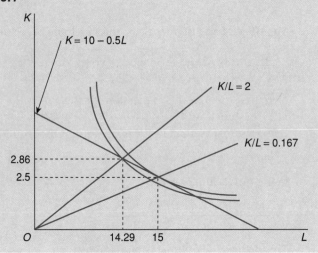

Long-run total cost and the expansion path

We are now in a position to derive a curve relating the total cost of producing X to its level of output: *a total cost curve*. As we have seen, the assumption of cost minimisation ensures that, in these circumstances, the outlay on factors incurred in producing a given output level will be that underlying the isocost curve that is tangent to the relevant isoquant.

Each equilibrium point in KL space, such as A, B or C in Figure 9.2, is a point on the firm's **expansion path**. This path is defined as the locus of equalities between *mrts* and input price ratios, or tangencies between isoquants and isocost curves at different levels of cost, and therefore output.

The long-run total cost function links cost, total outlay or factors, with output on the assumption that factor proportions have been chosen in such a way as to minimise costs. We therefore relate costs to corresponding output levels *along the expansion path* in order to derive this function.

Figure 9.3(a) shows the long-run total cost curve (LTC) when returns to scale are constant. It is derived from Figure 9.2 where the production function was drawn to display this property. Equiproportional increases in outlay on factors lead to equiproportional increases in their quantity devoted to producing X, and hence to equiproportional

Figure 9.3

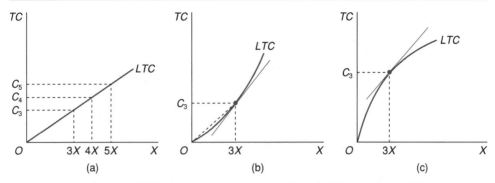

Long-run total cost curves (LTC) showing (a) constant returns to scale (this curve is explicitly derived from Figure 9.2 by relating the value of each isocost curve to that of the isoquant tangential to it), (b) decreasing returns to scale, (c) increasing returns to scale. At a particular level of output, average cost is given by dividing total cost by output (e.g. $C_3/3X$). Long-run marginal cost at any level of output is given by the slope of the total cost curve at that level of output.

increases in output. The long-run total cost curve in this case is, therefore, an upward-sloping straight line. Readers should satisfy themselves that a production function that everywhere displays decreasing returns to scale produces a long-run total cost curve that slopes upwards at a rate that increases with output, Figure 9.3(b), and that one that displays increasing returns to scale produces a long-run total cost curve that slopes upwards at a rate that decreases with output, Figure 9.3(c).

Box 9.2

The expansion path

We can develop the example used in Box 9.1 and derive the expansion path for the Cobb-Douglas production function

$$X = 10L^{0.75}K^{0.25} \tag{8.1.1}$$

With $r = £100$ and $w = £50$ in Box 9.1 we derived the efficient solution that $K/L = 0.167$. With $C = £1,000$ we found $L = 15$ and $K = 2.5$. Using the same technique as in Box 9.1, if we increase C to $£1,500$, optimal K/L will still (obviously) be $K/L = 0.167$ but now $K = 3.75$ and $L = 22.5$. The implication here is clear: that the expansion path with our Cobb-Douglas function is linear and defined by the optimal K/L.

More generally we can use the general Cobb-Douglas function

$$X = AL^\alpha K^\beta \tag{9.2.1}$$

It is a simple generalisation from the logic set out in Box 9.1 that the marginal rate of technical substitution is

$$mrts = -\frac{\beta}{\alpha}\left(\frac{L}{K}\right) \tag{9.2.2}$$

→

With exogenous input prices fixed at w/r, efficient production requires

$$-\frac{\beta}{\alpha}\frac{L}{K} = w/r \tag{9.2.3}$$

so

$$\frac{K}{L} = -\frac{\beta r}{\alpha w} \tag{9.2.4}$$

Equation (9.2.4) implies that, for given input prices, w, r, the capital–labour ratio is, in this Cobb-Douglas case, the same at every tangency between isoquants and isocost lines. The expansion path is therefore a straight line for a Cobb-Douglas function, and, more generally, for all homothetic production functions. In the particular Cobb-Douglas case where $\alpha + \beta = 1$ and the production function is homogeneous of degree one, factor outlays will rise in proportion to output along this expansion path, and the long-run total cost curve will be linear.

Average and marginal costs in the long run

Two other cost/output relationships are implicit in Figure 9.3. There is a relationship between **average cost** and output and between **marginal cost** and output. Average cost is simply the total cost of producing a given volume of output divided by the volume of output. In terms of Figure 9.3, it is measured by the height of the total cost curve at any point divided by its distance from the vertical axis or, in other words, by the slope of a straight line drawn from the origin to that point on the total cost curve. As the reader will readily discern, when returns to scale are constant, average cost does not vary with output; when they diminish, average cost increases with output; when they increase, average cost systematically falls with output.

Now consider the relationship between marginal cost and output. Marginal cost per unit of output is the ratio of the additional cost incurred by making a small (in the limit, infinitesimal) addition to output, to that addition to total output. In terms of calculus it is the derivative of the cost function (9.2). It is thus measured by the slope of the total cost curve – in just the same way as the marginal propensity to consume a good is given by the slope of an Engel curve (Chapter 2) and the marginal productivity of labour is given by the slope of the short-run production function. It should be obvious from Figure 9.3(a) that when returns to scale are constant, marginal cost is equal to average cost and does not vary with output. Figure 9.3(b) implies that decreasing returns to scale involves marginal cost increasing with output and exceeding average cost, while in Figure 9.3(c) we find marginal cost falling with output and being below average cost.

Long-run costs with varying returns to scale

Now we remarked in the previous chapter that there was no need to confine our attention to production functions that everywhere display the same returns to scale characteristics;

that it was quite conceivable that the technical conditions of producing a particular good were such as to result in increasing returns to scale at low output levels and decreasing returns at higher output levels. Such a production function is, in fact, most useful in the analysis of the behaviour of the competitive firm, as we shall see in Chapter 11, and the long-run cost curves implicit in it are worth consideration at this point.

In Figure 9.4, we draw the long-run total cost curve implied by such a production function, still assuming that factor prices are fixed to the firm. Total costs first increase with output at a decreasing rate and then at an increasing rate. Long-run average cost at first falls with output, and then rises; it reaches a minimum at level of output X^* where a straight line from the origin is tangent to LTC. As we have already said, long-run marginal cost at any level of output is given by the slope of the total cost curve. At first this too falls with output, and at levels of output lower than X^* is below average cost – as the reader should easily be able to verify by inspecting Figure 9.4. However, marginal cost begins to rise at X^{**} before output X^* is reached and becomes equal to average cost at X^*; at this level of output the slope of a straight line from the origin to the total cost curve is just equal to the slope of the total cost curve. Beyond X^* marginal cost continues to rise, and readers should satisfy themselves that marginal cost is above average cost at higher output levels than X^*. The relationships between long-run marginal cost, long-run average cost and output implicit in Figure 9.4 are displayed in Figure 9.5. The average cost curve (LAC) takes a form that is often called **U-shaped**, and is cut at its minimum point by a rising marginal cost curve (LMC). The reader will become very familiar with curves of this general shape in the chapters that follow.

| Figure 9.4 |

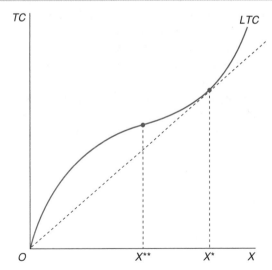

A long-run total cost curve showing first increasing and then decreasing returns to scale. Average cost is given by the slope of a straight line drawn from the origin to the curve. The slope of such a line, and hence average cost, is at a minimum at output X^* where the relevant line is tangent to the total cost curve. This straight line through the origin has the same slope as the total cost curve and hence, at output X^*, average cost and marginal cost are equal to each other. The slope of the total cost curve, and hence marginal cost, is at a minimum at output X^{**}, which is lower than X^*.

Figure 9.5

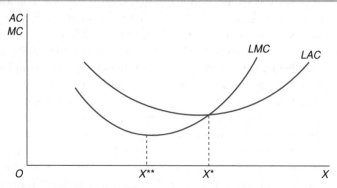

Long-run average and marginal cost curves implicit in Figure 9.4. Marginal cost cuts average cost from below at the minimum point of the average cost curve.

The short run

We can now investigate further the distinction between short and long run introduced in the last chapter. The curves with which we have been dealing so far are long run. They tell us how costs vary with output on the assumption that the firm may move freely to any point on its production function, that it may use any combination of inputs with equal ease, and that it always chooses the minimum cost combination. Movements such as this take time; the use of some inputs can be varied more rapidly than that of others. It is usually easier to hire more hourly paid labour than it is to order and install new machinery. It is usually easier to cut back on outlays on hourly paid labour than it is for the firm to rid itself of machinery once acquired. In ignoring such problems we were implicitly assuming that the firm had sufficient time to overcome them.

In contrast, we may define the 'short run' as that period of time over which the services of at least one factor input flowing to the firm are fixed as a result of past decisions. For the two-factor case it is usual to think of this fixed factor as being capital. Inasmuch as capital consists of machinery, it is physically fixed in place, owned or leased by the firm, and it is by no means straightforward to vary the amount of it. The labour force, on the other hand, is more likely to be on short-term contract, weekly or monthly, easily reduced by short-time working and dismissals and just as easily expanded by overtime and new hiring. Thus, we assume that, in the short run, only labour can be varied and capital is fixed.

This is nevertheless a naive assumption made, in the main, to keep the analysis simple. There is no particular reason why in any actual firm every type of capital should be only slowly variable and every type of labour rapidly variable. It is true that some types of labour are on short-term contract and easily hired and fired, but by no means all types. Equally, plant and equipment may be difficult to expand and contract quickly, but inventories of raw materials are just as much a part of capital and in some cases they may easily be adjusted. For any firm, there is a time horizon over which all inputs may be varied, but there are many, not just one, shorter horizons over which some inputs are fixed.

Moreover it is not necessarily the case that any type of labour may be varied more rapidly than any type of capital.

When in the following analysis we define the short run as the period over which labour but not capital inputs can be varied, we are not attempting directly to describe any kind of empirical reality. We are constructing a simplified special case in order to make certain analytic notions clear. Any attempt to apply the short-run/long-run distinction to a real-world problem that simply takes it for granted that there is a factor called labour whose services can be varied more rapidly than those of capital, and does not instead look carefully at the whole array of inputs involved in the particular situation to see which is the most easily varied, is likely to be misleading. We return to the topic again in Chapter 19.

Short-run cost functions

With the above caveat in mind, let us proceed to the analysis of **short-run costs** and their relationship to **long-run costs**. Just as the returns to scale characteristics of the production function underlie the shape of the long-run cost curves, so the nature of short-run cost curves depends upon the returns to the variable factor (labour in this simplified example) characteristics that it displays. We will explicitly analyse only the relatively complex case of a production function that displays increasing, followed by decreasing, returns to scale, but the reader will find it helpful to carry out the same analysis for at least one simpler case – say that of constant returns to scale.

We fix K at some historically given level K^* in Figure 9.6 and note that, given the prices of labour and capital, long-run cost minimisation would involve the firm producing at A.

| **Figure 9.6** |

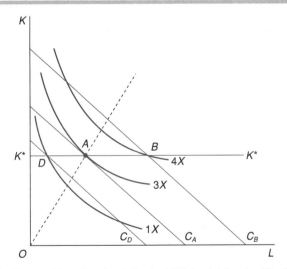

Given factor prices, the firm would produce level of output $3X$ at point A, using K^* units of capital services, even if it was free to vary the capital stock. With capital fixed at K^* any other level of output (e.g. $4X$ produced at B or $1X$ produced at D) will be produced at greater cost than it would be were the firm free to vary its capital input. C_D and C_B are the minimum short-run costs of producing $1X$ and $4X$. Note that the isoquants are here drawn to display first increasing and then decreasing returns to scale.

Figure 9.7

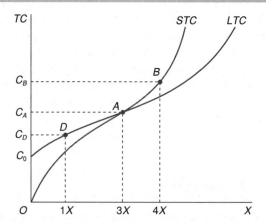

A short-run total cost curve for a particular level of the capital stock will be tangent to the long-run curve at A – corresponding to point A in Figure 9.6. C_0 here represents outlay on the services of K^* units of capital. It is a cost that must be met in the short run, even if output is zero.

If it wishes to vary its output over short periods it must move along the line K^*K^* rather than along the ray through the origin. We may construct a short-term total cost curve from Figure 9.6 by relating to one another the values of the isoquants and isocost lines that intersect K^*K^*. In this case, as we have drawn Figure 9.7, like the long-run curve, the short-run total cost curve displays first increasing and then decreasing returns, but these are returns *to the factor* and not returns *to scale*.

Now A represents a point that is both on the short-run total cost curve (*STC*) and on the long-run curve (*LTC*) as drawn in Figure 9.7. The level of output here is the only one for which short-run and long-run total costs of production are equal. The short-run total cost of producing any other level of output is higher than the long-run cost, for at any other point on K^*K^* the isocost lines *intersect* the isoquant and are not tangent to it. If, at level of output $3X$, the long-run curve and the short-run curve coincide, and at all other levels of output short-run costs are higher, there is obviously a tangency between the two curves at level of output $3X$.

The derivation of the short-run average cost curve and the short-run marginal cost curve from the short-run total cost curve is, analytically speaking, exactly the same exercise as the derivation of the relevant long-run curves and there is no point in repeating it explicitly. Because the long-run and short-run total cost curves touch tangentially at output $3X$ we may make inferences about the relationship between short-run and long-run average costs at that output, and between the two marginal cost curves. The average and marginal cost curves are drawn in Figure 9.8. First, the slopes of the two total cost curves are equal at A, in Figure 9.8, so short- and long-run marginal costs are equal at output $3X$. Immediately to the left of A the short-run total cost curve is less steeply sloped than the long-run curve, and to the right of A it is more steeply sloped. Hence, the short-run marginal cost curve (*SMC*) cuts the long-run curve (*LMC*) from below and to the left at level of output $3X$.

Figure 9.8

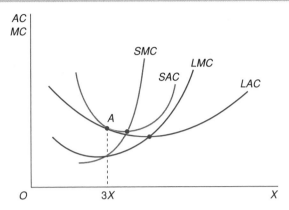

The relationship between long- and short-run average and marginal costs. The two average cost curves are tangent to each other at *A* – corresponding to point *A* in Figure 9.7 – while the two marginal cost curves intersect at the same level of output (3*X*).

Short- and long-run average costs coincide at this level of output, 3*X*, too, but here we have *tangency* between the two rather than an *intersection*. At any other level of output, total and hence average costs are higher in the short run than in the long run. Note that this does *not* mean that short-run average cost (*SAC*) is at a minimum at level of output 3*X*. The tangency of the two total cost curves means only that short-run average costs will fall *less rapidly* or rise *more rapidly* than long-run average costs as output expands, or contracts, not that they will necessarily rise in absolute terms. As Figures 9.7 and 9.8 are drawn, both short-run and long-run average costs are, in fact, falling at level of output 3*X*.

Short- and long-run average cost – the 'envelope'

Now we carried out the foregoing analysis on the assumption that there was a given level of capital that could not be varied. The amount we chose was quite arbitrary. There is in fact a different array of short-run curves for every level of the capital stock and, as the reader should see from Figure 9.9, the higher the level of the capital stock, the higher is the level of output at which the lines representing this stock (*K*K* and *K**K***) intersect the ray through the origin along which the long-run cost curves are derived. Hence the higher is the level of output at which the two total cost curves coincide. For every level of the capital stock there is a short-run average cost curve tangent to the long-run curve, and a short-term marginal cost curve intersecting the long-run curve. Figure 9.10 depicts a few of these curves, and its very appearance explains why the long-run average cost curve is often referred to as being the **'envelope'** of the short-run curves. As should be clear from the analysis presented earlier, the **'U' shape of the long-run average cost curve** in Figure 9.10 depends upon the assumption that we are dealing with a production function characterised by increasing returns to scale at low levels of output and decreasing returns to scale at higher levels. Such a production function was presented in Figure 9.6.

Figure 9.9

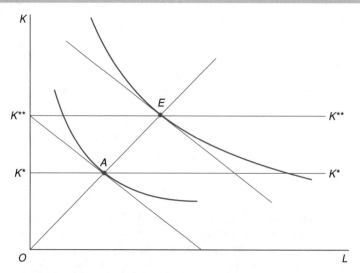

The higher the given level of the capital stock, the higher the level of labour input, and of output associated with the firm having the long-run cost minimising ratio of inputs. Point A here corresponds to point A in Figure 9.6. Point E is a similar point; it would yield a tangency between long-run and particular short-run total and average cost curves, the latter derived for a higher fixed level of capital services (K^{**}).

Figure 9.10

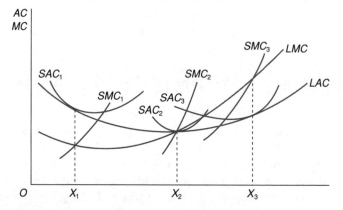

The long-run average cost curve is an 'envelope' of short-run average cost curves, each of the latter being derived for a different fixed level of capital services. There is a short-run marginal cost curve associated with each short-run average cost curve. It cuts the latter at its minimum point. It intersects the long-run marginal cost curve at the same level of output at which the short-run average cost curve is tangent to the long-run average cost curve. X_1, X_2 and X_3 are the output levels at which this happens for the three sets of short-run curves shown here. The curves labelled SAC_2 and SMC_2 are associated with a level of the capital stock which permits long-run average costs to be minimised. Hence SAC_2 equals LAC at the lowest point in the latter curve and SMC_2 intersects LMC where each curve cuts its associated average cost curve.

Fixed and variable costs

Now we have included outlays on capital services in the short-run costs with which we have been dealing. However, because capital input is fixed, outlay on it is fixed. It is often helpful to distinguish between the **fixed and variable** components of short-run costs. In the long run, of course, all costs are variable because, by definition, the level of all inputs can be varied as the firm desires. To obtain total variable costs from total short-run costs one simply subtracts the fixed outlay on capital. The short-run total cost curve depicted in Figure 9.7 and reproduced in Figure 9.11 cuts the vertical axis at C_0, for in the short run, at zero output, the firm must still pay this amount for capital services even if they are not utilised. To get the total variable cost curve (TVC), one simply shifts the short-run total cost curve (STC) down until it cuts through the origin, as shown in Figure 9.11. Since marginal cost measures the slope of the total cost curve, the distinction between variable and total cost does not affect the short-run marginal cost curve. After all, if fixed costs are fixed, then they do not vary with increments to output.

However, the distinction between fixed and variable costs is relevant to the discussion of average costs. If we average fixed costs over an increasing level of output, their contribution to overall average cost diminishes, as is shown in Figure 9.12. Average variable cost may be obtained from average overall cost by subtracting average fixed cost (AFC). Alternatively, the slope of a line drawn from the origin to the total variable cost curve in Figure 9.11 measures average variable cost. These two methods of obtaining the average variable cost curve are, of course, equivalent, and the minimum point of the average variable cost curve lies to the left of that of the overall short-run average cost curve. The marginal cost curve, of course, cuts both average cost curves at their minimum points. All

Figure 9.11

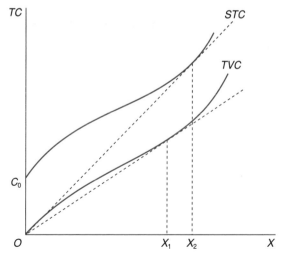

Total variable cost is equal to short-run total cost minus fixed costs (C_0). Average variable cost (the slope of a line drawn from the origin to TVC) is at a minimum at a lower level of output, X_1, than is short-run average cost (the slope of a line drawn to STC). The latter is minimised at X_2.

Figure 9.12

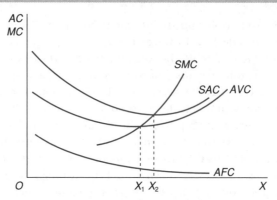

Average variable cost (*AVC*) is equal to short-run average cost (*SAC*) minus average fixed cost (*AFC*). The latter is simply a constant divided by an increasing level of output and hence declines systematically with output. Thus, *AVC* and *SAC* move closer together as output increases. The short-run marginal cost curve cuts both of these two curves at their minimum points at X_1 and X_2.

this is shown in Figure 9.12. Readers who doubt any of the foregoing propositions will find it helpful to derive them for themselves.

* From production to cost functions in the short run – a formal treatment

The relationship between production and cost functions in the short run can be brought out even more simply with the aid of calculus. In the short run, with capital costs fixed at C_0 ($r\bar{K} = C_0$), the total cost of function (9.1) becomes

$$C = wL + C_0 \tag{9.6}$$

and variable costs (*VC*) are given by wL.

The short-run production function is of course

$$X = f(L, \bar{K}) \tag{9.7}$$

which, since there is only one variable factor, can be respecified as

$$L = f^{-1}(X, \bar{K}) \tag{9.8}$$

In other words, with capital fixed, the level of output is unambiguously determined by employment only and vice versa. For given w, average variable cost (*AVC*) is therefore inversely associated with average product:

$$AVC = \frac{VC}{X} = \frac{wL}{X} \tag{9.9}$$

while short-run marginal cost is also specified as depending on the wage and the marginal product of labour.

$$\frac{\partial C}{\partial X} = w \frac{\partial L}{\partial X} \tag{9.10}$$

On this basis, we can discuss the relationship between average and marginal product and average and marginal costs. As we saw in Chapter 11, diminishing returns to a factor imply that average and marginal products both decline as output increases, with the former being *greater* than the latter. Diminishing returns thus also imply that average and marginal costs increase with output, with the former being everywhere *less* than the latter. Short-run curves such as those illustrated in Figures 9.8, 9.10 and 9.12, therefore, are all based on the assumption that returns to a factor are initially increasing, then constant, then diminishing as output increases.

The relationship between average and marginal cost will not in general remain constant as output changes. However, in the Cobb-Douglas case, marginal costs are a constant proportion of average costs, with

$$\frac{VC}{X} = \frac{wL}{X} \quad \text{and} \quad \frac{\partial C}{\partial X} = \frac{wL}{\alpha X}$$

so that

$$\frac{\partial C}{\partial X} \Big/ \frac{VC}{X} = \frac{wL}{\alpha X} \Big/ \frac{wL}{X} = \frac{1}{\alpha} \tag{9.11}$$

Concluding comment

Now the analysis of cost curves is quite tricky and if it was being carried out only for its own sake, it would be tedious as well. However, cost/output relationships such as those we have discussed here are a basic ingredient of the price and output decisions of the firm. We have now dealt with them in sufficient detail to begin discussing, in Part IV of this book, the entrepreneur's decision making about the quantity of output to be produced and the price at which it is to be sold. Readers who seek a deeper understanding of cost functions should read Chapter 10 next, but those who wish to defer mastering this material should proceed directly to Part IV.

SUMMARY

Cost functions

1. A central problem in the theory of the firm is to translate market prices of the individual factors of production into costs of production for output. In order to do this, assuming input prices to be given, we need to know:

    (a) the quantities of factor inputs chosen by the firm;

    (b) the underlying technical relationship linking the level of output to quantities of inputs. This is the long-run production function (dealt with in the previous chapter).

2. In order to determine the quantities of inputs chosen by the firm, we need a hypothesis about entrepreneurial motivation. We assume that decisions are made according to the

principle of cost minimisation. This implies that the firm minimises its outlay on the factors needed to produce any given level of output.

3. In geometric terms, cost minimisation occurs where an isoquant representing a particular level of output is just tangent to an isocost curve. This implies that costs are minimised where the marginal rate of substitution between inputs in production, the slope of the isoquant, is equal to the ratio of factor prices, the slope of the isocost curve.

4. The long-run total cost curve relates outlay on factors to output on the assumption that factor proportions have been chosen so as to minimise that outlay. Given input prices, assumptions about returns to scale in production technology yield precise implications about the long-run cost functions.

5. Long-run average costs are constant (the total cost curve is linear) with constant returns to scale, declining with increasing returns to scale, and rising with diminishing returns to scale.

6. Short-run average and marginal cost functions are the inverse of short-run average and marginal product functions. Diminishing returns to a factor imply that, in the short run, the average and marginal cost curves both slope upward.

7. Short-run average costs lie everywhere above long-run average costs except for a single point of tangency, at which the optimal choice of employment, given a fixed capital stock, happens also to yield the optimal choice of factor proportions. Short-run average costs are otherwise higher because at other output levels the firm is not using the optimal capital–labour ratio.

8. The long-run average cost curve is an 'envelope' which encloses all the short-run average cost curves drawn for different levels of capital.

PROBLEMS

1 Explain why

(a) short-run marginal cost is greater than or equal to long-run marginal cost;

(b) short-run average total cost is greater than or equal to long-run average total cost.

2 United Widgets plc has a production function which displays increasing returns in the output range from zero to X_1, constant returns from X_1 to X_2, and diminishing returns thereafter. What is the shape of the firm's long-run total cost curve? What is the relationship between long-run average and long-run marginal cost at levels of output between X_1 and X_2? Draw the long-run average and marginal cost curves for United Widgets.

3 A firm has the following short-run production functions:

Employment per week	Output per week
0	0
1	3
2	7
3	11.5
4	16
5	19
6	21

(a) Plot the average and marginal products of labour on a graph. Does this production function display diminishing marginal returns to labour eventually?

(b) If the wage is £5 per week, plot the short-run variable and marginal cost curves.

(c) If fixed costs are £10 per week, plot the short-run average and marginal cost curves.

4 A firm uses labour and capital to produce output, X. A new manager is appointed, who notes that, while each worker costs £5 per week and the weekly rental price of capital is £10, the marginal product of capital is 200 units of output per week. Can the manager conclude that the firm is minimising costs? If not, what actions should they take with regard to employment, the capital stock and output in order to rectify the situation?

5 Analyse the effect of an increase in the rental price of capital on average costs in the short run and in the long run. Is the impact greater in the short run or the long run? Why?

CHAPTER (10)

Production functions, cost functions, and the demand for factors of production

Key words and phrases

- duality; cost function
- substitutability between factors, fixed proportions technology, Shephard's lemma, perfect substitutability, Cobb-Douglas technology
- conditional factor demand functions
- elasticity of substitution
- normal and inferior factors

Introduction

We have seen in earlier chapters that the production function provides the essential link between factor markets and output markets. Thus, in Chapters 8 and 9 we showed how the production function could be used to translate information about factor prices into information about the short-run and long-run behaviour of costs of production. In Chapter 18 we use this relationship again, this time to relate the firm's demand for factors of production to the behaviour of the price of its output. In each case we are simply viewing the same set of interrelated profit-maximising decisions from different perspectives.

The production function is clearly a key relationship in the theory of the firm, just as the utility function is a key relationship in the theory of consumer behaviour. Nevertheless, particularly when it comes to empirical work, the key role of the production function presents problems; and though this book deals only with economic theory, we are concerned that its readers learn economic theory which is helpful in analysing and understanding the real world.

The problems to which we refer here arise because the data on the characteristics of actual production functions are always hard, and often impossible, to obtain. They run parallel to the problems caused for applications of the theory of consumer choice by our inability to measure consumers' utility functions directly. Here, as with the theory of consumer choice, that body of analysis known as **duality** *theory* is extremely helpful. We saw in Chapter 4 that the application of this idea enabled us to obtain useful results directly from data on consumer income and expenditure volumes on particular goods, without having any knowledge of the utility function. In the production function area, the analogous variables are output levels and outlays on factor purchases. Just as analysis of the expenditure function pays large dividends when dealing with consumer behaviour, so too does analysis of the cost function when producer behaviour is under study.

Now the mathematical techniques underlying duality theory are more complicated than others used in this book, and so this chapter, which sets out the basics of this theory as it applies to production, is more difficult than those which have come before it. Moreover the real benefits from mastering the techniques in question arise in empirical work, or in the treatment of certain theoretical questions, only a few of which have been treated in this book. Hence, though the material dealt with here is a vital part of the training of any economist, and should therefore command the attention of readers who intend to carry their studies further, we have written this chapter so that, if readers so choose, they may omit it without detracting in any large measure from their ability to read the rest of the book.

The essence of duality theory is that all aspects of a firm's production technology which are relevant to the economist can be summarised in a simple way in its cost function. This deceptively simple and apparently purely technical statement has important implications for the way we analyse firms' output and input choices. For example, optimal factor inputs can be derived directly from the cost function, without reference to the cumbersome isoquant–isocost apparatus that we developed in Chapter 9. Input demands at a given level of output, and given input prices, can instead be derived by differentiating the cost function with respect to these input prices. Moreover we shall also see that the slopes of input demand curves are themselves given by the second derivatives of the cost functions with respect to their prices, and that average and marginal cost curves can be shown to shift with input prices according to the derivatives of the cost function with respect to output and input prices. These points are fairly hard to establish, and we rely to some extent on specific examples rather than general proofs to present them in this chapter.

As we have already noted, a further reason for taking duality theory seriously is its usefulness in empirical work. Applied economists working, for example, on problems of public policy frequently find that the policy prescription depends on the shape of production technology. However, it is often hard to get reliable information on factor inputs, at least in an appropriate form. For example, the available data on labour inputs may cover the number of workers, but not control for skill level, hours worked or the intensity of effort. Problems are even more serious in the case of capital, where the evaluation of the flow of services yielded by a capital stock is particularly tricky. The value of capital is often hard to measure, and information about capacity utilisation is hard to obtain. Firms typically have more information about costs. Duality theory shows us how to make inferences about the shape of production technology, for which data are sparse and poor, using cost relationships, where data are more readily available and reliable.

From production to cost functions in the long run

Before coming to grips with duality theory proper, we first run through the formal analysis, analogous to that of utility theory in Chapter 2, in which we deduce the implications of cost minimisation for enterprise choice of output and input volumes.

It will be remembered that costs are defined as

$$C = wL + rK \tag{10.1}$$

The cost *function* relates costs of production to input prices and the volume of output on the assumption that the firm's choice of inputs, K^* and L^*, is optimal, i.e. cost minimising. The cost function,

$$C = C(X, w, r) \tag{10.2}$$

is therefore derived as the solution to a formal cost minimisation problem.

We can think about linking costs to output for given input prices in two ways. The first is to fix the level of cost at, for example, $\bar{C}$, and then to find the maximum output which can be produced at that level of cost. Alternatively one can fix output at, say, X^*, and find the minimum level of cost, given input prices, at which that quantity can be produced. The two methods are analogous and provide an identical solution, at the tangency between the isocost and isoquant curves. This is illustrated in Figure 10.1. As we noted in

Figure 10.1

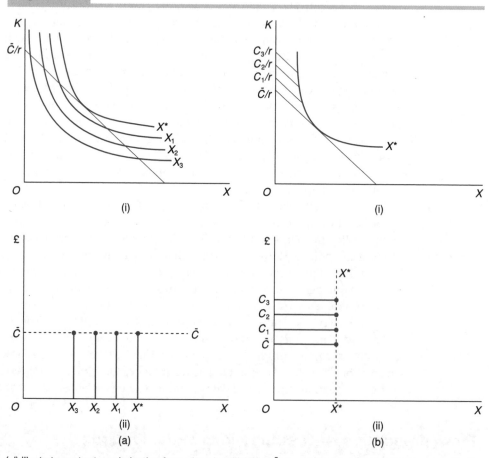

(ai) illustrates output maximisation for a given level of cost $\bar{C}$. As can be seen from (aii), X^* represents the greatest output that can be obtained for $\bar{C}$; X_1, X_2 and X_3 are outputs produced with inefficient capital–labour ratios. (bi) illustrates cost minimisation for a given level of output. There are numerous factor combinations available to produce X^*, costing C_1, C_2 and C_3 for example. The cheapest is $\bar{C}$, the lowest point in (bii).

Chapter 9, every point on the long-run cost curve is associated with an optimal capital–labour ratio, or *choice of technique*, which occurs at the tangency point. Here, the ratio of input prices equals the marginal rate of technical substitution (*mrts*) between the inputs.

Starting with our first method, if we fix the level of cost at $\bar{C}$, the cost-minimisation problem becomes an output-maximisation problem, namely, to maximise

$$X = f(L, K) \tag{10.3}$$

subject to

$$\bar{C} = wL + rK \tag{10.4}$$

We can therefore form the Lagrangian

$$H_1 = f(L, K) + \lambda_1(\bar{C} - wL - rK) \tag{10.5}$$

where λ_1 is the Lagrange multiplier. The first-order conditions are

$$\frac{\partial H_1}{\partial L} = \frac{\partial X}{\partial L} - \lambda_1 w = 0 \tag{10.6}$$

$$\frac{\partial H_1}{\partial K} = \frac{\partial X}{\partial K} - \lambda_1 r = 0 \tag{10.7}$$

$$\frac{\partial H_1}{\partial \lambda_1} = \bar{C} - wL - rK = 0 \tag{10.8}$$

From (10.6) and (10.7),

$$\frac{1}{\lambda_1} = \frac{w}{\partial X/\partial L} = \frac{r}{\partial X/\partial K} \tag{10.9}$$

We know from Chapter 9 that the expression $(w/(\partial X/\partial L))$ defines marginal cost in the short run (see equation (9.10)). Hence the Lagrange multiplier, λ_1, is equal to short-run marginal cost. We may interpret equation (10.9) as telling us that, if the firm is cost minimising, the marginal cost of increasing output must be the same whether it does so by using additional units of labour or additional units of capital $(r/(\partial X/\partial K))$. This result is intuitively appealing; if it did not hold, we could always in the long run increase output while holding costs constant, by switching to the input with lower marginal cost while reducing our use of the input with the higher marginal cost. In short, for a maximum, the contribution of the last unit of cost outlay to output must equal λ_1 for both inputs.

Rearranging terms in (10.9), we have

$$\frac{\partial X/\partial L}{\partial X/\partial K} = w/r \tag{10.10}$$

We know from Chapter 8 that the ratio of marginal products equals the slope of the isoquant, the *mrts* (see equation (8.7)). Hence since

$$\frac{dK}{dL} = -\frac{\partial X/\partial L}{\partial X/\partial K} \tag{10.11}$$

we have established that

$$\frac{dK}{dL} = -w/r \tag{10.12}$$

Output maximisation for a given cost requires that the ratio of relative input prices equals the marginal rate of technical substitution between them. This is the result we deduced geometrically in Chapter 9.

Precisely the same result can of course be obtained by minimising cost for a given level of output X. The problem here is to choose capital and labour inputs to

$$\min_{L,K} C = wL + rK \tag{10.13}$$

subject to

$$X = f(L, K) \tag{10.14}$$

The Lagrangian is

$$H_2 = wL + rK + \lambda_2(X - f(L, K)) \tag{10.15}$$

with first-order conditions

$$\frac{\partial H_2}{\partial L} = w - \lambda_2 \frac{\partial X}{\partial L} = 0 \tag{10.16}$$

$$\frac{\partial H_2}{\partial K} = r - \lambda_2 \frac{\partial X}{\partial K} = 0 \tag{10.17}$$

$$\frac{\partial H_2}{\partial \lambda_2} = X - f(L, K) = 0 \tag{10.18}$$

From (10.16) and (10.17) we derive

$$\lambda_2 = \frac{w}{\partial X/\partial L} = \frac{r}{\partial X/\partial K} \tag{10.19}$$

from which (10.12) can be derived as before. The results deriving the cost function from an output-maximising problem, subject to a cost constraint, are identical to those which emerge if the cost function is instead derived from a cost-minimising problem, subject to an output constraint.

Fixed proportions technology

We have already discussed in the previous chapter how the shape of the cost function is influenced by the returns to scale characteristics of the production function. In particular, constant, rising and falling long-run average costs are associated with, respectively, constant, diminishing and increasing returns to scale. We now begin to consider this relationship more formally, as well as the relationship between the degree of **substitutability between factors** and the shape of the cost function.

Consider first the case of zero substitutability between inputs, which was illustrated in Chapter 8, Figure 8.5(a). Suppose that the level of output is given by the minimum of γL and θK, where γ and θ are exogenous parameters which jointly determine the capital–labour ratio – that is, the ratio at which it would be impossible to reduce the input of either factor without reducing output, or, to put it in terms of Figure 10.2, the ratio at which the right angle in a representative isoquant occurs. The production function is therefore

$$X = \min(\gamma L, \theta K) \tag{10.20}$$

Figure 10.2   Fixed proportions and the choice of technique

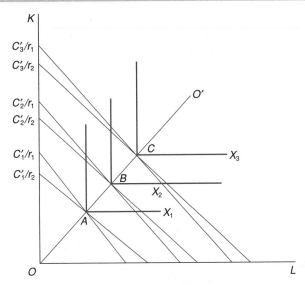

Fixed coefficient technology implies that the 'tangency' between the isoquant and isocost line always occurs at the kink, at *ABC* along the optimal capital–labour ratio ray *OO'*. The resulting long-run cost function is therefore linear because the production function displays constant returns to scale, and the choice of technique is not affected by input prices. However, costs themselves increase with input prices. For example, if capital costs rise from r_1 to r_2, the cost of producing X_1 rises. This can be seen by noting that, at the higher rental price of capital, the isocost curves passing through *A*, *B* and *C* cut the horizontal (labour) axis further to the right. Since wages are constant by assumption, this implies that factor outlays are higher.

and the isoquants are L-shaped as in Figure 10.2. To produce each unit of X, we therefore need both X/γ of labour and X/θ of capital, at a cost of w and r respectively. The minimum cost is therefore

$$C = \frac{Xw}{\gamma} + \frac{Xr}{\theta} \tag{10.21}$$

which can be rearranged as

$$C = X\left(\frac{w}{\gamma} + \frac{r}{\theta}\right)$$

This cost function can be used to illustrate formally the points made in Figure 10.2. The fixed coefficient technology we have envisaged here has constant returns to scale, so we expect the total cost function to be linear from the origin with respect to output, with average cost equal to marginal cost. From (10.21), we derive the marginal cost by taking the derivative with respect to output. This yields

$$\frac{\partial C}{\partial X} = \frac{w}{\gamma} + \frac{r}{\theta} \tag{10.22}$$

which is *constant* for given input prices. Dividing (10.21) by X generates average cost (C/X) which gives exactly the same expression as in equation (10.22). Hence, as expected, marginal and average costs are equal, and do not vary with output. We have therefore established formally that for a constant-returns fixed coefficient technology, the total cost curve is indeed linear.

We can also examine the relationship between costs and input prices at a given level of output. Differentiating (10.21) by each input price,

$$\frac{\partial C}{\partial w} = \frac{X}{\gamma} = L > 0 \tag{10.23}$$

$$\frac{\partial C}{\partial r} = \frac{X}{\theta} = K > 0 \tag{10.24}$$

We know from the production function that X/γ is the amount of labour services, L, and X/θ is the amount of capital services, K, being used to produce X units of output. Hence differentiating the cost function with respect to input prices reveals that an increase in the price of an input increases the minimum cost of producing a given level of output by the amount of the input being used. Minimum costs *always* rise when input prices increase. The increase in the minimum cost of producing X_1, when wages rise, is the employment level L_1 times the wage increase. Similarly, when capital costs rise the increase is given by that rise times the capital stock, K_1. This important result is an application of **Shephard's lemma**, which is one of the central findings of the so-called 'duality' literature. It establishes that the firm's demand for a factor at a given level of output can be expressed as the derivative of the cost function with respect to that input's price. This result is not, therefore, specific to the special case of fixed proportions.

Perfect substitutability

Let us now repeat the foregoing exercise on the assumption that labour and capital are perfect substitutes in the production process. As we saw in Chapter 8, the production function in this case takes the form

$$X = aL + bK \tag{10.25}$$

and the isoquants are straight lines, as illustrated in Figure 10.3. Since the inputs are perfect substitutes, a cost-minimising firm will choose that input which is cheapest per unit of output. If only labour is used, we require X/a units of employment to produce X units of output. Employment per unit of output is therefore $1/a$; the cost per unit of output is w/a. Similarly, if only capital is used, we require X/b units of capital to produce X units of output and the cost per unit is r/b.

The cost-minimising firm will, as we have said, choose the cheaper option, so the cost function is

$$C = \min\left(\frac{w}{a}, \frac{r}{b}\right) X \tag{10.26}$$

In defining technology here, we have once more assumed constant returns to scale, so, as with fixed coefficient technology, average costs and marginal costs are equal and

Figure 10.3   **Perfect substitutes and the choice of technique**

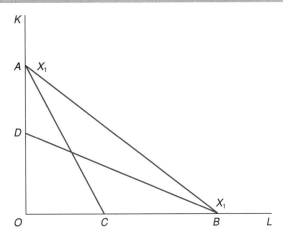

The isoquant X_1X_1 is a straight line which coincides with the isocost curve AB. Lines AC and DB are also isocost curves. When the (negative) slope of the isocost curve is less than that of the isoquant, as in AC, the cost-minimising firm uses only capital and produces X_1 at A. When the (negative) slope of the isocost curve is greater, as in DB, the firm produces using only labour, at B. When the slopes of the isoquant and the isocost curve are the same, as in AB, the firm produces anywhere along the isoquant AB.

constant, with given input prices. Thus, it is easy to show, by differentiating equation (10.26) with respect to X and by dividing it through by X, respectively, that

$$\frac{\partial C}{\partial X} = \min\left(\frac{w}{a}, \frac{r}{b}\right) = \frac{C}{X} \tag{10.27}$$

Moreover the 'derivative property' of the cost function which associates input demand functions at constant levels of output with the derivative of the cost function with respect to input prices – Shephard's lemma – holds for this functional form. Thus assuming no induced changes in technique, if the firm chooses to use only labour we have

$$\frac{\partial C}{\partial w} = \frac{X}{a} = L \tag{10.28}$$

and if it chooses only capital, we have

$$\frac{\partial C}{\partial r} = \frac{X}{b} = K \tag{10.29}$$

In this case too, therefore, we have established that the minimum cost of producing a given output increases when a factor price increases, by the amount of the input used times the change in its price.

Cobb-Douglas technology

Let us now consider, as a final illustration, the case where production technology is described by a Cobb-Douglas function

$$X = AL^\alpha K^\beta \tag{10.30}$$

The properties of this functional form were discussed at greater length in Chapter 11. Let us simplify the analysis without losing any of its content, by choosing the units in which inputs and output are measured so that $A = 1$, and let us maintain the assumption of constant returns to scale, so that $\alpha + \beta = 1$. The production function then becomes $X = L^{\alpha}K^{1-\alpha}$. Interested readers may wish to resolve the problem which follows with $(\alpha + \beta)$ not equal to one in order to establish for themselves the relationship between returns to scale and the shape of the cost function.

Let us now solve the minimisation problem,

$$\min_{L,K} C = wL + rK \tag{10.31}$$

subject to

$$X = L^{\alpha}K^{1-\alpha} \tag{10.32}$$

by forming the Lagrangian

$$H_3 = wL + rK + \lambda_3[X - L^{\alpha}K^{1-\alpha}] \tag{10.33}$$

Differentiating,

$$\frac{\partial H_3}{\partial L} = w - \lambda_3[\alpha L^{\alpha-1}K^{1-\alpha}] = 0 \tag{10.34}$$

$$\frac{\partial H_3}{\partial K} = r - \lambda_3[(1 - \alpha)L^{\alpha}K^{-\alpha}] = 0 \tag{10.35}$$

$$\frac{\partial H_3}{\partial \lambda_3} = X - L^{\alpha}K^{1-\alpha} = 0 \tag{10.36}$$

Rearranging terms

$$\lambda_3 = \frac{wL}{\alpha X} = \frac{rK}{(1 - \alpha)X} \tag{10.37}$$

so that

$$L = \frac{r}{w}\frac{\alpha}{1 - \alpha}K \tag{10.38}$$

and

$$K = \frac{w}{r}\frac{1 - \alpha}{\alpha}L \tag{10.39}$$

Substituting (10.38) into the production function

$$X = \left(\frac{r}{w}\right)^{\alpha}\left(\frac{\alpha}{1 - \alpha}\right)^{\alpha}K^{\alpha}K^{1-\alpha}$$

so

$$K = \left(\frac{r}{w}\right)^{-\alpha}\left(\frac{\alpha}{1 - \alpha}\right)^{-\alpha}X \tag{10.40}$$

Similarly, substituting (10.39) into the production function

$$X = L^{\alpha}\left(\frac{w}{r}\right)^{1-\alpha}\left(\frac{1 - \alpha}{\alpha}\right)^{1-\alpha}L^{1-\alpha}$$

so

$$L = \left(\frac{w}{r}\right)^{\alpha-1} \left(\frac{1-\alpha}{\alpha}\right)^{\alpha-1} X \tag{10.41}$$

Substituting these values for optimal L and K into the cost function, we obtain

$$C = wL + rK$$

$$= wXw^{\alpha-1}r^{1-\alpha}(1-\alpha)^{\alpha-1}\alpha^{1-\alpha} + rXr^{-\alpha}w^{\alpha}\alpha^{-\alpha}(1-\alpha)^{\alpha}$$

$$= Xw^{\alpha}r^{1-\alpha}(1-\alpha)^{\alpha}\alpha^{-\alpha}\left(\frac{\alpha}{1-\alpha} + 1\right)$$

$$= Xw^{\alpha}r^{1-\alpha}(1-\alpha)^{\alpha}\alpha^{-\alpha}\left(\frac{1}{1-\alpha}\right)$$

$$= Xw^{\alpha}r^{1-\alpha}(1-\alpha)^{\alpha-1}\alpha^{-\alpha} \tag{10.42}$$

At first sight, the cost function, equation (10.42), for the Cobb-Douglas production function seems complicated. However, it can be simplified to

$$C = Xw^{\alpha}r^{1-\alpha}B \tag{10.42'}$$

(where $B = (1-\alpha)^{\alpha-1}\alpha^{-\alpha}$), which is the dual of the original production function form. Studying (10.42), it comes as no surprise that if the output level doubles, the cost of production doubles, since we have assumed constant returns to scale. As in our previous two examples, if we derive the average and marginal costs, they are equal for given input prices, taking the value $w^{\alpha}r^{1-\alpha}B$.

To analyse the demand for inputs as their prices change, we take the derivatives of the cost function with respect to factor prices. Thus

$$\frac{\partial C}{\partial w} = \alpha Xw^{\alpha-1}r^{\alpha-1}B$$

$$= \frac{\alpha C}{w} \tag{10.43a}$$

Similarly,

$$\frac{\partial C}{\partial r} = (1-\alpha)Xw^{\alpha}r^{-\alpha}B$$

$$= \frac{(1-\alpha)C}{r} \tag{10.43b}$$

To establish the relevance of (10.43a) and (10.43b), we need to draw on material proved formally in Chapter 18. The factor weights, α and $(1-\alpha)$, in equations (10.43a) and (10.43b) represent the proportions in which the value of total output is distributed between wage payments to labour and rental payments to capital if the firm makes zero profits. To remind ourselves of how this result has arisen, accept that λ_2 in our cost-minimisation problem at the start of the chapter is in fact equal to the product price p. Then equations (10.16) and (10.17) show that in equilibrium the firm equalises the input price to the marginal product times the output price for each input. In the Cobb-Douglas case, this implies that $w = p\alpha X/L$, and $r = p(1 - \alpha)X/K$. Provided profits equal zero, so the entire value of output is exhausted by payment to factors of their marginal product, these can be rearranged to equal

$$\alpha = \frac{wL}{pX}; \ (1 - \alpha) = \frac{rK}{pX}$$

Hence, the Cobb-Douglas weights represent the shares of each factor in the value of output.

Returning to equations (10.43a) and (10.43b), αC is labour's share of costs, and $(1 - \alpha)C$ is capital's share of costs. As in our previous examples, $\alpha C/w$ therefore equals the number of workers and $(1 - \alpha)C/r$ the stock of capital used to produce total output. As with fixed coefficients and perfect substitutability, the minimum cost of producing a given output alters in response to change in input price by exactly the amount of the input used.

Conditional factor demand functions

We have so far illustrated how minimum costs change with output and with changes in factor prices on the basis of special assumptions about the nature of technology. Results on the first relationship have been associated with returns to scale, and results on the latter are associated with factor demands. The relationship between input prices and factor demands is potentially complicated because substitution effects away from relatively more expensive inputs (analogous to substitution effects in consumer theory) may be offset by scale effects via output adjustments resulting from changes in the relationship between cost and price (analogous to income effects in consumer theory). The duality approach allows us to avoid all this complexity and derive factor demands directly from the cost function, without having to worry about changes in output and the choice of technique (factor proportions). Given output, the value of the derivative of the cost function with respect to wages turns out to give us the optimal level of employment, and the derivative with respect to the rental price of capital yields the optimal level of the capital stock. These factor demand functions we shall refer to as **conditional factor demands**. In the balance of this chapter we outline more generally results on cost functions, input prices, and conditional factor demands. Profit-maximising factor demands, which take account of changes in output, will be analysed in Chapter 18. Students who seek formal proofs of the arguments which follow or wish to see the ideas developed are referred to Further Reading at the end of the book.

Costs when input prices change

The general cost function, $C = C(\bar{X}, \hat{w}, \hat{r})$, gives the minimum cost of producing output $\bar{X}$ when input prices are $\hat{w}$, $\hat{r}$, and L^*, K^* are the optimal values of factor inputs given those input prices. The first important property of this cost function is that the total cost of a given output will increase in proportion to a simultaneous equiproportional increase in both wages and the rental price of capital. For example, if the factor prices both double, the cost of producing $\bar{X}$ doubles, because the relative cost of the inputs remains constant and therefore the choice of technique does not alter. The only effect of proportional increases in input prices is therefore on costs; they do not influence relative factor demands at a given output level. We can say that the cost function is *linearly homogeneous* (or homogeneous of degree one) in factor prices in the same way as we spoke of linearly homogeneous production functions in Chapter 8. Similarly, since input demands are not affected by proportionate changes in wages and the rental price of capital, we can say that input demands (L^*, K^*) are homogeneous of degree *zero* in input prices.

A second important result, linking optimal input demand at a given level of output to the derivative of the cost function, has already been derived for special cases earlier in this chapter. *Shephard's lemma* tells us that

$$\frac{\partial C}{\partial w} = L^*; \frac{\partial C}{\partial r} = K^* \tag{10.44}$$

When wage rates increase by one penny, the minimum cost of producing the given level of output increases by L^* pence, and for an increase of r of one penny it increases by K^* pence. This result is of course equivalent to that developed on the demand side in Chapter 4 (see equation (4.17)) where we established that the compensated demand curve was the derivative of the expenditure function with respect to price.

This result is convenient because it enables us to analyse how costs change with input prices without direct reference to changes in the choice of technique and the underlying shape of the production function. Consider for example the extent to which costs change as wages alter. One might expect to have to take account of how capital is substituted for labour around the isoquant, and therefore to take account of the **elasticity of substitution** of labour for capital, but this turns out to be unnecessary. We define the elasticity of total cost with respect to wages in the normal way as

$$\varepsilon_w^C = \left(\frac{dC}{C}\right)\bigg/\left(\frac{dw}{w}\right)$$

$$= \frac{\partial C}{\partial w}\frac{w}{C} \tag{10.45}$$

Substituting from equation (10.44),

$$\varepsilon_w^C = \frac{wL^*}{C} \tag{10.46}$$

Hence total costs vary with wages according to the percentage of costs accounted for by the labour input. If the share of labour input in total costs is 50 per cent, total costs increase by 0.5 per cent if wages increase by 1 per cent. As the share of labour costs in total costs increases, the impact of a rise in wages on total costs increases proportionately.

The mathematics of duality therefore allows us to analyse extremely simply the underlying relationships between input prices and costs, without reference to the production function or a formal minimisation problem.

The cost function and conditional factor demand functions

As we noted above, it is important to stress the distinction between two sorts of factor demand function. The first, which is the topic of this section, relates optimal employment

Figure 10.4   **Conditional factor demand**

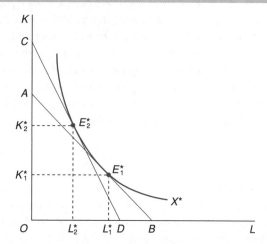

As the cost of capital falls or the wage rate increases, the isocost line shifts around the isoquant from AB to CD. The equilibrium choice of technique becomes more capital-intensive, moving from E_1^* to E_2^*, with optimal employment falling from L_1^* to L_2^* and optimal capital rising from K_1^* to K_2^*.

of labour and capital services to the wage rate and the cost of capital, *conditional* on the assumption that output is fixed. Hence the name given to factor demand functions of this sort: **conditional factor demand functions**. The second sort of input demand function takes account of changes in output as well as changes in the choice of technique when considering factor demand responses to changes in their price. We shall henceforth refer to this as a *profit-maximising factor demand function*, which is considered in detail in Chapter 18.

In this section, we are therefore concerned with how optimal input quantities and proportions alter with input prices as we move around an isoquant. The analysis is analogous to our discussion of Hicks compensated demand curves in consumer theory, when we analysed how the quantity demanded of our two goods changed with their relative price as we moved around the indifference curve (see Chapter 3). The slope of the isocost curve is the (negative) ratio of wages to capital costs, which increases with the wage rate. As the cost of labour relative to capital increases, cost-minimising firms substitute capital for labour around the isoquant; as in the case of consumer theory, so here too the substitution effect is always negative. This is illustrated in Figure 10.4.

Some properties of conditional factor demand functions

The degree to which input demands respond to changes in their relative prices, conditional on output, may be expressed as the elasticity of factor demand. As before, it is helpful to begin the discussion with reference to the two special cases of zero and infinite substitutability between the inputs.

Consider first the case of fixed coefficients, illustrated in Figure 10.2. Since the tangency between the isocost line and the isoquant always occurs at the kink of the latter, whatever the slope of the isocost line, factor proportions and input demands are not affected by

Figure 10.5

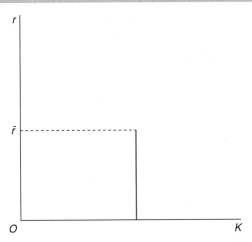

Demand for capital when inputs are perfect substitutes and output is given. The rental price of capital $\bar{r}$ is such that, for the given wage rate $\hat{w}$, the slope of the isocost curve $\hat{w}/\bar{r}$ exactly equals the slope of the linear isoquant, as along AB in Figure 10.3.

input prices. Since we cannot substitute between labour and capital, the demand for factors at each level of output is independent of input prices. In the example of production function (10.20), the optimal capital–labour ratio is always θ/γ, and the elasticity of conditional factor demand is zero. (Interested readers can derive this formally from the conditional input demand functions, (10.23) and (10.24).)

The results in the perfect substitutes case are equally transparent. The firm will use either only capital or only labour in its production process, unless the slope of the isocost line equals the slope of the isoquant, in which case the outcome is indeterminate. The impact of factor prices on the capital–labour ratio, and hence the elasticity of factor demand, is thus discontinuous in this case. Consider an instance when input prices yield isocost line AC in Figure 10.3, with isoquant AB. As the cost of capital rises (as the cost of labour falls so the *relative* cost of capital rises), the isocost line AC swivels outwards. At a certain point, the slope of the isocost line equals that of AB, and the firm may start to hire some labour, though the actual choice of technique is indeterminate. If the cost of capital rises any further, the firm switches to using labour only in its production process, at the corner B in Figure 10.3. The resulting conditional demand for capital curve for a given level of output is drawn in Figure 10.5. Its elasticity is either zero at a rental rate below $\bar{r}$, or infinite at $\bar{r}$.

These zero and infinite substitutability cases are, of course, highly restrictive. In general, one might expect a smoothly downward-sloping conditional input demand curve, analogous to the compensated demand curve of Chapter 3. It is fairly straightforward to show this for the case of the Cobb-Douglas function. It is useful to start with the elasticity of substitution, defined in Chapter 8. Equation (8.8) provides a unit-free measure of the curvature of the isoquant, and therefore the extent to which factor proportions adjust with input prices. This elasticity is defined as the ratio of the proportionate change in factor proportions to proportionate changes in the marginal rate of technical substitution that occur as we move around the isoquant. Since cost minimisation implies equality between the marginal rate of technical substitution and the input price ratio, w/r, the elasticity of substitution also measures the proportionate change in the capital–labour ratio for a proportionate change in the ratio of input prices:

$$\sigma = \frac{\% \text{ change in } K/L}{\% \text{ change in } w/r} = \frac{\partial(K/L)}{\partial(w/r)} \frac{w/r}{K/L} \tag{10.47}$$

In this case of Cobb-Douglas production function, where isoquants are smoothly convex to the origin as in Figure 10.4 and where, crucially, the elasticity of substitution is unity (see equation (8.27)), we may immediately see that a one per cent increase in the relative cost of labour leads to a one per cent rise in the capital–labour ratio. As we might expect from the conditional demand functions (10.43a) and (10.43b), optimal inputs therefore smoothly decline with input prices for a given output in the Cobb-Douglas case.

We may establish these results more formally. Recall that we showed in equation (10.44) that the derivative of the cost function with respect to the input prices yields input demands. We have also established that, provided isoquants are convex to the origin, conditional input demands diminish with input prices, or

$$\frac{\partial L}{\partial w}, \frac{\partial K}{\partial r} < 0 \tag{10.48}$$

But by the standard rules of differentiation,

$$\frac{\partial L}{\partial w} = \frac{\partial(\partial C/\partial w)}{\partial w} = \frac{\partial^2 C}{\partial w^2} \tag{10.49}$$

and

$$\frac{\partial K}{\partial r} = \frac{\partial(\partial C/\partial r)}{\partial r} = \frac{\partial^2 C}{\partial r^2} \tag{10.50}$$

Hence we may say that, if the cost function is concave with respect to input prices, then the conditional input demand functions must be downward sloping with respect to input prices; $\partial L/\partial w$ and $\partial K/\partial r < 0$ if $\partial^2 C/\partial w^2$ and $\partial^2 C/\partial r^2 < 0$.

The information summarised in equations (10.49) and (10.50) implies that we may derive the conditional input demand *functions* with respect to input prices directly from the cost function in an extremely straightforward way. They are merely the second derivatives of the cost function with respect to the input price. Thus, returning to the examples given at the start of this chapter, if technology has fixed coefficients, so that the relevant cost function takes the form of (10.22) with optimal employment given by equation (10.23) and optimal capital by (10.24), we may derive the conditional input demand equations from the second derivatives of the cost function:

$$\frac{\partial L}{\partial w} = \frac{\partial^2 C}{\partial w^2} = 0 \tag{10.51}$$

$$\frac{\partial K}{\partial r} = \frac{\partial^2 C}{\partial r^2} = 0 \tag{10.52}$$

Hence we establish formally the point made earlier, and more discursively, via Figure 10.2 that the demand for factors is independent of input prices when there is perfect complementarity between inputs.

The conditional input demand functions cannot be determined using differential calculus for the case when capital and labour are perfect substitutes because the cost function is not continuous, and as we have seen in Figure 10.5, the conditional input demand functions are also discontinuous. However, for the Cobb-Douglas case, the cost function is given by equation (10.42) and optimal employment and capital by equations (10.43a) and (10.43b). The conditional input demand functions are therefore given by

$$\frac{\partial^2 C}{\partial w^2} = \frac{\alpha(\alpha - 1)C}{w^2} < 0 \tag{10.53}$$

$$\frac{\partial^2 C}{\partial r^2} = \frac{(1 - \alpha)(-\alpha)C}{r^2} < 0 \tag{10.54}$$

As we noted above, conditional factor demands decline as factor prices increase when isoquants are convex to the origin, as they are in the case of Cobb-Douglas technology.

The effect of changes in input prices on average and marginal costs

From the perspective of output supply decisions, discussed below in Part IV of this book, the long-run average and marginal cost curves reflect the most important characteristics of the cost function. The bulk of this chapter has been spent investigating the ways in which total costs and conditional factor demands vary with wages and the rental price of capital, but the implications of this analysis for marginal and average costs are also worth considering. We shall now discuss these matters.

We have already established that the elasticity of total costs with respect to wages, for example, is given by the share of the wage bill in total costs (see equation (10.46)). The same result must clearly hold for average costs, since the level of output enters both the top and bottom of the elasticity formula. Hence, if the elasticity of average costs with respect to wages is ε_w^{ac}, at a given level of output, X^*,

$$\varepsilon_w^{ac} = \frac{\partial (C/X)}{\partial w} \cdot \frac{wX^*}{C} = \frac{1}{X^*} \frac{\partial C}{\partial w} \frac{wX^*}{C}$$

$$= \frac{\partial C}{\partial w} \frac{w}{C}$$

$$= \frac{wL^*}{C} \tag{10.55}$$

The same argument holds for a change in capital costs, $\varepsilon_r^{ac} = rK^*/C$. Hence an increase in either input price always shifts the average cost curve upwards because the share of each input in total costs is clearly positive.

However, the upward shift will be a proportionate one only if the share of labour costs in total costs is constant as output changes. This will occur if technology is *homothetic*, and expansion paths are therefore linear in capital–labour space. In this case, the vertical upward shift in the long-run average cost curve will be in the same proportion for every level of output. Hence the output level at which average costs reach a minimum will remain unchanged. In other cases the upward shift will not necessarily be proportionate and the level of output at which average costs reach a minimum may alter.

The effects of a change in input price on long-run marginal cost can, logically speaking, be positive or negative, depending on a further property of the production function: whether the input whose price has changed is '**normal**' or '**inferior**'. (As we shall see, the terms are used here exactly as they are in consumer theory.) Consider the effect of an increase in the wage on marginal cost, *mc*. We know that

$$\frac{\partial(mc)}{\partial w} = \frac{\partial^2 C}{\partial X \partial w} \tag{10.56}$$

By the rules of differentiation

$$\frac{\partial^2 C}{\partial X \partial w} = \frac{\partial^2 C}{\partial w \partial X}$$

and we also know from Shephard's lemma that

$$\frac{\partial C}{\partial w} = L^*$$

Hence

$$\frac{\partial(mc)}{\partial w} = \frac{\partial L^*}{\partial X} \tag{10.57}$$

The direction of the change in marginal cost at a given level of output when wages increase therefore depends on how optimal employment adjusts as output changes, starting at that initial level of output. There are two possible cases. If labour is a *normal input*, in the sense that optimal employment increases when output increases, then $\partial L^*/\partial X > 0$ and marginal cost rises with wages.

However, this is not the only logically possible case. Suppose we have a production process in which it is efficient to reduce the labour input as output expands. Labour is in this case an *inferior input* in precisely the same sense as a good whose demand falls with income is an inferior good. In these circumstances $\partial L^*/\partial X$ will be negative and marginal cost will fall as the wage increases. Precisely the same line of argument applies to an increase in the cost of capital. Marginal cost will rise if capital is a normal input, but fall if it is an inferior input.

The results just established may once again be illustrated by referring to two of the three special case technologies which we have analysed throughout this chapter. If the production function displays fixed proportions technology, the cost function is given in equation (10.21) and marginal cost in (10.22). The change in marginal cost when wages rise is given by

$$\frac{\partial(mc)}{\partial w} = \frac{\partial^2 C}{\partial X \partial w} = \frac{1}{\gamma} > 0 \tag{10.58}$$

This is an intuitively obvious result. Since labour is a normal input with fixed coefficient technology, marginal costs must clearly increase with the cost of labour. In the case of perfect substitutes the discontinuity of the cost function once again leaves us unable to analyse changes in marginal cost using differential calculus. With the Cobb-Douglas production function, and therefore a cost function as given by (10.42), marginal costs are

$$\frac{\partial C}{\partial X} = w^\alpha r^{1-\alpha}(1-\alpha)^{\alpha-1}\alpha^{-\alpha} = \frac{C}{X} \tag{10.59}$$

and the change in marginal cost with respect to wages is given by

$$\frac{\partial^2 C}{\partial X \partial w} = \alpha w^{\alpha-1} r^{1-\alpha} (1-\alpha)^{\alpha-1} \alpha^{-\alpha} = \frac{\alpha C}{wX} > 0 \tag{10.60}$$

As we would expect with smooth isoquants, convex to the origin, and an elasticity of substitution of unity, labour is here a normal input and increased wages raise marginal cost.

Concluding comment

We have sought in this chapter to give readers an introduction to recent developments in production and cost theory. In particular, we have focused on the way that traditional propositions in the theory of supply, for example that input demand curves slope downwards, can be derived directly from the cost function without reference to the underlying shape of production technology. While recognising that many of the arguments we have presented are subtle and difficult, it is hoped that they give an insight into economists' methods and into the assumptions underlying the traditional relationships we postulate when analysing questions about production decisions and costs.

SUMMARY

Production functions, cost functions, and the demand for factors of production

1. The essential insight of duality theory on the production side is that all aspects of a firm's technology can be summarised in its cost function. Hence for example optimal factor inputs can be derived without reference to isoquants and isocost curves; input demands can be derived directly from differentiating the cost function with respect to input prices.

2. In equilibrium, if the firm is minimising its costs of production, the marginal cost of increasing output must be the same whether it does so by using additional labour or capital inputs.

3. The change in the minimum cost of production at a given level of output when the price of an input increases is the amount of the input used times the change in its price. This is an application of Shephard's lemma, linking factor demand to the derivative of the cost function with respect to input price.

4. Conditional factor demand functions are the factor demand functions derived when output is taken as constant. Hence they abstract from issues of scale effects in enterprise adjustment to changes in factor price and focus only on substitution effects.

5. The total cost of a given output will increase in proportion to a simultaneous proportional increase in all factor input prices. The cost function is therefore linearly homogeneous in factor prices.

6. If the cost function is concave with respect to factor prices, conditional factor demand will be inversely related to factor price. Conditional factor demand functions can be shown to be the second derivatives of the cost function with respect to factor prices.

7. An increase in a factor price always leads to an increase in average costs. The upward shift will only be proportionate to the price increase, however, if the share of the factor in total costs is constant as output expands (e.g. if technology is homothetic).

8. The effect of an increase in a factor price on long-run marginal cost can be positive or negative depending on whether the input affected is normal or inferior. Normality implies that optimal use of the factor increases when output rises. Long-run marginal costs fall as factor prices increase if the use of the factor declines as output rises; the factor input is, in this case, said to be inferior.

PROBLEMS

1 Examine the effect of an increase in the cost of labour on marginal costs in the short run and in the long run. Under what conditions will the long-run marginal cost curve shift down?

2 Suppose that the production function takes the form $X = \min(10L, 5K)$ and that a competitive firm faces a wage rate of £60 per week and a weekly capital rental of £32.

(a) How much must the firm spend to produce 100 units of output, and what is the average cost of production when $X = 100$?

(b) What is the incremental cost of producing the 101st unit of output?

(c) What happens to the cost of producing 100 units of output if the wage rate and the rental cost of capital rise by 25 per cent each? What happens to the average and marginal cost?

(d) What happens to the cost of producing 100 units of output if the wage rate increases by £1, or if the cost of capital increases by £1?

3 Suppose that the weekly production function takes the form $X = 2L + K$, with the firm facing a weekly wage rate of £100 and capital rentals of £300.

(a) Will the firm use any labour at all in the production process?

(b) Suppose that output of X is 500 units per week. What are marginal costs? What are average costs?

(c) Suppose that the wage rate increases by 60 per cent. What happens to the cost of production? What happens to average and marginal cost?

4 The firm faces a long-run production function (for output per week)

$$X = 10L^{1/2}K^{1/2}$$

and input prices of £100 per week for labour and £200 per week for capital rental.

(a) What are the firm's cost-minimising levels of employment and capital stock if it produces 200 units of output?

(b) What if it produces 400 units of output? What are long-run average and marginal costs in each case (i.e. if output = 200 and 400)?

(c) Suppose that the firm becomes more efficient technically, so that the production function becomes

$$X = 11L^{1/2}K^{1/2}$$

What happens to total, average and marginal costs if output equals 200? If output equals 400?

(d) What happens to the capital–labour ratio if output equals 200 and the wage rate increases by 10 per cent? What happens to total and marginal costs?

PART IV

BASIC THEORY OF THE FIRM

CHAPTER (11)

Perfect competition

Key words and phrases

- profit maximisation, perfectly competitive or price-taking firm
- revenue functions, total, average and marginal revenue
- short-run marginal cost curve and short-run supply curve, long-run supply, entry and the industry supply curve, increasing, constant and diminishing returns to scale
- natural monopoly
- linearly homogeneous production functions
- indivisibility of managerial inputs, normal profits; differences in efficiency
- marginal and intra-marginal firms
- pecuniary economies and diseconomies of scale, economies internal and external to the firm

Introduction

We shall be concerned, in this part of the book, with the decisions of firms about how much to supply to the product market. One of our major interests will be the relationship between the demand for a product, associated with its price in competitive markets, and the quantity that a firm chooses to produce. This can be contrasted with the focus, in Part VI of the book, on the relationship between product demand and factor demand. The precise relationship between product demand and production can be shown to depend on the structure of the market in which the enterprise operates and upon the motivation of those who take the relevant decisions. In this part of the book we shall concentrate on competition and monopoly, before going on to discuss a variety of forms of imperfect competition and alternative company objectives. In Part V of the book we introduce the idea that the output or price decision of any one firm is interdependent with that of other firms. In what follows, we shall assume that firms are motivated to maximise profits, except in Chapter 14, where we examine the implications for supply behaviour of certain alternative assumptions about enterprise objectives. Strategic interdependence, while being core to the functioning of many markets, is largely ignored in this part of the volume.

This chapter outlines the theory of supply in a competitive industry. In this chapter we derive supply curves at the level of the firm and that of the competitive industry first under some rather special assumptions about technology and factor price behaviour and then more generally. In Chapter 12, we shall introduce the price and output decisions of a monopolist.

The profit-maximisation hypothesis

The **maximisation of profits** is not the only conceivable motive for the operator of a firm, whom we designated earlier as the 'entrepreneur'. However, if the entrepreneur is a utility-maximising individual who gains utility solely from the consumption of goods and services obtained on the market, then maximising profit is consistent with achieving that end. To the extent that an individual draws satisfaction from less tangible factors, such as power, the esteem of friends and neighbours and so forth, it is possible to construct arguments that suggest that the size of the firm (perhaps measured by the value of sales) or the rate of growth of the firm would be more appropriate variables to maximise. Moreover, when one recognises that the world in which any actual firm operates is far from being a certain one, so that it is seldom clear which particular decision among the alternatives available will indeed result in maximum profits, motives based upon acquiring security, cutting down the effort put into decision making and such, also begin to look appealing.

A part of the literature of that field of economics known as *industrial organisation* is devoted to careful analysis of the questions just raised about motivation, but we shall not take these matters any further in this text. Because we assumed that consumption alone yielded utility when dealing with the consumer, and because we are going to adopt, albeit usually implicitly, the assumption that uncertainty about the future does not exist when dealing with the firm, consistency suggests that we assume profit maximisation as well. It is not an uncontroversial assumption about motivation, but it does yield relatively simple and useful analysis. Its implications are worth pursuing for that reason alone. Moreover, in the last analysis, any firm, whatever the motivation of its owners and managers, must earn profits if it is to survive. There must always be an element of profit seeking in the behaviour of any firm and it is not perhaps unreasonable to approximate this with the simplifying assumption of profit maximisation. Remember, though, that the following pages do not represent a comprehensive survey of the theory of the firm, dealing as they do mainly with the theory of the profit-maximising firm operating in conditions of certainty.

The perfectly competitive firm's demand function

We will now analyse the so-called **perfectly competitive firm**, sometimes called a **price-taking firm**. As the latter name implies, the firm is one that takes the price of its output and of its inputs as given and makes decisions only about the volume of its output and the quantities of inputs it will employ.

It is usual to think of the price-taking firm as being a sufficiently small part of the industry of which it is a member that its own activities could not possibly have a noticeable effect on the price of the industry's output. A single farm producing a particular crop is the archetypal example here, which is one of the reasons why agricultural economists

Figure 11.1

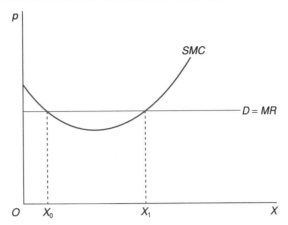

For a perfectly competitive firm the demand curve is infinitely elastic. Marginal revenue therefore equals price. Profits are maximised in the short run where marginal cost cuts the marginal revenue curve from below (at output X_1). At output X_0 marginal cost cuts the marginal revenue curve from above and losses are maximised. Figure 11.2 presents the same analysis in terms of total revenue and total cost functions.

find the perfect competition model so attractive and useful. The demand curve for output that such a firm faces takes the form of a horizontal line at a given price such as that depicted in Figure 11.1. The curve is characterised by an infinite price elasticity of demand, since the smallest cut in its selling price will lead to an infinite increase in the quantity that the firm can apparently sell.

Competitiveness is often associated not only with a very large, and potentially infinite, number of suppliers, but also with each operating under broadly the same conditions. By this last phrase we mean that information about technology is freely accessible, so that everyone can in principle choose the same techniques of production, and that there are no restrictions on new firms starting to trade on the market, nor on existing firms leaving the market if they are unable to earn an adequate return. In the real world, of course, these conditions are rarely satisfied in full, but the perfectly competitive model is nevertheless useful. It provides both an idea of the outcome to which a market with large numbers of firms, free entry and exit of traders, and free access to information and technology would tend, and a standard by which outcomes in other market structures can be judged.

Total, average and marginal revenue

The **revenue function** faced by the firm describes the relationship between **total revenue** (or the total value of sales) and output. Calculus is particularly useful in bringing out the relationship between revenue, revenue per unit of production and incremental, or marginal, revenue. Revenue, R, depends upon the quantity of output sold and its price:

$$R = R(X) = pX \tag{11.1}$$

We define **average revenue** as revenue per unit of output (R/X), which obviously equals price. The average revenue curve therefore relates price to output, and is the firm's *inverse demand curve*.[1] **Marginal revenue** is the increment to revenue generated by the sale of an additional unit of output, and can therefore be derived formally as the derivative of the revenue function with respect to output. In the general case, where we allow for price to vary with output along the inverse demand curve, marginal revenue is given by

$$MR = \frac{\partial R}{\partial X} = p + X \frac{\partial p}{\partial X} \tag{11.2}$$

where $\partial p / \partial X$ is the slope of the inverse demand curve faced by the firm. However, in a perfectly competitive market, the demand curve is horizontal, as in Figure 11.1. The slope of the inverse demand curve is zero and marginal revenue equals price. Hence for perfect competition, *and for perfect competition only*, the marginal and average revenue curves coincide, as in Figure 11.1. Since in competition $\partial R / \partial X = p$, which is a constant by assumption, the revenue curve, denoted *TR* in Figure 11.2, is a straight line with slope p. If we wish to think of this analysis in terms of the elasticity of demand, we may note that the elasticity of demand, e, is defined as $(\partial X / \partial p)(p / X)$. If we multiply the right-hand side of (11.2) by $1 = p/p$, we obtain

$$MR = \frac{\partial R}{\partial X} = p \left(1 + \frac{X}{p} \frac{\partial p}{\partial X} \right)$$

which we may rewrite as

$$MR = \frac{\partial R}{\partial X} = p \left(1 + \frac{1}{e} \right) \tag{11.3}$$

Figure 11.2

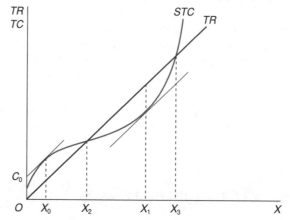

Short-run profits are maximised where short-run total cost is at a maximum distance below total revenue. This is at level of output X_1 where the slopes of the two curves are equal (i.e. where marginal cost equals marginal revenue) and the slope of the total cost curve is increasing. At X_0 the slopes of the two curves are equal, but here costs exceed revenue and the slope of the total cost curve is falling. Hence short-run losses are maximised here.

This equation is one of the fundamental relationships in the theory of the firm, and gives another way of thinking about the perfectly competitive firm's demand curve. In competition e is infinite, and therefore marginal revenue equals price.

It is worth repeating explicitly that average and marginal revenue are not in general the same; they just happen to be equal when the demand curve that the firm faces is horizontal. When price does not vary with the volume of sales, then marginal revenue (the amount added to total revenue per unit of output when a small addition is made to output – and hence to sales) is simply price per unit of output. If the price the firm received did vary with output – for example, when the firm faced the market demand curve, which would be downward sloping – this would not be the case. The behaviour of firms differs with market structure precisely because market structure can affect the slope of the demand curve faced by each individual firm, and therefore the impact of particular output decisions on the revenue to be earned by it.

Box 11.1   ## More on marginal revenue

For readers who prefer concrete, rather than general, functions we can derive the relationship between marginal revenue, the elasticity of demand and price with a simple linear demand function, $X = 100 - p$, and its inverse, $p = 100 - X$. Total revenue (R) is

$$R = pX = 100X - X^2 \tag{11.1.1}$$

Marginal revenue (MR) is

$$MR = \frac{dR}{dX} = 100 - 2X = 100 - X - X \tag{11.1.2}$$

Using the demand function it follows that

$$MR = p - X \tag{11.1.3}$$

The elasticity of demand (e) is

$$e = \frac{dX}{dp} \cdot \frac{p}{X}$$

For our demand function

$$e = -1\frac{p}{X}$$

i.e. $-X = \dfrac{p}{e}$ \tag{11.1.4}

Combining this expression with the expression for MR:

$$MR = p - X = p + \frac{p}{e} = p\left(1 + \frac{1}{e}\right) \tag{11.1.5}$$

This is the same expression as (11.3) derived in the text.

The firm's short-run supply curve

What, then, about profit maximisation? First, let us consider the **short-run** situation. There are two equivalent geometrical ways of finding the level of output at which profits are maximised in the short run. They are depicted in Figures 11.1 and 11.2. Consider first Figure 11.2 where a short-run total cost curve that displays at first increasing and then decreasing returns to labour, is set alongside the total revenue curve. Profits are equal to total revenue minus total costs which, in terms of Figure 11.2, is the vertical distance between the two curves. This distance is obviously at a maximum at output level X_1, where the total cost curve is below the total revenue curve and their slopes are parallel to each other. At any lower level of output, revenue is rising faster than cost, and at any higher level it is rising more slowly. Note that, by a similar argument, maximum losses would be made at output X_0.

Now we know that the slope of a 'total' curve defines a 'marginal' curve. If it is a condition of profit maximisation that the slope of the total revenue curve be equal to that of the total cost curve, then this also means that *marginal cost should be equal to marginal revenue*. This could take place at either X_0 or X_1 in Figure 11.1, but output X_0 is one that maximises losses. It is also a condition of profit maximisation then that the *marginal cost curve cuts the marginal revenue curve from below*. This, of course, is at a level of output at which there are diminishing returns to labour. We have here an example of the condition asserted in Chapter 8, that the firm will always operate in the region of the production function characterised by diminishing returns to a factor.

Now for a price-taking firm, marginal revenue and price are equal to one another. Thus, in the short run, a profit maximising price-taking firm will fix output at that level whose marginal cost of production (on the upward-sloping segment of the marginal cost curve) is equal to market price, with one qualification that we must now discuss.

It is always open to the firm to produce nothing at all, and there are circumstances where this is the most profitable (in the sense of being the least costly) thing it can do. In the short run, the firm must always pay its fixed costs, regardless of its level of output. It incurs variable costs only if it produces output, and it is easy to construct a case in which both the total cost curve and the total variable cost curve lie above the total revenue curve at every level of output. In such a case price is below both overall average cost and average variable cost at any positive level of output. Figure 11.3 depicts just such a situation. If this firm *must* produce something then it will certainly maximise profits (that is, minimise losses; the terms are synonymous) at output X_1, where marginal cost and marginal revenue are equal. However, by producing X_1, it would make greater losses than it would incur if it produced nothing at all. If it produced nothing, it would lose only its fixed costs, whereas by producing X_1 it is making a loss on its variable costs also. Unless a firm can reduce its losses by producing, it will not produce, and it can do this only if the price it receives for its output exceeds the minimum value of average variable cost.

At any price above this level, which just covers average variable cost, profit-maximising output is found by inspecting the marginal cost curve, but below this level the firm will produce no output at all. Notice what has just been said: above the minimum point of the average variable cost curve the marginal cost curve relates the firm's profit-maximising output to price. Since the firm is a profit maximiser, this will be its actual output. Hence, for the individual competitive firm in the short run, above the minimum point of the average variable cost curve, **the marginal cost curve is its supply curve.**

Figure 11.3

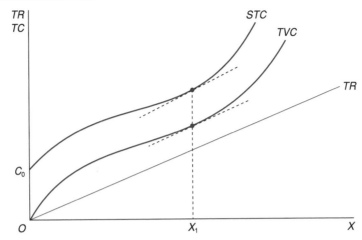

If total revenue is everywhere below total variable cost, then losses are greater at output X_1 (where they are nevertheless minimised for any positive level of output) than they would be if the firm produced nothing and incurred a loss of C_0 – its fixed costs.

Box 11.2   **The shut down decision**

To illustrate the decision to shut down we can compare two firms that compete in the same market. Both firms are *price takers* and sell their output at £20 per unit. This implies that the total revenue function is $R = 20X$ and $MR = 20$. For firm 1 the total variable cost function is

$$TVC_1 = 0.5X_1^3 - 8X_1^2 + 48X_1 \tag{11.2.1}$$

For firm 2 the total variable cost function is

$$TVC_2 = 0.5X_2^3 - 10X_2^2 + 75X_2 \tag{11.2.2}$$

The interested reader can confirm that these functions display TVC curves of the same shape as in Figure 11.3. Both firms have fixed costs of £35. Marginal costs are

$$MC_1 = \frac{dTVC_1}{dX_1} = 1.5X_1^2 - 16X_1 + 48 \tag{11.2.3}$$

$$MC_2 = \frac{dTVC_2}{dX_2} = 1.5X_2^2 - 20X_2 + 75 \tag{11.2.4}$$

It is up to the reader to confirm that these MC curves are U shaped. As the MC curves are quadratic functions, profit maximising by setting $MC = MR$ will give two apparent solutions for each firm: $X_1 = 2.21$ or 8.46 and $X_2 = 3.88$ or 9.46. The larger outputs in both cases are the ones in which MC cuts MR from below, and so is profit maximising. The smaller outputs imply MC cutting MR from above, and so it is profit minimising.

The actual profits earned can be found by substituting the profit maximising outputs into revenue and cost functions:

$$\pi_1 = 20(8.46) - 0.5(8.46^3) + 8(8.46^2) - 48(8.46) - 35 = -2.06 \qquad (11.2.5)$$

$$\pi_2 = 20(9.46) - 0.5(9.46^3) + 10(9.46^2) - 75(9.46) - 35 = -83.68 \qquad (11.2.6)$$

Clearly both firms are making losses. But only firm 2 should close down in the short run, i.e. with immediate effect. If firm 1 closed down, and consequently produced an output of zero, it would still have to pay fixed costs of £35. As revenue would be zero, because of zero output, losses would be worse than 2.06 from trading at profit maximising output. If firm 2 closed down it would reduce its losses from 83.68 to 35, i.e. it is rational to close down.

We can draw this same conclusion by comparing average variable cost with price. For firm 1:

$$AVC_1 = TVC_1/X_1 = 0.5X_1^2 - 8X_1 + 48 \qquad (11.2.7)$$

$$AVC_2 = TVC_2/X_2 = 0.5X_2^2 - 10X_2 + 75 \qquad (11.2.8)$$

For firm 1 there are some output levels that allow AVC_1 to be less than price, i.e. the firm will be able to cover its variable costs, a requirement for short-run commercial viability. But for firm 2 there are no output levels that allow AVC_2 to be less than price, i.e. firm 2 will not be able to cover its variable costs. To see this conclusion we find the output levels that minimise AVC and compute the AVC involved:

$$\frac{d(AVC_1)}{d(X_1)} = X_1 - 8 = 0 \qquad (11.2.9)$$

$$\frac{d(AVC_2)}{d(X_2)} = X_2 - 10 = 0 \qquad (11.2.10)$$

Substituting $X_1 = 8$ and $X_2 = 10$ into the AVC function we find: $\min(AVC_1) = 16$, $\min(AVC_2) = 25$. As price is £20 the conclusion is that firm 1 is commercially viable but firm 2 is not.

* A formal treatment

Supply decisions for competitive firms can be analysed particularly simply with the aid of calculus, which also offers a more general interpretation than our previous geometric approach. Algebraically, the firm chooses output to maximise profits, which equal revenue minus costs. Profits are given by

$$\pi = pX - wL - rK \qquad (11.4)$$

which, following our discussion of cost functions in Chapter 8 and of revenue functions above, we can respecify as

$$\pi = \pi(X) = R(X) - C(X) \qquad (11.5)$$

The first-order condition for maximisation is

$$\frac{\partial R}{\partial X} - \frac{\partial C}{\partial X} = 0 \tag{11.6}$$

which, in the case of competition when marginal revenue equals price, reduces to

$$p - \frac{\partial C}{\partial X} = 0 \tag{11.7}$$

The first-order condition states that profits are maximised at a level of output where *marginal cost equals price*. This is, however, only a *necessary* condition for profit maximisation. We derive the *sufficient* condition from the second derivative of the profit function (11.5). The second-order condition is

$$\frac{\partial^2 \pi}{\partial X^2} = \frac{\partial^2 R}{\partial X^2} - \frac{\partial^2 C}{\partial X^2} < 0 \tag{11.8}$$

In competition, the slope of the inverse demand curve faced by the firm is a constant (equal to zero) so $\partial^2 R / \partial X^2 = 0$. Sufficiency therefore hinges on the sign of the second derivative of the cost function, which must be positive, as we saw in Figures 11.1 and 11.2. Hence profits reach a maximum provided, at the point where price equals marginal cost, marginal costs are increasing with output. If we interpret our cost functions as relating to the short run, when only labour input is variable, we will remember, following the analysis of Chapter 8, that rising marginal cost is implied by diminishing returns to labour. Note also that we can also think about the firm's output decision directly in terms of the impact of a changing production level on profits. An example is illustrated in Figure 11.4 of the quadratic profit function implied by the revenue and cost functions of Figure 11.2.

Figure 11.4

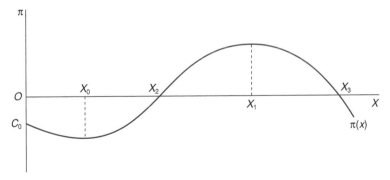

The profit function implied by the cost and revenue functions of Figure 11.2. Profits reach a minimum at X_0 and maximum at X_1, and equal zero at X_2 and X_3. Profit maximisation implies that the firm chooses X_1, where marginal revenue equals marginal cost.

Price determination in the short run

We are now in a position to investigate how the price, taken as given by the individual firm, is in fact determined, at least in the short run. The market demand curve for X may be obtained by summing up the individual demand curves derived in Part I (using the constant real income rather than constant money income curves if we wish to deal with a fully employed economy). Just as the individual's demand curve tells us how much that agent will buy at a given price, so the market demand curve tells us how much all the individuals in the market for X will together buy at a given price. By analogous reasoning, we may derive the short-run market supply curve for X on the assumption that input prices are constant for all producing firms, regardless of their output. The short-run marginal cost curve above the minimum point of the average variable cost curve tells us how much X any individual firm will supply at a given price. Adding up the amounts of X over all firms tells us how much the whole industry will supply. Figure 11.5(b) portrays the relevant market supply and demand curves. Their intersection at p^*, X^* determines the overall output of X and its price. This is the price which is given to the individual firm whose situation is depicted in Figure 11.5(a). At this price, the consumption plans of consumers and the output plans of firms are just compatible. We have an *equilibrium* situation.

Now the situation for the particular firm shown in Figure 11.5(a) has it producing X_1 at the going market price. Since the average cost of producing that level of output is AC_1, the firm is clearly making a total profit of $(p^* - AC_1)X_1$. A number of questions now arise. First, suppose we look at the behaviour of this firm over a rather longer time period. Would it still be the case that this is the level of output it would choose? Once it is free to vary its

Figure 11.5

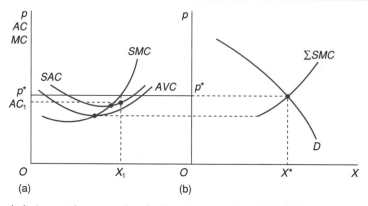

The short-run industry supply curve, when factor prices are given, is the horizontal sum of each firm's marginal cost curve above the minimum point of each firm's average variable cost curve (ΣSMC). The interaction of supply and demand at the industry level determines industry output at X^* and price at p^*. At this price the individual firm produces X_1 units of output and makes a total profit of $(p^* - AC_1)X_1$. Note that, to keep the diagram manageable, the scale on the horizontal axis of panel (b) is greatly reduced from that which is used on the same axis panel (a), so that a given horizontal distance from the origin of (b) represents a greater volume of X.

capital inputs, might there not be some other level of output that was more profitable at that price? Second, the supply curve used to determine the market price was obtained by adding up the marginal cost curves of all firms in the industry. It is valid to aggregate individual short-run marginal cost curves in this way only if we assume that input prices do not vary even when all firms in the industry vary their output levels. We have also been assuming that there is a given number of firms in the industry. Now, over a time period where the individual firm cannot vary its capital stock, it is quite reasonable to make this latter assumption. But what determined how many firms were in the industry in the first place? When we consider a horizon long enough to make all factors of production variable, we must also consider the possibility of firms entering and leaving the industry. In short, we must consider the determination of price and output in the long run.

The firm and the industry in the long run

The foregoing analysis showed, with input prices constant, that the short-run supply curve of the perfectly competitive firm is that section of its marginal cost curve which lies above its average cost curve. For purely expositional purposes, let us first consider the supply behaviour of already existing firms in the long run, though in practice it will be impossible to distinguish between capital expansion by existing firms and entry of new ones. If, still holding factor prices constant, we assume that entry is impossible and simply substitute the long-run total cost, average cost, and marginal cost curves for their short-run counterparts in the arguments embodied in Figures 11.1, 11.2, and 11.5, the firm's **long-run supply** curve is given by that section of its long-run marginal cost curve that lies above the minimum point of the long-run average cost curve. This conclusion also follows from a straightforward reinterpretation of the cost function embedded in equation (11.5) as a long-run relationship. However, it does not follow from this that the **industry's long-run supply curve** is simply some horizontal summation of the individual firms' supply curves. The reason is that, in the long run, each firm is free to vary the quantities of all the inputs that it uses, and if existing firms can do that, then they can, if they choose, leave the industry, while new firms can **enter** it. In the long run, therefore, the number of firms in the industry is variable. As we noted above, this is a second crucial characteristic of a competitive market structure.

In order to carry our analysis further, suppose that there are no special resources or limited skills necessary to produce X, so that the production function underlying the cost curves of the particular firm we have been considering is available to any firm. Suppose also that each firm is able to buy its inputs at the same price as any other. It then follows that the short-run and long-run cost curves for any firm will be identical to those for any other. For the remainder of this chapter, we assume that technology displays **increasing**, then **constant**, then **diminishing returns to scale**, so that the *long-run average cost curve is U-shaped*.

In order to appreciate the importance of the possibility of entry by new firms to the behaviour of a competitive industry in the long run, it is helpful to consider first a hypothetical situation in which entry is not possible. Consider, in the light of this assumption, Figure 11.6. Here we show the short- and long-run cost and supply curves for a typical firm in the industry. It is assumed in drawing this figure that the firm is in a situation in which price is equated to both long-run and short-run marginal cost, so that, given the

Figure 11.6

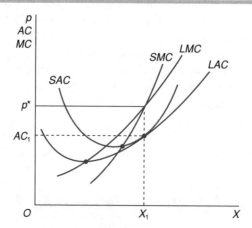

Suppose that price is given by p^*. At this price the typical firm will, in the long run, wish to sell X_1 of X. At this scale of output there are associated short-run average and marginal cost curves, the latter cutting the long-run marginal cost curve from below at output level X_1. As this figure is drawn, the firm makes positive profits at an output of X_1. From the point of view of the industry, this cannot be a long-run equilibrium situation.

price ruling in the market, the firm has the right-sized plant. If this is true of each firm, there will be no internal tendency for them to change their outputs at all: each one will be making profits of $(p^* - AC_1)X_1$ – the maximum available. Such a situation as we have depicted in Figure 11.6 could exist only if there were no entry into the industry. If the technology underlying the production function is readily available to all-comers, and if anyone may enter the industry, existing firms would not be allowed to remain undisturbed in that situation, if they were ever in it in the first place.

The profit which each firm is depicted as making is the difference between revenue and outlay both on the wage bill and on the rental of all its capital equipment. It is a pure surplus, because any 'normal rate of return' is already included in the rental price of capital. This profit is a rate of flow of extra income that is available simply as a result of being in the industry. If we start with barriers to entry, and then remove them, new firms will obviously be attracted by the existence of this profit and will set up in the production of X. By assumption, they can now costlessly enter the industry. Only when such profit is completely competed away will there be no further entry.

The means by which such profit is competed away are easily analysed. As each new firm enters the industry its output must be added to the output of the firms already in the industry. Because the market demand curve for X slopes downwards, the market price of X will fall as industry output is increased in this way. Firms will continue to enter the industry until market price has fallen to such an extent that no profits are being made by any firm. At this point, with neither entry nor exit, each firm may be said to be of equilibrium size and the industry to contain an equilibrium number of firms. As readers should be able to satisfy themselves, when the industry is of equilibrium size, the output of each firm in it will be lower than in what we now know to be the non-equilibrium situation depicted in Figure 11.6.

Now the foregoing description of profits being competed away after the removal of some unspecified barrier to entry of new firms serves the purpose of emphasising the important role played by the number of firms in the industry in determining the properties of the long-run competitive supply curve. It should not be taken literally as a description of a process often encountered in the real world. In an industry in which entry was always possible, it is unlikely that any firm would put itself in a position such as that depicted in Figure 11.6. If market price was ever high enough to create positive profits, the firm would realise that they would attract other firms into the industry and that they would be competed away. Hence the firm would not expand its capacity along its long-run marginal cost curve. It would foresee the arrival of new entrants and realise that it would be left with too much capacity to produce efficiently its share of the industry's long-run equilibrium output once they started producing. Hence the firm would avoid getting itself into this overcapacity situation in the first place, and at most would move along its short-run supply curve in order to take advantage of any temporary rise in output price above its long-run equilibrium level. We analyse the role of firms' expectations about the behaviour of others, upon which we merely touch here, in more detail in Chapters 15 and 16.

Now the industry's long-run equilibrium output level, at which there is neither entry nor exit, must be such that the price facing each firm in the industry just enables it to cover its costs while maximising profits. Maximum profits mean that marginal cost must equal price and zero profits mean that average cost must equal price. Marginal and average cost are only equal to one another at the minimum point of the average cost curve. Thus, if firms are free to come and go in the industry, the price of output will always return to this same level in the long run. The long-run supply curve for the industry will be a horizontal line at the minimum value of long-run average cost for any firm in the industry, as we show in Figure 11.7, and each firm will produce an output of X^{**}.

Figure 11.7

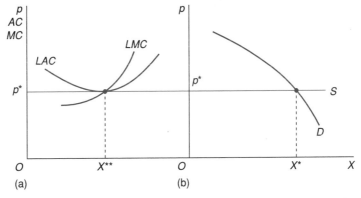

The existence of positive profits will entice new firms into the production of X. If factor prices are constant and all firms are equally efficient, price will always tend, in the long run, to be equal to the minimum attainable level of long-run average cost. Hence the long-run industry supply curve will be horizontal at this price. Each firm will produce X^{**} at price p^*.

The properties of the competitive industry

So far, we have assumed that each firm has identical technology with increasing, constant and then diminishing returns to both labour and to scale. Each firm therefore faces identically shaped long-run and short-run U-shaped average cost curves. Each firm also faces the infinite elasticity of demand which means that in perfect competition, price equals marginal revenue. On these assumptions, we have deduced that profit maximisation leads each firm to select the level of output at which marginal cost equals price. The price of goods sold on competitive markets therefore reflects the incremental costs of producing the last unit of output. It will be shown in Part VIII of this book that this sort of output rule can be associated with efficiency in the allocation of resources.

Alternative assumptions about returns to scale

The returns to scale characteristics of the firm's production function that underlie the U-shaped long-run average cost curve assumed above play an important role in the theory of perfect competition, and this is best seen by examining what would happen if these characteristics were different.

Consider, first of all, the long-run average and marginal cost curves of a firm that faces diminishing returns to scale at every level of output. They will be as depicted in Figure 11.8. Clearly, at any price above p^*, say p_1, this firm will be making positive profits. If every firm, actual and potential, faces the same cost conditions, the existence of positive profits will lead to an expansion of the industry. This expansion should go on until each firm is producing at the lowest point on its long-run average cost curve, but that would be at a level of output approaching zero. The prediction that an industry will end up in the long-run situation of having a number of firms approaching the infinite, each producing an

Figure 11.8

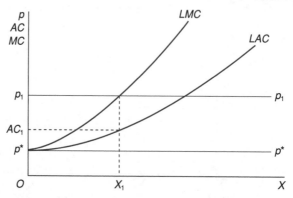

For a firm which experiences diminishing returns to scale at every level of output, the minimum point on its average cost curve is arbitrarily close to the vertical axis. In perfect competition, with all firms equally efficient, each such firm would end up making zero profits at an output approaching zero. The assumptions of consistently decreasing returns to scale together with that of equally efficient firms are not useful in the context of perfect competition.

output verging on zero, does not make much empirical sense, and we may rule this case out on these grounds alone. If the perfectly competitive firm is to have a finite equilibrium size in the long run, then the minimum point on its average cost curve must not coincide with the vertical axis.

When the firm's production function is everywhere characterised by constant returns to scale, its long-run average and marginal cost curves coincide and are horizontal lines. This case produces indeterminate rather than nonsensical results at the level of the analysis of the individual firm. In Figure 11.9 the long-run equilibrium price at the industry level is given at p^*, and the demand curve faced by the individual firm will be horizontal at that price, coinciding at every point with the firm's marginal and average cost curves. Thus, the number of firms in the industry and their sizes are left indeterminate in this case. One firm or many could equally efficiently produce the whole industry's output. Constant returns to scale at the level of the firm cannot be reconciled with a useful analysis of the behaviour of the individual perfectly competitive firm, at least not in terms of the simple analysis upon which we base this chapter.

Finally, consider the case of the individual firm benefiting from continuously increasing returns to scale. The appropriate cost curves are depicted in Figure 11.10. This case, though empirically plausible, is incompatible with the existence of perfect competition. When there are continuously increasing returns to scale up to the level of output that will satisfy the entire market demand for the industry's output, one firm can produce the whole industry's output at a lower average cost than can two or more firms, and that firm could therefore always undercut and drive out any smaller firms that tried to compete with it.

We have here what is known as **natural monopoly** and the perfectly competitive model may not be applied in this case. The theory of monopoly, dealt with in the next chapter, is the appropriate device to use in its analysis, and we shall take up the topic again there.

Figure 11.9

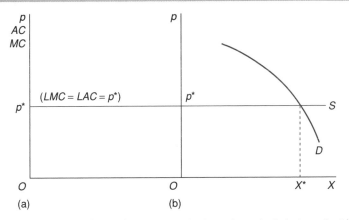

If all firms are equally efficient and experience constant returns to scale, industry output is determinate at X^*. However, the firm's output is indeterminate since the marginal cost, average cost and marginal revenue curves coincide when zero profits are being made.

Figure 11.10

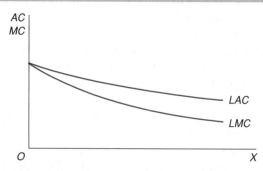

When returns to scale are always increasing, long-run average cost falls continuously and marginal cost is below it. There is no meaningful price and output equilibrium to this case in the context of perfect competition. Increasing returns to scale naturally lead to monopoly.

Box 11.3 | ## Returns to scale and profitability

To illustrate the relationship between returns to scale characteristics and profitability we can consider two firms: firm 1 has decreasing returns scale and firm 2 has increasing returns to scale. For the first firm the production function is

$$X_1 = 10L_1^{0.4}K_1^{0.4} \tag{11.3.1}$$

and for the second firm

$$X_2 = 10L_2^{0.6}K_2^{0.6} \tag{11.3.2}$$

The connection between exponent values and returns to scale in a Cobb-Douglas function was explored in Chapter 9. Assume that both firms sell their output at a price of £20 per unit, in which case the revenue function is $R = 20X$. In addition we can assume that capital costs are £100 per unit, and the wage rate is £50. These factor prices imply that total cost (C) for both firms is

$$C = 100K + 50L \tag{11.3.3}$$

The profit function for both firms is the difference between revenue and cost:

$$\pi = 20X - 100K - 50L \tag{11.3.4}$$

Using the production functions we can therefore define

$$\pi_1 = (20)10L_1^{0.4}K_1^{0.4} - 100K_1 - 50L_1 \tag{11.3.5}$$

$$\pi_2 = (20)10L_2^{0.6}K_2^{0.6} - 100K_2 - 50L_2 \tag{11.3.6}$$

We can find the profit-maximising solution by differentiating with respect to K and L and setting the derivatives equal to zero:

$$\frac{\partial \pi_1}{\partial L_1} = 0.4(200)L_1^{0.4}L_1^{-1}K_1^{0.4} - 50 = 0 \tag{11.3.7}$$

$$\frac{\partial \pi_1}{\partial K_1} = 0.4(200)L_1^{0.4}K_1^{0.4}K_1^{-1} - 100 = 0 \tag{11.3.8}$$

$$\frac{\partial \pi_2}{\partial L_2} = 0.6(200)L_2^{0.6}L_2^{-1}K_2^{0.6} - 50 = 0 \tag{11.3.9}$$

$$\frac{\partial \pi_2}{\partial K_2} = 0.6(200)L_2^{0.6}K_2^{0.6}K_2^{-1} - 100 = 0 \tag{11.3.10}$$

Using (11.3.7)–(11.3.10):

$$\frac{8X_1}{L_1} - 50 = 0 \tag{11.3.11}$$

$$\frac{8X_1}{K_1} - 100 = 0 \tag{11.3.12}$$

$$\frac{12X_2}{L_2} - 50 = 0 \tag{11.3.13}$$

$$\frac{12X_2}{K_2} - 100 = 0 \tag{11.3.14}$$

Using (11.3.11) to (11.3.14) we can define profit maximising input levels for the two firms:

$$L_1 = 0.16X_1; \quad K_1 = 0.08X_1; \quad L_2 = 0.24X_2; \quad K_2 = 0.12X_2$$

Substituting these input levels back into the profit functions for the two firms:

$$\pi_1 = 20X_1 - 100(0.08X_1) - 50(0.16X_1) = 4X_1 \tag{11.3.15}$$

$$\pi_2 = 20X_2 - 100(0.12X_2) - 50(0.24X_2) = -4X_2 \tag{11.3.16}$$

It follows that firm 1 makes positive profits and firm 2 losses at all output levels. The only difference between the two firms is that firm one has decreasing returns to scale and firm 2 has increasing returns at all output levels. This conclusion is presented in general terms in the Appendix at the end of this chapter.

The U-shaped average cost curve and managerial inputs

The reader will by now appreciate the importance of postulating a U-shaped long-run average cost curve in the context of the theory of the perfectly competitive firm. It is only when the curve takes this form that the individual firm's output level is finite, positive and determinate. The following argument is often advanced as a plausible justification for using this type of cost function.

The production process is not solely an engineering matter; there are also administrative problems involved in getting goods produced. Someone has to organise the factors of production to ensure that they do end up co-operating in the technically most efficient manner, and someone must decide upon output levels and so forth. There is, in effect, a third input into our production process, namely, the managerial skill of the organiser of the firm, the entrepreneur. Thus, when a firm expands output by equiproportional increases in labour and capital services, this does not represent equiproportional increases in *all* inputs. Managerial skill is being held constant. If, at very low levels of output, this skill is underutilised, the firm will be able to do an increasingly effective job of organising capital and labour as output expands – to get, that is, decreasing average costs of production – up to a certain level. But, as output expands further, this same amount of organisational skill is likely to become increasingly overtaxed: hence at higher output levels there arises a tendency to rising average costs.

One we treat managerial skill as an input, there is a need to discuss how the entrepreneur is rewarded. The answer here, as we noted in Chapter 8, is that the reward comes out of the firm's profits. Competition is no longer assumed to bid these down to zero, but down to some minimal acceptable level known as **normal profits**. One can reconcile the existence of normal profits with the analysis set out in the previous chapter in two equally acceptable ways. First, one can note that the entrepreneur, if not working in one industry, would be in some other. Hence, to engage in organising a firm in the production of X, the profit that could have been earned by organising a firm in some other industry is being forgone. The normal profits available elsewhere are then a cost of production of X in addition to outlays on capital and labour. It then becomes reasonable to think of these as being included in the factors lying behind the firm's long-run cost curves. Alternatively, one may simply suppose that these normal profits, when spread over a sufficiently large equilibrium volume of output, make such a small difference between the minimum point on the firm's average cost curve and the price of output as to be negligible.

The notion of normal profits is not devoid of problems of its own, however. Two points in particular should be noted. Their basis is that entrepreneurial capacity represents an indivisible factor of production, but the 'entrepreneur' may just as well be a management team as an individual person. Once that is realised, the case for treating entrepreneurial capacity as indivisible begins to lose much of its initial appeal. Furthermore, the management decisions that need to be undertaken by those in charge of a firm operating in the kind of perfectly competitive industry we are envisaging here are trivial to the point of being negligible. Our analysis abstracts from all the uncertainty about markets, about technical change, about the behaviour of competitors, and so on, that make entrepreneurial activity so taxing in the real world. Thus, arguments to the effect that the indivisibility of entrepreneurial inputs lies at the root of the U-shaped long-run average cost curves that we attribute to perfectly competitive firms are better regarded as attempts to extend the logical completeness of an already rather abstract, but not for that reason irrelevant, model than as attempts to bring that model closer to reality.

Inter-firm differences in efficiency

Let us now turn to relaxing certain other assumptions made in the previous chapter. As we shall see, these are by no means as critical for the perfectly competitive model as is that of a U-shaped long-run average cost curve. When we made the assumption that all firms in the industry are equally efficient, the long-run industry supply curve turned out to be infinitely elastic at a price given by the minimum point of the typical firm's long-run average cost curve. One way of looking at this case is to note that, by adding firms to the industry, one is adding to the production process units of the third input, the skill of the entrepreneur, and that constant returns to scale are emerging at the level of the industry rather than at the level of the firm. This solves the indeterminacy of output problem at the level of the firm which arises when we postulate a **linearly homogeneous production function**, while retaining the result that long-run supply curves are horizontal.

But it may not be reasonable to assume that firms are in fact equally efficient. In practice some firms may be more efficient than others, and may be able to maintain their technological advantage, for example by keeping details of their production process secret, or because they have some locational advantage which other firms cannot obtain. Such efficiency differentials affect the shape of the industry supply curve, as we shall now see.

Assume that every firm already in a particular industry is observed to be making positive – or above normal – profits, so new firms will still be attracted into that industry. If the factors that make existing firms more efficient are specific to the particular industry in which they find themselves, rather than arising from general advantages that could be exploited in any industry, and if they are not available to newcomers, then the new entrants will be less efficient in the sense that the minimum long-run average cost of production that they can achieve will be higher than that incurred by those already there, even though they pay the same price for other inputs. The entry of new firms will bid down the price of output, and this will continue to fall until the least efficient firm in the industry is producing at the minimum point of its long-run average cost curve. This least efficient firm is often called the **marginal firm**, for obvious reasons. All other firms in the industry will operate with average costs lower than price.

The long-run equilibrium described here is depicted in Figure 11.11, and this diagram should be self-explanatory. The important implication of the analysis set out in the figure is that in this case the industry's long-run supply curve slopes upwards even when the number of firms varies. This is because as output expands, less and less efficient firms,

Figure 11.11

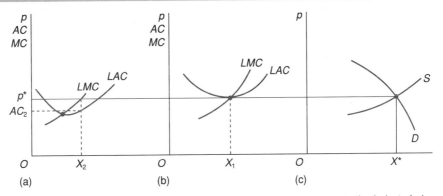

When all firms are not equally efficient, even when factor prices are constant, the industry's long-run supply curve with the number of firms variable (S) slopes upwards. Only the marginal firm, panel (b), makes no profits at its equilibrium output of X_1. Any intra-marginal (i.e. more efficient) firm such as that depicted in panel (a) will make positive profits at its profit-maximising level of output (X_2). Note that the intra-marginal firm does not produce at a scale of output that minimises long-run average cost, but at a larger scale with an average cost of AC_2.

with higher and higher average costs of production, enter the industry. At each level of output, equilibrium price is given by the minimum average cost of the marginal firm, and the higher the level of output, the less efficient is that marginal firm.

It might seem to follow from the foregoing argument that **differences in technical efficiency** will necessarily produce a dispersion of profits across firms in a competitive industry, with only the marginal firm earning zero profits. One must be careful here though. The advantage in technical efficiency enjoyed by a particular firm might arise because it has access to some particularly advantageous technology embodied in a trade secret, or some advantage in the location of its plant. If access to the secret, or the favourable plant site, is open to competitive bidding, the surplus of revenue over costs due to its being exploited will be paid to its owner, and not to the firm which uses it (unless that firm, fortuitously, happens to be the owner). In this case, even though the industry supply curve slopes upwards, each firm in the industry will make normal profits. Certain specific inputs, too short in supply to be available to all firms, will, however, be paid what are often termed 'rents', equal to the market value of the contribution they make to the value of the output of the firms that enjoy them. A fuller discussion of the concept of rent is contained in Chapter 19.

Finally, it should be noted that if some firms are more efficient than others because the entrepreneurs running them are in general more skilful, and if their greater skill could be utilised effectively in any industry, then the extra return yielded in the X industry should properly be regarded as a cost, because that extra return could also be earned elsewhere. In this case the industry long-run supply curve is a horizontal straight line, and there is no uniquely identified marginal firm.

Variations in factor prices in the short run

So far we have dealt with the effects on supply conditions of the technical characteristics of production within the industry and within firms. We have, throughout the analysis, held input prices constant. Let us now relax this particular assumption, and deal with the consequence of what are frequently called **pecuniary economies** and **diseconomies of scale**, which impinge upon firms' behaviour through the variations that they produce in factor prices. They are so called to distinguish them from **economies and diseconomies internal to the firm** that, being the consequence of increasing and decreasing returns to scale in the production function, are under the control of the firm itself (i.e. internal to its decision-making process). We will explicitly analyse pecuniary effects only in the case of an industry made up of equally efficient firms, but the reader might find it helpful to reproduce the analysis modified to fit the case of an industry where the firms vary in efficiency.

Consider first of all the effects of factor prices rising as the whole industry expands. If any particular firm is sufficiently small that no variations it makes in its scale of operations can influence factor prices, but if the industry as a whole is large enough relative to factor markets to bid up input prices when it expands, and bid them down when it contracts, then such factor price variations are outside the control of the firm, and hence are indeed external to its decision making. Because such variations result from changes in the industry's size, they may be referred to as internal to the industry.

Let us analyse an industry's short-run response to an increase in the demand for its product at any given price. In Figure 11.12 the industry demand curve shifts; each firm

Figure 11.12

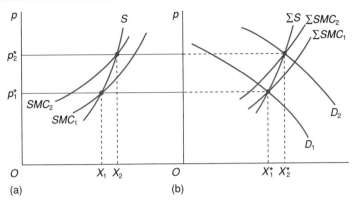

(a)   (b)

The short-run supply curve when prices of factors increase with an increase in their employment: industry demand increases from D_1 to D_2. Each firm attempts to move out along SMC_1 and hence industry supply tends to shift along ΣSMC_1. However, the price of the variable factor rises as output expands, shifting every firm's short-run marginal cost curve upwards. Equilibrium is re-established at X_2^* and p_2^*, as opposed to the initial equilibrium of X_1^*, p_1^*. Here the price of the variable factor is higher, so that each firm is on SMC_2 and the industry is on ΣSMC_2. The supply response of the firm from X_1 to X_2 is a mixture of a movement along a marginal cost curve and a shift of such a curve; which may be summarised into a movement along a curve such as S, which is the firm's short-run supply curve of X when the whole industry is expanding its output of X and the price of the variable factor of production increases with its utilisation. The industry's short-run supply curve is the sum over all firms of curves such as S, ΣS. It is more steeply sloped than the supply curve derived holding factor prices constant.

moves up its short-run marginal cost curve, and the industry as a whole moves up its short-run supply curve, which is of course just the sum of these short-run marginal cost curves. Now suppose that the effect of the increased demand for labour implicit in this move is to increase the price of labour. This might occur if the industry were a relatively large employer so that an increase in this demand for labour would lead to a tightening of the labour market overall. Then the short-run average and marginal cost curves of each firm are obviously shifted vertically upwards, as is the industry's short-run supply curve. We know this from Chapter 10 where it was established that the short-run marginal cost was the wage divided by the marginal product of labour. An increase in the wage therefore increases marginal cost proportionately.

The movement to a new short-run equilibrium in this case involves in part a movement along, and in part a shift upwards, of marginal cost curves, and the new equilibrium is to be found at a point such as $p_2^* X_2^*$ in Figure 11.12. Now we can perform the experiment of shifting the demand curve many times and the consequence will always be this combination of movements along curves and shifts of curves, the resulting equilibrium price and output combinations for the industry lying along a line such as ΣS, which may then be interpreted as the industry's short-run supply curve *when factor prices rise with output*. Such a curve will clearly be more steeply sloped than the summed marginal cost curves at any given level of factor prices. The reader can check that, were the price of labour to fall as output increased, the resulting short-run supply curve would have a shallower slope.

Factor price variations in the long run

Long-run supply relationships must be modified in a way similar to the short-run response when factor prices are allowed to vary. Output increases, the prices of both capital and labour services tend to increase, and so the minimum level of average cost attainable by any firm in the industry shifts upwards. Thus, the long-run supply curve derived from permitting the number of firms to vary acquires an upward slope. All this is shown, at the industry level, in Figure 11.13.

What happens at the level of the particular firm when, in the long run, factor prices increase as the industry expands is not altogether clear-cut. It is certain that each firm's cost curves shift upwards and also that, when the industry is in long-run equilibrium with an expanded number of firms, each firm will once more be producing at the minimum point of its long-run average cost curve. This much is clear, but what cannot in general be predicted is what will happen to the individual firm's scale of output. This is because one would not in general expect the prices of capital and labour to increase equiproportionately as the industry expands. As we saw in Chapter 9, the firm will change the proportions in which it employs labour and capital, sometimes called its *choice of technique*, towards the relatively cheaper factor. When factor proportions are thus changed it is not necessarily the case that the minimum point on the long-run average cost curve will occur at the same level of output at the two different sets of factor prices. It may, or may not. Everything here depends upon the specific nature of the production function.

Factor prices may fall rather than rise as output increases. This would happen if there existed some economies of scale in other industries producing inputs, or if the quality of inputs increased with their scale of use. If all firms are equally efficient, the long-run

Figure 11.13

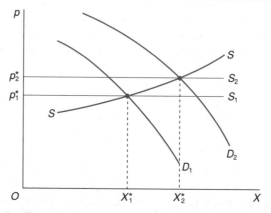

When all firms are equally efficient, but input prices vary positively with the industry's demand for them, a shift from D_1 to D_2 in the demand for X leads in the long run to an increase in the number of firms in the industry, and an increase in factor prices that shifts up the minimum point on each firm's average cost curve. Hence the long-run supply curve permitting the number of firms to vary, but holding factor prices constant, shifts up from S_1 to S_2. The industry's supply response is thus a mixture of a shift along such a curve and a shift up such a curve, and may be summarised in a movement from $p_1^* X_1^*$ to $p_2^* X_2^*$ along a curve such as S. This is the industry's long-run supply curve, when we permit the number of firms in the industry to vary and the prices of factors of production to rise systematically with output.

supply curve would then slope downwards. This is a point of some interest because it enables us to be precise about the extent to which average costs that fall as the level of output increases are compatible with competition. We have already seen earlier that falling average costs produced by increasing technical returns to scale – *economies internal to the firm* – lead to monopoly. So it is only when average costs fall as a result of declining input prices – as a result of *economies external to the firm* – that competition and decreasing costs are compatible.

Such external economies as these most often arise when we have a regionally localised industry requiring specialised skills on the part of its labour force. Thus, in the case of Britain during the Industrial Revolution, the localisation of the cotton industry in Lancashire, lace-making around Nottingham, and the pottery industry around Stoke, for example, led to a tradition among the local labour force that perhaps reduced the costs of training labour – hence effectively lowering the price of the services of skilled labour to individual firms. Moreover, the importance of this phenomemon tends to vary with the size of the industry, so that, for example, the advantages to a textile firm of locating in Lancashire now, as compared with, say, 100 years ago, have probably considerably diminished, as the scale of the industry in that area has diminished.

Perfect competition and the supply curve

Now in this chapter we have been discussing various aspects of the supply curve. We have seen that, as with the demand curve, there is no unique way of deriving a supply curve. Just as we could have demand curves for individuals and market demand curves, so we have here had firm and industry supply curves. Moreover, just as one gets different demand curves depending upon what it is that is conceptually held constant, so we have had different supply curves for the short run, for the long run, for constant factor prices and for variable factor prices.

Again, as with the demand curve, there is no uniquely correct way to define a supply curve; the appropriate choice must always depend upon the situation under analysis and hence upon one's assessment of which factors it is appropriate to hold constant in a particular instance. Nevertheless, the ability to generate a relationship between quantity supplied and price, to complement that between quantity demanded and price, so that the tools of supply and demand may be utilised, is an important one. *Of all the forms of industrial organisation that we will consider in this book, perfect competition is the only one that enables us to generate this relationship.*

* Appendix – returns to scale and profitability in the Cobb-Douglas case

The relationship between returns to scale, equilibrium output and profits in the long run for perfectly competitive firms can be illustrated formally using once again the example of the Cobb-Douglas production function. We therefore assume that the firm maximises profits,

$$\pi = pX - rK - wL \tag{11.9}$$

where

$$X = AL^\alpha K^\beta \tag{11.10}$$

but impose no restrictions on the degree of homogeneity of the production function (given by the sum of α and β).

The analysis in the previous chapter established that price must equal marginal cost in both the short and long run if profits are to be maximised. This condition may be written formally in the following two equations:

$$p = w\frac{\partial L}{\partial X} \tag{11.11}$$

and

$$p = r\frac{\partial K}{\partial X} \tag{11.12}$$

These equations say that price equals the extra outlay required to obtain the labour needed to increase output, holding capital constant, and the extra outlay required to obtain the capital needed to increase output, holding labour constant. The equations may be rearranged to show that firms hire labour up to the point at which

$$p\frac{\partial X}{\partial L} = w \tag{11.13}$$

and hire capital until

$$p\frac{\partial X}{\partial K} = r \tag{11.14}$$

These 'marginal productivity' conditions are studied in much greater detail in Chapters 10 and 18. For current purposes, we merely note that input factors are hired provided that the amount they add to revenue (marginal product times price) exceeds their cost.

Substituting equations (11.13) and (11.14) in (11.9), and remembering from Chapter 8 that in the Cobb-Douglas case $\partial X/\partial L = \alpha X/L$ and $\partial X/\partial K = \beta X/K$, we can derive

$$\pi = pX - \frac{p\alpha X}{L}L - \frac{p\beta X}{K}K$$

$$\pi = pX(1 - \alpha - \beta) \tag{11.15}$$

Then we may see at once that

$$\pi \gtreqless 0 \text{ as } \alpha + \beta \gtreqless 1 \tag{11.16}$$

With diminishing returns to scale ($\alpha + \beta < 1$), (11.16) shows that profits in a competitive firm are always positive. With increasing returns to scale, on the other hand, ($\alpha + \beta > 1$), long-run losses are technologically guaranteed for price-taking enterprises at any level of output. Perhaps the most interesting case is when the production function is linearly homogeneous, $\alpha + \beta = 1$. In this case the firm earns zero profits regardless of the level of output. These results are essentially those developed above in Figures 11.8, 11.10 and 11.9 respectively.

The profit function itself is *linearly homogeneous*, as defined in Chapter 8, when the production function is homogeneous of degree one. This can be checked by noting that multiplying the right-hand side of (11.10) through by a constant factor, k, raises profits by that same factor k; i.e.

$$pf(kL, kK) - rkK - wkL = k\pi, \tag{11.17}$$

when the production function is linearly homogeneous.

Three outcomes are formally possible in this case, only one of which we illustrated in Figure 11.9. In the first place, price could be higher than long-run marginal and average cost. Here the firm will have an incentive to increase its size indefinitely. Second, price could be below long-run marginal and average costs, and the firm would make losses at every conceivable level of production. Equilibrium output in this case is zero. Finally, we have the case illustrated in Figure 11.9, where market price is such that it equals long-run marginal and average cost. Equilibrium output in this case is indeterminate for the firm.

Factor proportions used in production are nevertheless determinate when technology is linearly homogeneous. Consider again the Cobb-Douglas production function. With linear homogeneity, i.e. $\alpha + \beta = 1$, then $\beta = 1 - \alpha$ and the function can be rewritten in the form

$$\frac{X}{L} = A\left(\frac{K}{L}\right)^{1-\alpha} \tag{11.18}$$

which is drawn to be concave in Figure 11.14. If the firm earns zero profits, dividing both sides of (11.9) through by L and setting profits equal to zero yields

$$0 = p\frac{X}{L} - r\frac{K}{L} - w \tag{11.19}$$

or

$$\frac{X}{L} = \frac{w}{p} + \frac{r}{p}\frac{K}{L} \tag{11.19'}$$

Figure 11.14

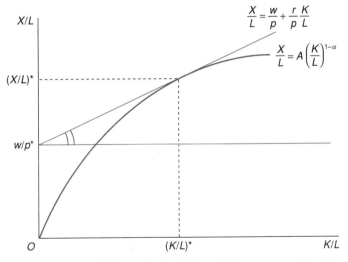

The choice of technique when production technology is linearly homogeneous. Even though the level of output is indeterminate (see Figure 11.9), the firm can still choose optimal factor proportions $(K/L)^*$ and labour productivity $(X/L)^*$ to maximise profit subject to production technology, which is assumed to be concave in $(X/L, K/L)$. Note that (X/L^*), or equilibrium output per unit of labour, minus the real wage is equal to the total return to capital per unit of labour.

This equation is drawn, for given p, r and w, as a straight line in Figure 11.14. Its slope is given by the rental price of capital divided by the product price, referred to as the *real rental price of capital*. Profits are maximised (at zero) where the line is just tangent to the transformed production function, that is, where the *marginal product of capital is equal to the real rental price of capital*. This solution yields a determinate value for output per unit of labour $(X/L)^*$ and for the capital–labour ratio $(K/L)^*$. Linearly homogeneous production functions are often used in empirical work despite the fact that they leave the size of the individual firm's output indeterminate, because one is still able to use them to analyse the choice of factor proportions, the *choice of technique* as it is often called, in competitive markets.

SUMMARY

Supply in competition

1. We assume that entrepreneurs are concerned to maximise profits. We consider alternative motivations in Chapter 14.

2. Firms in competition are price takers. Their demand curves are perfectly elastic, and marginal revenue is therefore equal to price.

3. Firms maximise profits at output levels where marginal revenue equals marginal cost. In competition, this implies an output level at which the firm's marginal cost equals market price. For profits to be a maximum rather than a minimum, we further require that the marginal cost curve be upward sloping at this level of output.

4. In the short run, a firm will cease production if price falls below average variable cost. It would lose less money by producing nothing and continuing to pay fixed costs than by producing output in these circumstances.

5. The competitive firm's marginal cost curve above its average variable cost curve is its short-run supply curve.

6. In long-run market equilibrium, there can be no incentive for entry and exit. Hence profits must equal zero and firms must produce where price equals average as well as marginal cost.

7. If all firms have the same cost curves and factor prices are given, the long-run industry supply curve will be horizontal. Demand factors will not influence the price at which price equals average and marginal cost for the individual firm, and output will vary with the exit and entry of firms as the market demand curve shifts.

8. The existence of a long-run equilibrium for the individual firm in perfect competition is particularly sensitive to assumptions about returns to scale. A determinate equilibrium is consistent only with a U-shaped long-run average cost curve.

9. The assumption that the long-run cost curve ultimately turns upwards is therefore crucial in determining the size of the firm. Justifications for diminishing returns to scale often appeal to administrative or managerial problems encountered as firms grow.

10. The existence of profits in the long run depends on returns to scale; they are positive with diminishing returns and negative with increasing returns.

11. Inter-firm differences in efficiency lead to a dispersion of profit among them, even in long-run competitive equilibrium. When firms vary in efficiency only the marginal firm – the least efficient supplier that can survive in the industry – makes zero profits.

12. The short-run industry supply curve is upward sloping, being the horizontal sum of firms' short-run marginal cost curves. If increases in industry supply bid up factor prices, the short-run industry supply curve will be more steeply sloped than the sum of marginal cost curves.

13. Reverting to the assumption that firms are equally efficient, if increases in long-run market supply bid up factor input prices, the competitive industry's long-run supply curve will be upward sloping. Conversely, declining factor costs with long-run industry supply increasing could, but need not, lead to a downward-sloping long-run supply curve. It is only with such 'external economies' of scale that competition and decreasing costs are compatible.

PROBLEMS

1 'The introduction of microtechnology will raise output and real wages.' 'The introduction of microtechnology will cause unemployment.' How does our analysis of the perfectly competitive market lead us to respond to these statements?

2 With price measured in £ per thousand units, and X being measured as thousands of units per week, a perfectly competitive industry faces a demand curve given by

$$p = 20 - 2X$$

and produces output at constant supply price of £1 per thousand units.

(a) Find, on the assumption that the area under the demand curve measures the total benefit accruing to consumers of X, the consumers' surplus accruing to purchases of X.

(b) Now suppose that a single firm takes over the whole industry, and that £1 per thousand units now represents its long-run marginal and average cost of producing X. Find:
   (i)   its output;
   (ii) the price of that output;
   (iii) the firm's profits; and
   (iv) the consumer's surplus accruing to purchasers of X.

(c) Suppose a sales tax of 10 pence per thousand units is levied on X. Recompute your answers to parts (a) and (b).

(d) Suppose a maximum price of £1.20 per thousand units is imposed by government decree. Recompute your answers to part (b).

3 Under what conditions will the long-run supply curve of the perfectly competitive industry be upward sloping?

Note

1. See Chapter 2 for a discussion of the inverse demand curve.

Monopoly

Key words and phrases

- downward-sloping demand curve, marginal revenue curve, demand elasticity and marginal revenue, positive profits
- relative inefficiency of monopoly
- returns to scale and natural monopoly, regulation, multipart tariff
- producer surplus
- price discrimination, perfect price discrimination, degrees of price discrimination

Introduction

The perfectly competitive firm faced a horizontal demand curve and was able to sell all it pleased at the going market price. The monopolistic firms we shall analyse in this chapter face **downward-sloping demand curves**. As we shall see, there is no unique set of influences which ensures that the demand curve faced by every monopolist is the market demand curve for its product, but for the moment it will suffice if the reader thinks of such a firm as being the sole seller of a good in an industry where, for one reason or another, the entry of competitors is quite impossible. In such a situation the market demand curve for the good does indeed become the demand curve that faces the monopolist.

The essence of monopoly power is that it enables the firm to raise its price because there are no other suppliers to whom consumers can turn when it does so: a firm cannot increase its price when there are alternative suppliers of an identical product willing to satisfy demand at the old price. Monopoly power of this type obviously exists when there is only a single firm in the market; but we shall discover below that such monopoly power can also exist when there are several firms supplying the market for a particular type of product provided that each firm's version of the product in question differs from that of other firms. This possibility implies that the monopoly model is a good deal more general than it seems at first sight.

Before taking up this matter, we shall extend our analysis of the single firm with monopoly power. There are other and more complicated ways than we have so far analysed for such a firm to use its market situation in order to increase profits. It may use pricing strategies more sophisticated than charging the same price for each unit of output sold in order to generate more profits from a given volume of output. Behaviour of this sort is referred to as **price discrimination**.

The demand curve, total revenue, and marginal revenue

The monopolist's demand curve is downward sloping, so the total revenue function is *not* an upward-sloping straight line along which revenue is proportional to sales. As we saw in Chapter 11, an average revenue curve is an inverse demand curve and if all we know about the demand curve itself is that it slopes downwards, a wide variety of shapes is available for the total revenue function. The property we require for the total revenue function is that straight lines drawn to it from the origin slope less steeply at higher and higher levels of output; the slope of such lines measures average revenue, which is, of course, demand price. Figure 12.1 displays a number of such curves and, curiously shaped though some of them are, all are compatible with a downward-sloping demand curve. The curve in Figure 12.1(c) is the one upon which we shall concentrate since it is derived from a straight-line demand curve, and the use of such a demand curve will make the exposition simpler. Simplicity is the only reason for preferring a straight-line demand curve, however; there is no theoretical or empirical reason for preferring it.

Now the reader will recall that as price falls and quantity demanded increases, total expenditure by consumers increases when the price elasticity of demand is in excess of unity; expenditure remains the same at unit demand elasticity and falls when elasticity is less than unity. Note that total expenditure by consumers is just the monopolistic firm's total revenue by another name, and consider the linear demand curve of Figure 12.2,

Figure 12.1

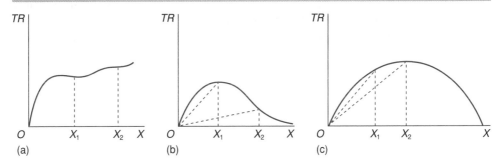

Three possible shapes for a total revenue curve associated with a downward-sloping demand (average revenue) curve. The slope of a straight line from the origin to any one of these curves falls systematically as output increases. The movement from X_1 to X_2 gives an example of this. Panel (c) shows the total revenue curve associated with a straight-line demand curve. Around level of output X_2, total revenue is constant as output varies. Thus, price must be changing in equal but opposite proportion to quantity and the elasticity of the demand curve must be unity at this point. At lower levels of output than X_2 demand must be elastic and, at higher levels, inelastic.

Figure 12.2   **A straight-line demand curve**

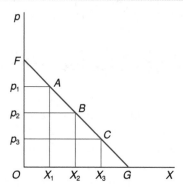

Its slope is constant at *OG/OF*. Halfway between *F* and *G*, at point *B*, the ratio *OX₂* to *Op₂* is equal to the slope of the curve, so its elasticity is equal to unity at this point. (*OFG*, *p₂FB* and *X₂BG* are similar triangles; *FB* equals *BG* and is half of *FG*. Thus, *X₂B*, which equals *Op₂* is half of *OF*, and similarly *OX₂* is half of *OG*.)

which has a constant slope d*X*/d*p*. As we pointed out previously, the own price elasticity of demand, e_p, is defined as $(\partial X/\partial p)/(X/p)$. At point *A* it is clear that *X/p* is smaller than $\partial X/\partial p$. Hence elasticity is greater than one and total revenue is increasing with quantity. By similar argument, at *C*, it is clear that *X/p* is greater than $\partial X/\partial p$. At this point elasticity is smaller than unity and total revenue is decreasing. At *B*, which lies halfway along the curve, $\partial X/\partial p$ and *X/p* are equal. Elasticity is unity at this point and total revenue is not changing with quantity. The straight-line demand curve encompasses all elasticities from infinity at its intersection with the vertical axis to zero at the horizontal, and the shape of the total revenue curve in Figure 12.1(c) reflects this.

The relationship between the demand curve, the **marginal revenue curve** and the price **elasticity of demand** can be established formally as follows. We noted in Chapter 11 that the slope of the total revenue function, **marginal revenue**, was given by

$$MR = \frac{\partial R}{\partial X} = p + X\frac{\partial p}{\partial X} \tag{12.1}$$

Since $\partial p/\partial X$ is always negative because demand curves slope down (provided the good in question is not a Giffen good), we know from (12.1) that *marginal revenue is less than price* at every level of output greater than zero. The marginal revenue curve therefore lies below the average revenue curve in Figure 12.2. We also saw that an alternative formulation of marginal revenue, in terms of the own price elasticity of demand, e_p, is

$$MR = \frac{\partial R}{\partial X} = p\left[1 + \frac{1}{e_p}\right] \tag{12.2}$$

Marginal revenue is therefore positive if the price elasticity of demand is less than −1 (greater in absolute value than 1), negative if it is greater than −1 (less in absolute value than 1), and zero if the elasticity of demand is (minus) unity.

| Box 12.1 | **The demand curve and price elasticity** |

To illustrate the relationship between the price elasticity of demand and a downward-sloping demand curve we can use the linear function

$$X = 100 - p$$

or $\quad p = 100 - X$ $\hspace{4cm}$ (12.1.1)

The price elasticity of demand is

$$e_p = \frac{dX}{dp}\frac{p}{X}$$

Using our demand function

$$e_p = -1\frac{100 - X}{X} = 1 - \frac{100}{X}$$ $\hspace{3cm}$ (12.1.2)

We can draw the following conclusions:

$$X = 0 \rightarrow e_p = -\infty$$

$$p = 0 \rightarrow X = 100 \rightarrow e_p = 0$$

$$p = 50 \rightarrow X = 50 \rightarrow e_p = -1$$

As an exercise readers can show that these conclusions imply that halfway down the demand curve $e_p = -1$ (as in Figure 12.2). Above this point on the demand curve demand is elastic and below this point demand is inelastic.

| Box 12.2 | **The determinants of marginal revenue** |

We can use the demand function in Box 12.1 to illustrate the determinants of a firm's marginal revenue. The inverse demand function is

$$p = 100 - X$$ $\hspace{4cm}$ (12.1.1)

This implies that a firm's total revenue is

$$R = pX = 100X - X^2$$ $\hspace{3cm}$ (12.2.1)

Readers can note that this revenue function is quadratic, which is always the case with a linear demand function. Marginal revenue is then

$$MR = \frac{dR}{dX} = 100 - 2X$$ $\hspace{3cm}$ (12.2.2)

Readers can confirm that, if the demand and marginal revenue functions are drawn on a conventional diagram, the two curves have the same vertical intercept, and that the (negative) slope of the mr curve is twice that of the demand curve. In addition note that $X = 50$ implies $MR = 0$, and that this output maximises total revenue.

Using the above definition for mr we can draw the following conclusions:

$$X < 50 \rightarrow MR > 0$$

$$X > 50 \rightarrow MR < 0$$

In Box 12.1 we defined the price elasticity for demand for the demand function being used here:

$$e_p = 1 - \frac{100}{X} \qquad (12.1.2)$$

So $\quad X < 50 \rightarrow e_p < -1$ or $|e_p| > 1$

$\qquad X > 50 \rightarrow e_p > -1$ or $|e_p| < 1$

Connecting these two sets of conclusions:

monopolist elastic demand $\rightarrow MR > 0$

monopolist inelastic demand $\rightarrow MR < 0$

We can illustrate these various findings in the following way (see Illustration 12.1). At an output of 50 units total revenue is maximised. This maximum total revenue implies $MR = 0$. At an output less than 50 units reducing price and increasing demand increases total revenue, which implies demand is elastic. At an output greater than 50 reducing price increases demand but total revenue falls, which implies demand is inelastic.

Illustration 12.1

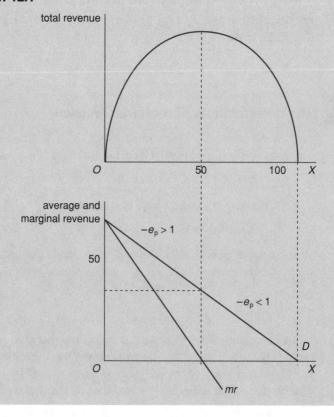

* A formal treatment of the relationship between demand and marginal revenue – some examples

To formalise the analysis depicted in Figure 12.2, consider the linear inverse demand curve

$$p = a - bX \tag{12.3}$$

for which the slope $\partial p / \partial X = -b$. From equation (12.1), we can calculate that marginal revenue is $(a - 2bX)$. The same result can be derived directly by differentiating the revenue function,

$$R = pX = aX - bX^2 \tag{12.4}$$

$$MR = \frac{\partial R}{\partial X} = a - 2bX \tag{12.5}$$

The total revenue function in this case reaches a maximum when $\partial R / \partial X = 0$, and therefore where $X = a/2b$. This is the point X_2 in Figure 12.1(c). It should be noted that, since the average revenue curve is $p = a - bX$ and the marginal revenue curve is $p = a - 2bX$, the marginal revenue curve always slopes twice as steeply as the demand curve when the latter is linear.

As to the price elasticity of demand, if we use equation (12.3) to substitute for p in the usual formula, and recall that $\partial p / \partial X = -b$, we get

$$e_p = \frac{a - bX}{bX} \tag{12.6}$$

When $X = a/2b$, the simple substitution into equation (12.6) confirms that the quantity at which total revenue is maximised in Figure 12.1(c) occurs where the price elasticity of demand is -1. Similarly it can be seen that when output is less than $a/2b$, the price elasticity of demand is less than -1, and when X exceeds $a/2b$, the elasticity is greater than -1.

An alternative form for the inverse demand curve addresses the need in much applied work to make the simplifying assumption that the elasticity of demand is a constant. We use this form in our analysis of monopolistic competition in Chapter 13. The family of curves with this convenient property takes the general form

$$p = AX^{-\alpha} \tag{12.3'}$$

Where A and α are positive, the slope of the inverse demand curve $(\partial p / \partial X)$ equals $-\alpha p / X$. The price elasticity of demand is therefore given by

$$e_p = \frac{p}{X} \frac{\partial X}{\partial p} = -\frac{X}{\alpha p} \frac{p}{X} = -\frac{1}{\alpha} \tag{12.6'}$$

which is, of course, a constant. Marginal revenue can be derived from the revenue function,

$$R = pX = AX^{1-\alpha} \tag{12.4'}$$

so

$$MR = \frac{\partial R}{\partial X} = (1 - \alpha)AX^{-\alpha} = (1 - \alpha)p \tag{12.5'}$$

The same result (12.5′) can be deduced by substituting the value of the elasticity of demand ($e_p = -1/\alpha$) in equation (12.2). Hence, though the elasticity of demand is a constant, marginal revenue is still everywhere below price.

A particular special case of the constant elasticity demand function is sometimes encountered, namely, when the elasticity of demand is assumed to be unity for every level of output. If we set $\alpha = 1$, we derive the demand curve

$$p = \frac{A}{X} \tag{12.3″}$$

with slope ($\partial p/\partial X$) equal to $-A/X^2$. The elasticity is therefore

$$e_p = \frac{p}{X}\frac{\partial X}{\partial p} = -\frac{X^2}{A} \cdot \frac{A}{X^2} = -1 \tag{12.6″}$$

It is clear from substituting the value of α in equation (12.5′) that marginal revenue in this case is zero at any level of output.

Profit-maximising price and output

There is no reason to suppose that a monopolist's cost functions differ in any qualitative way from those of a competitive firm and, with the exception that entry of new firms is ruled out, our previous analysis of the long-run/short-run dichotomy still holds.

There is no need for us to repeat all this then, and we may immediately analyse monopoly pricing in the long run. The analysis of short-run behaviour simply involves the substitution of short- for long-run cost curves in what follows. Figure 12.3 superimposes a long-run total cost curve upon the total revenue curve. Profits will be maximised where the vertical distance between the two curves is at its greatest (with revenue in excess of costs) and this occurs at output X_1, where the two functions have equal slopes. This statement about equality of slopes is another way of saying that profits are maximised where marginal cost equals marginal revenue. Figure 12.4 depicts the same profit-maximising solution in terms of explicitly drawn marginal cost and marginal revenue functions. As we have seen, for a monopolist, marginal revenue and price are not equal because the total revenue function is not a straight line through the origin. Indeed, if we call price by its other name, average revenue, it becomes obvious that a downward-sloping demand curve implies continually falling average revenue, with the marginal revenue curve everywhere below average revenue. This, be it noted, is *not* the same as saying that marginal revenue is always falling, as readers may prove for themselves by reproducing the relevant panels from Figure 12.1 and deriving the average and marginal revenue curves implicit in them, and as we establish more formally in a subsequent starred section of this chapter. These exercises justify our sticking for the most part to the special case of the straight-line demand curve for purposes of exposition; but they also warn of the dangers inherent in overgeneralising from analysis based upon it. In this case the marginal revenue curve is always downward sloping.

Now, what can we say about the properties of the long-run price and output decision of the monopolist set out in Figures 12.3 and 12.4? First, it shows **positive profits** being made equal to $TR_1 - TC_1$, as measured in Figure 12.3, or $(P_1 - AC_1)X_1$, as measured in Figure 12.4. That positive profits are earned is not a necessary consequence of monopolistic behaviour.

Figure 12.3

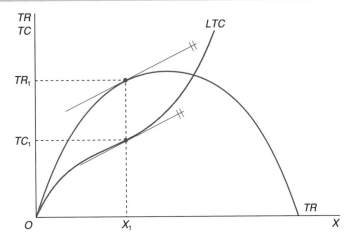

Long-run profit maximisation for a monopolist facing a straight-line demand curve, and endowed with a long-run cost function characterised by increasing followed by decreasing returns to scale. Maximum profits occur where the slopes of the two curves are equal (i.e. where marginal cost equals marginal revenue). Profit is equal to $TR_1 - TC_1$. So long as total costs increase with output, profit maximisation requires that output be fixed on the rising section of the total revenue curve, i.e. where the elasticity of demand for the product is greater than 1 in absolute value.

Figure 12.4

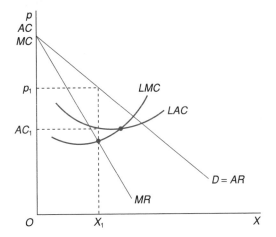

The profit-maximising monopolist will fix output where marginal cost equals marginal revenue at X_1 and charge the maximum price the market will bear for that quantity of output, p_1. This diagram repeats, in more familiar terms, the analysis set out in Figure 12.3. Profits are given by $(p_1 - AC_1)X_1$ which is equal to $TR_1 - TC_1$ in Figure 12.3.

Figure 12.5

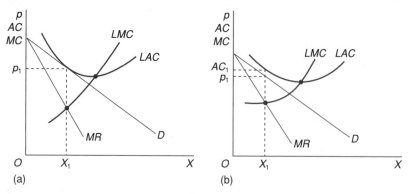

A monopolist whose profit-maximising level of output X_1 yields (a) zero profit, and (b) a loss of $(AC_1 - p_1)X_1$. In panel (a), if *LAC* is just tangent to *D*, then *MR* equals *LMC* at this level of output, for at this level of output the total revenue curve would just be tangent to the total cost curve from below.

It results from the assumption about costs and revenues which we have built into the diagrams and nothing else. Thus, in Figure 12.5(a) we have a situation in which the cost and revenue functions are such that the maximum available profit is zero, and in Figure 12.5(b) a situation in which losses would be made at any level of output, so that in fact no production would take place in the long run.

The second characteristic of Figure 12.4 worth noting is, however, a general property of monopoly behaviour (unless certain types of price discrimination to be dealt with below take place): the price charged is greater than marginal cost. Now, in perfect competition we noted that, in the long run, price is equal to long-run marginal cost. If it is the case that the monopolist's marginal cost curve is the same as that which would yield the long-run supply curve of a competitive industry, then the monopolist will charge more and produce less than a competitive industry.

This implication explains why economists often argue that a **monopolistic** market structure is **inefficient** relative to that of a competitive industry. The price of the good sold exceeds the incremental cost of producing it. We can think of monopolists as exploiting their 'monopoly power' (as sole source of supply) to restrict output and thereby driving up the price by creating an artificial scarcity. Moreover monopolists do not generally produce at the minimum point on their long-run average cost curve, though such an outcome is not *logically* impossible. For example, in Figures 12.3 and 12.4, the monopolist restricts supply below minimum efficient scale. One cannot rule out the possibility, however, that revenue and cost functions take a shape such that equilibrium output is to the right of the minimum point on the long-run average cost curve, or is even at the minimum itself. Readers might like to illustrate these cases for themselves.

We stress again that, because the monopolist produces where marginal cost equals marginal revenue, so long as marginal cost is positive, price and output will be at a level such that total revenue increases as output increases – a point where *the absolute value of the price elasticity of demand is greater than unity*. It is a common misconception that monopolists are particularly likely to exist where demand for products is inelastic. Any monopolist in such a situation can increase profits by curtailing output and raising price until an elastic segment of the demand curve is reached. Inelastic demand and profit-maximising monopoly (at least non-discriminating monopoly) are incompatible. The formula given above as equation (12.2) confirms this point. If elasticity lies between 0 and −1, it yields a negative value for marginal revenue, and so long as marginal costs are positive, the profit-maximising level of output cannot lie in such a region of the demand curve.

* A formal treatment of monopoly equilibrium

The formal maximisation problem faced by the monopolist has a similar structure to that of the competitive counterpart but, as we saw in the geometric sections, has rather different results because we can no longer assume that marginal revenue equals price. The firm chooses output as before to maximise

$$p = pX - wL - rK \tag{12.7}$$

subject to

$$X = f(L, K) \tag{12.8}$$

and, in addition, the inverse demand curve

$$p = p(X), \partial p/\partial X < 0 \tag{12.9}$$

Equation (12.7) can be reformulated in terms of revenues and costs:

$$p = R(X) - C(X) \tag{12.10}$$

where $C(X)$ can be either a short-run or a long-run cost function. We assume the latter henceforth and derive first-order conditions

$$\frac{\partial \pi}{\partial X} = \frac{\partial R}{\partial X} - \frac{\partial C}{\partial X} = 0 \tag{12.11}$$

and second-order conditions for a maximum

$$\frac{\partial^2 \pi}{\partial X^2} = \frac{\partial^2 R}{\partial X^2} - \frac{d^2 C}{dX^2} < 0 \tag{12.12}$$

Equation (12.11) is simply the conventional marginal revenue equals marginal cost condition which we have been using in our geometric exposition, and is formally identical to that derived for the competitive case.

The second-order conditions, however, are less restrictive here than under competition because we no longer require the marginal cost curve to be upward sloping at equilibrium. The slope of the marginal cost curve can be negative, provided that its value is more than offset by the negative slope of the marginal revenue curve. Given that marginal revenue is always diminishing with output ($\partial^2 R/\partial X^2 < 0$), an upward-sloping marginal cost curve ($\partial^2 C/\partial X^2$) is *sufficient* to ensure that inequality (12.12), the second-order condition, is satisfied, but it is not *necessary*.

Natural monopoly

So far, we have taken the structure of markets as given, and compared the outcomes of monopolistic and competitive behaviour in terms of prices, output, profits and consumer welfare. We have argued that monopoly yields higher prices, smaller output, and reduced consumer welfare when compared with competition. But this comparison is relevant only if competition is, in fact, a feasible alternative to monopoly, and this may not always be the case. As we saw in the preceding chapter, increasing **returns to scale**, if they continue to accrue up to the level of output which will satisfy the entire market demand for the industry's output, are incompatible with competition. In such a case, we have seen that one firm can always produce the industry's entire output more cheaply than two or more firms, and hence is in a situation of **natural monopoly**.

As we show in Figure 12.6, a monopoly can make a profit in the presence of continuously increasing returns to scale, but in the process it will restrict output and raise price above long-run marginal cost, imposing welfare losses on consumers. It should be noted, however, that any attempt to force a natural monopoly to mimic competitive behaviour, for example by the imposition of a price equals marginal cost rule along the lines discussed in Chapter 11, will lead the firm in question to make losses. The point is illustrated in Figure 12.6. Suppose that some regulatory authorities calculate that, given the demand curve for output D, the market will clear when price equals p^*. If these same authorities also enforce the output rule for the natural monopoly, that output must be chosen to equalise price and marginal cost. In this case, output will be X^*. Increasing returns to scale imply that the firm will always make a *loss* under these circumstances, equal to the area $abcp^*$ in Figure 12.6. This happens because, with increasing returns to scale, the long-run average cost curve lies everywhere above the long-run marginal cost curve. This technical consideration, rather than inherent inefficiency, will lead even well-run natural monopolies regulated by price equals marginal cost rules to make losses.

If the regulatory authorities whose existence we are here postulating are a government department of some sort, they might be provided with funds to subsidise the operation of a natural monopoly up to the level of the losses that would be generated by compelling

Figure 12.6

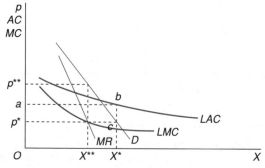

If a natural monopoly is forced to set price equal to marginal cost, it makes a loss of $abcp^*$. Left unregulated, it will produce X^{**} and sell it at p^{**}.

it to price at marginal cost. Or they might settle for forcing it to expand output as far beyond the profit maximising level as possible without incurring losses. A **regulation** of this sort would involve price being set equal to long-run average cost. In this case, output would be closer to the level that would prevail under a price equals marginal cost rule, but the outcome would still involve a higher price and less consumer welfare than under marginal cost pricing. Such approaches also ignore the incentive issues of how to motivate managers to minimise costs in a situation where losses will be subsidised or higher costs can be automatically passed on to consumers in the form of higher prices.

A third possibility, which might sometimes be feasible, would be for the natural monopoly to charge a **multipart tariff**. Under such a scheme, consumers would be charged for their actual consumption of the firm's output at its marginal cost of production, but, for the privilege of buying any of it at all, would have to pay a lump sum fee out of which the firm could at least cover its losses, or even make a profit. Such arrangements are not uncommon: for example, we are all used to paying a unit charge for the telephone calls we make from our homes and offices, and supplementing that with a monthly charge which gets us access to telephone service from those locations. They are, in fact, a form of **price discrimination**, a phenomenon whose economics we shall discuss later in this chapter.

Box 12.3   Natural monopoly

To illustrate the issues faced by a natural monopolist consider a firm that faces an inverse demand function

$$p = 100 - X \tag{12.1.1}$$

As shown in Box 12.2, with this demand function, marginal revenue is

$$MR = 100 - 2X \tag{12.2.2}$$

A natural monopolist experiences increasing returns to scale over all feasible output levels. To keep the mathematics as simple as possible we will assume a linear long-run average cost function rather than the non-linear form in Figure 12.6:

$$AC = 50 - 0.125X \tag{12.3.1}$$

With this *ac* function, total costs (*tc*) are

$$TC = X.AC = 50X - 0.125X^2 \tag{12.3.2}$$

Marginal cost (*MC*) is therefore

$$MC = \frac{\mathrm{d}(TC)}{\mathrm{d}X} = 50 - 0.25X \tag{12.3.3}$$

This *MC* function is positive for all outputs less than 200. From the demand function we are restricted to only economically meaningful positive prices. So economically meaningful output has to be less than 100 when $p = 0$. So our *MC* function is declining over all relevant output levels.

We can now consider three ways of determining this monopolist's output, as discussed in the text: profit maximisation, setting price equal to marginal cost, and two-part tariff pricing.

Profit maximisation

Setting $MC = MR$:

$$50 - 0.25X = 100 - 2X \tag{12.3.4}$$

$$X = 28.57$$

At this output level, selling price is

$$P = 100 - 28.57 = 71.43$$

Total profit is

$$\pi = 71.43(28.57) - 50(28.57) - 0.125(28.57^2) = 510.22 \tag{12.3.5}$$

The firm is making positive profits.

Price = marginal cost

Setting $p = MC$:

$$100 - X = 50 - 0.25X \tag{12.3.6}$$

$$X = 66.67$$

Selling price is

$$P = 100 - 66.67 = 33.33$$

Total profit is

$$\pi = 33.33(66.67) - 50(66.67) - 0.125(66.67^2) = -1667 \tag{12.3.7}$$

The firm is obviously making losses here.

Two-part tariff

If the monopolist is allowed to break even, i.e. earn zero profits, we can set price equal to average cost:

$$100 - X = 50 - 0.125X \tag{12.3.8}$$

$$X = 57.14$$

At this output level marginal cost is

$$MC = 50 - 0.25(57.14) = 35.715$$

If the monopolist charges this price total profit is

$$\pi = 35.715(57.14) - 50(57.14) - 0.125(57.14^2) = -1224.37 \tag{12.3.9}$$

This loss can be covered by a fixed charge to all consumers. So if there are 1,000 consumers in this market they will each be charged a lump sum fee of 1224.37/1000 = 1.23 to be allowed to purchase the product, following which each unit is bought at marginal cost.

Producer's surplus and the cost of monopoly

The negative impact of monopoly on what economists refer to as economic *welfare* is directly measurable in a rough and ready way with the aid of the concept of consumer's surplus introduced in Chapter 4 and the closely related concept of **producer's surplus**. It will be remembered that consumer's surplus was measured by the area under the demand curve above and to the left of the equilibrium price–quantity point. We can construct an equivalent measure of welfare for the supply side of the market. This is producer's surplus.

Consider first a typical competitive firm in long-run equilibrium, as depicted in Figure 12.7(a). The total cost that it incurs to produce its output is given by the area under its long-run marginal cost curve, and its total revenue is given by the area under its marginal revenue curve, which is in this case its horizontal demand curve. The difference between the two is the surplus the firm generates, its profit, or producer's surplus (which might, if the firm in question was producing at the minimum point of its long-run average cost curve, be zero). For the industry as a whole, producer's surplus is simply the sum of these surpluses generated by individual firms. The case we have depicted in Figure 12.7(b) to illustrate the concept is of an industry with firms of varying degrees of efficiency and the industry measure of producer's surplus is given by the area above the long-run supply curve, and below equilibrium price, the area $p*BC$.

Now consumer's surplus in this case is given by the area $ABp*$ (provided that we do not scrutinise too carefully the problems inherent in adding up the utilities of individual agents, and are willing to treat the market demand curve as the sum of individual Marshallian demand curves). The total benefit conferred on society by the activities of this industry may be thought of as the difference between the total utility derived by consumers from its products – the area under the demand curve to the left of $X*$ – and the total costs imposed by producing its output, or the area under the supply curve to the left of $X*$. This difference is the sum of producer's and consumer's surplus.

Now suppose that this industry was monopolised, with, however, a long-run marginal cost curve identical to the competitive industry supply curve. This case is illustrated in Figure 12.7(c). Output would be cut to X_m^*, price would rise to p_m^*, producer's surplus would increase to p_m^*DEC, but consumer's surplus would fall to ADp_m^*. The total benefit conferred by this industry would now be $ADEC$, an amount unambiguously smaller than that generated in the competitive case, and an amount which measures the monopoly's negative impact on welfare. This decline in total surplus is sometimes referred to as a **deadweight loss**.

Now the welfare measure we have developed here has the great advantage of being related to observable functional relationships such as demand curves and cost curves, but we had to cut some analytic corners to develop it. Some of these we noted during our exposition – for example, the use of Marshallian demand curve assumptions and our willingness to add up the utilities of different individuals – but there are other problems buried behind the analysis which we have left hidden. We defer further discussion of welfare issues until Chapter 23, but readers might like to come back to the analysis of this section when they have read those chapters to make up their own minds about how serious its shortcomings actually are.

Figure 12.7

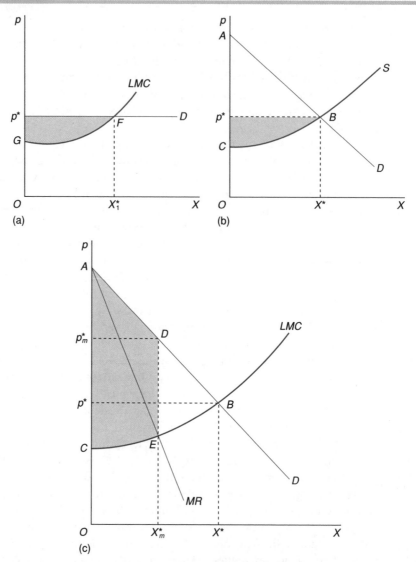

(a) The individual firm produces X_1^* at p^* and generates producer surplus equal to the shaded area p^*FG.

(b) At the level of the industry as a whole, producer surplus is given by p^*BC, and consumer surplus by ABp^*, and the total gain to utility by devoting resources to the production of X is given by ABC.

(c) When the production of X is monopolised, output falls from X^* to X_m^*, and price rises from p^* to p_m^*. Consumer surplus falls from ABp^* to ADp_m^*, producer surplus increases from p_m^*BC to p^*DEC, and the total gain from producing X shrinks by DBE. This decline in total surplus is referred to as a *deadweight* loss.

Price discrimination

From time to time in the previous discussion we have referred to the idea of price discrimination, which is closely associated with monopoly power. We shall now investigate this characteristic of monopoly in more detail. Price discrimination involves selling different units of the same good at different prices. It is a widespread phenomenon and we will consider it in two forms: first, charging different prices to different consumers and second, charging the same consumers different prices for different units of the good. Obviously these are not mutually exclusive practices – more complicated cases do indeed exist and may be analysed with the tools we shall now develop.

Suppose that, for some reason, the market for X facing the monopolist with whom we have so far been dealing were to expand by having a new group of consumers added to it. We would analyse the results of this by adding the demand of our new consumers to that of those already in the market, deriving the new marginal revenue curve and thereby solving for price and output. We do this in Figure 12.8. The only point here that is new to the reader is the discontinuity in the marginal revenue curve for the aggregate market. This arises because, at p_0, the price at which the new group of consumers comes into the market, there is a kink in the summed demand curve. There will therefore be a kink in the total revenue curve, as shown in Figure 12.9, and that implies a discontinuity in that curve's slope, in the marginal revenue.

The profit-maximising solution depicted in Figure 12.8, where marginal cost equals marginal revenue in the aggregate market, is an output of X^* sold at a price of p^*. Both groups of consumers are paying the same price for X; note that this implies that the marginal revenue accruing from selling to each group is different except in the special

Figure 12.8

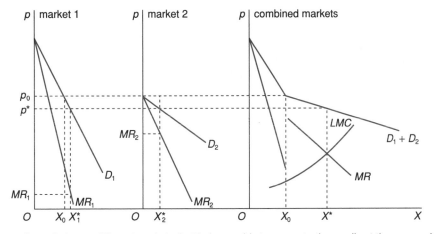

A monopolist sells in two different markets, but being unable to separate them sells at the same price p^* in both of them, X_1^* in market 1 and X_2^* in market 2. Thus, marginal revenue is different in the two markets and profits could be increased by charging different prices in the two markets and equalising marginal revenues. A unit of output withdrawn from market 1 and transferred to market 2 would add more to revenue in the second market than it subtracted from revenue in the first since at p^*, MR_1 is below MR_2.

Figure 12.9

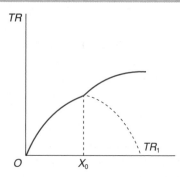

The total revenue curve implicit in summing the individual market demand curves of markets 1 and 2 in Figure 12.8 to get a total market demand curve. Up to output X_0, goods are sold only in market 1 and hence only TR_1 is relevant. However, at X_0, price is sufficiently low that purchasers in market 2 begin to buy the good. Hence, total revenue is now that earned in both markets, and there is a kink in the total revenue curve at this level of output that corresponds to the kink in the total demand curve. The slope of the total revenue curve (marginal revenue) thus increases discontinuously at output X_0. Note that this total revenue curve is derived on the assumption that the good X is sold at the same price in both markets. It is not relevant to the analysis that follows when different prices are charged in the two markets.

case where each group's elasticity of demand for X at that price is the same. Now marginal revenue is the addition to be made to total revenue from a small increment in the quantity sold (or the loss accruing from reducing quantity sold). As we have constructed Figure 12.8, holding output, and hence costs, constant, one could increase revenue by withdrawing units of X yielding a low marginal revenue from market 1 and selling them in market 2 where marginal revenue is higher. Gains would arise from doing this up to the point where marginal revenue was equated in the two markets. Such equating of marginal revenues, though, would involve charging different prices to the two groups of consumers: in short, there would be price discrimination between them.

Box 12.4   ## A single price monopolist

We can illustrate the loss of profits arising when a monopolist charges a single price in different markets that have different demand characteristics. The two markets can be defined by the following inverse demand functions:

$$p_1 = 100 - 2X_1 \tag{12.4.1}$$

$$p_2 = 80 - 0.5X_2 \tag{12.4.2}$$

The corresponding marginal revenues are

$$MR_1 = 100 - 4X_1 \tag{12.4.3}$$

$$MR_2 = 80 - X_2 \tag{12.4.4}$$

The reader can confirm that these functions define curves of the sort shown in Figure 12.8 for markets one and two.

To define the combined demand curve we must add quantities demanded, i.e. horizontally in terms of Figure 12.8. To sum in this way we must rearrange the demand functions to make demand the subject of the function:

$$X_1 = 50 - 0.5p_1$$

$$X_2 = 160 - 2p_2$$

For price greater than 80 there is no demand in market 2. So the combined demand curve is the market 1 demand curve for price above 80. This price corresponds to a demand of 10 in the first market. Below a price of 80 there is demand from both markets. So the combined inverse demand curve is

$$X = 50 - 0.5p, \quad X < 10 \tag{12.4.5}$$

$$X = 210 - 2.5p, \quad X > 10 \tag{12.4.6}$$

and the corresponding combined inverse demand curve is

$$p = 100 - 2X, \quad X < 10 \tag{12.4.7}$$

$$p = 84 - 0.4X, \quad X > 10 \tag{12.4.8}$$

The combined marginal revenue is therefore

$$MR = 100 - 4X, \quad X < 10 \tag{12.4.9}$$

$$MR = 84 - 0.8X, \quad X > 10 \tag{12.4.10}$$

The reader can confirm that this marginal revenue function produces a discontinuous curve of the form used in Figure 12.8. As an exercise the interested reader can define the combined total revenue curve equivalent to that defined in Figure 12.9.

Without loss of generality we can assume a constant marginal cost of 50. This defines a horizontal marginal cost curve rather than the upward-sloping curve in Figure 12.8. We can note from the combined marginal revenue function just defined that, with $X = 10$, $MR = 60$ with the first part of the function. This implies that with $MC = 50$ profit maximisation occurs on the second part of the mr function. To define profit maximising output we set $MR = MC$:

$$84 - 0.8X = 50$$

i.e. $X = 42.5$

From the combined inverse demand curve this output corresponds to a price of 67. Using the demand functions for the two markets, at this common price of 67 the demands in the two markets are: $X_1 = 16.5$ and $X_2 = 26$ (note that these two outputs sum to the original output of 42.5).

Using the demands in each market we can define the corresponding marginal revenues: $MR_1 = 34$ and $MR_2 = 54$. It follows that by producing the same global output the firm can increase revenue and profit by switching output from market 1 to market 2. This will increase the price in market 1 and reduce the price in market 2. For example by switching one unit of output the revenue loss in market 1 is 34 but the revenue gain in market 2 is 54, so the net revenue and profit gain is 20. By switching another unit of output the profit gain will be less than 20 but still positive. In short, by charging a single price the monopolist is not maximising profit.

Demand elasticity and price discrimination

A monopolist does not necessarily have the power to charge different prices to different people. It depends what good is being sold and how easy it is to identify and keep separate members of the two (or more) groups. If the good is such that one consumer can sell it to another after purchase at trivial cost in time and trouble, then discrimination is not possible, for any attempt to charge a higher price to one group would result in their having members of the lower price group make their purchases for them. Thus a cinema might offer a price discount to old age pensioners, but not a bookshop; a football ground might offer a discount to school children, but not a sweet shop. Readers can readily construct further examples of their own. If we assume that our two groups can be identified, and that the good is such that they can be kept from retrading it between them, it will pay the monopolist to charge them different prices. Moreover we may predict who will pay the higher price.

The reader will find it helpful to recall at this point that, just as the slope of the total revenue curve is equal to marginal revenue and just as the slope of the long-run total cost curve is equal to long-run marginal cost, so the area under the marginal revenue curve measures total revenue and the area under the long-run marginal cost curve measures long-run total cost. The reader should also recall the relationship between marginal revenue, price, and the elasticity of demand, equation (12.2).

If to maximise profits a discriminating monopolist is to equate marginal revenue between two markets, then the higher the absolute value of the elasticity of demand in either one of them, the lower will be the price. In terms of Figure 12.10, which reproduces

Figure 12.10   Price discrimination between two markets

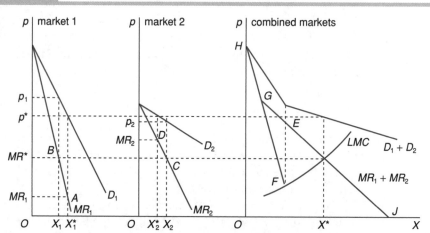

Prices are set in the two markets so as to equalise marginal revenue, so that p_1 is above p_2. The higher the elasticity of demand in a particular market, the lower the price charged. The increase in profits relative to charging the same price (p^*) in both markets is given equivalently by the areas ($CDX_2^*X_2 - ABX_1X_1^*$) or GEF. Sales in the first market contract from X_1^* to X_1 and those in the second market expand from X_2^* to X_2. There is no change in overall output X^* from the no price discrimination case and hence no change in costs of production. That is why revenue changes may be used to measure profit changes in this case.

Figure 12.8 and extends the analysis, the gain in profits from price discrimination is given by the area $CDX_2^*X_2$ minus the area $ABX_1X_1^*$. This is the gain in revenue from lowering price in market 2, minus the loss from raising it in market 1. Equivalently, it is given by the area *GEF* which is the difference between the area under the curve that is marginal to the summed demand curves of markets 1 and 2, and that under the summed marginal revenue curves of these markets. These two curves are *not* the same. The first is *HGFEJ* and the second is *HGEJ*. The first marginal revenue curve tells us how marginal revenue changes with quantity when *that quantity is sold to yield an equal price* in each market. The second deals with a situation when *that quantity is sold so as to yield the same marginal revenue*. The summed demand curve is irrelevant in the second case; it is the sum of the marginal revenue curves in the individual markets that is important.

This distinction is crucial when analysing the special case where the firm's marginal cost curve just passes through the discontinuity on the curve that is marginal to the summed demand curves. Here the inability to discriminate might lead to a price being set at which one group of consumers buys nothing. The ability to discriminate allows the latter group to be charged a lower price, and actually results in output increasing from the no discrimination situation. Readers will find it instructive explicitly to carry out the analysis for themselves.

Box 12.5   ## More on price discrimination

We can continue the example used in Box 12.4 to calculate the profit maximising prices that apply in the two markets. In the earlier box we set marginal cost equal to marginal revenue using the combined functions. This implied an optimal global output of 42.5. To allocate this global output to the two individual markets and calculate the different profit maximising prices that apply we set the individual marginal revenues equal to the combined profit maximising marginal revenue. We assumed a constant marginal cost of 50: hence the optimal combined $MR = 50$. From Box 12.4:

$$MR_1 = 100 - 4X_1 \tag{12.4.3}$$

$$MR_2 = 80 - X_2 \tag{12.4.4}$$

So for profit maximisation in the two markets

$$50 = 100 - 4X_1$$

$$50 = 80 - X_2$$

i.e. $X_1 = 12.5$ and $X_2 = 30$

(Note that these outputs sum to the global output of 42.5.)

Using the inverse demand curves from Box 12.4 we calculate the corresponding prices

$$p_1 = 100 - 2X_1 \tag{12.4.1}$$

$$p_2 = 80 - 0.5X_2 \tag{12.4.2}$$

i.e. $p_1 = 75$ and $p_2 = 65$. These output price combinations produce the maximum profit available to the monopolist.

Perfect price discrimination

To charge different prices to different groups of consumers is only one form that price discrimination can take. As we saw when we dealt with the theory of consumer's surplus, it is of the very essence that a consumer faced with a single price for a commodity gains from being able to purchase it; it is only marginal units purchased that are worth no more to consumers than they are asked to pay for them. Consider Figure 12.11 where a typical consumer's demand curve has been drawn, and let us make the Marshallian assumptions that permit us to treat the area under that curve as an approximate measure of the maximum amount that an individual would be willing to pay to obtain any particular quantity of the good. If the price is p_1, our consumer buys X_1 units of X spending in total p_1X_1, but would be willing to spend up to ABX_1O to obtain this quantity.

If the firm selling X was able to charge a different price for each unit bought, it could charge the area under the curve between A and C for the first unit, that between C and E for the second and so on. It would obtain a total revenue of $OABX_1$ from the sale of X_1 units, and would thereby increase its profits by ABp_1. Such **perfect price discrimination**, as it is called, would obviously be adopted by the profit-maximising firm if it was able to do so. Figure 12.12 shows what the situation would be from the point of view of the total market for X, rather than from that of the individual consumer (but still dealing with a demand curve based on Marshallian assumptions).

If the monopoly depicted there were able to price discriminate to perfection, its total revenue would be given by the area under the market demand curve for X, its total costs by the area under the long-run marginal cost curve; profits, the difference between the two, would obviously be maximised where the price of the last unit sold was just equal to long-run marginal cost. In this case, the market demand curve in effect becomes the firm's marginal revenue curve, rather than its average revenue curve. Note that in this case there is no deadweight loss associated with monopoly power. However, the outcome

Figure 12.11

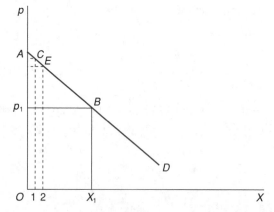

An individual's demand curve for X derived on Marshallian assumptions (cf. Chapter 4). A perfectly discriminating monopolist could acquire revenue of $OABX_1$ if it sold X_1 units of X to this consumer.

Figure 12.12

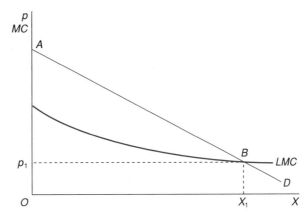

A profit-maximising perfectly discriminating monopolist would charge p_1 for the last unit of X that it sold and get a total revenue of ABX_1O. Equivalently, if it could operate a multipart tariff scheme it would charge p_1, i.e. long-run marginal cost per unit of X, and have available the area Ap_1B as the maximum amount it could collect by way of a fixed charge for the privilege of buying X at price p_1. Note that the downward slope of LMC in this diagram makes the firm a natural monopoly (cf. Figure 12.6).

differs from the competitive case in that the supplier captures all the consumer's as well as the producer's surplus.

In practice, monopolists rarely know everyone's separate willingness to pay for each unit of the good. Hence perfect discrimination is rare. But it is a limiting case of a very general phenomenon. Any consumer who faces a multipart tariff for the use of electricity or gas, or who pays a cover charge at a restaurant, is on the end of a discriminatory pricing scheme, as we shall now see.

Multipart tariffs

Perfect price discrimination appropriates to the seller of a good all the consumer's surplus that each consumer would get from buying it at a constant price. A two-part tariff for telephone service, gas or electricity, whereby a consumer can choose any quantity at a given price, after paying a rent for the right to receive any supply at all, takes some consumer's surplus in the form of this rental payment. If a profit-maximising seller knew the exact form of the consumer's demand curve, they could fix the rental equal to the area ABp_1 in Figure 12.12 and obtain exactly the effect of perfect price discrimination. Similarly for the restaurant that imposes a cover charge. Lack of perfect knowledge about the exact form of each customer's demand curve and the fact that it is expensive to acquire such knowledge even imperfectly – to say nothing of the administrative costs of running a different pricing scheme for every customer – leads such firms to set a uniform fixed charge, which leaves some consumers with a surplus, some with none, and persuades others to refrain from consuming the good at all where the charge is in excess of this surplus.

Price discrimination of the type just analysed can occur wherever it is possible for the seller to identify an individual consumer and to offer a two-part choice: whether to consume the good at all, and how much of it to consume, given that some is to be consumed. The possibility of imposing such a choice depends very much on the technical nature of the good being supplied. Telephone service, electricity and gas consumption require the installation of supply facilities in individual houses and factories; the consumption of a restaurant meal requires that a particular table be occupied. Hence rental, or cover, charges may be imposed. Readers are invited to think up further examples of their own where discrimination is possible. Doing so will not only help in understanding the foregoing analysis but also establish the ubiquity of the practice.

How much output will a discriminating monopolist of the type just described sell, and at what kind of price structure? To maximise profits, the first step is to set the price on the margin in such a way as to maximise the possible gain from charging a higher price for intra-marginal units. The possible gain in question is of course equal to the profits that would be made by a perfect price discriminator, and these are maximised, as we have seen, by setting price on the margin equal to marginal cost. In terms of Figure 12.12 output would still be equal to X_1 and price on the margin would be set at p_1, even if perfect discrimination were not feasible. How much of the consumer's surplus existing in the area ABp_1 the monopolist would appropriate, and with what kind of price structure, would depend upon how much was known about the shape of the demand curve and how ingenious the monopolist was at devising a suitable pricing scheme. The important implication here is that the monopolist who is able to price-discriminate by using multipart tariffs will produce exactly the same output as a perfectly competitive industry, if that monopolist's long-run marginal cost curve is indeed the same curve that would be the competitive industry's long-run supply curve. It is only monopolists who do not have the power to discriminate who will restrict output below its competitive level. Where price discrimination of the type just analysed is possible it is the amount of profits obtained (or consumer's surplus lost), and not the level of output, that differentiates the consequences of monopoly from those of competition.

This conclusion enables us to view natural monopoly, and the problems it presents, in a way rather different from that suggested by the analysis of simple monopoly pricing presented in the previous chapter. There, it seemed to be impossible for a natural monopoly to be forced to produce the competitive level of output without incurring losses. We can now see that, if it is possible for it to impose a multipart tariff, a natural monopoly will, of its own volition, produce the competitive level of output in order to maximise profits. However, it will, in the process, appropriate to itself the consumer's surplus that a competitive industry charging a single price would have left for its customers to enjoy. Thus the regulatory problem posed by a natural monopoly able to price-discriminate involves the distribution of consumer's surplus between the monopolist and its customers, and not its level of output.

Classifying types of price discrimination

It should be quite clear to the reader by now that the phrase 'price discrimination' covers a wide variety of behaviour. It is therefore useful to have labels that help us to classify the various pricing schemes to which that phrase applies. Such labels were proposed by A.C. Pigou, a student of Alfred Marshall, and his successor as Professor of Economics at Cambridge, who did much to extend and refine Marshall's contributions to microeconomics.

Pigou suggested that, though discriminatory pricing can take many specific forms, it could usefully be thought of as falling into three broad classifications.

To begin with, there is perfect price discrimination, a state of affairs in which the seller charges each buyer of their product a different price for each unit of that product, just equal to the marginal value to that buyer of that unit. Pricing behaviour of this type, which we analysed above and in Figure 12.11 above, under the label 'perfect price discrimination', Pigou called **price discrimination of the first degree**.

As we have seen, first degree price discrimination is a limiting case of a much broader class of pricing policies, usually involving facing each consumer with a multipart tariff in order to come as close as possible to a pricing scheme which is capable of appropriating to the seller all of the consumer's surplus accruing to each buyer. Pigou suggested that it was helpful to group such pricing schemes designed to approximate first degree price discrimination together, and classify them as **price discrimination of the second degree**.

An essential property of first and second degree price discrimination is that the same consumer is made to pay a different price for different units of the same product. But we began our exposition of price discrimination by considering a case in which this did not occur. There the firm was able to divide up the consumers that buy its output into separate sub-markets, and to charge different prices in those sub-markets. But within each sub-market, the individual consumer paid the same price per unit of output regardless of the amount bought. Pigou called pricing behaviour of this kind **price discrimination of the third degree**.

Now labels are just that. They do not add anything to the substance of economic analysis. But those which we have just discussed do provide a useful supplement to our vocabulary and enable us to discuss various types of price discrimination with greater clarity than would otherwise be possible. That is why they are widely used among students of industrial organisation, and why readers who pursue further studies in this branch of economics are likely to come across them with great frequency in the course of those studies.

Concluding comment

Perfect competition and monopoly between them do not provide a complete theory of firms' supply behaviour because they do not touch on problems arising from firms' interactions. Taking the demand curve that faces the firms as being given exogenously, the supply problem for each firm is to pick the point on that curve which will maximise profits; for the perfect competitor this involves choosing output alone, and for the monopolist it involves choosing a combination of price and output.

Lying behind the demand curve, whether of a monopolist or of a perfect competitor, are the prices of other goods. An implicit assumption behind the theories we have so far discussed is that the decisions taken by the firm under analysis have very diffuse effects on the demand curves facing other firms. If this assumption is granted, there is no need to consider the possibility of other firms reacting to the actions taken by the firm under analysis in such a way as to cause the demand conditions under which it is operating to change, and the theories of perfect competition and monopoly are adequate tools of analysis. However, if this assumption does not hold, and firms' demand curves do in fact become significantly interdependent in any circumstances, then these theories begin to break down. Oligopoly theory, aspects of which we will discuss in Chapters 15–17, represents an attempt to come to grips with such matters.

SUMMARY

Monopoly and price discrimination

1. Monopolists face the industry demand curve for their product and maximise profits at a level of output where marginal revenue equals marginal cost.

2. Marginal revenue is everywhere less than price for a monopolist because the demand curve slopes downwards.

3. Equilibrium output for the monopolist is determined where marginal revenue equals marginal cost. Profitability at that level of output depends upon the relationship between price and average cost. Unlike a competitive firm, a monopolist can co-exist with a production function displaying increasing, constant as well as diminishing returns to scale.

4. A monopolist's price always exceeds marginal cost. Monopolists can be thought of as restricting supply below the competitive level, in order to raise price.

5. From a Marshallian perspective, monopoly generates a deadweight loss for the economy relative to a competitive alternative.

6. Monopolies can arise because firms combine together to obtain monopoly power, or because increasing returns to scale are not exhausted by a single firm at an output sufficient to satisfy market demand. The latter case is referred to as 'natural monopoly'.

7. Attempts to force natural monopolists to imitate the competitive market outcome by setting price equal to marginal cost will lead to losses, because with increasing returns, marginal costs are less than average costs.

8. Natural monopolies, such as utilities, may require some form of regulation involving, for example, the imposition of average cost pricing. An alternative approach would be the application of a multipart tariff.

9. The monopoly model of the previous chapter showed firms exploiting their situation as sole supplier to raise prices. But markets permit monopoly power to be exercised in other ways. Two important possibilities involve price discrimination and product differentiation.

10. The simplest type of price discrimination, known as third degree price discrimination, occurs when the firm can divide its customers into groups and sell units of output at a price which differs between groups, but are the same within each group.

11. With third degree price discrimination, the monopolist equates marginal revenue between two (or more) markets. This implies that price will be lower the higher the absolute values of the elasticity of demand in the market in question.

12. First degree or perfect price discrimination occurs when the firm sells each unit of output at a different price. In this case, each consumer pays a different price for each unit of output, and the firm captures all consumers' surplus.

13. Second degree price discrimination occurs when a firm's pricing scheme approximates first degree discrimination. An important subset of such behaviour involves the use of multipart tariffs.

PROBLEMS

1 A firm in perfect competition faces the following total cost function:

$$C = 250X - 20X^2 + 2X^3$$

(a) What is the firm's supply function?
(b) At what output is marginal cost minimised?
(c) What is the firm's long-run equilibrium output and, assuming that every firm has the same cost function, price?
(d) In this long-run equilibrium, what is the value of profits?
(e) The firm is now a monopolist, with demand curve $p = 550 - 10X$. What are equilibrium price, output and profit?

2 How will the imposition on firms of a fixed charge per annum for the privilege of operating affect:

(a) the price and output set by a monopolist;
(b) the price and output of a competitive industry where all firms are equally efficient;
(c) the price and output of a typical firm in that industry;
(d) the price and output of an intra-marginal firm in a competitive industry in which some firms are more efficient than others?

In each case analyse short- and long-run responses.

3 A law is passed fixing, below the level currently prevailing, the maximum price that can be charged by a monopolist who produces good X. It responds by increasing output. Is this behaviour compatible with profit maximisation?

4 With price measured in £ per thousand units and X being measured in thousands of units per week, consider a monopolist producing X at a constant long-run marginal and average cost of £2 per thousand units, and selling to two groups of consumers whose demand curves are given by:

$$\text{Group 1} \quad p = 40 - 2X$$
$$\text{Group 2} \quad p = 20 - 2X$$

On the assumption that the monopolist cannot discriminate between the two groups, find:

(a) overall output;
(b) the price of output;
(c) the amount sold to each group of consumers; and
(d) profits.

Calculate all outputs to the nearest 10 units and prices and profits to the nearest penny. On the assumption that the monopolist can discriminate between the two groups, recompute your answers to (a), (c) and (d), and also find the prices at which it sells to the two samples of consumers.

5 Suppose a firm had a natural monopoly in the production of electricity and could impose an annual rental charge at a rate chosen by itself for the use of a meter without which no electricity could be used.

(a) If the firm wished to maximise profits should it set the price of electricity at marginal cost?
(b) Suppose the firm was prevented by law from charging a meter rental charge. Should this affect the profit-maximising price and output of electricity?

6 The short-run average cost curve of every firm in the industry is

$$C = 50 + (X - 50)^2$$

The firms sell to two types of consumer, type 1 and type 2. The demand curve for type 1 is $p_1 = 250 + 2X$, and for type 2 is $p_2 = 200 - X_2$. Calculate:

(a) output and price if the market as a whole is assumed to behave according to the assumptions of perfect competition;
(b) output, price and profit under pure monopoly;
(c) output, prices and profit under discriminating monopoly.

CHAPTER 13

Product differentiation and monopolistic competition

Key words and phrases

- Goods as bundles of attributes, similar but not identical goods, brands, brand loyalty, product differentiation, advertising, monopolistic competition, spatial economy, excess capacity, mark-up pricing

Introduction

We saw in the previous chapter that a monopolist may make positive profits in long-run equilibrium. We did not consider the question of why competitive firms did not spring up to compete these profits away. There are abundant reasons why a monopolist may be able to remain a monopolist, at least for a significant time. There may be legal barriers to other firms producing the same good as the monopolist; patent protection for the product; access to some trade secret that gives a significant cost advantage in producing the product; natural monopoly power when technology is characterised by increasing returns to scale; and so on. At the opposite extreme, if other firms can reproduce the product to perfection at no cost disadvantage, the industry becomes perfectly competitive. What about intermediate cases in which **a similar, but not identical, product** can be produced by other firms at no cost advantage? It is precisely with such a case that the theory of monopolistic competition seeks to deal, and we consider this model in the second part of the chapter.

We start by returning to theory of consumer behaviour, drawing on ideas first developed by Kevin Lancaster. In his approach, **goods** can be looked upon **as constituting bundles of attributes**, an approach to their definition that opens up the possibility of giving some sort of precision to ideas like 'similar but not identical goods'. There has always been an element of imprecision to this particular theory of firm behaviour that has limited its direct empirical applicability. Despite this, the theory remains of analytic interest, as we shall now see.

We still analyse the choice-making situation in terms of three basic components introduced in Chapter 2 – the objects of choice, the constraint upon choice and the tastes in terms of which the choice is made – but we consider them in a rather different way. We have thought in terms of the consumer deriving utility from the consumption of goods, and the constraint upon consumption being a financial one given by income and the prices of goods. The key to the new approach lies in looking more closely at the connection between the possession of goods and the derivation of satisfaction from their consumption. This allows us to analyse the idea of product differentiation.

Goods, attributes and choice

The 'goods' which are bought by consumers on the market are virtually never commodities that yield a single well-defined service to their purchaser. Instead, they have a number of attributes and it is reasonable to argue that it is these attributes which yield satisfaction in consumption, not the goods themselves. Thus a particular house or flat provides a whole variety of services to its occupier. It has a certain amount of floor space, a definite number of rooms, a particular quality of finish, a specific location relative to transport and recreational facilities, and so on; the list that one could draw up is virtually endless. Housing is a particularly complicated commodity to be sure, but even something as simple as a loaf of bread may be described in terms of attributes: its flavour, texture, colour, to say nothing of its nutritional characteristics, which are themselves a complex mixture of attributes.

Thus this approach to consumer theory views the objects of choice as being not the commodities which are available on the market, but their attributes. The utility function in terms of which choices are made deals not with bundles of goods, but with bundles of these attributes. What about the third ingredient of choice-making behaviour, the constraint upon choice? Instead of it being defined solely in terms of income and prices, it now must be defined in terms of income, prices and the technical characteristics of particular commodities available on the market. The demand for market goods and services is no longer to be regarded as the direct result of choice-making behaviour among bundles of such goods and services, but an indirect result of a more fundamental choice-making process.

The basic framework

Let us now look briefly at the way in which this new approach helps us to understand particular problems in economics. The reader will by now be used to our simplifying problems so as to render them tractable, and in this case we must simplify ruthlessly. We shall consider the case of a particular commodity, and shall assume that it has but two attributes. We shall also consider a highly artificial situation in which the consumer's volume of expenditure on that particular good is predetermined. In this way we can easily depict our problem in a two-dimensional diagram.

Let us then consider good X and treat it as having two attributes, R and S. The reader who wishes to give rather more concrete content to the analysis that follows may think of X as being baked beans, and R measuring the number of beans and S the amount of tomato sauce, or of X as nut chocolate with the two attributes being an amount of chocolate and a quantity of nuts. In Figure 13.1 we measure not quantities of a good along the axes, but quantities of a particular attribute: any point on Figure 13.1 denotes a particular combination of attributes of good X. Now suppose that there were three **brands** of X

Figure 13.1

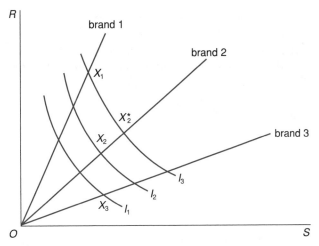

R and S are attributes of good X, and the indifference curves describe a consumer's tastes *vis-à-vis* those attributes. Three brands of X are available, each combining the attributes in different proportions. X_1, X_2 and X_3 represent quantities of these different brands of X that can be bought for a given outlay. If constrained to spend just that amount, our consumer will choose to buy X_1 of brand 1, since I_3 is a higher indifference curve than I_2 or I_1.

available to the customer, each of which mixed the attributes in different proportions, with the first brand having mostly attribute R and the third having mostly attribute S. Our consumer then can increase consumption of R and S in fixed proportions by moving out from the origin along any one of the three rays.

Associated with each point on any one of these rays is a price that must be paid to acquire just that combination of R and S. Tins of baked beans, if you like, have a price and, depending on the brand, contain different amounts of beans and sauce. In the artificial example which we are considering, we have endowed our individual with a fixed sum of money to spend on X, and with this sum that individual can just reach a particular point on each of the three rays. Let these points be X_1, X_2 and X_3 respectively. If our consumer is restricted to buying only one of the brands and is restricted to spending a fixed sum on that brand, then these three points represent the alternatives among which a choice must be made. They represent a highly discontinuous budget constraint. However, the important characteristic of the budget constraint as it is viewed in this approach is not its discontinuity, but the fact that it is no longer constructed on the basis simply of market data such as income and prices; the technical characteristics of particular goods also enter into it.

Tastes may be treated quite conventionally. We may draw an indifference map of the usual form which shows the consumer's preferences between bundles of attributes. Such a map, displaying a diminishing marginal rate of substitution between the attributes R and S, is drawn in Figure 13.1, and the consumer, as always, goes to the point on the budget constraint that yields the highest level of satisfaction. In this case the consumer has but three points to choose among, and as Figure 13.1 is constructed, it is point X_1 that is on the highest indifference curve.

Box 13.1	**Product differentiation: a simple example**

We can present a simple example of the characteristics framework that will be developed in more detail as the chapter progresses. Consider the market for breakfast cereals. Assume that only two brands exist in this market: to help presentation we can call these brands 'Fruity-nut' and 'Nutty-fruit'. Both brands have the same base cereal but, as their names suggest, they differ in their proportions of fruit and nuts. Fruity-nut has 15% total fruit content and 5% nut content, whereas nutty-fruit has 5% fruit content and 10% nut content. We can derive the characteristics rays, as presented in Figure 13.1 as follows, where F is fruit and N is nuts.

Fruity-nut: 3 times as much fruit as nuts
$$F = 3N \qquad\qquad (13.1.1)$$

Nutty-fruit: twice as much nuts as fruit
$$N = 2F \qquad\qquad (13.1.2)$$

Assume that a consumer spends on average £1 per month on breakfast cereal and that Fruity-nut is £1 for a 0.5 kg pack. Given the characteristics of Fruity-nut, this price and expenditure implies that our consumer can purchase 0.075 kg (i.e. 75 g) of fruit and 0.025 kg (i.e. 25 g) of nuts. This possibility is shown in Illustration 13.1. Our consumer derives the level of utility indicated by the I_1 indifference curve by buying Fruity-nut. This same level of utility can also be derived by consuming Nutty-fruit as long as 35 grams of fruit and 70 grams of nuts can be purchased. Given this required content our consumer must be able to buy (on average) 0.7 kg of Nutty-fruit per month, i.e. 70/0.1 = 700 grams of breakfast cereal or alternatively 35/0.05 = 700 grams of cereal. As expenditure is (on average) £1 per month the price of a 0.5 kg pack must be £0.71. In short, for our consumer, Nutty-fruit must be cheaper than Fruity-nut before purchase becomes rational.

Illustration 13.1

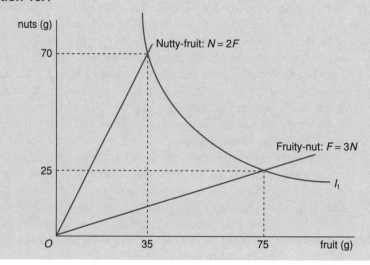

The conclusion just drawn about the required relative prices of the two brands of breakfast cereal follows because of our consumer's preference for fruit rather than nuts, in technical terms because of the MRS of the indifference curve I_1. For a different consumer, who has a greater preference for nuts rather than fruit, the indifference curves will be flatter and so the required price of Nutty-fruit will have to be greater to generate indifference between the two brands.

A simple application – brand loyalty

All this seems innocuous enough, and yet this analysis both makes predictions that are not given by the more conventional approach, and enables us to formulate questions about which that approach is silent. Consider first of all the simple question of the individual consumer's response to a fall in the price of a particular good. Conventional analysis predicts that as the price falls, more of the good in question will be bought, and that the bigger the price fall, the bigger will be the consumer's response. Consider, however, the consequences for the individual's behaviour of a fall in the price of just one brand of good X, say brand 2. The lower the price of this brand, the further out along the relevant ray does X_2 lie. However, unless it gets as far as X_2^* – the point at which the indifference curve passing through X_1 cuts ray 2 – there will be no effect whatsoever on our consumer's behaviour. Any price fall that enables the consumer to get beyond X_2^* will cause the entire consumption of X to be switched to this second brand.

Clearly this is a very different kind of individual response to that predicted by orthodox demand theory. Instead of a smooth and continuous movement from the relatively expensive good towards consumption of one whose price is falling, there is an all-or-nothing shift, the size of which is quite unrelated to the extent of the price fall. However, it should be noted at once that though the notion of a smooth downward-sloping demand curve is undermined here, it is only undermined at the level of the individual's behaviour. The aggregate demand for a particular brand of a good may still be smoothly downward sloping, but this property would come from the likelihood of different individuals having different tastes, and hence switching at different prices, to a brand whose price is falling.

Now the reader will have noted that in the foregoing discussion we referred to different 'brands' of X. The word did not crop up at all in our discussion of more conventional consumer theory. We derived demand curve for X on the assumption that it could be treated as a homogeneous product. However, product differentiation and the closely associated phenomenon of the use of brand names are widespread, and conventional consumer theory has considerable difficulty in dealing with them. To try to apply such analysis to the empirical study of the market, even for so uncomplicated a product as baked beans, immediately leads one to ask questions about whether it is satisfactory to treat all brands as if they were one homogeneous good, or whether each brand should be treated as a separate good. Only *ad hoc* answers are available to this question because the very notion of product differentiation has no place in conventional analysis. It starts after all by taking the product as given, as the basic object of choice. By treating the attributes of products as the basic objects of choice, the new approach enables us to talk about

product differentiation as involving goods mixing basic attributes in different proportions. In using it to analyse a consumer's choice between three brands of a particular
good, we have shown that there is no reason to expect that smooth substitution relationships will exist between brands of the same good. There is a range of price variation over
which the individual will continue to consume a particular brand of X; we have thus
given the notion of **brand loyalty** – the phenomenon of continuing to buy a particular
brand even though its price may have risen relative to others – a basis in economic theory,
a basis which it does not have in the more conventional approach.

An elaboration – combining brands

One assumption underlying the choice analysed in Figure 13.1 was that the consumer
was unable to get any mix of attributes other than those made available by consuming
one or another brand of X. The consumer was not able to mix brands. For some goods this
is a reasonable enough assumption, but not for others. If the only difference between
brands of baked beans was the ratio of beans to sauce in the tin, then by mixing the contents of different manufacturers' tins in different proportions, a much wider variety of
combinations of attributes can be obtained. Indeed, in terms of Figure 13.2, a constant

Figure 13.2

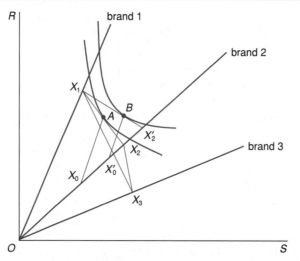

If brands can be mixed in order to obtain intermediate combinations of attributes, then a constant outlay
on X enables our consumer to obtain R and S anywhere along the lines $X_1 X_2$, $X_2 X_3$ and $X_1 X_3$. Given tastes,
the consumer will select combination A. If the price of brand 2 falls, this is equivalent to a fall in the price
of attribute S, since brand 2 contains relatively more of S than does brand 1. The consumer moves to
point B and, for a given outlay, unambiguously increases outlay on S. Whether this also involves buying
more of brand 2 is uncertain. Point A is reached by purchasing X_0 units of brand 2 and $A - X_0$ units of
brand 1. Point B is reached by buying X_0' units of brand 2 and $B - X_0'$ units of brand 1. As the indifference
curves are drawn, X_0' clearly exceeds X_0 so that more of brand 2 is bought. However, an indifference curve
could easily be drawn tangent to $X_1 X_2'$ at a point which would involve X_0' being less than X_0.

outlay could obtain any combination of attributes R and S along a straight line drawn between X_1 and X_2 by combining the first and second brand, between X_2 and X_3 by combining the second and third, and between X_1 and X_3 by combining the first and third. As the figure is constructed, however, the first and third brands would never be combined, since more of the good in question is always available in combinations involving brand 2. Given the tastes depicted in Figure 13.2, our individual will in fact combine brands 1 and 2 and settle at A. Should the price of brand 2 fall, a smooth substitution towards S will ensue, so long as this is not a Giffen attribute, but this may involve *either more or less* of brand 2 being purchased as is also shown in the figure.

This analysis is of interest for two reasons. First, it shows that the all or nothing nature of the response to a price change predicted in the previous section of this chapter is dependent upon the individual being unable to combine different brands of the same good in order to reach a personally preferred mixture of attributes, or at least unable to do so without incurring costs – which may be merely in terms of time and trouble – that more than offset any advantage that might be gained from so doing. Secondly, in showing that the demand for a particular brand of a good might fall as its own price falls, even though none of the attributes that make it up are inferior, the analysis warns us that the phenomenon of an upward-sloping demand curve might not be quite the practically irrelevant analytic curiosity that orthodox analysis of the Giffen good case might suggest.

Product differentiation and market research

The foregoing considerations lead us immediately into another problem area. It is not unreasonable to suppose that manufacturers of particular goods will find it much easier to vary the proportions in which their output combines various attributes than will individual consumers. Consider Figure 13.3. Our consumer with a given outlay to make on X will buy brand 1 so long as only three versions of the product are there to be chosen

Figure 13.3

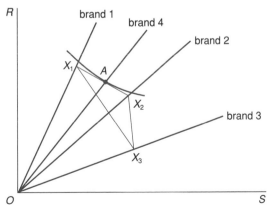

If, at going prices, enough consumers prefer R and S combined in the proportion given by A, it might pay a firm to introduce a brand 4 that would appeal to such consumers.

among. However, consider that combination of attributes that lies along the ray labelled 4. If some manufacturer can produce a new brand of X that combines R and S in these proportions, and offer it for sale at a price that enables our consumer to reach a point above and to the right of A for the given outlay, the consumer will switch to that brand. Given the particular tastes depicted in Figure 13.3, the consumer will be better off in so doing. If there are enough consumers with such tastes, and if it is technically feasible, there is a strong incentive for some firm, or firms, to produce brand 4.

The line of reasoning implicit in this very simple example helps us to understand two pervasive phenomena in everyday economic life. First, not every consumer will have the same tastes and hence we can begin to see why it will pay firms, and indeed even the same firm, to produce an array of brands of the same good, each one having slightly different attributes. Moreoever, there is no reason to suppose that any firm can possibly know *a priori* just how many of its potential customers prefer particular combinations of attributes in a particular product; but without such knowledge it would be all too easy to 'miss the market'. The importance of market research to firms becomes much easier to understand when we look at it in this light.

Box 13.2	**More on breakfast cereals**

Let us return to the breakfast cereal example introduced in Box 13.1. Assume that the prices of Fruity-nut and Nutty-fruit are respectively £1 and £0.71. Given the average monthly expenditure on breakfast cereal of £1, in principle consumers can mix the two brands and open up consumption possibilities defined by the frontier AB in Illustration 13.2. Given the consumer preferences defined by indifference curve I_1, the implication is that our consumer might maximise utility at (say) point C on this frontier on I_2.

An observant competitor might notice this gap and enter the market with a new brand of breakfast cereal, which for want of a better term we can call 'Super-nut'. This

Illustration 13.2

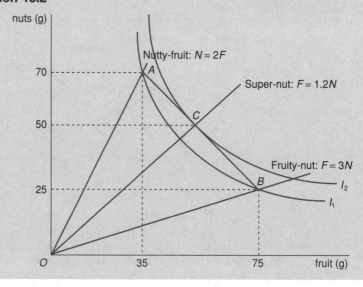

new brand might contain 15% fruit and 12.5% nuts, i.e. the same fruit content as Fruity-nut and more nut content than Nutty-fruit. The characteristics ray of this new brand will be defined by

$$F = 1.2N \tag{13.2.1}$$

as shown in Illustration 13.2. Our consumer will switch to this new brand as long as (say) 50 g of nuts can be purchased with the average £1 per month expenditure. Given the 12.5% nut content of super-nut this 50 g of nuts implies 50/0.125 = 400 g of overall breakfast cereal, i.e. 0.4 kg. This amount of breakfast cereal implies a price of £1.25 for a 0.5 kg pack. Note the higher possible price than either Nutty-fruit or Fruity-nut because of the greater nut content and the closer matching to our consumer's preferences. Assuming the higher price of Super-nut covers the extra cost of the nut content it would be rational for the new competitor to enter the market.

To prevent the greater competition implied by three firms rather than two the producer of Fruity-nut might itself introduce a new brand similar to Super-nut. Assuming consumer preferences are equally spread over the frontier AB in Illustration 13.2, this new brand will undermine the market for Nutty-fruit, in which case the producer might introduce a new brand with characteristics between Super-nut and Fruity-nut. This process of brand proliferation might continue until the extra revenues generated from a segmented market are equal to the extra costs of the product proliferation. Note that if new firm entry into a market is difficult the incentive for brand proliferation is undermined.

Advertising

If product differentiation and market research are phenomena that are illuminated by this new approach to consumer theory, it will come as no surprise to the reader to learn that it is also helpful in the analysis of **advertising**. Consider what the conventional analysis set out in previous chapters enables us to say about advertising. Consumers have given tastes *vis-à-vis* goods, and, given these tastes, do the best they can for themselves in the light of their incomes and the market prices that rule. Traditional analysis makes it difficult indeed to deal with advertising, for everything is presumed to be known to the consumer, but it does not take too much of a stretch of the imagination to realise that consumers in fact do not have perfect information. There is no reason to suppose that a consumer knows either the full array of prices ruling in the market at any time, or just who has what to sell. Clearly there is room for an industry that specialises in conveying such information, so that there is room for *informative advertising* in conventional analysis. But even quite casual observation soon convinces one that there is a lot more to contemporary advertising practices than conveying information about who has what to sell at what price. Estate agents' advertisements in local newspapers perform this role, but what about detergent advertisements on television? Prices and names of stockists are seldom, if ever, mentioned.

Such advertising is obviously aimed at persuading consumers to purchase one brand of a good rather than another, and since it hardly makes sense to suggest that consumers do not know their own tastes, the only way to fit such advertising into conventional analysis is to suggest that it is designed to change tastes, to shift the consumers' indifference maps. There is no need to dwell on the social and political implications of this interpretation. However, given conventional consumer theory, there is no other way of interpreting such advertising. The approach outlined in this chapter does leave room for an alternative interpretation without, however, ruling out the possibility that one of advertising's roles is to mould tastes.

If consumers do know their own tastes and advertising does not in fact change those tastes, then it must inform consumers about the objects of choice and about the constraints upon choice. Think of consumers having tastes for the attributes of goods, rather than directly for the goods themselves. Think also of different brands of a particular good combining attributes in different proportions so that the technical characteristics of particular brands are components of the constraint on the consumer's choice. There is no reason for us to suppose that consumers are familiar with the technical characteristics of each particular brand. We may then view advertising as informing consumers about what brands of a particular good are available, where, and at what price, and we can also think of it as informing them about the attributes of particular brands.

Thus, advertising that does not stress information about market prices and such, and which, in terms of conventional consumer choice theory, must be interpreted as having to do with an attempt to change tastes, may, in terms of this approach, be interpreted as informative. Consider, for example, car advertising that typically stresses such characteristics as fuel economy, passenger carrying capacity, manoeuvrability, acceleration, and so on. This is not to say that such advertising *must* be so interpreted, or that it is necessarily correct to interpret it so; only that an alternative hypothesis is available in the context of this new analysis. Which is correct is an empirical question that must await the formulation and performance of empirical tests designed to distinguish between them, but it is a strong point in favour of looking at goods in terms of their attributes that it opens up the possibility of formulating such tests.

Differentiated products and monopolistic competition

Let us now return to the issue of monopoly and monopoly power. We have seen that because consumers have different tastes, firms may choose to produce an array of goods which are similar but not identical. This yields the firm some element of monopoly power, in that the demand curve that it faces is not perfectly elastic. The model of **monopolistic competition** analyses the behaviour of firms and the industry in this case.

Thus consider a market with a large number of identical firms, each producing a slightly differentiated product in the sense discussed above of products which are similar, but not identical, at least in the mind of the consumer. As we have seen, differences in consumer preferences about the attributes of goods are one way to motivate the concept of product differentiation. Another is **spatial economics** which deals with the location of consumers and producers. Imagine that all consumers and producers of a particular good are located at different geographical locations. The consumer will buy from the producer who offers the lowest price, net of transport costs, to the consumer's specific location. By varying prices, producers can capture the custom of consumers located at different distances away from them. As one producer's price falls, the number of consumers who find that product the cheapest increases. As that producer's price increases, consumers from further away will begin to shop elsewhere, but the producer remains a relatively cheap supplier to consumers who are close by. Hence in such a spatial economy each firm faces a downward-sloping demand curve, even though there are numerous suppliers of an identical (except for the location of its production) product to the market. The situation of each monopolistically competitive firm may be portrayed just like that of a mono-polist, except that the demand curve facing the firm represents that for its own output and not the market demand for the output of the whole industry.

The firm in monopolistic competition

Figure 13.4 shows a firm in monopolistic competition in an initial long-run equilibrium position, producing where marginal revenue equals marginal cost and making profits equal to $(p_1 - AC_1)X_1$. Now suppose that it was possible for other firms to set up and produce a different brand of the same product under the same cost conditions as this firm. The effect of this would be both to make the demand curve for this firm's product more elastic at any particular price, and to shift the curve in to the left as customers are lost to these other firms. If there are no barriers to entry of new firms, this process would continue until there were no profits being made to attract new entrants. Thus, our original firm and all its competitors would find themselves in an equilibrium such as portrayed in Figure 13.5.

This equilibrium for the monopolistically competitive firm has the property that firms are constrained on the demand side of the market. By this, we mean that firms would like to sell more at the going price, but, because they have a downward-sloping demand

Figure 13.4

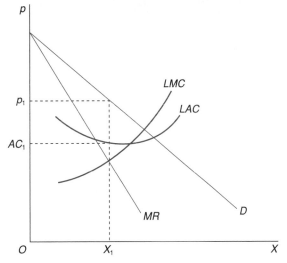

A monopolistic competitor in long-run equilibrium earning profits of $(p_1 - AC_1)X_1$. This diagram is similar in all respects to Figure 12.4.

Figure 13.5

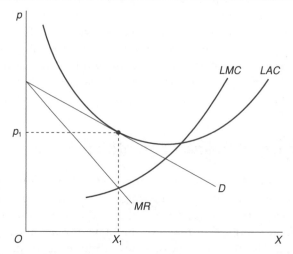

A typical monopolistically competitive firm in long-run equilibrium. The existence of positive profits attracts new firms, which produce a similar but not identical product to X. The expansion of such firms results in the demand curve for X shifting until it is just tangent to the firm's long-run average cost curve at p_1X_1. This figure is similar in every essential respect to the zero profit special case of a monopolistic firm portrayed in Figure 12.5(a).

curve, they can make additional sales only if price is reduced. This contrasts with the equilibrium for competitive firms, which are characterised as being able to sell as much as they want at the going price, and are constrained only by their willingness to supply.

Monopolistic competition and efficiency

A characteristic of the equilibrium portrayed in Figure 13.5 is that the firm is making no profits. It is in equilibrium at a level of output at which long-run average cost and price are equal. Because competitors are producing similar but not identical products, the demand curve facing each firm slopes downwards so that, with price being equal to average cost where profits are maximised, each firm is necessarily producing on the downward-sloping segment of its long-run average cost curve.

It is sometimes argued that a firm involved in monopolistic competition is inherently less efficient than its perfectly competitive counterpart, since it ends up producing output at more than minimum average cost. This finding does not necessarily hold in the case of pure monopoly, because, as will be remembered from the previous chapter, a monopolist simply produces where marginal revenue equals marginal cost without reference to the average cost curve. Monopolists could, in principle, produce at the minimum point of the long-run average cost curve therefore. A rough and ready intuition for this finding of 'excess capacity' under monopolistic competition is that there are 'too many firms' in long-run equilibrium. Since long-run average cost curves are U-shaped by assumption, and in perfectly competitive equilibrium every firm produces at the minimum of long-run average costs, an excess of firms implies that, in monopolistic competition, each firm produces less than its counterpart under perfect competition, and is therefore constrained to the downward-sloping part of the long-run average cost curve.

Box 13.3   ## More on the inefficiency of monopolistic competition

To explore the claimed inefficiency of a zero profit monopolistically competitive market we can develop a simple example. Assume a downward-sloping firm inverse demand curve:

$$p = a - X \tag{13.3.1}$$

We introduce a general term a here rather than an actual number as we want to solve for the value of a that generates zero firm profits. Given the logic outlined in the text the precise value of a is determined by the number of firms in the market. New firm entry produces a shift left in the demand curves of existing firms. This left shift can be produced as a fall in the value of our a parameter.

Assume the firm's long-run average costs curve takes the form

$$AC = 20 - 2X + 0.1X^2 \tag{13.3.2}$$

The firm's total costs are therefore

$$TC = AC.X = 20X - 2X^2 + 0.1X^3 \tag{13.3.3}$$

Long-run marginal cost is

$$MC = 20 - 4X + 0.3X^2 \tag{13.3.4}$$

The first issue is to find the output level that minimises AC. This can be found as the level X that makes the slope of the AC curve zero:

$$\frac{d(AC)}{dX} = -2 + 0.2X = 0 \tag{13.3.5}$$

This implies that efficient production requires $X = 10$.

For a monopolistically competitive firm in long-run equilibrium two conditions must hold: $AR = AC$ and $MR = MC$. The first condition generates zero profit; the second condition ensures this zero profit is the maximum obtainable.

AR = AC

$$a - X = 20 - 2X + 0.1X^2 \tag{13.3.6}$$

i.e. $20 - a = X - 0.1X^2$

MR = MC

$$a - 2X = 20 - 4X + 0.3X^2 \tag{13.3.7}$$

i.e. $20 - a = 2X - 0.3X^2$

Setting $20 - a = 20 - a$, i.e. ensuring that both conditions apply simultaneously:

$$X - 0.1X^2 = 2X - 0.3X^2 \tag{13.3.8}$$

$\rightarrow$

The only positive solution possible here is $X = 5$, i.e. half the efficient level. As stated in the text, this is the problem of too many firms. Using (13.3.6) this level of competition requires sufficient firm entry to generate a value of $a = 17.5$.

The reader is left to consider the following issues:

1. Out of long-run equilibrium the firm will earn positive profits. In the model used here this requires $a > 17.5$. The interested reader can show that with $a > 17.5$ the degree of excess capacity will fall.
2. Furthermore the very interested reader can show that with $a = 30$, the firm although earning significant positive profit will be operating a minimum AC, i.e. at full capacity.

* A more formal analysis

We can illustrate the above discussion with some simple calculus. We also draw on our formal analysis of the monopolistic firm to obtain a representation of the model of monopolistic competition using the example of a Cobb-Douglas production function.

We assume that the firm in monopolistic competition maximises profits

$$\pi = pX - rK - wL \tag{13.1}$$

subject to a Cobb-Douglas production function

$$X = AL^{\alpha}L^{\beta} \tag{13.2}$$

and downward-sloping output demand curve, which we write in inverse form:

$$p = p(X), \ \partial p / \partial X < 0 \tag{13.3}$$

We make no restrictions on returns to scale ($\alpha + \beta$), a priori. We established in Chapter 11 that, in competition, the price equals marginal cost condition could be rearranged to the labour hiring rule that price times the marginal product of labour, known as the marginal revenue product of labour, equals the wage (see equation (11.11)). Similarly we can derive the capital hiring rule for competitive product markets that the price times the marginal product of capital, known as the marginal revenue product of capital, equals the rental price of capital (see equation (11.12)).

These conditions, which are examined in more detail in Chapter 21, have to be modified somewhat when product markets are imperfectly competitive (see Chapter 22). In particular, the marginal revenue product terms ($p\partial X/\partial L$ and $p\partial X/\partial K$) must be specified differently because the addition to revenue from an additional unit of output is *marginal revenue*, not price, when competition is imperfect.

Hence the marginal revenue product of labour is marginal revenue times the marginal product of labour ($(p + X(\partial p/\partial X))(\partial X/\partial L)$). Denoting marginal revenue for the moment as *mr*, the equilibrium conditions are

$$MR\frac{\partial X}{\partial L} = MR\frac{\alpha X}{L} = w \tag{13.4}$$

$$MR\frac{\partial X}{\partial K} = MR\frac{\beta X}{K} = r \tag{13.5}$$

Substituting equations (13.4) and (13.5) into (13.1) yields

$$\pi = pX - \frac{MR(\alpha XL)}{L} - \frac{MR(\beta XK)}{K} \tag{13.6}$$

$$\pi = pX - MR(\alpha + \beta)X \tag{13.7}$$

As we have seen, firms in monopolistic competition which make positive profits are subject to competitive pressures which shift product demand curves inwards and make them more elastic. This process ceases when every (technologically identical) firm earns zero profits. Hence full market equilibrium requires that each firm's situation is characterised by

$$\pi = 0 \tag{13.8}$$

The two equations (13.7) and (13.8) therefore describe the equilibrium for the firm in monopolistic competition after entry has ceased. Combining them and rearranging terms yields

$$\frac{p}{MR} = \alpha + \beta \tag{13.9}$$

Thus, the firm must produce where $(\alpha + \beta)$, which is an index of returns to scale, equals the ratio of price to marginal revenue. We have already noted that, since demand curves slope downwards, marginal revenue is everywhere less than price (see Chapter 12, in particular equations (12.1) and (12.2)). Hence the left-hand side of equation (13.9) is greater than 1. This means that for (13.9) to hold, $\alpha + \beta > 1$; the firm must produce in the range of increasing returns to scale. We have therefore established that the firm's own equilibrium conditions in the face of a downward-sloping demand curve – the marginal revenue product equals the cost of the factor input – and the zero profit condition from free entry and exit, can only be satisfied simultaneously if the equilibrium occurs in the range of increasing returns to scale, when long-run average costs are diminishing. This result carries over to the case where production technology is not homogeneous, and as we have seen, is illustrated in Figure 12.6.

Mark-up pricing

A great attraction of the model of monopolistic competition is that it allows us to think about firms' pricing policies rather more explicitly than do the models of market structure dealt with earlier. In particular, it allows us to derive formally a '**mark-up**' model of **pricing**, in which prices are set as a multiple of average costs. This model is worth readers' attention for two reasons. First, much applied work in industrial organisation has dealt with the idea that output price is often set by adding a fixed mark-up to average costs, and it is by no means clear at first sight that such behaviour is compatible with profit maximisation. Certainly, the models of firm behaviour that we have considered so far give us no reason in general to predict such behaviour. It is therefore of some interest to see that, on certain specific assumptions, profit maximisation does indeed lead to fixed mark-up pricing. The analysis that follows will enable readers to see just what those assumptions are, and to form their own opinions about their plausibility.

Second, many macroeconomic models of the inflationary process see the link between labour-market conditions and the behaviour of money wages as being a crucial element in that process. Nevertheless, it is only one element, and must be supplemented by a theory of the relationship between labour costs and price if the so-called wage–price spiral is to be analysed. The idea of mark-up pricing has often been pressed into service to provide such a theory.

The analysis in question is most simply undertaken with the aid of a number of restrictive assumptions, some of which conflict with those made elsewhere in this chapter. In particular, it is helpful to focus on a monopolistically competitive industry made up of identical firms, each with constant average and marginal costs.

In order to make sense of this assumption, we are forced to assume also that some barrier to the entry of new firms into the industry exists, for under such cost conditions the typical monopolistically competitive firm will make positive profits at any positive level of output. Free entry would ensure that the 'zero profit' equilibrium depicted in Figure 13.5, where the demand curve is tangent to the average cost curve, would degenerate into a 'corner solution' in which the typical firm sold an infinitesimally small (in the limit zero) level of output at a price just equal to average and marginal cost.

Nevertheless, if we are willing to assume that the number of firms in the monopolistically competitive industry is exogenously given, we may then assume constant average and marginal costs of production and proceed to develop a model of mark-up pricing. In terms of the Cobb-Douglas production function, such as we set out above, constant returns to scale implies $\alpha + \beta = 1$. Unlike in perfect competition, where enterprise equilibrium is indeterminate with constant returns (see Chapter 11), the monopolistically competitive firm can achieve a determinate equilibrium level of output with constant average costs because the demand curve is downward sloping. As we know from Chapter 8, constant returns to scale means that long-run average costs equal long-run marginal costs, and we denote them by C. Let us assume that each firm faces a constant elasticity demand curve (see Chapter 12). We know from equation (12.2) that

$$MR = p\left(1 + \frac{1}{e}\right) \tag{13.10}$$

We also know that the monopolistically competitive firm produces where $MR = MC$. Hence in this case it produces where

$$p\left(1 + \frac{1}{e}\right) = LMC = LAC \equiv c \tag{13.11}$$

or

$$p = \left(\frac{1}{1 + (1/e)}\right) LAC \tag{13.12}$$

As we have assumed e is a constant, we can denote $(1/(1 + 1/e))$ as a constant $(1 + m)$. Hence

$$p = (1 + m)c \tag{13.13}$$

Equation (13.13) states that price is a mark-up (m) of long-run average cost, the size of the mark-up depending on the elasticity of demand. The more inelastic demand is, the greater the mark-up on costs to reach the selling price. The model of monopolistic competition, with some strong assumptions about entry conditions, not to mention demand and technology, therefore allows us to derive a simple *behavioural* model of how prices are set.

Criticisms of monopolistic competition

The foregoing analysis is appealing and popular, not least among economists seeking micro foundations for Keynesian macroeconomics, and among those looking for a theoretical framework within which to cast empirical studies of firms' pricing policies. It is not beyond criticism, however. In particular, its critics ask whether it adds anything to the monopoly model with which we dealt earlier. Monopoly differs from perfect competition in its analysis of the behaviour of the firm in one respect only: the monopolist's demand curve slopes downwards. So also does that of the monopolistically competitive firm, and in long-run equilibrium with freedom of entry it is just a special case of monopoly where zero profits are being made. The version of the model used to analyse mark-up pricing is yet another special case of monopoly, this one with constant returns to scale. If this analysis does add anything to our understanding of firms' behaviour, then, it must be because it tells us something about the interactions between firms in an industry, for it tells us nothing new about the individual firm.

But according to the critics there is a problem at this level too. The monopolistically competitive industry is made up of firms producing similar, though not identical, products that are therefore close, but not perfect, substitutes for each other. The question upon which, so they claim, the analysis founders is 'how close is close?' How do we define 'the market' which is our unit of analysis? For example, are different brands of tea similar products? And if they are, is coffee a sufficiently close substitute that we should talk about a 'beverage' industry? And if we do, are cocoa-producing firms part of it? The model does not tell us how to draw the boundary around an industry and hence leaves it up to the individual economist carrying out the analysis to decide whether to treat a particular group of firms as individual monopolies or as members of a monopolistically competitive industry. Since no one has ever suggested that there are no substitutes for an individual monopolist's output, and that changes in the price of those substitutes will not shift the demand curve, the critics argue that the notion of the monopolistically competitive industry adds little to our ability to understand firms' behaviour that is not already inherent in the theory of pure monopoly.

Concluding comment

In this chapter we have outlined a different approach to the analysis of consumer choice, based on the attributes of goods rather than the commodities themselves. This approach is rather more complex than that taken in our previous discussion, and suggests that individual demand curves may not be smoothly downward sloping after all. It also helps us to understand a number of 'real-world' phenomena not well explained by conventional consumer theory: brand loyalty, product differentiation and advertising.

We still analyse the choice-making situation in terms of three basic components – the objects of choice, the constraint upon choice and the tastes in terms of which the choice is made – but we consider them in a rather different way. We have thought in terms of the consumer deriving utility from the consumption of goods, and the constraint upon consumption being a financial one given by income and the prices of goods. The key to the new approach lies in looking more closely at the connection between the possession of goods and the derivation of satisfaction from their consumption.

The analysis of monopoly and competition seemed to indicate that the nature of price–quantity outcomes would depend upon the number of firms in an industry. Thus equilibrium in perfect competition, with a large number of firms, was characterised by price equalling the minimum of long-run average costs. In contrast, monopolistic markets had higher prices and smaller levels of output; output was set where marginal revenues equalled marginal cost, and price, given quantity, was determined on the demand curve.

One might have expected that 'intermediate market structures', with relatively few firms, would generate outcomes somewhere between these extremes. One important implication of the material presented in this chapter is that this perspective sometimes simplifies to the point of being misleading.

For example, the model of monopolistic competition suggests that market imperfections may also involve product differentiation and matters affecting the ease or difficulty of entry. As we see in the next section the framework for studying these complexities is much richer once we move to models of oligopolistic behaviour.

SUMMARY

Product differentiation and monopolistic competition

1. We analyse the behaviour of markets in which firms produce similar but not identical goods – differentiated products.

2. We first build on the conventional theory of consumer choice to explain product differentiation in terms of goods' characteristics.

3. This leads us to analyse the attributes or characteristics of goods as the basis of consumer satisfaction. Utility functions are therefore defined in terms of characteristics of goods, rather than their quantities.

4. Particular products or brands of products may be thought of as providing fixed combinations of attributes, each brand doing so in a different proportion.

5. There is no reason to conclude that there will be smooth substitution between brands as prices change. Rather there will be a range of price variation within which the consumer will show 'brand loyalty'; but once a certain price threshold is crossed, the consumer will shift to an alternative brand.

6. This all-or-nothing response to brands depends on the consumer not being able, at any feasible cost, to combine brands before consumption to achieve desired combinations of characteristics. But if this is feasible, then demand for a brand may decline or rise as its price falls.

7. The multiplication of brands observed in the real world may result from firms seeking to make available to consumers hitherto unattainable combinations of attributes.

Market research may be used to assist firms in establishing which missing combinations consumers desire.

8. Monopolistic competition is a form of market organisation in which entry and exit of firms is costless, but products are differentiated, that is, similar but not identical. The goods' characteristics approach is one way to motivate this assumption.

9. Firms in long-run equilibrium in monopolistic competition produce where marginal revenue and marginal costs are equal and here entry has driven prices down to equal long-run average costs. This implies that each firm is producing on the downward-sloping segment of its long-run average cost curve.

10. If we assume constant elasticity of demand and constant returns to scale, firms can be regarded as setting prices as a mark-up over long-run marginal and average cost, the extent of the mark-up being inversely related to the elasticity of demand.

PROBLEMS

1 'The theory of supply suggests that, as a rough and ready rule, the public authorities should keep their eye on the number of producers in an industry. When this becomes too small, public intervention will become necessary.' Discuss.

2 Are there any circumstances in which the firm in monopolistic competition can produce at a level of output at which the average cost curve is upward sloping? What do you conclude from your answer about the efficiency of monopolistically competitive industries?

3 With p measured as £ per thousand units and X measured as thousands of units per week, the market demand for X is given by

$$p = 20 - X$$

A group of small firms are able to provide X along a supply curve given by

$$p = 2 + 2X$$

(a) Find:
   (i)   the price of X; and
   (ii) the quantity of X.
(b) A large firm appears on the market which can produce X at a constant long-run marginal and average cost of £8 per thousand units. Find:
   (i)   the demand curve facing that firm;
   (ii) the price and output of the firm;
   (iii) the firm's profit;
   (iv) the overall output of X; and
   (v)   the quantity of X produced by the small competitive firms.

4 Consider a situation in which only one firm in a country produces a good X but in which foreign firms also provide X to the market under perfectly competitive conditions. How will the imposition of

(a) a flat rate tariff, and
(b) a ban on imports, affect the price, output and profits of the domestic firm?

5 Consider the industry described in question 3. Suppose that the monopolist who takes it over is a revenue maximiser instead of a profit maximiser. Recompute your answers to parts (b) and (c) of question 3.

6 Suppose that a firm in monopolistic competition faces a demand curve $p = 10/X^2$ and cost curve $C = 50 + 30X$. What is the mark-up of price on average cost? Suppose that the demand curve now shifts out, so $p = 20/X^2$. What happens to the mark-up?

Alternative theories of the firm

Key words and phrases

- corporate governance, different behavioural assumptions, revenue maximisation, minimum profit constraint, lump-sum tax
- labour-managed firm, maximising income per worker, backward-bending short-run supply curve, fixed costs, perfectly inelastic long-run supply curve
- entry and exit of firms as key factor leading to elasticity of industry supply

Introduction

The material on the theory of the firm dealt with so far in this book has assumed that the objective of the enterprise is to maximise profits. This assumption is justified with reference to the motives of individual entrepreneurs who seek to maximise their personal returns from carrying on business. But, as has been hinted on several occasions, this is not necessarily the most appropriate assumption about enterprise motivation in all circumstances. Even within capitalist firms, the relevance of profit maximisation is less obvious for large modern corporations where ownership and control of the firm are separated: the former in the hands of potentially diffuse shareholders and the latter vested in professional management. Many analysts have suggested that this separation provides a considerable degree of decision-making autonomy for managers, whose behaviour may in consequence deviate significantly from that implied by profit maximisation. Our first subject in this chapter is the problem of **corporate governance** which can emerge when the owners of firms are different actors from the people who manage them – hired managers. In fact, it is usually argued that modern market economies contain many mechanisms to ensure that, even though, unlike in our simple entrepreneurial model, owners and managers are not the same people, their objectives are brought into line. We go on to consider one example of what might happen if the motivation of owners and managers are not aligned. We follow William Baumol in examining a situation where owners are assumed to continue to maximise profits, but managers instead obtain their utility from their 'power' which is assumed to derive from the size of the firm. We further assume that the manager's choices guide the decisions of the company. This leads us to investigate the consequences of assuming that firms seek to maximise their size, measured by their sales revenue, rather than profits. This is only one among a variety of potential models analysing the implications of the separation of ownership from control on company behaviour.

We conclude the chapter by considering one example of a completely different sort of firm. Capitalist firms are not the only form of productive enterprise, even within capitalist economies. Numerous other forms of enterprise coexist – public corporations, consumer co-operatives, partnerships and workers' co-operatives – though typically these play a secondary role in the economy as a whole. Once we broaden our interest to non-Western economies, the range of enterprises is even larger, including the large socialist corporations which still characterise, for example, parts of Chinese industry, and less well-known institutions like producer co-operatives or Israeli kibbutzim. The assumption of profit maximisation is implausible for all of these organisations, though for a variety of different reasons. It is beyond the scope of the book to analyse fully the implications of **different behavioural assumptions** in all of these cases. We focus instead, in the final part of the chapter, on what is perhaps analytically one of the most interesting examples – referred to in the literature as the labour-managed firm. Such enterprises are run by, or at least in the interests of, their workers, and the framework we develop below therefore analyses behaviour of potential relevance to a wide variety of organisations, from the producer co-operatives of the West to the worker-managed firms that used to be typical in the former Yugoslavia.

We could argue indefinitely as to whether particular assumptions about enterprise objectives are appropriate or 'realistic' in various circumstances, but a priori debate about assumptions is rarely fruitful. It is more helpful to see whether alternative hypotheses about firms' objectives enable us to say anything about the way in which they might behave which is different from what is implied by profit maximisation. As we shall see, particularly in the case of labour-managed firms, differences in behaviour tend to be highly sensitive to differences in assumptions about enterprise objectives.

Corporate governance

In the 1930s, Berle and Means analysed a type of firm in which ownership and control were separated: the modern corporation. Their approach led some analysts to consider the behaviour of firms that were following the objectives of their managers rather than their owner, and we consider one such example below with the revenue maximising firm. However, it is useful to note that a major stream of modern economics, especially in the finance area, has developed to show how contracts can be developed and a variety of the characteristics of the market economy be brought to bear, to ensure that the incentives of management are more closely or fully aligned with those of owners. That is to say, that even when ownership and control are separated, managers can be given incentives that lead them to maximise profits in the way that would have occurred in the entrepreneurial firm.

The **corporate governance** problem in the modern corporation arises when ownership is separated from control and the objective of owners – profit maximisation – is different from that of managers, who are concerned instead with their own *private benefits*. If the owner could monitor perfectly the behaviour of managers, even the variation in objectives would not be a problem because the owners could force or induce managers to do what they wanted. The problem arises because of the asymmetry of information held by managers and owners; outside owners can never have full access to the information about corporate performance that is in the hands of managers. Thus, it is hard for them to establish whether poor results are a consequence of unforeseen circumstances or of managers exploiting firm profits for their own purposes. Whenever ownership and control are separated and information is distributed asymmetrically, firm-specific rents can be used to satisfy management's aims – for example, lower effort or managerial power, via the size of the firm – rather than profits.

However, a private ownership system also places limits on managers' discretionary behavior via external constraints from product and capital markets. These largely operate through the market for corporate control, and through the internal constraints imposed via statutes and monitoring by the owners themselves. In Anglo-Saxon countries, the constraints on managerial discretion are seen in large part to derive from stock markets. The quality of managerial decision-making and the extent of managerial discretion are an input in the choices of traders in equity markets, whose judgement on company performance is summarised in the share price. If the managerial team is thought to be incompetent or inefficient, the share prices will be reduced, putting pressure on managers to improve their performance. A persistently poor showing by a quoted company may also generate external pressure by encouraging a takeover bid. In this case, the stock market can be viewed as a market for corporate control, with alternative teams vying for the right to manage the enterprise. However, the effectiveness of these disciplines relies to some extent on the concentration of ownership. If ownership is highly dispersed, each individual owner has only a slight incentive to monitor effectively, and monitoring may be inadequate.

Governance also comes from the way that the managerial market operates, with managerial performance, pay and job prospects assessed by movements in share prices. Payment mechanisms such as management stock option schemes can also be put in place to align the incentives of owners and managers. In countries such as Japan or Germany, however, the mechanisms can be different, with less reliance on an adversarial market for corporate control and more extensive use of internal governance constraints. Ownership is typically highly concentrated into the hands of banks, funds or families who are granted board representation and undertake close monitoring of managerial performance directly, but may also rely on the managerial market and management incentive schemes.

It is widely argued that state owned firms are less efficient than privately owned ones, and this has led to the world-wide phenomenon of privatisation of former state assets. The previous discussion to some extent helps to explain why. It is hard for the state to imitate the market-based constraints on managerial behaviour. State-owned firms are not subject to private capital market disciplines, so neither the competitively driven informational structure nor the market-based governance mechanisms can be substituted for in full. State employees are usually civil servants and often do not compete in the wider managerial market, though many governments have recently tried to reduce the labour market segmentation between the public and private sectors. Moreover, though the government's ownership stake is concentrated, the state is rarely directly represented on the boards of public sector companies and usually does not have the capacity in the supervisory ministries to undertake the necessary scale and quality of monitoring.

Revenue maximisation in a competitive market

As we have seen, there are several reasons why **revenue maximisation** may be a plausible alternative to profit maximisation as an objective for certain types of firm. If managers are not the same people as owners, and the latter have only limited control over the former, we might expect to see the objectives of managers to some extent supplementing the goal of profit maximisation. Baumol has suggested that, while managerial rewards may not be closely associated with company profits, managers' power, authority and status in society will be related to the size of the firm which they control. Hence they will seek to maximise the size of the company. Note that this has the rather subtle implication that we are addressing issues which are implicitly dynamic – the growth of the firm – in the sales-maximisation approach, though the framework remains formally static.

Whatever the justification, it is unreasonable to postulate that the firm seeks to maximise its revenue and to leave it at that. A perfectly competitive firm, which faces a given price for its output can always increase its revenue simply by increasing output, at least up to the level of taking over the whole industry. However, we have already seen that when the perfectly competitive industry is in equilibrium with each firm maximising profits, the actual level of profits that will be made by a particular firm, unless it happens to have some special advantage not available to its competitors, will be zero. Thus, to expand output beyond this profit-maximising level for the sake of increasing revenue would involve the perfectly competitive firm in making losses.

The above argument has two important implications. First, because no privately owned firm can stay in business if it continually makes losses, the revenue-maximisation hypothesis does not, when taken by itself, make sense. It must be qualified by saying that firms seek to maximise sales revenue up to a level of output that ensures some minimum acceptable level of profits, which cannot be negative. The second implication follows immediately from this first one. The perfectly competitive profit-maximising firm is, as a result of market forces, put in a position of producing its output at a level which in the long run yields zero profits. Hence, it is already up against a **minimum** acceptable **profit constraint**, and its behaviour is going to be no different from that of a firm that seeks to maximise its sales revenue subject to that same constraint in perfectly competitive conditions.

This conclusion is of considerable interest. The conventional theory of the firm has often been criticised for the 'unrealistic' nature of its underlying assumptions, and the profit maximisation hypothesis in particular has been singled out for criticism along these lines. There are many who would regard the revenue-maximisation postulate as more acceptable, and yet we have now seen that, in the important case of perfect competition, without which we could not derive the supply curve which is so widely used in applications of simple microeconomics, the 'realistic' revenue-maximising hypothesis leads us to exactly the same conclusions about behaviour as does that of profit maximisation. Revenue-maximising firms behave 'as if' they were interested only in maximising profits, and may safely be analysed on the basis of this latter 'unrealistic' assumption. This illustrates a general principle first explicitly proposed by Milton Friedman and often invoked by economists in defence of their highly abstract models: namely, that debate about whether or not a model's assumptions are 'unrealistic' or descriptively 'inaccurate' is usually futile; the degree of conformity to reality of the conclusions it yields provides a more constructive basis for criticising a model.

The revenue-maximising hypothesis under monopoly

Now as it happens the revenue-maximisation hypothesis does not always yield the same results as does profit maximisation. Consider the case of monopoly. We have already seen that a profit-maximising monopolist whose marginal production costs are positive will choose a point on the demand curve for output where the absolute value of the elasticity of demand is greater than one. This means that such a firm could increase its revenue by lowering price and increasing output. So long as we were dealing with a typical case, in which maximum attainable profits were positive, the firm could do so without violating the requirement that it make some minimum level of profits. Thus, under conditions of monopoly, the revenue-maximising firm would produce a greater output than the profit-maximising firm. Just how much greater depends upon the cost conditions facing the firm.

Recall that sales revenue will be maximised at a level of output at which the elasticity of demand is equal to -1, and consider Figure 14.1 which depicts two possible cases. In panel (a) we depict a firm whose long-run average production costs are rather 'low' so

Figure 14.1

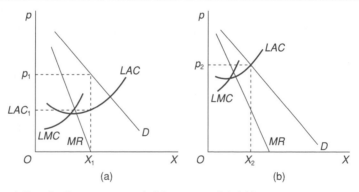

Two possible solutions for the revenue-maximising monopolist. (a) Long-run average costs are 'low' so the firm produces X_1 and sells it at p_1; at this point the elasticity of demand is -1 and profits are positive at $(p_1 - LAC_1)X_1$. (b) Long-run average costs are 'high' so the firm produces X_2 for sale at a price of p_2. At this output profits are zero and, because demand is still in the price elastic range, revenue is not at its unconstrained maximum. In either case, output is higher than the profit-maximising ($LMC = MR$) level.

The imposition of a lump-sum tax shifts the long-run average cost curve upwards by the amount of the tax divided by output, but does not shift the marginal cost curve. So long as the tax is less than $(p_1 - LAC_1)X_1$, its imposition will not affect the price and output of the firm (a); if the tax is greater than this amount, firm (a) will come to act like firm (b) and set its price equal to long-run average cost including the tax. The imposition of such a tax on firm (b), regardless of its amount, will shift the LAC upwards and will cause output to fall and price to rise.

that they are still below price at the level of output at which the elasticity of demand is equal to –1. This firm will settle at this level of output and will make positive profits. In panel (b) we depict a firm with rather 'high' average costs which become equal to price while output is still in the elastic range of the demand curve. If minimum acceptable profits are zero, this firm will settle at a level of output at which price equals average cost, and profits are zero. The literature on this topic has tended to concentrate on the latter case, in which the firm's output decisions are constrained by the minimum acceptable level of profit.

The effects of lump-sum taxes

It is worth noting that, in either case described above, the reaction of the firm to a **lump-sum tax** levied on its profits may be different from that of a profit maximiser, who will not react to the imposition of such a tax. After all, the price and output that maximise profits will also maximise profits net of some constant deduction unless the tax is greater than maximum profits, in which case the firm will simply go out of business. (More formally, lump sum impositions which are independent at the level of output and inputs do not affect the first-order conditions for maximisation.) In the case of the revenue-maximising firm depicted in panel (a) of Figure 14.1, the imposition of such a tax, depending upon its size, will either leave its price and output unchanged if net of tax profits are still positive, or cause it to lower its output to a point of higher profit if the amount of the tax is greater than the profit it was making at revenue-maximising price and output. In the case of the firm depicted in panel (b), the imposition of any such tax will cause it to lower output and to raise price. As with the profit-maximising firm, of course, it is possible to set the tax in question sufficiently high that the revenue maximiser will be driven entirely out of business by its imposition.

Now the point here, as in the previous two sections has been to show that the equivalence of the sales revenue-maximisation hypothesis and the profit-maximisation postulate that exists under assumptions of perfect competition does not exist under conditions of monopoly. Readers should note that this lack of equivalence was established, not by arguing about the relative degrees of 'realism' that might be attributed to the alternative *assumptions*, but rather by showing that there are circumstances under which they lead to *different conclusions* about the way in which we would expect to see firms behave. Whether the circumstances in question are sufficiently widely observed in the real world as to make the revenue-maximisation hypothesis an important alternative to profit maximisation is perhaps a moot point. Lump sum taxes are something of a rarity and real-world 'profit' taxes are typically levied on the rental rate earned by capital equipment owned by the firm as well as on any pure monopoly profit that it might be earning, and hence are not quite equivalent to the profits tax we postulated.

Nevertheless, if the foregoing analysis convinces the reader that there is an alternative theory of what it is that motivates firms to the simple pursuit of profit, that the theory in question does not always yield the same predictions about behaviour, that the profit-maximisation hypothesis should not therefore be taken for granted as a foundation for the theory of the firm, and that the ultimate test here is the empirical truth or falsity of the predictions yields by competing hypotheses, its presentation will have served its purpose.

Box 14.1	**A formal treatment of revenue maximisation**

For completeness, and to illustrate maximisation of a non-profit objective subject to a profit constraint, we end our discussion of sales revenue maximisation with a formal derivation of the result established geometrically in Figure 20.1(b). The revenue function may therefore be written compactly as $R = R(X)$. This function will be maximised where its derivative (marginal revenue) is zero, $\partial R/\partial X = 0$, and we already know that since $\partial R/\partial X = p(1 + 1/e)$, this maximum will be achieved when the elasticity of demand equals -1.

It is easy to establish formally the point illustrated above: that the level of output with revenue maximisation will be greater than with profit maximisation. Profits are maximised where marginal revenue equals marginal cost. Marginal costs are positive and marginal revenue will thus be higher at the profit-maximising level of output, where it equals marginal cost, than at the revenue-maximising level of output, where it equals zero. If marginal revenue is a decreasing function of output, which we usually assume it to be (but see Chapter 12 for possible exceptions to this usual case), production will be greater when revenue is maximised than when profits are maximised.

The argument can be extended to the case of a monopolist who maximises revenue subject to a minimum profit constraint, say π_0. The objective is to

$$\text{Max } R = R(X) \tag{14.1.1}$$

subject to

$$\pi = R(X) - C(X) \geq \pi_0 \tag{14.1.2}$$

The formal analysis which follows requires that revenue maximisation drives profits to the minimum set by the constraint, as occurs in Figure 14.1(b). This assumption means that (14.2) holds with equality, so we can use our previous constrained maximisation approach and form the Lagrangian

$$Z = R(X) + \mu(R(X) - C(X) - \pi_0) \tag{14.1.3}$$

where μ is the Lagrange multiplier. The first-order conditions are

$$\frac{\partial Z}{\partial X} = \frac{\partial R}{\partial X} + \mu\left(\frac{\partial R}{\partial X} - \frac{\partial C}{\partial X}\right) = 0 \tag{14.1.4}$$

$$\frac{\partial Z}{\partial \mu} = R(X) - C(X) - \pi_0 = 0 \tag{14.1.5}$$

From these we have

$$\frac{\partial C}{\partial X} = \frac{1 + \mu}{\mu}\frac{\partial R}{\partial X} = 1 + \frac{1}{\mu}\frac{\partial R}{\partial X} \tag{14.1.6}$$

Since the shadow price of the profit constraint on revenue is positive ($\mu > 0$), (14.1.6) implies that *marginal cost exceeds marginal revenue* in the equilibrium of the constrained revenue-maximising monopolist. Of course, marginal cost equals marginal revenue in the profit-maximising case, so provided that marginal revenue falls faster than marginal cost as output increases, we can deduce that output is greater in the case of the constrained revenue-maximising monopolist than in the profit-maximising case. Interested readers may go on to use this framework to analyse the effect of a lump sum tax on a sales revenue-maximising firm.

The competitive labour-managed firm – an introduction

When one thinks about institutions on the supply side of the product market, one of the most enduring (if economically somewhat marginal) is the producer co-operative. They have excited interest because of their democratic structures and because of potential benefits in terms of incentives. Such organisations, owned and run by their workforce, have existed in Western economies since the 1840s. There are more than 1,500 of them producing in the United Kingdom today, most of them small and concentrated in service activities. They are rather more common in France, Spain (clustered around the Basque town of Mondragon) and particularly in Italy, where around one employed person in 50 works in one of the more than 10,000 producer co-operatives. Workers' decision-making combined with *public* ownership also represented a significant tradition in Eastern Europe under socialism and particularly in Yugoslavia where all manufacturing industry used to be 'self-managed'. Our aim in this section of the chapter is to illustrate how economic theory can offer important insights into how this different form of productive organisation will make its supply decisions.

From a theoretical perspective, a **labour-managed firm** is an enterprise in which the labour force as a whole takes the economic decisions. This group undertakes the entrepreneurial role, and receives the surplus of revenue over cost, which they distribute amongst themselves according to some prearranged mechanism. We will assume that every worker has the same skills, and that the collective of workers has agreed to distribute the surplus, or pure profit, equally amongst the membership. The collective of workers is also assumed not to own the capital stock, but rather to be renting it at a market determined price. In the labour-managed firm, labour hires capital rather than capital hiring labour or an entrepreneur hiring both.

It should be noted that the analysis which follows focuses exclusively on the competitive case, so that the firm is assumed to be a price taker. The differences between the labour-managed and profit-maximising firms which we analyse below are not very different as we move from competitive to non-competitive market structures. Interested readers can establish this for themselves by studying some of the references given at the end of the book.

Maximising income per worker

For the economic analyst, one of the most important distinctions between labour-managed firms and their capitalist counterparts arises from the postulated objective of the organisation – to **maximise** average **income per worker** rather than profits. This maximand was first proposed by Benjamin Ward and may be defended by the argument that worker-members would always prefer outcomes with higher income to those with lower incomes. The case for income maximisation in labour-managed firms is straightforward. Economists usually assume that the group of entrepreneurs in charge of a firm (the group may have but one member) maximise their residual income. But since, in a capitalist enterprise, the size of this residual income, the firm's profit, does not depend upon the number of entrepreneurs in the group running the firm, the objective of maximising the amount of profit per entrepreneur can be reduced to the simpler objective of maximising profit. However, under labour management, when the labour force undertakes the entrepreneurial role, the quantity of output produced, and hence the amount of profit, varies with the size of the labour force. Hence the above mentioned simplification is no longer possible. The assignment of the entrepreneurial role to a productive factor, namely labour, implies that the maximisation of profit per member of the entrepreneurial group cannot be simplified to the maximisation of the enterprise's profits, pure and simple. The number of workers varies with output and, therefore, maximising income per worker is not the same as maximising profits. It is the former which is the natural goal for the labour-managed firm.

In the case of a labour-managed firm, it is normally assumed that the workers' collective exerts its control over economic decisions through a 'democratic process', but the nature of this process is here left deliberately vague. Critics point out that such a mechanism could be seriously inefficient in practice if internal dissension slows or prevents rational economic choices being made. We avoid these issues by assuming that authority can be divided between executive and policy-making powers. Our approach is consistent with the enterprise being run in accordance with the following arrangements. In the first instance, all members of the collective are assumed to be identical, in that they desire the labour-managed firm to maximise the same objective average earnings per head. The collective appoints a director who is given completely autonomous powers to execute this policy, subject to dismissal for failure. The labour force therefore exercises its control of the enterprise by determining the maximand, but the price and output decisions required to achieve this goal are taken in exactly the same way as in the capitalist firm.

Each labour-managed firm chooses simultaneously its own level of earnings and factor demands, including employment, subject to the constraints set by its own technology and the economic environment. For the most part, our attention in this book has been focused on the analysis of the firm in the long run. We did consider a short-run framework at the beginning of our study of the theory of competitive supply in Chapter 11, but it was quickly established that the pattern of results for the short run was duplicated in the long run, at least at the industry level. Since long-run models are more general than short-run ones, we concentrated on the former. In our analysis of the labour-managed firm, however, we adopt the short run as the principal 'period' of analysis, even though the main result which we shall establish – that the labour-managed firm always adjusts to a given product price change less than its capitalist counterpart – also carries through in the long run. Nevertheless, we use a short-run framework for much of what follows because it permits the main results to emerge in a particularly striking form, and one that is capable of both geometric representation and simple economic interpretation. The argument is generalised for the long run at the end of the chapter. In the analysis which follows we therefore assume, in the first instance, that the capital stock is fixed at a value, say $\bar{K}$. We also make the simplifying assumption that, in the short run, average and marginal products of labour *everywhere* decline with output. This assumption differs from that of an inverse U-shaped average and marginal product curve underlying the U-shaped short-run average cost curve derived in Chapter 9 and deployed in Chapter 11, but can be made at this point because, as for its capitalist counterpart, equilibrium for the labour-managed firm always occurs where technology displays diminishing returns to a factor.

Enterprise choices in the short run

In order to maximise average earnings in the short run, the labour-managed firm chooses output and employment subject to the constraints set by technology and the economic environment. If we denote earnings per head by y, these can be seen as comprising a notional wage per worker, w, and an (assumed) equal share of profit, π/L. Hence

$$y = w + \frac{\pi}{L} \qquad (14.1)$$

where $\pi = pX - wL - rK$ $\qquad (14.2)$

From this we derive the traditional maximand of the labour-managed firm,

$$y = \frac{pX - rK}{L} \qquad (14.3)$$

and average earnings are revealed to be average net product, or average revenue minus fixed costs per unit of labour. It can be seen by comparing (14.1) with (14.3) that the notional wage, w, plays no role in the economic decision making of the labour-managed firm.

The firm's choice is illustrated in Figure 14.2. The slope of the intersection of fixed costs $(r\bar{K})$ on the vertical axis to a point on the revenue function (which in the short run given a price depends only on the level of employment) is average earnings for that level of employment. The labour-managed firm wishes to maximise this average, and clearly will do so if it chooses level of labour input L^*, at the tangency between the production

Figure 14.2

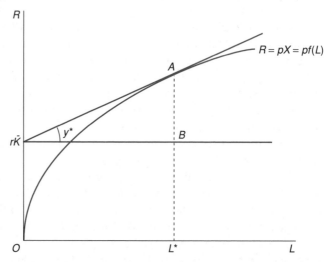

The labour-managed firm chooses employment to maximise average earnings, which equal revenue minus fixed costs $(r\bar{K})$ per worker. Earnings at each level of employment are therefore the slope of the line from the revenue function to the $r\bar{K}$ intercept. They are maximised at L^*, where earnings, y^*, equal the marginal revenue product of labour.

function and the average earnings line. At this point the slope from the intersection of fixed costs on the vertical axis to the revenue function is maximised. Here AB is revenue net of fixed costs, and y^* is earnings per worker. In equilibrium, earnings per worker equal the slope of the revenue function, which is in turn the marginal revenue product of labour.

* A more formal treatment

The algebra of income per head maximisation is subtly different from that of conventional profit maximisation, and helps us to develop additional geometric representations of the problem. The labour-managed firm chooses employment to maximise

$$y = \frac{pX - r\bar{K}}{L} \tag{14.3'}$$

subject to a short-run production function $X = f(L, \bar{K})$. Substituting $f(L, \bar{K})$ for X in equation (14.3), the first-order condition is

$$\frac{\partial y}{\partial L} = \frac{1}{L^2}\left(Lp\frac{\partial X}{\partial L} - pX + r\bar{K}\right) = 0 \tag{14.4}$$

which can be rearranged as

$$p\frac{\partial X}{\partial L} = (pX - r\bar{K})/L = y \tag{14.5}$$

Equation (14.5) appears at first sight to be the same as the labour hiring rule under capitalism, requiring the collective to add members until the marginal value product $(p\partial X/\partial L)$ of the last recruit equals the income that recruit generates. But appearances are misleading in this case. Wages, like other factor prices, are determined in the labour market under capitalism, and are therefore taken as given by the competitive profit maximisers. Average earnings are a choice variable for the labour-managed firm, however. The collective can choose the number of members it employs, and the rule governing this choice, as summarised in (14.5), is to increase the labour force only when this raises everyone's income. It is this maximum of income per head which occurs where earnings equal the marginal revenue product of labour.

Looking at it another way, the labour-managed firm will increase employment when a new member adds more to revenue per head than to cost per head. Denoting revenue per head by $G(= pX/L)$ and costs per head by $F(= r\bar{K}/L)$, the collective adds to the membership until $\partial G/\partial L = \partial F/\partial L$. We could draw G and F in value–employment space, in which case the equilibrium level of employment would be chosen where the slopes of the two curves were equal. A rearrangement of terms reveals that the slopes are in fact equal at the point where earnings equal the value marginal product of labour. Thus

$$\frac{\partial G}{\partial L} = \frac{Lp\partial X/\partial L - pX}{L^2} = \frac{1}{L}\left(p\frac{\partial X}{\partial L} - p\frac{X}{L}\right) \tag{14.6}$$

while

$$\frac{\partial F}{\partial L} = \frac{-r\bar{K}}{L^2} \tag{14.7}$$

Equation (14.6) tells us that the slope of the revenue per head function depends on the relationship between marginal revenue product and the average revenue product of labour at each level of employment. It will be negative given our assumption of diminishing returns to labour (see Chapter 8). Equation (14.7) indicates that fixed costs per head vary with employment along a rectangular hyperbola.

Income per head is maximised when increments to revenue per head from hiring one additional worker equal increments to fixed costs per head. If we therefore set $\partial G/\partial L = \partial F/\partial L$, this implies

$$\frac{1}{L}\left(p\frac{\partial X}{\partial L} - p\frac{X}{L}\right) = \frac{-rK}{L^2} \qquad (14.8)$$

or

$$p\frac{\partial X}{\partial L} = y \qquad (14.5)$$

A comparison of income-per-worker-maximising and profit-maximising firms

To compare the behaviour of income- and profit-maximising firms, we directly plot in Figure 14.3 the slope of the short-run earnings function (14.9′) as a function of employment. Inspection of Figure 14.2 should convince readers that this function will have an inverse U-shape. When the marginal revenue product of labour exceeds average earnings, average earnings will increase with employment, and the curve relating these two variables will be upward sloping. When the reverse holds, average earnings will be a declining function of employment. When marginal revenue product equals average earnings, earnings will have reached their maximum. All this is shown in Figure 14.3, which can now be used

Figure 14.3

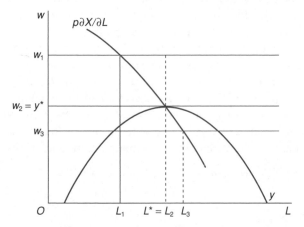

Average earnings for the labour-managed firm. With income maximisation, the firm always chooses (y^*, L^*). The profit-maximising firm chooses more, less, or the same level of employment (L_3, L_1, or L_2) depending on whether market wages are less than, more than or the same (w_3, w_1 or w_2) as average earnings (y^*).

to compare the behaviour of the labour-managed firm with that of its profit-maximising counterpart.

We know that the labour-managed firm chooses the income–employment combination to maximise the income per head of its labour force (y^*, L^* in Figure 14.3). In contrast, a profit-maximising firm hires labour until the marginal revenue product of labour equals the wage (see Chapter 11). We can now show that the profit maximiser which has the same technology and faces the same market determined prices makes exactly the same short-run output decisions as the labour-managed firm *if profits are zero*. We know from equation (14.1) that if profits in the capitalist firm equal zero, earnings must equal the market wage. But if wages are the same as average earnings (for example, $w = w_2$ in Figure 14.3), the profit-maximising firm hires the same number of workers as its labour-managed counterpart because, at that point only, maximum earnings and the marginal revenue product line coincide. Thus, if labour management is introduced into a fully competitive economy where zero profits are being earned, this will have no effect on the allocation of resources (at least in the short run). This sort of result has led some economists to argue that competitive market forces are more important than specific institutional arrangements in determining the allocation of resources.

But the foregoing conclusion arises only in the zero profit case. If the equivalent profit-maximising firm was operating at a loss ($\pi < 0$), equation (14.1) indicates that wages must exceed the maximum feasible average earnings (when wages are $w_1 > y^*$ in Figure 14.3). If demand and cost conditions are such that the capitalist firm makes losses in the short run, these must be borne collectively by the worker entrepreneurs after the introduction of labour management and this will depress earnings. The labour-managed firm will then shift to producing a relatively greater output with a larger labour force than its profit-maximising counterpart ($L_1 < L^*$ in Figure 14.3), in order to spread the losses over a larger number of workers. This result may help to explain the tendency for labour-managed firms to emerge in declining sectors. In such conditions, labour-managed firms often give the impression of being overmanned relative to capitalist enterprises.

Finally, consider what would happen if labour management were to be introduced into a profitable capitalist firm. In this case, output would be reduced and wages increased. Positive profits imply that earnings will exceed the market wage after the introduction of labour management. (If $\pi > 0$ in equation (14.1.3), we have the case where $w = w_3 < y^*$ in Figure 14.3). In this case, labour-managed firms are employment restrictive, relative to their profit-maximising counterparts. In Figure 14.3 when $w = w_3$ we find $L^* < L_3$. Since positive or zero profits seem the most likely outcome for most industries most of the time, this analysis suggests that labour management will either have no effect on output and employment, or lead to reductions in output and employment relative to profit maximisation.

The short-run supply curve

We cannot derive the short-run supply curve for the labour-managed firm using its marginal cost curve, as we do in the competitive profit-maximising case because, as we have stressed above, in this instance, the opportunity cost of labour is not determined in the labour market, and hence is independent of the level of output, as it is in the profit-maximising perfectly competitive case. We must instead investigate the impact of changes in product price on output via its effect on employment decisions. We continue to make the assumption that the capital stock is fixed.

The adjustments of output to an increase in product price are illustrated in Figure 14.4. The labour-managed firm is shown to respond to an increase in product price by reducing output and employment in order to increase average earnings. Its **short-run supply curve** is therefore **backward bending**. This striking result has no counterpart in the case of the profit-maximising firm. With profit maximisation, an increase in price raises the value marginal product of labour relative to the market determined wage, which leads the firm to hire *more* workers in order to increase profits. In the labour-managed firm, the increase in price increases earnings more than it increases the marginal revenue product of labour because, given our assumption of diminishing returns to labour, the marginal

Figure 14.4

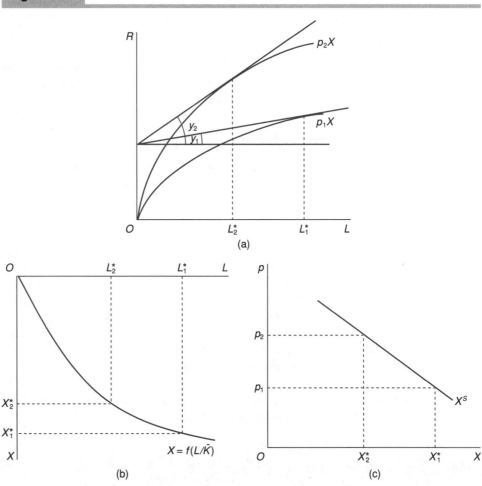

Supply under labour management. The supply curve of the income-maximising labour-managed firm is backward sloping (see (c)). In (a) we start at price p_1, with earnings of y_1, employment L_1^* and therefore output X_1^* via the short-run production function $x = f(L, \bar{K})$ of (b). If product price rises to p_2, maximum earnings rise to y_2 and employment declines to L_2^*. Via the production function (b), output also declines to X_2^*. The locus of price–output combinations – the supply curve – is illustrated in (c) and is backward bending by derivation.

product of labour (the slope of the revenue function) is always exceeded by the average product. This effect gives the firm an incentive to reduce its output.

The intuition behind the backward-bending supply curve under labour management is as follows. The average revenue per head of the labour-managed firm will increase as the membership declines because of diminishing returns to labour. It should be stressed that the assumption of diminishing returns to a factor, at least in the range of output and employment around the equilibrium, is required in order for average earnings to reach a maximum at all. Hence, the enterprise would seek to become as small as possible, say, in the limit one worker, to raise earnings if there were not a constraint imposed by **fixed costs**. These fixed costs force the firm to settle for a larger membership because, per capita, they are inversely related to employment. Any equilibrium must reflect a balance between these forces, where the marginal gain to the collective, in terms of revenue per head, of reducing membership exactly balances the marginal loss, in terms of fixed costs per head. An increase in product price does not affect the marginal loss from reducing membership. However, it increases the marginal benefit by raising revenue per capita at each level of employment. Thus the relaxation of the constraint imposed by fixed costs leads the co-operative to reduce membership, and therefore production, in order to raise average earnings.

A further difference between labour-managed firms and their profit-maximising counterparts in the short run concerns the impact of changes in fixed capital costs on output. Changes in fixed costs under labour management have an immediate effect on employment and therefore output in the short run, whereas under profit maximisation they have no effect. This result is illustrated in Figure 14.5. In terms of our previous

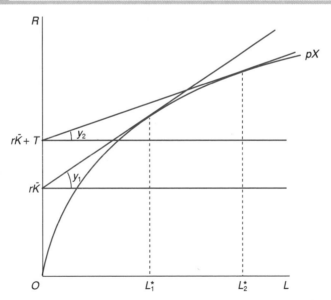

The response of the labour-managed firm to an increase in fixed costs because of the imposition of a lump-sum tax, T. By shifting the intercept with the vertical axis upwards, the increase in fixed costs increases employment from L_1^* to L_2^*, while reducing income from y_1 to y_2.

intuition, an increase in fixed costs, for example via a lump sum tax, raises the marginal loss to the firm of reducing employment without affecting the marginal gain. The collective therefore recruits more members in order to spread the new higher fixed costs over more workers. This result can be contrasted with that for the sales revenue-maximising monopolist.

Box 14.2 **A more formal treatment of the short-run supply curve under labour management**

The backward-bending supply curve can be derived more formally from the first-order condition for income maximisation, equation (14.4). In doing so we illustrate the role of the implicit function rule in simplifying the formal derivation of comparative static results. Let us set the slope of earnings function, $y = (pX - r\bar{K})/L$, equal to zero as in (14.4):

$$\frac{\partial y}{\partial L} = \frac{1}{L^2}\left(Lp\frac{\partial X}{\partial L} - pX + r\bar{K}\right) = 0 \tag{14.2.1}$$

Using the implicit function rule, we get

$$\frac{\partial L}{\partial p} = \frac{-\partial^2 y}{\partial L \partial p}\frac{\partial^2 y}{\partial L^2} \tag{14.2.2}$$

where

$$\frac{\partial^2 y}{\partial L \partial p} = \frac{1}{L}\left(\frac{\partial X}{L} - \frac{X}{L}\right) \tag{14.2.3}$$

and

$$\frac{\partial^2 y}{\partial L^2} = \frac{p}{L}\frac{\partial^2 X}{\partial L^2}, \frac{\partial y}{\partial L} = 0 \tag{14.2.4}$$

Hence our assumptions about technology imply that

$$\frac{\partial L}{\partial p} = \frac{(X/L - \partial X/\partial L)}{p\partial^2 X/\partial L^2} < 0 \tag{14.2.5}$$

because with diminishing returns to labour, $X/L > \partial X/\partial L$, and $\partial^2 X/\partial L^2 < 0$.

The slope of the supply curve, $\partial X/\partial p$, is determined (given $\partial L/\partial p$) via the short-run production function, and with $\partial X/\partial L > 0$,

$$\frac{\partial X}{\partial p} = \frac{\partial X}{\partial L} \cdot \frac{\partial L}{\partial p} = \frac{\partial X/\partial L(X/L - \partial X/\partial L)}{p\partial^2 X/\partial L^2} < 0 \tag{14.2.6}$$

This result highlights the role played by diminishing returns to labour in generating the backward-bending supply curve.

The labour-managed firm in the long run

Our analysis of the labour-managed firm in the short run suggests that such organisations may respond 'perversely' in the supply of output, reducing production as price increases and vice versa. This rather startling result is, in fact, an extreme version of the general argument, for the case of multiple inputs and outputs, that labour-managed firms always increase output by a smaller amount in response to given price changes than do their capitalist counterparts. We can see this by considering the behaviour of the labour-managed firm in the long run, when both labour and capital inputs can be varied simultaneously. For the moment, we maintain the assumption that there is neither entry into nor exit from the industry in question, whether firms are profit-maximising or labour-managed. This crucial assumption is relaxed in the following section.

Let us assume as before that the labour-managed firm maximises average earnings, in this case though, subject to the long-run production function. The formal problem is to maximise

$$y = \frac{pX - rK}{L} \tag{14.3}$$

subject to

$$X = f(L, K) \tag{14.9}$$

We can derive first-order conditions by substituting equation (14.9) into (14.3), and setting equal to zero the partial derivatives of the resulting expression with respect to employment and capital.

$$\frac{\partial y}{\partial L} = \frac{1}{L^2}\left(Lp\frac{\partial X}{\partial L} - pX + rK\right) = 0 \tag{14.4'}$$

$$\frac{\partial y}{\partial K} = \frac{1}{L}\left(p\frac{\partial X}{\partial K} - r\right) = 0 \tag{14.10}$$

Equation (14.4') is the labour hiring rule analysed above for the situation when the capital stock is variable, and equation (14.10) tells us that the labour-managed firm hires capital until its marginal value product ($p\partial X/\partial K$) equals its rental cost (r). This latter condition is identical to that governing the behaviour of conventional competitive profit-maximising enterprises (see Chapter 18). The change in maximand from profits to average earnings per head therefore affects the way in which the enterprise chooses employment but not the way in which it selects its capital stock.

It will be remembered that, since the labour force has undertaken the role of entrepreneur in labour-managed firms, it receives the entire flow of profits in its pay-packet (see equation (14.1)). Hence there is no pure surplus remaining in the labour-managed firm. First-order conditions (14.14') and (14.10), on the other hand, tell us that on the margin the remuneration of each factor, including its share of the profit in the case of labour, exactly equals its marginal revenue product. As we noted in Chapter 11, when factors are paid their marginal products, pure surplus, or profits, can equal zero only when the production function is linearly homogeneous at the equilibrium. Thus the labour-managed firm will achieve a long-run equilibrium only where the production function displays constant returns to scale.

The bulk of our analysis in this part of the book has been conducted under the assumption that the production function in the long run displays first increasing, then constant, then diminishing returns to scale. This assumption generates the by now familiar U-shaped long-run average cost curves used in Chapters 11 and 12. The argument above has established, assuming that the returns to scale characteristics of the production function do not vary with factor proportions, that *the labour-managed firm always operates at the level of production at which long-run average costs would be minimised if the enterprise were profit maximising.* The actual level of average payments to inputs (including the profits distributed to workers as part of average earnings) might be higher, lower, or the same as that achieved by the profit-maximising counterpart, depending on whether the latter organisation makes a profit, a loss, or just breaks even; but the labour-managed firm always produces at the output level at which the long-run average cost curve of the equivalent profit maximiser is at its minimum. The profit maximiser, of course, can produce anywhere to the right of that minimum point, depending on the relationship between marginal cost and price. This result is illustrated in Figure 14.6.

Our analysis of the competitive profit-maximising firm showed that in the absence of entry its supply curve is the long-run marginal cost curve, which is upward sloping in the relevant range. For the labour-managed firm, however, supply in the absence of entry is fixed at the point of constant returns, independently of the price which output fetches. Provided that returns to scale do not vary with the capital–labour ratio, the firm's **long-run**

Figure 14.6

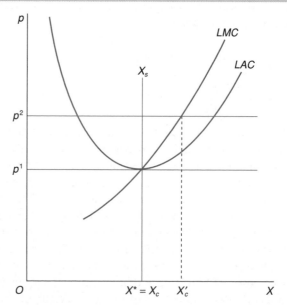

The labour-managed firm always produces at the output level where the production function displays constant returns to scale, denoted X^*. When price equals p_X^1, the competitive profit-maximising firm produces the same output, X_c, with profits equal to zero ($p_X^1 = LAC$). However, if the price is higher, say p^2, the profit maximiser produces at X_c^1, while the labour-managed firm continues to produce at X^*. The higher profits in the latter are paid to employees, raising earnings and therefore average payments to inputs. The labour-managed firm's long-run supply curve is therefore vertical at X^*.

supply curve is therefore **perfectly inelastic**, rather than being backward bending as was the case in the short run.

Labour-managed and profit-maximising firms with free entry

In our discussions of the long-run theory of competitive supply in Chapter 11, we noted that while it was logically possible to think of an industry supply curve from incumbent producers' long-run marginal cost curves on the assumption that there could be no entry, it was of no practical relevance. This was because firms would not make decisions about their scale of operations, the profitability of which would be undermined by the entry of new competitors. Hence a proper analysis of long-run **industry supply required that account be taken of entry and exit**.

In the light of this, it is important to stress that the analysis of the previous section, concerning the labour-managed firm in the long run in the absence of entry, was not undertaken in order to reach general conclusions about the shape of the industry supply curve. It was rather intended to illustrate that the perverse supply behaviour which we derived initially in our short-run analysis was not merely a consequence of special assumptions, in particular the assumption that the labour-managed firm had a fixed capital stock. We now see that such perversity was in fact a specific example of a quite general property of the behaviour of labour-managed firms, namely, their tendency to restrict employment relative to their profit-maximising counterparts whenever profits are positive.

In order to derive the long-run industry supply curve under labour management when entry is possible, we need to consider in more detail the motivations of worker-entrepreneurs. The discussion takes place on the assumption that all firms have identical technology. We have seen that the objective of the labour-managed firm is to maximise average earnings per head. On that basis, it is reasonable to suppose that individual worker-entrepreneurs will also be motivated by average earnings. They will therefore seek to form new labour-managed firms in activities where average earnings available exceed those that they are currently receiving, and to leave enterprises in which remuneration is below the rate available elsewhere in the economy. If we assume costless enterprise formation and closure, this means that there will be entry of new labour-managed firms into industries in which average earnings exceed remuneration elsewhere, and exit in industries for which the converse is true.

But we saw at the start of our discussion of labour-managed firms that there is a relationship between average earnings paid under labour management and the level of profits which would pertain in a capitalist environment. This relationship is given by equation (14.1) and states that average earnings exceed (are lower than) the wages which would be paid by the profit-maximising firm according to whether profits are positive (negative). Hence entry will take place into industries which would, if the firms were profit maximisers, be earning a positive profit, while exit will occur in industries which would, under profit maximisation, be loss-makers. These are precisely the same conditions for entry and exit that rule in the long run under capitalism.

Moreover the process which drives the system as a whole to equilibrium is also the same as under capitalism. Consider an industry in which earnings for some reason, say a favourable demand shift, exceed those available elsewhere in the economy. As we have argued above, supply adjustments by incumbent firms to such a new higher level of demand will be smaller than those of their profit-maximising counterparts, and may even be perverse. However, this increase in demand and its consequent higher output price create incentives for worker-entrepreneurs in other, lower-paying sectors to form new firms in the industry. As market supply is increased by their entry, price falls and the earnings of all firms in the industry decline. The process of entry, declining price and reductions in average earnings ceases when earnings in the sector are once again the same as those earned elsewhere in the economy.

The supply curve for a competitive labour-managed industry of identical firms is therefore perfectly horizontal, for exactly the same reasons as is the industry supply curve of profit-maximising firms. The previous discussion suggests, however, that the labour-managed economy may have to rely relatively more on entry and exit to ensure adequate supply responses to changes in demand than its profit-maximising counterpart. This will not cause problems if, as we assumed above, the process of entry and exit is costless. The adjustment of supply to demand or cost disturbances will be sluggish, however, which may cause problems if the process of entry and exit by worker enterprises is in fact a costly one.

Concluding comment

The discussion of the behaviour of firms in this book concentrates on examining the implications of profit maximisation under alternative assumptions about market structure. Our aim in this chapter has been to give a brief introduction to a parallel line of enquiry: examining the implications of alternative objectives for enterprise behaviour. For the most part, we have undertaken this analysis on the assumption that product markets are competitive, but as our discussion of revenue maximisation suggests, one can combine assumptions about alternative objectives and market structures to reproduce a set of results for these new organisations that parallel all those analysed in the literature on conventional firms.

One proposition that we have illustrated in this chapter is that the behaviour of firms in the marketplace depends on their objectives as well as on the structure of the market in which they operate. Firms that seek to maximise their revenue will be larger than conventional profit maximisers provided that they are monopolists. Labour-managed firms may respond perversely to an increase in their product price in the short run, and will in general adjust quantity in response to a change in price less than their capitalist counterparts. These results arise because in each case the new objective alters economic incentives on the margin. Even so, the equivalence of the equilibria of labour-managed and zero-profit capitalist firms shows that, at least in the competitive case, market forces can be as important as enterprise objectives in determining output decisions.

SUMMARY

Alternative theories of the firm

1. The problem of corporate governance arises when ownership and control are separated and managers have better information about the firm than owners.

2. The incentives of owners and managers can nonetheless be aligned through, for example, the market for corporate control or the market for managers.

3. Alternatively, if owners cannot control managers, firms may operate with objectives other than profit maximisation. Here we examine two: revenue maximisation, for firms concerned with their size rather than their profitability; and income per worker maximisation, for firms owned or run by their employees.

4. If markets are competitive, revenue maximisation leads to the same level of production as profit maximisation.

5. If markets are monopolistic, revenue maximising firms will produce a greater output than profit-maximising ones. Profits may be equal to or more than zero, but will always be less than under profit maximisation.

6. The imposition of a lump sum tax does not affect short-run supply in profit-maximising firms. However, it may lead to a reduction in the level of output of a revenue-maximising monopoly if the amount of the tax is greater than the initial level of profit.

7. Labour-managed firms (LMF) are assumed to maximise income per worker. In the short run, the competitive LMF hires labour to the point where the marginal revenue product of labour equals average earnings. The nature of equilibria relative to those under profit maximisation depends on the comparison between equilibrium average earnings and the market wage.

8. If average earnings exceed the market wage, the LMF produces less than its profit-maximising counterpart. The converse holds when the wage exceeds average earnings. The change in maximand does not affect output or employment when market wages and average earnings are equal, which occurs when profits in the profit-maximising firm are zero.

9. The competitive LMF has a backward-bending supply curve; as demand (and product price) increases, the quantity supplied is reduced in the short run.

10. Increases in fixed costs lead the competitive LMF to increase output in the short run.

11. In the long run, the competitive LMF always operates at a level of production at which long-run average costs would be minimised for the comparable profit-maximising firm.

12. The long-run supply curve for a competitive industry composed of identical labour-managed firms is horizontal. However, because of the possibility of output restrictions or perverse supply responses in the short run, this long-run adjustment relies on the role of entry and exit of new labour-managed firms.

PROBLEMS

1 Analyse the consequences of imposing a profits tax on a revenue-maximising monopolist if the tax also changes the minimum profit constraint faced by the firm. In what ways does this reaction differ from that of the profit maximiser?

2 Suppose technology is such that the labour-managed firm in the short run faces an average earnings curve which is inverse U-shaped, as in Figure 14.2. Use this short-run diagram to illustrate:

(a) the change in the level of earnings after an increase in price at the initial equilibrium level of employment;

(b) the change in the marginal revenue product of labour after an increase in price at the initial equilibrium level of employment;

(c) the new equilibrium level of earnings and employment after an increase in price;

(d) the new equilibrium level of earnings and employment after an increase in capital rentals.

3 A competitive labour-managed firm in the short run faces fixed costs of £100 per week and a weekly short-run production function, $X = 5L^{1/2}$. The market price of the output is £10.

(a) What is the level of employment which maximises average earnings per head? What do workers earn at that equilibrium?

(b) Suppose that price increases to £15. What happens to employment and to earnings?

(c) Suppose that capital costs increase to £150 per week. What happens to employment and to earnings?

(d) Suppose that the firm introduces new technology which increases average and marginal labour productivity, so that $X = 8L^{1/2}$. What happens to employment and to earnings?

4 Suppose that the competitive labour-managed firm uses two inputs in the short run (when capital is fixed at K_0), labour and material inputs M. The firm purchases materials at their market price, p_m. The objective of the firm is therefore to maximise

$$y = \frac{pK - rK_0 - p_mM}{L}$$

subject to the short-run production function $X = f(L, K_0, M)$ where $\partial X/\partial M > 0$, $\partial^2 X/\partial M^2 < 0$.

(a) What rule does the labour-managed firm use in determining its optimal level of material input? In what way does it differ from that of a profit-maximising firm?

(b) What is the effect of an increase in the price of material inputs on the demand for material inputs, on employment and on average earnings?

(c) Suppose the firm now faces an increase in product price. Is the short-run supply curve necessarily backward bending?

PART V

OLIGOPOLY AND STRATEGIC INTERACTION

CHAPTER 15

Oligopoly: an introduction

Key words and phrases

- interdependence among producers' decisions, collusive and non-collusive behaviour
- duopoly as a special case of oligopoly
- kinked demand curve, cartels, incentives to cheat, retaliation

Introduction

In this chapter we extend our treatment of price and output determination under imperfect competition to consider a more thorough analysis of the interaction of producers. Because inter-firm interactions in imperfect markets take many forms, *oligopoly* theory, whose name refers to 'competition among the few', lacks unambiguous results of the sort we developed for competition and monopoly. Instead, we have a variety of results derived from different behavioural assumptions, with each model potentially relevant to certain real-world situations, but not to others. Our aim in this and the following chapter is to provide an introduction to some of the more important models available, and a unifying framework which helps to highlight the sources of their differences.

Collusive and non-collusive behaviour

Models of enterprise decision making in oligopoly derive their special character from the fact that firms in an oligopolistic industry are, and know that they are, **interdependent**. In competitive markets, there are enough other producers that each firm can safely ignore the reactions of rivals to its decisions when it makes its own output choices. This is not necessarily the case where there are only a few producers; and two broad approaches may be taken to solve the problem created by this fact.

First, oligopolists may be thought of as agreeing to co-operate in setting price and quantity from the outset. **Collusive** models deal with this sort of behaviour. Firms agree to act together in the setting of price and quantity, and this, it will be seen below, leads to *exactly* the same outcome as would have emerged under monopoly. The widespread existence or possibility of emergence of such agreements between firms – the formation of *cartels* – further enhances the relevance of the monopoly model which we studied in Chapter 12. The monopoly model is relevant to any situation where the firms in an industry collude in the setting of quantity and price. However, in the presence of such collusion, the question still remains as to how the cartel's monopoly profits are divided among participating firms. The likelihood of arguments over this matter is high, and this has led economists to predict that collusive groups such as industry-wide cartels face severe internal pressures which might lead to their collapse. Such instability is often observed in cartelised industries in practice.

The second broad approach to analysing oligopoly is based on the assumption that firms do not co-operate, but instead make their decisions on the basis of guesses about the variables to which their competitors are reacting and about the nature and form of the reactions in question. Models dealing with such behaviour are referred to as **non-collusive** because, though in equilibrium the expectations of each firm about the reactions of rivals are realised, the parties never actually communicate directly with each other about their likely reactions. In the extreme, we shall see that models of this type can imply competitive behaviour.[1] Hence even simple oligopolistic models without price discrimination or product differentiation can span the range from the monopoly to the competitive outcome. The first arises when firms collude, and the second emerges as a limiting case of non-collusive behaviour.

In order to simplify our analysis we shall often assume that there are only two firms in the industry – a situation called **duopoly**. Results will sometimes be extended to the case of more than two firms, however, where such generalisations yield additional insights. In this chapter we shall first introduce the oligopoly problem in more depth than we have so far and outline one of the earliest, and not entirely satisfactory, attempts to resolve it – the kinked demand curve model. We shall proceed from there to develop the collusive model in some detail, considering the situation in which two firms combine to form a cartel, and set price and output jointly. We shall show why this solution tends to be unstable.

The oligopoly problem

The theories of perfect competition and monopoly have in common the assumption that the decisions taken by any particular firm have such diffuse effects on the environment in which other firms operate that the firm under analysis can safely neglect their likely reaction to its behaviour when it makes its decisions. However, it is easy to think of circumstances in which this is not a sensible assumption. In particular, when a small number of large firms dominate a particular industry and produce identical or closely substitutable products, one would expect the likely response of other firms to be a major factor influencing any price or output decision. Such a state of affairs is central in the theory of oligopoly.

The study of oligopolistic markets is inherently more difficult than that of competitive and monopolistic ones because it deals with the ways in which firms interact with each other, as well as with consumers. Profit maximisation is a fairly straightforward affair in the models discussed in earlier chapters. Given their (known) demand and cost functions, firms choose output at the level which equalises marginal revenue and marginal cost. In what follows we shall assume that the fact that there are only a few producers does not qualitatively affect the cost side of this equation. However, the firm's perspective on the revenue side is very different under an oligopolistic market structure. The oligopolistic firm must always allow for the fact that the relationship between the price which it charges and the quantity that it can sell depends on the behaviour of its competitors which will in turn depend upon its own decisions. It cannot, therefore, take its demand curve as given.

Consider two firms producing a homogeneous (non-differentiated) product and selling it at a common price. Suppose that one firm is considering raising its price and wishes to know the impact on its sales of doing so. It cannot answer that question without knowing how the other firm in the industry will react. For example, if the other firm leaves its price unchanged, our first firm will lose most if not all of its customers. If, on the other hand, the other firm takes the opportunity to raise its price by the same amount, both firms will lose some sales, the total loss being given by the slope of the industry demand curve. Should the other firm react by increasing its price by even more than our firm, then the latter might even gain additional sales from its price increase. The situation would obviously become even more complicated if the products that the firms produced were differentiated.

The fundamental point here is that oligopolistic firms cannot take their own demand curves as given when they make their decisions. They must make assumptions about the way in which their competitors will react to their own actions and about the effects of those reactions on their own sales. But if firms cannot take their demand curves as given, they cannot calculate marginal revenues and therefore determine their profit-maximising levels of output. Hence a general indeterminacy lies at the heart of the oligopolistic market structure, and we have, indeed need, numerous oligopoly models, each representing different assumptions about how small numbers of firms in an industry might interact with one another. We shall now outline the **kinked demand curve** model of oligopoly which further illustrates the problems we have been discussing here.

An illustration of the oligopoly problem: the kinked demand curve

This model was originally devised by Paul Sweezy to explain the apparent fact that, in oligopolistic markets, prices once set as a mark-up on average costs (see Chapter 13) tend not to change. However, the model also deals in a simple way with the manner in which expectations about the behaviour of competitors might influence decision making in oligopolistic markets, and it is this aspect of it upon which we focus.

The basic properties of the model are set out in Figure 15.1, and are derived in the following way. We deal with a firm, one of a small group of firms producing closely related products, which produces output X_1 and sells it at price p_1. Consider the demand curve for this product. If the prices charged by competing firms are held constant, then we have a conventional demand curve such as DD. This curve has been drawn with a relatively shallow slope to reflect the fact that some of the other goods whose prices are being held constant are close substitutes for X. It is by no means obvious that the producers of these close substitutes will set their prices independently of the price of X. We can draw another demand curve for X that reflects the response of quantity demanded to price, on the assumption that other firms would also alter their prices in the same direction as the price of X when it was varied. Such a curve would obviously be more steeply sloped than DD and in Figure 15.1 it is drawn as dd. There is a marginal revenue curve for each of these demand curves, and they are labelled as MR and mr respectively.

Figure 15.1 **The kinked demand curve model of oligopoly**

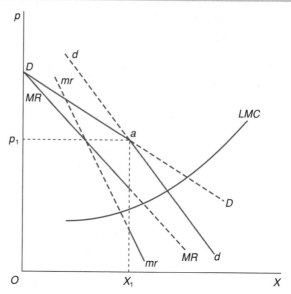

With price fixed at p_1 the firm believes that, if it raises price, other firms will not follow suit. Hence the response of quantity demanded of X to such a move will be relatively large. However, the firm believes that others will follow a price cut so that the response of quantity demanded to such a move will be relatively small. Thus the firm thinks itself confronted by a demand curve kinked at point a, and hence as facing the discontinuous marginal revenue curve $MR - mr$. Note that cost fluctuations that do not shift LMC outside the discontinuity in the marginal revenue curve will not result in the firm changing either price or output.

Now suppose that the firm takes the view that its competitors will react asymmetrically to a price change: that they will follow a price cut but will not follow a price increase. Then the demand curve that faces the firm will appear to be given by Dad, a kinked relationship. There is an element of a priori plausibility about this demand curve because, if one firm out of a small group of firms raises its price, all the others who at the old price were happy with the volume of sales they were enjoying, would see that volume of sales increase without their doing anything. Hence they might be expected to be reluctant to follow a price increase. On the other hand, one firm lowering its price would take customers from them if they did not respond. Hence, to avoid this possibility, these other firms would be likely to follow a price cut. And not only is there a priori plausibility here; there is also a certain amount of evidence from questionnaires circulated to firms that they do indeed tend to expect their competitors to react this way – not following a price increase, but following a price cut.

If the demand curve which a particular firm thinks it faces does indeed take the form of Dad, then it will also think of the marginal revenue curve which it faces as being a discontinuous relationship. Readers who are uncertain as to why there should be this discontinuity in the marginal revenue curve should construct for themselves the total revenue curve implicit in a kinked demand curve such as Dad. They will find that, at the level of output corresponding to the kink, there is a kink in the total revenue curve. Its slope will discontinuously become less at that level of output and this is equivalent to saying that marginal revenue will discontinuously become lower.

As we have drawn Figure 15.1, the firm's long-run marginal cost curve passes through the discontinuity in the marginal revenue curve and so the firm is in equilibrium at price p_1 and X_1. Note that, in this situation, fluctuations in costs that do not take the marginal cost curve out of the range of discontinuity in the marginal revenue curve will not result in price changes.

The analysis looks appealing then, and yields the prediction that for an oligopolist, the price of output will be relatively rigid in the face of cost changes. The model does not, however, explain how that particular price and quantity, rather than any other, happened to get established. Nor is there any way of knowing where equilibrium will be re-established if the marginal cost curve moves out of the discontinuity in the marginal revenue curve. In other words, Figure 15.1 gives us a portrait of a particular situation in which a firm might find itself, but contains no information as to how the situation in question arose in the first place. For this reason, the kinked demand curve model is best regarded as an illustration of the oligopoly problem, rather than a systematic solution to price and output determination in such a market structure.

Collusive behaviour – cartels

The kinked demand curve model is one in which firms do not co-operate in setting output or price. Rather they make assumptions about their rivals' behaviour, which in equilibrium are realised. We can regard any *non-co-operative* or *non-collusive* outcome of this sort as being a situation in which the firms have decided to compete with one another in the oligopolistic market.[2] However, there is an alternative strategy to competition when there are only a few suppliers, and it is one in which the profits earned by each firm will be higher. Firms could agree to *collude* with one another, so they would form a **cartel**, the purpose of which would be to maximise their joint profits.

Once firms agree not to compete with one another, but rather to collude, they have to agree on two matters. The first is a rule for the setting of output and price in the industry as a whole. The second is a mechanism for the allocation of profits and the division of output among themselves. In fact, we have already seen the solution to the first stage of this problem. It was provided in the context of a single firm in Chapter 12, but that solution can, as we shall now see, be generalised.

Figure 15.2 depicts the essentials of the behaviour of a duopolistic cartel, in which two firms have agreed to collude with one another in order to maximise their joint profits. Suppose that the market demand curve for X is given by the curve DD in Figure 15.2(c). If industry profits are to be maximised, then industry marginal revenue must be equated to industry marginal cost, just as in the case of the conventional single firm monopolised industry. The curve labelled MR is the relevant marginal revenue curve, while the industry long-run marginal cost curve is obtained by horizontally summing the long-run marginal cost curves of the individual firms depicted in Figures 15.2(a) and (b). Hence, industry profit-maximising output is determined at X^*, while price is given by p_1. Each firm then agrees to produce that quantity of output at which its marginal cost is equal to that of the industry at the aggregate profit-maximising level of output, so that firm 1 produces X_1 and firm 2 produces X_2.

Figure 15.2

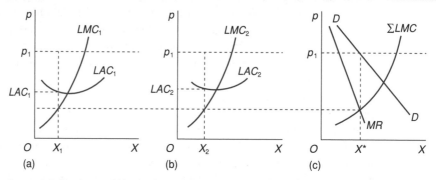

A two-firm cartel, firm 1, panel (a), and firm 2, panel (b), collude to fix price and output at the industry level to maximise their joint profits, panel (c). Each firm takes p_1 as given, and hence has an incentive to cheat on the cartel arrangement by expanding its output up to the point at which its long-run marginal cost equals p_1.

Suppose that the industry's rule for dividing up profits was simply that each firm kept the revenue raised from its own sales. Though there is no logical necessity that such a rule be adopted, it does have the merit of requiring no machinery to administer it and hence would be a likely one for a cartel to adopt. In that case, the profits accruing to firm 1 would be given by $(p_1 - LAC_1)X_1$ and to firm 2 by $(p_1 - LAC_2)X_2$.

Notice that the essential property of the agreement between the firms which we are discussing here is that each one of them takes as given to it the industry's output price which is determined by a joint profit-maximising output decision taken in collusion. Each individual firm, from its own narrow vantage point, becomes a price taker, and hence p_1 becomes its marginal revenue. Inspection of Figure 15.2 will confirm that p_1 is obviously and necessarily greater than the marginal cost of production to either firm at the levels of output which each of them must maintain if industry-wide profits are to be maximised. Hence, each firm has an incentive to increase its output a little in order to increase its profits at the expense of the other; in other words *each firm has an* **incentive to cheat**.

Box 15.1 | **Collusion and cheating: an example**

To illustrate the problem of cheating with a cartel consider a market that has an inverse market demand function

$$p = 100 - X \tag{15.1.1}$$

If the firms in this market form a cartel this inverse market demand function becomes the cartel's average revenue function. Corresponding to this average revenue function is the cartel's marginal revenue function

$$MR = 100 - 2X \tag{15.1.2}$$

We can assume the market is a duopoly in which the two firms have identical costs. For the first firm

$$TC_1 = 2X_1 + 0.25X_1^2 \qquad (15.1.3)$$

so $\quad AC_1 = 2 + 0.25X_1 \qquad (15.1.4)$

and $\quad MC_1 = 2 + 0.5X_1 \qquad (15.1.5)$

with equivalent definitions for firm 2.

To understand the construction of the cartel's MC curve consider Illustration 15.1. At a marginal cost of 2 both firms have zero output: hence for the cartel zero output has an MC of 2. With an output of 4 both firms have an MC of 4. Hence with a cartel output of 8, i.e. 4 from each firm, the cartel's MC is 4. More generally therefore the cartel's marginal cost is

$$MC = 2 + 0.25X \qquad (15.1.6)$$

Illustration 15.1

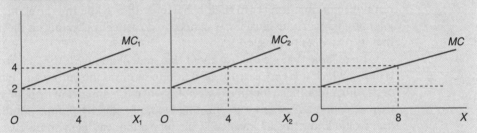

As the firms have identical marginal costs the cartel MC with a two firm cartel has the same intercept but half the slope. With a three (identical) firm cartel it has the same intercept but a third of the slope, etc. With different firm marginal costs the same logic is used but the horizontal sum is more complex. The interested reader can derive the cartel MC directly from the marginal cost functions for the two firms.

If the cartel maximises profit it sets $MC = MR$:

$$2 + 0.25X = 100 - 2X \qquad (15.1.7)$$

which implies $X = 43.56$. At this cartel output:

$$p = 100 - 43.56 = 56.44$$

As the firms have identical costs they divide the cartel output equally by setting

$$MC_1 = MC_2 = MC = 2 + 0.25(43.56) = 12.89 \qquad (15.1.8)$$

$$12.89 = 2 + 0.5X_1 = 2 + 0.5X_2 \qquad (15.1.9)$$

Hence: $\quad X_1 = X_2 = 21.78$.

With a cartel each firm earns a profit of

$$\pi = 56.44(21.78) - 2(21.78) - 0.25(21.78)^2 = 1067.111 \qquad (15.1.10)$$

→

But producing these cartel outputs does not maximise individual firm profits as $p > MC$, i.e. $56.44 > 12.89$. If firm 1 follows the cartel price but sets $p = MC_1$

$$56.44 = 2 + 0.5X_1 \qquad\qquad (15.1.11)$$

i.e. $X_1 = 108.88$.

This increase in output is obviously unsustainable and so will lead to a break-up of the cartel and a fall in price.

Cheating and retaliation

The foregoing analysis shows that the attraction of collusion from the point of view of firms is that it leads to higher levels of profits. However, that analysis also suggests that collusive agreements are inherently *unstable*, in that once firms have agreed to act collectively in a cartel, they each have an incentive to cheat on the agreement in order to raise their own profits further. Such cheating could be successful provided that other firms do not notice or do not react to their behaviour. Thus while the cartel outcome maximises joint profits, each individual firm can hope to do better by cheating on the bargain, provided that its rival does not respond.

Is there more that we can say about this state of affairs? If the industry under analysis is one in which it is very easy for each firm to monitor the output and the pricing policies of the other (or others, for this result holds when the number of firms is greater than two), then of course any attempt at cheating would be met by prompt **retaliation**, and each firm would know this in advance. If the retaliation was likely to involve price cutting by its competitors, then each firm would come to think of itself as facing a kink in its demand curve at its current price and output level, and the kinked demand curve model would become relevant to its behaviour. Note though that the analysis in question is now modified and expanded because we now have a way of explaining how price and output are determined in the first place. Even so, many other kinds of retaliation aimed at keeping cartel members in line – other than simple price cutting – are possible in the real world, depending upon the nature of the particular industry. A price-cutting airline might well find itself having difficulty in obtaining landing rights at key airports; or, under private medical care systems, the doctor who charges less than the medical association's 'recommended' fees sometimes loses hospital privileges. These are but two examples of the way in which cartel pricing arrangements may be enforced without resort to retaliatory price cutting.

Of course, to consider retaliatory action at all presupposes that the cheater gets caught, and not in every industry does each firm find it easy to police its competitors. Surreptitious discounts to particular customers, preferential after sales service involving, for example, 'secret warranties', priority delivery dates to particular favoured customers, are but a few of the more obvious ways in which firms who wish to cheat on cartel agreements may act in order to keep hidden what they are doing. All economic theory can say in general about these matters is that an agreement among firms to collude so as to maximise industry profits *automatically* creates an incentive for participants to cheat if they can. Whether they will do so, by what methods, and to what extent, whether their cheating will be detected, and if so by what means it will be punished – all these matters depend upon the nature of the specific case under analysis.

Concluding comment

The central problem faced by a firm in oligopoly is that its decisions affect the price and quantity choices of its rivals. We have seen that one solution to this problem from the perspective of firms is to co-operate in the setting of output and price in order to maximise joint profits. Solutions of this sort in principle provide the best feasible equilibrium outcome for firms, provided that they can resolve the threat of instability from cheating. However, they also represent an undesirable outcome from the perspective of consumers, who suffer losses in consumer surplus, and of society, which bears a deadweight loss. All this was analysed in Chapter 12. It is these costs to the consumer that underlie legislation in many countries against collusive agreements within industries, usually put under the umbrella name of *competition policy*.

SUMMARY

Oligopoly – an introduction

1. The oligopoly problem arises because, when there are only a few suppliers to a market, the demand for the product of one firm depends significantly on the price and output decisions of its competitors.

2. There exists no single set of results for market equilibrium under oligopoly. Equilibrium outcomes depend on assumptions about enterprise behaviour.

3. Fundamental behavioural assumptions concern whether firms choose to collude in setting output and price, or to compete with each other.

4. One approach has firms acting independently, but making assumptions about the reactions of their rivals to their own strategy. A simple example is the kinked demand curve model, in which firms assume that their competitors will follow them in cutting, but not in raising, price.

5. When firms collude, the oligopolistic equilibrium is the same as under monopoly. Collusion of this sort is referred to as forming a cartel.

6. Cartels are, however, unstable, in that individual members can raise their profits by cheating on the cartel agreement, provided other firms do not notice or seek to punish them.

PROBLEMS

1 'The kinked demand curve is a model of price stability but not price determination.' To what extent do you agree with this statement?

2 Suppose that a duopolist holds the following beliefs about the behaviour of a rival.

(a) If the duopolist makes 'small' changes in price, say within 10 per cent of the current price, either up or down, the rival will not react.

(b) If the duopolist makes 'large' changes in price, the rival will match the changes exactly.

Derive the average and marginal revenue curves implied by these beliefs. What are the implications of these beliefs for output and price setting?

3 Consider an industry with five suppliers. One is very large relative to total supply, with the capacity, in the relevant price range, to supply a significant proportion of market supply on its own. The remaining suppliers comprise two middle size firms and two that are relatively small. The largest and smallest firms each have relatively low (constant) unit costs, but average costs are somewhat higher for the two middle size firms. Discuss the problems that the five suppliers will face in forming and maintaining a cartel.

4 A market has an inverse demand function defined by

$$p = 200 - 0.5X$$

Two firms exist in this market that have identical total costs. For firm 1 these are defined by

$$TC_1 = X_1 + 0.5X_1$$

with an equivalent definition for firm 2.

(a) If these two firms form a cartel, define the cartel's, marginal cost function.

(b) What is the cartel's profit maximising output and the profit earned?

(c) How much will firm 1 sell if it cheats on the cartel?

Notes

1. See below, Chapter 16.
2. The reader should note that the word 'compete' is here being used in a much more general sense than in Chapter 11 where perfect competition was analysed. There the stress was on price-taking behaviour and free entry and exit of firms to and from the industry. In the context of oligopoly theory 'competitive behaviour' simply means non-collusive behaviour.

Oligopoly and strategic interaction

Key words and phrases

- Cournot model, output as the strategic variable, Cournot equilibrium, expectations, isoprofit curve, reaction function
- Bertrand model, price as the strategic variable, Bertrand equilibrium
- price leadership
- leader and follower, Stackelberg model, Stackelberg equilibrium
- collusion, contract curve, conjectural variations

Introduction

The type of collusive behaviour discussed in the previous chapter is only one possible response to the problems faced by firms operating in industries with only a few rivals. It is also possible for the individual firm to take independent decisions about output and/or price, but to make them conditional upon assumptions about the behaviour of its rivals. This basic idea underlay the analysis of the kinked demand curve, set out in Chapter 15, but it is, as we shall now show, capable of being carried a good deal further.

In this chapter we shall first of all analyse the **Cournot model**, in which the firm's **basic decision variable is its output**. Second, we shall consider the case in which price replaces output as the key variable set by the firm – the **Bertrand model**. Third, we will consider a class of models in which firms do not collude, but make their moves in sequence, so that followers can react to leaders. Here the **Stackelberg model** will receive a good deal of attention. As the reader has probably guessed, each of these models is named after the economist who developed it. Once we have discussed them, we will compare the properties of the equilibria they yield to those produced by collusive behaviour, thus returning, at a more sophisticated level, to some of the issues dealt with at the end of the previous chapter.

The Cournot model

The kinked demand curve model made the *ad hoc* assumption that the firm believes that its competitors will follow a price cut but not follow a price increase. The **Cournot model** focuses not on price, but on quantity responses. It is based on the assumption that the firm is expected *not to respond at all* to changes in the output decisions of its rival. Thus firm 1 chooses its output, say X_1, on the assumption that the output level of firm 2, X_2, is fixed. Similarly, X_2 is chosen on the assumption that X_1 can be treated by firm 2 as given. This is analogous to the assumption made in competitive markets that firms make their decisions without reference to the reactions of their rivals, and makes obvious sense in oligopolistic markets where there are a relatively large number of firms. The assumption appears rather strange in the limiting case of duopoly, but it must be remembered that in the **Cournot equilibrium**, when quantities are not changing, the **expectations** of each firm about the reactions of its rival will in fact always be realised.

Box 16.1	**The strategic interaction of Cournot oligopolists**

Consider a market that has the inverse market demand function

$$p = 100 - X \tag{16.1.1}$$

where X is total industry output. If we restrict analysis to a duopoly we can define industry output as the sum of the two firms' outputs:

$$X = X_1 + X_2 \tag{16.1.2}$$

Substituting into the demand function:

$$p = 100 - X_1 - X_2 \tag{16.1.3}$$

With Cournot oligopolists this formulation allows us to define demand curves for the two firms. For firm 1 output decisions are made assuming firm 2 does not respond, i.e. firm 1 assumes that X_2 will not change (an assumption that may of course be incorrect). With this assumption we can write firm 1's demand curve as

$$p = (100 - \bar{X}_2) - X_1 \tag{16.1.4}$$

where $\bar{X}_2$ is the assumed fixed level of firm 2's output.

We can now derive firm 1's marginal revenue curve:

$$TR_1 = pX_1 = (100 - \bar{X}_2)X_1 - X_1^2 \tag{16.1.5}$$

so $\quad MR_1 = \dfrac{\partial(TR_1)}{\partial X_1} = (100 - \bar{X}_2) - 2X_1 \tag{16.1.6}$

These demand and marginal revenue functions are drawn in Illustration 16.1. In principle we could use an MC curve in this diagram and maximise firm 1's profit. But the complexity of strategic interaction renders use of a diagram such as this counter-productive. From (16.1.6) we can see that the strategic interaction links firm 2's output with firm 1's AR and MR curves. An increase in X_2 will shift AR_1 and MR_1 in

Illustration 16.1

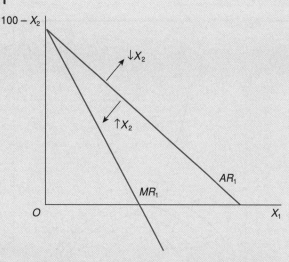

to the left, i.e. the vertical intercept of the curves shifts down. This reduces profit maximising X_1. This reduction in X_1 shifts firm 2's AR and MR curves and hence induces an increase in X_2. This induced increase in X_2 will shift AR_1 and MR_1 to the left and hence induce a secondary change in X_2. The complexity of this interaction renders a diagram such as Illustration 16.1 impractical. For this reason the analytical tools used to analyse oligopoly are isoprofit curves and reaction functions.

Isoprofit curves and reaction functions

The Cournot model is best explained diagrammatically with reference to isoprofit curves and reaction functions. An **isoprofit curve** for firm 1 is the locus of points in (X_1, X_2) space defined by different levels of output for both firm 1 and firm 2 which yield the same level of profit to firm 1. In duopoly, the profits of each firm depend on the output decision of its rival because the price obtained for the good depends on industry output $(X_1 + X_2)$. Isoprofit curves are concave to the axis of the firm to which they relate, with the level of profits declining with the height of the isoprofit curve above the horizontal axis. A family of isoprofit curves is illustrated in Figure 16.1. Note that, if firm 2 produces nothing, firm 1 is a monopolist, output is M_1 and the isoprofit curve corresponding to monopoly profits is, in essence, a point on the axis at M_1. Similarly, M_2 represents monopoly output for firm 2.

In order to analyse the Cournot equilibrium, we need to consider the impact of a change in firm 2's output upon the quantity produced by firm 1, and vice versa. The relationships through which we summarise these interactions are called **reaction functions**: firm 1's reaction function tells us how firm 1 will change output in response to a change in X_2, and firm 2's reaction function will tell us how firm 2 will respond to a change in X_1. We assume that both firms seek to maximise profits and that the industry as a whole faces

Figure 16.1

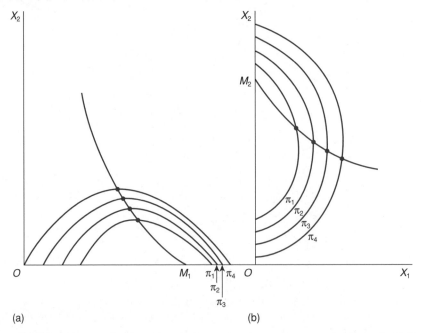

(a) illustrates a family of isoprofit curves for firm 1, which are concave to the X_1 axis, while (b) illustrates analogous curves for firm 2. The level of firm 1's profits rises as we move closer towards the X_1 axis ($\pi_1 > \pi_2 > \pi_3 > \pi_4$) and correspondingly for firm 2's isoprofit map. The output of X_1 at which profit is maximised for firm 1 increases as the output of firm 2 is reduced, and vice versa. At M_1 (M_2) the output of X_2 (X_1) is zero, and firm 1 (firm 2) makes monopoly profits. These points of maximum profit, given the other firm's output, define a reaction function: see Figure 16.2.

a downward-sloping demand curve along which price varies with the quantities produced by both firms, that is, the sum of X_1 and X_2. With the Cournot behavioural assumption that firms take the output of their rival as given, an increase in X_2 lowers the price both firms receive from the market, lowers the marginal revenue obtained by firm 1 at each level of output, and therefore, for given marginal cost, leads firm 1 to reduce output; and similarly for firm 2, which suggests that the reaction functions for both firms are backward bending.

The argument is illustrated in Figure 16.2. For a given level of output of firm 2, say X_2^1, firm 1 seeks to maximise profits, which entails choosing an output level X_1^1 which yields the lowest isoprofit curve consistent with X_2^1, at the tangency between π_1^1 and X_2^1. If firm 2 increases its output level to X_2^2, the highest level of profit attainable is at output level X_1^2 at the tangency between π_1^2 and X_2^2. The locus of the tangencies between given values of X_2 and isoprofit lines therefore plots out the reaction function for firm 1. This is of course the locus of maxima of the isoprofit curves and as we saw is backward bending. If one does the same analysis for firm 2, starting by taking output of firm 1 as constant at, say, X_1^3, we derive firm 2's reaction function as the locus of maxima of firm 2's isoprofit curves.

Figure 16.2

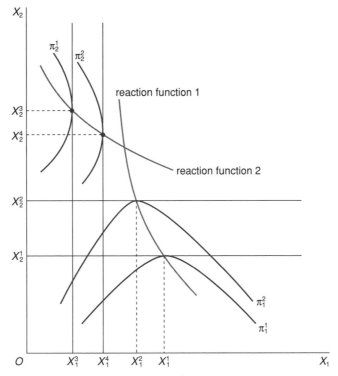

Firm 1 maximises profits at π_1^1, by choosing X_1^1 when firm 2 chooses X_2^1. Its optimal output declines to X_1^1, yielding π_1^2 when firm 2 increases output to X_2^2. The locus of these maxima of the isoprofit function is therefore firm 1's reaction function. Symmetrically, firm 2 maximises profits at π_2^1 by choosing X_2^3 when firm 1 chooses X_1^3 and will reduce output to X_2^4 in response to firm 1's increase of output to X_1^4.

Box 16.2   **Deriving Cournot isoprofit curves**

We can use the demand function introduced in Box 16.1 to derive Cournot isoprofit functions. The inverse demand function is

$$p = 100 - X_1 - X_2 \tag{16.1.3}$$

Firm 1's total revenue is therefore

$$TR_1 = pX_1 = 100X_1 - X_1^2 - X_1X_2 \tag{16.2.1}$$

If we assume a constant marginal cost of 10 and zero fixed costs, it follows that total costs are

$$TC_1 = 10X_1 \tag{16.2.2}$$

Hence we can write the profit function

$$\pi_1 = TR_1 - TC_1 = 100X_1 - X_1^2 - X_1X_2 - 10X_1 \tag{16.2.3}$$

Illustration 16.2

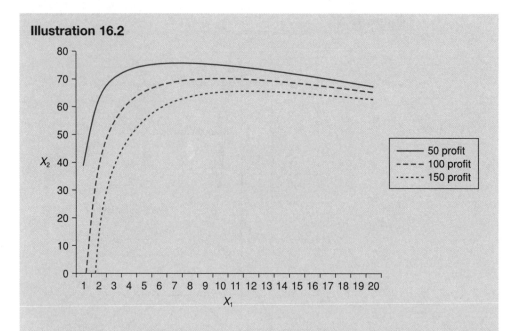

If we fix π_1 at a particular level we can then derive the isoprofit function for this profit level. In general terms with π_1 fixed at $\bar{\pi}_1$ we can write (16.2.3) as

$$\bar{\pi}_1 = 90X_1 - X_1^2 - X_1X_2 \tag{16.2.4}$$

Rearranging this function:

$$X_1X_2 = 90X_1 - X_1^2 - \bar{\pi}_1$$

and $X_2 = 90 - X_1 - \bar{\pi}_1/X_1$ (16.2.5)

Function (16.2.5) defines a Cournot isoprofit function for a particular level of $\bar{\pi}_1$. For a fixed level of profit it defines the relationship between X_2 and X_1. We can use any standard software to plot this isoprofit function for differing levels of profit. This is shown in Illustration 16.2 for three levels of profit: 50, 100 and 150. It is clear that, in general terms, the shape of these curves is the same as those drawn in Figure 16.1. In addition note the results reported in the text:

1. As profit increases the isoprofit curve approaches the X_1 axis.
2. As profit increases the peak of the isoprofit curve shifts to a higher level of X_1.

Each reaction function therefore plots the profit-maximising level of output for each firm given every conceivable expected value of production which could be chosen by its rival. The **Cournot equilibrium** is reached when the expectation of each firm about its rival's output choice proves to be correct. Clearly, this occurs at the intersection of the two reaction functions, where each firm is choosing to produce exactly the level of output which its rival expects. This mutual realisation of output expectations is illustrated at output levels (X_1^*, X_2^*) in Figure 16.3. Readers should note that industry output $X = (X_1^* + X_2^*)$ is greater than under pure monopoly (M_1 or M_2), and therefore price must be lower than the monopoly price. This establishes the result that, even when there are only two

Figure 16.3

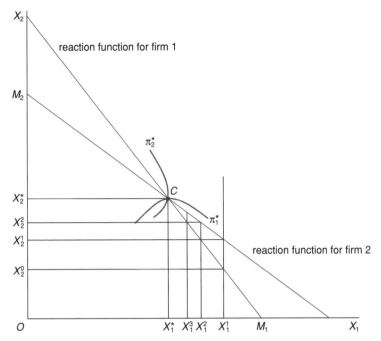

The Cournot equilibrium point C at the intersection of the two reaction functions. At this point, the expectations of each firm about the behaviour of its rival are confirmed. Suppose instead that firm 1 chooses X_1^1. Firm 2 responds with X_2^1, but at that output level, firm 1 would choose X_1^2. Expectations are therefore not confirmed; 2 chooses X_2^2 and 1 responds with X_1^3. The process continues until X_1^*, X_2^* is reached. The process is stable provided that 1's reaction curve is steeper than 2's. Note that in this case the reaction functions are drawn as straight lines mainly to keep the diagrammatic analysis manageable; but see the following formal analysis.

firms, non-collusive behaviour leads to higher consumer welfare (via lower prices) but lower company profits than collusive behaviour.

We can also illustrate the path of adjustment towards equilibrium implied by Cournot behaviour in Figure 16.3. If we arbitrarily start with the assumption that firm 1 chooses X_1^1, profits are maximised for firm 2 at the point where X_1^1 intersects firm 2's reaction function at X_2^1. But this output pair (X_1^1, X_2^1) is not a Cournot equilibrium because firm 1's expectation of firm 2's behaviour is not confirmed by firm 2. Firm 1 chose X_1^1 because it expected firm 2 to produce X_2^0, but in fact it produced X_2^1. The process of adjusting output in order to maximise profits (i.e. along the reaction function) in response to unrealised expectations about the output choice of rivals will stop when expectations are mutually consistent, at (X_1^*, X_2^*) where the reaction functions cross.

The process described here is *stable*, in the sense that, from any initial starting point on either firm 1 or firm 2's reaction function, it will lead to the Cournot equilibrium. This will be so, provided that firm 1's reaction function is steeper than firm 2's reaction function. Readers can prove for themselves, however, that when the relative slopes of the two curves are reversed, Cournot behaviour and profit maximisation lead away from the point of intersection of the two reaction functions from any initial starting point, except the intersection itself. In this case, the equilibrium is said to be unstable.

Box 16.3	**Deriving Cournot reaction functions**

In Boxes 16.1 and 16.2 we have set out all the information we need to derive Cournot reaction functions. The inverse market demand function is

$$p = 100 - X_1 - X_2 \tag{16.1.3}$$

Total revenue functions for the two firms are

$$TR_1 = pX_1 = 100X_1 - X_1^2 - X_1X_2 \tag{16.3.1}$$

$$TR_2 = pX_2 = 100X_2 - X_2^2 - X_1X_2 \tag{16.3.2}$$

If each firm has the same constant marginal costs of 10 and zero fixed costs

$$TC_1 = 10X_1 \tag{16.3.3}$$

$$TC_2 = 10X_2 \tag{16.3.4}$$

So the profit functions are

$$\pi_1 = TR_1 - TC_1 = 100X_1 - X_1^2 - X_1X_2 - 10X_1 \tag{16.3.5}$$

$$\pi_2 = TR_2 - TC_2 = 100X_2 - X_2^2 - X_1X_2 - 10X_2 \tag{16.3.6}$$

Each firm now chooses its own output level to maximise profit:

$$\frac{\partial \pi_1}{\partial X_1} = 100 - 2X_1 - X_2 - 10 = 0 \tag{16.3.7}$$

$$\frac{\partial \pi_2}{\partial X_2} = 100 - 2X_2 - X_1 - 10 = 0 \tag{16.3.8}$$

Using conditions 16.3.7 and 16.3.8 we can derive the Cournot reaction functions (CRF_1 and CRF_2) for the two firms. Using 16.3.7:

$$CRF_1: \quad X_1 = 45 - 0.5X_2 \tag{16.3.9}$$

Using 16.3.8:

$$CRF_2: \quad X_2 = 45 - 0.5X_1 \tag{16.3.10}$$

We can interpret CRF_1 in the following manner: firm 1 observes the second firm's output level, assumes this remains unchanged and calculates its own profit maximising output accordingly. An equivalent interpretation applies to CRF_2.

As considered in the text, the Cournot equilibrium occurs where these reaction functions intersect. Formally we can solve CRF_1 and CRF_2 as two simultaneous equations. For example, substituting RF_2 into RF_1:

$$X_1 = 45 - 0.5(45 - 0.5X_1) = 22.5 + 0.25X_1 \tag{16.3.11}$$

$$X_1 = 30$$

Using CRF_2, $X_1 = 30$ implies $X_2 = 30$; any other result would have been wrong here because the two firms are identical and so will have the same equilibrium outputs, i.e. the same equilibrium market shares. More generally if the firms are different they will

Illustration 16.3

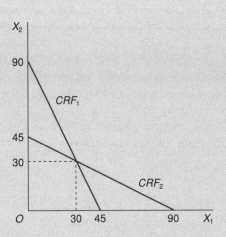

have different equilibrium outputs. For example if the firms have different marginal costs the firm that is more efficient (with a lower marginal cost) will have a higher equilibrium output (a higher market share). This result occurs as long as the cost differences are relatively small. With a large cost difference the inefficient firm will be unviable. This is an interesting characteristic of the Cournot model that seems to apply in practice. It shows that inefficient firms in an oligopolistic market might survive, with relatively small market shares, as long as the inefficiency is not too great and as long as they behave as Cournot oligopolists. The interested reader can show this result by working through the example developed here but with different firm marginal costs.

The two Cournot reaction functions derived here and the equilibrium outputs are shown in Illustration 16.3. Note that in general terms this is the same as Figure 16.3 in the text, but without the underlying isoprofit curves. In particular note that CRF_1 is steeper than CRF_2. This implies that the equilibrium outputs are stable and that if the market is out of equilibrium it will converge to the stable Cournot equilibrium.

* A more formal treatment of the Cournot model

The more mathematically inclined student can obtain a better understanding of the subtleties of the Cournot model from the following general formalisation and example. In the duopoly case, the profits of each firm depend on the level of output of both because output price is given by the industry demand curve. If the industry inverse demand curve is

$$p = p(X) = p(X_1 + X_2) \qquad (16.1)$$

where X is industry output, the profits of the two firms are given by

$$\pi_1 = p(X_1 + X_2)X_1 - C(X_1) \qquad (16.2)$$

and

$$\pi_2 = p(X_1 + X_2)X_2 - C(X_2) \qquad (16.3)$$

where $C(\cdot)$ represents each firm's cost function.

The Cournot assumption is that each firm chooses its output level taking the output of its rival as given. Hence firm 1 chooses X_1 to maximise π_1 given X_2, and firm 2 chooses X_2 to maximise π_2 given X_1. In each case, this maximum occurs where

$$\partial \pi_i / \partial X_i = 0, \ i = 1, 2 \tag{16.4}$$

There is a different value of X_i for every assumed value of $X_j (i \neq j)$, each representing the maximum of a particular isoprofit line as illustrated in Figure 16.1.

In this example, let us make the particularly simple assumptions that the demand curve is linear; that costs have a fixed element F and a constant marginal cost, c per unit of output. Hence, the demand curve is

$$p = a - b(X_1 + X_2) \tag{16.5}$$

and

$$C(X_1) = F + cX_1; \ C(X_2) = F + cX_2 \tag{16.6}$$

Then the profit functions are

$$\pi_1 = aX_1 - bX_1^2 - bX_2X_1 - F - cX_1 \tag{16.7}$$

$$\pi_2 = aX_2 - bX_1X_2 - bX_2^2 - F - cX_2 \tag{16.8}$$

Rearranging equation (16.7) yields the equation for firm 1's isoprofit curve:

$$X_2 = \frac{a - c}{b} - X_1 - \left(\frac{\pi_1 + F}{bX_1} \right) \tag{16.9}$$

which, for each value of π_1, yields an inverse U-shaped line concave to the X_1 axis. This is firm 1's isoprofit curve as depicted in Figure 16.1. Similarly for firm 2, the equation of the isoprofit line is

$$X_1 = \frac{a - c}{b} - X_2 - \left(\frac{\pi_2 + F}{bX_2} \right) \tag{16.10}$$

We can derive firm 1's reaction function by maximising π_1 in equation (16.7) taking X_2 as given. Profits are maximised where

$$\frac{\partial \pi_1}{\partial X_1} = a - 2bX_1 - bX_2 - c = 0 \tag{16.11}$$

which can be rearranged to yield the familar marginal revenue $(a - 2bX_1 - bX_2)$ equals marginal cost (c) relationship. From equation (16.11) we can derive the relationship between X_1 and X_2 when profits are maximised:

$$X_1 = \frac{a - c}{2b} - \frac{X_2}{2} \tag{16.12}$$

This is firm 1's reaction function and in the range where profits are positive it is linear when demand and marginal cost curves are linear. Similarly, we can derive firm 2's reaction function by maximising π_2 in equation (16.8) taking X_1 as given. Hence

$$\frac{\partial \pi_2}{\partial X_2} = a - 2bX_2 - bX_1 - c = 0 \tag{16.13}$$

which gives us a relationship between X_2 and X_1,

$$X_2 = \frac{a-c}{2b} - \frac{X_1}{2} \tag{16.14}$$

This is firm 2's reaction function. The two reaction functions are *symmetric* because we have assumed that the firms face the same structure of demand and cost equations.

The Cournot equilibrium occurs where the two reaction functions intersect, or at the solution to the simultaneous equation system (16.12) and (16.14). Substituting (16.12) into (16.14) yields

$$X_2 = \frac{a-c}{2b} - \frac{a-c}{4b} + \frac{X_2}{4} \tag{16.15}$$

so that

$$X_2 = \frac{a-c}{3b} \tag{16.16}$$

Substituting back into equation (16.12) yields

$$X_1 = \frac{a-c}{3b} \tag{16.17}$$

Since demand and cost conditions are assumed to be identical in this example, and the reaction functions are symmetric, the firms divide the industry output between themselves equally. The equilibrium is also stable. The slope of firm 2's reaction function $(\partial X_2/\partial X_1 = -\frac{1}{2})$ is less in absolute value than the slope of firm 1's reaction function $(1/(\partial X_1/\partial X_2) = -2)$. Industry output is $X = X_1 + X_2 = (2(a-c)/3b)$, while price is $(a+2c)/3$.

This equilibrium solution can be compared with the result under pure monopoly, where there is only one producer, say firm 1, producing X_1. Setting $X_2 = 0$ in equation (16.5) gives industry output as $X_1 = ((a-c)/2b)$ from equation (16.12) and the monopoly price as $p = (c+a)/2$. Hence output is greater and price lower in the Cournot equilibrium as compared with the pure monopoly outcome. Moreover it will be shown at the end of the chapter that, if we assume additional producers to have the same cost structure as those already in the industry, industry output expands and price falls as the number of firms increases. For example, readers can prove for themselves that, if there are three producers in the industry, each will supply $((a-c)/4b)$ and market supply will be $(3(a-c)/4b)$. The larger the number of firms, the closer are output and price to the competitive level.

More on the non-collusive approach

Several widely discussed alternatives to the Cournot model of non-collusive equilibrium have emerged in the literature. The one we shall now discuss is due to Bertrand, who argued that if price rather than quantity is the strategic variable to which firms react, and if their product is homogeneous, then price will fall to the competitive level, even if the market is duopolistic. The firm charging the lower price will always end up supplying the whole market, and therefore, so the argument goes, firms will continue to undercut each other while price exceeds marginal costs. Such price competition ceases only when the competitive price which equals marginal cost has been reached and, under conditions of constant marginal costs, profits have fallen to zero. Bertrand interprets his finding that price interaction can lead to zero profits as pointing to the likelihood of collusive rather than non-collusive equilibria emerging. We shall now discuss his model in detail.

The Bertrand model

Bertrand's approach is, as we have already noted, similar to that of Cournot, except that he assumes each firm chooses **price rather than output**, and makes that decision on the assumption that its rival will keep its price constant. Three fairly straightforward assumptions of the Cournot model, taken over by Bertrand, have considerable significance for the results generated by his model. The assumption of product homogeneity is crucial in the Bertrand framework, and the results change when it is altered. In particular, product differentiation allows positive profits to be sustained in equilibrium. The **Bertrand model** also requires the assumption that each firm has sufficient capacity to supply the entire market; there may be no equilibrium if each of the two firms does not have sufficient spare capacity. Finally it is critical to assume that firms face identical cost curves; otherwise the one which faces lower marginal costs will always end up supplying the entire market. Here we assume that, at given input prices, marginal cost is constant and equal to average cost.

Bertrand's analysis can be developed with the use of isoprofit curves and reaction functions. However, prices rather than quantities are on the two axes. Also, as illustrated in Figure 16.4, isoprofit maps for each firm are convex rather than concave to the axis of the firm in question. This is the case because, starting at the right of the minimum of any isoprofit line, say π_1^1 in Figure 16.4, firm 1 must cut price in order to maintain profits in response to its rivals' price reductions. Profits decline as we move to lower and lower isoprofit curves. The reaction function for each firm is the locus of points at which profits are maximised for firm 1 when the price of firm 2 is taken as given, and vice versa for firm 2. It is therefore the locus through the minimum of the relevant U-shaped isoprofit curves, and is upward sloping for both firms.

The **Bertrand equilibrium** is achieved when each firm's expectations about the price behaviour of its rival are realised. Hence in Figure 16.4, if firm 1 expects firm 2 to charge p_2^1, it will choose p_1^1 on its reaction function in order to maximise its profits at that price. But at p_1^1, firm 2 will actually charge p_2^2, on its own reaction function. Provided that firm 1's reaction function has a steeper slope than that of firm 2, this iterative procedure will lead the firms to the Bertrand equilibrium, which is where the two reaction functions intersect. This is labelled as point B in Figure 16.4. Since their products are assumed to be homogeneous, each firm must charge the same price in equilibrium. If they did not, the one offering the lower price would actually get all the demand. Hence the equilibrium must be characterised by equal prices, and therefore lie on a 45° line beginning at the origin.

Moreover the equilibrium price must equal the (assumed identical) marginal cost of each producer. This is because, if the equilibrium price exceeds marginal cost, and firm 1 believes that firm 2 will not alter its price in response to a price cut by firm 1 (the Bertrand behavioural assumption), then firm 1 will always cut its price, because in doing so it will capture the entire market. Exactly the same argument applies to firm 2. This incentive to cut price is eliminated only when the two firms charge an identical price equal to marginal cost, and industry profits are zero.

Bertrand competition therefore leads us to the perfectly competitive solution despite the small numbers of firms in the industry. This is a formalisation of an important, if

Figure 16.4   The Bertrand model

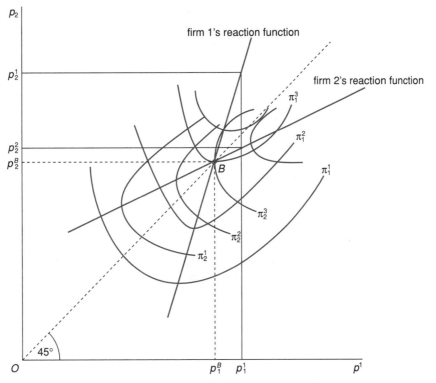

In the Bertrand model isoprofit curves are convex to the relevant firm's axis, with profits increasing as we move out. The reaction functions are the loci of minima of each firm's isoprofit curves and are upward sloping. The Bertrand equilibrium is at the intersection of the two reaction functions, at B, yielding equal (competitive) prices p_1^B and p_2^B along the 45° line.

hotly contested, argument in economics, to the effect that competition over price can lead to zero profits, even if there are very few firms in the industry. Its relevance to real-world situations depends in part on one's evaluation of the assumptions of the model – price rather than quantity competition, product homogeneity, no capacity constraints, identical firms and the Bertrand behavioural assumption that the rival's price is taken as given – but that relevance is ultimately an empirical question, the discussion of which lies beyond the scope of this chapter.

It should be noted that the Bertrand model points to the possibility that firms will collude to avoid its zero profit equilibrium. Clearly if non-collusion and competition lead firms to a zero profit outcome, the formation of cartels will seem even more attractive to the two parties than in the Cournot case, where, though each party earns less than when joint profits are maximised, it does at least earn positive profits. The point is illustrated in Figure 16.4, where we note that at the Bertrand equilibrium, B, the firms' isoprofit curves intersect. The two firms depicted could both raise profits by moving in a northeasterly direction, that is, by agreeing to raise price. One can derive a contract curve (as explained) as the locus of tangency points between isoprofit curves along which industry profits are maximised. There would be a tendency to cheat in a price collusive equilibrium since, if a firm believes that its rival will keep price constant while it reduces price, it can thereby capture the entire market. Collusive equilibrium in prices therefore tends to be unstable in the same way as in output-based cartels. However, to the extent that price is a more easily monitored variable than output, cartel arrangements that involve price fixing may be easier for their members to monitor.

Box 16.4 **Deriving Bertrand reaction functions**

In Box 16.3 we derived Cournot reaction functions. We can now go through a similar exercise and derive Bertrand reaction functions and the equilibrium they result in. Of course the difference is that with a Cournot model firms choose outputs assuming that competitor outputs are unchanged, but with a Bertrand model firms choose prices assuming competitor prices are unchanged. This difference implies that profit functions must be written completely in terms of firm prices rather than firm outputs.

Assume an oligopoly made up of two identical firms. As the firms are identical we can construct a profit function for firm 1 and use this as a model for firm 2's profit function without going through a detailed derivation. Firm 1's demand curve is

$$X_1 = 100 - p_1 + p_2 \tag{16.4.1}$$

Note here:

1. The effects of p_1 and p_2 on X_1 are of opposite sign. This implies the two products are substitutes.
2. The effect of p_1 on X_1 is the same (in absolute terms) as that of p_2 on X_1. This characteristic is reasonable as the firms produce identical products. With differentiated products we might expect a smaller (in absolute terms) effect of p_2 on X_1 compared with p_1 on X_1.

Firm 1's total revenue function is

$$TR_1 = p_1 X_1 = 100p_1 - p_1^2 + p_1 p_2 \tag{16.4.2}$$

We can assume, as in Box 16.3, that both firms have the same constant marginal costs of 10 and zero fixed costs. Firm one's total costs are

$$TC_1 = 10X_1 = 10(100 - p_1 + p_2)$$
$$1000 - 10p_1 + 10p_2 \tag{16.4.3}$$

The substitution using (16.4.1) to eliminate X_1 from the cost function is necessary because with the Bertrand model firms choose prices not outputs. Using the cost and revenue functions we can write firm 1's profits as

$$\pi_1 = TR_1 - TC_1 = 100p_1 - p_1^2 + p_1 p_2 - (1000 - 10p_1 + 10p_2)$$
$$110p_1 - p_1^2 + p_1 p_2 - 10p_2 - 1000 \tag{16.4.4}$$

Firm 2 has an equivalent profit function:

$$\pi_2 = 110p_2 - p_2^2 + p_1p_2 - 10p_1 - 1000 \tag{16.4.5}$$

Note the general structure of these profit functions that one firm's decisions affect the other firm's profits, i.e. there is strategic interaction because we are dealing with an oligopolistic market.

We choose profit maximising firm prices by differentiating the profit functions and setting the first derivatives equal to zero:

$$\frac{\partial \pi_1}{\partial p_1} = 110 - 2p_1 + p_2 = 0 \tag{16.4.6}$$

$$\frac{\partial \pi_2}{\partial p_2} = 110 - 2p_2 + p_1 = 0 \tag{16.4.7}$$

We use these results to formulate the Bertrand reaction functions (BRF_1 and BRF_2). From (16.4.6):

$$BRF_1: \quad p_1 = 55 + 0.5p_2 \tag{16.4.8}$$

Using (16.4.7):

$$BRF_2: \quad p_2 = 55 + 0.5p_1 \tag{16.4.9}$$

We can interpret BRF_1 in the following way: firm 1 observes firm 2's price, assumes this will remain unchanged and sets its own profit maximising price accordingly. A similar interpretation can be made for BRF_2.

The Bertrand equilibrium is the set of prices that are stable and so do not result in a competitor price change. This equilibrium is found where the two reaction functions intersect. Solving BRF_1 and BRF_2 as two simultaneous equations:

$$p_1 = p_2 = 110$$

Note that equilibria p_1 and p_2 are the same. Any other possibility is not feasible with identical firms. This equilibrium is shown in Illustration 16.4. Note that the two

Illustration 16.4

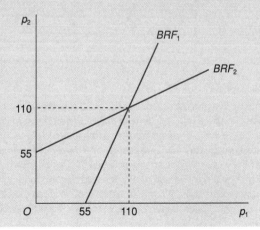

→

> Bertrand reaction functions are the same general shape as in Figure 16.4 in the text. It will be seen that if (for example) firm 2 cuts price below 110, firm 1 will follow with a price cut but firm 1's price cut will be less than firm 2's. From firm 2's reaction function this allows firm 2 to increase price, and so price increases will converge on the equilibrium.

Price leadership

Our third non-collusive model also deals with the interdependence problem by making specific assumptions about how firms will behave. In this model there is one *dominant firm* from which all others take the lead as far as pricing policy is concerned. The dominant firm takes the reactions of the other firms into account when making its decision about price and output, but they take the dominant firm's price as given in settling on their own behaviour. The phenomenon involved here is therefore called **price leadership**.

Consider Figure 16.5. In panel (a) we have the market demand curve for X, and a long-run market supply curve derived from the behaviour of a group of perfectly competitive firms. For simplicity we assume that given factor prices lie behind this curve and that it

Figure 16.5 **Price leadership**

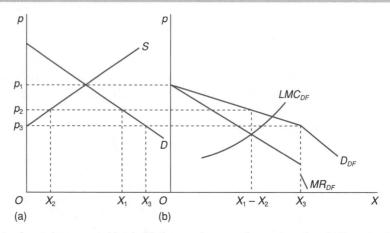

The industry demand curve, combined with the supply curve of a number of perfectly competitive firms, is depicted in panel (a). The demand curve of the dominant firm D_{DF} is derived by subtracting the competitive supply curve from the industry demand curve. Faced with this demand curve in the long run, the dominant firm equates marginal cost (LMC) to marginal revenue (MR_{DF}). Price is determined at p_2, competitive firms supply X_2, total demand is given by X_1, and the dominant firm sells $X_1 - X_2$. Note that, unless it can produce a positive output at price less than p_1, the equilibrium price in its absence, the dominant firm will not exist. Thus, a firm can achieve dominance only if it has a significant cost advantage. If its profit-maximising price was p_3 or below, the dominant firm would be the only firm in the industry.

derives its upward slope from declining efficiency of new firms as supply expands. Now suppose that a new relatively large (and hence 'dominant') firm was considering entering the market for X. How would it view the demand conditions it faced? Clearly at a price p_1, the already existing competitive firms would supply the entire market and the dominant firm would be able to sell nothing. However, were it to set its price at p_2, below p_1, less efficient competitive firms would drop out of the market. Those remaining would supply X_2, leaving $X_1 - X_2$ to be sold by the large firm. In other words, the quantity demanded from the dominant firm at any particular price is found by taking the market demand at that price and subtracting from it the quantity that would be supplied by the competitive firms. Obviously, at price p_3 the resulting demand curve becomes the market demand curve. There is a kink in the dominant firm's demand curve at this point and hence a discontinuity in its marginal revenue curve. This is *not*, however, the same type of kinked demand curve as we met in the previous analysis, as ought to be obvious. As we have drawn Figure 16.5 the price/quantity solution that emerges is one at which price is fixed at p_2 by the large firm. The total amount demanded is X_1, of which the dominant firm supplies $X_1 - X_2$, leaving X_2 to be supplied by small firms at the going price.

As well as explaining how price is determined, this model yields several interesting insights. First, a dominant firm can emerge only if it is capable of producing a 'substantial' proportion of the industry's output at a lower price than would emerge under competition among relatively small firms. The example of the supermarket in comparison with small groceries as a purveyor of retailing services comes to mind here. Second, it is not just existing competitors that affect the elasticity of a demand curve facing a firm, but potential competitors as well. Thus, a downward-sloping demand curve facing a firm is by no means necessarily synonymous with the market demand curve for the good in question – *even if that firm is the sole producer of the good in question*.

To make this point quite clear consider Figure 16.6, which is a variation on the theme developed in Figure 16.5, which differs from Figure 16.6 in two ways only. First it is

Figure 16.6

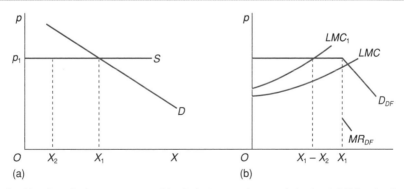

Price leadership when the long-run competitive industry supply curve is horizontal. If the dominant firm's marginal cost curve is given by *LMC* it produces the whole industry's output, but sells it at the competitive price p_1. If it is given by LMC_1 it sells a proportion of the industry's output, $X_1 - X_2$, at the competitive price with competitive firms selling X_2. In neither case does the dominant firm have any monopoly power, even when it is the only firm in the industry.

assumed that all small firms are equally efficient and second it is assumed in drawing its marginal cost curve as *LMC* that the large firm's cost advantage is such as to permit it to take the whole market for *X*. Nevertheless, this firm, even as the sole producer of *X*, has no power to raise its price above p_1. That is to say, a sole seller of a good who is in that position simply by virtue of a cost advantage is far less a 'monopolist' than one whose advantage stems from some legal barrier to competition. The latter, but not the former, can treat the market demand curve as the relevant one.

Another variation on Figure 16.6 is also worth considering. Suppose the large firm's marginal cost curve lay at LMC_1. It would produce a large part of the industry's output, but would in fact be a perfect competitor as far as its pricing behaviour was concerned.

Stackelberg equilibrium

The Cournot model discussed earlier is based on the idea that each firm takes its rival's output as given when choosing its level of production. Stackelberg analysed what would happen if one firm understood the structure of the Cournot model sufficiently well to work out how the other firm would react, and then used this information to improve upon its position in the equilibrium. Stackelberg thus analysed not 'price leadership' but 'quantity leadership', and we shall term this sophisticated firm the '**leader**' and its more naive rival the '**follower**'.

The **Stackelberg model** can then be developed as an extension of the Cournot framework. Firm 1, which we shall take to be the leader, seeks to maximise profits in the knowledge that firm 2, the follower, will treat firm 1's output decision as given. Hence firm 2 will always make decisions along its reaction function, while firm 1 maximises profits subject to firm 2's reaction function. The resulting **Stackelberg equilibrium** is at the tangency between firm 1's isoprofit curve and firm 2's reaction function, point *S* on Figure 16.7.

A comparison of the Cournot and Stackelberg equilibria gives us some intuition about how the leader firm uses its better knowledge to its own advantage. In the Cournot model, each party takes the behaviour of the other as given and adjusts output in response to disappointed expectations until an equilibrium of consistent expectations is reached (point *C* in Figure 16.7). In the Stackelberg model, firm 1 knows that firm 2 behaves in this way. It therefore chooses it output level, X_1^S, above that implied by its own Cournot reaction function in order to maximise profits subject to firm 2's reaction function. Given its expectation of X_1^S, firm 2 then responds with X_2^S, as firm 1 calculated that it would. Firm 2 in turn finds that its expectation of firm 1's behaviour is confirmed. Firm 2 is therefore misled into thinking that it is in a Cournot equilibrium, though it is producing less than X_2^C and therefore has lower profits ($\pi_2^3 < \pi_2^2$). Firm 1 on the other hand is producing more than the Cournot equilibrium ($X_1^S > X_1^C$) and is therefore earning higher profits ($\pi_1^2 > \pi_1^3$).

Industry profits are still not maximised at the Stackelberg equilibrium – both sides could gain from a move in a south-westerly direction along *EE'* in Figure 16.7. However, one suspects that the leader might be less sympathetic to the formation of a cartel in these circumstances than it would be under Cournot or Bertrand conditions, particularly if the rival's behaviour is hard to monitor.

Finally, note that, if both firms seek to be leaders, the Stackelberg model cannot yield an equilibrium. If both firms understand the other's Cournot behaviour, then they will either agree to collude or will enter a price war to determine who will act as leader and who as follower. The incentives for them to seek the former solution are obvious.

Figure 16.7 Stackelberg equilibrium

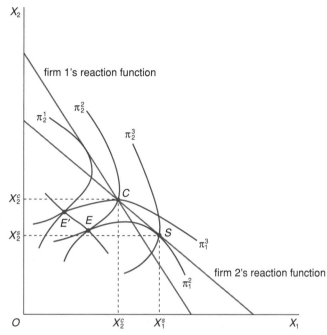

If firm 1 is leader it chooses the level of output which maximises profit, given firm 2's reaction function, at X_1^s, where its isoprofit curve (π_1^2) is tangent to firm 2's reaction function. Firm 2 responds to this choice with X_2^s, and has profits of π_2^3. Firm 1 produces more output and correspondingly has higher profits, firm 2 less output and correspondingly lower profits, than at the Cournot equilibrium C.

Box 16.5 | **More on Stackelberg equilibrium**

In Box 16.3 we set out a simple worked example to show how a Cournot equilibrium can be calculated. We can use the same example to calculate a Stackelberg equilibrium. The earlier framework was based on two identical firms. The inverse market demand function was

$$p = 100 - X_1 - X_2 \tag{16.1.3}$$

For firm 1 the key features were

$$TR_1 = pX_1 = 100X_1 - X_1^2 - X_1X_2 \tag{16.3.1}$$

With constant marginal costs of 10 and zero fixed costs

$$TC_1 = 10X_1 \tag{16.3.3}$$

So $\quad \pi_1 = TR_1 - TC_1 = 100X_1 - X_1^2 - X_1X_2 - 10X_1 \tag{16.3.5}$

As the two firms have identical cost and revenue functions,

$$\pi_2 = TR_2 - TC_2 = 100X_2 - X_2^2 - X_1X_2 - 10X_2 \tag{16.3.6}$$

Maximising profits allowed derivation of the two Cournot reaction functions:

$$CRF_1: \quad X_1 = 45 - 0.5X_2 \tag{16.3.9}$$

$$CRF_2: \quad X_2 = 45 - 0.5X_1. \tag{16.3.10}$$

We can now allow firm 1 to be a strategic leader but still keep firm 2 as a follower. The leader will not simply assume firm 2's output will remain constant and react to firm 2's decisions after they occur. Instead it will anticipate firm 2's reactions before they occur. It will be seen that this proactive behaviour by firm 1 allows it to earn extra profits at the expense of the follower firm. In terms of formal theory, firm 2's reactions to firm 1 are described by its reaction function CRF_2. If firm 1 anticipates firm 2's reactions it can use CRF_2 to predict what X_2 will be for any level of X_1. If firm 1 substitutes CRF_2 into its profit function it can predict X_2 rather than simply reacting to firm 2's decisions:

$$\pi_1 = 100X_1 - X_1^2 - X_1(45 - 0.5X_1) - 10X_1$$
$$= 45X_1 - 0.5X_1^2 \tag{16.5.1}$$

Firm 1 can now maximise profit anticipating firm 2's reactions in advance:

$$\frac{d\pi_1}{dX_1} = 45 - X_1 = 0 \tag{16.5.2}$$

So the Stackelberg equilibrium output for firm 1 is $X_1 = 45$. Using RF_2 firm 2 will respond to this output level with

$$X_2 = 45 - 0.5(45) = 22.5$$

It will be recalled from Box 16.3 that the Cournot equilibrium was $X_1 = X_2 = 30$. So with firm 1 being a leader there is an increase in output at the expense of firm 2, as we expect in a Stackelberg model. We can calculate the other key features of the two equilibria as follows:

Cournot $\quad \pi_1 = \pi_2 = 900; \quad X = 60, p = 40$
Stackelberg $\quad \pi_1 = 1012.5; \pi_2 = 506.25; X = 67.5; p = 32.5$

So the leader gains profit at the expense of the follower as we would expect. But note also industry output (X) increases and price (p) falls: hence consumers benefit from strategic leadership.

* A formal treatment of the Stackelberg model

The difference between the Cournot and Stackelberg models and the consequences for industry output and price can be illustrated formally. We return to the example we used for the Cournot model, with a linear demand curve (equation (16.5)), and a linear cost function (equation (16.6)). Firm 1's profit function is therefore

$$\pi_1 = aX_1 - bX_1^2 - bX_2X_1 - F - cX_1 \tag{16.7}$$

while firm 2's reaction function is

$$X_2 = \frac{a-c}{2b} - \frac{X_1}{2} \tag{16.14}$$

In the Stackelberg equilibrium, firm 1 chooses X_1 to maximise (16.7) subject to the constraint that firm 2 chooses X_2 on its reaction function (16.14). We therefore substitute (16.14) into (16.7) and maximise profits:

$$\frac{\partial \pi}{\partial X_1} = a - 2bX_1 - \left(\frac{a-c}{2}\right) + bX_1 - c = 0$$

$$X_1 = \frac{a-c}{2b} \tag{16.18}$$

Substituting into equation (16.14), we derive X_2 as

$$X_2 = \frac{a-c}{4b} \tag{16.19}$$

If we compare this with our solution to this example of the Cournot model (equations (16.16) and (16.17)), we note that the leader is producing more and the follower less than at the Cournot equilibrium. Interested readers are invited to prove for themselves that firm 1 also earns higher profits, and firm 2 lower profits, than at the Cournot equilibrium. In this particular example, industry output is also higher and price lower than in the Cournot equilibrium. The more general case is analysed in the following section.

Collusive and non-collusive behaviour compared – the contract curve

The Cournot model analyses one possible way in which firms might interact in oligopolistic markets. However, as we have seen, while each firm maximises its own profit at the Cournot equilibrium (given its assumptions about the output choice of its rival) industry profit is not maximised. Output is greater, and price lower, than it would be if the industry were monopolised. This is shown diagrammatically in Figure 16.3, where the isoprofit curves of the two firms (π_1^*, π_2^*) cut each other at the Cournot equilibrium, point C. Each firm could increase profits (move to an isoprofit curve closer to its own axis) by moving in a south-westerly direction (reducing output), provided that its rival responded in kind. But outcomes of this sort cannot be attained if Cournot behaviour is assumed. The alternative behavioural assumption is that firms **collude** in setting quantity and price in order to maximise joint profits.

When two firms collude it is reasonable to suppose that they will reach an agreement under the terms of which it will not be possible to make one of them better off without making the other worse off. If they had not reached such an agreement, then at least one of them could propose a change in the terms of the contract between them which would make the proposer better off without harming the other, and it is hard to see why such a proposal should be resisted. This fundamental principle of voluntary contracting will also underlie much of our analysis of trade unions in Chapter 20, and of the economy as a whole in Chapter 21, as well as this discussion of collusive oligopolies. In each case, equilibria which satisfy this principle are said to lie on a **contract curve**.

For the case of collusive firms we construct the contract curve by considering the isoprofit curves and reaction functions developed earlier. We noted there that, starting in a Cournot equilibrium, say C in Figure 16.3, both firms could increase their profits by moving in a south-westerly direction. The potential advantages of collusion will be exhausted, and such moves cease, when they are unable to find another combination of outputs which would allow for an improvement in the profits of one while not reducing the profits of another. This is satisfied only when the isoprofit curves are tangential. The locus of all such tangencies is the contract curve for the two firms, and is illustrated in Figure 16.8.

Collusive equilibria always lie somewhere on the contract curve, though their precise location depends on the agreement about the allocation of profits made when the cartel is formed. For example, suppose we start at the Cournot equilibrium, C, and the two firms agree to collude on the basis that firm 2 receives exactly the profits that it would earn under the Cournot solution (π_2^2), while all the incremental profits from the cartel accrue to firm 1 (which gains $\pi_1^1 - \pi_1^2$). The collusive equilibrium will be on the contract curve at E. If firm 2 shares in the gains that cartelisation brings to the producers (though not of course to consumers), the actual equilibrium will lie somewhere to the north-west of E. It

Figure 16.8

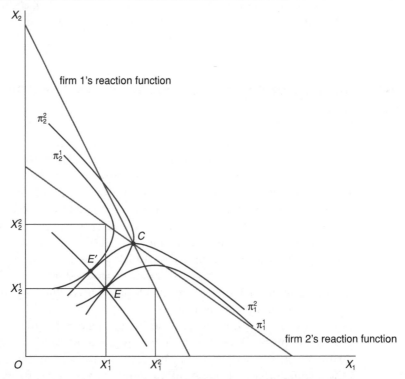

Isoprofit curves cross at the Cournot equilibrium (C) so profits can be increased for both parties by moves in a south-westerly direction. Profit-enhancing output changes are exhausted for both parties when isoprofit curves are tangential along the contract curve EE'. Collusive equilibria therefore lie along the contract curve, their precise location depending on the allocation of profits between the two parties to the bargain. As we move from E to E', the profits of firm 2 increase and those of firm 1 fall.

seems unlikely that any bargain would be struck which took the outcome beyond E^1, however, since beyond that point incremental moves along the contract curve reduce the profits of firm 1 below those that it would make in Cournot equilibrium.

The problem of cheating in a cartel can also be illustrated in this framework. Suppose that the cartel has agreed to distribute profits at (π_2^2, π_1^1) at point E on the contract curve. We know from the shape of the reaction function that, provided firm 1 believes that firm 2 will keep its output constant at the agreed level, X_2^1, it can increase its profits by expanding output. Indeed, firm 1's profits are maximised if firm 2 sticks to X_2^1, when firm 1 moves to X_1^2 on its reaction function. Similarly, if firm 2 believes firm 1 will keep its output constant at X_1^1, it will maximise its own profits on its reaction function at X_2^2. Hence while the cartel maximises *joint* profits, each individual firm can hope to do better by cheating on the bargain, provided that their rival does not respond.

It is left to the readers themselves to derive the contract curve for the Bertrand and Stackelberg cases, and to illustrate the problem of cheating in these frameworks. We return to the issue of cheating from a game theoretic perspective in the next chapter.

* Conjectural variations

Algebra allows us to derive most of the results obtained in previous sections, and some important generalisations of them, a good deal more simply than diagrams. It also allows us to categorise the various models in a unified framework based on assumptions about the reactions of a firm to the behaviour of its rivals. Our attention in this section is devoted to the models in which behaviour is directly concerned with quantities rather than prices.

For most of our discussion so far, we have assumed that firms have identical cost functions and that the number of firms (n) is two, but the analysis can be readily generalised to cover many firms, each with different costs. In general terms, a typical firm in the industry, denoted i, maximises the profit function

$$\pi_i = p(X)X_i - C_i(X_i) \tag{16.20}$$

where

$$\sum_{i=1}^{n} X_i = X \tag{16.21}$$

Profit maximisation implies that

$$\frac{\partial \pi_i}{\partial X_i} = p + X_i \frac{\partial p}{\partial X} \frac{\partial X}{\partial X_i} - \frac{\partial C_i}{\partial X_i} = 0 \tag{16.22}$$

We assume that the second-order conditions are satisfied ($\partial^2 \pi_i / \partial X_i^2 < 0$ for every firm), and note that equation (16.22) is a version of the familiar marginal revenue equals marginal cost condition, with the complication that marginal revenue depends upon both the slope of the industry demand curve ($\partial p / \partial X$) and the adjustment of industry output to the firm's output level ($\partial X / \partial X_i$). It is by considering alternative specifications of expectations about this latter term, $\partial X / \partial X_i$, that we can classify oligopoly models.

To get an intuitive grasp of the approach we shall use, start with the simple two-firm case where

$$X = X_1 + X_2 \tag{16.23}$$

so

$$\frac{\partial X}{\partial X_1} = \frac{\partial X_1}{\partial X_1} + \frac{\partial X_2}{\partial X_1} = 1 + \frac{\partial X_2}{\partial X_1} \tag{16.24}$$

The adjustment of industry output to firm 1's output, $\partial X/\partial X_1$, can therefore be broken into two parts, $\partial X_1/\partial X_1$, which of course equals unity, and the response of X_2 to a change in $X_1(\partial X_2/\partial X_1)$. The same reasoning in the more general case (equation (16.21)) leads us to the equation

$$\frac{\partial X}{\partial X_i} = \frac{\partial X_i}{\partial X_i} + \frac{\partial X_j}{\partial X_i} = 1 + \lambda_i \tag{16.25}$$

where X_j refers to the sum of the output of all firms other than i. If there are only two firms, $X_j = X_2$ and $\lambda_i = \partial X_2/\partial X_i$.

In order to choose an output level from equation (16.22), each firm must evaluate $\partial X/\partial X_i$, which we now see involves making an estimate of, or a 'conjecture' about, the value of the term λ_i (or $\partial X_2/\partial X_1$ in the two-firm case). λ_i is therefore referred to as the **conjectural variation** term. This term captures a key property of the various models which we have discussed, and derives directly from the interdependence of firms in an oligopolistic market. If we divide equation (16.22) through by price and rearrange terms, we obtain

$$\frac{p - \partial C_i/\partial X_i}{p} = -\frac{X_i}{X} \frac{X}{p} \frac{\partial p}{\partial X}(1 + \lambda_i) = \frac{s_i(1 + \lambda_i)}{e} \tag{16.26}$$

where s_i is the share of firm i in industry output (X_i/X) and e is the price elasticity of demand ($-(p/X)/(\partial p/\partial X)$). The term on the left-hand side of the equation is the difference between price and marginal cost expressed as a ratio to price. It is often referred to as the *price–cost margin* and used as an indicator of monopoly power. Equation (16.26) therefore tells us that the proportional mark-up of price to marginal cost increases with a firm's market share and λ_i, and decreases with the (negative) elasticity of demand.

The conjectural variation term in equation (16.26) can be used to categorise outcomes in terms of various market structures. In order to set our frame of reference, let us start with the case of perfect competition, where the market price is given to each firm and demand equals supply at zero profit. If one firm considers reducing its level of output, it does so on the assumption that market price remains unchanged. This can only occur if the industry output remains unchanged, which implies that other firms will make up its output reduction exactly. The derivative $\partial X_j/\partial X_i$ therefore equals -1, and this is the value of conjectural variation term for every competitive firm. When $\lambda_i = -1$ for all firms, equation (16.26) reduces to

$$p - \partial C_i/\partial X_i = 0 \tag{16.27}$$

which is the familiar price equals marginal cost condition for firms in a competitive industry.

The Cournot model is based on the opposite to the competitive assumption that each firm believes that its rivals will *not* respond to its own quantity adjustments. Hence, in this case the conjectural variation is assumed to be zero for all firms. From equation (16.26), we can derive the price–cost margin in the Cournot case as

$$\frac{p - \partial C_i/\partial X_i}{p} = \frac{s_i}{e} \tag{16.28}$$

If we go on to assume that firms have the same cost curves ($C_1(X_1) = C_2(X_2) = \ldots = C_n(X_n)$), we know that firms will be of the same size because they each face an identical profit-maximising condition, equation (16.22). Hence if there are n firms in the industry, the market share of each is $1/n$ and (16.28) can be further simplified to

$$\frac{p - \partial C_i / \partial X_i}{p} = \frac{1}{ne} \tag{16.29}$$

From this formula we note the point asserted above, that the price–cost margin in the Cournot equilibrium declines as the number of firms increases. We can also establish formally from (16.29) that the outcome approximates the competitive equilibrium as n increases towards infinity.

In the case of collusion, each firm knows that its rivals will follow suit if it increases or decreases output by an amount sufficient to leave market shares constant. This implies that the rival will react by altering output exactly in proportion to the current ratio of their market shares. Hence if there are only two firms, $\partial X_2 / \partial X_1$ is simply the ratio of their current market shares, X_2 / X_1. More generally, in a collusive market

$$\lambda_i = \frac{1 - s_i}{s_i} \tag{16.30}$$

If we substitute this into equation (16.26), we find for identical firms that

$$\frac{p - \partial C_i / \partial X_i}{p} = \frac{1}{e} \tag{16.31}$$

which rearranges to the simple monopoly condition, marginal revenue equals marginal cost. Thus as we saw earlier collusive outcomes yield the monopoly output and price.

Finally, the Stackelberg model is characterised by the fact that the leader and the followers have different conjectural variations. The followers behave as do all firms in the Cournot model, and therefore the conjectural variation term for them is zero. The situation for the leader is more complicated because it builds its knowledge about the followers' reactions into its decision making. If we consider the two-firm case, firm 1 as leader knows that the follower, firm 2, will adjust output in response to its level of production according to the second firm's reaction function. The conjectural variation term for the leader is therefore given by the slope of firm 2's reaction function. This took the value of $-\frac{1}{2}$ in the worked example of the previous section (see equation (16.14) where $\partial X_2 / \partial X_1 = -\frac{1}{2}$) and, more generally, depends on the sum of each follower's reaction to the leader's output change.

Concluding comment

We have seen in this chapter that there is no single answer to what industry output and price will be when firms are interdependent. The possibilities range from the competitive outcome of a Cournot model with many firms or a Bertrand model with homogeneous products to the monopoly equilibrium characteristic of the cartel. The key factors influencing the nature of the equilibrium achieved are whether firms collude or compete; whether, if they compete, they do so over quantity or price; and whether they do so on equal terms or with one firm having an advantage that it can use to exercise leadership, or obtain a dominant status. In the following chapter we shall reinterpret many of these ideas in terms of the theory of games. In particular, we will show that the equilibria of non-collusive models such as that of Cournot or Bertrand are equivalent to the Nash equilibrium concept of game theory, thereby showing that these models have a firm and appealing intellectual basis. We shall also analyse the instability of the collusive equilibria as a feature of a game known as 'the prisoners' dilemma'.

SUMMARY

Oligopoly and strategic interaction

1. The Cournot model assumes that each firm takes the level of output of its rival as given in choosing its own. In equilibrium, the expectations of each firm about the output choice of its competitor are realised. Equilibrium occurs where the two firms' reaction curves intersect.

2. Even when there are only two firms, a duopoly, non-collusive behaviour such as that modelled by Cournot leads to higher consumer welfare but lower profits than collusive behaviour.

3. In the Bertrand model, firms compete as they do in the Cournot model but over price rather than quantity. When products are not differentiated, the Bertrand equilibrium is the same as would be attained under perfect competition.

4. In addition to behavioural assumptions about whether or not to collude, and whether over price or quantity, the order in which firms take decisions can influence equilibrium. An example of an oligopoly model in which the order of play matters is that of price leadership. Here a dominant firm sets price and the smaller 'competitive fringe' choose their own supply as price takers.

5. The leader–follower approach was applied to a Cournot framework by Stackelberg, who established that if one firm, the leader, understood the market well enough to anticipate the reactions of its rival, it could use this information to increase its profits. Equilibrium occurs here where the 'leader's' isoprofit curve is tangent to the 'follower's' reaction function.

6. The relationship between collusive and non-collusive equilibria can be analysed with the help of a device called the contract curve.

7. In the final starred section of this chapter it was established that, as the number of firms tends to infinity, the Cournot equilibrium tends to the competitive outcome.

PROBLEMS

1 There are two identical firms in an industry, 1 and 2, each with cost function $C_i = 10X_i$, $i = 1,2$. The industry demand curve is $P = 100 - 5X$ where industry output, X, is the sum of the two firms' outputs ($X_1 + X_2$).

(a) If each firm makes its output decisions on the assumption that the other will not react to its choices (the Cournot assumption), what is the equilibrium output for each firm? What is the equilibrium price?

(b) Suppose that each firm takes it in turn to choose its level of output, on the assumption that the other's output level is fixed. Would the process of adjustment be stable?

(c) Suppose that firm 1 introduces a cost-saving innovation, so that its cost curve becomes $C_1 = 8X_1$. Firm 2's cost curve and the industry demand curve are unchanged. What happens to the equilibrium quantity produced by each firm and to market price?

2 Suppose the two firms in question 1 are now playing a Stackelberg game, with firm 1 as leader and firm 2 as follower. What are the equilibrium levels of output and industry price? How does your answer change if firm 1 has the cost function given in 1(c)?

3 'Since we know that firms compete over price rather than quantity, the theory of oligopoly suggests that outcomes will approximate those of perfect competition, even when there are only a few suppliers in the industry.' Discuss.

CHAPTER 17

Game theory

Key words and phrases

- Non-co-operative and co-operative games, payoff matrix, strategies, dominant strategy
- dominant strategy equilibrium, Nash equilibrium, Cournot equilibrium, multiple equilibria
- the prisoners' dilemma, one-shot game, repeated game, finite and infinite repeated game, reputation, credibility, tit-for-tat
- sequential game, game tree, entry deterrence, predatory pricing, perfect equilibrium, sub-game
- pre-commitment
- pure and mixed strategies, battle of the sexes

Introduction

In this chapter, we offer a brief introduction to the theory of **games**; a framework of analysis devised to study the decisions of economic agents who are aware that their actions are interdependent. Game theory enables us to analyse the strategic interaction of economic agents, an important example of which is the interaction of firms in oligopoly situations. We saw in the previous two chapters that traditional oligopoly theory yields a variety of possible answers to questions about how firms choose output and price when there are only a few interdependent suppliers, but it does not offer much help when we ask which is the best model to use in any particular case. Game theory may offer a possible way out of this dilemma, as well as enriching our understanding of how firms interact when their decisions are interdependent.

Game theory is concerned with the strategic elements of economic agents' behaviour and the rewards or *payoffs* that they expect to obtain. It can be used to analyse any sort of interaction which involves playing to a strategy, from chess or card games to arms limitation negotiations. For simplicity, we confine ourselves to games in which there are only two decision makers, referred to as *players* (a *two-person game*) and where the returns to playing the game are not fixed in advance (a *non-constant sum* game). An important classification of games is between those in which the players cannot make binding agreements among themselves, termed **non-co-operative** games, and games in which they can, termed

co-operative games. As the reader might guess, this classification parallels the distinction between non-collusive and collusive models made in previous chapters. In this chapter we focus primarily on non-co-operative games, and spend more time on co-operative games in Chapter 20.

Dominant strategies

The first concept needed in order to grasp the essential features of game theory is that of a **payoff matrix**. Suppose two players, firms 1 and 2, play some game according to certain moves, or **strategies**, for example by choosing various levels of output or price. If we restrict our attention to output choices, we can consider the payoff matrix in Figure 17.1, where strategies A and B for each firm represent different output choices, given known demand and cost conditions, and the numbers in the boxes represent the payoffs, in this case profits, to each firm from following each strategy.

The payoffs in Figure 17.1 have been chosen so as to provide the game with an obvious solution. Payoffs to firm 1 precede payoffs to firm 2 in each box. Let us consider the choices of firm 2. If firm 1 plays strategy A, it will choose to play strategy A as well because its payoff is greater (500 > 300). Moreover, if firm 1 plays strategy B, firm 2 will still choose strategy A because its payoff is still greater (250 > 125). So firm 2 will always choose strategy A. Turning to firm 1, if firm 2 plays strategy A firm 1 will receive higher profits by playing strategy A as well (500 > 250). If firm 2 chooses strategy B firm 1 will also choose strategy A to maximise its payoffs. Hence both firms always choose strategy A, which is therefore termed the **dominant strategy**. A dominant strategy is a strategy which produces at least as high a payoff as any other strategy in response to any strategy played by the other player. If, as in this example, both players have dominant strategies then the equilibrium must be the state of affairs achieved when both play their dominant strategies. This is called the **dominant strategy equilibrium**, and is given by the strategies (A, A) and payoffs (500, 500) in Figure 17.1. It can be seen that given the payoffs in Figure 17.1, there is only one dominant strategy equilibrium; the equilibrium here is said to be *unique*. As we will see below, this is not necessarily always the case.

Payoffs need not take a form such that rival firms each have a single dominant strategy. For example, if we consider the payoff matrix set out in Figure 17.2, firm 1 chooses strategy C in response to firm 2's strategy C, but strategy D in response to strategy D. Firm 2, on the other hand, has a dominant strategy, always preferring strategy C (because if firm 1 chooses strategy C, C yields firm 2 350 > 300 and if firm 1 chooses strategy D, C yields firm 2 450 > 400). There is therefore no dominant strategy equilibrium with this pattern of payoffs; firm 1's decision is contingent on firm 2's choice of strategy.

Figure 17.1   Payoff matrix with dominant strategy

		Firm 2	
		Strategy A	Strategy B
Firm 1	Strategy A	500, 500	300, 300
	Strategy B	250, 250	125, 125

Figure 17.2 **Payoff matrix for Nash equilibrium**

		Firm 2	
		Strategy *C*	Strategy *D*
Firm 1	Strategy *C*	500, 500	350, 300
	Strategy *D*	300, 450	400, 400

Nash equilibrium

The American mathematician John Nash developed an equilibrium concept which is weaker than that of the dominant strategy to deal with cases of the sort just described. The strategies of the two players are said to yield a **Nash equilibrium** if each strategy chosen maximises payoffs given the other player's choice. In a Nash equilibrium, no player has incentives to change their strategy if no other players do.

It is easy to see that the pair of strategies (*C*, *C*) yield a Nash equilibrium for the payoff matrix in Figure 17.2. If firm 1 plays strategy *C*, firm 2 will choose strategy *C* (500 > 300). Similarly, if firm 2 plays strategy *C*, firm 1 will respond with *C* (500 > 300). Hence strategies (*C*, *C*) are mutually consistent given the choice of the other player, and are therefore a Nash equilibrium.

There are no other Nash equilibria in Figure 17.2. For example, consider the strategy pair (*D*, *D*). If firm 1 plays strategy *D*, firm 2 responds with strategy *C*. But we know that if firm 2 plays strategy *C*, firm 1 will also choose strategy *C* instead of confirming firm 2's expectations at *D*. Hence the strategy pair (*D*, *D*) is not a Nash equilibrium. We can think of a Nash equilibrium as involving expectations on the part of each player about strategies of the other with the characteristic that, once each rival has played its own choice, neither wishes to change its strategy because the expectations upon which its choice depended have been realised.

If we think of output strategies, a Nash equilibrium involves a pair of production levels for which each rival's expectation about the behaviour of the other is confirmed. When we characterise a Nash equilibrium for output strategies in this way, we immediately recognise that we have described the **Cournot equilibrium** discussed earlier. Recall that, in the Cournot duopoly model, firms choose output on the basis of expectations about their rival's production, and that equilibrium occurs where both sets of expectations are mutually consistent. The notion of the mutual consistency of optimal strategies, we have now seen, is also at the heart of the Nash equilibrium. The formal equivalence of these equilibrium concepts has led analysts in recent years to conflate them, referring to the equilibrium of the Cournot model as the Cournot–Nash equilibrium. This analysis also establishes that the Cournot equilibrium, contrary to the view formed from the rather naive behavioural interpretation of the classical oligopoly model, is firmly grounded as an optimal outcome of strategic interaction. Bertrand equilibria also satisfy the Nash equilibrium criterion.

The Nash equilibrium is not necessarily unique, however. Moreover it is easy to conceive of games whose payoffs take a form in which no Nash equilibrium exists. The existence

Figure 17.3　**Two Nash equilibria**

		Firm 2	
		Strategy *C*	Strategy *D*
Firm 1	Strategy *C*	350, 350	350, 300
	Strategy *D*	300, 450	400, 400

Figure 17.4　**A payoff matrix with no Nash equilibrium**

		Firm 2	
		Strategy *E*	Strategy *F*
Firm 1	Strategy *E*	350, 300	300, 350
	Strategy *F*	300, 350	350, 300

of more than one Nash equilibrium is illustrated in Figure 17.3. We note that, as before, the top left-hand element of the payoff matrix is a Nash equilibrium. If firm 1 plays *C*, firm 2 chooses *C*. But if firm 2 chooses *C*, it is optimal for firm 1 to choose *C* as well. But the pair of strategies (*D*, *D*) also constitute a Nash equilibrium. Suppose firm 1 plays strategy *D*. From Figure 17.3 it is clear that firm 2 will then choose strategy *D*. This choice is consistent with firm 1's choice of *D*, in that if firm 2 chooses *D*, *D* is also firm 1's optimal strategy. Hence the payoff matrix in Figure 17.3 has two Nash equilibria.

Now let us illustrate the possibility that a payoff matrix may have no Nash equilibrium at all. Consider the matrix illustrated in Figure 17.4, and let firm 1 choose strategy *E*. Firm 2 would then choose strategy *F*. If firm 2 chooses strategy *F*, however, firm 1 will now choose strategy *F* in preference to *E*. So there exists no Nash equilibrium in which firm 1 plays strategy *E*. What if firm 1 plays strategy *F*? Firm 2 will now choose strategy *E*, but given the choice of strategy *E* by firm 2, firm 1 will choose strategy *E*. Once again there exists no Nash equilibrium if firm 1 chooses strategy *F*. The same result would clearly apply if we started our analysis by considering the strategy selected by firm 2. Thus, though the Nash equilibrium concept weakens the requirements we must impose on the payoff matrix in order to achieve a dominant equilibrium, it still leaves open the possibilities of **multiple equilibria**, and the absence of any equilibrium. We consider ways to resolve these difficulties at the end of this chapter.

The prisoners' dilemma

We can use game theory to investigate questions about cheating in a cartel. The appropriate analytical framework here is a game known as **the prisoners' dilemma**, which was originally formulated with reference to the behaviour of two suspects being interviewed in separate rooms about their involvement in a major and a minor crime. Each is given the option of confessing and thereby implicating the other, or of refusing to confess. The two suspects are forbidden to communicate with each other. If both suspects stay silent, they will be convicted of the minor offence but without a confession there is not enough evidence to convict either of the major crime. If either talks while the other does not, the one who remains silent will get a long sentence for the major crime, and the one who talks a lighter one for 'good behaviour'. They both get a long sentence (although with some remission) if they both confess.

The game is called the prisoners' *dilemma* because, even though both suspects are better off (i.e. receive shorter jail sentences) if *neither* confesses, the incentives of the game are such that *both will confess*. This result arises from the fact that, if one looks at the suspects' individual strategies, each is separately better off to confess whether or not the other does likewise. The Nash equilibrium of this game (and in this case the dominant strategy) leads to an outcome – of both confessing – in which the welfare of the players could be increased if the players were allowed to communicate and collude. In that case they would agree to remain silent. Thus the Nash equilibrium does not necessary lead to the best possible outcome from the perspective of the players.

The general structure of the prisoners' dilemma game is applied to the case of a cartel in Figure 17.5. Suppose firms 1 and 2 have entered a cartel which yields monopoly profits of £1,200, which they divide equally. This payoff is entered in the bottom right-hand area of the payoff matrix. Now let each firm realise that, if its rival keeps its production constant, it can raise its own profit, say to £800, by expanding production and assume also that, if the rival stuck to the agreement and kept its production constant, it would then receive £200 in profits. Assume also, however, that if the rival responded by increasing production as well, the two firms would ultimately reach a Cournot–Nash equilibrium where profits to each are lower, at £300. This payoff is entered in the top left-hand area.

The game set out in Figure 17.5 has exactly the perverse properties that we previously described for the prisoners' dilemma. Industry profits are maximised when both firms stick to the cartel. However, each perceives itself as being potentially able to do better by cheating, provided that its rival does not respond. Indeed, cheating is the dominant strategy in this case. For example, firm 1 makes higher profits by cheating, whether firm 2 responds by cheating or not. The same is true for firm 2. This is because the rewards perceived to be available when both parties cheat are greater than those accruing to the firm which sticks to the cartel agreement when the other cheats. Mutual cheating is thus the dominant strategy, though of course both parties would be better off staying in the cartel. Our analysis of these sorts of pressures formalises and clarifies our earlier conclusions about the tendency for cartels to be unstable.

Figure 17.5 **The prisoners' dilemma**

		Firm 2	
		Cheat on cartel	Stick to cartel
Firm 1	Cheat on cartel	300, 300	800, 200
	Stick to cartel	200, 800	600, 600

Box 17.1   Oligopoly and the prisoners' dilemma

We can set out the Cournot oligopoly model used in Chapter 16 in an explicitly game theoretic framework. In Box 16.3 the following model was used. The inverse demand function for identical Cournot duopolists was

$$p = 100 - X_1 - X_2 \qquad (16.1.3)$$

With both having a constant marginal cost of 10 the Cournot reaction functions are

$$CRF_1: \quad X_1 = 45 - 0.5X_2 \qquad (16.3.9)$$

$$CRF_2: \quad X_2 = 45 - 0.5X_1 \qquad (16.3.10)$$

Equilibrium output was $X_1 = X_2 = 30$. Market price is therefore 40. With zero fixed costs, equilibrium profit was 900 for each firm.

The incentive for our Cournot duopolists to create a cartel and also cheat on a cartel can be outlined in the context of Illustration 17.1. If the two firms form a cartel we can analyse the resulting equilibrium as a pure monopolist. If firm 1 is a monopolist (i.e. if $X_2 = 0$), from CRF_1 the profit maximising output is 45. If firm 2 is a monopolist it will also have an output of 45. If the two firms form a cartel they will therefore share an output of 45. This is shown in Illustration 17.1 as the line connecting the two end points of the reaction functions. This line shows all the possible ways of sharing the output of 45. As the firms are identical they will divide the cartel output equally, i.e. produce 22.5 each. But with either firm producing 22.5 they both have an incentive to increase their outputs to maximise their individual profits. This individual profit maximisation is shown by the firm's reaction function. So, with firm 2 keeping to the agreement to produce 22.5, firm 1 maximises profit by producing 33.75, i.e. where $X_2 = 22.5$ intersects with CRF_1.

We can now calculate the prices and profits with these various outputs. With the cartel output of 45 (using the demand function) selling price is $p = 55$. So cartel profit, with zero fixed cost, is

$$\pi = p(X) - MC(X) = 2475 - 450 = 2025 \qquad (17.1.1)$$

Illustration 17.1

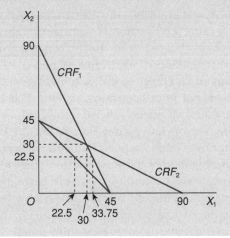

$\rightarrow$

As the two firms are identical, this cartel profit is divided equally, so $\pi_1 = \pi_2 = 1012.5$.

With firm 1 cheating on the cartel by maximising its individual profit, $X_1 = 33.75$ and $X_2 = 22.5$: industry output (X) is therefore 56.25. So selling price (p) is 43.75. The profits for the two firms are

$$\pi_1 = 43.75(33.75) - 10(33.75) = 1139.06 \tag{17.1.2}$$

$$\pi_2 = 43.75(22.5) - 10(22.5) = 984.375 - 225 = 759.38 \tag{17.1.3}$$

If firm 2 cheats, but firm 1 keeps to the cartel agreement, the profits of the two firms are reversed. It follows that a cheating firm is better off than with a cartel, and a non-cheating firm is worse off than with Cournot competition.

Bringing these profits together into a payoff matrix equivalent to Figure 17.5, we can produce Illustration 17.2. Inspection of this payoff matrix reveals that it is a prisoners' dilemma game with the dominant equilibrium that both firms cheat on the cartel. In a more general analysis, i.e. with generalised demand and cost functions, this link between standard oligopoly theory and the prisoners' dilemma game is maintained. The interested reader can prove this general result.

Illustration 17.2

		Firm 2	
		Cheat on cartel	Stick to cartel
Firm 1	Cheat on cartel	900, 900	1139.06, 759.38
	Stick to cartel	759.38, 1139.06	1012.5, 1012.5

Optimal cartel bargaining

In Box 17.1, and also while discussing oligopoly, we made the claim that identical firms will divide cartel profit equally. To substantiate this claim we can make a small detour into the area of co-operative game theory, which is a departure from the rest of this chapter, which concentrates on the principles of non-co-operative game theory. The key contribution in this area is known as the Nash bargaining solution, which is a general result about the efficiency of joint bargaining activity. This bargaining solution was developed by the same American mathematician, John Nash, who developed the equilibrium concept used in non-co-operative game theory. But the two ideas should not be confused. The Nash bargaining solution claims that optimal bargaining involves players co-operating to achieve the highest possible joint rewards. These highest possible rewards are then divided between the players according to relative bargaining power.

To develop this idea we will initially assume that a cartel is made up of two identical firms, i.e. the assumption made in Box 17.1. In this case we can reasonably assume that the two players have the same bargaining power. The Nash bargaining solution then says that the two firms in the cartel will maximise the product of the payoffs to the firms. In general terms we can formulate this as follows:

$$N^E = (\pi_1 + x)(\pi - \pi_1 + x) \tag{17.1}$$

N^E stands for the Nash formulation with equal bargaining power. The payoff to firm 1 is $(\pi_1 + x)$ and $(\pi - \pi_1 + x)$ is the payoff to firm 1. In this formulation x is the minimum payoff available to the two firms. In terms of oligopoly theory this is either the positive profits earned in a Cournot–Nash equilibrium or the zero profit earned in a Bertrand–Nash equilibrium. In either case x is the profit earned if there is no cartel. The element π is the *total extra* profit available to be shared between the firms if a cartel is formed. Of this total extra profit an amount π_1 is distributed to firm 1, and so an amount $(\pi - \pi_1)$ is distributed to firm 2. So the general formulation N^E in (17.1) is the product of the payoffs to the two firms from forming a cartel. The Nash bargaining solution says that π_1 should be chosen to maximise N^E. Hence we differentiate N^E with respect to π_1 and set the first derivative equal to zero:

$$\frac{dN^E}{d\pi_1} = \pi - 2\pi_1 = 0 \tag{17.2}$$

For those who find differentiating (17.1) difficult because of the brackets, it is straightforward to remove the brackets by multiplication and so derive (17.2). Using (17.2) it is clear that optimal bargaining with identical firms involves $\pi_1 = 0.5\pi$, i.e. firm 1 has half the extra profit from the cartel. This was the result we used in Box 17.1.

Now we can introduce a Nash bargaining model in which two firms with differing bargaining power form a cartel. It is reasonable to assume that if firms are identical they must have the same bargaining power. So this more complex analysis must be based on firms differing in some way, e.g. different efficiency levels and so different sizes. This possibility can be introduced into the model defined in formulation (17.1) by introducing different minimum firm payoffs (x_1 and x_2) rather than a single parameter x. In addition the relative bargaining power can be modeled using a single parameter μ. Hence we can define the product of the payoffs as formulation (17.3):

$$N^U = (\pi_1 + x_1)^\mu (\pi - \pi_1 + x_2) \tag{17.3}$$

where N^U refers to the Nash formulation with unequal bargaining power. Using (17.3) we can think of two particular cases:

1. Firm 1 has less bargaining power than firm 2: $\mu < 1$ and $x_1 < x_2$.
2. Firm 1 has more bargaining power than firm 2: $\mu > 1$ and $x_1 > x_2$.

As with the equal bargaining case we find the value of π_1 that maximises the joint payoff. Differentiating (17.3) with respect to π_1 and setting the first derivative equal to zero:

$$\frac{dN^U}{d\pi_1} = (\pi - \pi_1 + x_2)\mu(\pi_1 + x_1)^{\mu-1} - (\pi_1 + x_1)^\mu = 0 \tag{17.4}$$

Simplifying (17.4) we can suggest that with unequal bargaining the first firm's extra profit from forming a cartel is

$$\pi_1 = \frac{\mu}{1 + \mu}(\pi + x_2) - \frac{1}{1 + \mu}x_1 \tag{17.5}$$

To simplify analysis of (17.5) we can use the two special cases just identified of firm 1 having more or less bargaining power. In particular we can set parameters using the values of $\mu = 0.5$ and $\mu = 2$. In addition with $\mu = 0.5$ we assume $x_2 = 2x_1$ and with $\mu = 2$ we assume $2x_2 = x_1$.

$\mu = 0.5$: substituting in values implies $\pi_1 = (1/3)\pi$ and so $\pi_2 = (2/3)\pi$
$\mu = 2$: substituting in values implies $\pi_1 = (2/3)\pi$ and so $\pi_2 = (1/3)\pi$.

It is clear therefore that if we depart from the assumption of identical firms, optimal cartel bargaining involves an unequal distribution of cartel profits.

Repeated games

Once the instability of cartels has been formulated as a prisoners' dilemma game, it raises the question of whether there is any way to play the game in order to ensure a different, and perhaps more realistic, outcome. After all, firms do in practice sometimes solve the co-ordination problem involved in running a cartel, via either formal or informal agreements, while Figure 17.5 suggests that such an outcome cannot occur. There has been considerable analysis of this problem, and it has led to the realisation that the appropriateness of characterising cheating as the dominant strategy depends above all else on whether the game is played just once, or is played over and over again an infinite number of times.

The element of time is missing from the prisoners' dilemma game and so, therefore, is the idea that strategies chosen today can affect behaviour in the future. For example, in the original prisoners' dilemma, neither suspect has to consider the effect of making a confession on future relations with the other suspect. In the jargon of game theory, the prisoners' dilemma is a **one-shot game**. Suspects put in different interrogation rooms by the police might, in practice, behave differently from the manner indicated by our formulation of the game, not least because of fear on the part of each about the reaction of their former partner in crime when they have the opportunity to renew their acquaintance. To put it in terms of the framework of the game itself, our prisoners have to allow for the possibility that a confession made now may lead to punishment meted out by the other the next time the game is played: for example, by the other confessing in order to ensure the conviction of the other even when not to do so would otherwise be rational.

Many games can reasonably be thought of as being played over and over again by the same players. Such games are called **repeated games**. The fact of repetition broadens the strategies available to the players, because they can make their strategy in any current round contingent on the others' play in previous rounds. This introduction of the time dimension permits strategies which are damaging to be punished in future rounds of the game. It also permits players to choose particular strategies with the explicit purpose of establishing a *reputation*: for example, by continuing to co-operate with the other player even when short-term self-interest indicates that an agreement to do so should be breached.

However, one of the most important results yielded by game theory is that repetition in and of itself does not necessarily resolve the prisoners' dilemma. Take, for example, the case illustrated in Figure 17.5, in which cheating is the dominant strategy for both firms. Suppose now that each firm knows that, instead of joining the cartel only once, it will play the game a total of five times. Suppose also that each firm seeks to maximise the discounted sum of its profits over the five-game horizon. Collusion is still the joint profit-maximising outcome for the two players in each round and therefore across the five rounds together, but repetition for a predetermined finite number of plays does nothing to help them to achieve it. This is because, though each player actually plays forward in sequence from the first to the last round of the game, that player needs to consider the implications of each round up to and including the last, before making their first move. In game theory terminology this involves using backward induction, i.e. starting at the end of a game and working backwards through it.

In choosing its strategy using backward induction each firm starts by considering the final round of the game and then work backwards. Once we realise this, it is immediately clear that the fifth and final round of a repeated game would in fact be identical to a one-shot game and would lead to exactly the same outcome. Both firms would cheat on the cartel in the fifth round of our game. But, looking forward to this outcome at the start of the fourth round, each firm would find it profitable to cheat in that round as well. It would gain nothing from establishing a reputation for not cheating if it knew that both it and its opponent were bound to cheat next time. As we work back towards the first round of the game, the same argument applies at every step. The fact that both firms will cheat in the final round thus undermines any alternative strategy: for example, building a reputation for not cheating, as the basis for establishing the collusive outcome. In short, no strategy that involves not cheating will make sense at any stage in the game; cheating remains the dominant strategy for each player in each round.

The critical feature of the foregoing example is that the game is repeated for a fixed, finite number of times; it is a **finite repeated game**. The knowledge that the game will have a final round, and that the dominant strategy for both players in that round is to cheat, is the factor which undermines the prospects for attaining collusive outcomes in earlier rounds. The potential influence of a threat *not* to collude in future as a method of enforcing collusion in earlier rounds is negligible because both players can work out from the properties of the final round that neither would, in any event, choose to stick to the collusive agreement in that or any earlier round of the game. In an infinitely repeated game, however, there is no final round in which the players no longer have an incentive to maintain their reputations. In such a game, there is always a next time in which a rival's behaviour can be influenced by what happens this time, so solutions to the problems presented by the prisoners' dilemma are feasible.

Credibility and punishment in cartels

Now let us assume that there is no final round for the game. Suppose that the game is to be played for an infinite number of times. In such an **infinite repeated game**, it becomes feasible for one player to influence the behaviour of the other players through their own strategy.

In the context of the cartel problem, the repeated prisoners' dilemma game problem for the two firms is how to achieve co-operation – the joint profit maximum in each period – when both parties have an incentive to cheat on any agreement. In considering strategies to resolve this dilemma, the firms need to consider two issues – how can cheating be detected, and what punishment will deter it? Successful collusion, as we shall now show, depends on the balance between the gains available to a cheating firm relative to the costs which the other firm can impose on it as a punishment for cheating. These factors also arose in our discussion in the previous chapter, in which successful collusion was shown to be related to matters such as the number of firms in the industry, or the similarity of the underlying cost structures of the different suppliers.

The gains realised by cheating depend in part upon the length of time that elapses before the individualistic behaviour is discovered. The more firms there are in the market, the greater the gain to any one of them from cheating in each round of the game. Any single firm's own marginal revenue from cheating will be large relative to marginal cost since an increase in supply by one relatively small-scale producer will not greatly influence market price. Moreover, since price will not change greatly if one firm cheats, cheating would be hard to detect, and the culprit hard to identify. Detection is also more complicated when demand is highly variable between periods. In such circumstances, sales for a particular period may fall below a firm's agreed share of the cartel's production quota for either one of two reasons: because of insufficient demand or because some other firm is cheating. The difficulty in discriminating between these phenomena can encourage firms to cheat in such circumstances. Finally, the ability to detect cheating will be affected by the ease of checking on competitors' behaviour. Institutional arrangements can be set up to facilitate this by encouraging the parties to a cartel agreement to monitor each other's activities. In some sectors, industry chambers of commerce or trade groups might play such a role.

The second element in resolving the prisoners' dilemma is the formulation of a punishment strategy. In a two-firm case, for example, firm 1 has to inform firm 2 of how it will react if it detects cheating, so that firm 2 can take the cost of the punishment into account when it is considering whether or not to cheat. Such information could be transmitted by public announcement. For example, one sometimes encounters a pledge posted in some shops to refund the difference if a customer is able to purchase the same good at a lower price elsewhere. This can be interpreted as a public threat by the firm posting the pledge immediately to respond in full to any price cutting by a rival. Information might also be transmitted as a by-product of observed behaviour. Thus a firm might consistently react to cheating by a competitor by undercutting the competitor in question by the same amount by which it had itself been undercut. Once this response had been observed a number of times, the firm in question would have established a **reputation** for a rapid and aggressive response to cheating on the agreement. The latter possibility means that cartels can rely on informal mechanisms rather than written agreements to enforce their rules.

However, it is not always enough for a firm to announce a punishment strategy in order to influence the behaviour of rivals. The strategy that is announced must also be **credible**, in the sense that it must be understood to be in the firm's self-interest to carry out its threat at the time when it becomes necessary. For example, consider a two-firm cartel supported by an agreement between the firms to punish cheating by cutting price and increasing output so that the culprit is driven out of business. Suppose that firm 2 is a relatively smaller producer than firm 1, with higher costs. It is not clear that firm 2 would ever be in a position to carry out such a threat; at least, in order to do so, it would have to sustain greater losses for longer than would firm 1. Firm 1 would probably dismiss the announced punishment strategy as non-credible. In short, punishment strategies in and of themselves do not resolve the prisoners' dilemma in an infinite repeated game, unless they are seen by all parties to be credible.

This possible solution to the instability of cartel arrangements with an infinitely played prisoners' dilemma game is an example of what has come to be called the 'folk theorem' among game theorists. This theorem states that with a repeated prisoners' dilemma game co-operation can be the best response to another player's cooperation (an example of this is shown in Box 17.3 below). But while co-operation, i.e. cartel stability, is one Nash equilibrium in a repeated prisoners' dilemma game there are many other Nash equilibria. For example, in the game described in Figure 17.5, firm 1 might say that it will stick to the cartel on odd plays of the game but cheat on even plays. Given this announced strategy it can still be optimal for firm 2 to stick to cartel arrangements because any deviation from this co-operation by firm 2 will be punished by complete non-co-operation by firm 1. So the folk theorem says that co-operation in a repeated prisoners' dilemma game is possible but not inevitable.

Box 17.2 ## Most-favoured-customer clauses

In addition to repeat play and credible punishment, cartel stability can be promoted in other ways. These other strategies involve changing the payoffs in a one-shot prisoners' dilemma game. One such method involves the use of most-favoured-customer clauses. In terms of the payoff matrix set out earlier in Figure 17.5 we can view 'stick to cartel' as charging a 'high price' and 'cheat on the cartel' as charging a 'low price'. But now consider a promise, made by both firms, that if either firm sells in the future at a lower price than currently exists earlier customers that paid the higher price will get a refund of the price difference. This is not an example of corporate philanthropy or generosity, but is instead a way of changing the payoff structure of the one-shot game to promote cartel stability.

Using the example from Box 17.1 we can illustrate this impact of a most-favoured-customer clause. In outline the earlier example was:

cartel: $p = 55$, $X_1 = X_2 = 22.5$
firm 1 cheats on the cartel: $p = 43.75$, $X_1 = 33.75$.

With a most-favoured-customer clause the price difference of $55 - 43.75 = 11.25$ must be refunded on the 22.5 units of output sold at the higher price. This refund implies a loss in revenue of $11.25 \times 22.5 = 253.125$. The profit for the cheating firm therefore goes down by this much with the clause in place. The resulting payoff matrix is shown in Illustration 17.3. The original profit from cheating was 1139.06 in Box 17.1. Having to refund 253.125 reduces this profit to 885.94. With this lower profit the game is no longer a prisoners' dilemma and there are now two Nash equilibria. If both firms cheat this is stable and if both firms stick to the cartel this is stable. In short, a most-favoured-customer clause can promote cartel stability but this does not preclude a Cournot–Nash equilibrium. Which Nash equilibrium is likely to occur depends on, among other things, the expectations of the players. This is a matter addressed later in this chapter.

Illustration 17.3

		Firm 2	
		Cheat on cartel	Stick to cartel
Firm 1	Cheat on cartel	900, 900	885.94, 759.38
	Stick to cartel	759.38, 885.94	1012.5, 1012.5

Tit-for-tat

The foregoing discussion suggests that in order to develop stable co-operative cartels, participating firms need to select simple criteria that will establish whether cheating has occurred, and credible rules to guarantee that punishment will be meted out. Moreover, because it is possible that mistakes will be made in detecting cheating (if, for example, the effects of unexpected shifts in output demand are misinterpreted as the result of cheating), the severity of punishment should be kept to the minimum required to deter the act of cheating. Such a conclusion is also consistent with the need to ensure credibility.

The American political scientist Robert Axelrod used experimental methods to investigate punishment strategies. Consider an infinite repeated game between two firms in which the payoff matrix in each round takes the form represented in Figure 17.5 (p. 344). Each firm's strategy is as follows. In the first round, it chooses to co-operate rather than cheat, but in subsequent rounds it will only persist with this strategy provided that the other firm co-operated in the previous round. If the other firm cheated in that round, the first firm will cheat in the current round, even if cheating would not otherwise be its best strategy. Cheating by either firm in the previous round is therefore immediately punished by cheating, by the other, in this round. This strategy is referred to as **tit-for-tat**.

Tit-for-tat satisfies a number of criteria for successful punishment strategies. It carries a clear threat to both parties, because it is one of the simplest conceivable punishment strategies and is therefore easy to understand. It also has the characteristic that the mode of punishment it implies does not itself threaten to undermine the cartel agreement. This is because firms cheat only in reaction to cheating by others; they never initiate a cycle of cheating themselves. Nonetheless it is a tough strategy, in that cheating is never allowed to go unpunished. Perhaps most significantly, the tit-for-tat strategy offers speedy forgiveness for cheating, because once punishment has been administered the punishing firm is willing once again to restore co-operation. Hence firms which play tit-for-tat do not bear grudges.

For all these reasons, tit-for-tat can represent an effective strategic solution to the prisoners' dilemma if the game is infinitely repeated. It does, however, have one significant weakness. If information is imperfect so that it is hard to detect whether a particular outcome is the consequence of unexpected external events such as lower demand than forecast, or cheating, tit-for-tat has the capacity to set up a chain reaction of negative responses to an initial mistake.

Box 17.3 Tit-for-tat in the Cournot model of oligopoly

We can illustrate the logic of tit-for-tat decision making using the prisoners' dilemma game, based on the Cournot model, used in Box 17.1. Let's assume, for the moment, that the discount rate for future payoffs is 10 per cent and that both firms use a tit-for-tat logic. In this case if both firms stick to the cartel the payoff can be written as

$$V_{cartel} = \frac{1012.5}{1.1} + \frac{1012.5}{(1.1)^2} + \frac{1012.5}{(1.1)^3} + \ldots \tag{17.3.1}$$

If one firm decides to cheat on the cartel it will obtain a one-period higher payoff but following this will not be trusted by the other firm. As both firms are using tit-for-tat this implies that following the one-period higher payoff both firms will cheat, i.e. compete against each other. The payoff to the cheating firm can in this case be written as

$$V_{cheat} = \frac{1139.06}{1.1} + \frac{900}{(1.1)^2} + \frac{900}{(1.1)^3} + \ldots \tag{17.3.2}$$

It is easy to confirm that after two plays of the game V_{cheat} is greater than V_{cartel}, but after three plays V_{cartel} is greater than V_{cheat}, i.e. it requires minimal repeat playing to generate stable cooperation with a tit-for-tat strategy.

This analysis of tit-for-tat can be generalised for any discount rate (r). In which case, using the same one-shot payoff values:

$$V_{cartel} = \frac{1012.5}{1 + r} + \frac{1012.5}{(1 + r)^2} + \frac{1012.5}{(1 + r)^3} \ldots \tag{17.3.3}$$

We can solve this infinite series in the standard manner. Multiplying both sides of (17.3.3) by $(1 + r)$:

$$V_{cartel}(1 + r) = 1012.5 + \frac{1012.5}{1 + r} + \frac{1012.5}{(1 + r)^2} + \ldots \tag{17.3.4}$$

Subtracting (17.3.4) from (17.3.3) allows us to cancel the infinite series:

$$V_{cartel} - V_{cartel}(1 + r) = \frac{1012.5}{1 + r} + \frac{1012.5}{(1 + r)^2} + \frac{1012.5}{(1 + r)^3} + \ldots$$

$$-1012.5 - \frac{1012.5}{1 + r} + \frac{1012.5}{(1 + r)^2} - \ldots$$

Hence

$$V_{cartel} = \frac{1012.5}{r} \tag{17.3.5}$$

Using the same logic with V_{cheat}:

$$V_{cheat} = \frac{1139.06}{r} - \frac{239.06}{(1 + r)r} \tag{17.3.6}$$

So a cartel will be stable, if both players play tit-for-tat, when $V_{cartel} > V_{cheat}$, i.e.

$$\frac{1012.5}{r} > \frac{1139.06}{r} - \frac{239.06}{(1 + r)r} \tag{17.3.7}$$

This implies $(1 + r) < 1.89$. So in the Cournot oligopoly example used here the discount rate can be very high, i.e. at least 89 per cent, before cartels become unviable.

Sequential games

The prisoners' dilemma is a game in which both players make their moves simultaneously. If we consider our original two prisoners, the essence of the game is that neither knows what the other has chosen before having to make their own move. The police, it will be recalled, used two interrogation rooms rather than one. The same simultaneity of decision making applied to the cartel version of the game represented in Figure 17.5. In practice, many games are actually played in sequence, with one player's move following that of the other. As we saw in the previous chapter, oligopoly theory also allows for a sequence of moves, with, for example, the equilibrium outcome for a particular firm in the Stackelberg equilibrium depending on the order of play. The price leadership model also relied upon a sequencing of decisions, with the dominant firm setting price and the competitive fringe then determining their level of output. In this section we extend our discussion of game theory to the analysis of **sequential games**. The framework is then applied in the following section to questions of entry and entry deterrence.

We saw that simultaneous decision making in a game could be represented with reference to a payoff matrix. However, we need a more complicated diagram to represent alternative choices in a game with several rounds, in which the action taken by one player in this round depends on the action taken by the other player in the previous round. A simple

Figure 17.6   **Dominant strategy payoffs in game tree form**

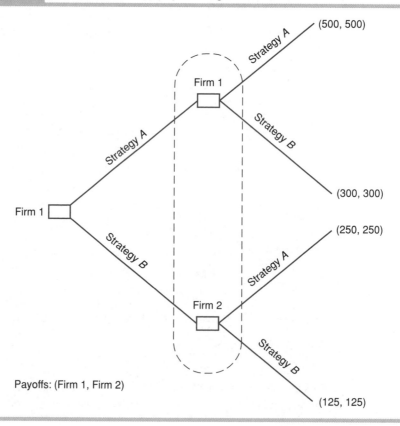

Payoffs: (Firm 1, Firm 2)

representation is a **game tree**, which represents the alternative strategies and payoffs for each player in each round as a tree whose complexity increases with the passage of time. For example, the payoff matrix of Figure 17.1 could instead be represented by the game tree in Figure 17.6. The small boxes, referred to as decision nodes, represent points at which a choice or decision has to be made. In this framework, a strategy encompasses the sequence of actions that each player plans to take at every decision node. Strategies and actions are the same if each player has only one decision node. Figure 17.1 described a game in which both firms made their moves simultaneously, and the dotted line around the two decision nodes in Figure 17.6 is drawn because firm 2 cannot distinguish between them at the time when it makes its own decision. If the game had been sequential, so that firm 1 chose between strategy *A* and *B* and then firm 2 made its choice, the dotted line would have been omitted.

Entry deterrence and predatory pricing

In earlier chapters we analysed the key role played by entry in keeping down prices and preventing the exploitation of monopoly power. We also noted in Chapter 13 that free entry was a critical element in leading the model of monopolistic competition to produce industry-wide excess capacity. In these models, however, entry was a transparent issue because we assumed that it was costless for firms to enter and, we might have added, to leave a profitable market. Once we recognise that there may be costs of entry or exit, however, it becomes necessary to analyse the way in which firms choosing to enter a market take account of both set-up costs and the financial consequences of failure. In this section, we shall use the framework of sequential games to analyse the problem faced by a potential entrant who must decide whether or not to enter a market which is currently monopolistic. The result, as we shall see, will depend in part on the likely response of the current supplier – the incumbent firm – to the threat of entry.

Our earlier discussions of game theory have highlighted the importance of the information available to the players. We shall commence as before with the assumption that our two firms – the *incumbent* and the *potential entrant* – are fully informed about the payoffs available under different strategies. The question of imperfect information and the analysis of situations where one player knows more than another will be taken up in Chapter 25. The traditional approach to the question of **entry deterrence** was outlined by Sylos-Labini, who argued that entrants would make their decision on the assumption that the incumbent would not alter its level of production as a consequence of entry. Readers will note the analogy between this *Sylos-Labini postulate* and the Cournot assumption that, in duopoly, each firm takes the other's output as given. This postulate implies that incumbent firms can set their own output level in order to influence the choices of potential entrants. Attention is here focused on finding the so-called *limit output* and *limit price*, the values of those variables which will just deter potential entry.

There is a problem with this approach, however. It has incumbents deliberately forgoing profits now, by holding down their price to ward off the threat of entry which, if their strategy is successful, will never materialise. However, suppose that a potential entrant sees through this strategy, and decides to enter anyway. Our previous discussion of the prisoners' dilemma suggests that, post-entry, the two firms now in the market will ultimately find a way to collude and to share industry profits. Hence the potential entrant will perceive that the incumbent's limit price does not in fact give a credible signal about how the incumbent will behave after its entry into the market. This leads to a general insight, to the effect that monopolists cannot always effectively threaten price wars against entrants to secure their position, because potential entrants are able to calculate that such a response by an incumbent in the event of entry might hurt the incumbent more than would agreeing to collude with the entrant.

These verbal arguments can be formalised in terms of the game tree of Figure 17.7. The entrant firm can choose to enter or to stay out of the market. The incumbent can choose to collude with the entrant post-entry, or to compete with the entrant. We assume in Figure 17.7 that monopoly profits are 500, and that entry costs the entrant 50. If there is entry and the two firms collude, we assume that they agree to split the profits equally. If the incumbent competes post-entry, we assume that both firms can only break even. Hence if the incumbent does choose to compete, the entrant makes a loss if entry is costly.

This game has two Nash equilibria, at (200, 250) where there is entry and at (0, 500) where there is not. Consider first what transpires if the potential entrant decides to stay out. In that case the incumbent does not in practice have to choose between collusion and competition, though we do need to identify a box in order to test the Nash equilibrium; the appropriate one in this case is competition. This choice confirms that a decision to stay out is a characteristic of an equilibrium, because if the incumbent is indeed going to compete, the entrant will choose to stay out. This equilibrium rests on a threat of competition by the incumbent which is never in fact put to the test. The second Nash equilibrium is achieved when the entrant does in fact enter the market. In this situation, the incumbent will in fact choose to collude (250 > 0). This is a Nash equilibrium because, if the incumbent is going to collude, the entrant will always choose to enter (200 > 0).

Though, formally speaking, there are two Nash equilibria in this game, in practice we are very unlikely to observe the one in which the potential entrant is scared off by the

Figure 17.7 **A sequential game of entry deterrence**

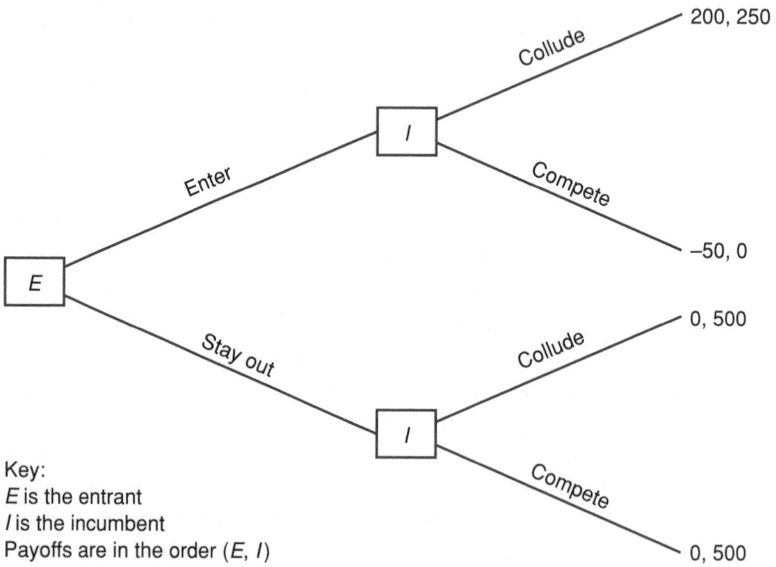

Key:
E is the entrant
I is the incumbent
Payoffs are in the order (*E*, *I*)

incumbent's threat to compete. As we suggested above, the entrant can work out that the incumbent will never actually act competitively if entry takes place. Once it has, it is nearly as much in the incumbent's interest as the entrant's to reach a collusive accord. Hence the threat to compete is not *credible* in this game, and we will actually reach the (entry-collusion) equilibrium. This process of ruling out Nash equilibria which are not credible is referred to as determining the game's **perfect equilibrium**. In the vocabulary of game theory, an equilibrium is perfect if the strategies which characterise it are in equilibrium not only in the game as a whole (as with our two Nash equilibria for the entry deterrence game) but also in each **sub-game** of the game. In Figure 17.7, there are two sub-games, with the second beginning with boxes marked *I*. Collusion dominates competition in this sub-game, and implies that the alternative Nash equilibrium in which the incumbent competes and the entrant stays out is not a perfect equilibrium.

Credibility and commitment

The problem for the incumbent firm in the foregoing analysis is that it cannot credibly pre-commit to competing with the entrant once entry has taken place. Output or price strategies pre-entry appear to have no effect on the entrant's evaluation of post-entry profits. There is here an implicit, though perhaps reasonable, assumption that output or price is easily varied, so the incumbent just cannot convince an entrant that they will not be altered if circumstances change. However, there may well exist some instruments other than price which the incumbent cannot alter so easily post-entry, and whose current setting can have the effect of deterring the entrant. The incumbent, that is to say, may find ways to **pre-commit** itself to actions which will damage the gains to entry. This implies finding a way of altering the payoffs irreversibly so that the entrant will perceive that it will indeed be in the interest of the incumbent to carry out its threat to cut prices if entry does take place.

For example, the incumbent might construct a large new factory in which the marginal costs were low, so that, with this additional capacity, it could continue to make considerable profits post-entry without colluding. Such a move would increase the return to the strategy of competing after entry in Figure 17.7. In this case the threat of competition would become credible in the second sub-game, and successful deterrence would become the perfect equilibrium for the same. This conclusion has the intriguing corollary that if the incumbent actually builds the new factory, it will never be required to use it because the entrant will never enter. Extra capacity will have been developed solely to ensure that the incumbent's threat of competition is credible.

Mixed strategies

Up to now in this chapter we have viewed strategies as involving a player choosing a single specific action. In the earlier cartel analysis a firm chooses to stick to the cartel OR to cheat on the cartel. This choice of single strategy was sometimes viewed in a complex manner, as for example when backward induction is used. But this complex decision was still based on choosing the best single strategy. In game theory terminology this single strategy approach is known as the analysis of **pure strategies**. The resulting equilibria we have analysed up to now should, strictly speaking, be called *pure strategy Nash equilibria*. This pure strategy approach to game theory can yield powerful results, the core of which have been examined up to now in this chapter. But pure strategies can have difficulties in two circumstances: when a game has more than one pure strategy Nash equilibrium, and when a game has no pure strategy Nash equilibrium. The first of these possibilities was indicated above when considering most-favoured-customer clauses (see Box 17.2). These clauses change the payoffs in a prisoners' dilemma game to generate a non-prisoners' dilemma context in which two pure strategy Nash equilibria exist. In this situation cartel stability is possible but not inevitable.

A slightly different approach to choosing a strategy can help when there exist multiple pure strategy Nash equilibria or when no such equilibrium exists. This different approach is based on the use of **mixed strategies**. A mixed strategy is based on not choosing a specific action but on being able to choose among different actions. For example, in the earlier prisoners' dilemma analysis of cartels a firm might choose to support the cartel 50 per cent of the time and break the cartel agreement 50 per cent of the time. This implies that with mixed strategies we can assign probabilities to a particular set of actions. When this is done any equilibrium that results is called a *mixed strategy Nash equilibrium*.

Consider the game set out in Figure 17.8. For reasons that will become apparent shortly this is called a '**battle of the sexes**' game. In a non-economic context, players one and two are usually viewed as a couple that want to spend time together. Options 1 and 2 are two ways of going out together, e.g. a film and a sporting event. If players one and two do different things there is a zero payoff. If they do something together there is a positive payoff. But player one prefers option 1 and player two prefers option 2. So both doing option 1 together generates payoffs of 2 and 1 for, respectively, players one and two, whereas option 2 generates payoffs of 1 and 2. In this game there are two pure strategy Nash equilibria: option 1/option 1 and option 2/option 2. To this extent the battle of the sexes game is similar to the most-favoured customer game considered earlier in the chapter.

This game has a possible economic application to the choice of technologies under some circumstances, specifically in situations where it is in the players' interests to choose the same rather than incompatible technologies. Two real world examples of this arise with respect to computer operating systems and (somewhat obsolete now) video technology. Thus, and ignoring the open source Linux system, two main computer operating systems, Apple and Microsoft Windows, are currently available commercially, with Windows having an overwhelmingly dominant position in the market. When a person buys a computer, an important issue is the availablity of software compatible with that

Figure 17.8   **Battle of the sexes game**

		Player two	
		Option 1	Option 2
Player one	Option 1	2, 1	0, 0
	Option 2	0, 0	1, 2

being used by others, and in a two-person context, if both choose the same system, there is no chance of this need not being met, because software writers will simply respond to their joint need. This is called a network effect in economics. Similar network effects were evident with video technologies, which is why VHS came to dominate the market rather than Betamax. In a simple game theory context this presence of network effects and problems of incompatible technologies can produce a battle of the sexes game.

Using the payoffs in Figure 17.8 consider the possibility that there is a 75 per cent chance that each player chooses option 1 and therefore a 25 per cent chance of choosing option 2. The *expected* payoffs are then:

Player one, going across the rows of the payoff matrix

Option 1: $0.75 \times 2 + 0.25 \times 0 = 1.5$
Option 2: $0.75 \times 0 + 0.25 \times 1 = 0.25$

Player two, going down the columns of the payoff matrix

Option 1: $0.75 \times 1 + 0.25 \times 0 = 0.75$
Option 2: $0.75 \times 0 + 0.25 \times 2 = 0.5$

In short, player one has a higher expected return from option 1 ($1.5 > 0.25$) and player two also a higher expected return from option 1 ($0.75 > 0.5$). So, given the choice probabilities we can conclude that option 1 is the mixed strategy Nash equilibrium.

This analysis can be easily generalised. Define:

p_1 = the probability that player one chooses option 1,
$1 - p_1$ = the probability that player one chooses option 2,
p_2 = the probability that player two chooses option 1,
$1 - p_2$ = the probability that player two chooses option 2.

Using the payoff structure in Figure 17.8, we can specify the following expected payoffs:

Player one

Option 1: $p_2 \times 2 + (1 - p_2) \times 0 = 2p_2$
Option 2: $p_2 \times 0 + (1 - p_2) \times 1 = 1 - p_2$

Player two

Option 1: $p_1 \times 1 + (1 - p_1) \times 0 = p_1$
Option 2: $p_1 \times 0 + (1 - p_1) \times 2 = 2 - 2p_1$

We can draw the following conclusions:

Option 1 is chosen, i.e. is the mixed strategy Nash equilibrium when

$2p_2 > 1 - p_2$ i.e. $p_2 > 1/3$
and $p_1 > 2 - 2p_1$ i.e. $p_1 > 2/3$

Option 2 is the mixed strategy Nash equilibrium when

$2p_2 < 1 - p_2$ i.e. $p_2 < 1/3$
and $p_1 < 2 - 2p_1$ i.e. $p_1 < 2/3$

Using this more general analysis it is clear why the earlier example that assumed each player had the probability 0.75 of choosing strategy one produced option 1 as an equilibrium. This probability is above the required threshold. But this is not the end of the mixed strategy story, even at a simple level, because a mixed strategy equilibrium may not always exist. If $p_2 > 1/3$ and $p_1 < 2/3$ or $p_2 < 1/3$ and $p_1 > 2/3$ incompatible choices will be made. In the earlier economic example different technologies will be chosen and in the domestic version of the battle of the sexes an argument might ensue.

Also there is one further possibility, namely that $p_2 = 1/3$ and $p_1 = 2/3$. In this case there is no stable equilibrium. Instead the game's outcome will vary over time as players use those probabilities to make random choices about which strategy to play in any instance. Such behaviour may nevertheless have a meaningful and quite reasonable interpretation. For example, in the domestic version of the battle of the sexes game it means that in the *long-run* option 1 is chosen by person one two-thirds of the time and by person two one-third of the time. In other circumstances, however, involving for example a single purchase of a particular technology, the only interpretation would be that the choice in question was made randomly, which does not say a lot about human perception and understanding.

The possibly random nature of decision making poses one more question, for many readers may find it hard to accept a literal interpretation of such behaviour, in which, for example a person seems to be deciding what do in any particular instance by, as it were, simply tossing a coin or rolling dice. It is hard, on the face of it, to find much plausibility in such an interpretation of behaviour. But there is an alternative way of thinking about the use of probabilities to randomise behaviour that makes more intuitive sense: thus, where actions taken by one player are used by others as indicators of that player's beliefs or expectations, it may be to that player's strategic advantage to resort to random behaviour in order to make their actions less predictable. Interpretations of mixed strategy analysis along these lines are often quite appealing.

Concluding comment

As a framework for analysing strategic interactions among interdependent economic agents the theory of games has a large number of potential applications in economics, a few of which have been examined in this chapter. Game theory of course adds nothing to our understanding of situations when there are no strategic interactions among economic agents, as, for example, in competitive or monopolistic markets. It comes into its own in situations where there are only a few economic agents, whose decision making is inherently interdependent. An obvious and fruitful field of application is therefore oligopoly theory, and we have found in this chapter that many of the insights of Chapter 16 have been capable of clarification, refinement and extension with the aid of game theory. We have also been able to give traditional oligopoly analysis, set out in Chapter 16, firmer theoretical foundations by showing the equivalence that exists between the concepts of Cournot or Bertrand equilibrium used there, and the Nash concept of equilibrium that arises in the theory of games. Similarly we have shown that the prisoners' dilemma game provides a framework that enables us to think clearly about the long-standing conjecture that cartels tend to be unstable.

We conclude by drawing attention to a distinction which must be observed when deducing policy conclusions from oligopoly models. Our analysis of oligopoly in the previous chapter involved us in making frequent references back to issues of consumer welfare. Thus the cartel outcome was seen to be monopolistic, with an associated deadweight loss, and the collapse of a cartel was viewed as beneficial from the point of view of consumers. In this chapter, we have looked at the outcomes of games only from the perspective of the participants in those games. We saw, for example, that the prisoners' dilemma posed a threat to collusion, and we investigated strategies whereby firms could restore and enforce their cartel. When we moved on to entry deterrence, we addressed the question of how incumbent firms might successfully retain their monopoly power in the face of the threat of entry. It is appropriate to end this chapter with an explicit reminder that once we leave the world of perfect competition, we lose the identity of interest between consumers and producers. So the benefits to firms in oligopoly that arise from finding strategies to enforce collusive behaviour might well be at the expense of consumers.

SUMMARY

Game theory

1. Game theory models strategic interaction among economic agents. This chapter focuses on games in which players cannot make binding agreements among themselves – non-co-operative games.

2. Players choose strategies that give different payoffs depending on the strategies played by their rivals. The relationship between strategies played and payoffs is summarised in a payoff matrix.

3. There are numerous possible equilibria for games. If players can find mutually consistent strategies that yield at least as high a payoff as any other, we have a dominant strategy equilibrium.

4. Players might instead be in a position where they have no incentive to change their strategy given the strategy of the other players. This is known as the Nash equilibrium concept. It is formally equivalent to the equilibrium concept of the Cournot and Bertrand models.

5. The instability of a cartel can be modelled as a prisoners' dilemma game. The payoff matrix has a structure which ensures that cheating is a dominant strategy for both players.

6. Cheating continues to dominate in a repeated prisoners' dilemma game with a finite horizon because the knowledge that both players will necessarily cheat in the final round prevents the emergence of collusive outcomes in earlier rounds.

7. In an infinite repeated game, firms can achieve the co-operative outcome in a prisoners' dilemma, provided they use strategies which punish cheating. An important example is the tit-for-tat strategy.

8. Sequential games allow players to make their moves in order. They can be used to analyse questions of entry deterrence and predatory pricing. We find that incumbents will not keep prices down now to prevent future entry when in practice it will not be profitable for them to compete rather than collude with their new rivals once these have entered. Hence predatory pricing is not a credible strategy in such circumstances.

9. Such sequential games may have several Nash equilibria. A perfect equilibrium is one in which its strategies are credible at each stage of the game.

10. Predatory pricing may become rational if the incumbent can make a credible threat to cut prices post-entry. One way to establish credibility would be to increase capacity so that the incumbent could continue to make profits while competing with a newly entered rival.

11. A useful way to analyse games with multiple equilibria is to adopt a mixed strategy framework.

PROBLEMS

1 The prisoners' dilemma game offers insights into the incentives to cheat of agents who will not be placed in the same situation again, such as two criminals whom we can presume will not again be partners in crime. These insights carry over to the case where two suppliers are operating temporarily in a particular market, and have formed a cartel in order to maximise their short-term joint profits. Discuss the ways in which the argument will have to be modified if the two parties to the cartel know that they will be facing each other on the same market for many periods to come.

2 'The common characteristic of the Cournot model is that it assumes a common pattern of reaction by competitors in each period which, despite the fact that the expected reaction does not in fact materialise, is never altered. This assumption that firms never learn from their past experience is excessively naive.' Discuss with reference to the distinction between Cournot behaviour and the Cournot equilibrium, and in the light of the insights that game theory yields about the character of the Cournot equilibrium.

3 Cournot duopolists face the inverse demand function $p = 200 - 0.5X$, where p is selling price and X is the total output of both firms. Long-run marginal costs are a constant 50 for both firms.

   (a) Along the lines suggested in Box 17.1 construct the payoff matrix if the two firms 'stick to a cartel' and 'cheat on a cartel'. Confirm that the payoffs involved define a prisoners' dilemma game.

   (b) If both firms adopt a tit-for-tat strategy, what is the maximum discount rate that is consistent with cartel stability? (Hint: use Box 17.3.)

4 The following payoff matrix defines a 'hawk–dove' game. It is commonly used in biology to analyse the behaviour of two species that can be either aggressive or non-aggressive in food acquisition. In economics the same payoff structure can apply to a situation of aggressive or non-aggressive negotiation.

		Player 2	
		Hawk	Dove
Player 1	Hawk	−1, −1	2, 0
	Dove	0, 2	1, 1

   (a) Identify the pure strategy Nash equilibria in this game. (Hint: there are two.)

   (b) Identify the mixed strategy Nash equilibria and the critical probabilities that define the stable equilibria.

PART **VI**

FACTOR MARKETS

CHAPTER 18

Factor demand

Key words and phrases

- physical product, revenue product, factor outlay (or cost) curve, value of marginal product, marginal revenue product
- substitutability between factors, elasticity of factor demand
- factor payments, Euler theorem,
- monopsony, marginal factor cost
- discriminating monopsony, elasticity of labour supply, overtime payments

Introduction

In previous chapters, we used revenue and cost functions to analyse the way in which profit-maximising firms choose the price and quantity of their output. As we saw in Chapter 10, implicit in these output market choices are decisions about the demand for factor inputs. In this chapter we analyse the input (or factor) demand problem, allowing changes in output as well as the choice of technique (or choice of factor proportions) to influence factor demands when input prices vary. Input demand curves of this sort may be termed *profit-maximising* factor demand curves. Let it be clear that we are not here analysing new or different decisions taken by the firm. We are looking at exactly the same decisions with which we dealt earlier when analysing the output market, but from a different perspective; from the point of view of the market for the inputs used by the firm. We start by analysing input demand on the assumption that product markets are perfectly competitive. We go on to consider the consequences for factor markets of product and factor market imperfections; monopoly and monopsony.

Physical products and revenue products

It is convenient to begin where we began before, with the two-input production function (Figure 18.1), but this time with the aim of deriving the demand curve for a factor of production rather than with the aim of deriving cost functions and from them a supply curve for output. The relationship between price and quantity is not uniquely defined

Figure 18.1

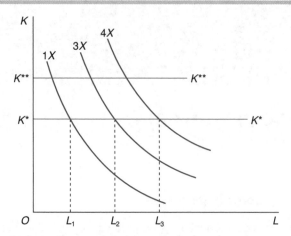

A production function displaying first increasing then decreasing returns to scale and two short-run paths along which output can be expanded holding capital fixed – K^*K^* and $K^{**}K^{**}$.

merely by the term 'demand curve'. We must specify what other things there are that we are holding constant before we can be precise in this respect. We will concern ourselves initially with deriving the demand curve for labour of a perfectly competitive firm *in the short run*: that is to say when the amount of capital services in the production process is given and when the price of output is given. Thus, we are concerned with what happens to the price that the firm is willing to pay for labour as it moves along a path such as K^*K^* in Figure 18.1.

The first step in the analysis involves investigating what happens to the 'physical productivity' of labour as its quantity is varied: the marginal product of labour, $\partial X/\partial L$. If the short-run production function is assumed to display increasing, then constant, then diminishing returns *to a factor*, as in Figure 18.2(a), the average (physical) and marginal

Figure 18.2

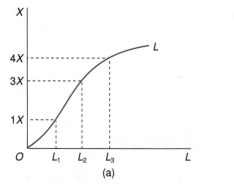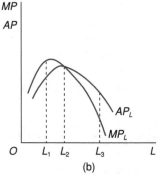

(a) The short-run production function implied by Figure 18.1.

(b) The average and marginal (physical) product of labour curves (AP_L and MP_L) implicit in panel (a).

(physical) product curves will take the shapes illustrated in Figure 18.2(b). As we noted in Chapter 9, these short-run average and marginal (physical) product curves are exact (inverse) analogues of the short-run average and marginal cost curves. Thus L_2, the employment level at which the average product is at its maximum in Figure 18.2(b), generates an output level of $3X$ in Figure 18.2(a), which is the level of output, given output prices, at which short-run average costs are minimised, for example X_2 in Figure 9.12.

We assume that the firm is concerned not with physical productivity for its own sake, but rather with the profits it can make from its productive activities. It is therefore the *revenue* that a factor generates, rather than the physical output it creates, which is ultimately of interest. Our productivity measures therefore have to be changed from physical to value terms. **Physical products** must be transformed into **revenue products**. This is done in Figure 18.3, where we multiply units of output, X, by the price, p, which is a constant since we are considering a perfectly competitive firm. Given that the level of capital inputs, and hence cash outlay on capital inputs, is constant, profits will be maximised if total revenue minus total outlay on labour is maximised. If we assume a constant price for labour, total outlay on that output is proportional to the quantity of it employed, and we may draw a straight line *total* **factor outlay (or cost) curve** in Figure 18.3.

Profits are then maximised where the *slope* of the total factor cost curve is equal to the *slope* of the total revenue curve, that is, where marginal revenue product is equal to marginal factor cost. In this case, constancy of the price of X means that we may also refer to the marginal revenue product of labour as the **value of the marginal product** of labour.

Now readers will no doubt have been struck by the similarity between this analysis and that by which the short-run supply curve of the individual firm was derived in Chapter 11. What we have been doing here is to look at exactly the same set of conditions which we

Figure 18.3

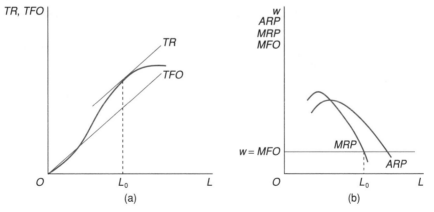

(a) Profits are maximised where the vertical distance between the total revenue (*TR*) and total outlay on the factor (*TFO*) is maximised, that is, at the level of employment L_0 where their slopes are equal.

(b) An alternative portrayal of the profit-maximising level of employment. Here the marginal revenue product of labour (*MRP*) is equal to marginal outlay on labour (*MFO*). Since the wage rate is given at w, *MFO* is constant and equal to w.

discussed there from a different point of view. We said in Chapter 11 that profits would be maximised where marginal cost was set equal to marginal revenue. Short-run marginal cost of production is given by the extra outlay on labour per unit of output necessary to produce a small addition to output. As we saw, it therefore equals the marginal outlay on labour per unit of labour divided by the marginal product of labour; or, to put the same point in other words, short-run marginal cost is the additional cost of employing an extra unit of labour divided by the amount that that unit will add to output.

The point can be made much more simply with algebra. Using our previous notation, the condition that price equals marginal cost for the competitive firm can be written as

$$p = MC \equiv \frac{w}{\partial X/\partial L} \tag{18.1}$$

But we have just shown that, when looking at the factor market, profit maximisation requires that marginal factor outlay, the wage in a competitive labour market, must equal the **marginal revenue product** of labour, i.e.

$$w = p\frac{\partial X}{\partial L} \tag{18.2}$$

Obviously (18.2) is equivalent to (18.1), and can be derived from it by multiplying both sides of (18.1) by $\partial X/\partial L$.

Factor demand in the short run

If the perfectly competitive firm will always set its employment of the variable factor at a point where its marginal revenue product equals the price of that factor, then this curve becomes the firm's short-run demand curve for the factor. This is a mirror image of the proposition that the firm's short-run supply curve of output is its short-run marginal cost curve. The firm's shut-down condition, namely, that the firm will not produce at all if the product price is less than average cost, also has a corollary for the demand for labour curve: the firm will not hire a factor if its average revenue product is less than the price of the factor divided by the product price. Note also that, for the equality of marginal factor outlay and marginal revenue product to be consistent with profit maximisation, the latter curve must cut the former from above. Thus, the firm will always be operating at a level of output where returns to labour are diminishing. This point was made earlier in Chapter 11, during our discussion of the firm's short-run supply decision.

The *industry's* short-run demand curve for labour will not just be the sum of the firm's demand curves. When analysing the individual firm, it makes sense to hold the price of output constant, but when we consider the whole industry expanding its labour input, and hence its output of X, we must remember that this will affect the price of X. This price will fall as output expands so long as the demand curve for X does not shift. Hence, the *industry's* demand curve for labour in the short run will be more steeply sloped than the sum of the *firm's* marginal revenue product curves. The latter slopes downwards only because the marginal productivity of labour diminishes. The industry's demand curve slopes more steeply because, in addition, the price of X falls as the industry's output increases. Figure 18.4 illustrates this.

Figure 18.4   **A short-run industry demand curve for labour**

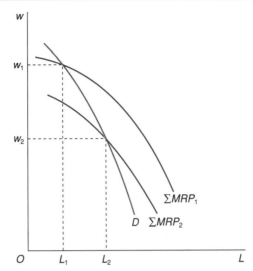

It is more steeply sloped than the sum over all firms in the industry of their marginal revenue product curves at a constant output price because, as employment and hence output increases, the price of output falls. Thus, when the wage rate falls from w_1 to w_2, the summed marginal revenue product curve shifts down from ΣMRP_1 to ΣMRP_2 and employment increases from L_1 to L_2. The industry's demand curve for labour is given by D.

Box 18.1   **Industry factor demand in a competitive market: a simple example**

We can apply the logic set out in Figure 18.4 using a simple example. Consider a competitive industry with an inverse market demand function

$$p = 100 - X \tag{18.1.1}$$

where p is selling price and X is total demand. The aggregate short-run production function for all the firms in the industry is

$$X = 10L - 0.01L^2 \tag{18.1.2}$$

where L is labour input. Note that this is short-run because output is determined by labour alone; other inputs are fixed, and their effects are incorporated in the coefficient values (10 and 0.01). Given this aggregate industry production function, marginal product is

$$MP_L = \frac{dX}{dL} = 10 - 0.02L \tag{18.1.3}$$

It is clear that there is diminishing marginal productivity in (18.1.3) as MP_L is declining in L. The aggregate marginal revenue product is

$$MRP_L = PMP_L = 10p - 0.02Lp \tag{18.1.4}$$

Assume that the industry is initially in equilibrium with a selling price of 30.49 and hence demand of 69.51. With a wage rate of 300.631, setting $w = MRP_L$, labour demand is 7, and with this industry labour force output is 69.51. Now assume that the wage rate falls to 203.098; the response is for firms to maximise profit by setting $w = MRP_L$ i.e. firms will increase employment. The extra employment results in an expansion of industry output and hence a fall in selling price. The fall in selling price reduces MRP_L for each level of employment and so reduces the demand for labour. The firm and industry adjustment process continues until the fall in selling price is consistent with the labour demand decision. The details of this adjustment process will depend on, among other things, the extent to which firms anticipate the fall in market price. The new equilibrium involves $L = 8$, and hence $X = 79.36$, and from the demand function $P = 20.64$. With this new market price the aggregate marginal revenue product is

$$MRP_L = 206.4 - 0.4128L \qquad (18.1.5)$$

Setting $w = MRP_L$ results in industry employment of 8.

Illustration 18.1

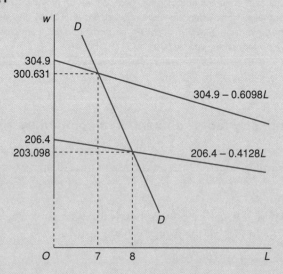

The shift in equilibrium is shown in Illustration 18.1. The two aggregate MRP_L curves are defined along with the assumed wage rates and industry labour demands. The resulting short-run industry demand curve for labour is shown as D. To define this labour demand curve we specify MRP_L as above:

$$MRP_L = 10p - 0.02Lp \qquad (18.1.4)$$

Use the inverse demand curve (18.1.1) to remove p to create a function D that shows how MRP_L shifts at each industry output, and hence market price:

$$D = 10(100 - X) - 0.02L(100 - X) \qquad (18.1.6)$$

Using formulation (18.1.6) we transform industry output into industry labour demand using the aggregate production function:

$$D = 10[100 - (10L - 0.01L^2)] - 0.02L[100 - (10L - 0.01L^2)]$$

Multiplying out the brackets and simplifying:

$$D = 1000 - 102L + 0.3L^2 - 0.0002L^3 \qquad (18.1.7)$$

This final expression is our short-run industry labour demand function. Although it is cubic, over the relevant range involving positive values of D it is effectively linear, as shown in Illustration 18.2, which plots D for values of L up to 10. Hence the simplified diagram shown as Illustration 18.1 has D as a straight line.

Illustration 18.2

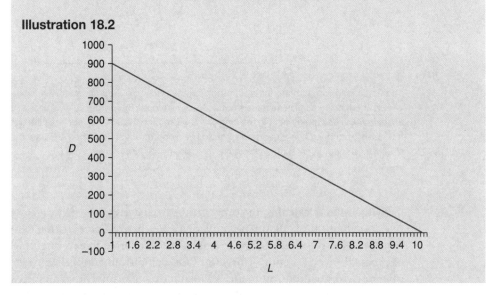

* The firm's factor demand in the long run

The interesting question remains of how the demand for a particular factor changes in the long run, when both inputs can vary simultaneously. A higher level of the capital stock, say K^{**} in Figure 18.1, may involve, at any given level of labour input, a higher total, average and marginal physical productivity for labour. If it does, then as a consequence, in the long run the firm's demand for labour will be more elastic than it is in the short run, provided that output price is held constant.

As we have seen, a fall in the price of labour involves more labour being employed by the firm, even if capital cannot be varied: costs of production unambiguously fall and at a given price output expands. However, as we saw in Chapter 8, an increase in the employment of labour is usually assumed to *raise* the physical productivity of capital. In other words, the derivative of the marginal product of capital with respect to labour is positive, i.e.

$$\frac{\partial^2 X}{\partial K \partial L} > 0 \qquad (18.3)$$

Figure 18.5

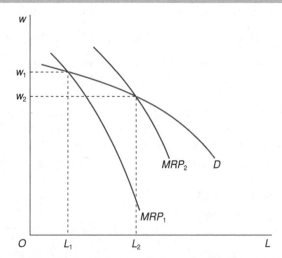

The firm's long-run demand for labour, holding the price of output constant. An increase in employment of labour following a fall in its price from w_1 to w_2 increases the productivity of capital and hence leads to an increase in its employment in the long run, thus shifting the MRP of labour to the right. The firm's long-run demand curve, D, is a compound of a shift along and a shift of the MRP curve and hence is more shallowly sloped, generating a change in the demand for labour from L_1 to L_2.

By the rules of calculus, the other cross partial derivative $(\partial^2 X/\partial L \partial K)$ must also be positive and identical to (18.3). The converse case, when the cross partial derivatives are both negative, is also conceivable in principle, and is referred to as a case in which the factors of production are 'inferior'. This latter case is empirically unlikely, however, for if we had inferior factors of production, this would, for example, imply that an increase in the capital stock *reduces* the marginal product of labour. We henceforth rule out this analytic curiosity by assumption. A fall in the price of labour, with the output price given, therefore leads to an increase in the marginal revenue product of capital.

With a given supply price for capital services, employment of capital will increase in the long run, and the short-run marginal revenue product curve of labour will shift to the right. The long-run demand curve for labour, then, is the result of movements along and shifts in the same direction of the short-run curve, and hence is more shallowly sloped. This is illustrated in Figure 18.5.

Industry demand for labour

The analysis of the industry's long-run demand for labour is less clear-cut than that of the firm because we must drop the assumption that output price is given. Two considerations now affect the marginal revenue product of capital services when the quantity of labour employed varies, and these operate in opposite directions. Increased labour input increases capital's *physical productivity*, but expanding industry output lowers the price of output and hence drives its *productivity in revenue terms* downwards. The net effect of these two

Figure 18.6

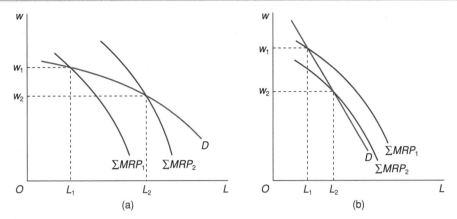

(a)   (b)

D is the industry's long-run demand curve for labour. (a) *D* will slope more shallowly than *ΣMRP* if, when the wage rate falls from w_1 to w_2, the consequent expansion of employment and output and the fall in output price on balance increase the revenue productivity of a given stock of capital. More capital inputs will be used, *ΣMRP* of labour will shift to the right and employment will increase from L_1 to L_2. (b) *D* will slope more steeply than *ΣMRP* if a fall in the wage rate from w_1 to w_2 produces responses that lead to a fall in the revenue productivity of a given stock of capital. In this case, a cut in capital input shifts *ΣMRP* of labour to the left, though employment still increases from L_1 to L_2.

tendencies may go either way. We may end up with more capital employed and hence have a long-run industry demand curve for labour that, though more steeply sloped than the simple summation of firms' demand curves, is nevertheless more shallowly sloped than the short-run industry demand curve. On the other hand, it is possible for the demand for capital actually to fall, and for the long-run demand curve for labour to be less elastic than the short-run curve. Figure 18.6 illustrates both cases.

The effect of a fall in the price of labour on the demand for capital depends on the relative importance of two offsetting tendencies. First, there is a tendency for labour to be substituted for capital and hence for the demand for capital to decrease, but second, there is a tendency for output to increase and the demand for capital to increase. If the first tendency dominates, the amount of capital used will fall in the long run, the physical productivity of labour at any scale of input will diminish, and the industry's long-run demand for labour will be less elastic than the short-run curve along which the level of capital utilisation is held constant. Such a situation will be associated with a degree of **substitutability between factors** that is high relative to the **elasticity of demand** for output. Cases where the long-run demand curve for labour is more elastic than the short-run curve will occur where substitutability between factors is relatively low and the elasticity of demand for output is relatively high.

Influences on the elasticity of factor demand

As we saw in Chapter 8, substitutability has to do with the extent to which the ratio in which capital and labour will be used changes in the long run when the ratio of their prices changes. A higher degree of substitutability involves a greater change in the capital–labour ratio for a given change in the price ratio of inputs. In terms of isoquants, the flatter they are – the less convex towards the origin – the greater is the degree of substitutability between factors. The concept of substitutability is important because the extent to which factors are substitutes for one another has a great deal to do with determining the degree to which the long-run industry demand for a particular input is sensitive to its own price.

It should be immediately obvious that, other things being equal, the greater the degree of substitutability between factors of production, the more elastic will be the demand for a particular factor. However, as we have seen, the long-run response of the demand for a particular factor – let us take the case of labour – to a change in its price does not consist solely of a substitution of labour for capital at a given level of output. A fall in wages leads to a fall in marginal production costs and hence to a fall in output price and an increase in the volume of output. Clearly, the larger the increase in output as a result of a given fall in the wage rate, the greater will be the resulting change in the demand for labour for a given degree of substitutability between labour and capital. There are two steps between a change in the wage rate and a change in output. The first step is a fall in output price, and the larger is that part of production costs made up of payments to labour, the larger will be the fall in output price as a result of a given fall in the wage rate. The second step is the response of the demand for output to a change in its price, and the more elastic the demand for output the greater will this response be.

Thus, for a given price of other inputs, the greater the degree of substitutability between labour and these other inputs, the greater is the proportion of production costs made up of wages, and the more elastic the demand for the final output, the more elastic will be the demand for labour. However, there is no reason to treat the price of other inputs as necessarily remaining constant. If a fall in the price of labour causes the demand for other inputs to increase in the long run, then the less effect this increase in demand has on the prices of other inputs, the smaller will be the extent to which the effect of a fall in wages on output price will be offset by price increases of other inputs. If the fall in wages leads to a fall in demand for the other factor, then the smaller the effect this has on their prices the less tendency is there for substitution towards labour as a result of the initial fall in wages to be offset. In short, to the three influences on the elasticity of demand for labour already derived, we must add a fourth, namely, the elasticity of supply of other factors. The higher this is, holding other influences constant, the higher will be the elasticity of demand for labour.

Factor payments, the value of output and the Euler theorem

Lying behind the various demand curves for labour whose properties we have been considering in this chapter is the marginal productivity of labour. We could, of course, just as easily have concerned ourselves with the demand for capital, for from a formal point of view the two pieces of analysis are absolutely identical. This observation leads us into a problem area that at one time much concerned economists and even now is worth some brief discussion. Consider again the firm in the long run. Suppose that in terms of Figure 18.7 the firm is in long-run equilibrium employing L_1 units of labour services at a wage rate of w_1. Implicit in the assumption that the firm is in long-run equilibrium is the

Figure 18.7

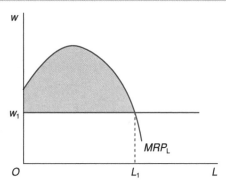

The marginal revenue product of labour. The wage bill is given by $w_1 L_1$, leaving the shaded area available for payments to capital. If factor payments exhaust the value of output, this area should equal $r_1 K_1$ in Figure 18.9.

proposition that a certain flow of capital services is also being utilised, the marginal revenue product of which is also equal to the price of capital services. In terms of a production function diagram, the firm is at a position such as A in Figure 18.8 where the marginal rate of substitution between factors is equal to the ratio of their prices.

Associated with the employment of capital services at a rate K_1 is a marginal revenue product curve for labour that passes through the long-run demand curve at $L_1 w_1$ and is derived by moving along the line $K_1 - K_1$ in Figure 18.8. Now, the area under this marginal revenue product curve between the vertical axis and L_1 measures the total revenue accruing to the firm at its equilibrium output level. (If output at L_1 is X_1, then the area under the marginal revenue product of labour curve is the integral from zero to L_1 of $p\partial X/\partial L$, which equals revenue at X_1, pX_1.) Since payments to labour amount to $w_1 L_1$, it is clear that an amount equal to the shaded area in Figure 18.7 is left over to make payments to capital. (The return to the factor that is fixed in the short run is often called a *quasi-rent*

Figure 18.8

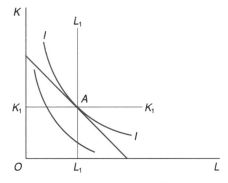

The firm in long-run equilibrium at point A, with employment of labour at L_1 and of capital at K_1. The ratio of factor prices is given by the slope of the isocost line and equals the ratio of the marginal productivities of the inputs given by the slope of the isoquant at point A.

Figure 18.9

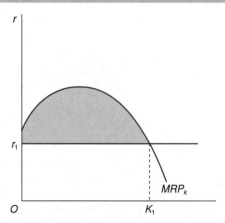

The marginal revenue product of capital, where r is the rental price of capital, outlay on capital is $r_1 K_1$, leaving the shaded area available to meet the wage bill. If factor payments exhaust revenue, this area should be equal to $w_1 L_1$ in Figure 18.7.

for reasons that we shall go into below.) An exactly parallel argument may be developed in terms of the demand for capital services. Variations in the marginal revenue product of capital as one moves along a line such as L_1–L_1 in Figure 18.8 may be plotted in a diagram exactly similar to Figure 18.7. Figure 18.9 is such a diagram; here the area $r_1 K_1$ represents payments to capital and the shaded area then becomes what is left over to meet the wage bill. Now we may put an interesting question: are the alternative measures of wage payments and capital payments depicted in Figures 18.7 and 18.9 consistent with one another? Do **factor payments** exhaust the value of output?

This is a question which bothered economists for many years. It seemed to boil down to a technical question about what kind of production function had the properties which would, in general, ensure that the sum of the marginal revenue product of each factor of production multiplied by the quantity of that factor being utilised, when added up over factors, would just turn out equal to the value of output. To put it in symbols for the two-input case, under what circumstances will it be the case for a competitive firm engaged in producing X that

$$pX = p\frac{\partial X}{\partial K}K + p\frac{\partial X}{\partial L}L \tag{18.4}$$

or, dividing through by output price,

$$K\frac{\partial X}{\partial K} + L\frac{\partial X}{\partial L} = X \tag{18.5}$$

If we ask what are the mathematical properties of a production function that will guarantee that the above equality always holds, the answer given by the so-called **Euler theorem** turns out to be a production function which is *homogeneous of degree one*. Among its other properties such a function everywhere displays constant returns to scale – as we mentioned in Chapter 8.

If we were forced to require that the production function take on the rather restrictive mathematical characteristic of homogeneity of degree one before payments to factors add up to the value of output, we might regard a theory of the demand for factors of production based on perfectly competitive profit-maximising behaviour with a certain amount of scepticism. However, notice that the question 'do factor payments exhaust the value of output?' is the same question as 'do total costs equal total revenue?' When the question is put this way it becomes apparent that it does not concern only the production function but also the way in which firms behave. Suppose that the area under the marginal revenue product curve of labour is less than total expenditure on factors of production at that scale of output. The firm of which this was true would leave the industry since it would be making long-run losses. Firms would continue to leave the industry until such long-run losses had been eliminated. Similarly, if the area under the marginal revenue product curve of labour were to exceed total factor payments as measured by their prices times the quantity of them employed, then this would imply the existence of positive profits, price would be above long-run average cost, and firms would enter the industry until these profits were eliminated.

So long as each firm has the same production function, then profit-maximising behaviour ensures that each firm will achieve just that level of output at which factor payments do indeed exhaust revenue. That is to say, each firm will produce at zero profits at the minimum point of its long-run average cost curve, but that is precisely a point at which cost per unit of output is neither rising nor falling, a point at which returns to scale may be said to be constant.

In an industry in which different firms are of different levels of efficiency this will be true only of the marginal firm, of course. All others will be earning positive profits, and factor payments will not exhaust their revenues. There is no need to elaborate further on all this. We have already been through the analysis in some detail in Chapter 11. The important point to notice here is that whether or not factor payments exhaust the revenue of a perfectly competitive firm is a question that must be answered with reference to market behaviour and not just to the technical nature of the production function.

Box 18.2

The so-called 'adding up' problem

We can illustrate the so-called 'adding up' problem in a fairly straightforward manner. Assume we have a firm with a production function that exhibits constant returns to scale. Using a simple Cobb-Douglas formulation the production function takes the form

$$X = 10L^{0.8}K^{0.2} \tag{18.2.1}$$

The production function in (18.2.1) is homogeneous of degree one as $0.8 + 0.2 = 1$. The marginal products for the firm are

$$\frac{\partial X}{\partial L} = 8L^{-0.2}K^{0.2} \tag{18.2.2}$$

$$\frac{\partial X}{\partial K} = 2L^{0.8}K^{-0.8} \tag{18.2.3}$$

→

Using formulation (18.2.2):

$$MP_L = \frac{8L^{0.8}K^{0.2}}{L} = 0.8\frac{X}{L}$$

Using formulation (18.2.3):

$$MP_K = \frac{2L^{0.8}K^{0.2}}{K} = 0.8\frac{X}{K}$$

It follows that the marginal revenue products are

$$MRP_L = p.MP_L = 0.8\frac{pX}{L} \tag{18.2.4}$$

and $\quad MRP_K = p.MP_K = 0.2\frac{pX}{K} \tag{18.2.5}$

In general terms we can specify the firm's total costs as labour costs plus capital costs:

$$TC = wL + rK \tag{18.2.6}$$

In competitive conditions we know that a firm maximises profit by setting $w = MRP_L$ and $r = MRP_K$. The firm's total costs function is then

$$TC = (MRP_L)L + (MRP_K)K \tag{18.2.7}$$

Using the specifications for the marginal revenue products in (18.2.4) and (18.2.5) we can therefore write the total cost function as

$$TC = \left(0.8\frac{pX}{L}\right)L + \left(0.2\frac{pX}{K}\right)K$$

i.e. $\quad TC = 0.8pX + 0.2pX = pX \tag{18.2.8}$

As pX is the firm's total revenue we can conclude that with our Cobb-Douglas production function, which is homogeneous of degree one, total cost is equal to total revenue in competitive conditions, i.e. our firm makes zero profit. In short we have the so-called 'adding up' problem in which total factor outlays are equal to the value of the output produced. It is left to the interested reader to work through the logic presented here with a Cobb-Douglas production function that is not homogeneous of degree one, i.e. that exhibits increasing or decreasing returns, and show that profits will not be zero.

* The firm's factor demand in the long run – a formal analysis

At several points in previous chapters (see for example Chapter 10), we have referred to the solution of an enterprise's general maximisation problem, in which the firm chooses the level of production and the factors to be employed on the basis of output and input prices and its knowledge of production technology. In this section we provide an algebraic representation of this problem and its solution, analogous to our previous uses of constrained optimisation to describe utility maximisation.

The firm seeks to maximise

$$\pi = pX - rK - wL \tag{18.6}$$

subject to the production function

$$X = f(L, K) \tag{18.7}$$

We can therefore form the Lagrangian

$$H_3 = pX - rK - wL + \lambda_3(f(L, K) - X) \tag{18.8}$$

with first-order conditions

$$\frac{\partial H_3}{\partial L} = -w + \lambda_3\frac{\partial X}{\partial L} = 0 \tag{18.9}$$

$$\frac{\partial H_3}{\partial K} = -r + \lambda_3\frac{\partial X}{\partial K} = 0 \tag{18.10}$$

$$\frac{\partial H_3}{\partial X} = p - \lambda_3 = 0 \tag{18.11}$$

$$\frac{\partial H_3}{\partial \lambda_3} = f(L, K) - X = 0 \tag{18.12}$$

From equation (18.11) we note that the Lagrange multiplier λ_3 is in fact equal to the output price. Substituting into (18.9) and (18.10) yields the conditions discussed less formally earlier:

$$p\frac{\partial X}{\partial L} = w \tag{18.13}$$

$$p\frac{\partial X}{\partial K} = r \tag{18.14}$$

Equation (18.13) is of course the same as (18.2), and with (18.14) states that profit-maximising competitive firms will hire inputs until the marginal revenue product of that input equals its price.

Finally, it should be noted that equations (18.9), (18.10) and (18.11) imply

$$p = \lambda_3 = \frac{r}{\partial X/\partial K} = \frac{w}{\partial X/\partial L} \tag{18.15}$$

This equation states that the marginal cost of producing output, by using either more labour or more capital, should be equal to the price of output if profits are to be maximised.

Equations (18.13) and (18.14) are implicit factor demand functions. We can make these functions explicit if we consider the special case of the Cobb-Douglas production function. Rather than re-solve the whole problem with $X = AL^\alpha K^\beta$ replacing $X = f(L, K)$ as equation (18.7), we can instead simply substitute the partial derivatives with respect to labour and capital into the first-order conditions (18.13) and (18.14). Since we know from Chapter 8 that $\partial X/\partial L = \alpha X/L$ and $\partial X/\partial K = \beta X/K$ if the production function is Cobb-Douglas, these two equations can be rewritten

$$p\frac{\alpha X}{L} = w$$

and

$$p\frac{\beta X}{K} = r$$

which yield

$$L = p\frac{\alpha X}{w} \tag{18.16}$$

$$K = p\frac{\beta X}{r} \tag{18.17}$$

the labour and capital input demand equations. It can be seen by inspection that, with this specification of technology, the demand for both factors *increases* with output and with output price, but *declines* with the price of the input. Previous chapters have stressed the first two relationships but here we shall concentrate on the third. Hence, denoting optimal values with a star, we can deduce that

$$\frac{\partial L^*}{\partial w}, \frac{\partial K^*}{\partial r} < 0 \tag{18.18}$$

i.e. that factor demands fall with their prices, holding output price and the volume of output constant. As we established previously, this point generalises to any production technology, provided only that the marginal physical product of the input diminishes as the input increases.

We now offer a formal analysis of how the firm adjusts inputs in response to a change in their price – the comparative statics of factor demand. Consider the two first-order conditions

$$p\frac{\partial X}{\partial L} - w = 0 \tag{18.13'}$$

$$p\frac{\partial X}{\partial K} - r = 0 \tag{18.14'}$$

If we take a total differential of these two equations, allowing both capital and labour to vary, we derive

$$\frac{\partial X}{\partial L}dp + p\frac{\partial^2 X}{\partial L^2}dL + p\frac{\partial^2 X}{\partial L\partial K}dK - dw = 0 \tag{18.19}$$

$$\frac{\partial X}{\partial K}dp + p\frac{\partial^2 X}{\partial K\partial L}dL + p\frac{\partial^2 X}{\partial K^2}dK - dr = 0 \tag{18.20}$$

From (18.20)

$$dK = \frac{dr - \dfrac{\partial X}{\partial K}dp - p\dfrac{\partial^2 X}{\partial K\partial L}dL}{p\partial^2 X/\partial K^2}$$

Substituting for dK in (18.19):

$$\frac{\partial X}{\partial L}dp + p\frac{\partial^2 X}{\partial L^2}dL - dw + \frac{\partial^2 X}{\partial L \partial K}\frac{\partial K^2}{\partial^2 X}dr - \frac{\partial^2 X}{\partial L \partial K}\frac{\partial K^2}{\partial^2 X}\frac{\partial X}{\partial K}dp - p\frac{\partial^2 X}{\partial L \partial K}p\frac{\partial^2 X}{\partial L \partial K}\frac{\partial K^2}{p\partial^2 X}dL = 0$$

yields

$$dp\left(\frac{\partial X}{\partial L} - \frac{\partial^2 X}{\partial L \partial K}\frac{\partial K^2}{\partial^2 X}\frac{\partial X}{\partial K}\right) - dw + \left(\frac{\partial^2 X}{\partial L \partial K}\frac{\partial K^2}{\partial^2 X}\right)dr + dL\left(p\frac{\partial^2 X}{\partial L^2} - p\left(\frac{\partial^2 X}{\partial L \partial K}\right)^2\frac{\partial K^2}{p\partial^2 X}\right) = 0$$

Multiplying through by $p\partial^2 X/\partial K^2$ yields

$$p\frac{\partial^2 X}{\partial K^2}\left(\frac{\partial X}{\partial L} - \frac{\partial^2 X}{\partial L \partial K}\frac{\partial K^2}{\partial^2 X}\frac{\partial X}{\partial K}\right)dp - p\frac{\partial^2 X}{\partial K^2}dw + p\frac{\partial^2 X}{\partial L \partial K}dr$$

$$+ \left(p^2\frac{\partial^2 X}{\partial L^2}\frac{\partial^2 X}{\partial K^2} - p^2\left(\frac{\partial^2 X}{\partial L \partial K}\right)^2\right)dL = 0$$

(18.18)

If we first consider the effect of an increase in wages on employment in the long run, on the assumption that prices and capital costs remain constant, i.e. $dp = dr = 0$, (18.18) simplifies to

$$p\frac{\partial^2 X}{\partial K^2}dw - \left(p^2\frac{\partial^2 X}{\partial L^2}\frac{\partial^2 X}{\partial K^2} - p^2\left(\frac{\partial^2 X}{\partial L \partial K}\right)^2\right)dL = 0$$

so that

$$\frac{dL}{dw} = p\frac{\partial^2 X/\partial K^2}{D}$$

(18.22)

where

$$D = \left(p^2\frac{\partial^2 X}{\partial L^2}\frac{\partial^2 X}{\partial K^2} - p^2\left(\frac{\partial^2 X}{\partial L \partial K}\right)^2\right)$$

Equation (18.22), describing the behaviour of the competitive firm in response to a change in wages, can be given a simple intuition. Starting with the term D in equation (18.22), we know that if there are diminishing returns to any factor, its marginal product declines with output. Hence, since second-order conditions require diminishing returns to each factor, we know that $\partial^2 X/\partial K^2$, $\partial^2 X/\partial L^2 < 0$ and their product, $(\partial^2 X/\partial L^2)(\partial^2 X/\partial K^2)$, must therefore always be positive. But, whatever the sign of the cross partial derivative $(\partial^2 X/\partial L \partial K)$, its square must always be positive, and output price too is always assumed to be greater than zero, so the sign of D is thus at first sight indeterminate. However, as is established in most texts in mathematical economics (see Further Reading), and as mathematically inclined readers may wish to prove for themselves, second-order conditions imply that

$$D > 0$$

(18.23)

This condition can be interpreted as showing that, in equilibrium, profits must be decreasing with respect to changes in both capital and labour. Hence, given (18.20), we know that employment will always be decreased if the wage is increased, provided only that the production function is concave. Hence we have deduced that if equilibrium employment is L^*,

$$\frac{dL^*}{dW} < 0$$

provided

$$\partial^2 X/\partial K^2 < 0 \text{ and } D > 0$$

The impact on the demand for one input of a change in the price of another can be evaluated by considering dL/dr from equation (18.18) on the assumption that $dp = dw = 0$. We therefore derive

$$p\frac{\partial^2 X}{\partial L \partial K}dr + \left(p^2\frac{\partial^2 X}{\partial L^2}\frac{\partial^2 X}{\partial K^2} - p^2\left(\frac{\partial^2 X}{\partial L \partial K}\right)^2\right)dL = 0 \qquad (18.24)$$

Hence

$$\frac{dL^*}{dr} = \frac{-p(\partial^2 X)/(\partial L \partial K)}{D} \gtreqless 0 \text{ as } \frac{\partial^2 X}{\partial L \partial K} \gtreqless 0 \qquad (18.25)$$

This ties down our previous informal discussion of 'inferior inputs', where we identified the determining role of the cross partial derivative on the effect of an increase in one input price on the demand for another input. If we assume that an increase in the quantity of one input increases the marginal product of the other, i.e. $\partial^2 X/\partial L \partial K > 0$, then increases in the first input price will reduce the demand for the second input. However, in the case of an 'inferior' input, when $\partial^2 X/\partial L \partial K < 0$ and the marginal product of one factor declines with increasing usage of the other, input demand will actually increase with increases in the price of the other.

Factor demand under monopoly

For the product market monopolist, just as for the perfectly competitive firm, the demand for factors arises as a corollary of profit-maximising price and output decisions, and not as the solution to some separate and distinct set of problems. Moreover, the basic nature of the decision is the same as that of the competitive firm. The employment of any factor of production will be expanded just as long as profits are increased by so doing, that is to say, as long as the expansion adds more to revenue than it does to costs. In short, the condition that marginal revenue product be equal to marginal factor costs underlies the monopolist's demand for factors just as it does that of the competitive firm, and is but another way of stating the product market condition that marginal cost should be equal to marginal revenue.

The monopolist's factor demand curves

However, this is not to say that the monopolist's behaviour does not differ at all from that of a competitive firm. If the monopolist is a price taker in the market for factor inputs, and their supply price does not vary with the quantity purchased, then the market price of the input is equal to marginal factor cost, and this side of the market is the same as it was in our analysis of the competitive firm. To the competitive firm, though, the price of output and marginal revenue are identical. Thus the short-run demand curve for the factor which related its marginal revenue product to the quantity of it utilised was obtained by multiplying the factor's marginal physical product by a constant output price. Marginal revenue product was equivalent to the value of the factor's marginal product. To the monopolist, price declines with output, and marginal revenue is less than price. The value of the marginal product of a factor of production employed by a monopolist is obviously marginal product multiplied by price, but marginal revenue product is obtained by multiplying marginal physical product by marginal revenue. The two magnitudes are different for a monopolist, marginal revenue product being always the lower of the two.

Figure 18.10 shows the two relationships, the difference between them reflecting in the factor market the gap between the price of output and the marginal revenue accruing from the sale of one extra unit of output. If the demand curve for output faced by the monopolist was the same as that which would be faced by a competitive industry, the production function was the same as would characterise that industry, and the wage rate w_1 was the same as would face a competitive industry, then such a competitive industry's short-run demand curve for labour would be given by the value of the marginal product curve in Figure 18.10 and its employment of labour would be equal to L_2 instead of L_1, the quantity employed by the monopolist. This tendency of the monopolist to curtail the use of factor inputs relative to what might be demanded by a competitive industry is simply a reflection in the factor market of the tendency to restrict output relative to a level that would be realised by a competitive industry.

There is little to be said about the monopolist in the long run. The demand for a particular factor may be more or less elastic in the long run than in the short run,

Figure 18.10

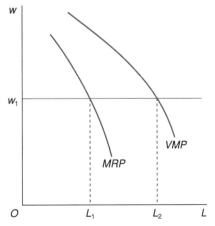

For a monopolist, marginal revenue is below output price. Hence, the marginal revenue product or *MRP* (marginal physical product times marginal revenue) of a factor is below the value of its marginal product or *VMP* (marginal physical product times output price).

depending upon the outcome of two competing tendencies. A fall in the price of one factor leads to more of it being used and hence raises the marginal physical product of the other factor. It also leads to increased output and lower marginal revenue. The net effect of these competing tendencies can lead either to an increase or a decrease in the quantity of the other factor employed. Thus a monopolist's long-run demand curve for a factor of production may either be more or less elastic than the short-run relationship.

Finally, it should be noted that the question of factor payments exhausting revenue does not arise in the context of monopoly. If it just happens that the monopolist's profit-maximising price for output equals long-run average cost of production, then factor payments will equal revenue. If positive profits are made then they obviously will not. As with perfect competition, what happens in this regard is a matter of the firm's behaviour and not simply of the nature of the production function.

| Box 18.3 | **Value of marginal product and marginal revenue product** |

We know from basic monopoly theory that if a monopolist has a linear demand curve the marginal revenue curve is also linear and twice the slope of the demand curve (in absolute terms). Does the same relationship apply for the value of marginal product and marginal revenue product curves of a firm with a monopoly position in its output market? Intuition might suggest that if the marginal product curve is linear then the relationship between the *VMP* and *MRP* curves might be viewed as equivalent to the relationship between a monopolist's *AR* and *MR* curves. This box explores this issue.

A monopolist has a general linear inverse demand function

$$p = a - bX \tag{18.3.1}$$

where p is selling price, X is demand, and a and b are the vertical intercept and slope of the curve. It follows that total revenue is

$$TR = pX = aX - bX^2 \tag{18.3.2}$$

Hence marginal revenue is

$$MR = \frac{dTR}{dX} = a - 2bX \tag{18.3.3}$$

This shows the standard conclusion that with a linear demand curve the *MR* and *AR* curves have the same vertical intercept (i.e. a) and the *MR* curve has twice the absolute slope (i.e. $-2b$ rather than $-b$).

Assume that, in general form, the monopolist's short-run production function is

$$X = cL - dL^2 \tag{18.3.4}$$

where L is labour input. This implies that the marginal product of labour is linear:

$$MP_L = \frac{dX}{dL} = c - 2dL \tag{18.3.5}$$

We can now define the value of marginal product and marginal revenue product functions:

$$VMP_L = p(MP_L) = (p)c - (p)2dL \tag{18.3.6}$$

$$MRP_L = MR(MP_L) = (MR)c - (MR)2dL \qquad (18.3.7)$$

Using the demand function (18.3.1) and the marginal revenue function (18.3.3) we can rewrite these expressions for VMP_L and MRP_L:

$$VMP_L = (a - bX)c - (a - bX)2dL \qquad (18.3.8)$$

$$MRP_L = (a - 2bX)c - (a - 2bX)2dL \qquad (18.3.9)$$

In turn we can eliminate X from these expressions by using the production function. Substituting in (18.3.4) and collecting terms:

$$VMP_L = ac - (bc^2 + 2ad)L + 3bcdL^2 + 2bd^2L^3 \qquad (18.3.10)$$

$$MRP_L = ac - (2bc^2 + 2ad)L + 6bcdL^2 + 4bd^2L^3 \qquad (18.3.11)$$

We can make the following observations about (18.3.10) and (18.3.11). First the vertical intercepts are the same. Setting $L = 0$ results in $VMP_L = MRP_L = ac$. This is clearly equivalent tot he relationship between AR and MR that have the same vertical intercept. But this is where the similarity ends. It is clear that VMP_L and MRP_L are non-linear, instead they are cubic. The relationship between (18.3.10) and (18.3.11) is not obvious in the general form presented here. To explore this relationship we can parameterise the functions by assuming the following values: $a = 100$; $b = 1$; $c = 10$; $d = 0.01$. Using these parameter values in (18.3.10) and (18.3.11):

$$VMP_L = 1000 - 102L + 0.3L^2 + 0.0002L^3 \qquad (18.3.12)$$

$$MRP_L = 1000 - 202L + 0.6L^2 + 0.0004L^3 \qquad (18.3.13)$$

Illustration 18.3 plots (18.3.12) and (18.3.13) for relevant values of L. The two functions appear linear, and over relevant values of L the slope of MRP appears to be twice that of VMP (in absolute terms). In short we can draw VMP and MRP as if they are equivalent to AR and MR, when AR and MR are linear, but we should realise that this is a local not global characteristic.

Illustration 18.3

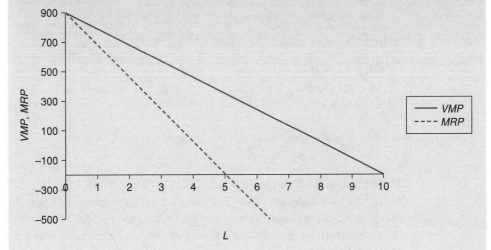

* A formal treatment

We previously referred to the general maximisation problem for the firm in imperfect competition choosing its factor inputs simultaneously with its output. In this section we offer a formal treatment of that problem, analogous to that already undertaken for the competitive firm. Instead of choosing output levels to maximise profits, as in equations (15.7)–(15.12), we focus instead on the choice of inputs, K and L. The optimisation problem is therefore to maximise

$$\pi = pX - wL - rK \tag{18.23}$$

subject to

$$X = f(L, K) \tag{18.24}$$

and

$$p = p(X) \tag{18.25}$$

Rather than once again solve the full constrained optimisation problem by forming a Lagrangian, in this case we illustrate an important simplification. The constrained problem can be simplified to an unconstrained problem by substituting equations (18.24) and (18.25) into (18.23), yielding

$$\pi = p(X)f(L, K) - wL - rK \tag{18.26}$$

This can be maximised with respect to L and K, without reference to the output decision. In effect this is the approach we used in our formal treatment of the labour-managed firm in Chapter 14. This approach yields first-order conditions

$$\frac{\partial \pi}{\partial L} = \frac{\partial p}{\partial X}\frac{\partial X}{\partial L}X + p\frac{\partial X}{\partial L} - w = 0 \tag{18.27}$$

and

$$\frac{\partial \pi}{\partial K} = \frac{\partial p}{\partial X}\frac{\partial X}{\partial K}X + p\frac{\partial X}{\partial K} - r = 0 \tag{18.28}$$

Hence

$$\left(p + X\frac{\partial p}{\partial X}\right)\frac{\partial X}{\partial L} = w \tag{18.29}$$

and

$$\left(p + X\frac{\partial p}{\partial X}\right)\frac{\partial X}{\partial K} = r \tag{18.30}$$

are the hiring equations for labour and capital respectively. As noted in Chapter 13, the expression $(p + X\partial p/\partial X)$ is marginal revenue, which is everywhere less than price because the demand curve slopes down $(\partial p/\partial X < 0)$. Equations (18.29) and (18.30) are therefore the counterparts to the monopolistic case of the competitive first-order conditions derived earlier in this chapter, namely equations (18.13) and (18.14). They state that factors will be hired until their marginal revenue product is equal to the cost of hiring them. Because $(p + X\partial p/\partial X) < p$ for all X, the factor demand implied by a given value of the input price is always less under monopoly than under competition.

Monopsony

The analysis carried out so far has been of the demand side of the market for a factor of production; and whether the firm under consideration is a competitor (as in the last chapter) or a monopolist (as in this one), as far as the market for output is concerned, the assumption has been made throughout that factor inputs are purchased competitively. That is to say, each firm we have considered has been assumed able to buy as much as it pleases of any factor of production at a given price, a price presumably determined in some broader market for the factor in question of which the firm under analysis makes up a small part. In other words, the firm faces a horizontal supply curve of the factor.

There is no need to restrict our analysis of factor markets to such a situation any more than, when discussing product markets, it was necessary to restrict ourselves to dealing with a firm which could sell all it pleased at a given price. Just as we can think of a particular seller of a product being faced with a downward-sloping demand curve for output, so we can think of a particular purchaser of a factor of production being faced with an upward-sloping supply curve for that input, so that the price paid for the input varies with the quantity purchased. Such a purchaser is called a **monopsonist**.

Faced with an upward-sloping factor supply curve, the firm must distinguish between the price (i.e. the average cost) of the factor on the one hand, and the marginal cost of obtaining it on the other. The total factor outlay curve associated with the horizontal supply curve that underlay the analysis of the last chapter would clearly be a straight line through the origin. Figure 18.11 shows an upward-sloping factor supply curve (a straight line for simplicity) – which may be termed an *average factor outlay* (or *average factor cost*)

Figure 18.11

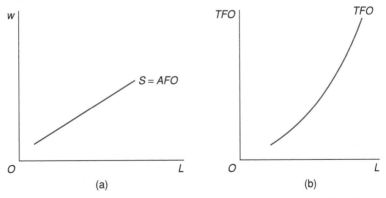

(a) An upward-sloping supply curve of labour yields (b) a total factor outlay curve that slopes upwards at an increasing rate. Hence, marginal factor outlay lies above the factor supply curve.

curve – as well as the associated total factor outlay curve. Total factor cost here increases at an increasing rate with the quantity of the input purchased, and the slope of the total factor cost curve is everywhere steeper than the slope of a straight line drawn to it from the origin. That is to say, **marginal factor cost** everywhere lies above the market price of the factor. Though Figures 18.11 and 18.12 show the relationship in question for the special case of an upward-sloping, but linear, factor supply curve, the reader must bear in mind that its properties, though analytically very convenient, are those of a case that is every bit as special as the straight-line demand curve which we used in Chapter 12 when we considered the behaviour of a monopoly seller of a good.

The profit-maximising firm will purchase that flow of inputs for which marginal revenue product equals marginal factor outlay and will choose the price which it pays for that quantity as the minimum which it needs to pay in order to obtain it: that is to say, the price it pays will be given by the factor supply curve. All this is shown in Figure 18.12 with L_1 units of labour being employed at a wage rate of w_1. Just as it is inappropriate to refer to the monopolist's marginal cost curve as a supply curve since it does not relate quantity supplied to price, so it is inappropriate to refer to the monopsonist's marginal revenue product curve as a demand curve for a factor. A further parallel with monopoly in the product market is worth noting here: as compared with perfect competition, monopsony leads to a restriction of input use just as monopoly leads to a restriction of output. Figure 18.13 shows the combined effects of these tendencies for a firm that is both monopolist in its product market and monopsonist in its factor market. Perfect competition in both markets would result in the market price of the factor being set at w_1 and L_1 of it being employed. The combination of monopoly and monopsony results in a lower price of the factor (w_2) and a smaller quantity of it being utilised (L_2).

Figure 18.12

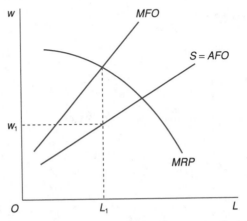

A monopsonist equates marginal factor outlay to marginal revenue product in order to determine the profit-maximising level of employment for a factor, L_1, in this case, paying it the wage rate given for that quantity by the supply curve, w_1, in this case.

Figure 18.13

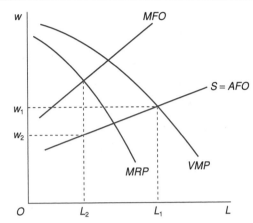

A monopsonist in a factor market who is also a monopolist in the product market employs less labour at a lower wage than would a competitive industry. The latter would equate the value of labour's marginal product to the wage rate and would employ L_1 at a wage rate of w_1, while the former equates marginal factor outlay to marginal revenue product, thus employing L_2 of labour at w_2.

Box 18.4

Monopsony and competitive firms

To compare the employment practices of a monopsonist with those of competitive firms we can use a simple example. Assume that labour supply is defined by the supply function

$$w = 20 + 0.5L \tag{18.4.1}$$

This implies that total labour costs are

$$wL = 20L + 0.5L^2 \tag{18.4.2}$$

in which case the marginal factor outlay on labour is

$$MFO_L = \frac{d(wL)}{dL} = 20 + L \tag{18.4.3}$$

Interested readers can satisfy themselves that these supply and *MFO* functions are consistent with those drawn in Figure 18.13.

We can assume that the output market is governed by an inverse demand function

$$p = 100 - X \tag{18.4.4}$$

which is also the average revenue function for the monopolist. The marginal revenue of the monopolist is therefore

$$MR = 100 - 2X \tag{18.4.5}$$

Finally, the short-run production function of the monopolist is assumed to be

$$X = 10L - 0.01L^2 \tag{18.4.6}$$

which is also the aggregate production function for the competitive firms. This short-run production function implies that the marginal product of labour is

$$MP_L = 10 - 0.02L \tag{18.4.7}$$

We can now define our *VMP* and *MRP* functions:

$$VMP_L = (p)MP_L = (100 - X)(10 - 0.02L) \tag{18.4.8}$$

$$MRP_L = (MR)MP_L = (100 - 2X)(10 - 0.02L) \tag{18.4.9}$$

A profit maximising monopsonist sets $MRP_L = MFO_L$. We indicate the monopsonist decision using a subscript M on output and employment:

$$(100 - 2X_M)(10 - 0.02L_M) = 20 + L_M \tag{18.4.10}$$

Rearranging expression (18.4.10) indicates profit maximising output as a function of employment for a monopsonist that is also a monopolist:

$$X_M = \frac{980 - 3L_M}{20 - 0.04L_M} \tag{18.4.11}$$

Profit maximising competitive firms operate where $VMP_L = w$. We indicate the competitive equilibrium using subscript C:

$$(100 - X_C)(10 - 0.02L_C) = 20 + 0.5L_C \tag{18.4.12}$$

$$X_C = \frac{980 - 2.5L_C}{10 - 0.02L_C} \tag{18.4.13}$$

A general analysis of expressions (18.4.11) and (18.4.13) is somewhat tedious and does not warrant the conclusions drawn. To indicate these conclusions we will grossly oversimplify with the arbitrary solution involving $X_M = 2$ and $X_C = 1.5X_M = 3$. With these outputs:

$$L_M = 321.92; \quad L_C = 389.34$$

Using the labour supply function, these labour demands involve wage rates of

$$w_M = 180.96; \quad w_C = 214.67$$

These results are consistent with those reported in the text. A monopsonist with monopoly power in its output market pays lower wage rates and has lower employment levels than equivalent competitive industry.

Discriminating monopsony

As readers may well have suspected, the parallels between product market monopoly and factor market monopsony run further than we have so far taken them. Thus, we can have **discriminating monopsony** in the factor market. Consider a situation in which a monopsonist has two sources of supply for a particular factor input, sources of supply that can be kept separate in the sense that it is impossible for the owners of the services from one source to begin to provide them instead by way of the other source. Then, as we

Figure 18.14

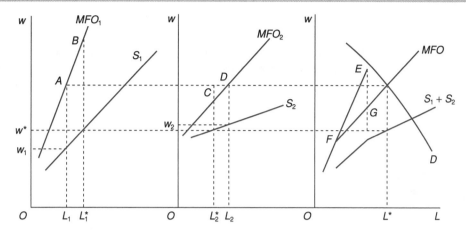

A firm which buys its labour in two markets will employ L^* units of it at a wage of w^* if it cannot discriminate between markets. If it can discriminate, it will equate marginal factor outlay in the two markets. The
wage rate will fall to w_1 in the first market with employment falling from L_1^* to L_1; in the second market,
wages will rise to w_2 and employment will expand from L_2^* to L_2. The overall level of employment will
remain the same, the increase in expenditure on labour in the second market is given by $CDL_2L_2^*$, and the
cut in expenditure in the first market is $ABL_1^*L_1$. The gain in profits from being able to discriminate is given
by the difference between these two areas, or equivalently by the area EFG, which is the difference between
the area under the marginal factor outlay curve that corresponds to the summed factor supply curves of
the two markets – which is relevant in the no discrimination case – and the area under the summed
marginal factor cost curves of the two markets, which is relevant when discrimination takes place.

show in Figure 18.14, it will pay our monopsonist to equate the marginal costs of obtaining the factor from each source of supply and this will result in different prices being paid
to factors obtained from the two sources.

The argument here is exactly parallel to that already set out when we discussed the
price and output behaviour of a discriminating monopolist. Suppose our monopsonist
initially was unable to discriminate between the two sources of supply. The same price
would then have to be paid to each unit of the factor regardless of where it was bought.
But the marginal cost of obtaining an extra unit of input from market 1 is, in these circumstances, higher than it is in market 2. If the monopsonist acquires the power to pay
different prices in the two markets, profits can be increased by reducing purchases in the
first market and increasing purchases in the second, thus cutting down on the total outlay
on this particular factor without reducing the quantity of it available for employment. As
readers will see from Figure 18.14, this results in the factor price being lower in the market
where the **elasticity of labour supply** is lower.

It is often asserted that discriminatory wage fixing in the labour market between men
and women may be explained by the fact that women, having fewer alternatives for
employment than men, face any potential employer with a less elastic supply curve for
their services. However, other factors contributing to lower productivity on the part of
female workers must also be taken into account before concluding that wage differentials
between men and women in the same occupation are to be taken as prima facie evidence
of the existence of discriminating monopsony.

Now the price discrimination in the factor market just discussed is a particular kind of price discrimination. Factor markets apparently provide scope for paying a particular provider of a factor service a different price for different units of it. **Overtime payment** arrangements for workers are an example of such behaviour. As with perfect price discrimination in the product market (see Chapter 12), the more finely monopsonists can separate from one another the services they are buying, and pay a different price for each of them, the more closely will the quantity of the input bought approach the competitive solution. In terms of Figure 18.13, a perfectly discriminating monopsonist would buy L_1 of labour, paying w_1 for only the last unit of it, and lower prices for each intermediate unit, always provided the output market was competitive.

Box 18.5   ## A discriminating monopsonist

In line with Figure 18.14 we assume that a monopsonist can hire labour in two sub-markets. For markets one and two the supply functions are

$$w_1 = 10 + L_1 \tag{18.5.1}$$

$$w_2 = 20 + 0.5L_2 \tag{18.5.2}$$

Using the logic set out in Box 18.4 these supply functions imply the following marginal factor outlays:

$$MFO_1 = 10 + 2L \tag{18.5.3}$$

$$MFO_2 = 20 + L_2 \tag{18.5.4}$$

The interested reader can confirm that these supply and *MFO* functions are consistent with those drawn in Figure 18.14. To sum these functions we must remember that we are adding up horizontally (in terms of Figure 18.14), not vertically. We must therefore rearrange the expressions to make L the subject of the equations. Using (18.5.1):

$$L_1 = w_1 - 10 \tag{18.5.5}$$

and using (18.5.2):

$$L_2 = 2w_2 - 40 \tag{18.5.6}$$

Using (18.5.3):

$$L_1 = 0.5MFO_1 - 5 \tag{18.5.7}$$

and using (18.5.4):

$$L_2 = MFO_2 - 20 \tag{18.5.8}$$

Constructing the combined supply function
Observe from (18.5.1) and (18.5.2) that for wage rates between 10 and 20 only labour in sub-market 1 is supplied, but for wage rates above 20 labour is supplied from both sub-markets. The combined supply curve is therefore

$$L = w - 10, \qquad\qquad 10 < w < 20 \tag{18.5.9}$$

$$L = w - 10 + 2w - 40 \qquad w > 20 \tag{18.5.10}$$

Expressing these functions with w as the subject of the equations:

$$w = 10 + L \qquad\qquad 10 < w < 20 \qquad\qquad (18.5.11)$$

$$w = (50/3) + (1/3)L \qquad\qquad w > 20 \qquad\qquad (18.5.12)$$

Constructing the combined MFO function

Using a similar logic:

$$L = 0.5MFO - 5, \qquad\qquad 10 < MFO < 20 \qquad\qquad (18.5.13)$$

$$L = 0.5MFO - 5 + MFO - 20 \quad MFO > 20 \qquad\qquad (18.5.14)$$

Hence

$$MFO = 10 + L \qquad\qquad 10 < MFO < 20 \qquad\qquad (18.5.15)$$

$$MFO = (25/1.5) + (1/1.5)L \qquad MFO > 20 \qquad\qquad (18.5.16)$$

Assume that the inverse demand for labour (i.e. the MRP) is defined by the function

$$w = 100 - L \qquad\qquad (18.5.17)$$

We can now analyse the two possibilities of a non-discriminating monopsonist and a discriminating monopsonist.

Non-discriminating monopsonist

To maximise profit the demand function (18.5.17) is set equal to the combined MFO function (18.5.16):

$$100 - L = (25/1.5) + (1/1.5)L \qquad\qquad (18.5.18)$$

i.e. $L = 50$

To acquire $L = 50$ requires a wage rate of

$$w = (50/3) + (1/3)50 = 33.33$$

Note that this wage rate is above 20 and so involves labour supply from both sub-markets. With this wage rate the supply in these sub-markets is

$$L_1 = 33.33 - 10 = 23.33$$

$$L_2 = 2(33.33) - 40 = 26.66$$

These two labour supplies add up to the aggregate labour demand, ignoring rounding errors.

Discriminating monopsonist

The discriminating monopsonist once again maximises profit and so wants a total labour force of 50, but now can offer different wage rates to labour in the two sub-markets. To calculate these different wage rates it makes the marginal factor outlays the same, any deviation from this implies lost profit opportunities. With a labour force of 50 the combined MFO from (18.5.16) is

$$MFO = (25/1.5) + (1/1.5)50 = 50$$

Setting the *MFO* in the two sub-markets equal to 50, i.e. using (18.5.7) and (18.5.8),

$$L_1 = 0.5(50) - 5 = 20$$

and $L_2 = 50 - 20 = 30$

To obtain these employment levels requires different wage rates of

$$w_1 = 10 + 20 = 30$$

$$w_2 = 20 + 0.5(30) = 35$$

Note that compared with the non-discriminating case, wage discrimination results in employment levels in the first sub-market being lower (20 rather than 23.33) and in the second sub-market being higher (35 rather than 26.66). In addition note that wages are lower in the first sub-market (30 rather than 33.33) and higher in the second sub-market (35 rather than 33.33). These results are consistent with the general analysis presented in Figure 18.14.

Concluding comment

In this chapter we have been concerned with the demand for factors of production, and the determination of their prices, and have simply taken supply conditions for granted. The general decision as to whether to work or not, and for how long, is clearly one element that underlies the supply of labour to a particular firm or industry. Similarly, capital equipment cannot be made available for leasing out to firms unless someone refrains from current consumption in order to acquire such equipment. Thus, the analysis of saving behaviour set out in Chapter 5 is of some relevance in dealing with the supply of capital equipment to particular firms or industries. However, when the decision to work has been taken, or the decision to acquire savings, and hence perhaps capital equipment, there still remains the issue of whom to work for, and to whom to rent capital equipment. Thus, we still need to say something about influences on the supply of factors of production to particular firms and industries. This topic provides the subject matter of the next chapter. We consider institutions on the supply side of the labour market in more detail in Chapter 20.

SUMMARY

Factor demand

1. The short-run factor demand curve is derived from the factor's marginal revenue product curve. Profits are maximised where marginal revenue product (MRP) is equal to marginal factor cost, and since the competitive firm will set employment of its variable factor at this point, the MRP curve becomes the short-run factor demand curve.

2. The firm's short-run factor demand curve slopes downwards only because of the assumption that marginal factor productivity diminishes: the so-called law of diminishing returns. For the *industry*, however, we cannot hold the price of output constant

as output changes. We must allow for an inverse relation between output price and quantity, and the industry short-run factor demand curve will be steeper than the sum of firms' short-run factor demand curves.

3. A fall in factor price unambiguously leads to an increase in output at a given output price. Moreover it can be shown that the cross partial derivatives of the production function are equal. Since we assume they are non-negative a decrease in one factor price increases the quantity demanded of both inputs. The firm's long-run factor demand curve is therefore more shallowly sloped than the short-run curve.

4. For industry long-run factor demand, output price is no longer given. Increasing the input of one factor still increases marginal physical productivity of the other but expanding industry output lowers price and tends to lower the revenue productivity of the other factor.

5. The net outcome of these two effects, and the elasticity of long-run factor demand, depends on the degree of substitutability between factors and the elasticity of demand for output. There is no reason to treat the price of other inputs as given as the price of any one of them varies, and the elasticity of demand for one factor is also influenced by the elasticity of supply of other factors.

6. Quasi-rents accruing to factors fixed in the short run will equal total revenue less returns to the variable factor. These will also equal the fixed factors' marginal product times quantities with constant returns to scale. However, where total payments to factors do not just exhaust total revenue, firms will enter and leave the industry until profits are zero. If all firms have the same production function, yielding the usual U-shaped long-run average cost curve, profit maximising behaviour ensures factor payments exhaust revenue.

7. The monopolist, like the competitive firm, sets marginal revenue product equal to marginal factor cost. If the monopolist is a price taker in the market for factor inputs then market input price equals marginal factor cost.

8. However, although the value of marginal product (VMP) is equal to marginal physical product multiplied by price, price (average revenue) declines with output and is greater than marginal revenue. VMP is therefore greater than marginal revenue product (equalling marginal physical product times marginal revenue). At a given factor price the monopolist restricts factor use relative to the competitive firm.

9. In the long run, changes in factor price lead to changes in marginal physical product and in usage of all factors but changes in output also alter marginal revenue. The monopolist's long-run factor demand may be more or less elastic than in the short run, depending on which of these two effects is the stronger.

10. Monopsonistic firms facing upward-sloping factor supply schedules have marginal factor cost everywhere above average factor cost (factor price). Equating marginal factor cost to marginal revenue product determines the profit-maximising level of factor employment. Monopsony leads to restriction of factor use relative to the competitive outcome.

11. The *discriminating* monopsonist will equate the marginal factor cost of obtaining factor inputs from various sources of supply, thereby reducing total outlay on a factor without reducing the quantity available for production. This will result in factor price being lower in markets where the elasticity of factor supply is low.

PROBLEMS

1 Discuss the assertion that input demand of the firm is merely the mirror image of output supply.

2 'In competitive equilibrium, workers always earn less than their average product.' Discuss.

3 A firm uses 8 units of labour and 24 units of capital to produce 24 units of output. If there are constant returns to scale and the marginal product of labour is 1.5, what is the marginal product of capital? Will it be greater or smaller if technology instead displays diminishing returns to scale?

4 Analyse the effect of an increase in the price of capital on the demand for labour when the elasticity of substitution between labour and capital is low and the elasticity of the demand for output is high.

5 Use a Cobb-Douglas production function ($X = L^\alpha K^\beta$) to illustrate the propositions that, provided the firm can reach an equilibrium,

   (a) Euler's theorem (equation (21.25)) holds when a homogeneous production function displays constant returns to scale;
   (b) there will always be a positive profit in a competitive firm which has a homogeneous production function with returns to scale less than one, and which pays its inputs their marginal products;
   (c) there will always be a positive profit in a monopoly which faces a linearly homogeneous production function.

6 What will be the effect on the following of fixing a minimum wage above the market equilibrium level:

   (a) employment in a perfectly competitive industry in which all firms are equally efficient;
   (b) the number of firms operating in that industry;
   (c) employment in a particular firm in that industry; and
   (d) employment in a firm that, prior to the fixing of the minimum wage, faced an upward-sloping supply curve of labour?

7 A monopsonist in the labour market faces a relatively inelastic supply of female labour and hence pays its female employees a lower wage than its male employees even though the two groups are equally productive. What will be the effect on

   (a) the wage level paid to women;
   (b) the number of women employed;
   (c) the wage level of men; and
   (d) the number of men employed, of legislation forcing the firm to pay the same wage to all employees?

8 Suppose, at a given wage rate, there is unemployment in a particular competitive industry of a certain type of labour. Will government policies of

   (a) subsidising its wage, and
   (b) subsidising the rental price of capital equipment, result in an increase in the employment of that type of labour?

CHAPTER 19

Factor supply

Key words and phrases

- flows of factor services, stocks of factors
- supply to the firm, the industry and the market
- transfer price, rent, quasi-rent, human capital
- income and leisure, unearned income, wage rate, backward-bending supply curve of labour
- overtime pay, all-or-nothing choice
- household production, production opportunity locus, market opportunity locus
- functional distribution of income, personal distribution of income

Introduction

In the last chapter we analysed various aspects of the theory of the demand for factors of production. Of course the price of a particular productive input, just like that of any output, is determined by the interaction of both demand- and supply-side considerations. We have dealt with the firm's demand and the industry's demand for factors of production, very much taking the supply side of the market for granted. In this chapter we introduce the supply side of the factor market before going on in the next chapter to consider the impact of institutions on the supply side of the labour market like trade unions, which may lead the market processes to be replaced by a bargaining outcome.

Flows, stocks and their relationship

Recall at the outset the nature of the units in which we measure factor inputs. The production function relates a **flow** of output to a flow of inputs. Labour is measured in units such as man-hours per week, capital in terms of machine-hours per week, and so on. The demand for factors discussed in the last two chapters has also been for inputs measured in such units. However, when we think of the level of employment of labour in a firm or industry, or the amount of capital it utilises, we usually think in terms of **stocks**: the number of men and women on the payroll, or the number of machines of particular types that the firm has on hand. Clearly, a given increase in inputs to production may be realised in many ways: by working the existing stock, be it capital or labour, more intensively; by increasing the stock and working each unit at the same rate as before; or by some combination of the two. Similarly, the flow of inputs can be reduced by short-time working, by reduction of the number of employees and machines, or by a combination of these methods. The analysis of the last two chapters, which implicitly assumed that there was one and only one way to increase or decrease the quantity of any input, and one price – or marginal factor cost – at which this was possible, greatly simplified the nature of the problem that any firm has to solve.

There is no reason why the costs of obtaining more inputs by taking on more employees, or by buying more machines, should be the same as those involved in lengthening working hours. For example, to get more capital services by utilising a given stock of machines more intensively might involve maintenance difficulties; buying new machines might involve the firm in costs of ordering and installing them. On the labour side, the cost involved in inducing workers to put in more hours may be a higher overtime wage rate, but associated with an addition to the labour force in a firm are administrative costs having to do with each employee's tax and social security contributions, and so on.

We raise these problems now although we are not going to go on and analyse them. Nevertheless, the reader ought to be aware that a whole set of interesting economic problems is involved if one is to proceed carefully from an analysis of the demand for the services of factors of production to conclusions about the level of employment, in any firm or industry, of labour or of machines or indeed of any other stock that yields a flow of productive services. As before, so in this chapter we will make the simplifying assumption that there is a unique relationship between the number of employees which a firm or industry has and the hours of labour services which go into its production process, and we shall make a similar assumption about the relationship between capital inputs and the stock of machines. Thus, when we talk about the supply and demand for labour, we talk of both hours and people, and when we talk about capital we talk about machine-hours and machines. This will greatly simplify the exposition of the following analysis without, it is hoped, making it also too misleading. Nevertheless, a whole set of interesting problems is bypassed by making this assumption.

Supply to the firm and the industry

With this caveat in mind then, let us consider the factors that determine the nature of the supply curve of a productive input. The first question that must come to mind is surely 'supply to whom?' We must distinguish between the supply curve of an input as it appears from the point of view of a particular firm, of an industry and, indeed, of the economy in general, given that not working is a viable alternative for some inputs.

The more narrowly we define the entity to which factor services are being supplied, the more alternatives there are open to their owners and hence, one would suppose, the more elastic the supply curve. Thus, if we consider by way of example the supply curve of a particular type of labour to a typical perfectly competitive firm, each worker has the alternative of working for some other firm in the same industry at the going wage rate. If the firm is indeed 'typical' of the industry, there is no reason why any worker should have a preference for working for this firm rather than any other, and hence there is no reason to accept a lower wage in order to work for it. Nor, of course, is there any reason why any worker in the industry should remain with any other firm if the one whose supply curve we are studying were to be paying even slightly more than the going wage rate. In short, one would expect the supply curve of labour to this particular firm, and to every other in the industry, to be perfectly elastic at the going market wage rate.

There is nothing specific to the behaviour of labour in this analysis. One can equally well think of the owners of machines, or factory buildings, or land, or any other productive resource, deciding to whom to lease that resource and, if they have no reason to prefer one firm in the industry to another, a perfectly elastic supply curve at the going payment rate for the resource will be the result in the long run. The argument here is, as the reader will have realised, exactly parallel to the reasoning that underlies the perfect elasticity of the demand curve that faces the perfectly competitive firm in the output market. In the short run, obviously, such inputs cannot so readily be transferred from one firm to another, so that the short-run supply curve of inputs even to a single firm might have a positive slope to it (indeed, being vertical in the limit), this supply curve becoming horizontal as time passes.

When we come to look at factor supply from the point of view of the industry, matters immediately become more complex. We cannot easily ignore the possibility that the owners of a particular resource might have a personal preference for having it used in one industry rather than in another. The most obvious reasons for such preferences arise when we consider labour, for conditions of work may be more pleasant in one industry than in another; though such differences can exist between firms in the same industry, they are likely to be greater and hence more important across industrial boundaries. Moreover what are or are not 'pleasant' working conditions is to some degree a matter of taste for the individual worker, involving preferences for the type of work, etc., and tastes are likely to differ in this respect.

Though differences of taste about employment are most obviously relevant in the case of labour, they can also affect the choices made by owners of other factors when they decide to which industry they might be allocated. Thus, the owners of a hall (to pick a less usual example) may have a taste for the performing arts that would lead to them permitting it to be used for live performances of plays or classical music at a lower rent than would be required for it to be used as a cinema or a bingo hall.

Furthermore, differences in the alternatives available elsewhere, to what, from the point to view of one particular industry, are different units of the same input, might affect its elasticity of supply. Just because two units of a resource are equally productive in one industry does not mean that they are equally productive in alternative uses. Two halls may be equally suitable for bingo, but because of their acoustic properties only one might be a viable theatre. Two people may be equally productive as pop singers, but because of differences in education may have completely different alternative job opportunities: one might otherwise be a lawyer, and the other a lorry driver.

Transfer price and rent

Thus, some resources are more specific to a particular industry than others, and some will work in a particular industry at a lower rate of payment than others, either because of a subjective preference for employment in that industry on the part of their owners, or as a

Figure 19.1

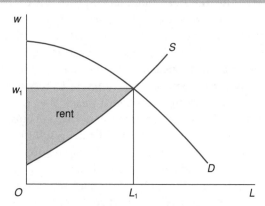

The demand for and supply of labour to a particular competitive industry. The L_1th worker is being paid exactly transfer earnings. At any wage below w_1 the worker would leave the industry, and is the marginal worker at that wage. The shaded area represents the total amount of payments to labour that represent rents, payments above transfer earnings.

result of an objective inability to work more productively elsewhere. We call the price at which a particular unit of a resource will come into industry its **transfer price** or *transfer earnings* to that industry. We would expect this price to rise *on the margin* as more resources are brought in to any particular industry, those whose owners find it particularly congenial to be in that industry being available at a lower price than those for which there are more attractive alternatives.

Now given a competitive industry demand curve, the equilibrium price of any factor in a particular use is determined. As should be apparent from Figure 19.1, at this equilibrium price only the marginal unit of the resource is being paid its transfer price – indeed this statement is just a way of defining the term *marginal unit*. Every other unit is being paid more than would be necessary to keep it in this particular use. The amount by which the price it receives exceeds its transfer price is called a '**rent**'. There is a close relationship between such a 'rent' and the notion of consumer's surplus which we explored earlier in this book. Consumers of a good receive a 'surplus' from being able to obtain all but the last unit of it at a price below the maximum which they would be willing to pay to obtain them; the owners of a productive resource receive a rent because they are paid more for the services of that resource than the minimum price at which they would be willing to provide them to a particular industry. Just as discriminating monopolists appropriate some or all of the available consumer surplus to themselves, so clearly would a discriminating monopsonist be appropriating rents to itself.

Now how much of the payment to a particular factor of production is made up of transfer earnings and how much of rent clearly depends upon the elasticity of its supply curve. As we have seen in our analysis of the firm, a perfectly elastic supply curve involves all factor payments being transfer earnings; and at the opposite extreme, a perfectly inelastic supply curve would mean that all payments are rents, for the resource would be available in the same quantity even at zero price. These two extreme cases are depicted in Figure 19.2.

Figure 19.2

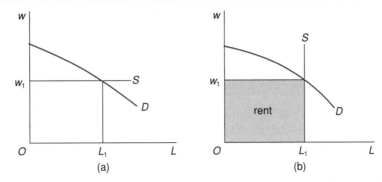

(a) When the supply of labour to an industry is perfectly elastic, all wage payments are transfer earnings.

(b) When the supply is perfectly inelastic, all payments are rents, since a perfectly inelastic supply curve implies that all workers in the industry would be there even for zero wages.

Quasi-rent

When might a resource be in completely inelastic supply to a particular industry? Only when it is specific to the technology of that industry and has no alternative use elsewhere. Readers will recall that in the short run, the quantities of some productive resources available to any particular firm are fixed. From the point of view of their owners then, they cannot be moved elsewhere and hence have no alternative use. In the short run, the income accruing to them has the character of a rent. In the long run, of course, the owners of such resources can move them in and out of particular uses and considerations of transfer earnings enter into the determination of their earnings in any use. Hence, returns to factors fixed in the short run are often referred to as **quasi-rents**. As far as capital equipment is concerned, the rental price to be paid for it is a fixed cost in the short run, and a firm whose quasi-rents are insufficient to meet this fixed cost is making a loss. To the extent that the rental price of capital equipment represents a 'normal' rate of return to the owner of the equipment, then it is apparent that 'making a loss' and 'making less than a normal rate of return' are synonymous phrases.

Though it is usual to think of such factors as machinery as being the inputs whose services yield quasi-rents in the short run, the same concept is also helpful in dealing with labour income. Labour services, after all, are not some kind of homogeneous raw input. They consist of the application of many different kinds of skills to the production process, skills that can only be acquired by the worker making an investment of time and trouble, to say nothing in some cases of forgone income, in their acquisition.

To the extent that a worker's skills are specific to the production process of a particular firm, the return to that skill in the short run is just as much a quasi-rent as is the return to a machine; the alternative is not to utilise the skill. Thus the difference between earnings as a skilled worker and as an unskilled worker is a quasi-rent accruing to the specific skill. If that skill is specific to a particular industry and there is short-run mobility of workers between firms then, from the point of view of any firm, the wages represent transfer earnings, though from the point of view of the industry they contain an element of a quasi-rent. Now all this amounts to saying that for some problems it is illuminating to treat the ownership of skills by a worker as analogous to the ownership of machines: to treat these skills as **human capital** and to view their acquisition as an act of investment.

The individual's supply of labour

For the remainder of this chapter we apply the theory of choice to aspects of the supply of a factor – labour. In particular, we consider the choice of an individual member of the labour force as to how many hours of work per week will be undertaken. As always, we need to know about three matters in order to set the problem up in manageable form – the objects of choice, the constraints upon choice, and the tastes which govern the choice.

The analysis that follows will concentrate upon investigating the consequences for the outcome of this choice problem of variations in the nature of the constraint that faces the individual. We shall show how the constraint's form varies when such complications as overtime payments, a fixed length working week, and the possibility of household production are taken account of, and we shall examine the effects of such variations on the individual's labour supply behaviour.

The nature of the choice problem

Consider first the objects of choice involved in the labour supply decision. At first glance one might think of each member of the labour force being faced with a choice between work and leisure, but a moment's reflection makes it apparent that only one item is in fact being chosen. When hours to be worked have been selected, the number of hours available for leisure are already determined and vice versa. In mentioning work and leisure we are specifying only *one* of the objects of choice, and in our analysis it is convenient to deal explicitly with leisure and hence implicitly with work. Our individual gives up leisure, and receives wage payments in recompense. **Income** – the ability to purchase consumption goods – is gained and **leisure** is sacrificed. The objects of choice here are therefore income and leisure.

We measure income along the vertical axis of Figure 19.3 and leisure along the horizontal axis. Now let us consider the constraint upon the individual's choice. First of all there is the obvious physical constraint that limits the number of hours of leisure available in a week to the number of hours that there are in a week. This point is given by L_0 on the horizontal axis of Figure 19.3.

Working is only one source of income, and there is no reason why any person cannot also receive **unearned income**. Such income receipts are common indeed in a modern economy in which the state provides a number of services to individuals. Free education for children, health insurance – the benefits of which are unrelated to contributions – and so forth, are all part of income, but receipt of them does not depend in any way upon hours worked. More traditional forms of unearned income accruing from ownership of wealth belong here as well. Thus, there is no reason to suppose in general that the level of income associated with not working, i.e. with L_0 hours of leisure per week, is zero. In Figure 19.3 it is assumed to be Y_0 and the budget constraint is drawn vertically up to this

Figure 19.3

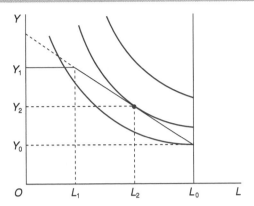

The choice between combinations of income, Y, and leisure, L. Note that hours worked may be measured moving to the left from L_0. If we read the diagram from right to left in this way, it depicts the choice of the best available combination of a 'good' (income) and a 'bad' (work). The individual here chooses to work $L_0 - L_2$ hours for a wage income of $Y_2 - Y_0$. See note 2 on p. 26 on the use of Y to denote income.

level of income. Beyond this point, however, more income can only be obtained by working and hence by sacrificing leisure.

Each hour worked increases income by the hourly wage that the individual can command. Hence the slope of the budget constraint above point L_0Y_0 is given by the wage rate, with a negative sign of course, showing the rate at which income can be substituted for leisure. It is clearly not possible to continue the constraint to cut the vertical axis since no individual can work every hour of the week without some 'leisure' time being devoted to eating and sleeping. Thus there is a cut-off at some minimum amount of leisure L_1 and an associated maximum income level of Y_1. Thus, the constraint on the choice we are analysing is characterised as a kinked relationship such as shown in Figure 19.3. The continuity of the constraint over the range $L_0Y_0 - L_1Y_1$ implies that the individual may choose the length of the work week. This is obviously too simple for direct application to modern labour market institutions. Despite this degree of simplification, however, the analysis is of considerable interest.

As to the individual's tastes, if income and leisure are both goods in the sense that more of one of them, without sacrifice of the other, increases satisfaction, then we are safe in characterising them by a conventional indifference map. One may object to this on the grounds that perhaps the first few hours work a week may actually be a pleasant alternative to the boredom implicit in complete idleness, and prefer indifference curves that actually become upward sloping at high levels of leisure as in Figure 19.4. But reflection on the results developed in Chapter 2 makes clear that this extra complication adds nothing to the analysis that follows, so we ignore it from now on. This is not to say, though, that the assumption underlying it lacks plausibility.

The formal solution to the choice problem portrayed in Figure 19.3 is obvious enough. Our worker will consume L_2 hours of leisure per week at the going wage, hence working $L_0 - L_2$ hours for an income of Y_2.

Figure 19.4

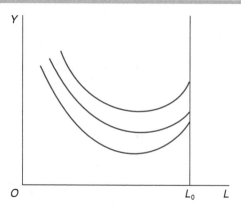

The indifference map implicit in the assumption that, after a certain point, leisure becomes a 'bad'. Moving to the left from L_0 the individual would be willing to pay for permission to work for the first few hours.

Variations in the wage rate

We are now in a position to see how the individual's supply of working hours changes in response to changes in the constraints under which they are chosen. First let us derive the supply curve of effort as a function of the **wage rate**. As the wage rate rises the mid-sector of the budget constraint becomes steeper, pivoting on point Y_0L_0, as in Figure 19.5(a). The

Figure 19.5

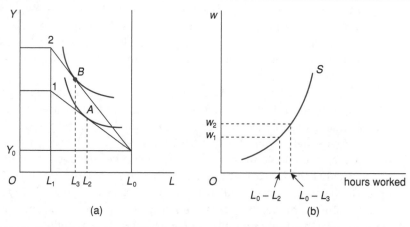

(a)
(b)

The wage rate rises from w_1 to w_2 and the equilibrium moves from A to B. More income is demanded but less leisure. If income and leisure are indeed substitutes, the supply curve of labour slopes upwards as shown in panel (b).

'price' of income falls, and, provided only that it is a normal good – hardly a proviso to argue about – the amount of it demanded rises as our individual moves from *A* to *B*. However, we are mainly interested in what happens to the demand for leisure and hence the supply of hours worked. To put the matter in the language of consumer theory, this is a cross effect rather than an own price effect. If income and leisure are substitutes, then hours worked will increase with the wage rate, but if they are complements, hours worked will actually fall. The former case, with its upward-sloping supply curve of hours worked is shown in Figure 19.5; the latter with a **backward-bending supply curve** is shown in Figure 19.6.

Now if there were only a substitution effect to consider here there would be no problem. A fall in the price of income would be synonymous with a rise in the price of leisure. It is because there is an income effect at work that we run into ambiguity. We examine this matter more closely in Figure 19.7. After the wage rate rises, we carry out a Slutsky compensating variation (see Ch. 3) on our individual's budget constraint by lowering unearned income until we reach constraint 3. Clearly, the overall response to this rise in the wage rate can be broken down into a movement from *A* to *C*, a substitution effect, and a movement from *C* to *B*, an income effect. If leisure were an inferior good, there would be no ambiguity in the individual's response: the negative income effect and the negative substitution effect would reinforce one another to produce an upward-sloping supply curve of labour. However, to think of leisure as being an inferior good is implausible, to say the least. If it was such a good, we would expect to observe the longest hours being worked for wages by those whose unearned incomes were highest! If leisure is a normal good though, the income effect on hours worked of an increase in the wage rate operates in the opposite direction to the substitution effect and may or may not outweigh it. This is why an individual's supply curve of labour services as a function of the wage rate may either be upward sloping or backward bending.

Figure 19.6

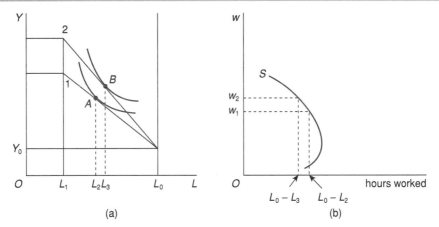

(a) (b)

The wage rate rises from w_1 to w_2 and the equilibrium moves from *A* to *B*. More income is demanded, but in this case the indifference map is drawn so that income and leisure are complements. Thus we get the backward-bending supply curve of labour depicted in panel (b).

Figure 19.7

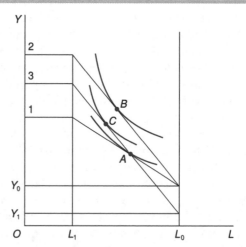

The movement from *A* to *B* involves a substitution effect from *A* to *C* and an 'income effect' from *C* to *B*. The compensating variation to get from constraint 2 to 3 may be thought of as involving a cut in unearned income from Y_0 to Y_1.

Overtime payments

We may look at **overtime payment** arrangements in the light of the foregoing analysis. They are a form of price discrimination, by which we mean that a different price is paid for different units of the same item (see Chapter 12), and can prevent the supply of labour from falling as its price rises. Consider Figure 19.8 and suppose that our typical individual, at the going wage rate on constraint 1, was supplying $L_0 - L_2$ hours of work. Now suppose that the employer wished to induce our individual to work longer hours. One course of action would be to offer the same wage rate for all hours worked up to $L_0 - L_2$ and a higher rate thereafter.

In terms of Figure 19.8, the effect of this is to kink the budget constraint at *A*, making it more steeply sloped above and to the left of this point (constraint 3). But if *A* was initially an equilibrium point, there must exist a point on a higher indifference curve, such as *C*, which also lies on the more steeply sloped segment of the constraint, the movement to which is motivated by a pure Slutsky substitition effect.

The price discrimination involved here clearly reduces the real income of the wage earner relative to what it would have been had the same wage rate been received for every hour worked. This is easily shown. In Figure 19.8, at the original wage rate, the individual is on indifference curve I_1, and hence at a level of utility exactly equivalent to that which would have been attained with an unearned income of Y_1. The difference between this and Y_0 measures the surplus that accrues from working at the wage rate in question. Were the wage rate simply to go up so that a new budget constraint was given by 2, then this change would be equivalent to an increase of $Y_2 - Y_1$ in unearned income. However, if the

Figure 19.8

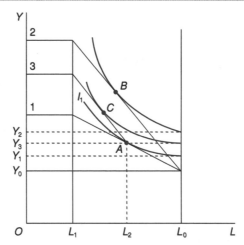

If the wage rate rises, the individual moves from A to B with a gain in utility equal to that yielded by an increase of $Y_2 - Y_1$ in unearned income. Such a movement as that from A to B may or may not involve an increase in hours worked. If the new wage rate is introduced as an overtime only rate, we have a pure substitution effect from A to C, an unambiguous increase in hours worked, but the gain in utility is here only equivalent to $Y_3 - Y_1$.

new rate is an overtime only rate, the gain is reduced. It is equivalent to an increase in unearned income of only $Y_3 - Y_1$. It is perhaps small wonder, therefore, that the length of the basic working week is so often a bone of contention in wage negotiations between unions and employers.

Now overtime payments are by no means the only arrangement that can introduce a kink into the budget constraint. National Insurance contributions levied as a proportion of income up to a maximum amount, and income tax which begins to bite above a certain threshold income level, to give but two other examples, also have this effect. Readers who wish to be sure that they have mastered the material just presented might find it helpful to analyse these cases for themselves.

The effect of fixing the length of the working week

Now the reader will no doubt have been somewhat concerned that our analysis so far has dealt with an individual who is able to choose the length of the working week to the very minute. In fact, of course, the length of the basic working week tends to be institutionally determined. The effect of this is to present the individual with an **all-or-nothing choice**. They can work $L_0 - L_2$ hours at the going rate or not at all. Such a choice is depicted in Figure 19.9. Our individual will work if the point L_2, Y_2 lies on a higher indifference curve than the point L_0, Y_0, otherwise not. If the length of the basic working week is given at a fixed wage, but there is flexibility in the worker's choice of overtime hours, then we may be back with the analysis of marginal choices. Figure 19.10 deals with this case.

Figure 19.9

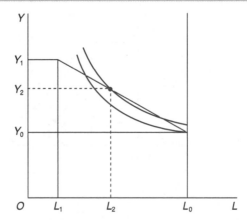

If the length of the working week is fixed by the employer along with the wage offered, the individual is faced with a choice between two income–leisure combinations L_0, Y_0 and L_2, Y_2. As this figure is drawn, the latter is on the higher indifference curve and the individual will choose to work.

Figure 19.10

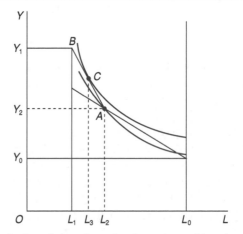

If the individual is permitted a free choice of overtime hours beyond $L_0 - L_2$ at an increased wage rate, the constraint is given by the point L_0, Y_0, and any point along the line AB linking L_2, Y_2 and L_1, Y_1. As the indifference map is drawn here, the individual moves to point C and works $L_3 - L_2$ overtime hours. Note, though, that if the indifference curve passing through A had been drawn to slope more steeply than the continuous section AB of the constraint, our individual would have refused to work overtime.

Household production – the simple case

Our analysis has so far taken it for granted that an individual's opportunities to sacrifice leisure in order to generate income all lie in the labour market. This is a gross oversimplification. Work carried on within the home, including housework, does not generate

Figure 19.11

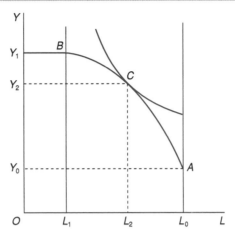

Household production. If leisure may be transformed into income by devoting time to household production, and the individual has no access to the labour market, then $L_0 - L_2$ hours of work will be carried out at home to produce $Y_2 - Y_0$ of income.

cash income but it surely generates income in kind. The tools we have developed in this chapter may be extended easily enough to encompass the important phenomenon of **household production**.

Consider Figure 19.11. As before we endow our individual with a certain amount of unearned income Y_0, and recognise the existence of some minimum requirement of leisure L_1. Suppose, however, that our individual is excluded from any organised labour market, but is permitted to trade off leisure in return for income by engaging in household production along the curve AB. This curve is known as a **production opportunity locus**. It is drawn concave to the origin, thus implying that the first units of time devoted to household production are more productive than later ones, that our agent's productivity in household activity falls as more time is devoted to it – that the activity is subject to diminishing returns (see Chapter 8). If we superimpose our individual's indifference map on Figure 19.11, we may solve for the utility-maximising allocation of time between leisure and household production at point C.

Household production and the labour market

Let us now remove the restrictions that keep this individual out of the organised labour market, while leaving open as before the opportunities for household production characterised by AB. How should we now construct the budget constraint? Note first that any point along AB is still available to be chosen. Note secondly, and crucially, that the agent is not compelled to make an 'either–or' choice between household production and participation in the labour market. Working time can be divided among these two activities and leisure. These two observations imply that our individual may choose a level of household production, say that given by point D' in Figure 19.12, and starting at that

Figure 19.12

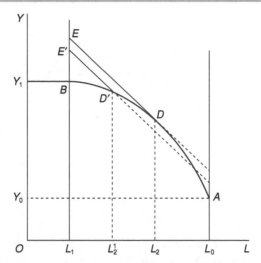

Household production in the presence of market opportunities. If the individual engaged in household production also has access to the labour market, then there is a market opportunity locus such as E' passing through every point, such as D' on the production locus AB. The market opportunity loci here have the slope of minus the wage rate, and the highest available one, E, is just tangent to AB at D.

point begin to supply labour in the organised market along a straight line such as $D'E'$, whose slope is given by the market wage rate. This line is known as a **market opportunity locus**, and it will be apparent that the analysis of previous sections has already made extensive use of this device drawn for what now appears as the special case in which the agent under analysis devotes no time to household production. In that case the market opportunity locus does in fact originate at point A.

Now if the agent can select any point along the production opportunity locus AB, there is, for a given market wage rate, a market opportunity locus beginning at every point along AB. The agent's utility-maximisation problem involves choosing the best combination of leisure, household production and work in the organised market, and part of its solution must involve the choice of a level of household activity that permits the most satisfactory market opportunity locus to be attained. Since our individual attains higher and higher levels of satisfaction as we move upwards and to the right in Figure 19.12, that market opportunity locus must be the one that lies furthest out from the diagram's origin. In turn that must be DE, the market opportunity locus just tangent to the production opportunity locus. Any other market opportunity locus having the same slope as DE, and starting at a point on the convex production opportunity locus AB, must lie below and to the left of DE. Our individual will devote no more than $L_0 - L_2$ of time to household production, because moving to the left beyond L_2, more income can be generated by supplying services in the organised labour market than by devoting them to further household production. Thus, for our individual, whose household production opportunities are described by AB, and who faces a market wage ratio given by the slope of DE (or $D'E'$), the overall budget constraint on the labour–leisure choice is given by ADE.

Figure 19.13

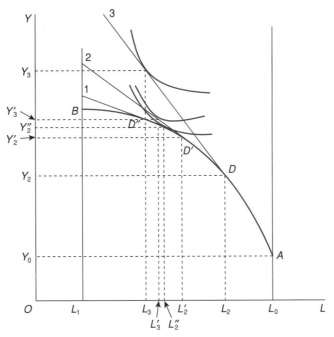

Market opportunity loci 1, 2 and 3 are drawn for successively higher market wage rates. 1 is tangent to AB at D'', and the individual's tastes are such that $L_0 - L_2''$ is devoted to producing $Y_2'' - Y_0$ at home, and no time is supplied to the market. At the wage underlying 2, tangency occurs at D', $L_0 - L_2'$ is devoted to producing $Y_2' - Y_0$ at home, and $L_2' - L_3'$ in the labour market generates $Y_3' - Y_2'$ of income. At the wage underlying 3, tangency occurs at D, $L_0 - L_2$ yields $Y_2 - Y_0$ from household production, and $L_2 - L_3$ of labour time is sufficient on the labour market to generate $Y_3 - Y_2$ of income.

The individual's tastes may be such that, at the given wage rate, the best available choice lies somewhere along the segment AD, and hence involves staying at home. However, if we were then to allow the market wage rate to rise, a critical level would eventually be reached at which the individual would be tempted to enter the labour market. Moreover, once in the market, if the experiment of increasing the market wage is continued, the individual will respond by systematically reducing the amount of time devoted to household production. This effect occurs because, as the market wage rate increases, the market opportunity locus gets steeper, so that the point (D in Figure 19.12) at which it is tangent to the production opportunity locus moves down the latter to the right. Figure 19.13 shows what is involved here.

Household production and the labour supply function

Now this analysis of household production is of considerable empirical importance because of the implications it yields for the form of the individual's supply function

Figure 19.14

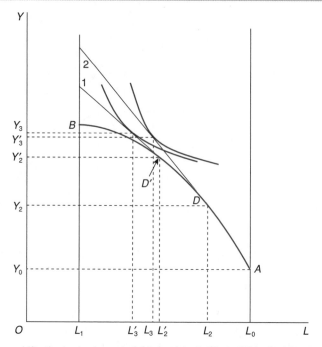

As the market wage shifts the budget constraint from 1 to 2, this individual's tastes are such that consumption of leisure rises from $O - L_3'$ to $O - L_3$. Nevertheless, because household production time is reduced from $L_0 - L_2'$ to $L_0 - L_2$, the amount of time offered on the labour market increases from $L_2' - L_3'$ to $L_2 - L_3$.

of labour to the organised labour market. The earlier analysis of this chapter ignored household production. That analysis yielded the prediction that, given the plausible assumption that leisure is a normal good, the individual's labour supply function might well be backward bending, and more generally was likely to display considerable insensitivity to the wage rate. Consideration of household production softens this conclusion. When the market wage rate is in the region at which an individual engaged only in household production will be induced to enter the labour market by a small increase in that variable, the supply of labour (to the organised market) is unambiguously positively related to the market wage. Moreover, as the market wage rate increases beyond that level, the individual may substitute market-oriented labour against household production activities, as well as against leisure. Thus the likelihood of an increase in the wage rate inducing an increase in the supply of labour to the formal market is increased by the availability of household production opportunities. Indeed it is quite possible for both the supply of labour outside the household, and the consumption of leisure, to increase at the expense of household production as the market wage rises. Figure 19.14 is drawn to depict this possibility.

Factor prices and the distribution of income

In this chapter, we have been concerned with the supply of factors of production to firms and industries. In the last chapter we dealt with the demand for factors of production. Hence we have the ingredients of a theory of factor prices and hence of factor incomes. Is this theory sufficient to tell us about the distribution of income? The brief answer to this question is: between factors, yes, but between people, no. We have the ingredients of a theory of the **functional distribution of income**, but not of the **personal distribution**. Before one can say anything about the distribution of income among people on the basis of a theory of factor pricing, we must have a theory which explains how the ownership of factors of production is distributed among people.

The theory alluded to above that treats the acquisition of particular productive skills as investment in human capital tells us something about the way in which the ownership of labour services might be acquired. Moreover the acquisition of machinery and such, as well as that of human capital, requires that current consumption be deferred. Hence the elementary analysis of saving behaviour set out in Chapter 5 is also relevant to the theory of factor ownership. Though we may have acquired some insights into some of the matters which will influence it, we are far from being able to produce a coherent overall model for the distribution of income between people. Readers should not expect too much from the analysis developed in this book in attempting to understand the overall distribution of income among people in any economy.

However, this is not to say that distribution is an unimportant matter for economics, just that it is not thoroughly understood. As we shall see in Part VII, where we deal with the workings of the economic system as a whole, questions concerning distribution are an important element to be taken into account when we try to appraise the success or otherwise of the way in which a market economy works, and put an important limit on the amount that we can say about such matters.

SUMMARY

An introduction to factor supply

1. Changes in factor demand may result in the factor stock being changed with each unit working at the same rate as before, by working the existing factor stock more or less intensively, or by some combination of the two.

2. For the competitive firm, although the short-run supply of factors to it may be inelastic, we expect the long-run supply to be perfectly elastic. At the industry level, however, differences among factors available from elsewhere in the economy may affect elasticity of factor supply. Two resources that are equally productive in one industry may not be so in another.

3. We expect the transfer price of resources to rise in the margin. The payments to factors other than the marginal one includes elements of transfer payment and rent, the division between which is determined by the elasticity of the factor supply curve.

4. Returns to factors fixed in the short run are referred to as quasi-rents since their short-run supply is fixed and they cannot be put to alternative use. The wage differential

between non-skilled and skilled labour can therefore be seen as a quasi-rent accruing to *human capital*.

5. One major application of the theory of choice is to the supply of labour. To analyse this problem, the indifference curves are drawn in leisure–income space, with work derived as a residual from leisure. The real wage rate defines the market trade-off between income and leisure.

6. Maximising utility as a function of leisure and income yields an equilibrium in income–leisure space where the indifference curve is tangential to the budget constraint.

7. Changes in the wage rate alter the slope of the budget constraint. If leisure is a normal good the income effect of an increase in the wage rate on the supply of labour operates in the opposite direction to the substitution effect and may, but need not necessarily, outweigh it, producing a backward-bending labour supply curve.

8. We can model overtime payments as a form of price discrimination under which a different price is paid for different units of labour. This leads to a kink in the budget constraint. Labour supply decisions in the region of the kink are dominated by the substitution effect.

9. Household production generates income in kind if it is the sole opportunity for work. Hours worked are now determined at the tangent of the indifference curve and the production opportunity locus, which usually is assumed to exhibit diminishing returns to labour.

10. When working time can be divided between household production and the labour market, the solution to the agent's utility-maximisation problem is determined as follows. As the market wage increases the individual may substitute market-oriented labour against household production as well as leisure. The possibility of a backward-bending labour supply curve is softened since the supply of labour outside the household and the demand for leisure may both increase at the expense of household production.

PROBLEMS

1 What is the relationship between

   (a) the elasticity of factor substitution and the elasticity of demand for labour?
   (b) the elasticity of demand for the product and the elasticity of demand for labour?
   (c) the ratio of labour costs to total costs and the elasticity of demand for labour?
   (d) the elasticity of supply of other inputs and the elasticity of demand for labour?

2 Discuss what the four propositions derived in question 1 (Marshall's laws of derived demand) tell us about the factors likely to influence the relative success or failure of unions in attaining wage increases for their members without causing substantial job losses.

3 Suppose that income and leisure are perfect substitutes. Use indifference curve and budget line diagrams to illustrate the cases when:

   (a) the individual will work for every hour available;
   (b) the individual will not work at all;
   (c) the individual will work an indeterminate number of hours.

4 An individual is known to increase the hours per week worked when non-wage income is decreased. What will happen to the hours worked if

(a) a proportional income tax is levied on wage income?
(b) a proportional income tax is levied on total income?
(c) a proportional tax on wage income is used solely to finance an increase in non-wage income?

Would any of your answers differ if the individual were known to decrease working hours when non-wage income decreased?

5 Discuss the impact of an increase in the marginal rate of income tax on the individual's supply of labour, on the assumption that leisure is a Giffen good. What are the implications for the market wage rate and employment level? Under what conditions will the labour market be unstable?

CHAPTER ⟨20⟩

Labour markets – trade unions and bargaining

Key words and phrases

- trade union
- wage rate, volume of employment
- monopoly union, wage bill, rent, expected utility, representative worker, union–non-union wage differential
- bargaining, efficient bargaining, contract curve, labour hoarding, featherbedding, threat point
- Stone–Geary function

Introduction

In previous chapters we have analysed factor markets in general, but have not considered in any practical detail the operation of actual input markets, either for capital or for labour. Some issues concerning the functioning of the capital market have, however, already been raised in Chapters 5 and 6. Our purpose in this chapter is to focus on the labour market, taking explicitly into account from the outset the existence of one of its more notable institutions, **trade unions**. The supply and demand apparatus that we have built up in previous chapters will form the basis for our analysis of how trade unions – institutions operating on the supply side of the labour market – influence the determination of wages and employment.

Alongside firms, trade unions are among the most pervasive institutions formed by economic agents in pursuit of their economic interests, though in many countries levels of unionisation have been in decline in recent years. Nonetheless negotiations between firms and unions still represent an important institutional feature in many countries, and allow us to return to the analysis of bargaining introduced in Chapter 17. As with firms, our analysis will concentrate on what unions do, rather than why people form them, though the positive wage differential paid to unionised workers which we derive in the models which follow might give a clue here. Our main purpose in this chapter is to analyse labour market behaviour – the determination of employment and wages – in the presence of unions.

Trade unions are of course complex organisations operating at many levels and with objectives in the social and political as well as the economic sphere. It may therefore at first appear that, while trade unions are too important a form of economic organisation to ignore, they are also too complicated to analyse with the narrow tools of economics. One thing we hope to show in this chapter is just how far even simple tools of economic analysis can in fact take our understanding of relatively sophisticated organisations such as unions.

An overview of union behaviour

Part of the reason why unions are formed by workers is to influence the **rates of pay** and the **level of employment** in a firm, an industry or even perhaps the economy as a whole. In a competitive industry made up of identical firms, however, we know that, if they operate at the level of the firm, unions will be unable to affect the competitive equilibrium. If technology is freely available, any firms which agree to higher pay for unionised workers will be driven out of business because they will face higher costs than their competitors. Hence, unions can influence equilibrium outcomes only if there are intra-marginal profits (or rents) available to be distributed. For example, if a competitive industry's output supply curve is upward sloping because the lowest cost technology is not freely available to every entrant, rents will be available in intra-marginal firms. As we saw in the previous chapters, rents will also be available when product markets are imperfect and in particular when they are monopolised. It will be helpful to begin with the case in which a single trade union faces a single employer in an industry – the monopoly–monopsony situation introduced in Chapter 18 – but it must be stressed that the essential feature sustaining the emergence and existence of the union is the existence of rents in the industry, initially appropriated entirely by the producer, but in principle partially available to workers through the exercise of bargaining power by their trade union. A product market monopoly simply provides a special case of this general situation.

In our analysis of output markets, we distinguished between traditional models of imperfect competition, and more recent treatments of oligopoly which have arisen from the application of game theory. As we shall explain below, a parallel dichotomy arises in the economic analysis of trade unions. Traditional models begin with the perception of the union as a monopolist on the supply side of the labour market, while more recent models which use game theory explicitly take account of the bargaining process between management and unions. The former approach extends the analysis of Chapters 15 and 16; the latter extends the analysis set out in Chapter 17 for the case of *co-operative games*.

As we mentioned above, one way to view a union is as analogous on the labour supply side to a monopolist in the product market who faces a given demand curve. The resulting model is referred to as the **monopoly union** *model*, and provides the framework of analysis for the first part of this chapter. The traditional model of the monopoly firm has it setting output price, and permitting output to be determined on the demand curve. A monopoly union is thought of as setting the wage, and allowing the employer to choose labour input as its profit-maximising level. In contrast, *bargaining models* assume that unions have control over employment as well as wages, and are therefore able to push firms off their labour demand curves in order to achieve mutually beneficial collusive outcomes. Wage and employment determination in bargaining models are discussed in the second part of this chapter.

Basic analysis of the monopoly union model

In the monopoly model the union is assumed to operate by restricting the supply of labour to the firm so as to ensure that, in order to obtain labour, the firm must pay the union-determined wage. The mechanisms whereby the supply of labour can be restricted by a union range from direct control of employment, as in the cases of doctors, actors and, until recently, printers, through the exercise of social pressure which prevents workers from offering to supply labour at below the union rate, to strike activity. Whatever the mechanism, in the monopoly union framework the union sets the wage, and the firm in effect faces a supply of labour curve which is perfectly elastic at that wage.

Now of course a union could not attract members if the *union wage*, let us call it w_u, was not higher than workers could obtain elsewhere. This latter level of pay we term the *alternative wage*, w_a. Depending on the nature of the broader economy in which the union operates, this alternative wage could represent the level of pay available to workers in non-unionised sectors, or, if the entire economy is unionised, the level of unemployment benefit. For present purposes, the key point is that we presume the union is always able to maintain pay above the alternative wage:

$$w_u > w_a \tag{20.1}$$

How, then, does the union choose its desired wage level, w_u? If a monopoly union was interested in the level of wages alone, it would be able to raise them to any value that it wished (subject to the constraint imposed by the employer's demand for labour). Simple wage maximisation would lead to the absurd outcome of the industry employing only one worker for an essentially infinitesimal period of time per week, with the wage paid equalling the intercept of the labour demand curve with the wage axis. Here, though, the benefits to prospective members in terms of wages are obviously more than offset by losses in terms of employment. This argument tells us that unions will be interested in employment as well as pay targets, and that they might be viewed as maximising a utility function (U^u) in wages and employment, of the form

$$U^u = U(w, L) \tag{20.2}$$

Here we assume that the marginal utility the union gains from both wages and employment is positive but diminishing in the conventional way (see Chapter 2). This preference function can be represented by standard convex-to-the-origin indifference curves, such as I_1, I_2 and I_3 in Figure 20.1. The monopolist's demand for labour curve, which as we showed in Chapter 18 is its marginal revenue product curve (*mrp*), represents the constraint on the union's wage–employment choice. The outcome of the union's maximisation problem is at the tangency between the union's indifference curve and the firm's labour demand curve. The union will therefore fix its wage at w_u which is, by assumption, higher than the alternative wage w_a. The effective labour supply curve faced by the firm is $w_a w_u$, and it chooses employment L_u, just the amount desired by the union.

Figure 20.1

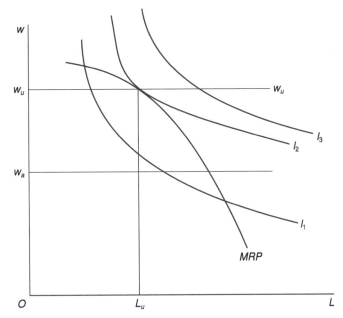

The monopoly union equilibrium is (w_u, L_u) at the tangency of the union indifference curve between wages and employment and the monopolist's labour demand curve, *MRP*. The union wage is assumed to exceed the alternative wage, w_a.

Wage bill maximisation

The foregoing analysis is interesting as far as it goes, but it does not go very far. In particular it says next to nothing about the shape of the union's preferences. A number of attempts have been made to specify the union's objectives more precisely. Thus John Dunlop proposed, as a rough and ready approximation, that unions seek to maximise the **wage bill** paid to their members. The utility function in this case takes the form

$$U^u = w_u L \tag{20.3}$$

The implications of this hypothesis are illustrated in Figure 20.2. The rectangle formed by the choice of any wage–employment combination on the labour demand curve, *mrp*, gives the wage bill (*wL*) for that level of output. The labour demand curve is therefore analogous to the demand, or *average revenue* curve, in product market monopoly theory, where the rectangle formed under the demand curve gives total revenue. Associated with this labour demand or 'average wage bill' (*awb*) line is therefore a marginal wage bill line (*mwb*) which plots the increment to the total wage bill created by reducing the wage sufficiently to lead the firm to employ an additional worker. The marginal wage bill line is exactly analogous to the marginal revenue curve in monopoly theory, and lies everywhere below the average wage bill line because the fall in wage required to permit an additional worker to be employed reduces the wage for all other employees as well.

Figure 20.2

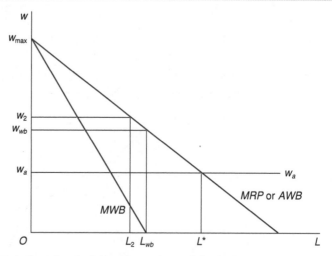

For wage bill maximisation when the labour demand curve is linear, the union chooses the wage rate, w_{wb}, at which the marginal wage bill equals zero, at the point where the wages are half the maximum available (w_{max}). The firm then chooses employment to be L_{wb}. We assume that $w_{wb} > w_a$. If the wage were raised to w_2, employment would fall to L_2.

As we have drawn it in Figure 20.2, with a linear labour demand curve, the marginal wage bill line bisects the angle made by the average wage bill line with the vertical axis. The wage bill is maximised where the marginal wage bill is zero, at (w_{wb}, L_{wb}). At this point, wages are half the level of their maximum value (w_{max}), the level that would be chosen in the absurd case in which the union was concerned with wages alone.

While the wage bill maximisation idea enables us to be more precise than general utility maximisation, its arbitrary nature can be easily illustrated. First, there are no forces within the model to ensure that the wage consistent with wage bill maximisation actually exceeds the alternative wage. It is therefore conceivable that, if pursued, this maximand would lead unions to a choice as unlikely as that of wage maximisation – setting the union wage below the alternative wage. It is hard to see how the union could attract members in such a case.

Nor is this the only problem with wage bill maximisation. Figure 20.2 illustrates clearly the gains and losses from unionisation. Suppose that there existed a market clearing equilibrium wage of w_a in the absence of the union, at which employment would be L^*. The wage-bill maximising union would restrict the supply of labour by $L^* - L_{wb}$ workers, forcing up the wage by ($w_{wb} - w_a$) in Figure 20.2. Thus OL_{wb} workers gain ($w_{wb} - w_a$) each, while ($L_{wb}L^*$) workers lose their jobs. The gainers and losers here are not the same people, and there is no reason to suppose that wage bill maximisation leads to a balancing of the opposing gains and losses from unionisation to which workers would agree. Furthermore, there is no way of knowing whether a further reduction in employment, from L_{wb} to L_2, would be sufficiently beneficial to the L_2 workers who retain their jobs at the new higher wage w_2 to compensate them for the relatively low probability ($L_{wb} - L_2$)/L, of losing their job if they agree to such a new union policy. In short, wage bill maximisation is, upon close inspection, an *ad hoc* and unsatisfactory hypothesis about union motivation.

Box 20.1

Rent maximisation

Unions provide a *mark-up* on the alternative wage. A simple way to ensure that is to modify the wage bill maximisation objective, by assuming that the union maximises the total **rents** earned by its members, net of the alternative wage. This gives us a union utility function

$$U_u = (w_u - w_a)L \tag{20.1.1}$$

In effect, this function has the union maximising the value of its monetary 'profits', where the alternative wage can be viewed as the 'marginal cost' to the union of supplying an incremental worker to the firm. The outcome here is exactly analogous to the standard profit-maximising result for the monopolistic firm. The union will maximise rents when the 'marginal revenue' from supplying an additional worker, which we have already seen is the *mwb*, equals the 'marginal cost', the alternative wage. This equilibrium is shown in Illustration 20.1 using the same labour demand curve and alternative wage as in Figure 20.2. Rents are maximised at (w_R, L_R), at the level of employment where the marginal wage bill equals the alternative wage. Because the alternative wage is positive, rent maximisation always implies a lower level of employment and a higher rate of pay than wage bill maximisation. (This result is exactly parallel to that yielded by the product market monopolist model which has the firm unambiguously producing on the elastic segment of its demand curve.)

Illustration 20.1

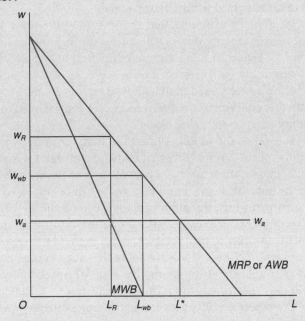

With rent maximisation, the union chooses the wage (w_R) at which the increment to the wage bill exactly equals the incremental cost of supplying an additional worker, which is the alternative wage. The firm then chooses the level of employment to be L_R. In this model, w_R is always greater than w_a. Moreover, rent maximisation always implies a higher level of pay and lower level of employment than wage bill maximisation.

* Maximising expected utility of the representative worker

A criticism of the wage bill maximisation hypothesis was that it gave us no framework for analysing how to weigh the losses of workers who lose their jobs when the union begins to operate against the gains of those who receive higher wages. At first sight, it would appear that this argument applies with even more force to the hypothesis of rent maximisation, because the number of losers and the benefits to the gainers are always greater in this case than under wage bill maximisation. In fact, we will establish that rent maximisation is a perfectly rational objective for workers who weigh up potential income gains against possible job loss, provided that workers are assumed to be *risk neutral*, in the sense defined in Chapter 7. (Risk neutrality, it will be remembered, refers to the case when the individual is indifferent between a sure payment and a risky one which yields the same expected value. Risk aversion, in contrast, refers to the case when the individual prefers the sure payment to a risky one yielding the same expected value.)

Our approach in this section will be to derive an objective for the union by building from assumptions about individual preferences concerning wages and employment. The model explicitly takes account of the potential benefits and costs of joining a union as viewed by workers before the union begins to operate. Potential members are thought of as weighting possible outcomes by the probabilities of their occurring, and treating the resulting sum of expected payoffs as the utility to be gained from joining the union. The approach therefore is an application of the ideas set out in Chapter 7, and, as there, is called **expected utility** *maximisation*.

We start by assuming that every employed worker in a non-unionised industry is required to join the union, which fixes the maximum membership of the union at L^*, in terms of Figure 20.2. We also make the simplifying assumptions that individual workers obtain utility (with respect to the activities of their union) solely through the rate at which they are paid, and that all workers are identical in this regard. Hence, as far as the union is concerned, the preferences of a **representative worker** can be described by a utility function in wages, $U(w)$.

The job of the union is to ensure that, for every worker, the expected value of this utility function across different employment states is maximised. There are two possible outcomes for the worker as a consequence of the union's activity. They can be employed in the industry at the union rate, w_u, or can be displaced and forced to move to another industry in which the ruling rate for the job is the alternative wage. As we argued above, if we denote employment in the unionised industry by L_u, the probability that the representative worker remains employed is L_u/L^* and the expected return from their employment is $(L_u/L^*)U(w_u)$. The activities of the union could instead force the worker to work in another industry at the alternative wage. The probability of this occurring is $(L^* - L_u)/L^*$ and the expected return for this outcome is $(L^* - L_u)/L^*(U(w_a))$.

The expected utility function of the representative worker (U_r^u) can therefore be represented by

$$U_r^u = \frac{L_u}{L^*}U(w_u) + \left(\frac{L^* - L_u}{L^*}\right)U(w_a) \tag{20.4}$$

We can rearrange terms to yield

$$U_r^u = \frac{L_u}{L^*}(U(w_u) - U(w_a)) + U(w_a) \tag{20.5}$$

This allows a particularly simple representation of the effect of the union, because it will be remembered that in the absence of the union, $w_u = w_a$ and the representative worker has a probability of employment at the alternative wage equal to one. The second term on the right-hand side of equation (20.5) thus represents the representative worker's level of utility attainable in the absence of the union. The *gains* for the representative worker in joining the union are described by the first term on the right-hand side of equation (20.6), the expected value of the utility surplus resulting from the union mark-up of wages above the alternate wage. It is this which we assume that the union seeks to maximise for each worker.

The objective for the union is therefore to maximise the representative worker's expected gain from unionisation, $U_r^u - U(w_a)$, for each worker. We therefore multiply the representative worker's utility function net of the base level of utility by L^* to derive the *union's expected utility function,*

$$U_u = L_u(U(w_u) - U(w_a)) \tag{20.6}$$

Recall our general analysis of equilibrium in the monopoly union model (see Figure 20.1). We there established that equilibrium levels of pay and employment in a monopoly union model are determined at the tangency between the union's indifference curve and the firm's demand for labour curve. This in turn implies that, in equilibrium, the slope of the labour demand curve, $\partial L/\partial w$, must equal the slope of the union's indifference curve. The union's utility function contains wages and employment, and we know from Chapter 2 that the marginal rate of substitution between them will equal the ratio of their marginal utilities $(\partial U/\partial w)/(\partial U/\partial L)$.

We can establish this result formally by viewing the union as choosing wages and employment to maximise the general utility function

$$U^u = U(w, L) \tag{20.2}$$

subject to the labour demand curve which we can write for this purpose in the form

$$L = L(w) \tag{20.7}$$

where we know that employment falls as the wage declines $(\partial L/\partial w < 0)$. Maximisation yields the general first-order condition that

$$-\frac{\partial U/\partial w}{\partial U/\partial L} = \frac{\partial L}{\partial w} \tag{20.8}$$

which of course describes an equilibrium of the sort illustrated in Figure 20.1.

We now apply this general approach to the case when the union's utility function takes the expected utility form. If we assume that union preferences are described by equation (20.7), the specification of the left-hand side of the general first-order condition (20.8) may be made more precise as follows. The derivative of the expected utility function with respect to wages is $L\partial U/\partial w$ and with respect to employment is the bracketed term $(U(w_u) - U(w_a))$. Hence in this case the first-order condition (20.8) takes the form

$$-\frac{L\partial U/\partial w}{U(w_u) - U(w_a)} = \frac{\partial L}{\partial w} \tag{20.9}$$

The equilibrium level of employment and wages therefore depends on the specification of the representative worker's utility function with respect to wages $U(w)$. In this probabilistic context, this function indicates the worker's attitude to risk. We can illustrate this argument with an example.

Suppose that the marginal utility of incremental wages is constant, which would imply that the underlying utility function is linear in income. This means that the individual is risk neutral. If the representative individual's utility function, U_n^u takes this simple linear form,

$$U_r^u = w \qquad (20.10)$$

then the expected utility function (20.6) becomes

$$U^u = L_u(w_u - w_a) \qquad (20.11)$$

This is of course identical to the utility function under rent maximisation (which we discussed in Box 20.1). Maximising rents yields the equilibrium described in Illustration 20.1, in which the marginal wage bill equals the alternative wage. The marginal wage bill is the derivative of the wage bill with respect to employment ($\partial(wL)/\partial L$). Thus in equilibrium

$$mwb = \frac{\partial(wL)}{\partial L} = w_u + \frac{L\partial w}{\partial L} = w_a$$

which holds when

$$w_u - w_a = -L\partial w/\partial L \qquad (20.12)$$

Rather than using the formal condition implied by Illustration 20.1, we can instead derive (20.12) directly from the first-order condition (20.9), as follows. If the individual's utility function is just the wage (equation (20.10)), $\partial U/\partial w = 1$, $U(w_u) = w_u$ and $U(w_a) = w_a$. Hence the first-order condition can be rewritten

$$\frac{-L}{w_u - w_a} = \frac{\partial L}{\partial w}$$

which rearranges to

$$w_u - w_a = -L\frac{\partial w}{\partial L} \qquad (20.12)$$

This establishes that, if we had explicitly drawn the union's rent-maximising utility function in Illustration 20.1, it would have been tangent to the average wage bill at exactly the equilibrium point (w_R, L_R). We therefore obtain a formal link between the two diagrammatic approaches used above: the utility-maximisation approach of Figure 20.1, in which equilibrium is located at the tangency between the labour demand curve and the union's indifference curve; and the monopoly union approach of Figure 20.2, in which the union appears to choose the wage and employment level without direct reference to the utility function.

As we noted in discussing Illustration 20.1, the objective of rent maximisation implies lower employment and higher wages than the objective of wage bill maximisation. We can now see that this is because workers who are risk neutral are willing to risk their jobs relatively more in return for a higher wage differential than they would if they are risk averse. If we assume some degree of risk aversion, the slope of the indifference curves will become relatively steeper at any wage–employment combination, and we move to an

Figure 20.3

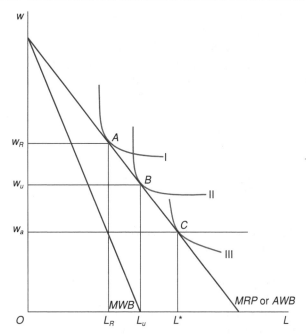

Expected utility maximisation with a variety of attitudes to risk. Risk neutrality yields indifference curves such as I, and the rent-maximising outcome at A. Some degree of risk aversion in individual utility functions implies indifference curves such as II, with an equilibrium at B. Finally, if the workers are unwilling to accept any risk of job loss, the union's indifference curve must be at III and the union is unable to attain any increase in wages.

equilibrium with higher employment and lower wages, such as point *B* in Figure 20.3. In the limit, where workers are unwilling to bear any risk of job loss in order to obtain a higher wage, the union's indifference curve will yield a tangency at the alternative market clearing wage. The expected utility framework therefore suggests that the extent of the **union–non-union wage differential** and the resulting loss of jobs, for a given labour demand curve, depends on the attitude of individual workers to risk.

The monopoly union model – a final comment

The monopoly union model sheds some light on how unions are likely to operate, and the conditions under which their actions are most likely to be successful. While we have been unable to tie down union objectives precisely, the previous section has yielded insights into one likely important determinant of those preferences, namely the attitude of individual union members to employment and wage risks. The expected utility approach argues that the union will seek to attain a positive differential between the union and alternative wages, while keeping the resulting loss in employment as low as possible given that differential. This suggests that the unions will be more successful, the more *inelastic* is the demand for labour curve in the region at which the market would clear in the absence of the union. (In the region where the rent-maximising union will set the wage, of course, the demand for labour will, as we have seen, always be elastic, for exactly the same reasons as a product market monopolist always operates on the elastic part of the demand curve; see Chapter 11.) As we saw in Chapter 18, the demand for labour is derived from product demand, and will be more inelastic the more inelastic the demand for the product, and the lower the degree of substitutability between labour and capital. When we combine this result with the incentives for unions to restrict factor supplies, and the requirement that they operate in sectors where product markets are imperfect (so that there are rents to be shared), we get a surprisingly rich set of insights into how and where unions will be most effective.

Bargaining between unions and firms

The monopoly union model starts from the premise that unions can control the supply of labour at their chosen wage rate (in particular, preventing workers offering to work for less than the union rate) but are unable to influence the level of employment directly. That is assumed to be chosen by the firm in order to maximise its profits given the union wage. This framework has the obvious attractive feature that outcomes always lie on the labour demand curve. However, it has the less obvious drawback that such outcomes fail to offer the best available wage–employment combination, in terms of the utility yielded to the two parties. As we shall now see, for any given point on the labour demand curve, one can find an outcome with lower wages and higher employment at which the union's utility is increased and the firm's profitability is not affected. Alternatively, we can find outcomes at which the firm's profitability is increased while the union's utility remains unchanged. The essential characteristic of these outcomes is that they result from the union and the firm **bargaining** over wages and employment *simultaneously*, with each agreeing to stick by the negotiated wage–employment contract. Such outcomes cannot be achieved in the monopoly union framework because it is assumed that unions fix wages and firms the level of employment in separate decisions.

It is not necessary to alter our analysis of the union to any great extent in order to model a more general bargaining process. We shall simply revert to the general assumption that the union maximises some utility function in wages and employment such as (20.2), without recourse in the first instance to specific functional forms. The big difference in bargaining models comes in the treatment of the firm, which is now assumed to be an active participant in the bargaining process rather than simply choosing employment at a wage unilaterally set by the union. As we saw in Chapter 18, the firm's labour demand curve is derived from a profit-maximising exercise with respect to employment. For a given wage, we deduce a particular level of employment at which profits are maximised. Suppose instead that we take as given the level of profit, say π_0, and consider the combinations of wages and employment which would yield the same level of profit. We can plot these combinations in wage–employment space to produce what is termed an *isoprofit curve* analogous to those derived in Chapter 16 in the duopolists' output space. A family of such curves is plotted in Figure 20.4. Because, for a given level of employment, and hence output, profits will rise as wages fall, these curves represent higher and higher levels of profit as we move down the diagram. Moreover each curve is at its maximum height where it cuts the labour demand curve. Starting at the maximum point on the

Figure 20.4

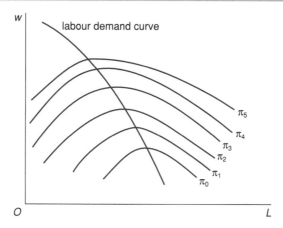

Each point on the labour demand curve is associated with an isoprofit curve, such as π_0, π_1, π_2, etc., which plots the levels of wages and employment at a given level of profit, i.e. π_0, π_1, π_2, etc. The isoprofit curve reaches its maximum height at the wage–employment combination on the labour demand curve. Higher and higher points on the labour demand curve are associated with lower and lower levels of profit ($\pi_0 > \pi_1 > \pi_2$, etc.).

curve, to increase employment at a given wage will certainly reduce profit. Therefore to hold profits constant, the wage must fall as employment rises. Similarly to cut employment and output at a given wage also reduces profits: hence to keep profits constant, the wage must fall as we move to the left of the demand curve.

Efficient bargaining

The analysis of **efficient bargaining** is now straightforward, and parallels our formulation of joint profit maximisation by cartels in Chapter 17. If we look back to Figure 20.1, we can remind ouselves that in the monopoly union framework, wages and employment are determined at the point of tangency between the union's indifference curve and the labour demand curve, point *A* on Figure 20.5. We can clearly achieve wage–employment outcomes which raise either the firm's profits (by moving to a lower isoprofit curve) or the union's welfare, or both, by moving to a point at which the level of employment is higher and the wage rate lower than under the monopoly union outcome. Such equilibria are indicated by points such as *B* or *C* in Figure 20.5. We cannot say exactly which outcome bargaining will lead us to. However, we do know that the situations in which neither the firm nor the union can be made better off without the other party to the negotiations being made worse off are all characterised by the fact that the slope of the union's relevant indifference curve is equal to the slope of the firm's relevant isoprofit curve. Points *B* and *C* in Figure 20.5 characterise such situations. The locus of all such points we again refer to as the **contract curve** and we now develop its analysis for firm–union bargains below. (See also Chapters 7 and 22 for further applications of the contract curve idea.)

Figure 20.5

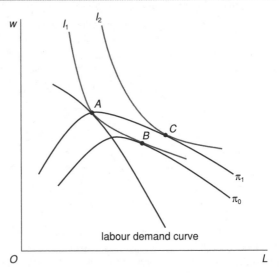

Bargaining as against monopoly union outcomes. If we suppose the union's indifference curves to take the form I_1, I_2, the monopoly union equilibrium occurs at point A. However, this is not the best conceivable bargain for either party. The union could attain the same level of satisfaction while the firm earned higher profits at B, while the converse is true at point C. In general, bargaining equilibria are characterised by tangency between the firm's isoprofit curve and the union's indifference curve.

Consider first the determination of the union–firm curve's end points. In our discussion of the monopoly union case, we indicated that unions would be unable to attract members, and hence to control the supply of labour, at any wage below that available in alternative lines of work. This sets a floor to the wage level to which firms can push unions, at the alternative wage, w_a. This wage level is depicted in Figure 20.6. Conversely, however powerful the union, it cannot raise wages and employment so high that the firm is driven out of business. We can denote the firm's minimum acceptable level of profit by $\pi_{\min}$. There is of course an isoprofit line associated with this minimum profit level, $\pi_{\min}$, and we draw it in Figure 20.6. The part of the contract curve along which bargains between unions and firms can be struck therefore lies above w_a and below the isoprofit curve $\pi_{\min}$. This is the segment XY in Figure 20.6.

In order to press our analysis further, we need to know about the relative bargaining power of the union and the firm. As the firm becomes relatively more powerful, it can force the union to accept lower levels of utility, towards point X in Figure 20.6. Similarly, as the union becomes more powerful it can extract an increasing proportion of the firm's profit for its members, shifting the outcome of bargaining along the contract curve towards point Y in Figure 20.6. To say more about the outcome than this requires an explicit theory of the bargaining process which we shall introduce in the following section.

For the moment, let us assume that relative bargaining powers are fixed so that the union is unable to obtain utility greater than I_1 in Figure 20.6. In the monopoly union framework we developed earlier, to obtain this utility level the union would fix a wage of w_u, and the firm would set employment on the demand curve at L_u. Now suppose we

Figure 20.6 Union–firm bargaining

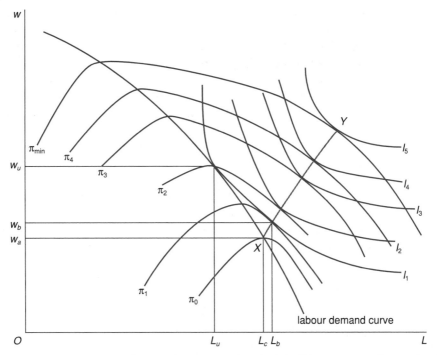

The contract curve is the locus of tangencies between the union's indifference curves (I_1, I_2, ...) and the firm's isoprofit curves (π_0, π_1, ...) between the minimum acceptable level of pay for the union (w_a) and the minimum acceptable level of profits for the firm (π_{min}): the segment XY. The precise point on the contract curve chosen depends on the relative bargaining power of the two sides. As the firm becomes relatively more powerful, outcomes move along the contract curve towards X. In the monopoly union model, unions decrease employment and raise wages relative to the competitive outcome (w_a, L_c), attaining an equilibrium such as (w_u, L_u). If we suppose the attainment of I_1 represents the union's relative bargaining power, employment is greater and wages less with efficient bargaining (w_b, L_b). Indeed, employment exceeds that attained under competition.

move to efficient bargaining. Since we have fixed the union's utility level at I_1, the benefits from efficient bargaining must by assumption then accrue entirely to the firm, which can raise its profits from π_2 to π_1. The efficient bargaining equilibrium is characterised by a higher level of employment and lower pay, at (L_b, w_b), than obtained in the monopoly union case. This result arises because the union is assumed to gain higher utility from greater levels of employment as well as higher wages. In this bargaining framework which allows the union to trade employment against wages, it will therefore agree with firms to settle on an outcome beyond their labour demand curve.

It should be noted that in Figure 20.6 we have drawn the relevant section of the contract curve, XY, as upward sloping in wage–employment space. As a result, the equilibrium level of employment in efficient bargaining exceeds that which would arise from a competitive labour market ($L_b > L_c$). Firms earn less profit under efficient bargaining than in the competitive case, however, because wages as well as employment are higher ($w_b > w_a$,

$\pi_1 < \pi_0$ in Figure 20.6). For this reason, efficient bargaining models are often seen as describing the '**labour hoarding**' or '**featherbedding**' considered characteristic of unionised industries, which are said to overemploy labour and therefore to have relatively lower labour productivity. In this framework, overemployment arises from the union's interest in employment as well as wages and its assumed ability to enforce agreed levels of employment as well as pay on the firm.

However, contract curves are not necessarily always upward sloping. A backward-bending contract curve is illustrated in Figure 20.7. As we shall show more formally in the next section, the slope of the contract curve can be associated with the relative weights attached by the union to wages and employment in its utility function. Roughly speaking, if the union weights employment heavily relative to wages on the margin, the contract curve will be upward sloping, as in Figure 20.6. In this case, increased union power leads to higher employment. Conversely, if the union weights wages relatively more highly, the contract curve will be backward bending as in Figure 20.7 and equilibrium employment under efficient bargaining will be less than the competitive level ($L'_b < L'_c$). With backward-sloping contract curves, increased union power acts to reduce employment and to increase wages.

Figure 20.7

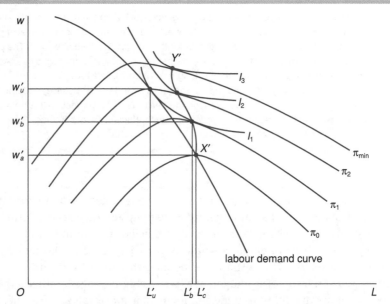

The contract curve is the locus of tangencies between the union's indifference curves (l_1, l_2) and the firm's isoprofit curves (π_0, π_1). In contrast to Figure 20.6, the union is here assumed to attach relatively more weight to wages than to employment, so the contract curve $X'Y'$ is backward bending. If the union's utility level is fixed at l_1, that which would be attained at the monopoly union solution w'_u, L'_u, efficient bargaining will increase employment to L'_b and reduce the wage to w'_b. However, with a backward-bending contract curve, employment is less than L'_c, the amount that would rule at the alternative wage, w'_a.

* Bargaining theory

As with our analysis of oligopoly, game theory can yield considerable additional insights into the interactions between unions and firms. The monopoly union model closely parallels the non-collusive games developed in Chapter 17. Indeed, alert readers will have recognised precisely the structure of a Stackelberg game in the premise that unions can control the supply of labour at a given wage but the firm chooses the level of employment. It is our intention in this chapter, however, to extend our use of game theory in order to formalise the outcome of *collusive* bargaining processes. We therefore concentrate our attention on how firms and unions combine to choose wages and employment jointly through efficient bargaining. We use the Nash bargaining solution, or the *Nash fixed threat point* model, in this analysis, an approach which we have already applied to the discussion of cartels in Chapter 17.

The game which we assume that unions and firms play takes the following form. As in Chapter 16 and 17 two players *co-operate* in order to achieve the highest possible joint rewards, which they then divide between themselves according to their relative bargaining powers. 'Rewards' in this context are defined relative to **threat points**, the payments which each party would receive in the absence of any binding agreement. If we follow our previous notation, the firm's threat point is therefore its shutdown level of profit, π_{min}, while the union's threat point is the utility derived at the competitive outcome (w_a, L_c), termed U^u_{min}. Nash deduced, from axioms about the outcome, that the solution to a game of this type is provided by the *maximisation of the product of the union's and the firm's utility increments above their respective threat points*. We can therefore investigate the properties of Nash co-operative equilibrium by analysing the first-order conditions of the joint maximisation problem.

Let us suppose we can represent the relative bargaining power of the firm as against the union by the parameter μ. The Nash approach leads the union and the firm to maximise the product of their respective gains above the threat points:

$$N = [\pi - \pi_{min}]^\mu [U^u(w, L) - U^u_{min}] \tag{20.13}$$

Maximisation with respect to wages and employment yields two first-order conditions which can be rearranged to yield

$$-\frac{\partial U/\partial L}{\partial U/\partial w} = \frac{1}{L}((mrp) - w) \tag{20.14}$$

where (mrp) is the marginal revenue product of labour. Equation (20.14) defines the contract curve. The left-hand side defines the slope of the union's indifference curve in wage–employment space. To understand the right-hand side, we must consider the firm's profit-maximising behaviour. If, in order to keep the analysis simple, we abstract from fixed costs, we can define profits as

$$\pi = pX - wL \tag{20.15}$$

so that for a given level of profits, π_0, the equation of an isoprofit curve for a monopolist on the product market is given by

$$w = \frac{pX - \pi_0}{L} \tag{20.16}$$

The slope of the isoprofit curve is given by

$$\frac{\partial w}{\partial L} = \frac{L(mrp) - (pX - 1)}{L^2}$$

$$= \frac{L(mrp) - wL}{L^2}$$

$$= \frac{1}{L}((mrp) - w) \tag{20.17}$$

The right-hand side of equation (20.17) is therefore the slope of the isoprofit curve. Interested readers will note the parallels with the analysis of the labour-managed firm in Chapter 14. Equation (20.14) is the algebraic version of the condition we deduced geometrically in Figure 20.6, that the contract curve is the locus of points at which the union's indifference curve is tangent to the firm's isoprofit curve. As we can see by inspection of (20.14), in general we cannot say whether the contract curve is upward sloping or backward bending.

Different union objectives and efficient bargaining

A fairly simple representation of union and firm preferences allows us to examine the impact of different assumptions about the union utility function on the shape of the contract curve. We will first assume that firms go out of business if profits become negative, so that the firm's threat point, π_{min}, equals zero. The firm's relative bargaining power we continue to represent with the parameter μ. In specifying union preferences we adopt a version of a functional form widely used in demand theory, namely the **Stone–Geary function**, in which utility is the weighted product of the arguments of the function. Thus:

$$[U^u(w, L) - U^u_{min}] = (w - w_a)^\gamma L^\theta \tag{20.18}$$

Alert readers will note the similarities between the functional form of equation (20.18) and the Cobb-Douglas function which we have already employed.

The Nash product of utility increments under these conditions can be written as

$$N^1 = [\pi]^\mu (w - w_a)^\gamma L^\theta \tag{20.19}$$

This of course is merely a particular specification of the general Nash product (20.13), given (20.19) when $\pi_{min} = 0$. Maximising N^1 with respect to wages and employment and simplifying yields the first-order condition

$$w = w_a + \left(\frac{\gamma}{\mu}\right)\frac{\pi}{L} \tag{20.20}$$

$$(mrp) - w = -\left(\frac{\theta}{\mu}\right)\frac{\pi}{L} \tag{20.21}$$

Combining these equations yields the contract curve

$$[(mrp) - w] = -\frac{\theta}{\gamma}(w - w_a) \tag{20.22}$$

which can be rearranged to the convenient form

$$w = \frac{\gamma}{\gamma - \theta}(wrp) - \frac{\theta}{\gamma - \theta}w_a \tag{20.23}$$

The slope of this curve depends on the relationship between the weight attached to the union's utility function to wages (γ) and that attached to employment (θ). We can distinguish three cases, each of which is illustrated in Figure 20.8. If the union attaches more weight to employment than wages ($\theta > \gamma$), since mrp is a decreasing function of employment, equation (20.24) establishes that the contract curve will be upward sloping, such as the locus AC in Figure 20.8. More formally, differentiating (20.23) with respect to employment, we derive its slope, $\partial w/\partial L$:

$$\frac{\partial w}{\partial L} = \frac{\gamma}{\gamma - \theta}\left(\frac{\partial(mrp)}{\partial L}\right) \tag{20.24}$$

and $\partial(mrp)/\partial L$ is negative because of diminishing returns to a factor and downward-sloping product demand curves. Hence if ($\gamma - \theta$) is less than zero, the slope of the contract curve is positive. Conversely, if the union attaches more weight to wages than to employment ($\gamma > \theta$), equation (20.24) tells us that the contract curve will be backward sloping, for example the locus AC' in Figure 20.8.

Finally, the case of rent maximisation discussed above is also yielded by a special case of utility function (20.18), namely when $\theta = \gamma = 1$ (see equation (20.18)). Under this

Figure 20.8

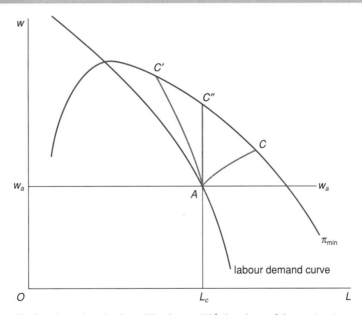

If the union's utility function takes the form $U^u = (w - w_a)^\gamma L^\theta$, the slope of the contract curve depends on the relative magnitudes of γ and θ. If $\theta > \gamma$, the contract curve is upward sloping, locus AC. If $\gamma > \theta$, it is backward bending, locus AC'. If $\theta = \gamma$, which holds if the union maximises rents, the locus is vertical at employment level L_c between the alternative wage and the minimum profit level, locus AC''.

assumption, the slope of the contract curve is infinity and this locus is therefore vertical. If we refer back to the original formulation of the contract curve under this specification, equation (20.22), when $\theta = \gamma = 1$ this reduces to

$$(mrp) = w_a \qquad\qquad\qquad (20.25)$$

Hence if the union's objective is to maximise rents and the framework for negotiation is efficient bargaining, employment will be fixed independently of the wage rate at the level where the marginal revenue product of labour equals the alternative wage at the competitive employment level L_c. The wage will be determined along the vertical contract curve above w_a according to relative bargaining powers, as illustrated by the locus AC'' in Figure 20.8.

Concluding comment

In this chapter, we have shown that the simple framework which we derived to analyse the behaviour of single economic agents, be they consumers or firms, can be extended to more complex organisations such as trade unions. Moreover the fact that we were unable to identify with any degree of precision an objective for such organisations proved to be only a limited drawback for our analysis.

A number of unambiguous predictions have emerged from this work, of which the most important is that unions act to push wages above the level which would pertain in a competitive market. This result holds for all sensible specifications of the union's objectives, including formulations which explicitly take account of the possibility that such wage-increasing activities may reduce the level of employment. In general, the greater the stress placed on the level of remuneration by the union, the greater will be the mark-up over the competitive wage that the organisation will achieve.

We were unable, however, to conclude unambiguously that wage increases also act to reduce employment. Rather, it emerged that the outcome here depends on the bargaining framework in which unions and firms operate. If the union is unable to control the determination of employment, their wage-increasing activities must reduce the level of employment. If employment as well as wages are open to negotiation, we enter a bargaining framework in which sufficiently high stress on employment in the union's preferences can lead to a greater level of employment than would pertain under competition.

SUMMARY

The economic analysis of trade unions and bargaining

1. Traditional models analyse trade unions as monopolists on the supply side of the labour market, restricting the supply of labour to raise wages above the market clearing rate.

2. To analyse union behaviour we need to make assumptions about union preferences with respect to wages and employment. One approach is to assume that unions seek to maximise the wage bill paid to their members. In this case, the union chooses a wage

rate where the marginal wage bill equals zero. If the labour demand curve is linear, this is half the maximum possible wage.

3. A second assumption is that unions maximise the mark-up of wages over the market (or alternative) wage. With this maximisation of rents, unions set wages so as to equalise the marginal wage bill to the alternative wage. The equilibrium wage is higher in this case than under wage bill maximisation.

4. Unions might also maximise the expected income of their members given by the wage paid in the employed and unemployed states, each multiplied by the probability of their occurring.

5. We can gain further insights into the plausibility of these three assumptions when we analyse the union's attitude to risk. Rent maximisation is consistent with risk neutrality, and wage bill maximisation with some degree of risk aversion.

6. The monopoly union model presupposes that bargaining between managers and firms is sequential, with the union setting wages and the firm then choosing the level of employment. However, if values for these two variables are chosen simultaneously, we move to a situation of efficient bargaining. Bargaining always leads to outcomes on the contract curve, the locus of points of tangency of the firm's labour demand curve and the union's indifference curve.

7. The precise point on the contract curve chosen by the two sides depends upon their relative bargaining power. Contract curves can be forward or backward sloping, depending on the union's attitude to risk.

8. In a co-operative game of this sort, the players co-operate to achieve the highest possible joint rewards, relative to their threat points, or worst acceptable outcomes. They then divide the joint spoils according to their relative bargaining power.

PROBLEMS

1 Suppose that in a monopoly union framework the union maximises its wage bill and the firm's labour demand curve can be approximated by a straight line.

(a) What happens to the level of employment and the wage paid if demand in the product market increases? What happens to profits?

(b) What happens to the level of employment and the wage paid if the firm introduces a technical innovation which increases the marginal physical product of labour at each level of output?

(c) Are these results altered if we assume that the firm maximises rents rather than the wage bill?

2 Suppose that the representative worker's utility function takes the form $U_r^u = w^\gamma$. Show that, if the union maximises expected utility, and unions and firms bargain according to the monopoly union model, the equilibrium level of employment declines as the value of the parameter γ increases.

3 Suppose in an efficient bargaining framework, the union and firm have attained a particular equilibrium on the contract curve.

(a) What is the effect on wages and employment of an increase in the alternative wage?

(b) What is the effect on wages and employment of an increase in product demand?

4 Suppose that a union and a firm operate in an efficient bargaining framework, with equal bargaining powers (so the term for bargaining power in the Nash product equals one). The union is assumed to have a utility function, specified net of its threat point, of the form $U = (w - w_a)L$. The firm gains satisfaction from profits according to the utility function $U(\pi) = \pi$ with the threat point, π_{min}, equal to zero.

(a) Derive the equation for the contract curve.
(b) Show that the level of employment is determined independently of the equilibrium value of wages.
(c) Show that changes in the degree of bargaining power affect wages but not employment.

PART VII

GENERAL EQUILIBRIUM AND WELFARE

CHAPTER ⟨21⟩

The exchange economy

Key words and phrases

- co-ordination of choices, partial equilibrium, general equilibrium, exchange economy, welfare economics, market failure
- auctioneer, endowments, box diagram, contract curve, core
- *tâtonnement*, excess demand, competitive equilibrium, coalitions, blocking coalitions
- equilibrium price vector, Walras' law
- existence, uniqueness, and stability of equilibrium
- planning

Introduction

We stressed at the very outset of this book that economics is about scarcity, and that scarcity implies that people must make choices. The relationship between this proposition and the analysis we have presented so far is surely clear to readers. Consumer theory deals with the choices of individual households and their consequences for behaviour. Similarly, production theory and the theory of industrial organisation have much to say about the choices of individual firms. Scarcity, however, is not merely a private phenomenon. It has a social aspect as well. Individuals can formulate plans about how to make the best use of the resources available to them, but unless those plans are compatible with those made by others, they will not be able to execute them. Hence, as hinted at the start, a coherent solution at the level of the economy as a whole to the problems posed by scarcity requires that the choices made by individuals be co-ordinated with one another.

In the preceding chapters we have had a good deal to say about the interaction of households and firms in markets, and many of the mechanisms we have analysed may usefully be thought of as operating to **co-ordinate the choices** which individual agents make. Thus, to cite the most obvious example, we have shown that equilibrium exists in a perfectly competitive market for a particular good where its supply and demand curves intersect; this state of affairs is one in which the plans of agents to buy the good in question are just compatible with those of firms to sell it, this compatibility being achieved by varying the price at which the good is traded. If, at some initial price, consumers plan to buy more of it than firms plan to supply, this incompatability between choices may be removed by raising the price, and vice versa. In this example, then, it is the price of the good being traded which moves to co-ordinate the choices of buyers and sellers.

Now the analysis of markets for particular goods and services is certainly interesting and useful but, when it comes to helping us to develop an understanding of the way in which individual choices are co-ordinated on an economy-wide basis, it does not go far enough. The theory of consumer behaviour shows that the consumer's decision about how much of any particular good to buy is not taken in isolation, but as part of an overall plan about how to allocate income over an array of available goods and services. At the same time the theory of the firm shows that the firm's output decision is taken simultaneously with others concerning the purchase of factors of production. Moreover, if the typical consumer's income is derived from the sale of productive services to a firm, then firms' factor market decisions will affect consumers' incomes and hence their choices about the purchase of goods and services. Clearly, there must be much more to the co-ordination of the choices of individual householders and firms than the interaction of supply and demand in a particular market.

Such analysis is usually referred to as **partial equilibrium** analysis. It concentrates upon the way in which choices in certain parts of the economy are made and co-ordinated, while neglecting the way in which solutions achieved in one market impinge upon others. Underlying it is the assumption that these interactions are sufficiently minor that to neglect them does not undermine the validity of the conclusions reached. If this assumption holds, then it is well worth making, for to neglect such interactions certainly enables us to achieve a degree of simplicity in our theorising that would not otherwise be attainable. There are no rules, however, which can always guarantee that partial equilibrium analysis may be validly applied to a particular issue. It is a matter for the judgement of the individual economist to decide when it is appropriate to hold 'other things equal', and indeed to choose which 'other things' they should be. There is, however, as we have just noted, one set of issues at least, where partial equilibrium analysis will not do. If one is concerned to understand the way in which market mechanisms do, or do not, work in order to achieve compatibility of agents' choices on an economy-wide basis, a '**general equilibrium**' analysis which focuses on the interaction of markets is required.

As readers may have already guessed, general equilibrium theory, the very purpose of which is to analyse the way in which the choices of individual consumers and firms are co-ordinated across markets on an economy-wide basis, is potentially very complicated. Such analysis must do everything that partial equilibrium analysis does, and more. It must deal with consumers' decisions about the demand for goods and services, and the supply of factors of production, and show how those choices impinge upon one another, and are rendered compatible among consumers. It must deal with firms' output supply and input demand decisions, and show how these are co-ordinated among firms. Moreover, since factor sales are the source of consumers' incomes, it must also show how the output market decisions of firms and consumers interact with their factor market decisions. Finally, and crucially, it must deal with all of these matters *simultaneously*. The fact that a particular market can reach an equilibrium, taking the prices from all other markets as given, tells us little about the possibilities for all markets to reach a state of general equilibrium.

A body of theory dealing with general equilibrium does indeed exist, and this and the next two chapters of this book will be devoted to expounding its essential properties. We shall develop the properties one step at a time. First, because many of its complexities arise from the interactions among consumption and production decisions, we shall abstract from these by considering an economy with no production, an **exchange economy** in which consumers trade, with one another, exogenously given endowments of goods. In this context we shall analyse the nature of a situation in which all agents' trading and consumption plans are compatible with one another, and say something about the mechanisms whereby such a state of general equilibrium might be achieved. We shall then complicate the analysis by introducing production, and having first analysed the nature of equilibrium in production, will proceed to bring the two sides of the economy together in order to display the characteristics of general equilibrium in an economy with production.

Once the properties of a production economy in general equilibrium have been set out we shall discuss the application of such analysis to so-called **welfare economics**, which confronts questions about the ethical desirability of various solutions to the scarcity problem. We shall ask whether the solution implied by our analysis is a desirable one, and discuss ways in which particular problems arising in the private sector of the economy might impinge upon its desirability. We shall also have some things to say in the next part of the book about the way in which government action might deal with the problems of **market failures**, and also about issues having to do with the distribution of income. We reserve to the final chapter of this book some discussion of topics in the theory of *public choice*, that branch of public economics which tries to explain not how economic policy decisions ought to be taken, but how in fact they are made in practice.

A simple exchange economy – the box diagram

In order to keep our analysis as clear as possible we shall initially confine our discussion to a so-called exchange economy: one in which agents are endowed with particular quantities of goods and services and trade them, but in which there is no production. We shall discuss the key characteristics of equilibrium in such an economy and also say something about the means whereby it might be achieved. In particular we shall discuss the role played by competitively determined prices in our economy and the activities of a somewhat mysterious entity usually referred to as the **auctioneer** in setting and changing them. As it happens, considerable simplicity can be obtained if we deal with an economy in which only two agents trade two goods. Though a two-person two-good economy with no production is far removed from anything one might conceivably encounter in the real world, it turns out that the critical features of general equilibrium in such an economy also occur in much more complex production economies with many goods, many agents and many inputs. Hence we surrender realism here in order to obtain a great deal of simplicity. Nevertheless, proofs of many of the key propositions in the chapters which follow rely on the assumption that there are a large number of traders, so it should always be remembered that our treatment here is meant to achieve clarity of exposition, not theoretical rigour.

Consider an economy in which two goods are made available to two consumers at constant rates per unit of time. There is no production, the goods in question simply being delivered from the outside, but our two consumers are allowed to exchange goods. The essential properties of this economy may be set out in a diagram, Figure 21.1. Let the goods with which the economy is endowed be called X and Y, and let us refer to the two consumers as A and B. In Figure 21.1 we measure quantities of X on the horizontal axis and of Y on the vertical. There is available to the economy a given amount, an **endowment**,

Figure 21.1

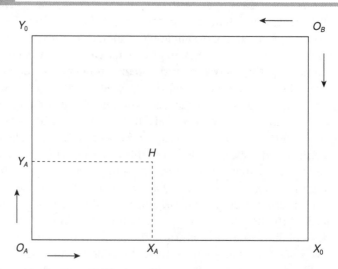

X_0 and Y_0 are the total quantities of X and Y available. Consumer A's consumption of the goods is measured from the bottom left-hand corner O_A and B's from the top right-hand corner O_B. Any point such as H represents a division of X and Y between the consumers that results in the available quantities of both goods being entirely consumed.

of X, X_0, and a given endowment of Y, Y_0, so let us close off the space above and to the right of the axes at these quantities, thus drawing what is usually referred to as a 'box'.

Let us measure the quantity of X available to consumer A (X_A) from left to right along the horizontal axis, and the quantity of Y available to that same consumer (Y_A) from bottom to top of the vertical axis. If we do this, it is immediately apparent that X_0 minus A's consumption of X gives us the amount of the economy's endowment of X left over for B to consume, and that Y_0 minus A's consumption of Y gives us the amount of Y left over for B. In other words, if we treat the bottom left-hand corner of the box as the origin relative to which A's consumption is measured, the top right-hand corner becomes the origin relative to which B's consumption may be measured. If we further impose the condition that A and B between them must consume the economy's entire endowment of goods, then we may interpret any single point within the box as representing simultaneously a combination of X and Y consumed by A and a combination of X and Y consumed by B. Thus, if A consumes X_A of X and Y_A of Y, then B will consume $X_0 - X_A$ and $Y_0 - Y_A$, so that the point labelled H will represent this joint consumption pattern. Any point within the box, including those lying on the axes, represents a feasible joint consumption pattern for our two agents, given the economy's endowments of X and Y.

The contract curve, trade and the core

We draw our two agents' preference patterns for X and Y in Figure 21.2. A's satisfaction increases as we move from bottom left to top right in this **box diagram** and B's increases as we move from top right to bottom left. We also draw a line linking the two origins of

Figure 21.2

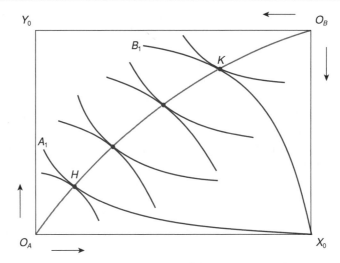

A's indifference map is drawn relative to O_A and B's relative to O_B. The contract curve $O_A O_B$ is a locus of points of tangency between the two indifference maps. At any point on it, it would be impossible to make one consumer better off without reducing the satisfaction of the other. If A begins with all the X and B with all the Y, voluntary trade will never move A below indifference curve A_1 or B below B_1. The equilibrium outcome of their trading would thus lie between H and K. This segment of the contract curve is known as the core of the economy.

the box and passing through all the points within it where indifference curves of our two agents are tangent to one another. As we saw in Chapters 17 and 20, loci of this sort are called **contract curves**. We have already remarked that any point within our box, including those on the axes, represents a feasible joint consumption pattern of X and Y that A and B could undertake. We may now subdivide these points into two groups, those which lie on the contract curve and those which do not, and it is helpful to do this because the economic significance of the two sets of points differs in an important way.

Consider first a typical point on the contract curve such as H in Figure 21.2. Suppose that, when the economy's endowment of X and Y arrived it was distributed between A and B so as to locate them at this point. Would there be any way of redistributing the economy's endowment of X and Y between A and B to which they would both consent? Clearly not, because if the redistribution in question involved a movement along the contract curve, one of our two agents would be moved to a lower level of satisfaction as the other gained, while if it involved a movement off the contract curve at least one, and perhaps both agents would see their level of satisfaction reduced. Now consider some point not on the contract curve, say X_0 in Figure 21.2 at which A has all the X and B has all the Y, and ask the same question. Here the answer is just as clearly yes, for A would consent to any redistribution of goods that involved a movement along indifference curve A_1 or to a curve that lay above it. Similarly B would consent to any redistribution that involved a movement along B_1 or to a curve lying above it. Clearly there is much scope within the area bounded by these two indifference curves to redistribute goods among our consumers so that both gain. Being maximising agents, they would both consent to such a redistribution.

Now note that, in the foregoing argument, point H stood for any point on the contract curve, and X_0 for any point off it. We have shown, therefore, that if goods are distributed between our consumers in such a way that they are not at a point at which their indifference curves are tangent to one another – are not on the contract curve – they can both gain from a redistribution of goods between them. We have also shown that, if they are at a point on the contract curve, no gains are available to both of them simultaneously. Hence if, when they receive their initial endowments, we permit our two agents to trade with one another until all mutually beneficial trades are exhausted, we may conclude that their activities will be such as to place them on the contract curve.

If we perform the experiment of permitting our consumers to start from every conceivable distribution of goods within the box, we can see that the contract curve links up all those distributions of goods between them which could possibly be attained if they freely contracted with one another to exchange goods. Now in any particular instance we can, if we specify the initial distribution of the economy's endowment, find the segment of the contract curve to which voluntary trade would lead. The distribution of goods actually reached in any instance would have to result in a gain (or at least no loss) in satisfaction to both parties. Thus, to refer back to Figure 21.2 again, there is a segment of the contract curve below and to the left of point H, and another above and to the right of point K, which would not be attainable if our agents were to start their trading from point X_0. Any point between H and K could, however, be reached by mutually agreeable trades beginning from X_0. This segment of the contract curve is usually referred to as the **core** of the economy, and its location must be defined not just with respect to the tastes of agents inhabiting the economy, and its overall endowment of goods, as is the whole contract curve, but also with respect to the initial distribution of that endowment between the two agents from which trading activity begins.

Competitive prices and the auctioneer

Readers will have been struck by the vagueness of our description, in the foregoing section, of the trading process underlying the movement from a point off the contract curve to a point on it, and we now turn to clarifying this matter. In principle one could conceive of a wide variety of rules under which two agents could bargain with one another, but here we shall consider what happens when the agents trade with one another at competitively determined prices. It is true, of course, that we normally associate competition with large numbers of traders being at work in a market, but the reader who treats our application of competitive notions to the highly artificial two-agent case as a simplification designed clearly to reveal the key properties of a market made up of many traders will not be misled.

We must begin our exposition by drawing attention to a puzzle. It is of the very essence of a competitive market that every agent operating in it has no control over prices. These are taken by every individual as given by 'the market' and treated as the basis for that agent's decisions about quantities. Consider our treatment of consumer theory in Chapter 2 above. There the typical consumer was treated as taking the prices of goods as given, and the demand curve we derived told us how the consumer's demand for a particular good would vary as its market price changed. Similarly, our analysis of the perfectly competitive firm in Chapter 13 treated it as a price taker choosing its quantity of output. But suppose that every market in an economy is to be treated as perfectly competitive. This implies that every agent in that economy is a price taker and, therefore, that no one within the economy sets prices. Who then sets prices? How do they change? This gap in the theory of competitive markets is a real one, and the standard way of filling it, which we shall now set out, though logically viable, leaves many economists extremely uncomfortable about the validity of blindly applying competitive market theories to the real world. The discomfort in question figures particularly prominently in debates about macroeconomic issues, and so we simply note it here rather than discussing it at any length.

The problem of price setting in a perfectly competitive market economy is usually dealt with by postulating that the system works as if it was presided over by an *auctioneer* who neither consumes nor produces goods, and whose sole job it is to set prices according to certain rules and to inform traders about them. The rules in question involve the auctioneer operating what is usually referred to as a process of **tâtonnement**, which in a pure exchange economy may be thought of as working as follows. When they receive their endowments of goods, agents come to a 'market' presided over by the auctioneer, and this entity suggests to them a list of prices for all the goods in the economy. Each agent then submits to the auctioneer a list consisting of the quantities of goods to be supplied and demanded by that individual at those prices. It is then the auctioneer's task to check these lists to see if the trades offered can all go through. If they cannot, if more (or less) of some good is being demanded than is available, then the auctioneer recognises that the market is not in equilibrium, that all agents' plans are not mutually compatible, and tries another set of prices. The new set of prices is not chosen at random, however. The auctioneer raises the prices of those goods for which the sum of agents' demands exceeds the economy's endowment, and lowers the prices of those for which demand falls short of the endowment.

This process of groping for an appropriate set of prices continues until one is found at which the sum of agents' demand for each and every good just equals the economy's endowment of it, at which the so-called **excess demand** for each good is zero. At this point the auctioneer permits trading to begin at this equilibrium set of prices, and agents may do so confident that all of their planned exchanges can indeed go through. It should be stressed that in our model of the perfectly competitive economy, the auctioneer never permits anyone to trade until equilibrium prices have been established. This assumption is crucial in the analysis which follows. One derives markedly different results if we assume that agents actually exchange goods at disequilibrium prices, referred to as *trading at false prices*, though models of this sort are beyond the scope of this book

Properties of competitive equilibrium

The process of *tâtonnement* we have described leads to a state of competitive equilibrium, and we can learn something about its properties by considering a two-person two-good exchange economy in which trade takes place according to the rules just set out. Figure 21.3 depicts such an economy, indeed the same economy described in Figure 21.2, in which its initial endowment of goods is distributed so that A has all the X and B has all the Y. Now let the auctioneer suggest a price for X in terms of Y which implies that our two agents can trade along a line such as I. Faced with such a budget constraint, A would wish to move to point L, consuming X_1 of X and Y_1 of Y. B on the other hand would wish to move to point M, consuming X_2 of X and Y_2 of Y. Obviously in this case the economy-wide

Figure 21.3

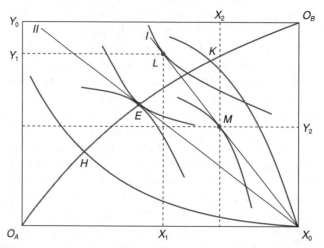

At the price ratio underlying *I*, there is an excess demand for *Y* and an excess supply of *X*. As the relative price of *Y* is increased, the price ratio pivots towards *II*. If each agent faces the same relative price for *X* and *Y*, as they would in a competitive market, their demands for *X* and *Y* will just take up the economy's endowment of these goods at a point such as *E*.

planned consumption of X $[(O_A - X_1) + (O_B - X_2)]$ falls short of its total endowment $(O_A - X_0)$, and planned consumption of Y $[(O_A - Y_1) + (O_B - Y_2)]$ exceeds its total endowment $(O_A - Y_0)$. In these circumstances the auctioneer would not permit our agents to attempt to trade with one another, but would instead try another lower relative price for X in terms of Y in order to eliminate the excess demand for Y and the excess supply of X. The line characterising the price ratio facing our two agents would thus pivot to the left of *I*. Such a process of price adjustment could continue for some time, but would cease when the excess demand for each good was eliminated and the planned quantities demanded of each good by each agent just sum up to the economy's endowment of those goods. Such a **competitive equilibrium** would occur at a point such as *E*, at a price ratio given by the slope of *II*.

In Figure 21.3 *E* represents a distribution of the economy's endowment of goods between *A* and *B* that would be attained if they traded as price takers in a competitive market in equilibrium, and the first point to be noted is that it lies on the economy's contract curve, and indeed on that segment of it which we termed the economy's core. Hence our competitive equilibrium represents a state of affairs in which it would be impossible to make one of our agents better off, in the sense of moving that agent to a higher indifference curve, without simultaneously making the other worse off. We shall have much to say about this property of competitive equilibrium later when we discuss welfare economics. It should also be noted that there is no reason to believe that point *E* represents a unique equilibrium for the economy. There may well exist other price ratios at which our two agents' plans would also be mutually compatible and hence on the contract curve. However, it is also true that the range of competitive equilibrium points is smaller than the range of points that lie within the economy's core. Readers may satisfy themselves of this by reproducing Figure 21.3 and drawing straight lines from X_0 to points *H* and K, the limiting points on the contract curve that lie in the economy's core. Clearly a competitive equilibrium at the price ratio implicit in either line would not be feasible. At the first of them there would exist an excess demand for X and an excess supply of Y and at the second an excess demand for Y and an excess supply of X.

Blocking coalitions and the core

The foregoing analysis offers a very specific description of how the economy achieves a general equilibrium. Each individual maximises utility subject to the constraint that the value of the bundle of goods demanded can be no greater than the value of that individual's endowment. The prices at which goods are valued here must also be such as to equate the market supply and demand for each good. Another way of thinking about how resources are allocated in an exchange economy is based on the notion of **coalitions** – groups of individuals – which are formed to **block** particular allocations. Consider again Figure 21.3, where the initial endowment is at X_0. We can conceive of the economy having two types of individual, A and B; so that A and B are now groups or coalitions of agents. In Figure 21.3, coalition A starts the game with all of X and coalition B with all of Y. The coalitions then consider alternative allocations of resources. If the best they can do is to share out the new allocation in such a way that each member of the coalition is no better off, and some members of the coalition are worse off with the new allocation than with the starting allocation, the coalition in question can always refuse to trade and thereby *block* the new allocation.

Now this argument deals with the activities of only a subset of the possible coalitions that could be formed in a multi-agent economy. Coalitions consisting of all As and all Bs and all As and Bs together only exhaust the possibilities when there are but two agents, A and B. More generally, any number of coalitions, consisting of any mixture of type A and B individuals are conceivable, and any one of these could be a blocking coalition.

We can now define the *core* more formally as follows. An allocation of resources is in the core if it represents a redistribution of resources from the initial endowment which cannot be blocked by any feasible coalition. If we revert to interpreting Figure 21.3 as representing a two-person economy, then the coalition consisting of person A will block any allocation below the indifference curve HX_0, and the coalition consisting of person B will block any allocation above the indifference curve KX_0. The coalition consisting of A and B will block any allocation between HX_0 and KX_0 which is not on the contract curve. The economy's core is therefore the segment of the contract curve between H and K in Figure 21.3.

Box 21.1	Competitive equilibrium and Walras' law

A competitive equilibrium occurs when demand equals supply for every good simultaneously. The list, or *vector*, of prices at which all markets clear will be called the **equilibrium price vector**, and the resulting quantities of goods the *equilibrium allocation of resources*. In this box, we provide a simple formalisation of the price-setting process, and discuss the concept of the core in yet more detail.

→

We can consider the *tâtonnement* process described earlier as a sequence of adjustments, or *iterations*, towards the equilibrium price vector. We can generalise the model to a large number of goods, so that g_i (for goods) represents the ith good, where $i = 1, \ldots, n$. Consumers are represented by the subscript $j = 1, \ldots, n$. The demand and supply of goods are denoted by the superscripts d and s respectively. Then the price-determining process can be described in the following way. The auctioneer selects one good relative to which the prices of all others are to be measured – the so-called *numeraire* of the system. This choice is quite arbitrary, because any good will serve the purpose equally well. Then the process of equilibrium price formation proceeds by steps.

Step 1

The auctioneer calls out an initial list of prices, the price vector $\mathbf{p}^1$, which contains prices $p_1^1 \ldots p_n^1$, with the price of the numeraire good relative to itself being, of course, equal to one.

Step 2

On the basis of these prices, consumers maximise utility given their initial endowment of goods, and derive their supplies and demands for each good g_{ij}^d and g_{ij}^s. At the level of each market, demand and supply for good i equal $\sum_j g_{ij}^d$ and $\sum_j g_{ij}^s$ respectively.

Consumers inform the auctioneer of these *notional demands and supplies*, but no trade takes place as yet.

Step 3

The auctioneer sums the demand and supplies for each good, and calculates the *excess demand*

$$ED_i = \sum_j g_{ij}^d - \sum_j g_{ij}^s \tag{21.1.1}$$

for each good, i. The auctioneer then alters the price vector according to the rule

$$p_i^2 - p_i^1 = \alpha(ED_i) \tag{21.1.2}$$

for every i, where α is a positive constant. The auctioneer therefore raises the price of goods in excess demand, and reduces the price of goods in excess supply. An adjustment process of this kind is referred to as *Walrasian*.

Step 4

The auctioneer calls out the new price vector, $\mathbf{p}^2$, and steps 1–4 are repeated again.

This process continues until the auctioneer changes no price, i.e. until $p^{k+1} = p^k$, where k is the number of iterations. This occurs of course where excess demands are zero for all goods. At that point, but not before, people are allowed to trade with one another.

The equilibrium price vector is therefore derived as the solution to n simultaneous equations: the excess demand functions for each good. However, in fact the equation system need be solved for only $(n - 1)$ relative prices, because we can always, as we have seen, choose a single price, that of the numeraire, to be fixed at some predetermined level. This result arises from what is known as **Walras' law**, which states that for each and every price vector the *sum* of excess demands for all goods, valued in terms of the numeraire, must equal zero. Individuals always spend their entire budget on goods, so that at any price vector the total value of each individual's excess demands for goods necessarily equals zero.

Consider the example of the two-good model discussed earlier. Walras' Law tells us that

$$p_X(X^d - X^s) + p_Y(Y^d - Y^s) = 0 \qquad (21.1.3)$$

Thus, if we have a certain value of excess demand in the market for good X, we must have excess supply to the same value in the market for good Y, and vice versa. Thus, in the two-good special case, we actually have only a single equation to determine a single equilibrium relative price between the two goods. Because we know that if the market for X is in equilibrium, the market for Y must also be in equilibrium, we cannot solve two excess demand equations for two prices, but only for a single relative price, the price ratio, p_X/p_Y.

More generally, in a system of excess demand equations, Walras' Law tells us that if $(n-1)$ markets are in equilibrium, then the nth market is also in equilibrium. We therefore have only $(n-1)$ prices for which to solve, and can fix the price of the nth good arbitrarily to any level. This nth good is, of course, the arbitrarily selected *numeraire* good referred to earlier.

The existence, uniqueness and stability of equilibrium

The analysis of general equilibrium raises three important technical issues: whether the general **equilibrium** actually **exists**, whether it is **unique**, and whether it is **stable**. We can introduce these issues only informally in this book, but interested readers with technical skills can follow up the analysis with more advanced texts listed in Further Reading.

The question of existence is fairly straightforward. In a general sense, we want to know whether the $(n-1)$ equation system of excess demand functions has a solution: the vector of $(n-1)$ equilibrium prices. In a two-good economy, we know from Walras' law that if demand equals supply in one market, excess demand will equal zero in the other. Therefore, we can think about the problem from the perspective of a single market, in which we will find an equilibrium if the demand curve is continuously downward sloping and the supply curve continuously upward sloping. (Strictly speaking, we also need to assume that the intercept of the supply curve with the quantity axis lies to the left of the demand curve's intercept in order to ensure that equilibrium exists at a positive price and quantity.) If for some reason there are discontinuities or gaps in the demand and supply curves, they may not intersect at any well-defined price and quantity, and there will be no competitive equilibrium.

If demand curves monotonically slope down and supply curves monotonically slope up, excess demand is everywhere a diminishing function of price. The rule for the auctioneer – change price in proportion to excess demand – will then ensure that, if we start out of equilibrium, price will converge towards its equilibrium value, and excess demand go to zero. Moreover that equilibrium will be unique.

However, consider a good which is a normal good at low levels of income, becomes inferior at higher levels of income and then reverts to being nomal. If the income effect outweighs the substitution effect of a price change in the relevant inferior range, the resulting demand curve could be downward sloping initially, then backward bending and finally downward sloping again. This case is depicted in Figure 21.4. We present it here as a logically conceivable case, which enables us to illustrate the possibility that there can exist multiple equilibria, and that not all of them need be stable. We do not mean to suggest in any way that it is empirically likely.

It will be remembered that the auctioneer's adjustment mechanism is to alter price according to equation (21.1.2) (see Box 21.1), raising price when excess demand is positive and reducing price when it is negative. In Figure 21.4. the segments of the excess demand function lying to the left of A and the right of B are *stable* with this adjustment mechanism, but the segment lying between these points is *unstable*. Consider first a disequilibrium situation in the segment to the left of A, for example, a price below p_X^1. Excess demand is positive in that region and so the auctioneer lowers price back to the equilibrium, p_X^1. The same analysis applies in the segment of the excess demand curve that lies to the right of B except that price converges to p_X^3. However, in the segment AB the auctioneer's adjustment rule takes the market further away from equilibrium at p_X^2 rather than towards it. For example, between A and p_X^2, the market is in excess supply so the auctioneer lowers price, which takes us even further from the nearest equilibrium, p_X^2. Similarly between p_X^2 and B the market is in excess demand so the auctioneer raises price, taking the system even further from the equilibrium. Market instability is therefore associated with a situation in which the demand or supply curves are perversely sloped, with the absolute value of the elasticity of demand greater than that of supply. It can be ruled out in an exchange economy if we assume that in general income effects do not outweigh substitution effects on the demand side of the economy.

Figure 21.4

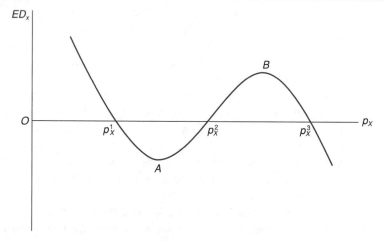

Excess demand for X as a function of p_X. As drawn, there are three equilibria in this market, at p_X^1, p_X^2 and p_X^3. The first and third of these are stable and the second unstable.

Market mechanisms and planning

The *tâtonnement* process described informally earlier and more formally in Box 21.1, is often interpreted as approximating the operation of a market economy in which the role of the auctioneer is played by 'market forces', namely the general realisation by traders that the market is either tight or slack, with prices being adjusted accordingly. It should be noted, however, that our formulation would also permit us to think of the job of the auctioneer being undertaken by planners. In principle, they could search for equilibrium prices in the manner outlined above, and then incorporate the equilibrium allocation of resources compatible with them in a national plan. A model of **planning** along these lines was discussed by Oskar Lange during the 1930s, and has since formed the basis for the analysis of so-called decentralised planning. It might be added that planning in practice bore little or no relationship to Lange's graceful equilibrium-seeking processes.

There are two important drawbacks to this method of price determination, however. The first concerns the motivation of economic agents. If, at the end of the day, the quantities to be bought and sold are set by planners, rather than freely chosen by individuals, there is no obvious reason for economic agents to act as if they are maximising their own utility functions at earlier stages of the iterative procedure. Motivating consumers, and particularly producers, to provide truthful information about how they would behave, therefore becomes a serious problem in a centrally planned economy. Secondly, the planners would face the problem of how to accumulate and process the huge quantity of information required to measure the demands and supplies for every good in the economy. In practice they are likely to be submerged by the sheer volume of information involved here. This assertion appears to be borne out by the operation of planning in the former socialist economies of Eastern Europe, where planners took numerous short cuts in the processing and accumulation of data about demands and supplies, with the consequence that the plans themselves were often internally inconsistent.

Concluding comment

The properties of a state of general competitive equilibrium in an exchange economy sketched out earlier in the two-person two-good case are rather general, holding indeed for any economy made up of a finite number of agents, as a large body of advanced mathematical economic analysis has shown. If a competitive equilibrium exists for an exchange economy, it will lie within the economy's core, so-called, and it will therefore involve a state of affairs in which no one agent, or coalition of agents, can be made better off utilising the resources available to it. If that equilibrium also lies on the economy's contract curve, and in the simple model we have considered here it clearly will, then that state of affairs will also involve no one agent or coalition of agents being able to be made better off except at the expense of another. Readers who pursue further studies in microeconomics beyond the level of this book will in due course come across many extensions of the simple analysis dealt with here. In the next chapter we shall extend the analysis in question in a particular direction and go on to discuss the nature of general competitive equilibrium in an economy in which production as well as trading takes place.

SUMMARY

The exchange economy

1. Our discussion thus far has concentrated on the maximising choices of individuals, and the co-ordination of these choices in particular markets. It has developed partial equilibrium analysis, in which equilibria have been derived holding certain factors constant.

2. General equilibrium analysis is concerned with questions of resource allocation in the economy as a whole, with the manner in which all markets attain equilibrium simultaneously.

3. The general equilibrium framework allows us to consider questions of efficiency and welfare for the economy as a whole, as well as issues of public policy.

4. If we assume no production, the process of exchange between two individuals can be analysed with reference to a box diagram. The possible outcomes of voluntary trade will be represented by the contract curve, along which the indifference curves of the two individuals are tangential to one another.

5. Given an initial endowment for each agent, the core of the economy is that segment of the contract curve that could be attained by voluntary trades.

6. We may think of prices in the competitive economy as being set by an auctioneer, who adjusts prices in response to excess demand in each market until equilibrium is reached. This *tâtonnement* process also leads to an outcome on the contract curve.

7. Another way to analyse resource allocation is in terms of coalitions of agents. An allocation of resources is in the core if it represents a redistribution of resources from some initial endowment which will not be blocked by any feasible coalition.

8. Formally, competitive equilibrium involves the existence of a price vector at which demand equals supply for all goods simultaneously. This vector can be thought of as being the solution to n simultaneous equations, comprising one excess demand function for each of the n goods.

9. Walrus' law states that for every price vector, the sum of excess demands must equal zero. This implies that if $(n - 1)$ markets are in equilibrium, the nth must be in equilibrium as well. We therefore need only solve the equation system for $(n - 1)$ relative prices, with the nth being the *numeraire* good.

10. Three important questions in general equilibrium theory are whether the equilibrium exists, is unique and is stable. The answers to all three depend upon the nature of underlying demand and supply functions.

11. The model of general equilibrium can also be used in the analysis of central planning processes.

PROBLEMS

1 You and a friend are on holiday on a remote island but you have forgotten to bring any food. A fixed supply of coconuts is the only thing available to eat. Show that any allocation of the coconuts is a point on the contract curve. What is the core of this contract curve? What allocation might you agree?

2 Consider a two-person/two-good exchange economy, illustrated by a box diagram as in Figure 21.2. Illustrate a three-step process of Walrasian adjustment to equilibrium from an initial endowment in which there is excess demand for good X and excess supply of good Y in the first step and the converse in the second step.

3 Let the excess demand function for good X take the form in the figure below.

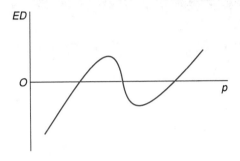

(a) Illustrate equilibrium price(s) in this market.
(b) Which equilibria are stable and which unstable?
(c) Discuss why the excess demand function may take this form.

4 If there are N markets in an economy and N − 2 of them are in equilibrium, what does Walras' law imply about the two markets that are not in equilibrium?

CHAPTER 22

General equilibrium with production

Key words and phrases

- production box, technical efficiency, contract curve, transformation curve, production frontier, constant returns to scale, concavity of production frontier, simultaneous equilibrium in production and consumption
- Robinson Crusoe (representative agent) economy

Introduction

In this chapter we shall extend our discussion of general competitive equilibrium to an economy in which the goods which consumers buy are produced, rather than simply being delivered from the outside. Even so, we shall assume that the economy has fixed endowments of productive inputs, capital and labour services. We shall also confine our analysis to a two-good economy in which the goods in question are produced using the two inputs. Moreover, in discussing the properties of competitive equilibrium in this production economy, we shall take it for granted that a *tâtonnement* process, such as we described in the last chapter, is at work to ensure that the equilibrium in question is in fact attained in that economy.

The production sector

Provided that we make the appropriate simplifying assumptions, we may analyse the production sector of the economy with the aid of a box diagram essentially similar to that deployed in the previous chapter.

Let us, therefore, assume that our two goods, X and Y, are produced by using the productive services of capital and labour. Let us also assume, as we did in our earlier analysis of the firm, that smooth production functions exist to translate input services into outputs of X and Y. Finally, let us assume that the quantities of factor services available to our economy are exogenously fixed.

In Figure 22.1 the quantity of labour service inputs (L) available to the economy is measured horizontally and that of capital services (K) vertically. If all available factor services are utilised and are fixed in overall quantity, we may measure inputs into the X industry

Figure 22.1   **A production box diagram**

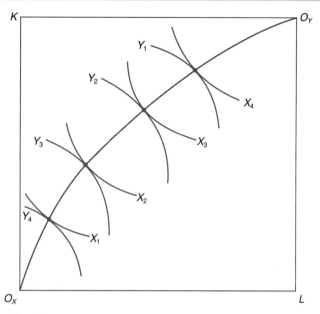

The lengths of the *K* and *L* axes represent the amounts of these two factor services available to the economy. Isoquants representing the output of *X* are drawn relative to the origin O_X and those representing the output of *Y* relative to the origin O_Y. $O_X O_Y$ is a production contract curve and the economy will be in equilibrium somewhere along it if output takes place under competitive conditions. Figure 22.2 is directly derived from Figure 22.1.

from an origin at the bottom left-hand corner, and for the *Y* industry from the top right-hand corner. Any point within the box represents an allocation of factors between the two industries. We may draw the production functions for the two industries as isoquant maps – just as we drew the indifference maps of our individuals in Chapter 21 – so that any point within the box is also associated with particular levels of output of *X* and *Y*. Any point within the **production box** is, therefore, an allocation of productive resources in the economy, describing the shares of the two industries' outputs in total production, their respective capital–labour ratios and the amounts of labour and capital used in each.

The locus of tangencies between isoquants is directly analogous to the **contract curve** of our previous analysis. At any point on this locus, given the output of *X*, the output of *Y* is the maximum attainable, and vice versa. Thus, on this locus, **technical efficiency**, not just for each industry, but for the whole production side of the economy, is achieved.

There are good reasons to suppose that competitive equilibrium in production would involve the two industries in being on the contract curve. Exactly as in the case of consumer exchange in the previous chapter, a *tâtonnement* process will ensure that the ratio of factor prices will adjust until the capital and labour markets clear simultaneously. The argument can also be made in terms of the individual firm's optimisation process. A competitive factor market would have each unit of a particular factor of production being paid the same amount for its services regardless of the firm or industry employing it.

Moreover, in an industry that is competitive *vis-à-vis* both output and factor markets, each factor receives a payment equal to the value of its marginal product, which is the marginal physical product of the factor multiplied by the price of the output to whose production it is contributing.

Now it will be remembered that the slope of an isoquant at any point measures the ratio of the marginal physical products of the two factors. It tells us by how much K must be increased in order to keep production constant in the face of the withdrawal of a small (in the limit, infinitesimal) quantity of L. If each factor of production gets the same payment in each industry, the ratio of the payments going to each factor must be the same in both industries, and this ratio must be equal to the ratio of their marginal physical products in both industries, if firms are competitive profit maximisers. At the same time we have assumed that all factors are fully employed. It is only at those points at which the isoquants of Figure 22.1 are tangent to each other that all these conditions are satisfied.

Again, note that we have said that a competitive equilibrium in production will involve an allocation of factors of production between industries that lies on the contract curve. We have said nothing about where on that curve it might lie, nor indeed is there anything which we can say about this on the basis of the information so far given.

Production possibilities and the transformation curve

The ultimate aim of our analysis is to bring the consumption and production sectors together and to study the properties of their joint equilibrium. The next step towards this goal is the construction of the **transformation curve**. Consider Figure 22.1 once again. Each point in the box lies on both an X-isoquant and a Y-isoquant. Competitive equilibrium involves being on the contract curve and we may take the information implicit in that curve and display it in another way. In Figure 22.2 we measure quantities of X on the horizontal axis and Y on the vertical and draw the *transformation curve* which shows how the output of X and Y varies as we move along the production contract curve, i.e. how X is 'transformed' into Y. The point at which this transformation curve cuts the Y-axis on Figure 22.2 corresponds to the X-origin of the box diagram and the point at which it cuts the X-axis corresponds to the Y-origin. Because this transformation curve for a competitive economy is derived from the contract curve, along which, for any output of Y, the output of X is maximised given the resources available in the economy, and vice versa, it may also be referred to as a *production possibility curve*, or **production frontier**.

In general, the shape that this competitive equilibrium transformation curve will take depends upon the nature of the production function. It has been drawn concave to the origin in Figure 22.2, but there is no general technical necessity for it to have this shape. Increasing returns to scale in one or both industries would lead to the curve being convex over some of its range, and if they were strong enough, over all of its range.

However, **constant returns to scale** will be assumed throughout the following analysis and it is easy to show that, given constant returns to scale, the production possibility curve is indeed concave to the origin. Figure 22.3 presents the relevant box diagram. Consider the straight line drawn between the origins in this case. It is technically feasible to vary the outputs of X and Y along this line, and since each industry is characterised by constant returns to scale, the rate at which output of X would have to be sacrificed for Y,

Figure 22.2

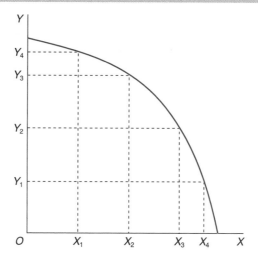

A competitive economy's transformation or production possibility curve. It shows, for given factor avail-ability and technology, the maximum output of X attainable for a given output of Y. Its slope at any point measures the marginal cost of producing X in terms of units of Y. It is derived from Figure 22.1 by reading off the values of the X and Y isoquants as the output moves along the contract curve from O_X and O_Y, and plotting pairs of these, e.g. X_1Y_4, as points on the transformation curve.

Figure 22.3   **A production box diagram**

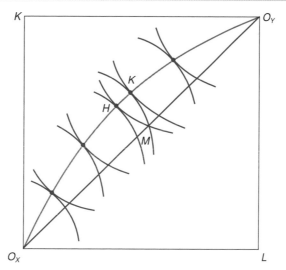

With constant returns to scale, successive equidistant moves along the diagonal drawn between O_X and O_Y involve equal changes in the output of X and equal changes in the output of Y. For any point on the diagonal such as M, except the two origins, a higher output of X or Y or both can be obtained by moving to the appropriate segment of the contract curve, HK in the case of point M. Figure 22.4 may be derived from Figure 22.3.

i.e. the rate at which X would be transformed into Y, would be the same at every point on it. Thus, a straight-line transformation curve relating the output of X to that of Y, such as has been drawn in Figure 22.4, would correspond to moving along this diagonal.

Only two points on this diagonal are also on the contract curve – the two origins. For any other point on the diagonal it is possible to move to the contract curve and increase the output of at least one good without reducing the output of the other. Thus, relative to point M on the diagonal, anywhere between H and K on the contract curve involves higher output of X (at K) or Y (at H) or both. In terms of Figure 22.4, then, except at its intersection with the axes, the transformation curve derived from the contract curve lies outside the straight line derived from this diagonal, and hence must be generally concave in shape. This transformation curve is the production possibility curve, and is, as we have seen, the one that is relevant for a competitive economy. Only in the limiting case in which the contract curve itself was the diagonal would the production possibility curve be a straight line.

Such a state of affairs would arise if the production functions of the two industries were such that, at a given ratio of factor prices, each one used the two factors of production in the same proportion at any level of output. This would hold if all firms in each industry had identical homothetic constant return to scale production functions (see Chapter 8). If this rather stringent condition does not hold, then, with constant returns to scale in each industry, the **production frontier is concave** to the origin.

Figure 22.4

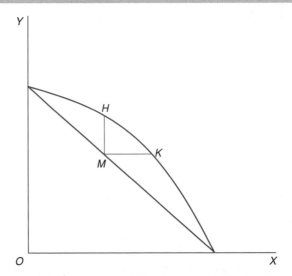

Movement along the diagonal in Figure 22.3 involves a constant ratio of changes in the outputs of X and Y. Hence the straight line on which M lies is constructed by reading off the values of the isoquants as we move up this diagonal. Because M represents a combination of output of X and Y that can be exceeded by moving to the contract curve, any point on this straight line, except those at which it meets the two axes, lies inside that implied by the contract curve. Hence, the production possibility curve, given constant returns to scale, will be generally concave to the origin except in the limiting case when the contract curve itself is a diagonal.

Simultaneous equilibrium in consumption and production

Production and consumption equilibria are brought together in Figure 22.5. Here we explicitly assume constant returns to scale, competitive equilibrium, and full employment of all resources, and draw the transformation curve concave. The key to understanding Figure 22.5 lies in grasping the fact that the slope of the transformation curve at any point measures the rate at which one good must be sacrificed in order to obtain more of the other. This slope then measures the marginal cost of X in terms of Y (and its inverse thus measures the marginal cost of Y in terms of X). But in perfectly competitive equilibrium the supply price of any good is equal to its long-run *marginal* cost of production. Therefore the slope of the transformation curve also measures the ratio of the prices at which the two goods will be supplied by competitive industries. Hence a simple competitive economy, such as the one which we are considering, will be in equilibrium when the outputs of the two goods are at levels at which the ratio of their prices, as given by the slope of the transformation curve, is such as to put our two consumers into equilibrium at a point on the consumption contract curve.

Such a situation is depicted in Figure 22.5. The equilibrium level of output is given at O_B with the ratio of the supply price of X to that of Y equal to W/V. We construct a consumption box diagram having one of its two origins at the equilibrium point on the transformation curve and the other at the origin relative to which the transformation

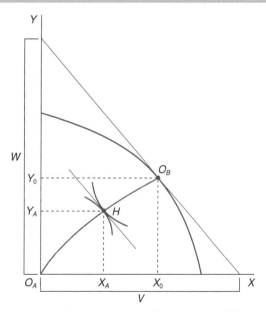

General equilibrium in the two-good/two-person/two-factor model. W/V measures the ratio of the marginal cost of and hence supply price of X to that of Y. The aggregate output mix is given at point O_B. Consumer A consumes X_A of X and Y_A of Y, while B consumes $X_0 - X_A$ of X and $Y_0 - Y_A$ of Y. Note that the slope of the indifference curves at H, which gives the ratio of the demand price of X to that of Y, must be equal to W/V.

Figure 22.6 The production box diagram

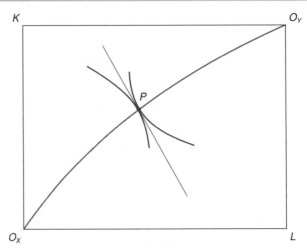

Point P corresponds to O_B in Figure 22.5. The slope of the isoquants at this point gives the ratio of the price of labour services to that of capital services. Since the levels of output and the prices of output are both given by the analysis set out in Figure 22.5, and since factor payments exhaust output, the level of payments to factors of production is thus set. Given the ownership of factors, which is taken as exogenously determined in this analysis, the distribution of income is determined. This distribution must be such as to enable each consumer to be in equilibrium at point H in Figure 22.5, if the whole economy is to be in equilibrium.

curve is drawn. Within this box diagram the consumers' indifference curves cut the contract curve at H, their slopes at this point being equal to the slope of the transformation curve. Consumer A thus consumes X_A of X and Y_A of Y while B gets $X_0 - X_A$ and $Y_0 - Y_A$.

How does this distribution of consumption between the two consumers get settled? Consumers in this economy also own factor services and derive their incomes from selling them to firms. The point O_B of Figure 22.5 corresponds to a point such as P on Figure 22.6 where the slopes of the isoproduct curves tell us what the relative payment rates for capital and labour will be. Values of the isoquant tell us the levels of output. Since factor payments exhaust output where there are constant returns to scale, factor payments are fully determined at this point. Hence, our situation of general equilibrium has the following property: the ownership of factor services, given exogenously, is distributed in such a way that the distribution of income corresponding to the output mix given by O_B is just such as to permit our two consumers willingly to achieve the consumption mix corresponding to point H. It is also, of course, implicit here that different distributions of resource ownership can result in different output mixes.

Box 22.1 **The Robinson Crusoe economy**

The two-agent, two-input, two-output model which has provided the basis of our analysis so far relies on one simplification in particular which, for some purposes, turns out to be unhelpful. It takes supplies of inputs to the economy as given. It cannot, therefore, be used to deal with any questions having to do with economic agents' labour leisure choices. An alternative simple model is available to cope with issues such as these, and, as we shall see, it also enables us to gain extra insights into certain questions about the uniqueness and attainability of competitive equilibrium.

The economy in question is inhabited by just one agent, and that is why it is often referred to as a **Robinson Crusoe economy**. Though it is severely oversimplified, having diverse activities on different sides of the market being undertaken by a single individual, its logic in fact at many points carries over to an economy inhabited by many consumers and producers. That is why it is also known as a **representative agent economy**, one in which the choices of its single inhabitant are representative of those which would be made by the inhabitants of a much more complex structure. But the model's most attractive feature for purposes of this chapter is that it enables us to consider a case in which the supply of inputs, in this case labour, is determined within the model, rather than being given exogenously, without unduly complicating the economy.

On the supply side of his economy, we assume that Robinson Crusoe uses a single input, L, to produce output X. Hence, he may also be thought of as a consumer, who buys X and sells L. To bring out the relevance of his decisions to the general competitive case we make the artificial assumption that Robinson Crusoe is a price taker, making decisions on the basis of prices set by a Walrasian auctioneer who obeys an adjustment rule such as was described earlier by equation (21.1.4). The auctioneer initially chooses $(w_1 p_X^1)$. As a producer, Robinson Crusoe therefore seeks to maximise profits subject to a short-run production function which is assumed to display strictly diminishing returns. The maximisation problem is, therefore, maximise with respect to X and L

$$\pi = p_X^1 X - w^1 L \tag{22.1.1}$$

subject to

$$X = f(L) \tag{22.1.2}$$

with first-order conditions

$$p_X^1 \partial X / \partial L - w^1 = 0 \tag{22.1.3}$$

or

$$\partial X / \partial L = w^1 / p_X^1$$

Diagrammatically, equation (22.1.1) can be rearranged in (X, L) space as an isoprofit map,

$$X = \frac{\pi}{p_X^1} + \frac{w^1}{p_X^1} L \tag{22.1.4}$$

which for a given wage and price can be plotted as a series of positively sloped parallel lines, with higher intercepts on the X-axis being associated with higher levels of profit. In Illustration 22.1(a), we draw Robinson Crusoe's production decision for the given wage–price ratio, which is to choose the (X, L) combination which generates

→

Illustration 22.1

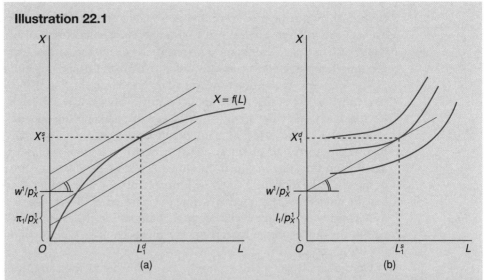

(a) Robinson Crusoe faces production function $X = f(L)_1$ with labour input measured in the negative quadrant. Given an isoprofit line with slope w^1/p_X^1, he chooses X_1^s and L_1^d to obtain the maximum available profits, π_1.

(b) As consumer, Crusoe has unearned income I, and real wages w^1/p_X^1. He chooses (L_1^s, X_1^d).

the largest volume of profit consistent with the available technology. Crusoe, therefore, chooses X and L at the tangency of the highest available isoprofit line with the short-run production function, which is at a point where equation (22.1.3) is satisfied. We denote this combination (X_1^s, L_1^d), with the profits earned being π_1. This economy yields positive profits despite the assumption of 'competition' (price-taking behaviour) because there are diminishing returns to labour (see Chapter 11) and therefore, in this one input case, to scale as well.

Now consider Crusoe as a consumer. Given w^1 and p_X^1, he chooses X and L to maximise

$$U = U(L, X) \tag{22.1.5}$$

subject to

$$p_X^1 X = I + w^1 L \tag{22.1.6}$$

where I is some 'unearned' income endowment (see Chapter 5). The first-order condition here is

$$\frac{\partial U/\partial X}{\partial U/\partial L} = w^1/p_X^1 \tag{22.1.7}$$

Diagrammatically, we can represent utility function (22.1.5) by convex indifference curves, with the budget constraint (22.1.6) being rearranged to a budget line as follows:

$$X = \frac{I}{p_X^1} = \frac{w^1 L}{p_X^1} \tag{22.1.8}$$

Illustration 22.2

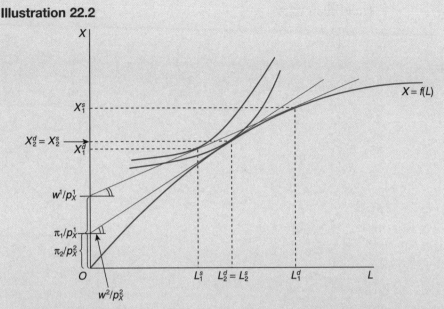

At initial price vector (w^1, p^1_X), we have excess demand in the labour market and excess supply in the goods market. The auctioneer therefore raises the real wage, for example to (w^2, p^2_X). With these prices, and the associated level of profits, demand equals supply in both markets simultaneously.

For any given I, say I_1, Crusoe chooses (X^d_1, L^s_1) in Illustration 22.1(b), at the tangency between the budget line (22.1.8) and the highest available indifference curve which satisfies condition (22.1.7).

Let us now make the assumption that all the profits earned by Crusoe in production are spent in consumption. Profits are fully paid out as 'unearned' income, so that in the example above, $\pi_1 = I_1$. We can, therefore, bring the demand and supply sides of the Crusoe economy together in Illustration 22.2 to illustrate price determination. At the initial prices (w^1, p^1_X), Robinson Crusoe finds that the demand for labour, L^d_1, exceeds the supply, L^s_1. As we would expect from Walras' law, he simultaneously discovers that his supply of goods exceeds demand.

The auctioneer will also have this information, and, acting on Walrasian principles, will raise the wage and lower the product price, calling out a new higher real wage (w^2/p^2_X). As we have drawn it, these are equilibrium prices, with demand equal to supply in both the goods and money market. However, one could equally imagine the case of overshooting, in which the second price vector generates excess supply in the labour market, with excess demand in the goods market. The Walrasian price-setting mechanism would still ultimately ensure that, provided the indifference curves were convex to the origin and the production function was strictly concave, a price vector would be found at which excess demands were zero in both markets.

This diagram allows us to investigate in more detail the role of technical assumptions in ensuring the uniqueness of competitive equilibrium. Consider, for example, the case where technology is characterised by constant returns, as illustrated in Illustration 22.3(a). We can see that in the Robinson Crusoe economy, there is a point

Illustration 22.3

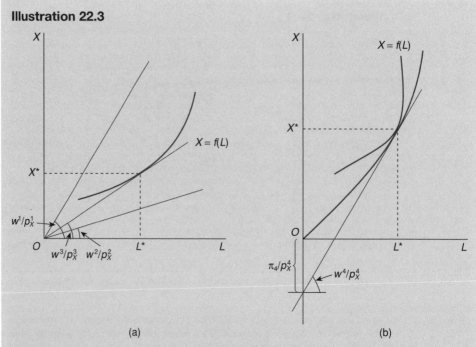

(a)   (b)

(a) With constant returns, the Walrasian adjustment procedure is unable to isolate the competitive equilibrium (X^*, L^*). Desired output supply and labour demand is always either infinite (with w^2, p_X^2), zero (with w^1, p_X^1) or indeterminate (with w^3, p_X^3).

(b) With increasing returns, tangency between the isoprofit line and the production function occurs where profits are negative, for example at π_4 (in fact, at a profit minimum). Crusoe always chooses an infinite output supply and labour demand, whatever the real wage.

of competitive equilibrium, at (L^*, X^*). However, the Walrasian auctioneer will not be able to get the economy to that equilibrium point. Suppose that the auctioneer calls out a real wage such as w^1/p_X^1. Crusoe the producer will find that profits are maximised where output and employment are zero. If the auctioneer responds to the goods shortage and employment glut by reducing the real wage, for example to w^2/p_X^2, optimal output and, therefore, labour demand for Crusoe the producer becomes infinite. If, by chance, the auctioneer isolates the equilibrium real wage w^3/p_X^3, Crusoe will find that the level of profit is independent of the level of output and employment, and is always zero. Crusoe's product supply and labour demand decision is therefore indeterminate in this case. Unless Crusoe the producer happens by chance to choose (L^*, X^*) when the auctioneer calls out (w^3, p_X^3), general equilibrium cannot be achieved.

A related problem arises in the case of increasing returns, illustrated in Illustration 22.3(b). The production function in this case is strictly convex, so that at every conceivable real wage combination tangency between the isoprofit line and the production function yields a loss. It appears to Robinson Crusoe, the producer, that he can in fact raise profits by increasing output and employment indefinitely, so that the first-order tangency conditions will never be satisfied. Though there is a competitive equilibrium at (L^*, X^*), the Walrasian price-setting mechanism once again is unable to lead Crusoe the producer to select that allocation.

In the case of constant returns, the excess demand functions for the two markets are therefore discontinuous, with small changes in relative prices at certain points leading to abrupt shifts from excess demand to excess supply and vice versa without necessarily reaching the point where excess demand equals zero. With increasing returns, the labour market is locked into a situation of excess demand and the goods market into one of excess supply, with no adjustment of price leading to sufficient changes in excess demands for them ever to reach zero. These non-convexities in production are, therefore, associated with non-existence of competitive equilibrium.

One can imagine similar arguments applying to the demand side. If employment and goods are perfect substitutes, so that the indifference curves are straight lines, we have an analogous argument to the case of constant returns. There will be discontinuities in the resulting excess demand functions and the competitive equilibrium may not be attainable by a *tâtonnement* process. If the indifference curves are not smoothly convex, we may have a case of multiple equilibria, as illustrated in the previous chapter, Figure 21.4. If, in addition, Crusoe has a backward-bending supply of labour curve for some relevant part of the range of the real wage, one or several of the equilibria must be unstable. Interested readers may wish to develop the appropriate diagrams for these cases themselves.

Now in the preceding few pages we have barely begun the analysis of the representative agent economy. To take matters further here in any detail would be to move beyond the scope of this book. Readers should note, however, that having made labour supply endogenous, the next logical development of the representative agent economy is to make the supply of the capital with which Robinson Crusoe works the outcome of his own saving decisions. Just as we have here explicitly incorporated a version of the labour supply analysis developed in Chapter 19 into a general equilibrium model, so this latter step would involve incorporation of a version of the intertemporal choice analysis of Chapters 5 and 6.

To take such a step would, as some of our readers may already be aware from their work in macroeconomics, turn our static general equilibrium model into a device capable of analysing certain basic features of economic growth. As those readers will also be aware, this is only the first of a series of extensions which have been made of this 'representative agent' model by macroeconomists. It has in fact become an extremely important analytic device in the whole area of growth and business-cycle analysis, providing a prime example of the ever-strengthening links between macroeconomics and the microeconomic analysis developed in this book.

Concluding comment

In this chapter we have concentrated on describing some of the attributes of competitive equilibrium in a simple two-factor/two-good/two-person economy (though in the immediately preceding section we have dealt with aspects of the 'Robinson Crusoe' case in order to explore certain aspects of general equilibrium analysis a little more deeply). Needless to say, the attributes of so simple an economy would not be of much interest if they did not carry over to much more complex cases of many more goods, factors and persons. It would be far beyond the technical scope of this book to prove that they do so, but readers may accept that this can be, and has been, proved by others. The basic implication of the analysis of competitive equilibrium which we have carried out for a special simple case is this: if consumers maximise utility and if perfectly competitive firms maximise profits, then there usually exists a set of market prices that will render all their individual plans compatible with one another and with the overall constraint imposed on the economy by available resources and technology. In short, the price mechanism operating in a market economy can, at least in principle, provide a coherent solution to the social problem of scarcity.

The above-mentioned solution is coherent in the sense that factors are allocated, income is distributed, and consumption goods are chosen in mutually consistent patterns, but whether such a solution is desirable is another question. The mere fact that it might exist tells us nothing about this matter. Nevertheless, questions about whether monopoly or competition does more to promote economic welfare, about the consequences of various tax and subsidy schemes for economic welfare, and so forth, are surely worth asking. Once the prior question of what constitutes economic welfare is settled, economic models of the type dealt with in this chapter may be used in many attempts to get to grips with these questions. We shall discuss these issues in the next chapter.

SUMMARY

General equilibrium with production

1. For an economy with a given endowment of productive resources we can construct a production box analogous to the exchange box of the previous chapter. Points along the contract curve represent the maximum attainable output for each industry, given the output of the other.

2. In competitive equilibrium, factors of production will be allocated along the production box contract curve.

3. The transformation curve or production possibility curve is derived from the contract curve. Given constant returns to scale the curve is concave to the origin. The slope of the curve measures the marginal cost of one good in terms of the other and is called the marginal rate of transformation.

4. In a two-person, two-good, two-input world, general equilibrium occurs at a point on the transformation curve, where the slope of the indifference curves of the two individuals are tangential to one another, and to the slope of the transformation curve. Both the marginal rates of substitution and the marginal rate of transformation are equal to the ratio of product prices.

5. We can also describe competitive equilibrium and the *tâtonnement* process with production in terms of a representative agent (Robinson Crusoe) model. In this model, in competitive equilibrium, the real wage equals both the marginal rate of substitution between income and leisure, and the marginal productivity of labour.

6. In the Robinson Crusoe model the Walrasian process of *tâtonnement* cannot necessarily find the equilibrium price vector if the production function displays constant returns. The equilibrium in question does not exist with increasing returns.

PROBLEMS

1 Explain how, in a two-input/two-output economy, the allocation of resources might be improved if the (common) marginal rate of substitution for X and Y held by each of the two consumers were not equal to the marginal rate of transformation. By what mechanism is the condition ($mrs = mrt$) satisfied in a competitive equilibrium?

2 In a two-good/two-factor economy with a fixed quantity of factors, what happens to the transformation curve between the goods if a tax is imposed on the use of one factor in the production of one good

   (a) in a situation of perfectly competitive equilibrium in all markets in which there are no monopolies and no other taxes;

   (b) in a situation in which the use of the other factor in the production of the same good is already taxed?

3 Suppose that Robinson Crusoe regards employment and goods as perfect substitutes on the demand side, and produces with a decreasing returns technology.

   (a) Does the Crusoe economy have a competitive equilibrium?

   (b) Illustrate the process whereby the Walrasian auctioneer adjusts real wages in order to find it.

   (c) Draw the excess demand functions for the goods and labour markets.

Welfare economics

Introduction

Up to now in this book we have dealt with questions about how consumers and firms will behave in various situations, and about the logic linking the predictions which we make about such behaviour to assumptions about the motives underlying it. These are **positive questions**, so-called. A prediction about behaviour is either right or wrong, and can be checked against data. A conclusion either follows from a set of assumptions or it does not, and the logic of an argument can be checked for its validity. This is not to say that such checks are always easy to perform. Real-world data are often ambiguous and difficult to interpret, and long chains of logical argument are frequently hard to assess for rigour. However, their outcome does not depend on any ethical stance that the economist carrying them out might bring to the task. Economist *A* might believe that self-interested utility-maximising behaviour is morally deplorable, while economist *B* might regard it with approval, but both would be able to agree on the assumptions necessary to derive from it the prediction that the quantity demanded of a commodity will increase as its price falls, and both, on consulting the same set of data, would be able to agree about whether or not this prediction was confirmed.

Positive economics is not the whole of the subject, however. We often wish to go beyond the description of a particular situation and pass judgement on it, to say that it is desirable or undesirable. We may also want to compare alternative situations and say something about their relative merits. Finally, and crucially, we may want to design economic policies intended to eliminate undesirable characteristics of an economy and replace them with desirable alternatives. In short, economics sometimes deals with **normative** as well as **positive questions**, and these form the subject matter of **welfare economics**. This chapter is intended to provide an introduction to this body of analysis. In order to discuss normative questions, one must have norms. Our first task, therefore, is to describe an ethical principle widely used as a basis for welfare economics. This is the so-called **Pareto criterion**. When this has been described, we shall use it to assess the desirability of the state of general competitive equilibrium analysed in the last two chapters, and to compare such an equilibrium with one that might arise if some sector of the economy were to deviate from the competitive ideal.

In the course of this analysis it will become apparent that the Pareto criterion does not enable us to make comparisons between situations where questions about alternative income distributions are crucial. We shall conclude this chapter with a detailed discussion of this issue and of situations in which markets seem to 'fail', in the sense that the operation of competitive mechanisms appears, in the light of the Pareto criterion, to need a little help from well-designed policies in order to achieve socially desirable ends. We also return to the issue of market failure in Chapter 24.

The Pareto criterion and Pareto optimality

There can be no competely objective basis for selecting criteria upon which judgements about the superiority of one social situation over another may be made. Inevitably there is a normative element present in such a judgement and the discussion of normative criteria is more the business of moral philosophers than of economists. Welfare economics usually bypasses detailed normative debate by taking the *Pareto criterion* as its starting point. This criterion states that if, when the resources available to a society are reallocated among alternative uses, the *economic welfare* of at least one member of society is increased without that of any other member being reduced, then the economic welfare of that society has increased. An increase or decrease in an individual's economic welfare simply involves a movement from a lower to a higher indifference curve or vice versa. A **Pareto optimal** situation is then said to exist when it is no longer possible to reallocate resources so as to increase the economic welfare of one individual except at the expense of another.

This criterion is to some extent controversial. It identifies the welfare of society solely with the welfare of the individuals that make up the society. This is a defensible position but there are ethical systems which invest society itself, or groups within society (such as social classes) with a moral importance that is distinct from that attaching to individuals. In terms of such systems the Pareto criterion is at best inadequate and at worst meaningless.

Even granted the individualist ethic, the Pareto criterion is far from providing a complete guide to economic policy. It says nothing about the extent of the superiority of one situation over another, nor does it enable us to distinguish between alternative situations, both of which may be Pareto superior to some starting situation, but which involve the welfare of different individuals being increased. A resource reallocation that makes a poor person better off by a pound a year and lowers the welfare of no other member of the community represents a movement to a Pareto superior situation, but so does a reallocation that makes a rich person better off by the same amount if no one else's welfare is altered. The Pareto criterion gives us no way of choosing between the two reallocations. Even though most of us would agree that questions about distribution are of central importance to the assessment of alternative situations, the criterion has nothing to say about the distribution of economic welfare between individuals. There are in general as many non-comparable Pareto optimal situations as there are distributions of income. In short, the Pareto criterion tries to distinguish between questions concerning what is usually termed the allocative efficiency of a particular economic situation and those dealing with the justness, or otherwise, of the income distribution ruling in that same situation. The distinction here is certainly one that can be made in principle, but, in practice, because payments to owners of factors of production are an integral part of the mechanism whereby a market economy allocates resources, questions about allocation and distribution tend to turn up together, as we shall see in due course.

Nevertheless, a standard that does not enable us to make all the judgements we might want to make may be useful for some purposes and it is worth looking at the implications of the Pareto criterion in more detail. In particular, it is worth showing that a situation of competitive equilibrium such as was described in the last chapter is Pareto optimal, a situation in which it is impossible to make one person better off without making someone else worse off.

The Pareto criterion and competitive equilibrium in an exchange economy

Consider once again the simple exchange economy analysed in Chapter 21. It was described in terms of a simple box diagram such as we have drawn here as Figure 23.1. Let M represent any point not on the contract curve and hence an allocation of consumption goods between individuals that is inconsistent with **competitive equilibrium**. By moving from M to any point in the economy's core, that is any point on the contract curve between H and J, it is possible to make at least one or, in all but the limiting cases

Figure 23.1

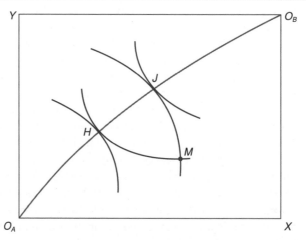

For any point, such as M, off the contract curve, there is a segment of the contract curve (HJ) a movement to which would make at least one consumer better off without making the other worse off.

of H and J, both individuals better off. Hence any such move would take us to a Pareto superior situation. Note that this does not say that a move to *any* point on the contract curve from M involves an improvement of welfare. Points to the left of H and to the right of J involve one individual being made better off and the other worse off and hence are not comparable to M using the Pareto criterion.

However, it is the case that, for every point in our box diagram that is *not* on the contract curve, there is at least one point *on* the contract curve that is Pareto superior to it. Moreover, any point on the contract curve is Pareto optimal. Consider point H in Figure 23.1, and let it represent any point on the contract curve. To move away from this point by leaving the contract curve will involve at least one and perhaps both individuals in a loss of economic welfare, while to move away from it up or down the contract curve involves the welfare of one individual being increased at the expense of the other.

Recall, however, that in Chapter 21 we showed that a situation of competitive equilibrium in this simple exchange economy would lie on the contract curve, and indeed within the economy's core. It must now be apparent to the reader that, according to the Pareto criterion, a competitive equilibrium is a desirable state of affairs; indeed, it is a Pareto optimal situation. In a simple exchange economy, the condition for Pareto optimality that the economy be on its contract curve implies that society's economic welfare is at *a* maximum (not the unique maximum) where the *marginal rates of substitution between goods are equalised among different consumers*.

The reader should note that this conclusion about the social desirability of being on the contract curve should not be extended by analogy to the cases of collusion between firms, or firms and unions, discussed in Chapters 17 and 20. In these cases there is a sense in which being on the contract curve maximises the welfare of those colluding, but emphatically not that of society as a whole.

Pareto optimality in production

The foregoing conclusion about the optimality of competitive equilibrium also holds for an economy with production. This is best shown by first considering the production sector of the economy in isolation, and then bringing it together with the consumption sector. Figure 23.2 reproduces the production box diagram analysed earlier. If it is possible to increase the output of one good without decreasing the output of another, it is possible to increase economic welfare. In this sense the Pareto criterion ensures that there is no waste in the allocation of inputs to alternative uses. The application to Figure 23.2 of arguments analogous to those made about the exchange economy described in Figure 23.1 should readily convince the reader that for any point not on the production contract curve there is at least one point on the curve at which the output of at least one of the goods is higher without that of the other being reduced. It should also be obvious that it is impossible to move along the contract curve without reducing the output of one good while that of the other is increased. Thus, as far as production is concerned, points on the contract curves (and of course all competitive equilibria lie on the contract curve) are required for Pareto optimality. The second condition for Pareto optimality is therefore that *marginal rates of technical substitution between inputs are equalised* between alternative uses. This argument, of course, amounts to a reaffirmation of a point made earlier: namely that the transformation curve for a competitive economy also represents its production frontier.

Figure 23.2

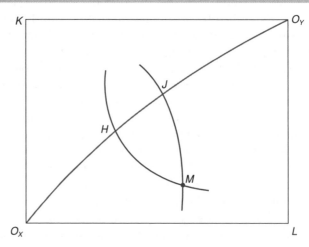

For any point off the contract curve such as *M*, there is a segment of the curve (*HJ*) movement to which will permit the output of at least one good to be increased without reducing the output of the other.

The foregoing argument reaffirms that the transformation curve between *X* and *Y* derived earlier (cf. Figure 22.1) specifies for any level of output of *Y* what is the maximum output of *X* it is physically possible to produce, and vice versa. It divides the area of a figure such as 22.2 into a region below and on the curve which contains bundles of *X* and *Y* whose production is feasible with available resources and technology, and a region which contains bundles whose production is not feasible. Thus, it represents the economy's production frontier, as we have already noted.

The Pareto optimality of competitive equilibrium in a production economy

Now we saw earlier that a situation of competitive equilibrium would result in each good's market price being equal to long-run marginal cost. The economy's competitive equilibrium production pattern was thus at a point on the production frontier where the ratio of the goods' marginal production costs equalled the ratio of their market prices. It remains to show that such a situation is Pareto optimal.

In terms of our simple model, this is best done by considering a situation in which the market price of one of the two goods differs from its competitive level. There are many ways in which this could happen. The output of one good could be monopolised and a monopolist, other than a perfect price discriminator, could set price above marginal cost. Or a government could impose a per-unit sales tax (subsidy) on the output of a competitive industry, thus raising (lowering) its price to consumers above (below) long-run marginal cost. In analysing such matters we must assume that the recipients of monopoly profits are also consumers; or that the proceeds of a tax (costs of a subsidy) are redistributed to (collected from) consumers as lump sum additions to (deductions from) their incomes. If we did not do so we would have to deal with the complexities that arise when the income accruing to members of an economy differs from the economy's output, and the analysis of such complexities would simply distract attention from the matter now to be dealt with.

We wish to show that an equilibrium situation in which the price of one good differs from its long-run marginal production cost is not Pareto optimal. We shall explicitly deal with a situation in which the price of Y is initially above marginal cost because its production is either monopolised or taxed, but readers should satisfy themselves that consideration of a subsidy to X would produce identical analysis. Figure 23.3 shows an equilibrium situation for an economy in such a situation. The key feature of Figure 23.3 as far as the current analysis is concerned is that the ratio of the market prices of X and Y differs from that which competitive equilibrium would produce. Monopoly pricing or a tax on Y raises its price above its competitive level so that the ratio of the prices of X and Y comes to fall short of the ratio of their marginal production costs. It should go without saying that when these ratios differ consumers will allocate their expenditure between the two goods in accordance with relative market prices, and not in accordance with relative marginal costs of production.

Recall that the slope of an indifference curve measures the rate at which the consumer is just willing to trade one good for another to maintain satisfaction, or welfare, constant; the slope of the production frontier measures the rate at which it is physically possible to substitute one good for the other. If production of Y is monopolised or taxed, this leads both of our individuals to consume Y and X in quantities such that the amount of X that they are willing to give up for extra units of Y exceeds the amount that must in fact be

Figure 23.3

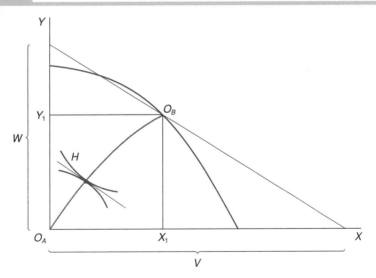

General equilibrium when the price of Y is above its competitive level, as a result of either monopoly pricing or the imposition of a tax. The ratio of the market price of X to that of Y is given by W/V and falls short of the ratio of their marginal production costs at (X_1, Y_1). The consumers' marginal rate of substitution between X and Y is given at H by the ratio of their market prices. More Y is in fact being sacrificed on the margin to obtain X than consumers are willing to sacrifice. The market price of X relative to that of Y is below its marginal cost of production in terms of Y, and a Pareto gain in welfare is possible by substituting Y for X in production and consumption, given the distribution of income ruling at H.

given up as far as the technical conditions of production are concerned. Clearly then, a substitution of Y and X in production could lead to a Pareto superior situation as long as the consequences of such substitution for the distribution of income between the two consumers were offset in some way. Whenever the marginal rate of substitution between goods in consumption differs from that in production, a Pareto gain in welfare is possible. When the two rates of substitution are equal and the other conditions already discussed are satisfied, no such gain is possible. The final condition for Pareto optimality is therefore *equality between the marginal rate of transformation in production between goods and the (common) marginal rate of substitution* at which individuals trade those goods.

Box 23.1 | ## Competitive equilibrium and Pareto optimality

In this box, we will bring together the key implications of Paretian welfare analysis for general equilibrium of the economy. We have derived the conditions for Pareto optimality – that outcomes occur on the relevant contract or production possibilities curves – and noted that those conditions are satisfied in competitive equilibrium. We can look at the relationship between competitive equilibrium and Pareto optimality in a slightly different way, by referring to the conditions which have to be satisfied for each to be achieved simultaneously.

The material developed in the previous sections of this chapter can be summarised as follows. Pareto optimality is attained for pure exchange when

$$mrs^A_{xy} = mrs^B_{xy} \tag{23.1.1}$$

Marginal rates of substitution between goods are equalised across all consumers (A and B in the two-person case). In the production sector we additionally require that

$$mrts^X_{LK} = mrts^Y_{LK} \tag{23.1.2}$$

that marginal rates of technical substitution between inputs (labour and capital) are equalised across activities. Finally, the so-called *grand criterion* for simultaneous optimality in production and exchange is that

$$mrt_{XY} = mrs^A_{XY} = mrs^B_{XY} \tag{23.1.3}$$

The marginal rate of transformation of goods in production equals the (common to all consumers) marginal rates of substitution between the goods.

It is easy to see that these three conditions will always be satisfied in competitive equilibrium. Condition (23.1.1) will be satisfied because individuals face a common equilibrium price rate, Px/Py, to which utility maximisation leads each separately to equalise their marginal rate of substitution. Similarly, condition (23.1.2) is satisfied because firms face a common wage rate–capital cost ratio, w/r, at which profit maximisation leads them to equalise the marginal rate of technical substitution between inputs. Finally, condition (23.1.3) is satisfied because individuals face the *same* common equilibrium price ratio, Px/Py, as firms face in the two industries when choosing outputs so as to equalise price and marginal cost. The fact that both Pareto optimality and general competitive equilibrium imply conditions (23.1.1), (23.1.2), and (23.1.3) suggests that there is a close relationship between the two, indeed that competitive equilibrium is Pareto optimal.

The two fundamental theorems of welfare economics

The relationship between competitive equilibrium and Pareto optimality in the allocation of resources is summarised in what economists call *the two* **fundamental theorems of welfare economics**. The first of these theorems, which we have in fact derived in Box 23.1 states that, in a situation of perfectly competitive equilibrium, the allocation of resources will be Pareto optimal.

A formal derivation of the second theorem is beyond the technical scope of this book. Suffice it to note that it follows from the analysis of competitive equilibrium developed in Chapters 21 and 22. It was shown there that, with given resource endowments and consumer tastes (and in the case of a production economy, technology too), a wide variety of **competitive equilibria** are attainable, each one being related to a different initial distribution of endowments among agents.[1] But it was also shown that any **competitive equilibrium** lies on the contract curve and therefore represents a Pareto optimal situation. The second theorem of welfare economics builds on these results and states that any Pareto optimal allocation of resources that is logically feasible in a particular economy may be obtained as the outcome of competitive market processes, provided that the economy's initial endowment of resources can be redistributed in an appropriate fashion among agents. The reader should note that the phrase 'appropriate fashion' hides a great deal here. In particular it is vital to the validity of the second theorem that any taxes and transfers required to reach some desired distribution of endowments are 'lump sum' in nature and unrelated to the outcomes of agents' market activities.

The two fundamental theorems of welfare economics are of considerable importance. The first of them establishes a presumption in favour of competitive market mechanisms if a Pareto optimal allocation of resources is considered desirable. And though the Pareto criterion, in and of itself, is silent on the matter of **distributional justice**, *equity* as it is sometimes called, the second theorem tells us that if we do wish to achieve a particular distribution of economic welfare there is no logical need to sacrifice Pareto efficiency in the allocation of resources. If 'appropriate' distributional policies are put in place, competitive markets can apparently be relied on to provide Pareto optimality in the allocation of resources while preserving equity.

The Pareto criterion and distributional questions

As the reader may well suspect already, whatever may be true in principle, in practice things are not quite as simple as the two theorems of welfare economics seem at first sight to make them. It is difficult to imagine a real-world economy that relies only on tax and transfer systems which impose burdens or distribute largesse in amounts independent of agents' market activities. Also, it turns out that the conditions under which real-world economies can be expected to conform to the competitive ideal are stringent to the point of being unrealistic. Given these two facts of life, government intervention in the economy often becomes easy to defend, and such intervention frequently has a simultaneous influence on the allocation of resources and the distribution of income. The implications of these observations are discussed in considerable detail in the remainder of this chapter as well as the following one.

The most obvious difficulty with the Pareto criterion, and one to which we have already referred, is its silence on the matter of the distribution of income. It is all very well to distinguish between allocative **efficiency** on the one hand and **distributive justice** on the other, and to have a criterion that deals only with the former, but payments made to factors of production are an integral part of the allocative mechanism. A competitive equilibrium may be optimal, but the movement to an optimal situation from a non-optimal situation is not the same thing as a movement to a socially superior, or preferred, situation. Such a movement may well involve making someone worse off. Consider again the example we used in Chapter 11 in which some such distortion as monopoly pricing or a tax leads to the price of Y exceeding its competitive value. The removal of such a distortion leads to an increase in the demand for Y and hence in the demand for the factor of production that is particularly heavily used in the production of Y. The factor's price will rise and the incomes of its owners increase, perhaps, though not necessarily, at the expense of reducing the incomes of the owners of the other factor. This is shown in Figure 23.4.

Figure 23.4

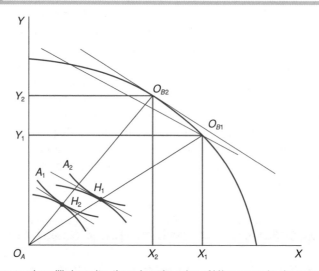

The change in the general equilibrium situation when the price of Y is restored to its competitive level. This figure depicts the *possible* outcome of such action, but not, in every detail, the *necessary* outcome. First, equality between the ratios of the goods' market prices and marginal production costs is restored in the move from $X_1 Y_1$ to $X_2 Y_2$. This must happen if the tax was the only source of discrepancy here. Figure 23.4 is drawn so that the structure of output shifts towards Y and the distribution of income changes in such a way as to reduce A's welfare. Point H_2 lies on a lower indifference curve for A than does point H_1. Note here that A's indifference map is drawn relative to O_A and hence does not shift between the two situations. This reduction in A's welfare is not a necessary outcome of the removal of the tax but it is a logically possible outcome. Hence, though the movement from the first situation to the second takes us from a non-Pareto optimal to a Pareto optimal situation, we cannot say that it represents a movement to a Pareto superior situation. Someone has been made worse off in the shift.

Some illustrations

A moment's reflection should convince the reader that the problem of making judgement about alternative situations in which the welfare of one group rises (or falls) at the same time as the welfare of others falls (or rises) commonly arises in the real world. In Figure 23.4 the utility level of A, whose consumption is measured from the origin O_A, is lowered if the economy moves to the optimal situation. Has the economy's welfare improved?

Consider as a practical example a country in which airline service is provided by a government-regulated monopoly, which, as a condition of being allowed to maintain its monopoly power, uses some of the excess profits extracted from heavily travelled routes to subsidise the provision of loss-making services to more remote areas. Suppose it is proposed that the government take steps to end the airline monopoly and open up the industry to competition. If this step is taken, one might expect users of heavily travelled routes to benefit from the fact that fares there would fall. However, those living in more remote areas might face a sharp increase in travel costs, or even the loss of all airline service, and their welfare would fall. And what judgement would one make about the fall in the income of shareholders in the monopoly airline? How would one weight these issues in deciding whether or not to implement the proposal in question?

Or consider what might be involved in a plan to flood a mountain valley in order to enhance the water supply of some distant city. To carry through the plan would make the city dwellers better off, but the welfare of people living in the valley would be reduced. Can one make a decision about cases like these without assuming from the start that the welfare of one group is to be given greater weight in the decision-making process than that of another? Economists have developed the analysis of **compensation criteria** in an attempt to avoid the necessity of making judgements about whose welfare is to be given priority in just such instances. As we shall now see, this analysis can help, but it does not provide a complete solution to distributional problems, and it may raise questions in readers' minds about interpersonal comparisons of utility (see Chapter 4).

Compensation criteria

Two compensation criteria have been proposed in order to enable us to judge the desirability of making changes that cause some people to gain and others to lose. The first suggests that a move from one situation to another would be desirable if those who gain from the move were able to compensate those who lose and still remain better off after the move. The second criterion suggests that the same move would be undesirable if the losers were able to compensate the gainers for remaining in the initial position and still themselves be better off than they would be if the move were to be made.

Unfortunately, these criteria do not cover all possible cases, for it is easy to construct examples in which it is simultaneously possible for the gainers to compensate the losers if a move is made (indicating the move is desirable) and for the potential losers to compensate the potential gainers if the move is not made (indicating that the move is not desirable)! However, this does not always happen, and it will be convenient to discuss an unambiguous case first of all.

Consider once more the two-person/two-input/two-output, general equilibrium model developed in previous chapters. In that model, just as the production box diagram yields

Figure 23.5

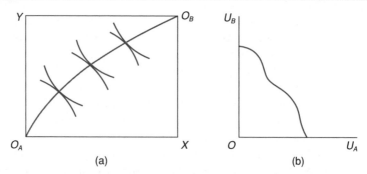

Panel (a) shows a consumption box diagram. Panel (b) shows the utility possibility curve generated by moving along the contract curve. We can say that, as B's utility decreases, A's increases as we move along the curve. However, if we are dealing with ordinal utility functions we cannot say by how much. Thus the utility possibility curve slopes downwards, but not at any defined rate, and is drawn as a wavy line in panel (b) to remind the reader of this.

a production frontier, so, once the outputs of X and Y are determined at a point such as O_B in Figure 23.3, does the consumption box diagram yield an analogous relationship that might be called a **utility possibility curve**. Such a relationship, derived in Figure 23.5, measures the maximum level of utility that A may obtain, given the level of utility made available to B and given a particular output mix of X and Y.

There exists one such utility possibility curve for every point on the production frontier. Since any reallocation of resources involves a change in the outputs of X and Y we may think of it as shifting the utility possibility curve.

Whether we can say a particular thing about the desirability of any reallocation depends not only upon how the utility possibility curve is shifted by it, but also upon which point on the original curve we start from and upon which point on the new curve we arrive at. Let us look at some of the possibilities, dealing with the simple example of the restoration of the price of one good to a competitive level. One logically possible (but not logically necessary) consequence of the removal of monopoly or of a tax is a reallocation of resources which results in a pattern of output such that, for any given level of utility attained by A, B could attain a higher level.

Such an unambiguously outward shift of the utility frontier is shown in Figure 23.6. If, beginning at D, the removal of the tax results in the economy generating a consumption pattern that puts our two individuals at a point on the new frontier between E and F, then the new situation is unambiguously Pareto superior. But what if the new consumption pattern were to lie at G? Here A would be worse off than initially with U_{A2} rather than U_{A1}. But B could sacrifice utility by giving consumption goods to A until the latter was enjoying the same level of utility as initially while B was still better off. That is, the consumption pattern *could* move to E, and here we would have a situation in which one person (B) was better off without the other (A) being worse off. Equally, in order for A *to persuade B* to remain in the initial situation it would have to be possible to increase B's utility to at least U_{B2} in that starting situation while leaving A better off than at point G. This is clearly impossible. Thus, the new situation meets both compensation criteria and according to them would be judged superior to the original one.

Figure 23.6

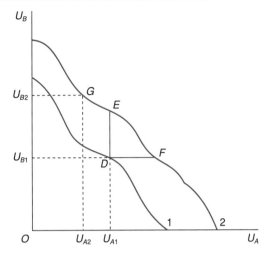

There is a different utility possibility curve for every composition of output, for every point on a given production frontier. In terms of Figure 23.4, a movement from a structure of output such as $X_1 Y_1$ to $X_2 Y_2$ produces a new utility possibility curve. It is possible (though not necessarily the case) that the new curve lies everywhere outside the old one. If we start at D and the change in output results in a shift to some point on the segment EF of the second utility possibility curve, then the shift is unambiguously desirable from a Pareto point of view. Both consumers are made better off. However, if we go, say, to point G, A is made worse off and we cannot say that G is Pareto superior to D. However, B could bribe A and make A better off than at D and still be left with a gain. Moreover, there is no way that A could bribe B to move back to the first situation. Hence, according to the compensation criteria, the move from utility possibility curve 1 to 2 is desirable.

Even in so clear-cut a case as this, though, one might have qualms about accepting that the move from D to G represented an unambiguously desirable step to take. It is *possible* to move from G to E, and hence it is *possible* to achieve a situation Pareto superior to that ruling at D. However, unless, after the move is made, the gainers are *actually* taxed and the losers *actually* compensated so as to move to E, the achievement of a Pareto superior situation is only a possibility, not an established fact. To accept the possibility of compensation as a sufficient criterion for regarding a change as desirable, rather than insisting that compensation be carried out, involves one in making stronger judgements than strict application of the Pareto criterion would permit.

In short, if a cost–benefit analysis of a particular economic project finds that the benefits outweigh the costs, but that these accrue to different people, the decision to proceed with the project without insisting that the losers be compensated by the gainers involves a comparison of the economic welfare of the two groups, the very thing that the Pareto criterion seeks to avoid. To return to the example given earlier, if a valley is to be flooded to improve the water supply to a city, the inhabitants of the valley must actually be compensated to a level at which they willingly acquiesce in the flooding if the project is to be judged as constituting a Pareto improvement in society's economic welfare.

The compensation criteria in an ambiguous case

In any event, the two compensation criteria we have been discussing may well produce contradictory results. One example will suffice to demonstrate this point. It hinges on the perfectly straightforward proposition that there is no particular reason why the removal of a tax on one good should result in an unambiguously outward shift of the **utility frontier**. Hence, what we have here is not just an analytic curiosity, but an illustration of an extremely important limitation on the practical usefulness of compensation criteria. Suppose consumer A found Y a relatively unappealing good. Then to substitute Y for X in production could well result in A's maximum attainable level of utility falling. Such a situation is depicted in Figure 23.7. It is possible that the removal of monopoly or of a tax on Y could result in a reallocation of resources and redistribution of income between A and B such that there was a movement from D on utility frontier 1 to G on utility frontier 2. In this case B could certainly compensate A for making the change with a shift to point F. However, A could simultaneously compensate B for not making the change by a shift to point E.

Figure 23.7

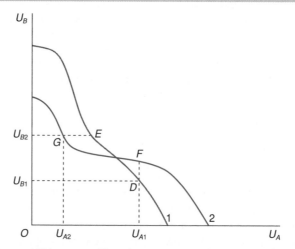

A change that involves a shift in composition of output can produce a new utility possibility curve that crosses the old one, and then the compensation criteria can prove contradictory and hence unhelpful. Suppose we start at D in the first situation and shift to G in the second. Consumer B can bribe A to accept the move by permitting a move to F, where A can enjoy U_{A1} just as at D, while B is left better off. However, once at G, A could bribe B to return to the original situation. In that situation, point E is available and here U_{B2} is available to B, just as it is at G, while A is better off than at G where U_{A2} is obtained.

The utility frontier

We may use the utility possibility curve construction to set out more clearly the nature of the distributional problem with which we have been dealing. For every point on the production frontier, there is a utility possibility curve derived from the relevant consumption

Figure 23.8

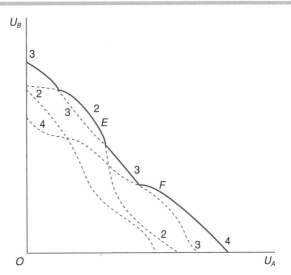

The derivation of the utility frontier. For every point on a given production possibility curve we have a different utility possibility curve. The potentially infinitely large number of such curves is reduced to four here only for the sake of geometric clarity. The utility frontier shows us the maximum amount of utility available to A given the utility available to B, and given, not a particular structure of output, but a particular set of productive resources. It is thus made up of those segments of the individual utility possibility curves that lie outside any other. This frontier is drawn here as a continuous curve and the segments of the utility possibility curves that lie inside the frontier as dotted curves.

contract curve. In principle, we can derive every such curve and plot them in a figure such as Figure 23.8. Some of these curves will lie entirely inside others; others will criss-cross one another, and not necessarily only once. In just the same way as, in Chapter 8, we derived the isoquant as a boundary showing the *minimum* quantities of factors of production required to produce a given level of output, so in Figure 23.8 we derive an overall utility frontier from all these utility possibility curves. It shows what is the maximum level of utility available for A given a certain level of utility for B, when fixed quantities of factors of production are available to be reallocated between the production of various goods. Thus, in terms of Figure 23.8 the movement from E to F not only represents a re-allocation of utility in favour of individual A; it also represents a reallocation of resources such that the output mix changes from that underlying utility possibility curve 2 to that underlying utility possibility curve 4.

The distribution of welfare

The overall utility frontier of Figure 23.8 shows clearly why the Pareto criterion does not permit us to make all the judgements about the performance of an economic system that we might want to make. Every point on it is **Pareto optimal** and, without making explicit judgements about the distribution of economic welfare between our two individuals, we

Figure 23.9

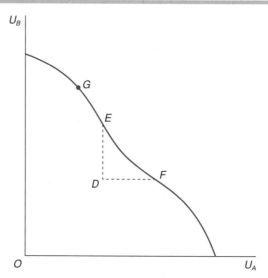

For any point inside the utility frontier, such as *D*, there is a segment of the frontier *EF*, any point on which is Pareto superior to *D*. However, a point such as *G* is not Pareto superior to *D* since *A* is worse off there. Despite the fact that *G*, like every point on the frontier, is a Pareto optimal point while no point within the frontier is, we cannot say that the achievement of Pareto optimality is always desirable in and of itself.

cannot choose between them. But can we at least say that, since every point on the frontier is Pareto optimal, we should nevertheless aim economic policy at being somewhere on the frontier rather than inside it, and avoid discussing distribution in this way? Inspection of Figure 23.9 will readily confirm that we cannot do so. It would only be possible to say this if it were the case that every point on the frontier was **Pareto superior** to every point within it, and this is not true. For any point within the frontier, such as *D*, there is certainly a segment *EF* of the frontier that is made up of Pareto superior points, but a point such as *G* is not Pareto superior to *D*. To move there involves making someone worse off. Depending upon the judgements that one might make about the **distribution of welfare** between the two individuals whose situation is depicted in Figure 23.9, one might well regard point *D* as superior to *G* even though it is non-Pareto optimal. Thus, there can be no overall implication from the foregoing analysis that the achievement of Pareto optimality can always be regarded as desirable as an end in itself!

The story which we have been telling is abstract and complex, but it has a very clear-cut moral. It is, in general, impossible to make judgements about social welfare without also making judgements about the distribution of income. Allocative efficiency is not the only factor to be taken into account in judging a particular social situation or a particular form of social organisation. Its achievement puts one on the utility frontier, but the desirability of a particular distribution of utility between individuals must still be judged. Such judgements must involve the application of ethical criteria. That *does not* mean that they are arbitrary by any means, but it does mean that economics alone does not provide a sufficient basis for making them.

Concluding comment

If there existed a market for every scarce resource; if all the costs and benefits of every aspect of productive activity were reflected in market transactions; and if there were no need to provide a background of enforceable legal arrangements, then one could talk about the Pareto optimal properties of competitive equilibrium without qualification. Even then, though, all the ethical problems concerning distribution that we have raised would remain to qualify one's judgements about the desirability of one such equilibrium relative to another. However, as soon as one considers the desirability, indeed, in some cases the necessity, of providing public goods, and as soon as one recognises the many ways in which the costs and benefits of various aspects of economic activity can escape the market and appear as 'externalities', then it becomes apparent that the solutions to such problems have both allocative and distributional consequences which require analysing together, and that the interconnectedness of these problems is inherent in the operation of a market economy.

Thus the analysis that we have been pursuing in the last three chapters of this book in no way implies that an economy free of any government intervention is in any sense the 'best' economy. Nor does that analysis provide any blanket justification for all the many different sorts of government intervention in economic life that one might encounter in practice. Rather it provides a set of analytic principles that enable coherent judgements to be made about the allocative, but *not the distributive*, aspects of such intervention, or absence thereof. It does not provide all the answers to all the questions one might raise about these issues, but that does not mean it is useless. The very fact that it helps us to think coherently about the type of issues we have discussed above surely means that it is a great deal better than nothing.

SUMMARY

Welfare economics

1. The Pareto criterion provides a means of assessing the desirability of various resource allocations. A Pareto optimal situation is one in which it is not possible to reallocate resources in such a way as to make one person better off without making another person worse off.

2. The Pareto criterion does not provide a complete guide to economic policy making. It cannot indicate the extent to which one situation is superior to another, nor provide answers to questions concerning the desirability of reallocations in which the welfare of one agent is increased at the expense of another.

3. Pareto optimality is attained in a two-person/two-good exchange economy when the allocation of resources is on the contract curve. The key condition for Pareto optimality in such an economy is that each individual's marginal rate of substitution between the two goods be the same.

4. Pareto optimality in production implies that output occurs along the production box contract curve. A condition for Pareto optimality in production is therefore that marginal rates of technical substitution are equalised between inputs.

5. The so-called grand criterion for Pareto optimality in a production economy is that the marginal rates of substitution between goods in consumption for each individual equal the slope of the production frontier, the marginal rate of transformation between goods in production.

6. The first fundamental welfare theorem states that the allocation of resources attained by a competitive market economy in equilibrium will be Pareto optimal.

7. The second fundamental welfare theorem states that any Pareto optimal allocation may be attained as the outcome of a competitive market process, provided that an appropriate initial pattern of endowments among agents is first put in place.

8. The Pareto criterion is silent on the matter of the distribution of income. In many policy problems, comparisons of situations in which one group's position is improved at the expense of another must be made.

9. Economists have sought to avoid making judgements about whose welfare should be given priority, by the use of compensation criteria.

10. One compensation criterion has it that a move from one situation to another would be desirable provided those who gain from the move are able to compensate those who lose and still remain better off.

11. A second criterion has it that the losers should not be able to compensate the gainers for remaining in the original situation and still be better off than they would have been if the move had been made.

12. In some situations, these two criteria produce an unambiguous result. However, it is easy to construct ambiguous cases. The problem can be illustrated with reference to the utility frontier.

13. It is, in general, impossible to make judgements about social welfare without making judgements about the distribution of income.

PROBLEMS

1 In a perfectly competitive economy, there are two individuals, A and B, and two goods, X and Y, each in fixed supply. Before trading commences A has no X and B has no Y. Under what circumstances will they be at the same point after trading? Will the outcome be Pareto efficient?

2 Using a two-person/two-good exchange model, show with diagrams that:
   (a) the competitive equilibrium is Pareto optimal;
   (b) every Pareto optimal allocation can be sustained as a competitive equilibrium if a suitable redistribution of endowments is made.

3 (a) What assumptions must you make about the demand curve facing a monopolist in order to interpret the area under it as measuring the total gross benefit accruing to consumers from consuming its output?
   (b) What assumptions must you make in order to interpret the area under the long-run marginal cost curve as measuring the total cost to society of having the monopolist's output produced?
   (c) If the area under a monopolist's demand curve did measure the total benefit to society of consuming its output and the area under the long-run marginal cost curve did measure the total cost to society of producing the output, would the profit-maximising price and output

decision result in the net benefit to society of the monopolist's activities being maximised? Would your answer change if the monopolist were able to indulge in perfect price discrimination?

4 In an otherwise distortion-free, perfectly competitive economy, the production of X is monopolised and the firm producing X makes positive profits for its owners. Consider the effects on the distribution of income and allocation of resources of the following suggested actions:

(a) taxing the profits made in the production of X and distributing them to the rest of the community;

(b) subsidising the production of X so that the firm produces the level of output that would be produced by a competitive industry;

(c) a combination of (a) and (b).

Which action would you prefer to see taken? Would your preference be influenced by the knowledge that the owners of the firm in question were the otherwise penniless inhabitants of an orphanage?

5 Suppose that society is able to construct a social welfare function which allows us to rank distributions of welfare between individuals. In a two-person world, this social welfare function can be represented by convex to the origin social indifference curves in utility space. Suppose that the utility frontier takes the form illustrated in Figure 23.9. Draw and explain the case when points such as G, E or F in Figure 23.9, which are on the utility frontier and Pareto optimal, are regarded as socially inferior to another point, call it H, which is not on the utility frontier and is therefore not Pareto optimal.

Note

1. Recall, for example, that, in the pure two-person two-good exchange economy in Chapter 21, any point on the contract curve portrayed in Figure 21.2 was attainable, depending on how goods X and Y were divided among the two consumers before trade was allowed to begin.

PART VIII

MISSING MARKETS

CHAPTER 24

Taxes, externalities and public goods

Key words and phrases

- enforcement of property rights and contracts, taxation, sales tax, income tax, poll tax, second best principle
- externalities, pollution, Coase theorem
- public goods, non-rivalry, non-excludability, Lindahl equilibrium, free rider problem, government

Introduction

The Pareto optimal properties of a perfectly competitive equilibrium lie at the root of a great deal of work on economic policy problems. At one time the existence of this property was widely regarded as providing an argument in favour of competitive capitalism as a form of economic organisation. It would be hard nowadays to find a professional economist willing to defend such a position, at least when it is put so baldly, but it is worth looking more closely both at the nature of the competitive economy whose properties we have been studying and, at the nature of the optimum we have been considering. To do so will help us better understand the relevance of the Pareto criterion to real-world economic problems and, crucially, the limits to that relevance; or the circumstances in which markets 'fail' to allocate resources in a Pareto efficient way.

In this chapter we shall consider in turn aspects of what the notion of Pareto optimality has to say about the design of taxation systems, and about the pervasive group of policy issues which, in everyday parlance, are labelled *pollution problems*. Finally we shall discuss the problems created by *public goods*. We continue with the theme of market failure in the following two chapters of this section. In the next chapter, we consider the consequences of a situation in which consumers and producers do not have sufficient information to make with certainty their maximising decisions. This can be viewed as a consequence of missing markets, for example the markets for future goods that would be required for rational intertemporal choices along the lines discussed in Chapter 7. In the final chapter, we outline some topics in public choice, a branch of public economics that tries to explain, not how economic decisions ought to be taken, but how in practice they are made.

Taxation and Pareto optimality

No form of economic organisation exists in a social vacuum. A competitive market economy needs, at the very least, a framework of **law concerning property rights and contracts**, if it is to function smoothly, and laws need enforcing. This is the minimal necessity for its operating, but even the provision of this bare necessity would require the use of real resources: police and court officials must be fed, clothed and housed. Thus **taxes** must be levied in order to provide the necessary resources. Far from being some kind of interference with the operation of a competitive economy, the levying of taxes must, therefore, be a necessary condition for its existence.

As we have already seen in Chapter 23, to levy a tax on sales of one good leads the ratio of the market prices of goods to depart from the ratio of their marginal costs of production, and hence to a less than Pareto optimal allocation of resources. In terms of the analysis presented in the last chapter, the solution to the problem might appear to be simple: levy a **sales tax** at the same rate on each good, or, what apparently amounts to the same thing, levy an **income tax**.

There are two objections to this. First the impression of an income tax as a non-distorting tax arises from a rather special property of our model. The model assumes that the supply of productive resources to the economy is given. In general we would not expect this to be the case. We would expect the supply of labour to vary with the wage rate received; indeed we have analysed some of the factors underlying this phenomenon in Chapter 19, and have considered some of the general equilibrium implications in the case of the Robinson Crusoe economy analysed in Chapter 22.

Once we permit the owners of labour services to choose between work and leisure, we open up another area of choice where a tax can be distorting. An income tax ensures that workers will receive less for their marginal hour of work than those who purchase their output would be willing to pay for it. It is equivalent to levying a tax on every good in the economy except leisure, and hence leads to a misallocation of resources just like any other specific tax. The only tax that will not involve some such distortion is a tax which does not affect any choice about resource allocation. It must be levied as a lump sum and be independent of any consumption pattern or work pattern. The only such tax appears to be a **poll tax**, and even that is suspect if one takes the view that family size, and hence the future supply of labour, is partly the result of choices based on economic factors! Besides, it would be hard to find anyone willing seriously to defend using a poll tax as the sole source of government revenue from the point of view of distributional equity. In short, even in the most competitive economy conceivable, taxes have to be levied, and they are going to affect a great many things including the allocation of resources.

Moreover taxes are not the only potential source of distortion in the economy and, in addition to raising revenue, they may themselves be used to offset other distortions. For example, if the price of one particular good is already too high relative to its long-run marginal cost of production because the output of that good is monopolised, then to tax each good equally will leave resources misallocated. In this case, it would be appropriate to levy taxes on other goods at a higher rate in order to offset the effect of the initial monopoly. What is an appropriate pattern of taxes is dependent upon the initial pattern of resource allocation in an economy and there are no general rules to be laid down. There can be no general presumption in favour of an income tax over a sales tax on specific goods as a means of raising revenue or, indeed, in favour of any other particular pattern of taxation.

The second-best principle

The implications of the foregoing arguments are easily summed up and are of considerable importance. An economy which was completely free of distortions, including those arising from taxes, would achieve Pareto optimality, but such an economy is a figment of the economist's imagination, not a practical possibility. Governments are necessary, do exist, and do need to collect revenue. The problem, then, is not to design an economic policy regime that will deliver a Pareto optimal allocation of resources, a *first best* allocation as it is called. Rather it is to design a system that will get the economy as close as possible to such an allocation, given the fact that taxes must be levied and do distort resource allocation. It is to achieve, in the terminology that economists have adopted, a **second best** solution to the problem. Moreover, to the extent that economic policy has distributional goals and effects, these too must be weighed when policy is designed. We shall return to these distributional issues in the next chapter.

Externalities and absence of markets

Allocative (and distributive) problems also arise when so-called **externalities** are under analysis. Such effects can involve both costs and benefits and arise whenever an important, but nevertheless so far implicit, assumption of our analysis of competitive equilibrium is violated. In formally analysing the competitive equilibrium model we assumed that there were two, and only two, scarce resources; and in identifying its equilibrium properties with a Pareto optimal allocation of resources we took it for granted that there was a perfect market for every scarce resource available to the economy. Externalities arise whenever there is a scarce resource for which there is no such perfect market, and this is quite a common phenomenon in any actual economy. Indeed it lies at the heart of the so-called problem of **pollution**.

A simple example will illustrate the nature of the problem. Consider a river which is utilised by two groups of economic agents: fishermen for fishing and manufacturers for discharging waste materials. The river is clearly a productive resource, but not necessarily scarce. It is a property of rivers that they can absorb a certain amount of waste material without their capacity to support life in their waters being affected, and as long as the amount of waste disposal undertaken is below this limit, the river, though productive, is nevertheless free. By free, we mean that there is enough of it to meet all demands being put upon it without any need to choose among alternative uses.

But now suppose that for some reason the manufacturers along the river expand their output and with it the volume of their waste disposal up to a level at which it affects fishing prospects. Part of the cost of the new higher level of manufactured output is clearly the fish lost to fishermen. However, this is not captured in the private costs of production facing manufacturers and, if they are profit maximisers (and are not fishermen), will be ignored by them. What has happened is that a resource that once was free has become scarce as the demand for its services has increased, but has not had a market price attached to it.

From the point of view of allocative efficiency, the marginal *private* cost facing manufacturers, upon which the pricing of their output is based, falls short of the marginal *social* cost upon which price ought to be based if an optimal allocation of resources in the Pareto sense is to be achieved. The output of manufacturers is thus too high, and the costs involved in lost fish are borne by fishermen instead of by the consumers and producers of manufactures. These costs are *external* to the market for the goods in whose production they are actually incurred.

Now one can have external benefits as well. Suppose the activities of manufacturers enhanced the fish-bearing capacity of our river in such a way that when manufacturing expanded so did the output of fish. In this case the private benefits of expanding manufactured output would fall short of the social benefits, since the greater yield in fish would not enter into the cost calculations of the manufacturers (unless they were also fishermen). Their output would fall short of a Pareto optimal level. Indeed, everything in the foregoing analysis – and that which is to follow – is simply reversed in the case of external benefits and so there is no need to deal with the latter as a different case.

Box 24.1 **Externalities and the theory of the second best**

We can use the discussion on externalities to illustrate the second best principle considered above. It will be recalled that the theory of the second best concerns what happens when one or more optimality conditions are not satisfied. If one optimality condition is not satisfied, it is possible that the next best solution involves changing another variable away from what is usually assumed to be optimal. This means that with some unavoidable market failure in one activity, there can actually be a decrease in efficiency due to a move toward greater market perfection in another area that is connected in some way to the first activity. In theory, at least, it may be better to let two market imperfections cancel each other out rather than make an effort to remove either one. Note the complexity here that different market failures can exist simultaneously, rather than separately as might be suggested by textbook discussion. We can use the existence of externalities as one possible market failure.

Consider a simple example that can be used to illustrate the complexities of multiple but connected market failures. A monopolist produces output that is considered necessary for non-economic reasons, e.g. the product is considered essential for national defence. But when producing the product a negative externality (e.g. pollution) is generated. Note that because of the non-economic justification this market failure is unavoidable. A different branch of government may examine the monopoly position of the producer and suggest a breaking up of the producer into competitor firms. This shift to a competitive market structure increases industry output and hence increases the negative externality. To control the externality, given the national defence requirement, it is globally preferable to allow monopoly production, i.e. a second market failure.

Consider Illustration 24.1, which depicts the very special, not to say empirically unlikely, case in which monopoly pricing would precisely offset the negative externality. In this diagram MC_P is private marginal cost for the monopolist and so the supply curve for an equivalent competitive industry. The curve MC_S is the social marginal

Illustration 24.1

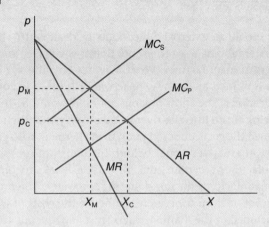

cost. The vertical distance between MC_S and MC_P is the cost of the negative externality. Curve AR is the monopolist's average revenue and the equivalent competitive industry's market demand curve. MR is the marginal revenue corresponding to AR. A profit maximising monopolist produces X_M at price p_M. An equivalent competitive industry produces X_C at price p_C. The optimal production, taking account of the externality is X_M, i.e. the optimal solution is generated by combining two market failures. Note this solution may be more efficient than, for example, governments taxing competitive supply to raise MC_P to MC_S because of the costs of collecting taxes. Of course in reality the cost of a negative externality may not be precisely the size to generate optimality with a monopoly. But this does not remove the general second best idea that the more efficient solution may involve combining failures.

The theory of the second best has been used in the area of international trade to justify the development of customs unions. In this case the exogenous market failure is a trade distortion from another country outside the customs union. But the same principle applies whenever market failures co-exist and one is considered immovable. Consider the area of health, which might be viewed as a positive externality (e.g. the management of contagious disease) and also a social factor that makes good health beyond economic justification. The promotion of health obviously involves, in some circumstances, drug use. But drug advice involves considerable hidden information. We shall see from the discussion of adverse selection in the following chapter that competitive supply with hidden information can involve high quality activity being driven from a market. Hence the positive externality, and the hidden information, might be managed by government regulation and/or non-competitive provision. In an otherwise optimal economy regulation and non-competitive production imply deviations from optimality. But with the co-existence of other market failures (e.g. externalities and information asymmetries) this need not be the case.

The general implication of the theory of the second best is that with multiple and connected market failures, economists need to study the details of any situation before recommending an improvement in market perfection in one area, based on apparently general rules that may impact on global efficiency.

Property rights and the Coase theorem

How should an external diseconomy be dealt with? The answer obviously is to *internalise* the external cost so as to ensure that it is taken into account by the producers and consumers of manufactures. What may not be quite so obvious in the river example is that there is more than one way to accomplish this, each of which has different distributional implications. The most obvious solution would be to charge the manufacturers for discharging waste into the river in such a way that their outlay on waste disposal expenses reflected the costs imposed upon the fishermen, who could then be compensated for their losses. Alternatively, one could think of instituting a scheme whereby fishermen paid the manufacturer a certain sum for each fish taken from the river, thereby compensating the manufacturer for not polluting the water. The more waste disposal undertaken, the less revenue from fishermen and hence the costs of waste disposal would again come to be included in the manufacturers' cost and revenue calculations.

The second of these two solutions sounds unfair to fishermen, but that is because we have described our example in a particular way. We have had manufacturing expand to cause the externality problem; but suppose manufacturers had always maintained a given level of waste disposal and it was fishermen who found this level of disposal a hindrance to expanding their activities? In that case it would seem more reasonable for fishermen to pay the manufacturer to reduce its activities rather than to ask the manufacturer to compensate the fishermen.

The point here is that, so long as the cost of manufacturing operations in terms of fish, or the cost of fish in terms of manufactured goods, is reflected in the cash revenues and outlays of firms involved in these activities, then correct (from a Pareto point of view) decisions about resource allocation will be made. It is the distributional consequences of the above two solutions that differ. In the first case we are essentially suggesting that the fishermen become owners of the river and rent out its waste disposal services to manufacturers, while in the second case that manufacturers become the owners of the river who may then sell fishing rights.

We have here an illustration of the so-called **Coase theorem** (named after its originator, Professor Ronald Coase of the University of Chicago), which says that, provided property rights in scarce resources are freely exchangeable in competitive markets, the distribution of their ownership among agents is irrelevant to ensuring their efficient use. However, it must be understood that this proposition relies on the assumption that transactions in competitive markets are essentially costless to implement.

In the foregoing example it is indeed feasible to think of solving the 'externality' problem by vesting in someone or other property rights in the resource that has become scarce, that is the river, and then allowing for market transactions among the parties involved, the manufacturers and the fishermen (and the owner of the river if not a member of one or the other groups), to solve the problem of allocating the resource.

Not all 'pollution' problems can, as a practical matter, be dealt with in this way. Consider for example the case of a group of householders who have been using the airspace around their homes to provide themselves with fresh air and peace and quiet, but who now find that an airport is to be set up in the vicinity. In this case, the airlines operating from the airport would use that same airspace for absorbing the kerosene fumes and the noise emitted by their aircraft, thus reducing its capacity to provide fresh air and peace and quiet. The problem here is formally similar to the one considered earlier, but problems of allocating property rights in airspace, and of monitoring its use so that it can be charged for, are altogether more difficult. In this case, the problem as a practical matter might better be tackled by some direct form of government intervention, perhaps by levying taxes on aircraft movements, or by enforcing regulations concerning permissible noise levels and so on.

Box 24.2   ## An application of the Coase theorem

We can continue the example set out in the text to illustrate the Coase theorem, and also draw out a number of problems with its use. Assume that a manufacturing company pollutes a river that affects the fish stocks available to a commercial fish firm. To simplify presentation we assume that the manufacturer is a price taker in its output market, in which case $p = MR$. The private marginal costs of the manufacturing firm can be assumed linear:

$$MC_P = a + bX \tag{24.2.1}$$

where X is the manufacturing firm's output. The cost of the externality can be modelled as depending on the manufacturing firm's output:

$$C_{EXT} = cX \tag{24.2.2}$$

Hence the social marginal cost is

$$MC_S = MC_P + C_{EXT} = a + bX + cX = a + (b + c)X \tag{24.2.3}$$

If we ignore the externality the manufacturer maximises profit by setting $MR = MC_P$:

$$p = a + bX \tag{24.2.4}$$

i.e. the privately optimal output is

$$X_P = \frac{p - a}{b} \tag{24.2.5}$$

The socially optimal level of output (X_S) is defined where $p = MC_S$:

$$p = a + (b + c)X \tag{24.2.6}$$

i.e. $\quad X_S = \dfrac{p - a}{b + c} \tag{24.2.7}$

It is clear that as $b + c > b$ then $X_S < X_P$ as we would expect.

We can now explore how the Coase theorem suggests we might attain X_S. First assume that the fishing firm owns the river, i.e. has the property right. In this case the manufacturer starts with $X = 0$ and pays for the right to pollute, i.e. pays to increase output. The two firms will be able to come to an agreement if the amount the manufacturing firm is willing to offer is at least as large as the amount the fish farm is willing to accept. The *maximum* the manufacturing firm is willing to offer to produce one unit of output, and hence pollute the river because of the one unit, is the profit it would have earned. This maximum amount is therefore

$$\Delta\pi = MR - MC_P = p - a - bX \tag{24.2.8}$$

→

The *minimum* the fish firm would be willing to accept is the cost of the externality because it could then afford to clean the river. This minimum amount is therefore

$$C_{EXT} = cX \qquad (24.2.9)$$

Agreement between the two firms is therefore possible when (24.2.8) is at least as large as (24.2.9):

$$p - a - bX \geq cX \qquad (24.2.10)$$

This implies the following manufacturing output (X_1) if the fish firm owns the river:

$$X_1 \leq \frac{p - a}{b + c} \qquad (24.2.11)$$

By comparing (24.2.11) with (24.2.7) we can see that the manufacturing firm will be willing to pay the fish farm to pollute until $X_1 = X_S$, i.e. until socially optimal output is reached.

Now we can assume that the manufacturing firm owns the river. In this case the fish farm will pay the manufacturer not to pollute, i.e. will pay for less manufacturing output. The *minimum* the manufacturer is willing to accept to reduce output by one unit is the profit it would have earned on that unit of output as defined in (24.2.8). The *maximum* the fish firm is willing to pay is the cost of the externality as defined in (24.2.9). Any higher payment by the fish firm would be irrational as it would then be cheaper to clean the river independent of any agreement. So when the manufacturer owns the river, agreement is possible when (24.2.9) is at least as large as (24.2.8):

$$cX \geq p - a - bX \qquad (24.2.12)$$

Rearranging implies the following manufacturing output (X_2) if the manufacturer owns the river:

$$X_2 \geq \frac{p - a}{b + c} \qquad (24.2.13)$$

Comparison of (24.2.13) and (24.2.7) indicates that the fish farm will be willing and able to pay the manufacturer to reduce output until $X_2 = X_S$, i.e. until socially optimal output is achieved.

In short it follows that it does not matter who owns the river, i.e. who owns the property right, as long as one of the parties does. Ownership plus private bargaining produces socially optimal output. But note an important omission from this example. It has been assumed that agreement between the firms is possible without incurring any transaction costs. At a minimum these transaction costs will involve bargaining time costs and possibly legal advice costs. But also we have assumed one polluting party and one party being polluted. If we have many parties on both sides, which may be geographically dispersed, transaction costs will rise accordingly. It is left to the reader to show that with transaction costs our output levels X_1 and X_2 will diverge from X_S; X_1 falls and X_2 rises. In addition there is some level of transaction costs that makes private bargaining impossible. With transaction costs it may be more efficient for the state to manage externalities, or it may be only the state that can manage externalities if private bargaining is irrational.

Public goods

The awkward external effects arising from aircraft noise to which we have referred earlier also provide an example of a class of phenomena that bear the label **public goods**, though given that it is disutility rather than utility that is involved in this particular example, perhaps it would be better to use the phrase 'public bad' to describe this. In order to see what is involved here, it is best to begin by discussing that theoretically clear-cut case to which economists refer as a *pure public good*.

The first distinguishing feature of such an entity is that its consumption is characterised by what is called **non-rivalry**. By that we mean that consumption of a good by one agent does not affect its availability to be consumed by any other. Usually, if one person consumes a good – a loaf of bread, or a cup of coffee, say – then it is used up by that act and rendered unavailable to others. But (and here we cite the most often used example of a public good) consider, by way of contrast, the services that a lighthouse provides to sailors. The consumption of its extremely useful services by the crew of one vessel has no effect whatsoever on their simultaneous availability to others. Moreover the services of the lighthouse also display the other defining characteristic of a public good – namely, **non-excludability** of potential consumers: given that the lighthouse is sending out its signal, there is no feasible physical way of preventing anyone within range of it from observing that signal and benefiting from the information it provides.

If it is impossible to prevent anyone consuming a particular good, it also becomes impossible to sell it in the normal way. Market mechanisms are therefore unlikely to lead to its provision. And yet, if potential consumers would gain more from a public good than they would from the goods and services that would have to be given up to produce it, a Pareto improvement in the allocation of resources can clearly be generated by getting the public good produced. The pure public good is thus a potential source of market failure just as externalities are. Now it is not difficult to state the principle which should be applied in deciding how much of a public good should be produced to arrive at a Pareto optimal allocations of resources – to follow through on our original example, in deciding how many lighthouses, with what range of visibility, should be built and operated.

Note first of all that provision of *any* good, whether public or not, should be carried up to the point at which the marginal benefit to consumers of providing an extra unit of it just equals the marginal cost of doing so. Public goods present no particular difficulties on the cost side of this equality. The marginal cost of extending a lighthouse's range is neither more nor less difficult to compute than the marginal cost of baking an extra loaf of bread. But public goods present novel problems on the benefit side. The marginal benefit accruing from bread consumption is measured by the sacrifice that the consumer of the marginal loaf of bread is willing to make to consume it, and that in turn is conveniently assessed by the price that the consumer in question is willing to pay. But when the supply of a public good is increased on the margin, the property of non-rivalry that characterises its consumption implies that *every* agent to whom it is available simultaneously gains. Each of those consumers would be willing to make an individual sacrifice in order to obtain their own gain. The *sum* of those sacrifices over all consumers therefore measures the marginal benefit accruing from providing an extra unit of a public good. If output is set so that this sum is equal to the good's marginal production cost (and the economy is otherwise distortion free), a Pareto optimal amount of it will be forthcoming.

The free rider problem

But how is the sacrifice in question to be implemented so that whoever is providing the public good is able to obtain from consumers the wherewithal to buy the resources necessary to produce it? One theoretically viable solution would be: (a) to get potential consumers of a public good to declare its value to them, or indeed to declare a schedule of the value to them of having successively increasing amounts of it; (b) to have some agency – perhaps a club to which potential consumers voluntarily belong – collect and process this information, along with data on production costs, in order to settle on the optimal amount of the good in question; and (c) to levy dues on potential consumers in accordance with their already expressed willingness to pay for the public good. Such a procedure would produce what is known as a **Lindahl equilibrium** – named after Erik Lindahl, the Swedish economist who first suggested this solution – in the provision of the good.

There is, however, a fatal flaw here, arising from what is known as the **free rider problem**. All potential consumers, knowing that the size of a future liability hinged upon their initial estimate of the benefit accruing to them from the good, would have an incentive to understate that benefit. Indeed, each would be tempted falsely to declare that, to them, the good was worthless, while hoping that the good would be provided anyway at the expense of others. The information provided at step (a) above, then, would be unreliable. The value of the benefits that the good would provide would be systematically understated, and if it were treated as accurate at step (b), the public good would be under-provided. The appropriateness of the term 'free rider problem' in this context will now be clear. Each potential consumer acts in the hope of receiving a 'free ride' at the expense of all the others, and this leads to a 'problem' inasmuch as insufficient resources are devoted to producing the public good, with a resulting sub-optimal allocation of resources.

Public goods and government intervention

All in all, where a pure public good is potentially available, it is difficult to avoid the conclusion that market mechanisms will fail to provide a Pareto optimal allocation of resources. Some form of **government** intervention is required if such an allocation is to be achieved. It should be stressed, though, that the government intervention required involves estimating and then articulating the demand for the good in question, because it is on the demand side of the market where the difficulty arises. The public good problem does not give rise to the need for government involvement in production. To return to the example of lighthouses for a moment, it might be necessary for government to express a willingness to pay for their services, but given that commitment, it would be quite feasible to contract out their construction and operation to private profit-making enterprises. This is not to say that the matter must be handled this way. Perhaps a government lighthouse service would be the preferred solution for administrative reasons; but it would not be dictated by anything inherent in the nature of public goods.

We hinted earlier that aircraft noise in the vicinity of an airport provides an example of a 'public bad', and it should now be clear why we did so. There is certainly non-rivalry involved. The fact that one household is deafened by aircraft flying overhead does not in any way reduce the problems of its neighbours next door; and the non-excludability problem turns up in the guise of its being impossible for one household to benefit from a reduction in noise without its neighbours also gaining. A moment's thought will also convince the reader that to attempt to solve the problem of aircraft noise by a system of voluntary self-assessed payments from households to airlines in return for noise abatement measures would be subject to free rider problems. So, as we remarked at the end of the preceding section, some form of government intervention by way of taxes or direct regulation of aircraft operations seems to be called for here.

The pure public good (or bad) is a limiting case of a rather widespread class of phenomena. The problems for the functioning of markets it presents spring by and large from the non-excludability characteristic rather than non-rivalry. Sports events, concerts, theatre performances, and so on, all have a large element of non-rivalry in consumption about them, at least up to the capacity of the stadium or hall where they take place, but the fact that potential consumers may be made to pay to get into the venue is enough to ensure that there are no problems in excluding those unwilling to do so. This, in turn, enables their promoters to reap the revenue necessary to put the events on (and also enables economists to make the case that their provision can be left to the private sector). The services of highways and bridges too, where the possibility of non-rivalry arises, may be charged for by levying tolls, and even the costs of television and radio programming may be recouped by way of licence fees levied on the use of receivers. But in the latter case, the difficulty of enforcement within a particular jurisdiction and the fact that signals may in any case have a range beyond the jurisdiction in question, begin to raise questions about the excludability of potential consumers.

There is very little that can be said in general about specific examples such as these. Each case needs to be analysed and dealt with on its own merits. The point we would stress here, though, is that the existence of public goods and bads is yet another factor tending to militate against any comfortable belief that the operation of market mechanisms will in and of itself necessarily lead to a Pareto optimal allocation of resources. Without some form of government intervention, public goods will tend to be underprovided, and public bads overprovided, relative to a Pareto optimal situation.

Concluding comment

Providing the basic framework of law and order required for markets to function in the first place (which the reader will now recognise as a special case of the public good problem); coping with externalities of various sorts; supplying public goods and eliminating public bads: none of these interrelated activities, it would now appear, can be 'left to the market'. Government is, that is to say, an integral part of economic life. But, as we noted earlier in this chapter, government has to be paid for. Taxes, therefore, have to be raised. Moreover the actions which governments take to raise taxes, and indeed to influence the allocation of resources, are bound to affect the incomes of individuals. We cannot avoid discussing distributional matters. We shall take them up in the next chapter, and they will also figure prominently in the final part of this book, which applies some elementary microeconomic principles to analysing the behaviour of government itself.

SUMMARY

Taxes, externalities and public goods

1. Taxation is required to support the functions of government, such as law and order. But taxes distort individual choice, most notably concerning the supply of labour. Only lump-sum taxes are non-distortionary in their impact.

2. Pareto optimality implies that interventions should be non-distortionary but such an outcome is unrealistic. In practice, policy makers must get as close as is feasible to the Pareto optimal allocation. They should seek a second best allocation.

3. Externalities occur when the activities of one agent influence the welfare or productivity of another without the exchange being mediated through the market mechanism.

4. The market mechanism leads to overproduction of goods that generate negative externalities, because producers of such goods do not take into account their external effect when making their production decisions. The market leads to underproduction of goods with positive externalities.

5. The Coase theorem states that externality problems will be internalised provided property rights are freely exchangeable, and that the distribution of those rights does not affect the efficiency of resource use.

6. Public goods are characterised by non-rivalry in consumption and non-excludability.

7. A Pareto optimal output of a public good is attained where its marginal cost equals the sum of its consumers' marginal willingness to pay. Lindahl equilibrium can be achieved if each consumer declares a schedule of values of the public good to them at each level of production.

8. The free rider problem arises because all consumers know that their future bill for the public good depends on their declared willingness to pay for it. They also know that the good's suppliers cannot prevent them from consuming it. They will therefore be tempted to state that the good's value to them is zero.

9. Government intervention may therefore be required on the demand side of the market for a public good. This does not imply that its provision by government is necessary.

PROBLEMS

1 Should airline operators be surcharged on their landing and take-off fees at airports, the proceeds being redistributed to the inhabitants of nearby houses as compensation for their being disturbed by aircraft noise? If aircraft are forbidden to operate from a particular airport at night, should airline operators be compensated for the resulting losses by a tax levied on the inhabitants of nearby houses whose amenities are thereby improved?

2 Discuss the view that the only tax which the government should use to raise revenue is a poll tax, because it has no effect on economic choices.

3 Discuss the relative merits of controlling negative external effects such as pollution by:
   (a) setting up markets to internalise the external cost;
   (b) taxes or subsidies to eradicate the gap between marginal private and marginal social cost;
   (c) direct regulation of the quantity of the externality produced.

CHAPTER 25

Economics of information

Key words and phrases

- asymmetric information, adverse selection, hidden characteristics, moral hazard, hidden action
- market for lemons, sequential game, collapse of market
- quality choice, uninformed and informed consumers
- signals, human capital, sheepskin effect, screening, pooling equilibrium, separating equilibrium, hidden action, managerial incentives, principal agent problem

Introduction

Almost all the discussion in this book has been based on the assumption that the economic decision makers had all the information required to make their maximising decisions with certainty. The principal exception was in Chapter 7, where we considered how agents made decisions in the face of risk. We showed there that choices could still be taken rationally when the consequences of decisions were not known with certainty, provided that agents were able to attach a probability distribution to alternative outcomes. We used this framework of expected utility maximisation to consider the emergence of markets in the bearing of risk–insurance markets. We also introduced some of the problems which can emerge in such markets when the information held by the two parties to the trade is not symmetric: problems of moral hazard and adverse selection. We now return to these issues, and readers would be wise to refresh their memories about the contents of Chapter 7 before taking their current study further.

The assumption to which we have stuck for most of this book, and which we will relax in this chapter, is that consumers and producers have sufficient information to make with certainty their maximising decisions. There are a number of circumstances in which this is not an entirely unreasonable assumption. For example, if markets are competitive, the information required for economic choice is contained in prices, and most current prices are generally available. The assumption is less convincing in an intertemporal world like that discussed in Chapters 5 and 6, where individuals are making choices about consumption across several periods. It also loses credibility in imperfectly competitive markets where, for example, firms need to know how their competitors will react to their decisions in order to make their own choices.

The idea of asymmetric information

In this chapter we are not concerned with general informational deficiencies which affect all economic agents equally. Rather we return to the case first introduced when we discussed corporate governance in Chapter 14, in which we focus on the situation when the absence of information is distributed asymetrically. The particular example used will be when consumers or producers do not know with certainty the quality of the products which they are buying. In such cases, the choices taken by one side of the market might impart information to the other about product quality. We began to think in Chapter 17 about such problems as being modelled in terms of sequential choices, in which moves by one party imparted information to the other players in the game. We shall sometimes take a game theoretic approach in this chapter. Even when we do not, readers should quickly be able to draw the parallels with the subject matter dealt with in the latter part of Chapter 17.

This chapter will examine two cases where **asymmetric information** is important. The first is due to pioneering work by the American professor George Akerlof. It looks at a product market and is concerned with a situation where the goods offered for sale can be either high or low in quality. The informational asymmetry involved derives from the assumption that the supplier knows the quality of the product, while the consumer does not. The consumer is forced to infer information about product quality from the pricing policies of suppliers. In this case the absence of correct information, or perhaps more realistically the high cost that consumers face in correctly ascertaining the true quality, causes low-quality goods to drive high-quality ones out of the market, or even to a collapse in the market itself. This is an example of **adverse selection**, when the side of the market which is uninformed finds that it is trading with precisely those suppliers with whom it does not want to trade, and is therefore being offered a product of a quality that it does not want to buy.

Adverse selection emerges in a situation when the informational asymmetry takes the form of one party knowing something about its own *characteristics* which the other party does not know. In the example discussed above, only the supplier knows whether a product is of high or low quality. This is sometimes referred to as the problem of **hidden characteristics**. This idea is related to, but not the same as, the problem of **moral hazard** in insurance markets which we introduced in Chapter 7. Both concepts refer to situations in which one side of the market has different information from the other. With moral hazard, the problem is that the asymmetry of information concerns the actions or behaviour which one side of the market takes, but which the other side cannot observe. An example given in Chapter 7 concerned actions to prevent a burglary in the event of the individual being insured. We found that this problem of **hidden actions** leads the uninformed side of the market (for example, insurance companies) to trade less than it would otherwise want because of fears about the consequences of its trading for the behaviour of the informed side (people buying insurance policies).

We will show in this chapter that in the case of *hidden characteristics* the uninformed side of the market (consumers who do not know product quality) also trades less than it would otherwise want, in this case because suppliers seek to palm off on them low-quality goods at high-quality prices. Here both the uninformed consumers and the suppliers of high-quality goods who cannot sell their products therefore have an incentive to transmit information that would encourage some trade to occur. An obvious response to this incentive is for the suppliers to *signal* to consumers the quality of their product. But this solution will not always work: for example, if the purveyors of low-quality goods understand the signalling process, they may seek to deceive consumers by emulating it.

Such problems as these are the subject of the second example of informational asymmetries discussed in this chapter, which draws on the work of Professor Michael Spence. The analysis here is applied to the labour market. It addresses the situation that arises when workers have significantly different levels of productivity, but when the firm hiring them does not know at the time when it recruits employees what their productivity level will be at work. We shall examine the implications of the assumption that, in such a situation, workers use education as a way to signal, rather than to improve, their efficiency. We will find that the signal works, in that under certain conditions the more able workers can indicate their productivity through their educational attainments. But signalling is ultimately wasteful because, though able workers earn more, total output is unchanged and education is not free.

The market for lemons

Akerlof's memorable example of the economics of adverse selection derives from an analysis of the market for second-hand cars. In practice such vehicles differ in a wide variety of ways, but we start by simplifying these differences to create only two categories of car – good and bad. Following American slang, good cars are referred to as plums and bad cars are referred to as lemons. There is assumed to be an informational asymmetry in this market: people selling cars know whether the vehicles in question are plums or lemons, but potential purchasers do not, or at least not until after they have made their purchase. Even then, they are not in a position to seek recompense from the sellers should they discover they have a lemon on their hands. This is therefore a case in which product quality characteristics are hidden from buyers.

We can illustrate the basic problem of the **market for lemons** with the aid of a simple example. Let us assume that the number of second-hand cars available for sale is fixed, and that everyone knows the proportion of cars that are lemons – say, one in two. The problem arises because though everyone knows that only half the cars are plums, only the seller knows whether their particular car is a plum or a lemon. The buyers must simply assume that they have a 50 per cent chance of buying a lemon. To simplify the analysis of the typical buyer's decision making in this case, let us assume that consumers are risk neutral. Suppose that, in this example, good cars have a value of £6,000 both to sellers and to buyers but that bad cars are worth only £2,000 to each party. There would clearly be no problem for the functioning of the market here if both sides had the same information. Equilibrium prices would emerge for the two types of car. But we have assumed that buyers cannot know product quality in advance, and cannot demand recompense for poor quality after the purchase once quality has been ascertained.

Clearly, the typical buyer will not offer to pay £6,000 for a car in this situation because they do know that only half the cars on the market are actually worth that much. A similar line of reasoning shows that it is irrational for a buyer to offer £2,000. The rational approach for the buyer would seem to be to follow the procedure outlined in Chapter 8, and offer the expected value of the car. This will be 0.5 times £6,000 plus

0.5 times £2,000, or £4,000. This price is equal to the average quality of cars available in the market. However, it is less than the value which the owners of plums attach to their vehicles, and they will never sell at this price. The only suppliers who would be willing to trade at £4,000 are the sellers of lemons.

The existence of the informational asymmetry under analysis here has the striking consequence of ensuring that plums will never actually be sold. The buyers can of course work all this out for themselves, and will realise that at the price which it seems rational to offer, the only cars that will be available to them will be lemons. Thus, the consumer will not offer more than £2,000 and the only cars traded will be lemons. This is frustrating for them since we have seen that they would in fact be willing to pay what suppliers want for plums, that is, £6,000, if only they could identify them. It is the fact that they cannot which leads to only lemons being offered for sale. The problem is rather general, and can still arise if there is a gap between how consumers and suppliers value cars. Thus, suppose that consumers continue to value the car types at £6,000 and £2,000 respectively, but that their sellers would accept £4,500 and £1,500. The average price the rational consumer is willing to pay is still less than that which sellers of plums will accept. However, if the proportion of lemons on the market was lower – say, only a third of all the cars on the market – sellers of plums would be willing to accept the offer of £4,667 which would be made by rational buyers. Obviously, the more lemons that are offered for sale, the lower the average quality of cars available, and the lower the price consumers will offer. Thus the less likely it will be that suppliers will offer the high-quality product. Low-quality cars therefore drive the higher-quality ones out of the marketplace, in the sense that, the more of them there are on sale, the lower the price consumers will be willing to offer for any car, and the less likely it is that good cars will be traded.

We can formulate the foregoing discussion as a **sequential game** along the lines introduced in Chapter 17. The game, which is represented in Figure 25.1, assumes that, at the outset, each hidden characteristic occurs with a 50 per cent probability and that buyers know this. The dotted line indicates that the buyer does not know the characteristics of the particular car they are offering to purchase when choosing the price, p, to offer for it. We assume that this price is chosen at the average quality (£4,000) of the good in question, however. It can be seen at once that the owners of plums will always reject this offer price; only lemons will be supplied.

Since the framework we have been analysing is so stylised, some readers may be worried that the results that we have just been discussing are more an artefact of the specific assumptions made than a rather general consequence of asymmetries in information. We shall therefore now relax one of the strongest assumptions, namely that there are only two types of car, and we shall see that the basic propositions we have derived above still go through in this more complex case. Let us therefore assume that instead of two levels of quality being available on the market – good and bad – there is a continuum of car types between good and bad. As before, the best quality of car is worth £6,000 to both buyers and sellers while the worst is worth only £2,000. Since there is an equal probability of selling or buying any level of quality in that range, the average level of quality, which we saw was also the price that the buyer was willing to offer for a car of unknown quality, remains unchanged at £4,000.

It can be easily seen that, under these more complicated conditions, the market will still collapse. As in our original market for lemons, £4,000 cannot be the correct equilibrium price. This is because it represents the consumer's rational offer price only provided

Figure 25.1 The market for lemons

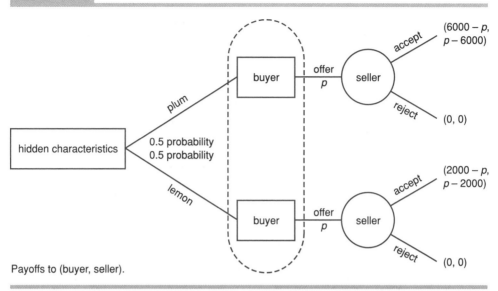

Payoffs to (buyer, seller).

that all cars will be put on sale. But we have seen that, at an offer price of £4,000, the value of the average quality of car on offer is actually going to be less than £4,000 for the simple reason that sellers will not put on the market cars the quality of which they value at more than £4,000. At an offer price of £4,000, only cars of value between £2,000 and £4,000 will be offered for sale, and the car of average quality will be worth £3,000. But by exactly the same reasoning, £3,000 cannot be the equilibrium price, because if it is offered the average quality of cars available will be reduced once again as the sellers who value their cars between £3,000 and £4,000 withdraw from the market. At an offer price of £3,000, therefore, the average quality of the cars still offered for sale is in fact worth only £2,500. The argument can run on in the same vein until the price comes down to the minimum of £2,000. At least in principle, at this price, there is a balance between average quality desired and offer price. However, at this price, the number of cars actually being supplied to the market, the very worst available, is minuscule, all others having been withdrawn because the price is too low.

This process whereby the **market collapses** is shown in Figure 25.2. This figure illustrates the choices made by buyers and sellers in terms of the price offered by the former, and the value of the average car offered by the latter. We can characterise buyers' behaviour in terms of a 45° line, because buyers will only offer a price equal to the average or expected value of the quality of car available. A degenerating price–average quality loop, described in words above, characterises the supply side of this market. At each price offered by buyers, sellers offer a different average quality of vehicle. Consider what happens as price rises. Average quality offered does not increase proportionately with price because though the value of the quality of the *marginal* car offered keeps pace with price as the price rises, the value of the quality of the *average* car rises more slowly. This is for the simple reason that cars whose quality is worth less than the price offered remain on sale as price rises. Hence at a price above £2,000 the slope of the supply relationship is steeper than 45°. The market can only find an equilibrium where demand equals supply,

Figure 25.2

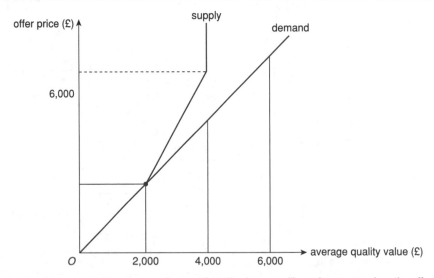

In the market for lemons with a cars continuum of quality, buyers will purchase cars when the offer price equals the average quality along the 45° demand line. However, sellers will only accept offers for which the price exceeds or equals the value of quality. Hence at an offer price of £6,000, the supply of quality on average is £4,000. The demand and supply curves intersect at the lowest available quality, at which price virtually no cars are exchanged.

and that is at the minimum supply price £2,000. At that price there will occur the smallest conceivable level of trade. In effect the market will not function.

Adverse selection, quality choice and informed consumers

In the foregoing analysis, the suppliers of used cars did not produce them, and had no control over the quality of the cars that they were offering for sale. It is interesting to see whether the lemon problem re-emerges when firms can **choose** product **quality**. We shall now investigate this question, and then go on to examine what happens when informational asymmetry affects some but not all potential consumers. This possibility opens up the chance that **uninformed consumers** can learn from the behaviour of their better-**informed** counterparts to prevent adverse selection.

As before, we assume that there are two qualities of good – high and low – and also initially that these different quality levels cannot be identified by any consumers prior to purchase. But now we suppose that suppliers incur costs in providing the two goods. Initially, though, we assume that the costs of producing a high- or a low-quality good are the same. As before, it will be rational for us to assess the goods on offer on the basis of their average quality and to set the price that consumers are willing to pay accordingly. The identical competitive firms on the supply side of the market can choose between supplying high- and low-quality goods; the proportion of high-quality goods supplied

Figure 25.3

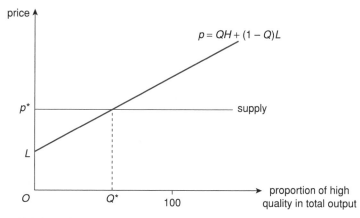

Quality choice with information asymmetry. The demand curve is given by the price consumers are willing to pay as average quality increases, and is upward sloping. Marginal costs are assumed constant and invariant with respect to quality. Equilibrium occurs at the intersection of the demand and supply curves, and determines both price and the proportion of high-quality goods produced.

is denoted by Q. Consumers will then offer an average price (p) equal to Q times their valuation of the high-quality good (H) plus $(1 - Q)$ times their valuation of the low-quality good (L). As the average quality of the goods on offer increases, consumers are willing to pay more. This relationship is drawn as the upward-sloping demand curve in Figure 25.3. Note that the slope of this curve is not inconsistent with the theory we derived in the first part of this book, because in Figure 25.3 the quantity demanded is not being derived as a function of price, *all other things being held equal*. Instead, the price consumers are willing to pay for the good rises because the expected quality of that good also rises.

Let us assume that competitive firms produce under conditions of constant cost, so that supply conditions in the industry are given by the horizontal supply line in Figure 25.3. Given these assumptions, the market has an equilibrium, at (P^*, Q^*), in which both product qualities are produced. It appears that the problem of adverse selection is resolved in this case, in the sense that some high-quality goods are produced.

It is unlikely, however, that differences in product quality are not reflected in costs. Let us therefore suppose instead that it costs less to produce a low- than a high-quality product. However, let us retain the assumption that the cost of supplying either the high- or the low-quality product is less than consumers are willing to pay for them. Now consider the situation faced by any producer if the value of Q is greater than zero. We have assumed the market to be competitive, so the firm believes that its own actions will have no effect on the rest of the market. In this case it is obviously more profitable for the firm to supply only the low-quality good.

This result follows because the firm will not be rewarded, and knows that it will not be rewarded, by a higher than average price if it produces any of the high-quality good. At the same time, being in a competitive market, the firm believes that its own behaviour will not affect the market equilibrium so that it will not be penalised in price terms if it abstains from high-quality production. But this argument applies to all firms, and consumers will know this. They will know that no firm has an incentive to supply the high-quality good. If the price they are willing to pay for the low-quality good is higher than the marginal cost of producing it, then only the low-quality good will be produced and traded. If this price is less than the marginal cost of supplying it, there will be no production or trade of any sort. These results will occur even if both firms and consumers would in principle be better off if the high-quality good were produced. Thus the basic lemons problem still arises when firms can choose the quality of the product they produce, if the cost of producing a high-quality product exceeds that of producing a low-quality product.

How are these results affected by changes in the character of the informational asymmetry? Suppose now that, instead of all consumers being uninformed, there exists a group on the demand side of the market which is informed about quality. As an illustration, let us assume that there are 100 consumers, and the proportion who are informed about the quality is denoted by i. Let us also assume that consumers have identical tastes and are willing to pay £5 for a high-quality good, but nothing for a low-quality one. Finally, let average and marginal costs of production be £3 for high-quality goods and £1 for low-quality ones. We know that all of the informed customers will pay up to £5 for high-quality goods, but will not purchase any low-quality ones. The outcome in this market depends on how the uninformed customers behave. Suppose first, for the sake of argument, that they decide not to buy the good at all. Then competitive firms will supply only high-quality products, making a profit of £200i. Our uninformed customers can thus calculate that if they stay out of the market, only high-quality goods will be produced. But in that case, they will not want to stay out of the market. They will want to purchase the goods as well because they can be sure that those supplied will be high quality. Hence everyone, both informed and uninformed, will be active in the market we have just described.

Let us now consider what firms will do if both the informed and the uninformed enter the market. If they supply only the high-quality good, they will sell to all customers and generate profits of £2,000 ((price − average cost) × the number of buyers). If, on the other hand, they supply only the low-quality good, they will not sell any to informed customers (who do not want to buy any low-quality goods), but will earn profits of £400$(1 − i)$ ((price − average cost of low-quality product) × the uninformed population). Whether or not firms will supply high-quality goods therefore depends on the proportion of the population that is informed. In this case, they will produce high-quality goods if $400(1 − i) > 200$ or to put it more simply if $i > 0.5$. In general, the high-quality good is more likely to be produced if there is a relatively high proportion of well-informed customers on the demand side of the market.

Note also that the proportion of well-informed customers required to ensure production of the high-quality good is positively related to consumers' willingness to pay for that quality. Suppose, in the above example, that we keep all other parameters unchanged, but assume that consumers are willing to pay £10 for the higher-quality good rather than £5. The condition that makes the production of higher quality attractive in this case is given by $i > 0.222$. There is clearly a trade-off between proportion of informed customers and the price they are willing to pay in making it attractive for firms to produce high-quality products. We can view this trade-off as arising because the firm is able to gain more from producing the high-quality good, and selling it to informed customers, when the price they are willing to pay is higher.

Adverse selection and moral hazard

The market for lemons model provides an example of how, if information is distributed asymmetrically, agents on the uninformed side of the market find themselves trading with exactly the wrong people. As we noted in Chapter 7, this problem arises in the market for insurance. We shall now investigate this matter further, taking the case of an insurance company which is offering insurance against car theft. To keep the structure of the argument close to that of the lemons example, we shall suppose that people can park their cars in one of two areas – where the probability of theft is high or low. Let us suppose that the insurance company cannot know the area in which particular people park, but merely the proportion of all cars which park in each area. The insurance company will set its premium according to the value of the expected rate of car theft in the two areas combined.

Following our previous logic, people who park in the safe areas would be unwilling to purchase insurance at this price. The pricing policy in question will thus lead to a disproportionate number of the company's policy holders being people who park in the more risky area. In this situation, however, the insurance company would not be able to meet the claims on its policies out of its premiums. Setting its price on the basis of the average probability of car theft will therefore be inappropriate, because the insurance company will not obtain a random sample of customers with such a pricing scheme. Instead there will arise an adverse selection among potential policy holders. Only those whose probability of suffering theft is higher than for the population as a whole will buy policies. In such a situation, the only viable pricing policy for the insurance company is to charge premia on the assumption that everyone parks in the high-risk area. In these circumstances, those who park in low-risk areas will remain uninsured. This failure of all consumer demand to be satisfied in market equilibrium is also characteristic of our previous example of adverse selection.

Readers are reminded that this problem of adverse selection is not the same as that of moral hazard. This latter problem arises, not because of asymmetries of information about the characteristics of customers, but because the very act of buying insurance affects the actions of those who have taken out the policy in such a way as to influence the probabilities of particular outcomes. We do not need to assume that there are different areas with different theft probabilities to which customers are committed before they buy insurance for problems of moral hazard to emerge in our insurance example. Even if the probability of car theft is the same throughout the country, we can suppose that it may be influenced by the actions of particular owners. For example, the amount of care that is taken in seeing that the car is locked when it is left parked affects this probability. Moral hazard arises when the existence of an insurance policy leads people to act in such a way as to increase the probability of the insured against eventuality actually occurring: for example, when being insured leads people to be less careful about locking their cars when parking than they would be if they were not insured.

Insurance companies respond to problems of moral hazard in ways quite different from problems of adverse selection. It is clear that people will take serious steps to prevent car theft if they are not insured against it. The more they expect to be recompensed for the financial consequences of theft, however, the weaker are their incentives to take the appropriate preventive measures. Because of this, insurance companies rarely offer full reimbursement against car theft. They typically insist that the insured must pay some amount in the event of any claim. Moreover they try to discriminate among different categories of insured according to the actions that they can be proved to be taking to avert car theft: for example, people who have installed alarms in their cars might expect to pay lower premiums for theft insurance than those who have not; those whose cars are kept in locked garages overnight similarly are charged less than those who park on the street; and so on.

Box 25.1

Adverse selection and insurance: a simple example

To illustrate and reinforce some of the key issues and consequences involved with hidden information we can develop a simple and somewhat stylised insurance example. Assume that two professional pianists want to insure their hands against possible damage that would reduce their income. If they can work as pianists their incomes would be 10,000 per period. If they damage their hands permanently their incomes would fall to 2,500 per period. For the moment we will assume that both pianists have the same utility of income function $U = y^{0.5}$, where y is income period. Based on discussion in Chapter 7, it is clear that the pianists are risk averse and so might increase utility by buying insurance. The utility levels are

$$U(10,000) = 100 \tag{25.1.1}$$

$$U(2,500) = 50 \tag{25.1.2}$$

Although both pianists have the same income potential they have different probabilities of damaging their hands because of exogenous life-style factors. Pianist one has a probability of hand damage of 0.4, whereas pianist two has a probability of 0.2. It follows that the expected utilities of their income possibilities are

$$EU_1 = 0.6(100) + 0.4(50) = 80 \tag{25.1.3}$$

$$EU_2 = 0.8(100) + 0.2(50) = 90 \tag{25.1.4}$$

Defining CE as a certain equivalent income, these expected utilities would be obtained with the following certain income levels:

$$CE_1 = 80^2 = 6,400 \tag{25.1.5}$$

$$CE_2 = 90^2 = 8,100. \tag{25.1.6}$$

Whether either pianist buys insurance depends on the price charged. As long as their incomes after insurance costs do not fall below the certain equivalent levels they would have earned without insurance then buying insurance cover will increase utility. The maximum insurance costs (C_1^{MAX} and C_2^{MAX}) are therefore

$$C_1^{MAX} = 10,000 - 6,400 = 3,600 \tag{25.1.7}$$

$$C_2^{MAX} = 10,000 - 8,100 = 1,900 \tag{25.1.8}$$

We know from the theory set out in Chapter 6 that if the insurance is fair a risk averse person will fully insure and so equalise payoffs in both states of the world. Recall that fair insurance involves the probability of a claim being equal to the price of a policy. Using our example we can therefore define the fair insurance equilibrium as involving insurance cover (V) that equalises income without and with hand damage. For pianist one:

$$10,000 - 0.4V_1 = 2,500 + V_1 - 0.4V_1 \qquad (25.1.9)$$

and for pianist two:

$$10,000 - 0.2V_2 = 2,500 + V_1 - 0.2V_2 \qquad (25.1.10)$$

In expressions (25.1.9) and (25.1.10) the left-hand sides define incomes after buying fair insurance without hand damage. The right-hand sides define incomes with hand damage: this is made up of basic income (2,500) plus insurance payout (V_1) minus insurance premium. Solving for the insurance cover implies $V_1 = V_2 = 7,500$. But although the same cover is bought the costs of the insurance differ: for pianist one this is $7,500 \times 0.4 = 3,000$, for pianist two this is $7,500 \times 0.2 = 1,500$, both of which are less than the maxima they would be willing to pay. We can therefore see that the revenue the insurance company receives is 4,500 (i.e. 3,000 + 1,500) and the expected payout is 4,500 (i.e. $7,500 \times 0.4 + 7,500 \times 0.2$). The insurance company is therefore viable as it is not making long-run losses.

The complexities of hidden information and adverse selection can now be introduced. The probability of claiming on a policy is not observable, i.e. hidden information exists. If the insurance company sets the price of the insurance sufficient to break even on average, but the two pianists pay the same price, we can see that the insurance is then unfair to the benefit of (high risk) pianist one and to the disadvantage of (low risk) pianist two. We can calculate the required insurance price and cover bought using three constraints:

1. insurance company profit is zero;
2. pianist one is fully insured;
3. pianist two spends the maximum that is rational on insurance.

Constraint 1 is a viability condition for the insurance company. Constraint 2 follows because compared with fair insurance the price for the higher risk pianist will go down. In response pianist one would want to increase demand for insurance but this would involve a higher income with damaged hands. The insurance company would not allow this possibility: hence the maximum insurance constraint for pianist one. Constraint 3 is somewhat arbitrary but reflects the fact that demand will decrease compared with fair insurance because of the higher cost involved. This allows us to show the key effects of hidden information.

Identifying the price of insurance as r, the three constraints can be formalised as follows:

$$rV_1 + rV_2 = 0.4V_1 + 0.2V_2 \qquad (25.1.11)$$

$$V_1 = 7,500 \qquad (25.1.12)$$

$$rV_2 = 1,900 \qquad (25.1.13)$$

Substituting (25.1.12) and (25.1.13) into (25.1.11) and rearranging:

$$7,500r - 1,100 - 0.2V_2 = 0$$

→

Using (25.1.13):

$V_2 = 1,900/r$

Hence

$$7,500r^2 - 1,100r - 380 = 0 \qquad (25.1.14)$$

This quadratic has one relevant solution: $r = 0.31$. Using this solution, $V_2 = 6,129.03$. This implies that with hidden information the (high risk) pianist one is fully insured, but the (low risk) pianist two buys less than full insurance. For pianist two, if their hands are not damaged, income would be $10,000 - 1,900 = 8,100$. If their hands are damaged, income would be $2,500 + 6,129.03 - 1,900 = 6,729.03$.

We can cover one final matter in this box. We have assumed up to now that the two pianists have the same utility function. This can easily be relaxed. Assume, for the sake of argument, that the (low risk) pianist two is more risk averse than pianist one, and has the utility function $U = y^{0.25}$. Intuitively we can understand this change in function as a change in tastes, or more precisely attitude to risk. Interested readers can plot the two utility functions and examine the difference between them. With the more risk averse function:

$$U(10,000) = 10 \qquad (25.1.15)$$

$$U(2,500) = 7.07 \qquad (25.1.16)$$

So the expected utility is

$$EU_2 = 0.8(10) + 0.2(7.07) = 9.414 \qquad (25.1.17)$$

This expected utility would be obtained with a certain income of

$$CE_2 = 9.414^{(1/.25)} = 7,854.82 \qquad (25.1.18)$$

It follows that the maximum insurance cost is

$$C_2^{MAX} = 10,000 - 7,854.82 = 2,145.18 \qquad (25.1.19)$$

Note that with greater risk aversion the maximum possible insurance cost increases. The new equilibrium can be calculated by changing the constraint (25.1.13) to

$$rV_2 = 2,145.18 \qquad (25.1.20)$$

Using the same procedure as that just used, we can specify the quadratic:

$$7,500r^2 - 854.82r - 429.036 = 0 \qquad (25.1.21)$$

This has one relevant solution that defines the equilibrium price for insurance as $r = 0.30$. Using this solution: $V_2 = 7,150.6$. This implies the not surprising conclusion that when pianist two is more risk averse the demand for insurance increases. But this increase in demand occurs with a reduction in the price of insurance, a somewhat counter-intuitive occurrence. Because of the adverse selection a greater proportion of insurance sales now come from low risk customers, hence the reduction in price. But the readers can satisfy themselves that pianist two is still not fully insured, i.e. is still worse off with damaged hands, just less so.

Solutions to adverse selection – signals

In all the examples of adverse selection we have discussed, the uninformed buyers have an incentive, which we have not yet considered, to learn more about the product. In the used car market, the market for lemons, it would pay buyers to find out about the quality of the particular car that they are considering buying. In practice, buyers in such markets are often able to do so, for example by taking the car for a drive and subjecting it to a road test. At the same time, sellers of high-quality cars have an incentive to inform buyers about the quality of what they are offering, because consumers would be willing to pay the asking price for a proven high-quality car. Such sellers can be expected, therefore, to attempt to send a credible **signal** to buyers about the quality of the particular car they are offering for sale.

In the second-hand car market, one way in which to transmit such a signal is by providing a full warranty to the purchaser of the vehicle. Such a warranty is, in effect, a promise by the seller to reimburse the buyer the full amount of their loss if the car does in fact prove to be a lemon. In our two-quality used-car market, a full warranty would involve a promise to pay the difference in value between a plum and a lemon, or £4,000. Buyers can be expected to understand that sellers of plums can afford to offer a full warranty, because they know it will never be taken up, but that sellers of lemons will not be able to make such an offer, because they would always have to pay out more than the value of the car they had sold as a consequence. A full warranty not only offers a costless way for high-quality suppliers to signal quality, but because buyers can work out that only suppliers of high-quality cars can make such an offer, the signal is also credible in the game theoretic sense that we discussed in Chapter 17.

In the foregoing example, then, sellers of plums can send a credible signal. But the problems associated with adverse selection are not always so simply eradicated. Suppose, for example, that the provision of a full warranty generates a moral hazard problem. The performance of a car subsequent to its sale may reasonably be assumed to depend not only on its quality at the time of purchase, but also on how it is driven by its new owner. By offering a full warranty, therefore, the seller provides the buyer with an incentive to drive the car poorly, or perhaps to maintain it inadequately, thereby increasing the probability that the warranty will be exercised. Indeed, the very offer of warranties by sellers of plums is likely to lead to an increase in the number of bad drivers among their buyers. We noted above that suppliers of insurance may react to the threat of moral hazard by leaving some residual element of risk to be borne by the insured. A parallel argument in this case would suggest that the sellers of high-quality cars will not after all offer a full warranty, but rather a partial one. Unfortunately this attempt to deal with the moral hazard problem reopens the original adverse selection problem once again. A partial warranty does not offer the credible signal of quality provided by a full warranty since buyers might reason that a supplier is only offering a partial warranty because of a fear that they will be called upon to pay out once the car has been sold. Hence buyers will deduce that the car on offer might after all be a lemon; the signal embodied in the offer of warranty is no longer credible if the warranty is a partial one.

In summary, there are occasions when the provision of credible signals can help markets operating with asymmetries of information to perform better. However, in practice such signals may be hard to design and then transmit. In the following section we provide an example of a situation when signalling can actually lead such a market to perform less well.

Signalling in the labour market

It is well known that better-educated people on average earn higher incomes than do worse-educated people. Many economists regard this differential as the major factor in explaining people's willingness to undertake education. The so-called **human capital approach** to the analysis of the demand for education sees each individual evaluating whether the return to education in terms of increased expected future income is sufficient to compensate for the costs involved, including the income forgone as a result of choosing to study for a while rather than work. This approach obviously presumes that more highly educated people are more productive. If they are not, it is argued, firms will not be willing to pay them more than the less educated and there will exist no individual incentives to become better educated.

But it has sometimes been argued, for example, that some aspects of higher education contribute little or nothing directly to the skills that will later be required in the workplace. (Readers of this book may find comfort in the knowledge that remarks along these lines are more commonly addressed to subjects like classics, archaeology or literature than to economics, though they may also wish to reflect on the justice of this evaluation.) When asked to explain why graduates earn more than non-graduates, those who doubt the practical benefits of university education can reply that a degree is not so much a measure of an education-induced improvement in productivity, as it is a signal to potential employers that a person is of high ability.

There is some empirical support for this signalling explanation of the wage differences associated with educational attainments, coming from the quantitative evaluation of the so-called **sheepskin effect** by American labour economists.[1] Empirical estimates of the economic returns to education revealed that there was a large jump in the estimated returns from the graduating year of high school relative to those associated with earlier years. On one calculation these returns were three times as great as for those who had abandoned education just one year earlier, without receiving any formal diploma. It seems unlikely that this final year in the classroom had three times the effect on a worker's productivity as the one preceding it; indeed, explicit calculations of the productivity gains by Professor Weiss of Boston University indicate that they are in the order of 1–2 per cent for each year of education. It seems more promising to look for explanations of the high returns from staying in high school until graduation in the fact of the receipt of the diploma itself; the sheepskin effect.

There are two possible explanations available as to why people who are already of high ability (and therefore high productivity) take the trouble actually to obtain degrees or diplomas. The first is that the schools and universities at which they study have screened their ability as part of their admissions procedure, and that future employers are happy to accept the judgement of these institutions and thereby avoid the costs of replicating this **screening** procedure. This explanation seems more plausible when applied to university education rather than to the education sector as a whole. But suppose that there exists an asymmetry of information so that employers are unable to screen the ability of candidates at any reasonable cost prior to recruiting them. In this situation, the second explanation may become appropriate, namely, that to obtain a diploma or degree is a credible signal which potential employees can send to firms to show that they are in fact high-productivity workers. This explanation was first developed by Professor Michael Spence.

In Spence's model, what in the real world is a continuum of potential abilities and productivities is stylised into two types of workers; those with low and those with high ability (type 1 and type 2 respectively). The marginal products of each are denoted a_2 and a_1; $a_2 > a_1$. We shall assume in what follows that half the labour force has high productivity, and the remainder low productivity. If both workers and firms were fully informed about labour quality, the resulting model would amount to a straightforward extension of the ideas introduced in Chapter 21. Firms would pay each type of worker a wage equal to their marginal product. Thus in equilibrium, we would have

$$w_2 = a_2 > w_1 = a_1 \qquad\qquad (25.1)$$

However, suppose instead that the distribution of information between workers and firms is asymmetric. To be precise, suppose that workers know their own ability, but that firms are not, and cannot be, privy to that information, at least prior to the employment decision. Moreover assume that firms cannot recover from recruitment errors by firing the workers who do not have high ability. This would be the case, for example, if the economy in which the firms operate had very onerous statutory redundancy payments. In that case, if the firms do not know whose marginal product is high and whose is low, they will have to offer all workers an average wage equal to the expected value of the productivity level of the labour force as a whole. In our example, this is $(a_1 + a_2)/2$. This offer could, in principle, yield an equilibrium if both types of worker were willing to accept the average wage. Adverse selection problems, similar to those encountered in the lemon market, will, however, emerge if high-productivity workers are unwilling to offer themselves for work at a wage below their marginal product.

It is, in any event, clearly in the interest of high-quality workers to discover a credible way to signal firms about their level of ability. Let us therefore examine whether educational attainment represents such a signal. We denote the amount of education obtained by each type of worker by e, and the cost per unit of education by d, each subscripted by worker type. Hence education costs low-productivity workers $d_1 e_1$ and high-productivity workers $d_2 e_2$. In order to focus attention solely on the signalling dimension of education, we follow Spence and assume that education has no effect on employee productivity. The model that results from these assumptions has two distinct equilibria, referred to as the **pooling equilibrium** and the **separating equilibrium**. In the former equilibrium, each type of worker makes the same choice about education and there is no signalling. In the latter, workers of different ability make different choices of the level of education. They are thus *separated* by ability, so educational attainment can serve as a credible signal to employers. Which equilibrium will in fact be reached depends on the relative costs of education to high- and low-productivity workers, as we shall now show.

We start by assuming that it is more expensive for high-ability workers to be educated than for low-ability ones. In this case, both types of worker will choose not to be educated at all and firms pay the average wage, $(a_1 + a_2)/2$, regardless of the educational level. The reasoning here is as follows. Since it is cheaper for low-ability than for high-ability workers to obtain education, and the firm knows this, it assumes that both quality types are equally likely to undertake education. Since the expected quality of workers who have and have not been educated is the same, firms will offer both groups a wage equal to the average marginal product of the two groups. Both types of worker will calculate that there will therefore be no material benefit to undertaking education. Hence since the activity is costly to both, neither type of worker will choose the education strategy.

Let us now assume instead that, though education is costly for both types of worker, it is more costly for individuals of low productivity. This might be because, for example, individuals of higher ability do not have to work so hard on their courses in order to attain their diplomas or degrees, and hence can afford to spend some proportion of their time at an educational establishment working to earn some extra money. Is this assumption consistent with an equilibrium in which high-ability workers are more educated and paid more, while low-productivity workers do not seek education? If such a separating equilibrium was achieved, we would find that each labour type was paid its marginal product (equation (25.1)). This would certainly be equilibrium behaviour for firms because, if via signalling they receive correct information about worker productivity, equation (25.1) is consistent with profit maximisation.

But is such behaviour rational for the two types of worker? Let us start with the high-productivity workers. They will undertake education only if the benefits exceed the costs. The gain to them in the hypothesised separating equilibrium is the difference between high and low wages, which, given equation (25.1), equals $(a_2 - a_1)$. But we are further supposing that people can either be educated ($e = 1$) or not educated ($e = 0$), and that the cost of education for able workers is given by d_2. Thus one condition under which our separating equilibrium will exist is

$$a_2 - a_1 - d_2 > 0 \tag{25.2}$$

Now consider the low-productivity workers. In the separating equilibrium, their pay is a_1 and they receive no education. Do they have an incentive to send a false signal by becoming educated? Their wage gain in this case would be $(a_2 - a_1)$, and their cost would be d_1. Low-productivity workers would not therefore undertake education provided that

$$d_1 - (a_2 - a_1) > 0 \tag{25.3}$$

holds. Without being certain that this is the case for every conceivable value of the as and the ds, we know that provided $d_1 > d_2$ there do exist values of the six parameters of our model for which equations (25.2) and (25.3) can be satisfied simultaneously. Hence provided the benefits of education exceed the costs for high-productivity workers, but are simultaneously less than the cost facing low-ability workers, a separating equilibrium will exist.

One might be tempted to conclude from this that by providing information about hidden characteristics, signalling can indeed play a useful role in solving problems created by asymmetric information. It is therefore salutary to reflect that, in the Spence model, signalling may in fact make the outcome worse. To see this, think about the level of output that would have emerged without signalling in a situation in which high- and low-productivity workers were willing to accept the same wage. Workers would have all been employed and each would have been paid a wage equal to the expected value of their marginal product. The total wage bill and the output level in this case would be the same as in the separating equilibrium made possible by signalling. However, it is more costly to get to this separating equilibrium because, to achieve it, half the labour force would have to undertake expensive educational activities that do not in any way affect their productivity, or the economy's total output. Therefore, if the separating equilibrium of this model characterised an economy, it would be one in which net national output was less than one where signalling was absent. The separating equilibrium in this example is one in which able workers gain, but net output is reduced, by signalling.

Hidden action and managerial incentives

The final 'economics of information' topic to be considered in this chapter involves consideration of **hidden action** and **managerial incentives**. This takes up a number of themes first considered in Chapter 14 under the general heading of corporate governance. As already discussed in this chapter, the general issue with hidden action, or moral hazard, is that the benefits that follow from the production of a particular good or service depend on the actions taken. But because the actions are 'hidden' they cannot be observed by any party who is not producing the good or service. This non-observability of actions is what defines the standard **principal agent problem**. The usual approach to this problem is to claim that the 'principal' must construct appropriate incentives for the 'agent'. This is how the topic of corporate governance treats relations between a firm's owners (the principals) and managers (the agents). It is an introduction to this issue of agent incentives that is the subject matter of this section.

We can assume that managers of a company obtain utility from income and on-the-job leisure:

$$U = U(y, L) \tag{25.4}$$

In a standard manner we can describe these managerial preferences in terms of indifference curves, as shown in Figure 25.4. In this diagram the utility level U_0 defines a reservation utility, or participation constraint. If utility falls below this level, managers will leave

Figure 25.4

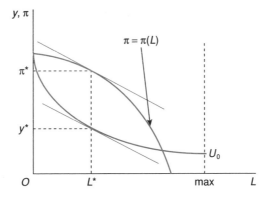

Indifference curve U_0 defines the minimum utility needed by managers. Given the profit constraint defined by $\pi = \pi(L)$, the maximum profit owners can generate is $\pi^* - y^*$ with managers having on-the-job leisure of L^*.

the firm. But in addition to obtaining income and on-the-job leisure managers must earn profits for the owners of the firm. In general terms firm profits will be a function of on-the-job leisure:

$$\pi = \pi(L) \tag{25.5}$$

It is perhaps obvious that more managerial leisure implies lower firm profits, i.e. $\partial\pi/\partial L < 0$. But if we make a somewhat standard assumption of diminishing returns to managerial effort the constraint will be concave from below in Figure 25.4, i.e. increasingly lower levels of leisure will be associated with smaller increments in terms of profit gained.

The owner decision can now be set out as maximising profit after managerial payments subject to paying managers enough to keep their services, or more formally:

$$\text{max: } \pi - y \tag{25.6}$$

$$\text{s.t.: } U = U_0 \tag{25.7}$$

In terms of Figure 25.4 the solution to this constrained optimisation problem is solved as the level of L that maximises the vertical distance between the profit constraint and U_0. Using standard logic it should be obvious that this level of L is defined where the slopes of the profit constraint and U_0 are the same, i.e. L^*. So optimal managerial payments are y^* and owners receive returns of $\pi^* - y^*$.

This analysis is obviously unrealistic because scope for hidden action exists, i.e. owners cannot observe L. In these circumstances, if managers receive a flat salary this provides no incentive not to take on-the-job leisure. If managers exploit this possibility the result would be low firm profits. It is therefore in the owners' best interests to introduce appropriate incentives. Such performance-related pay can take many specific forms, but a simple version will be considered here. We will assume that some profits are distributed to owners (d) and that managerial income is the profit not distributed:

$$y = \pi - d \tag{25.8}$$

The owners' problem is then to determine the level of distributed profits (d). Consider Figure 25.5: if an amount d_1 is distributed to shareholders the profit constraint will shift down vertically by this amount. This creates a new constraint that is vertically below the original. Managers will then choose the level of L that maximises utility on this new constraint. The resulting utility will be above U_0, and so is not optimal from an owner's perspective. Optimality requires that distributed profits be increased until only minimum managerial utility is possible. This is shown as the amount d^* in Figure 25.5, which shifts the profit constraint down vertically by this amount. Managerial utility maximisation will then result in L^*, i.e. the same level as with full information in Figure 25.5.

It would appear, therefore, that owners can set up incentive mechanisms that control managerial moral hazard. But while performance-related pay is widely used, it is not universal. This indicates that problems might exist with the analysis presented here. Two such problems might be relevant. First, Figure 25.5 assumes that owners can identify profit potential at different levels of distributed profit and the level of managerial utility U_0. If activities are complex and many managers exist these assumptions may not be appropriate. In these circumstances it might be more realistic to view owner–manager relations as a bargaining game, as in Chapter 17, rather than owners setting up an incentive system to which managers respond. The second potential problem with Figure 25.5

Figure 25.5

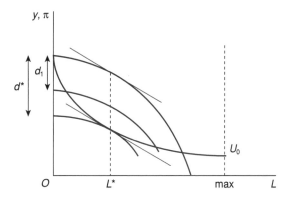

With a managerial incentive scheme based on managers keeping profit above that distributed to share-holders, owners can potentially motivate managers in an optimal manner. With profit distributions of d^* the profit constraint shifts vertically down by this amount and managers maximise utility on U_0 and have on the job leisure of L^*. This solution is the same as that generated with full information.

is the potential presence of managerial risk aversion. We have assumed that the level of utility U_0 is unchanged when payments are certain and with performance-related pay. This unchanged U_0 is appropriate if managers are risk neutral. But with risk aversion any income uncertainty will reduce managerial utility. If managers are very risk averse this might undermine any incentive system. The issues involved here are explored in Box 25.2.

Box 25.2 **Incentive schemes and risk averse managers**

In this box the issue of managerial risk aversion will be explored in more detail. If owners introduce an incentive scheme, to control managerial moral hazard, along the lines suggested in the text:

$$y = \pi - d$$

In reality, once the distribution figure is fixed, there are two reasons why manage-rial income might vary. The first involves decision over on-the-job leisure, i.e. man-agers will choose L to maximise utility given the value of d. The second reason is that exogenous environmental factors can affect π and from this the level of income. If managers are risk averse this environmental uncertainty will reduce utility.

To explore these issues consider Illustration 25.1. The diagram is largely the same as that used in the text. If profit distributions were zero, managers would maximise utility on indifference curve U_1. With optimal profit distributions managers max-imise utility on U_0. Note the characteristic here that for a fixed level of leisure (L^*) the slopes of the indifference curves are the same at different income levels. This is a necessary requirement with risk neutrality, and if income varies with exogenous

Illustration 25.1

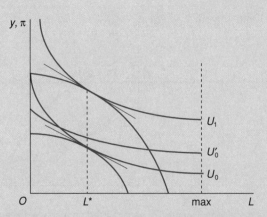

environmental factors. The implication is that the willingness to substitute leisure for income is not influenced by the level of income. But now consider indifference curve U_0': this is flatter at the level of leisure L^*. In this case, as income goes down (i.e. as profit distributions increase) any change in income induces a much larger change in on-the-job leisure. A flatter indifference curve like this exists if managers are risk averse. In this case optimal profit distributions are lower and managerial income is higher. In the limit the indifference curve U_0 might be so flat that any profit-related incentive scheme might be demotivating for managers.

Concluding comment

In this chapter, we have provided some striking examples of the proposition that it is not merely the fact of uncertainty, but the distribution of information between economic agents, which can influence economic behaviour. Moreover we have begun to see cases in which the operation of a free market for a good does not necessarily lead to desirable or efficient outcomes, because the quality of product on offer is known only to one side of the market before the trade is undertaken. We have also seen examples in which markets fail to function at all, and in which markets have more than one equilibrium. It is also notable that these problems do not arise because of market power, as was the case in our discussion of monopoly and oligopoly. We have found that adverse selection can arise in markets that are competitive.

SUMMARY

Economics of information

1. In this chapter, we focus on situations in which information is distributed asymmetrically between economic agents.

2. Adverse selection occurs when the informational asymmetry takes the form that characteristics are hidden. Moral hazard occurs when actions are hidden from the other party to a trade.

3. In his original analysis of the market for lemons, Akerlof showed that if there are two product qualities only the cheaper, or low-quality, product will be offered for sale. This happens because while buyers must rationally offer the expected price, sellers will only accept their reservation price, which will be higher than average for high-quality goods.

4. When, instead of just two, there is a continuum of different qualities, the market will collapse. The supply and (upward-sloping in quality space) demand curve intersect only at the minimum conceivable price and quality.

5. Manufacturers may be willing to supply both low- and high-quality products despite cost differences in manufacture if some consumers are informed about quality. In such a world, price can act as an indicator of quality.

6. Problems of adverse selection give suppliers an incentive to provide credible signals about the quality of their product. In the original lemons example, a full warranty would suffice. However, this may not always be feasible, for example for reasons of moral hazard.

7. Spence's model of signalling in the labour market views education as a way for able people to signal their productivity to potential employers. In the so-called pooling equilibrium, each type of worker makes the same choice of education and there is no signalling. In the separating equilibrium, high-quality workers undertake education and low-quality ones do not. The successful screening that arises from this signal supports wage differentials between the two skill levels.

8. Since education is assumed not to affect productivity, net national output is lower in the screening equilibrium.

9. Moral hazard, or hidden actions, also characterises principal–agent problems, for example the relations between a firm's owners and managers. In the absence of appropriate incentives, managers will not maximise owners' profits.

10. This problem can be solved with appropriate incentives for managers – in our example that they are rewarded with some share of the profits.

PROBLEMS

1 Suppose a second-hand car dealer supplying good-quality cars offers a warranty for parts but not for service. Would that be sufficient to signal quality? Would they be better advised to offer a warranty for labour as well?

2 Discuss the problem that an insurance company faces in setting the premium for car insurance. What pieces of information about the policy holder would the insurance company like to collect? Do they concern characteristics of the policy holder or actions?

3 Suppose that high-productivity workers have a marginal product of £5,000, low-productivity ones of £2,000. What will the firm pay in the pooling equilibrium? We suppose that workers can either become educated or not educated. Education costs £2,500 for high-productivity workers and £3,500 for low-productivity ones. Is there a pooling equilibrium? Will there be a pooling equilibrium if the costs of education are reversed (i.e. they are £2,500 for low-productivity and £3,500 for high-productivity workers)?

Note

1. The obscure name is a reference to the fact that diplomas were once made of sheepskin (vellum).

CHAPTER 26

Public choice

Key words and phrases

- economics as policy maker's toolkit
- self-interested policy makers, disinterested policy makers, public choice, costly information, voting paradox, voting, transitivity of preferences, individual vs community
- median voter, majority voting, uniformly distributed preferences, single peaked preferences
- income redistribution, skewed income distribution, productivity differences, Laffer curve, public goods, poll tax
- inequality, the franchise, growth of the welfare state
- single issue and multiple issue elections, interest groups, coalitions, rent seeking

Introduction

Chapters 23 and 24 set out analysis designed to help us form judgements about the outcomes which a market economy generates. Armed with such judgements, and an understanding of how the economy operates, we are, in principle at least, in a position to design economic policies to improve those outcomes. It is helpful to know that it may sometimes be possible to eliminate a negative externality, or to ensure that a positive externality is internalised and then exploited, by a readjustment or perhaps extension of the structure of property rights, and that, if the readjustment of property rights is impossible for some reason, then a suitably designed set of indirect taxes and subsidies might be used to the same effect. It is also useful to understand what a public good is, and why market mechanisms might underprovide such things. And though we have seen that it is impossible to address matters of income distribution without applying ethical criteria, this very knowledge is at least helpful to clear thinking about an important set of social issues.

There is a long tradition of treating **economic analysis as a policy maker's toolkit**, indispensable to anyone wishing to intervene in economic life in order to improve economic efficiency and distributive justice. The creation of such a toolkit was high on the agenda of the economists who created the body of knowledge which earlier chapters of this book have expounded, and this knowledge is often deployed for such purposes.

It is hard to imagine how current debates about global warming, for example, could be conducted without the concept of externalities, or how a multitude of policy decisions about such mundane matters as road building, or the provision of street lighting, could be taken in a coherent fashion without some understanding of the nature of public goods, and without reference to the principles of cost–benefit analysis. And without knowledge of how suppliers of factors of production respond to changes in the rewards they command, we could not have much confidence that any policy designed to redistribute income would in fact end up having its desired effect.

But the reader must not infer that making economic policy involves nothing more than the application of well-understood theoretical principles by well-meaning governments intent only on promoting economic welfare and distributive justice among their fortunate citizens. It may be that the politicians who enact the legislation underpinning economic policy are driven by a desire to help others when they enter public life, and that the bureaucrats who execute policy on their behalf are public-spirited people strongly motivated to be of service to others. But politicians and bureaucrats are not automata. They are people, just as the consumers, workers, entrepreneurs and so on, who operate in the economy's private sector are people.

Though we have not, in the foregoing pages, denied that private sector agents are capable of acting out of altruism, we have not found it necessary to refer to such motives in analysing their behaviour. Quite the contrary. The postulate of self-interested behaviour in various guises – utility maximisation, profit maximisation, and so forth – has provided so useful a basis for explaining and helping us make predictions about a wide variety of circumstances that we have not found it necessary to go beyond it.

At the very least it is intellectually awkward to treat the making of economic policy as nothing more than a matter of the application of well-understood principles by an altruistic government to promoting the economic welfare of private agents who are themselves self-interested. To do so involves making diametrically opposite simplifying assumptions about people's behaviour depending upon whether they inhabit the economy's public or private sector. And matters are not improved if we reflect that in the economies we inhabit, although not every private sector agent is a politician or bureaucrat, every politician or bureaucrat is, after all, a private sector consumer.

This consideration in and of itself provides a powerful argument for taking a different view of the matter, and for analysing the policy-making process as also involving **self-interested** behaviour on the part of politicians and bureaucrats. Instead of treating policy makers as **disinterested** 'philosopher kings', or 'benevolent despots', it might be interesting instead to treat them as maximising agents, doing the best they can for themselves. If the predictions that such an approach yields are patently false, then we may abandon it, but if it yields interesting insights into the policy-making process, then an important new line of economic enquiry is opened up. Proponents of the analysis of **public choice** – as the application of the self-interested maximising postulate to explaining the formation and execution of economic policy is usually known – claim, with considerable justification, that it does indeed pass the all-important test of throwing new light on real-world phenomena. In the remainder of this part we shall present some of the results yielded by this body of analysis so that readers may make up their own minds about the matter.

The first fact of real-world policy making to which public choice analysis draws our attention is that, at least under democratic forms of government, policy makers have to get elected. In this chapter we shall investigate some implications of this fact. This leads us to consider questions about why people bother to vote at all, and suggest that this simple question does perhaps test the limits of the applicability of simple economic analysis. We shall then go on to analyse the so-called **voting paradox**, which reveals that the outcome of votes on complicated issues can sometimes depend on the way in which the choices are formulated. We then shall go on to discuss the nature of, and some applications of, the so-called **median voter** theorem, which has proved to be a fruitful source of insights into policy-making questions. Finally, we consider the implications of the fact that **information is costly** to voters, leading to the emergence of interest groups, and from there to **rent seeking**.

Why vote at all?

It is a fact of life that in a popular election or referendum the vote of any one individual has only the slightest chance of affecting the outcome. On the other hand, there are certain costs involved in **voting**. It is necessary to register to vote, and to take the time and trouble to visit the polling place and cast a ballot. Why, then, does anyone bother to vote in the first place? We are not aware of any convincing economic arguments that reconcile these considerations with the fact that large numbers of people do, nevertheless, vote in elections of all sorts.

The best that can be done to deal with this fact is to explain it away by postulating that many agents have a 'taste' for participating in the democratic process, and that the very act of voting yields them satisfaction enough to outweigh the costs they incur. But this is not a very good 'best', for it amounts to saying no more than that people who vote must be presumed to gain from doing so. Even so, we are not quite at a dead end here, because, given a distribution of the 'taste' for voting across the population, it still makes sense to postulate that people are more likely to vote in elections whose outcome will have important consequences for them than in others (and are more likely to vote the higher the chances that, by doing so, they will affect that outcome).

The facts that voters do seem to turn out in larger numbers for national, rather than local, elections, and that more people also seem to turn out in elections that are expected to be closely contested, are at least consistent with the postulate that self-interest influences the decision to vote on the margin. The fact that some democracies levy fines on those who do not cast ballots in elections, thereby inducing higher turnouts, suggests that self-interest sometimes needs support from extra incentives to produce behaviour deemed to be socially desirable, and incidentally lends further support to the postulate that it is at work in political processes.

The voting paradox

A further difficulty about applying economic analysis to voting among individuals is also worth noting at this point. The difficulty in question is often referred to as the **voting paradox**. It illustrates vividly the danger of taking it for granted that the analytic tools which have been developed for the case of a single individual may always safely be applied to a community of individuals on the assumption that the group as a whole may be treated 'as if' it was itself an individual. Results derived for Robinson Crusoe, the representative agent, may sometimes be useful when applied to the economy as a whole, as we have seen in Chapter 22, but not always.

The voting paradox can arise when we consider a community made up of agents with different tastes, though as we shall see in a moment, it need not necessarily do so. It can be illustrated by considering a society made up of only three agents (or, a little more realistically, three equally sized groups of agents) whom we may label 1, 2 and 3. Suppose they have to choose among three competing, indeed mutually exclusive, outcomes *A*, *B* and *C*. For example, if we were dealing with a municipality deciding what to build on a prime city-centre site, the alternatives might be an art gallery (*A*), a sports arena (*B*), or a hospital (*C*). Suppose our three groups of voters had tastes that could be arranged as follows, where the symbol > signifies 'is preferred to'.

Group 1 $A > B > C$
Group 2 $B > C > A$
Group 3 $C > A > B$

Clearly, any kind of ballot that presented the voters with the three alternatives simultaneously would lead to a tie among them.

But matters would be even more confusing if those voters were presented successively with choices between pairs. If the choice were between *A* and *B*, then groups 1 and 3 would outvote 2, and *A* would be selected. If instead, it were between *B* and *C*, then groups 1 and 2 would outvote 3 to select *B*. These two votes would appear to reveal a preference ordering within our community, of the following kind:

$A > B, B > C$

Applying the idea of transitivity of preferences, a *sine qua non* of 'rational' individual preferences (see Chapter 3), would lead to the conclusion that therefore

$A > C$

But if we put this to the test by way of a ballot, it is clear that groups 2 and 3 would outvote group 1, and produce a majority in favour of *C*.

In short, the kind of **transitivity of preferences** which we take for granted when dealing with **individuals** need not arise when we consider **communities**. Nor is the example here particularly outlandish. Return for a moment to the specific examples we gave of *A*, *B*, and *C*: the art gallery, the sports arena and the hospital. Would not the 'arts and leisure' fanatic have the tastes we have characterised as belonging to group 1, the 'anti-cultural/elitist' those of group 2, and the 'anti-athletic' those of 3; and don't we all know individuals that might fit into each category?

Box 26.1   **Arrow's impossibility theorem**

An important generalisation of the voting paradox was developed by Kenneth Arrow and is known as Arrow's impossibility theorem. This theorem states that there is NO voting mechanism that generates transitive social preferences if four conditions hold. Usually these four conditions are viewed as defining an ideal voting mechanism. The four conditions are:

1. *Unrestricted domain*: in principle any particular set of individual preferences that are complete and logical should be allowed. The implication here is that no voting rule should rule out certain rational preferences.
2. *Non-dictatorship*: no powerful individual should be able to determine social preferences so that they reflect the preferences of this powerful individual.
3. *Pareto principle*: if there is a choice alternative a that is preferred by all individuals to an alternative b then social preferences should rank a above b.
4. *Independence of irrelevant alternatives*: the social ranking of two options a and b should depend only on a and b, not on an alternative option c. So, for example, if $a > b > c$, but then the position of c changes such that it becomes socially most preferred, this should not affect the relative ranking of options a and b.

Arrow's theorem says that any voting rule based on (1)–(4) will always produce non-transitive social preferences. So, for example, if conditions (1), (3) and (4) hold, logical social preferences require dictatorship. Or if (2)–(4) hold, logical social preferences require that some (rational) people are not allowed to vote. It is inappropriate to offer here a proof of this theorem; interested readers can find a formal proof in many more advanced texts. All that is required here is to recognise the fundamental insight of Arrow's impossibility theorem: that if we want transitive social preferences, the voting mechanism must relax at least one of Arrow's conditions, and as such will not be ideal.

The median voter

Be that as it may, much public choice analysis sets these difficulties aside, takes it for granted that all eligible voters will participate in elections, and assumes that tastes are not so diverse as to lead to voting paradoxes. It then asks what kind of policies will emerge if those who design and implement them must first win an election. A frequent starting point for such analysis is the so-called **median voter** theorem, which is no less important for being rather obvious. The theorem in question rests on the simple proposition that, under a **majority voting** system, victory goes to the candidate, or programme, which can attract the support of 50 per cent plus one of the voters. To extract predictions from this proposition about how the preferences of the electorate might affect the conduct of policy, it is necessary to make certain simplifying assumptions.

Suppose, then, first of all that our election is about a single issue – for the sake of simplicity let us say 'income redistribution'. Let it also be the case that candidates in the election are sufficiently eager for re-election the next time round, and that their behaviour is sufficiently easy to monitor, that voters can and do rely on winning candidates to carry out their promises upon assuming office. Suppose finally that we may arrange all of the voters in the population in order with respect to the degree of income redistribution they desire, starting at one extreme with zero, and moving to some maximum amount. Let it also be the case that each voter will cast their ballot for the candidate who promises the degree of income redistribution closest to that which that particular voter desires. This particular assumption about voters' tastes and voting behaviour is important, because it rules out the voting paradox, as we shall explain in a moment.

Figure 26.1

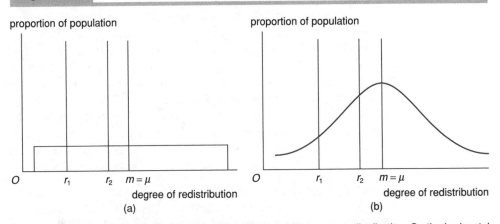

Two possible representations of a given population's 'taste' for income redistribution. On the horizontal axis we measure the degree of income redistribution, on the assumption that this can be measured by a scalar, and on the vertical axis the proportion of the population favouring a particular degree of income redistribution. In panel (a) we depict a so-called uniform distribution, under which an equal proportion of the population favours each feasible degree of redistribution, and in panel (b) a single peaked, but symmetrical distribution, under which tastes are bunched towards the centre of the feasible range, but equally spread out on either side. In each case the mean of the distribution equals its median.

In Figure 26.1 we portray these desires, measuring desired degree of income redistribution on the horizontal axis, and the proportion of voters desiring a particular degree of income redistribution on the vertical axis. Though nothing hinges on the matter at this point, we consider two frequently used postulates about the distribution of voters' preferences. In Figure 26.1(a) we draw a **uniform distribution** – with an equal proportion of voters preferring each given degree of redistribution – and in Figure 26.1(b) a distribution which is **single peaked** and *symmetrical*, with voters' preferences being bunched around a central value but equally distributed on either side. In each case the preference of the *median voter*, the voter relative to whom half of remaining voters prefer more and half less income distribution, is indicated by point m on the horizontal axis.

Now consider the choice of election promise on the part of any particular candidate. Suppose the candidate promises a degree of redistribution $r_1 < m$. Clearly this promise cannot win the election, because if it is made, some other candiate could enter with a promise of r_2, lying between r_1 and m, and take a majority of votes. This argument will hold true for any promised degree of redistribution less than m. It will also, quite obviously, hold true for any promised degree of income redistribution greater than m. In short, in this election, the candidate who promises exactly to satisfy the preference of the median voter for **income redistribution** by promising m will win. The same result would hold true for any election held over any single issue where voter preferences could be described and ordered as they are in Figure 26.1.

To see why the voting paradox has not arisen in this analysis, consider the following simplified version of it. Suppose we presented our voters with a choice among only three alternative degrees of income redistribution: little (A), moderate (B) and high (C). Our assumption about their preferences would enable us to place them in three groups: those who prefer no, or only a little, income redistribution for whom $A > B > C$; those in favour of a high degree of it, for whom $C > B > A$; and those favouring a moderate amount, whose tastes would have to be categorised as $B > A = C$, in order to capture the idea that movement away from their preferred position in *either direction* was equally distasteful to them. In this case, as the reader will quickly see, a vote between A and C will end in a tie, and any pairwise choice involving B will result in it winning – the taste of the 'median voter', that is to say, will dominate the outcome.

We have departed from the voting paradox in this case because the typical voter's preferences for alternatives are assumed to become weaker, the further away they are from that voter's most desired outcome. We have therefore assumed away voters whose first choice is a 'little' income redistribution, but who, denied that, would then rather have a 'lot' of it than a 'moderate' amount, and voters desiring a 'lot' of redistribution, whose second choice is a 'little'. This assumption about preferences seems quite reasonable given the nature of the matter being voted on; and the general lesson to be drawn here is that whether the voting paradox is important, or whether it may safely be assumed away, probably depends upon the particular matter about which a social choice is being made.

Even so, there is not a great deal to be inferred from so general a version of the median voter theorem as we have considered here. Some commentators argue that the tendencies it highlights explain why democracies tend to produce 'middle of the road' governments regardless of the 'left' or 'right' wing credentials of the political parties that contest elections. They may be right, but it is a long way from the simple mechanics of a single-issue election, whose winner can be guaranteed to carry out the letter of a policy promised when still a candidate, to the complexities of multiparty contests in a multi-issue world with less than perfect *ex post* accountability on the part of the victors. More to the point here, however, is that, when combined with certain other specific assumptions about the economic environment, the median voter theorem yields some intriguing implications about the politics of income redistribution. That is one reason why we chose this issue rather than any other to lend concreteness to the foregoing exposition, which forms a basis for the analysis to which we now turn.

The median voter and income redistribution

The preceding section established that, in any majority vote about a single issue, it is the median voter who will control the outcome. Suppose, then, we consider votes on the matter of income distribution, and assume that all voters, including the median, are interested in maximising their own after-tax-and-redistribution incomes. Suppose also, to keep the analysis manageable, that taxes can be levied only in proportion to income, and redistributed in equal lump sums to each and every member of the population. This particular simplification is not quite as 'unrealistic' as it may seem at first sight, because one way in which income redistribution can be, and indeed commonly is, accomplished in the real world is through the provision of tax-financed public goods. It is, as we saw in Chapter 24, the very essence of such goods that no one can be excluded from consuming them, and that the consumption of one member of the community does not reduce the good's availability to others. Hence, if a public good is provided through taxation, it is reasonable to think of the sum collected in taxes as being redistributed in equal amounts (albeit in kind rather than cash) to all members of the community.

IF t is the tax rate, and μ the arithmetic average, or *mean* income of the community, then tax payments per head in the community, and hence lump sum receipts from redistribution, whether in cash or in kind, call the amount T, will be given by the simple formula

$$T = t\mu \qquad (26.1)$$

The median voter's own tax liability, let us call it T_m, when their before-tax income is equal to M will be given by

$$T_m = tM \qquad (26.2)$$

Clearly, the only object of political choice in this world is the tax rate t, and the question we must address is what value for t would the income maximising median voter choose, given that the voter's after-tax income, call it Y_m, is given by

$$Y_m = t\mu + (1 - t)M \qquad (26.3)$$

The answer here, as the reader will soon discover, can be very 'unrealistic' and can depend upon how before-tax income is distributed among the population.

Suppose first that it is distributed symmetrically, and can be described by a relationship such as we draw in Figure 26.2. It is a property of such a symmetrical distribution that its median value equals its mean or, in terms of the above formula, $\mu = m$. In this case, it is obvious that any value for t between zero and one will yield the same value for Y_m, that the median voter is unable to benefit from income redistribution through the tax system. It is reasonable, then, to conclude that no attempt will be made to introduce it, and that the median voter will opt for a zero tax rate.

But now suppose that before-tax income is distributed asymmetrically, with a few voters having relatively high incomes, with the majority clustered at the low end of the distribution. We portray such a **skewed** *to the right* **distribution** in Figure 26.3, and note that it is a property of such a configuration that it leads to the mean of the distribution

Figure 26.2 **A symmetrical income distribution**

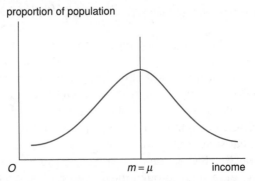

The vertical axis measures the proportion of the population having a particular income, and on the horizontal axis we measure income (as opposed to taste for redistribution as in Figure 26.1). In this case, mean income (μ) is equal to median income (m), and the voter in receipt of median income, whose views will dominate any election on the choice of the tax rate to apply to a proportional-income-tax-lump-sum-redistribution, has nothing to gain from a positive income tax rate.

Figure 26.3

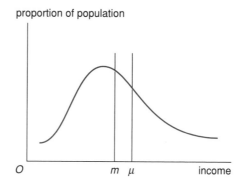

proportion of population

A skewed income distribution, with a relatively small number of agents having unusually high incomes. In this case the median voter's income (m) is below the economy's mean income (μ), and the median voter's after-tax-and-transfer receipts will be maximised by a tax rate of 100 per cent.

lying above its median. To put it in ordinary language, more than half of the voters in Figure 26.3 have a 'below average' before-tax income, or to put it more formally, $M < \mu$. In this case, it is obvious that the highest after-tax-and-redistribution income which our median voter can attain is the mean income for the economy as a whole, and that this would be had by setting a tax rate of 100 per cent, $t = 1$.

At first sight, the above results seem to cast considerable doubt on the empirical relevance of the median voter theorem. Tax rates in the world we live in (except for anomalies that sometimes inadvertently arise from the interaction of rather complicated tax and social security arrangements) invariably lie between zero and one, while the theorem seems to tell us that only one or the other of these extreme values will be chosen. As we shall now see, however, this result in fact derives from another characteristic of the simple model we have been analysing, namely, that the before-tax income of every agent is assumed to be given independently of the tax rate. Once this assumption is dropped, the implications of the median voter theorem become rather more interesting, as the following analysis shows.

The influence of the tax rate on mean income and tax revenue

Suppose then that we complicate our model economy by assuming that its inhabitants gain their incomes by working in co-operation with a given stock of capital equipment, and that differences in the rate at which they produce income stem from **productivity differences** among them, whose sources we need not specify for present purposes. Let it also be the case that the tastes of the inhabitants of this economy are such that the higher the wage rate they receive for their work, the more hours they will put in, and that the productivity of their efforts diminishes on the margin as more hours are worked. These assumptions allow us to draw Figure 26.4(a), which shows the relationship between mean before-tax income per head in our economy, μ, measured on the horizontal axis, and the proportional rate at which that income is taxed, measured on the vertical axis.

Figure 26.4

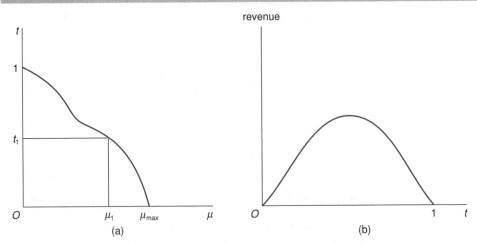

In panel (a) we depict the relationship between the economy's before-tax mean income (μ) and the proportional tax rate (t) on the assumption that the former depends inversely upon the latter. In this case, tax revenue is given by the area of a rectangle such as $t_1 \cdot \mu_1$. The relationship between tax revenue and the tax rate implicit in (a) is drawn as a Laffer curve in (b). Revenue at first rises, and then falls, as the tax rate is increased.

If income is left untaxed, then there is a certain determinate level of income μ_{max} which the average agent will generate, and it is a harmless assumption that, at a tax rate of 100 per cent, $t = 1$, that agent will not work at all, generating zero before-tax income. Between these two extremes there will be a generally downward-sloping relationship between the two variables, such as we draw in Figure 26.4(a), and at any tax rate we may obtain the tax revenue obtained by multiplying the tax rate as measured on the vertical axis by before-tax income as measured on the horizontal.

The resulting relationship between tax revenue and the tax rate is drawn in Figure 26.4(b). It is sometimes known as the **Laffer curve**, after Dr Arthur Laffer, an economist who, so legend has it, drew the relationship on a napkin in a Washington restaurant. Its important characteristic is that tax revenue reaches a maximum at a tax rate less than 100 per cent, reflecting an insight that has been familiar to economists for over 200 years – historians trace it to the writing of Jonathan Swift, best known nowadays as the author of *Gulliver's Travels*. This property of the Laffer curve tells us immediately that, even if the median voter in our economy wished to maximise the revenue available for redistribution (and as we shall see in a moment, the median voter would usually aim for less than its maximum), they would still opt for a fractional tax rate.

The median voter's problem

Continuing parallels with the analysis presented earlier in this chapter, let us assume that the distribution of skills in the economy is asymmetrical, with the median voter being less productive than the mean voter. The median voter is interested, among other things, in receiving tax-financed transfers, and the size of the transfer available to them is the amount of tax that can be raised from taxing the mean voter. Suppose the object of the median voter, who in this case will be the worker with median productivity among those eligible to vote, was to maximise their own disposable income. Then, in addition to receipts from the tax-transfer system, the median voter's own after-tax income would have to be considered. As we have already seen, where M is the median voter's before-tax income, and Y is the same voter's after-tax-and-transfer income, the sum to be maximised is

$$Y = t\mu + (1 - t)M \qquad\qquad (26.3)$$

We have seen that as t rises, the first term on the right-hand side here will first rise to a maximum and then begin to fall. The second term will unambiguously fall as t rises. This will be the case even if M is a constant that does not depend on the tax rate, and the effect will be accentuated if the median voter, like the mean voter, works less, the higher is that tax rate. The reader might note, though, that if the median voter does respond in this way, then they are presumably maximising not just after-tax-and-transfer income, but some utility function in which income and leisure are arguments. In this case the analysis being presented here, though not misleading, would not be quite rigorous.

The argument we have just presented suggests that, in an economy where the distribution of before-tax income is such that mean income lies above the median, where the tax-transfer system is subject to a majority vote, and crucially, where the amount of before-tax income generated is affected by the tax rate chosen by the electorate, the outcome will be a fractional tax rate lower than that which would maximise tax revenue.

Redistribution through the provision of public goods

It is nevertheless the case that, where income is redistributed in kind through the provision of **public goods**, these will tend to be 'overprovided' in the sense that their provision will be continued to a point at which their marginal cost of production will exceed the marginal social benefit which they yield.

This latter result comes about because the median voter will want public goods to be provided up to the point at which the marginal benefit from their services to them just equals the marginal cost as expressed in their own extra tax bill. But the marginal benefit in question will be the same for all members of the community, while under proportional taxation the marginal cost to the *mean* voter will be higher than that to the *median* voter. Hence public goods will be provided up to a point at which the benefit (added up over all voters) on the margin from providing public goods falls short of the cost (also added up over all voters) on the margin of providing them. A moment's reflection will enable the reader to see that, if public goods were financed by levying a tax of equal amount on each voter, rather than in proportion to income, this tendency to 'overprovide' public goods would be removed. This result provides the basis of the case for financing local government expenditures, which have a large public good element to them, by way of a '**poll tax**' rather than some other income- or wealth-contingent source of revenue.

Now, whatever readers may think about poll taxes – and in drawing attention to the above argument, we certainly do not mean to defend them – they must agree that the foregoing analysis is much more interesting than that which we initially developed on the assumption that levels of before-tax income were given independently of the tax rate.

Perhaps it is interesting enough to persuade the reader not to dismiss the median voter theorem out of hand. And the analysis in question may be taken a little further, as we shall now show.

Variations in productivity and the extent of redistribution

The median voter chooses the economy's tax rate by trading off one effect of that rate, namely, its influence on the revenue that can be extracted from the mean voter, against another, namely, its influence on the median voter's own after-tax but before-transfer income. Suppose we hold the first set of factors constant, but consider what happens as the median voter becomes less productive. This can be done by holding the mean productivity of workers in the economy constant by simultaneously fattening the right-hand tail of the distribution of productivity and shifting the peak of the distribution to the left, as we show in Figure 26.5. As these changes take place, the influence of the tax rate on the size of available income transfers remains the same, but the influence of the tax rate on the median voter's own after-tax earnings becomes smaller as that worker becomes less productive. Hence, under these new circumstances, the median voter's after-tax-and-transfer income would be maximised at a higher tax rate.

Some economists, notably Allan Meltzer and Scott Richards, have argued, using reasoning similar to this, that the higher the degree of before-tax-and-transfer income **inequality** in an economy, the greater will be the degree of redistribution built into its tax and transfer system. They have also argued that if inequality shifts over time, then in the presence of democratic institutions so will the extent of income redistribution. Finally, they have pointed out that in over the last 200 years there has been a marked tendency in Western countries for **the franchise** to be extended to members of successively lower

Figure 26.5

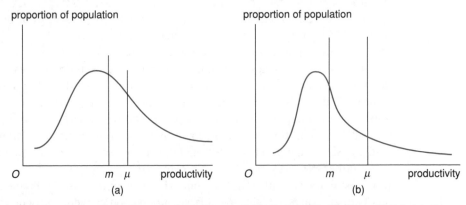

In panel (a) we draw a skewed income distribution much like that depicted in Figure 26.3 but, in this case, on the horizontal axis we measure agents' ability to produce income, rather than income itself. In panel (b) we depict a more skewed distribution, with a relatively fatter upper tail. The important feature illustrated in these two charts is that, as the distribution becomes more skewed to the right, the gap between its mean and median values becomes greater.

income groups, and that this has widened the gap between the incomes of the mean and median voters. They have speculated that the systematic **growth of the welfare state**, involving as it has increasingly high tax rates, and a greater and greater proportion of national income passing through the government sector for redistribution both in cash and in kind, may partly be understood as a result of this spread of the franchise.

The significance and limitations of the median voter theorem

Now the analysis we have presented in the last few pages has been based on highly simplified assumptions – too simplified, we suspect, for the tastes of many readers. Nevertheless, it does have two vital characteristics which ought to appeal to an economist. It relies solely on the postulate of maximising self-interested behaviour, and it makes concrete predictions about relationships among observable variables. Moreover we have seen that among the observable variables about which such predictions are possible, are included those having to do with taxes and transfers, to achieve government-sponsored income redistribution.

If readers will reflect for a moment on the nature of much everyday discussion of these matters, they will readily agree that the concepts of altruism and envy play a large role in those discussions. And yet median voter analysis suggests that we can discuss these issues without reference to these concepts. We do not have to think of politicians as altruistic, or voters as envious, in order to explain why income redistribution occurs in democracies. All we need postulate is that the same self-interested motives which have so much explanatory power in economic life are at play in what many term the political marketplace. This is a powerful insight that ought not to be neglected in any discussion of economic policy.

But for all that, there do seem to be limits on how far we can push median voter analysis. In particular, we were careful to specify in the earlier analysis that we were dealing with **elections** to decide a **single issue** about which the tastes of the electorate could be described in terms of a simple distribution. Real-world democracy is not usually like that. Elections do not directly decide policies, but rather return people to power who will then execute policies. Moreover the policies in question deal not with single but with **multiple issues**, and it is simply not possible to collapse the views of voters about multiple issues into a simple single index which can then be measured along the horizontal axis of diagrams such as Figures 26.1–26.5. There are, moreover, real problems to do with the amount of knowledge voters bring to the electoral process, given that it takes time and trouble to gather and process information. It is one thing to expect a hypothetical median voter to be informed fully about the consequences of setting a single proportional tax rate; it is quite another to expect a real-world voter to be equally well informed about the consequences of each item in the election manifestos of a number of political parties.

The most we can say for median voter analysis, then, is that it demonstrates the feasibility of applying the economist's hypothesis of self-interested maximisation to political processes, and that it perhaps yields some interesting 'broad-brush' insights into their functioning. We now go on to consider other profitable ways of deploying the idea of self-interest in the analysis of policy problems which do not suffer from the same limitations.

Costly information

In the real world, neither economic policy debates nor voting are typically about single issues. Political candidates and parties alike offer platforms – packages of policies – to the electorate, and the policies themselves are usually rather broadly specified, leaving the victors of the election a good deal of room for manoeuvre when it comes to their actual implementation.

The resources which agents have available to acquire and assess information about the promises of politicians, and then to decide on how to cast their votes, are strictly limited relative to the calls upon them. Voters' time and energy are, in the language of micro-economics, *scarce*, and it is reasonable to suppose that voters will allocate time and energy so as to maximise their product. This observation suggests that voters will become better informed about those aspects of policy which are likely to have a big effect on them, and will pay far less attention to analysing policies which will impinge only marginally upon them. If we carry this line of thought a step further, and allow for the possibility that voters might actively seek to influence the policies on offer from politicians, it clearly leads to the prediction that they will work hard to influence legislation that promises to yield them large benefits (or threatens to impose large costs upon them) but will put little effort into measures that will make only a minor difference to their own wellbeing.

Interest group politics

It follows from this that politicians seeking elected office will be likely to offer a menu of rather specific benefits, each of which is particularly important to a particular group among the electorate – an **interest group**, as it is often called – while ensuring that the costs of providing the benefits in question are as widely diffused as possible among the population. The importance of each particular benefit to the groups at which it is aimed stongly attracts the votes of their members, while the costs to them of providing benefits to other groups will be relatively small, and hence will not deter them from voting for their own particular programme. The successful political party, then, is one which can put together the largest **coalition** of interest groups in support of the policy menu it offers.

If the political process works along the lines just outlined, then it follows that there is a bias in political life towards a relatively large amount of government intervention in the economy. Everyone is tempted to support measures tailored to their own desires, measures in which they have a strong interest, but no one is strongly disposed to oppose the costs which the whole array of such measures imposes upon the community at large. For any particular member of the community, the extra cost imposed by a policy designed to satisfy one more particular interest group is rather small. Some economists also argue that the same reasoning helps to explain the seemingly chronic tendency of governments to finance their expenditure by running deficits rather than by levying taxes. Government borrowing is not a means of avoiding the imposition of taxes but of deferring it. Even government debts have to be paid eventually and they accrue interest in the interim. But if future tax payers are not currently enfranchised, they cannot vote to protect their own interests.

Now one must be careful about the morals that are drawn from the above arguments. They suggest that democratic politics in a world of self-interested voters might be biased towards producing large government, but it certainly does not follow that there is an anti-democratic bias to the type of analysis which yields this conclusion. To begin with, such analysis does not tell us that undemocratic government is free of tendencies to cater to interest groups. Consider the size of military budgets in military dictatorships, or the power of the bureaucracy in many erstwhile socialist dictatorships: are these phenomena not explicable in terms of the power of interest groups?

Our arguments do, however, draw attention to the way in which self-interest might work in a particular political context. Hence they provide a basis for debating ways in which democratic institutions might be reformed so as to improve their economic performance while preserving their political advantages. A very large segment of the literature in public choice analysis, particularly that associated with the name of James Buchanan, is devoted to seeking solutions to this problem by way of placing constitutional constraints on the conduct of economic policy. One does not have to agree with the particular solutions offered by this literature to concede that these problems are important and well worth discussion.

Rent seeking

The analysis to which we have just referred is extremely broad in scope, far too broad indeed to fit comfortably into a book like this one. However, one line along which it has been developed is worth a little more attention here. Politically active interest groups do not appear out of thin air, but usually arise out of some already existing affinity among their members. In the economic sphere, for example, owners and managers of firms, and/or their employees, operating in particular industries, form a natural base upon which interest groups might form in order to use the political process to seek advantages. Successful political activity might, for example, lead to direct subsidies for the industry concerned, or to the creation of market conditions conducive to the extraction of monopoly profits from customers. And once such conditions have been created, individual agents within such groups might be expected diligently to seek to maximise their own share of the advantages which accrue from them. Such behaviour, following the usage adopted by one of its early analysts, Ann Krueger, is generally termed **rent seeking**, with the word 'rent' being used to signify profit, or surplus above cost.

Concluding comment

We make no claim to have provided a comprehensive survey of the economic literature dealing with public choice in this final part of our book. Rather, we have tried to present a few examples of how the basic principle underlying that analysis yields insights into questions having to do with economic policy. The principle in question is a straightforward one: namely, that agents whose private behaviour may usefully be treated as the consequence of self-interested maximisation are likely to behave in the public sphere in a manner open to similar interpretation. The consumer, worker, or property owner who becomes a candidate for public office is not transformed into a different person by virtue of that fact; and the agent who casts a ballot in an election is the same agent who selects goods to consume when out shopping, and is just as likely to be pursuing self-interested motives when engaged in one activity as in the other. None of this means that we should become unduly cynical about economic (or any other) policy. Public choice analysis rests on the assumption that policy makers are no less self-interested than others, but it does *not* claim that they are any *more* self-interested.

Traditional approaches to policy analysis had it that the task of economics was complete if it first developed reliable means of predicting the way in which private sector agents would respond to various incentives, went on to develop criteria whereby disinterested policy makers could judge what behaviour was and what was not in the public interest, and then helped them design policies to promote that public interest. Public choice analysis tells us that such analysis is incomplete because the assumption that policy makers are disinterested is all too likely to be untrue. It suggests that economics has a further contribution to make to policy analysis: namely, to make us conscious of the incentives to which policy measures are a response, and to help us devise the means whereby the self-interest of voters and policy makers alike may be harnessed to produce beneficial rather than destructive outcomes.

Thus the message of this chapter is not that the material developed earlier in this book is erroneous. It is still useful to know that competitive markets tend to use resources efficiently, that monopolists tend to underprovide output relative to what might be socially desirable, that the existence of externalities and public goods poses problems which can be solved by government intervention, that the design of such intervention inevitably involves policy makers in value judgements about income distribution, and so on. What public choice analysis tells us is not that any of these conclusions is wrong, but only that a thorough understanding of them, though necessary, is not sufficient for intelligent discussion of economic policy issues. So long as economic policy is made by self-interested human beings, it is not sufficient for them to know what is in the public interest in order to get desirable policies enacted. It is also important that the private incentives which they face tempt them towards, rather than against, the enactment of such policies. And, as we have seen, such a state of affairs cannot be taken for granted. Its creation and maintenance present challenging policy problems.

SUMMARY

Voting and the median voter

1. Government activities can be analysed as maximising behaviour rather than as the actions of a disinterested or altruistic 'benevolent dictator'.

2. We assume in the discussion of *public choice* that politicians and bureaucrats are motivated by self-interest.

3. The voting paradox provides one example of a case in which voting among alternatives fails to yield transitivity of social preferences.

4. The median voter theorem states that under majority voting, the alternative chosen is that supported by 50 per cent plus one of the votes. It suggests that it is the median voter who will determine the outcome of an election.

5. If income distribution is skewed to the right so that the median income is less than the average, and taxation is to be used for redistribution, it seems at first sight that the median voter will choose a 100 per cent tax rate.

6. Ability differences complicate choice of tax rate if income differences arise from underlying variance in ability, and higher taxes reduce effort.

7. Tax revenue will reach a maximum at less than a 100 per cent tax rate. The relationship between tax revenue and the tax rate has an inverse U-shape and is known as the Laffer curve.

8. The less productive the median voter is, holding all other factors constant, the higher the tax rate at which their after-tax and transfer income is maximised. Hence the optimal degree of redistribution for the median voter will increase as the franchise is extended to successively lower income groups.

9. Information about the gains and losses from different policies is expensive to obtain. People will therefore be more knowledgeable about things that affect them directly, positively or negatively. This will lead politicians to offer a menu of specific benefits to particular interest groups.

10. Rent seeking involves the efforts of interest groups to maximise their advantages from political or quasi-political activity. For example, a group of firms trying to form a cartel but worried about prisoners' dilemma problems might club together to persuade the government to support the collusive price.

PROBLEMS

1 Is the assumption of self-interested behaviour on the part of individuals to be taken literally, or treated as a useful approximation? If the latter, how would you decide whether it is useful or not?

2 Discuss the relevance of the idea behind the Laffer curve – namely, that beyond a certain tax rate revenue will fall as the tax rate rises – to the design of sales taxes, income taxes, or property taxes.

3 Do the implications of analysis based on the median voter theorem justify the replacement of income taxes with a poll tax?

4 Are the conclusions yielded by traditional welfare economics about the desirability of government intervention in the provision of public goods affected by the observation that the provision of such goods may be a means of redistributing income?

5 Argue the case for and against the introduction of rent controls in a particular city from the point of view of

(a) existing tenants,
(b) existing landlords,
(c) owner occupiers who pay property taxes to the city,
(d) potential future renters and
(e) potential future landlords.

6 Which of the viewpoints articulated in your answer to question 5 are likely to have a politically effective interest group coalesce around them? Assess the likely outcome of the resulting political decision from the point of view of traditional welfare economics.

7 An old American political observation had it that, 'The tariff is the mother of trusts.' Explain this observation and assess its validity in the light of the analysis of rent-seeking behaviour.

8 In some cities, the supply of taxi licences is fixed by city government, and a secondary market in such licences exists.

(a) What factors will determine the price at which such licences trade?

(b) Taxi operators argue that taxi fares are reasonable because they are just making normal returns, while economists argue that that taxi fares are too high because supply has been artificially limited. Whom should we believe?

(c) Who, if anyone, has or does benefit from the regulations in question, and who if anyone is adversely affected?

(d) How would you devise a scheme for deregulating the taxi trade in this city which might be politically successful?

9 In some countries, strict, but marketable, output quotas for the production of, for example, milk, eggs and poultry are fixed by government. Consider the likely implications of such a scheme for the incomes of already established producers and newcomers to dairy and poultry farming, and the economic welfare of consumers, in the light of the arguments you developed in answering question 8. Unlike taxi rides, agricultural products are internationally tradable. What position on free trade in

(a) agricultural products and

(b) processed food products

would you expect the government of such countries to take?

FURTHER READING

Akerlof, G. (1970), 'The market for lemons: quality uncertainty and the market mechanism', *Quarterly Journal of Economics*.

Alchian, A. (1953), 'The meaning of utility measurement', *American Economic Review*, reprinted in W. Breit and H.M. Hochman (eds), *Readings in Microeconomics*, New York: Holt Rinehart and Winston, 1968.

Arrow, K.J. (1971), *Essays in the Theory of Risk Bearing*, Amsterdam: North-Holland.

Arrow, K.J. (1974), *The Limits of Organisation*, New York: Norton.

Atkinson, A.B. and Stiglitz, J.E. (1980), *Lectures on Public Economics*. Maidenhead: McGraw-Hill.

Auld, D. (1972), 'Imperfect knowledge and the new theory of demand', *Journal of Political Economy*.

Bailey, M.J. (1965), 'The Marshallian demand curve', *Journal of Political Economy*, reprinted in W. Breit and H.M. Hochman (eds), *Readings in Microeconomics*, New York: Holt, Rinehart and Winston, 1968.

Bailey, M.J. (1965), 'The welfare cost of inflationary finance', *Journal of Political Economy*, reprinted in K.J. Arrow and T. Scitovsky (eds) on behalf of the American Economic Association, *Readings in Welfare Economics*, Homewood, Ill.: Irwin.

Bain, J.S. (1962), *Barriers to New Competition*, Cambridge, Mass.: Harvard University Press.

Bator, F. (1957), 'The simple analytics of welfare maximisation', *American Economic Review*, reprinted in Breit and Hochman (eds), *op. cit.*

Bator, F. (1958), 'The anatomy of market failure', *Quarterly Journal of Economics*.

Baumol, W.J. (1959), *Business Behaviour, Value and Growth*, New York: Macmillan.

Baumol, W.J., Panzar, J.C. and Willig, R.D. (1982), *Contestable Markets and the Theory of Industry Structure*, New York: Harcourt, Brace, Jovanovich.

Becker, G. (1965), 'A theory of the allocation of time', *Economic Journal*.

Becker, G.S. (1975), *Human Capital*, 2nd edn, New York: Columbia University Press.

Bishop, R.L. (1964), 'A Zeuthen-Hicks model of the bargaining process', *Econometrica*.

Black, D. (1958), *The Theory of Committees and Elections*, Cambridge: Cambridge University Press.

Brown, A. and Deaton, A.S. (1972), 'Models of consumer behaviour: a survey', *Economic Journal*.

Buchanan, J. (1970), *The Public Finances*, 3rd edn, Homewood, Ill.: Irwin.

Buchanan, J. and Tullock, G. (1962), *The Calculus of Consent*, Ann Arbor, Mich.: University of Michigan Press.

Buchanan, J., Tollison, R. and Tullock, G. (eds) (1980), *Towards a Theory of the Rent Seeking Society*, College Station, Tex.: Texas A & M University Press.

Chamberlain, E. (1956), *The Theory of Monopolistic Competition*, Cambridge, Mass.: Harvard University Press.

Coase, R. (1960), 'The problem of social cost', *Journal of Law and Economics*, reprinted in Breit and Hochman (eds), *op. cit.*

Coase, R.H. (1937), 'The nature of the firm', *Economica*, reprinted in G.J. Stigler and K.E. Boulding (eds) on behalf of the American Economic Association, *Readings in Price Theory*, London: Allen & Unwin, 1953.

Cohen, K.J. and Cyert, R.M. (1965), *Theory of the Firm*, Englewood Cliffs, NJ: Prentice Hall, chs 4–6, 10–12, 15–17.

Courchene, T.J. (1980), 'Towards a protected society – the politicisation of economic life', *Canadian Journal of Economics*.

Cowling, K.G. and Waterson, M. (1976), 'Price cost margins and market structure', *Economica*.

Currie, J.M., Murphy, J.A. and Schmitz, A. (1971), 'The concept of economic surplus and its use in economic analysis', *Economic Journal*.

Cyert, R.M. and March, T.G. (1963), *A Behavioural Theory of the Firm*, Englewood Cliffs, NJ: Prentice Hall.

Deaton, A.S. and Muellbauer, J. (1980), *Economics and Consumer Behaviour*, Cambridge: Cambridge University Press.

Demsetz, H. (1959), 'The nature of equilibrium in monopolistic competition', *Journal of Political Economy*.

Diewert, W.E. (1971), 'An application of the Shephard duality theorem: a generalised Leontief production function', *Journal of Political Economy*.

Diewert, W.E. (1974), 'Applications of duality theory', in M. Intrilligator and P. Kendrick (eds), *Frontiers of Quantitative Economics*, vol. 2, Amsterdam: North-Holland.

Dixit, A.K. (1982), 'Recent development in oligopoly theory', *American Economic Review* (papers and proceedings).

Downs, A. (1957), *An Economic Analysis of Democracy*, New York: Harper & Row.

Dunlop, J.T. (1957), *The Theory of Wage Determination*, London: Macmillan.

Ehrenberg, R.G. and Smith, R.S. (1982), *Modern Labor Economics*, Glenview, Ill.: Scott, Foresman.

Estrin, S., Jones, D.C. and Sjevnar, J. (1987), 'The productivity effects of worker participation in the producers cooperatives of western economies', *Journal of Comparative Economics*.

Farber, H. (1986), 'The analysis of union behaviour', in O. Ashenfelter and R. Layard (eds), *Handbook of Labour Economics*, Amsterdam: North-Holland.

Ferguson, C.E. (1969), *The Neoclassical Theory of Production and Distribution*, Cambridge: Cambridge University Press.

Friedman, J.W. (1977), *Oligopoly and the Theory of Games*, Amsterdam: North-Holland.

Friedman, M. (1949), 'The Marshallian demand curve', *Journal of Political Economy*, 1971, reprinted in Breit and Hochman, *op. cit.*

Friedman, M. (1953), 'The methodology of positive economics', in id. *Essays in Positive Economics*, Chicago: University of Chicago Press.

Friedman, M. (1957), *A Theory of the Consumption Function*, Princeton, NJ: Princeton University Press for the NBER, chs 1–3.

Friedman, M. and Savage, L.J. (1953), 'The utility analysis of choices involving risks', *Journal of Political Economy*, 1948, reprinted in Stigler and Boulding, *op. cit.*

Frisch, R. (1950), 'Alfred Marshall's theory of value', *Quarterly Journal of Economics*.

Fuss, M. and McFadden, D. (1978), *Production Economics: A Dual Approach to Theory and Applications*, Amsterdam: North-Holland.

Green, H.A.J. (1971), *Consumer Theory*, London: Penguin.

Hall, R.L. and Hitch, C.J. (1939), 'Price theory and business behaviour', *Oxford Economic Papers*.

Harberger, A.C. (1957), 'Monopoly and resource allocation', *American Economic Review*.

Hartle, D. (1983), 'The theory of rent seeking – some reflections', *Canadian Journal of Economics*.

Heathfield, D.F. (1974), *Production Functions*, London: Macmillan.

Heidensohn, K. and Robinson, J.N. (1974), *Business Behaviour*, Deddington, Oxford: Philip Allan.

Henderson, A.M. (1947), 'The pricing of public utility undertakings', *The Manchester School*, reprinted in Arrow and Scitovsky (eds), *op. cit.*

Henderson, J.M. and Quandt, R.E. (1971), *Microeconomic Theory: A Mathematical Approach*, 2nd edn, New York: McGraw-Hill, ch. 3.

Hey, J.D. (1979), *Uncertainty in Microeconomics*, Oxford: Martin Robertson.

Hicks, J.R. (1941), 'The rehabilitation of consumer's surplus', *Review of Economic Studies*, reprinted in K.J. Arrow and T. Scitovsky (eds) on behalf of the American Economic Association, *Readings in Welfare Economics*, Homewood, Ill.: Irwin.

Hicks, J.R. (1946), *Value and Capital*, 2nd edn, New York: Oxford University Press, chs 1–3.

Hicks, J.R. (1963), *The Theory of Wages*, 2nd edn, New York: St Martin's Press.

Hirsch, B.T. and Addison, J.T. (1986), *The Economic Analysis of Trade Unions*, Boston: Allen & Unwin.

Hirschleifer, J. (1958), 'On the theory of optimal investment decision', *Journal of Political Economy*.

Ireland, N.J. and Law, P.J. (1982), *Economics of Labour-Managed Enterprise*, London: Croom Helm.

Johnson, H.G. (1971), *The Two Sector Model of General Equilibrium*, The Yrjö Jahnsson Lectures, London: Allen & Unwin, chs 1 and 2.

Kaldor, N. (1939), 'Welfare propositions of economics and inter-personal comparisons', *Economic Journal*.

Killingsworth, M.R. (1983), *Labour Supply*, Cambridge: Cambridge University Press.

Koopmans, T. (1957), *Three Essays on the State of Economic Science*, New York: McGraw-Hill.

Krueger, A.O. (1974), 'The political economy of the rent seeking society', *American Economic Review*.

Lancaster, K. (1966), 'A new approach to consumer theory', *Journal of Political Economy*.

Lancaster, K. (1971), *Consumer Demand: A New Approach*, New York: Columbia University Press.

Lancaster, K. and Lipsey, R.G. (1965), 'The general theory of the second best', *Review of Economic Studies*.

Leontief, W.W. (1966), *Input–Output Economics*, Oxford: Oxford University Press.

Lerner, A.P. (1934), 'The concept of monopoly and the measurement of monopoly power', *Review of Economic Studies*.

Little, I.M.D. (1957), *A Critique of Welfare Economics*, 2nd edn, Oxford: Oxford University Press.

Machlup, F. (1967), 'Theories of the firm, marginalist, managerialist, behavioural', *American Economic Review*.

Marris, R. (1964), *The Economic Theory of 'Managerial' Capitalism*, London: Macmillan.

Marshall, A. (1920), *Principles of Economics*, 8th edn, London: Macmillan, bk 3.

McDonald, I.M. and Solow, R.M. (1981), 'Wage bargaining and employment', *American Economic Review*.

Meltzer, A.H. and Richard, S.F. (1981), 'Rational theory of the size of government', *Econometrica*.

Nash, J. (1950), 'The bargaining problem', *Econometrica*.

Olson, M. (1982), *The Rise and Decline of Nations*, New Haven, Conn.: Yale University Press.

Oswald, A. (1982), 'The microeconomic theory of the trade union', *Economic Journal*.

Phlips, L. (1974), *Applied Consumption Analysis*, Amsterdam: North-Holland.

Rasmusen, E. (1989), *Games and Information*, Oxford: Blackwell.

Robbins, L.C. (1946), 'On the elasticity of demand for income in terms of effort', *Economica*, 1930.

Robinson, J. (1934), 'Euler's theorem and the problem of distribution', *Economic Journal*, reprinted in W. Breit and H.M. Hochman (eds), *Readings in Microeconomics*, New York: Holt, Rinehart and Winston, 1968.

Robinson, J. (1971), 'Rising supply price', *Economica*, reprinted in Stigler and Boulding (eds), *op. cit.*

Samuelson, P.A. (1947), *Foundations of Economic Analysis*, Harvard: Harvard University Press.

Scherer, F.M. (1980), *Industrial Market Structure and Economic Performance*, Chicago: Rand-McNally.

Sen, A.K. (1979), 'The welfare basis of real income comparisons: a survey', *Journal of Economic Literature*.

Sharkey, W.W. (1982), *The Theory of Natural Monopoly*, Cambridge: Cambridge University Press.

Shephard, R. (1953), *Cost and Production Functions*, Princeton: Princeton University Press.

Simon, H.A. (1957), *Models of Man*, New York: Wiley.

Spence, M. (1973), 'Job market signalling', *Quarterly Journal of Economics*.

Stigler, G.J. (1947), 'The kinky oligopoly demand curve and rigid prices', *Journal of Political Economy*, reprinted in G.J. Stigler and K.E. Boulding (eds) on behalf of the American Economic Association, *Readings in Price Theory*, London, Allen & Unwin, 1953.

Svejnar, J. (1982), 'On the theory of a participating firm', *Journal of Economic Theory*.

Sweezy, F.M. (1939), 'Demand under conditions of oligopoly', *Journal of Political Economy*, reprinted in Stigler and Boulding (eds), *op. cit.*

Tobin, J. (1965), 'Liquidity preference as behaviour towards risk', *Review of Economic Studies*, 1958. Reprinted in M.J. Mueller (ed.) *Readings in Macroeconomics*. New York: Holt Rinehart and Winston.

Tullock, G. (1987), 'Public choice', in J. Eatwell, M. Milgate and P. Newman (eds) *The New Palgrave, A Dictionary of Economics*, London: Macmillan.

Vanek, J. (1970), *The General Theory of Labour-Managed Market Economies*, New York: Cornell University Press.

Viner, H. (1931), 'Cost curves and supply curves', *Zeitschrift für Nationalökonomie*, reprinted in Stigler and Boulding (eds), *op. cit.*

Von Neumann, J. and Morgenstern, O. (1944), *Theory of Games and Economic Behaviour*, Princeton: Princeton University Press.

Ward, B. (1957), 'The firm in Illyria: market syndicalism', *American Economic Review*.

Waterson, M. (1984), *Economic Theory of Industry*, Cambridge: Cambridge University Press.

Weintraub, R.E. (1974), *General Equilibrium Theory*, London: Macmillan.

Williamson, O.E. (1964), *The Economics of Discretionary Behaviour*, Englewood Cliffs, NJ: Prentice Hall.

INDEX